THE IT GIRL

50 years as a woman working in the Information Technology industry

Published by Third Age Publishing Pty Ltd. Sydney NSW Australia.

THIRD AGE PUBLISHING

The IT Girl: 50 years as a woman working in the Information Technology industry

National Library of Australia Cataloguing-in-Publication Entry

Creator:	Ann Moffatt, author
Title:	The IT Girl: 50 years as a woman working in the Information Technology industry
ISBN:	978-0-6481668-6-3
Subjects:	Autobiography, computers, information technology

NATIONAL LIBRARY OF AUSTRALIA

A catalogue record for this book is available from the National Library of Australia

For my children and grandchildren, and for all the women in the IT profession who support each other to be the best they can be.

Cover picture: Ann Moffatt working from home for fpl in 1966, developing code for the analysis of data from the black box of the Concorde. The toddler is her daughter Claire.

Contents

Foreword by Steve Shirley

I **HAD THE PLEASURE** of working with the author for eight years starting in the 1960s when we both had young children. Ann was my company's Technical Director and I was – in theory at least– her boss. That was in an age when women were viewed as second class citizens requiring male authorisation for financial transactions and debarred from some professional activities. There were few part-time jobs with any intellectual challenge so it was usual for women to leave work on marriage or when their first child was expected. What a waste of skilled resources!

I founded Freelance Programmers (one of the UK's first high-tech start-ups) as a crusade for women returners rather than to make my fortune. Study after study has shown that women's two priorities in the workplace are flexibility and work/life balance. We provided these in the extreme.

Ann was dubbed the 'IT Girl', meaning both Information Technology and (the original meaning) attractive young woman with 'it' – sex appeal and an engaging personality. I often used my nickname Steve to get through the door before anyone realised that 'he' was a 'she'. I got teased with headlines about 'Steve and her birds' (bird also being Pom slang for a sexually attractive or promiscuous young woman).

Things have moved on since we both worked in that pioneering social enterprise. But today there is still an acute waste of female talent in an industry that is desperate to recruit and retain skilled staff. Freelance Programmers – and that is exactly what the company was in its early years – helped me, helped Ann, and helped hundreds of women to contribute to the IT industry.

The percentage of women in STEM (science, technology, engineering and mathematics) has been depressingly low in most countries, and sunny Australia is no exception. The pace of change towards a fairer and more diverse labour force remains slow. Massive changes in the workplace are needed if we are to move to gender equality.

Dame Stephanie Shirley CH DBE FREng FBCS
Henley-on-Thames, England
August 2020

Introduction

JUST ABOUT EVERBODY says they'd like to write a book about the story of their life. In my retirement I actually did so, and I'm very glad of it. It helps you remember things, and reminds you how chance meetings or events can totally change your life. It conjures up the what ifs and the maybes. I recommend it to you all. Don't just think about it, do it. And it's great gift to your family, including those yet to be born who you will never meet. It will ensure that they will meet you.

I have enjoyed my life immensely, and I have learnt a lot. I am reminded of the saying that 'experience is something you get just after you need it'. I have made my share of mistakes, but I have also done many things I am proud of. This my story.

I would like to thank all the people who have made my life what it has been. Even those who maybe were the cause of some of my problems. Life's rich tapestry and all that. In a long life you meet many people, and they all make you what you are.

There are a few people I would like to specifically mention. At the top of the list is my family. My parents Jack and Evelyn, my siblings Rosemary and Richard, and my children Claire and Stephen. I would like to thank two remarkable strong and independent women who each had a major influence on my life, Marjorie Errington and Steve Shirley. They showed me that anything is possible.

A special thanks to my editor, publisher and good friend Graeme Philipson, who turned my voluminous and meandering ramblings into the book you are now reading. Thanks to all my colleagues and friends who made contributions to and comments about the book, and who have supported me in my career and in my life.

And thanks to you for reading about my journey. I hope you find it enjoyable, and maybe even helpful.

Thanks to everyone.

Ann Moffatt
Queensland, Australia
July 2020

Prologue

I OFTEN WONDER if there is any single event that sets someone on their chosen path in life. My memory of this particular day in my life is still very vivid. It's as if that is the day my future began. Up until then other people were in charge of my life.

I can still see myself cycling along the ridgetop towards the aerodrome. It was July in England. A perfect summer day, the sort you remember when you think of an English summer, but which you rarely ever get. Seen through clouds of insects and pollen, the huge sun was dusty and yellow and high in the hazy blue sky. Big white fluffy clouds hung like the giant barrage balloons I remembered from the war.

All around were fields of ripe corn, the dusty yellow-gold colour that corn goes when it really should have been harvested. Here and there were patches of bright red poppies. My tightly curly hair was the same colour as the corn and the linen skirt I was wearing. I tried and tried to make my hair smooth and silky like the shampoo ads in the magazines, but no matter what I tried it did exactly what it chose to do.

I had been offered a job but I told my prospective employer that before I decided whether to accept the position I wanted to talk to someone who was already doing that sort of work.

My mind wandered on that warm summer day. I knew I had a bright future. I was going to have a career as a scientist where I was sure I would have an opportunity to make a difference to the world. It would be a career that would make me feel proud of my achievements.

I thought about how I had got to this place in my young life, where I felt my future was assured and I would be secure and valued. I thought about how different my life would be from now on, and how different it would be from the life of my parents and most people I knew, who seemed to have very mundane and uninteresting lives.

The sweet summer air smelled like my grandad's pipe tobacco when he first lit up. I felt good about life. I was just about to leave school and that made me a grown up. I would be earning a real salary and be paid monthly like a real professional.

But first I had to have that conversation.

1 My early life

I **WAS BORN** in the Queen Charlotte and Chelsea Hospital in the London suburb of Hammersmith on 11 July 1939, just two months before Hitler marched into Poland and started World War II. I was christened Ann Stafford Hill. Stafford was a family name given as a middle name to the first boy in each generation in my father's family. I was going to be Ian Stafford Hill. Ann seemed close enough.

My parents both came from Sunderland in northern England. My father John, always called Jack, was a carpenter who had marched from Tyneside to London in the famous Jarrow March in 1936 to escape the high unemployment that hit the north of England very hard.

My mother Evelyn Humble only ever worked for a few months, as a nursery maid for the wealthy family of Sir Arthur Dorman, one of the owners of Dorman Long. Sir Arthur had seven children, who needed a governess and three nannies. Each nanny had two nursery maids to do the menial work like changing nappies, emptying chamber pots and ironing the children's clothes.

Nursery maids were not allowed to touch the children and had to address even the smallest of them as 'sir' or 'm'lady'. Dorman Long was a very well known engineering firm that specialised in large projects including the Tyne River Bridge in Newcastle. It also built the Sydney Harbour Bridge.

My father found work as a jobbing carpenter on the first day he arrived in London, mainly working as a cabinet maker. His dream was to work for Waring & Gillow, then England's most famous furniture manufacturer.

WHEN MY FATHER got his first pay he rushed back to Sunderland and married my mother by special licence and brought her back with him to London. My mother expected a husband who would keep her and provide for her for all her life, which my father did.

She was dreadfully homesick in London at first and spent her days wandering the better suburbs looking for a house they could live in. They boarded for a short time with a wealthy family. One day the very generous lady of the house found my mother sitting on the front garden wall crying. She said the house was large enough because all her children had left home. She and her husband became my Auntie Bess and Uncle Jim and my godparents. They were great friends of our family for as long as they lived.

My mother insisted that my father provide a house for them both where they could start a family. They found a newly built house in Harrow, a location best known for the famous boys' public school of that name.

Harrow was established in the Middle Ages on one of the few high places in the flat Thames basin. It was about 12 miles north-west of the centre of London. To this day the train station is called Harrow-on-the-Hill. With two and a half bedrooms and a front and back garden, the house was more modest than my mother expected but all my father could afford, and far better than any house their own parents had ever lived in.

Because of minor heart problems my father did not get called up for war service. He was given a job mending aircraft that limped home damaged from the war. His carpentry skills were very useful. Up to that time fighter aircraft were made mainly of plywood and fabric and held together with glue. The new Spitfire was all metal, but the Hawker Hurricane was not.

My father worked at Northolt Airfield, three miles from our house. It was the oldest airfield in the Royal Air Force, dating from before World War I. In World War II it was a fighter base, the first to take Spitfires and the home of the famous Polish Squadron.

He rode to work on his pushbike and came home for lunch. One of my earliest memories was when I was about two. I had been taken to work by my father on the cross bar of his bike. He put me in the back seat of one of the aircraft for a morning nap.

When I woke up it was very cold and very noisy and very bright and I was hungry. I remember seeing a man with a funny hat sitting in front of me. I thought it must be my Daddy. I poked him in the back and when he turned round I said, "You're not my Daddy and I'm hungry." We were in the air. The pilot quickly turned the aircraft for home.

Dad went home crying and told my Mum he had put me in an aeroplane and it had taken off to war.

"Well you just go back and find my baby," said my mother. "And don't come back home until you've got her'. We were lucky that the pilot had only taken the plane up for a test flight. He had not looked in the rear seat and said he nearly had a heart attack when he saw me.

ANOTHER VIVID memory from the war is when I was about four. My mother was taking an afternoon nap and I heard a 'buzz bomb', a German V1 rocket, pass over our house. This happened a lot that year but this time the engine stopped. That was always the warning sign that they were about to crash land and explode.

Because we were near the fighter aerodrome at Northolt, our area was a target for anything Hitler could throw at us. We children were told that we had to listen for buzz bombs because they were not like the German planes that could be trapped in the chains hanging off the barrage balloons. When their engine stopped they fell straight down, destroying anything they landed on. They had a ton of high explosive in them.

I woke my mother when the noise of its engine stopped. I remember saying 'buzz bomb, buzz bomb' but my mother said if there was a buzz bomb we would have heard the air raid sirens. I just rushed off to rescue my teddy in the kitchen when the buzz bomb dropped onto the house two doors away, killing the five people inside. All our ceilings fell down and the glass was shattered in all our windows.

Soon the war was over and life was very different. There was no blackout and no air raid sirens. The bomb-damaged houses were gradually repaired. Our windows were replaced but the ceilings were still damaged and there was a huge crack in the wall that separated the sitting room from the dining room.

My Dad decided to knock that wall down and make one larger room. When the men came to repair our house they told my father he shouldn't have knocked the wall down without permission and now the whole house might have to be demolished. Dad apologised and said he was a carpenter and he knew what he was doing, and he got away with it.

Soon the bomb shelters were knocked down and removed from the streets. Life was returning to normal.

My Mum and Dad always seemed to be fighting about something. I was too young to understand what it was all about. Mum usually ended up in tears, leaving my father to feed me and get me to bed. I could hear the arguments continuing through my bedroom wall.

When I was seven my Mum started to get very big and Dad said she had to go to hospital to get me a little brother or sister. Eventually my mother came home with twins. I had a little brother, Richard, and a little sister, Rosemary.

The winter of 1947 was very cold. Life was tough in England with post war austerity. Food rationing was still in force. Mum spent a lot of time in tears saying she just couldn't cope and asking me to call a neighbour in.

I made myself useful by getting her things she asked for from around the house. She seemed to get fatter and fatter. My father usually made us dinner when he got home from work and the arguments continued.

When the twins were five months old they both got very sick. I think it was gastroenteritis. Our very concerned doctor said they might die. My mother and the twins were sent to a nursing home in the country. Dad and I visited at weekends sometimes, but it was a long way and we had no car. Only rich people did in those days.

After what seemed ages my mother and the twins came home. When the twins left they were babies who did little else but sleep and take their bottles. Now they were sitting up and chattering baby babble. They were real people that I could play with. I loved them very much.

After the twins were born my father got a job with the building division of well-known restaurant and hotel chain J. Lyons & Co. He started as a carpenter and was to work his way up to the position of building division manager.

I STARTED AT Roxeth Hill Primary School just before the war ended. I was five years old and very tall for my age. We were told to find another student to hold hands with so we could march in to school in pairs. Another tall girl named Kathleen Mann took my hand and we marched in together. We started a friendship that would last for more than 50 years.

I loved school. My best and favourite subject was arithmetic. I found it easy because it made so much sense. I was especially good at adding up the pounds, shillings and pence that Britain used for money until 1971. There were 12 pennies in a shilling and 20 shillings in a pound, so adding them up was tricky.

At least it was for many of the others. I had no trouble. Only when I did maths years later did I find this was called base 12 and base 20. I just carried the numbers across. It was easy.

At the end of the sixth grade we sat for our 11 plus exam. It was called that because that was the age of the students sitting it. Kathleen and I both got scholarships to the most prestigious girls grammar school in the county, Harrow County Girls School.

I was the first person in my family to go to grammar school, which were academically selective state schools. Both my parents had left school at 13, which was the legal age back then.

Although they were proud of me, my parents grumbled about having to buy school uniforms and provide money for school outings. Richard and Rosemary were eight years younger than me and were beginning to put a strain on the limited family finances.

Although we were both in the A stream, Kathleen was always ahead of me. She was very bright. She had always come first in the class in primary school and I had always come second. Her reports were full of praise for her achievements, while mine always said 'could do better'. I knew I would never do better than Kathleen and deep down I didn't want to.

We made a very striking couple, the two tallest girls in the class by far, me with curly, unruly corn blonde hair and Kathleen with gleaming dark brown hair in neat plaits down to her waist.

Kathleen and I made firm friends with two other girls, Barbara Cox (Babs) and Patricia Croft (Pat). Babs was slim and petite with straight blonde hair, the whitest skin and cornflower blue eyes. Pat was short and dumpy with a spotty complexion and mousy hair dragged back from her face in two bunches.

We four were inseparable. We formed a secret club and wore red pop bottle tops held on by the cork inserts on our fleecy lined, regulation navy blue school knickers to show our alliance. Everyone in our class knew of the alliance, even though we only showed the bottle tops to each other.

I wanted to be a scientist when I left school. Kathleen wanted to be a philosopher, and so studied Latin and Greek. Babs and Pat wanted to be secretaries.

We four spent every break from lessons talking seriously about the ways of the world. We helped each other with homework. On weekends we went on long bike rides. Other girls had started to try to attract boys, but we were happy with each other's company.

The boys from their local grammar school still tried to chat us up at the bus stop or whistle at us as we walked to the lacrosse field on sports day. It was against the school rules to speak to a boy while in school uniform so we would just blush and giggle.

2 A working girl

WHEN I WAS 12 I got my first job, doing a paper round. At first the man at the paper shop said he employed only boys to deliver papers, but I told him I could do anything boys could do and wasn't afraid of hard work.

He thought the best round for me was to deliver papers to a few posh houses that stood in their own enormous grounds on Harrow Hill. Although the round was ten miles long the sack of papers was light, not like the very heavy loads the boys had to carry round the poorer streets in the area where the houses were close together.

I was paid 3/6d, a shilling less than the boys were paid because the round delivered to just twelve houses. After giving my brother and sister sixpence each I still had 2/6d to spend.

The roads round the big houses were rough and stony and full of ruts. In autumn and winter, they were slippery with leaves fallen from the huge chestnut trees, and wet from frost and snow. Starting the round at 6am was great on the sunny summer mornings but on the dark winter days I often came home wet, cold and bleeding after falling off my bike and having to complete the round on foot pushing my bike.

After a year or so my mother decided the paper round was no job for a girl and got me a Saturday job at the local haberdasher's shop, working on the glove counter as she had done when she was a girl. The people in the shop were nice enough but I was the only young girl and my mother kept coming into the shop 'to see how I was going'. The bossy shop manageress paid the five shillings I earned to my mother. My mother gave me 2/6d and kept the other half 'to help with the housekeeping'.

MY SCHOOL WAS near a big department store. One day after school I decided to ask if they wanted a 'Saturday girl'. To my delight they wanted someone to work on the counter selling cosmetics and perfume. Although I was only 13 and didn't wear makeup I thought the job was much more interesting than selling gloves at the haberdasher's. And it paid more, a whole 7/6d.

All the shop girls had to parade in front of the manageress every day before the store opened. Deportment, clothes, hair, makeup and stockings were inspected. If clothes were crumpled or not in perfect condition or not strictly all black or black with a white blouse, girls were sent home to change and had a whole day's pay docked, even if they returned an hour later. Not to return after being sent home meant the sack.

The girls on the perfumery counter were beautiful. Most specialised in a specific brand of cosmetics which were used to make up their own faces to perfection. If the counter wasn't busy, one of the salesgirls would make my face up, watched by a ring of smiling customers. I felt very important while I was being made up. but when I saw my finished face in the mirror I would race off to the washroom to remove the heavy makeup, which I thought made me look like a clown.

That's when I met Miss Errington, the amazingly slim and stern faced buyer for the department. When she came over to perfumery to ask the head salesgirl for 'the figures', she bustled around the counters moving expensive goods to more prominent positions and even came behind the counter to attend to customers herself.

All the salesgirls stood up straight and tried to look very busy when Miss Errington was around. She would often take over a sale and recommend a more expensive cosmetic that was 'the latest thing' or 'what they are all wearing in Paris'. The customers treated Miss Errington with great respect. They even changed the way they spoke and put on a posh voice while they talked to Miss Errington and always bought what she recommended.

"See," Miss Errington would say when the customer had gone, "you can always sell up. Think of your commission gals!" All the salesgirls were on commission based on the money they rang up in the cash register. As a casual, I wasn't paid commission; I had to pass my sale over to a permanent assistant to cash up.

ON MY THIRD week in the job, just before lunchtime, I was told by the head salesgirl to take a piece of paper with 'the figures' over to Miss Errington. The head salesgirl checked me over even more intently than the manageress had when I first arrived that day.

"Miss Errington is a stickler for correct dress and good posture," said the head salesgirl. "She can be in a foul mood so watch what you say. Say as little as possible, answer questions politely and smile. You'll do," she said, giving me a little push.

Miss Errington's office was a tiny space in a corner between the wool department and buttons and zips. The desk was covered with scraps of paper with neat figures. There were also scraps of material, swatches of coloured fabric, and buttons and belts all jumbled up with lipsticks and tiny sample perfume bottles.

There was just enough room behind the desk for a tiny tatty swivel stool. Here Miss Errington sat, dressed always in black, hunched over the desk, legs twisted round the chair, pencil gripped between her teeth looking very grim. Her face was powdered stark lily white except for the wide red gash of shiny lipstick that defined her mouth. Her eyebrows had been plucked and redefined with a thin line of black eyebrow pencil. She seemed to the salesgirls like a giant black widow spider waiting to pounce on anyone who came near.

I said, "Hello. Why are you doing sums? I like doing sums!"

"Well I don't!" she said. "If you're so clever at doing sums, Miss, you can help me find out why I get a different answer each time I add this column of figures."

I quickly totted up the column. "£1543/10/4d."

"You're no use, that's a different figure again!" said Miss Errington. "Well it's right!" I said with confidence.

Miss Errington looked blacker than ever. I smiled broadly. "I'll check it again if you like, but I'll be right, I always am." I added the numbers again. "Yes, £1543/10/4d."

"Well, just for being cheeky add all these numbers on these five till rolls while I go to the powder room," said Miss Errington.

Why on earth should Miss Errington want till rolls added? I had supposed that the tills automatically added the amounts rung up and held a total somewhere. I noticed the rolls were not only for perfumery but also for haberdashery, wools, belts, headdresses and hosiery. When I added up the roll for perfumery. I realised how much money the department took. I knew roughly what the girls earned and, presuming naively that the difference between sales and salaries was profit, I couldn't believe that the store was making that much money, just on a Saturday morning.

By the time Miss Errington reappeared looking much relieved and smelling of fresh powder and perfume, I had added three of the rolls.

"Alright, you can stop now. What do you get?"

I told Miss Errington the totals. "Good girl, you really can add up accurately, and fast too. So can you subtract and multiply and divide and do percentages as well?"

"Of course I can."

"And you *enjoy* that stuff?" she asked incredulously.

"Yes. I'm going to be a scientist and scientists have to be good at maths. Miss Robinson, my headmistress, says I'm going to go to Oxford or Cambridge and I'll get a PhD and discover something very important. And anyhow, maths isn't just arithmetic. It's Algebra and Geometry and Calculus too and I'm good at those as well," I said, trying to impress.

"Well clever clogs, we are only a shop so percentages are the highest form of maths I have to do, thank goodness," said Miss Errington. "But if you are fast and accurate I'll save all my arithmetic for you to do on Saturdays so that I can get out and see what's happening on the counters.

"I hate maths and I'm no good at it. What I love is finding out what customers want and how much they are prepared to pay for it so we can make lots of money. Have you any idea what I do or am I just the grumpy old witch in the corner office? Oh, don't think I don't know what the girls say about me," she said.

I was embarrassed and wished I'd just kept my mouth shut as I'd been told to do. "They don't know the half of it. I've got a very exciting job. It's the best job in the world and pays very well. The only thing I don't like is all the bookwork. I need one of those 'electronic brains' that we read about in the newspaper. But it seems I might have found my 'brain'."

Although neither of us knew it at the time, Marjory Errington had found the daughter she'd always wanted and I had found a role model, a truly independent, professional woman who lived a non traditional life to the full. The friendship would last for over 50 years and across many continents.

I SOON LEARNED that Miss Errington's main job was buying goods from wholesalers that she thought the shoppers would buy, and pricing them to sell at a profit. Sometimes it was buying goods that would encourage shoppers to buy other goods that would sell at a profit. She was the store's buyer for cosmetics and perfumery, haberdashery, wools, belts, scarves, artificial flowers, bridal headdresses, hosiery and gloves.

Instead of going to the perfumery counter on the next Saturday I went straight to Miss Errington's office. True to her word, she had saved all her paperwork and the small desk was piled high with invoices and letters from wholesalers. There were also a number of large cardboard cartons of goods in the space behind the wool counter next to the office.

"Open up that box," said Miss Errington. "You'll find a packing note that tells you what the goods are and how many of each have been sent. As you unpack them, check them off the packing list. Make sure you count them carefully and note any differences in numbers. Each time you find a new item give the first one to me."

The box was full of artificial flowers that could be worn as a corsage to brighten up a suit or dress or could be attached to a hair comb and pinned in the hair for a dance. The packing note gave a vague description of each item. The flowers were tied with string into bundles of the same type. I wondered how they could ever be sold. They were all squashed up and looked just about good for the dustbin. I pulled out a bundle and handed one to Miss Errington.

"Well, what is it?" said Miss Errington.

"I think it's this one, 'Love in the mist'. It seems to be the only blue flower in the carton," I said. "The packing note says 24 blue and it looks like there are 24."

By the time I counted the bunch, Miss Errington had lovingly pulled the wrinkles out of the flower I had given her and it looked very pretty. She held it against her own black dress.

"What do you think: 3/6d or 2/4d? They cost ninepence each." My eyes widened, it seemed like stealing, buying a flower that cost ninepence and selling it at three or four times that price. Sure, you had to pay the salesgirls but that seemed like a very big difference. Miss Errington decided on 3/6d saying "We might have to mark them down for the sales. Blue is fashionable now but it might not be at the end of the season."

The goods in the box were unpacked, counted, admired and priced item by item. Sometimes there would be more items than stated on the packing note, sometimes fewer. I noted each discrepancy carefully.

I noticed each item had a little swing ticket on it with a price written in Miss Errington's beautiful copperplate handwriting. "Take those over to the counter. The girls will sort them out and price them and I'll show you how we do the maths," she said. I felt very important taking the bundles of flowers over to the department.

MISS ERRINGTON showed me how to match the packing note with the invoice, checking off items charged against items delivered. She told me to ignore over deliveries. "He's probably done that in the hope he'll get a bigger order next time," she said. But under deliveries were not ignored.

A piece of paper was stuck to the side of the invoice next to the column of prices. "Now here comes the maths," she said. "You have to check all the figures on the invoice. Multiply the number of goods received by the price and see if he's charged us the right total amount. Where he's under delivered write a line underneath showing the amount he has overcharged.

"I've written the sales price against each item, multiply that by the number of each item received and write it on the paper on the side. Take the wholesale price plus tax from the retail price and you'll get the profit. Work that out as a percentage of the wholesale price plus tax and you'll get the profit margin. Then add all the amounts except the profit margin to get the totals for the invoice as a whole then calculate overall profit as a percentage. Check the overall profit is more than 50%."

Miss Errington then dictated a letter to the wholesaler, which I wrote carefully in a triple carbon book, listing items invoiced but not received.

"Now do you think you can do all that by yourself?" asked Miss Errington. "This week I saved some goods to show you the whole process but usually I get the girls to unpack and count the stock in the week as each consignment comes in when they aren't so busy. They can pack up any returns too.

"I always check that what's been sent is what I ordered and price stuff myself but they ticket the goods and get them ready for the counter. If I write discrepancies and sales prices on the invoices can you write the letters to suppliers, do all the maths and take the invoices up to accounts?"

"Well it's really just simple arithmetic," I said. "I can do that. But how do you know what you've ordered and at what price?"

"It's all up here," said Miss Errington, pointing to her head. "The wholesalers rarely put one over me. Whatever you order and at whatever agreed price, it's what they send that matters and the price they charge. They make mistakes, they try to palm their old stock off to me, they charge the wrong price but I always have the upper hand. If there's nothing in writing I can send stuff back.

"Of course it's not like that when you're dealing with a big cosmetic firm like Elizabeth Arden. There you have to do an order on their own order sheet but then they do send the goods you've ordered. You still have to count them, of course, but the goods are always as specified."

I was beginning to see that there was more to running a store than just selling things over a counter. This was a whole new and exciting world and I felt I was right in the centre. After a few weeks, in addition to getting a pay rise to 12/6 every Saturday, Miss Errington would often have some samples for me so I always had a bottle of the latest perfume or a new lipstick or a pretty scarf or belt. I would share these items with my school friends, none of whom seemed to have as exciting a Saturday job as I did.

I talked about Miss Errington at home until my mother said "I'm fed up of hearing about her. She's only a jumped up shop girl." But I noticed that when my mother came into the store on a Saturday, she would speak in deferential tones to Miss Errington the same way she spoke to my headmistress at school, and she would smile proudly when she was told how much I was valued.

3 Mistakes do happen

ONE SATURDAY when I arrived at the store all was in chaos around Miss Errington's office. I had great difficulty even getting to the office as the spaces behind the counters were loaded with boxes and cartons of every description. The desk was littered with scraps of paper. I learned that Miss Errington had been battling flu all week and had phoned in on Thursday to say that she was too sick to come to work.

The head salesgirls from each of the departments were waiting for me. What was the problem?

"I'm mainly okay," said the girl from perfumery. "I've found the invoices for my orders and marked them up. They didn't need pricing cos they are all standard prices. There are a few sponge bags and cosmetic bags that need pricing, but I can do without those until she comes back."

"I can manage too," said the girl from wools. "Most of my stuff is just reorders of stuff we're already selling. I haven't heard that there are to be any price rises."

The story from hosiery and haberdashery was similar, but the girls from scarves and artificial flowers were more concerned. "It's nearly Easter," said the girl from artificial flowers. "That huge box is a gross of bridal head-dresses for the spring brides and I need them. If we don't sell them soon people will go elsewhere and we'll be left with them. They'll be out of fashion next season and we'll have to mark them down in the sale."

"I'm in the same boat with scarves," said the other girl. "I could wait till Monday but I'd prefer to have my new silk scarves out today, they are beautiful. You can price them, Ann. You know how she does it. We need them, Ann."

I felt flattered that the girls thought I could do the pricing but I'd never actually done it by myself. Miss Errington seemed to pluck prices out of the air and they often bore little resemblance to the wholesale price. She would often ask me what I thought about the price but I would always tell her she was right. Once, Miss Errington had asked me to price goods that had been delivered on a Saturday. She told me I had priced very conservatively. Yes, they would make a profit but people would pay more.

By now I understood the tax system and understood how much sales tax had to be added to the wholesale price before a profit would be made and there were often delivery charges to be considered too. I had no real idea what people were willing to pay for the goods but I thought the salesgirls should know that. If I just did the arithmetic and added a bit extra on 'for luck' then asked the girls what they thought, then I was sure I could at least get the 144 bridal headdresses out onto the counter.

The girls counted them. They were all in good condition and there were no returns. That simplified matters but it was a very large number of head-dresses all the same. What if Miss Errington had only ordered a dozen or half a gross? I decided to put the headdresses out a dozen at a time. If there had been over deliveries those not sold could be returned next week.

I carefully calculated the price. I did it again from scratch just in case I made an error, then added a bit for luck. I brushed my unruly blonde hair and put a headdress on. I looked at myself in the mirror above the desk. Yes, the headdress looked good for the price. I took a dozen over to the counter. Was the price reasonable? Very reasonable, was the reply.

I set about tidying the office and working through the piles of invoices. I decided I wouldn't push my luck and price the silk scarves. One look at the invoice told me they would be very expensive. A mistake there might be catastrophic. The head salesgirl from headdresses popped her head round the partition. "We've sold all those. They are going like hot cakes. We need more out on the counter now. I think we could put the price up a shilling or so too," said the head salesgirl.

I felt very pleased with myself. I agreed the price should be put up and gave the girl five dozen more. I now felt confident enough to price the scarves. I took the scarves out to the department. "That's very expensive," said the head salesgirl. "But I'll do my best."

Before lunch the girls from headdresses had sold six dozen. People were lining up at the counter to buy for friends. I agreed that the second six dozen be put out for sale. "Phew," said the head salesgirl from headdresses as she popped her head in to the office after the store closed. "What a day. Our sales figures are huge. Miss Errington will be pleased. I don't know what we'd have done without you, Ann."

THE NEXT WEEKEND there was another huge carton of bridal headdresses from Kleinworts outside the office. I said, "Good, you got some more. They sold so well last week."

"Well they would have done," said Miss Errington looking very stern, "at half cost price! Good job Rita on the counter added another shilling or we'd have caught a real cold!"

I was horrified. "How? What? What did I do?" I stammered.

"You made a simple arithmetic mistake," said Miss Errington. But she was smiling, rather than angry.

"You can't make an omelette without breaking eggs. The only people who never make a mistake are those who don't do anything, Ann. You do wonders. Accounts often check your arithmetic and tell me you rarely make a mistake. Before you came I was always being called up to the manager's office to explain my slip ups. Of course they didn't ever get near to sacking me, although they've often threatened, because they know that overall I make good profits for them."

I was crestfallen. Accounts had checked my arithmetic and found mistakes! I had priced 144 headdresses at half cost price! I'd lose the job I loved just as I was beginning to feel confident.

"I'll pay for them. I'll make up the losses." I was almost crying.

"Don't be silly. You'd have to work for at least a couple of years for no pay to come anywhere near to making up the loss. You're not yet 14, Ann. You'll make lots of mistakes. The secret is how to get over them. The girls have been taking orders for these headdresses all week. We've told everyone we'd put them on special and the next delivery will be at least four to five times the price, but people still seem willing to pay.

"Many have even paid totally up front just to ensure they get one. My problem has been to get old Manny at Kleinworts to find me another gross. He had to get onto his supplier in Poland. They must have had their girls sewing at all hours. I told him if I didn't get a gross by today he needn't bother. I can't imagine 288 brides in Harrow wearing the same headdresses but there you go.

"We'll charge just over three times cost. I agreed with Manny that he would pay sales tax. He won't of course, but that's his problem. He's noted on the invoice that he will, so we are in the clear. If they all go well we'll have made a huge profit and people coming in for headdresses have bought lots of other things so the management is very pleased.

"Mr Devonshire in Ladies Fashions has kitted out lots of bride's mothers who have said they bought their daughter's headdress here and they were sent back to buy a 'lovely silk scarf' from us to go with the outfit, so all those expensive scarves sold. I would never order anything that expensive. They were a try-on by the wholesaler but you spotted it. You charged the right price and now I know our customers are willing to pay that much. I'd never have been brave enough to charge a price that high."

I had learned a very important lesson early in life that would stand me in good stead in the future.

I LEARNED THAT Miss Errington had two main loves, apart from her job. Her first love was travel. She had been all over the world. She'd even been to Hong Kong for a trade fair and to Poland to stay with Manny's family on a ticket paid for by Kleinworts as a 'thank you' for selling so many of their headdresses.

She took every two week annual holiday in Europe and could speak several languages. She paid to stay in the best of the grand hotels of Europe with her large commission. If she spent a few days of her European holiday visiting a manufacturer for the store they would allow her to take a week off at Christmas so she could go skiing in Switzerland.

Her other love was Mr Scanes. Mr Scanes was the boss of Mr Richardson, who lived near our house and was highly respected by the local people, including my parents. He was 'The Man from the Prudential' and got right royal treatment when he came to collect the insurance money each week.

If Mr Richardson was important, his boss, Mr Scanes, who spent his days in the big office in the town, was even more important. Mr Scanes had more than 20 men like Mr Richardson working for him, each well respected by their community. Mr Scanes never visited homes unless somebody died, when he came to view the body and offer his condolences to the family even if they weren't insured by the Prudential.

Mr Scanes would also attend the funeral with Mr Richardson because he knew there was business to be done. At the grave he would discretely pass Mr Richardson's card to mourners saying it was fortunate the deceased was insured by the Pru and the family now had money to pay for a good send off and an annuity to support the wife and kids. If the deceased was not insured, Mr Scanes would say that it was such a pity and told mourners that they should take care not to be caught without insurance. In either case he would send Mr Richardson around to ensure they had catered for their family to ensure they had made provision for those left behind.

Mr Richardson would always manage to sell more insurance after a funeral. Yes, funerals were good for business and Mr Scanes would get a nice commission from the business Mr Richardson wrote.

Mr Scanes was married but his wife was 'frigid', according to Miss Errington. He would often come over to her cosy flat in Kilburn in the evening for a whiskey. Mr Scanes had his own cowhide chair in Miss Errington's flat, laid out with his pipe and tobacco pouch ready on the side table. They would play whist or chess or just sit and watch the fire, said Miss Errington. Mr Scanes was a true friend, a gentleman and a good conversationalist, according to Miss Errington.

MISS ERRINGTON arranged for me to work for the store in my school holidays. My family never went away on holiday. My father had two weeks off work a year. A day trip on a boat down the Thames to Southend once a year was the only treat my family could afford. We went on the same trip every year. Once at Southend we would take the little train along the lengthy pier to the town. We would walk along the promenade to the Kursaal, which was a funfair with roundabouts, dodgem cars and a Ferris wheel.

My father would buy us all fairy floss or ice cream. After three rides each it was back along the promenade to sit on the beach and eat lunch of boiled egg sandwiches made by my mother. If the tide was in there might be a paddle in the sea.

Although the Southend council had put a thin stretch of sand against the promenade wall so that it would look good on photos of people lounging on deckchairs, the beach was really mud flats in the Thames estuary. My young brother and sister always got muddy and the day out would usually end in tears as the mud spattered children were hurried onto the pier train to catch the boat home.

When I was younger, I had been sent to my Nana's in Sunderland or my Auntie Eleanor and Uncle Joe's in Newcastle. Uncle Joe had his own tailor shop so would take three weeks off at Easter and a month off in my summer holidays to take us to the Lake District. There my uncle and I, dressed in our Harris tweed jackets and plus fours made by Uncle Joe, would climb mountains roped together like the real mountain climbers. At other times we would play golf on the course by Derwentwater near Keswick. Uncle Joe bought me special child's size golf clubs. Auntie sat in the car knitting complex fairisle jumpers.

While staying with Auntie and Uncle in the summer I turned 12, I had been allowed to go with a group of local children to see 'The Day the Earth Stood Still' at the cinema. I felt scared when the space ship opened and the alien walked down the ramp. I made a grab at Brian Dolkin's hand in the dark for comfort. On the way home he tried rather inexpertly to kiss me.

That evening, after I had been sent to bed at 7pm as usual, I was discovered leaning out of the bedroom window in the bright sunlight of the early evening talking to boys. My aunt and uncle were worried. I was very pretty and had started to develop breasts. The thought that I might get pregnant while in their care was too much of a responsibility so they asked that I not be sent again.

Working at the store in the school holidays was better than going on holiday. Miss Errington made the school holidays fun. Most of the time was spent tidying out the stockroom or rearranging the showcases under the glass countertops. The shop girls took pity on me and gave me items that were no longer needed to take home.

Sometimes Miss Errington took me on buying expeditions. Most of the firms that supplied buttons, belts, haberdashery, flowers, headdresses and scarves were based in the East End of London. I was taken down narrow alleyways into dark, dank smoke filled back rooms that looked as if they hadn't changed since Dickens' times.

Most of the wholesalers were old Jewish men from Eastern Europe. They enjoyed wheeling and dealing with Miss Errington, who was businesslike and charming at the same time. She obviously enjoyed this part of her work and would tell me in great detail why and how she had got a good deal on the goods she had just ordered and how much profit and commission she would make. She told me that most of the goods were manufactured in Eastern Europe but some were 'finished' in sweat shops in the East End or in people's homes. 'Finishing' might consist of sewing buttons onto a white card carrying the wholesaler's logo or assembling belts from component parts.

We took our lunch in one of the many dockland pubs. Usually a cheese roll and a pickled onion would be washed down by a large tumbler of port for Miss Errington and lemonade for me. The pubs were full of old men. We hardly ever saw women except those working as barmaids behind the counter. Miss Errington told me that 'good' women didn't usually walk these streets without a man by their side, especially at night. This was where Jack the Ripper had murdered young girls of ill repute and he had never been found.

4 Boys

MY GROUP OF friends at the church youth club often chose to walk home from church in pairs holding hands or a boy would ask a girl to the Thursday 'hop' at the youth club. If a boy was really forward he would try to sneak a kiss as he delivered a girl to her garden gate. 'Good girls' ran away blushing and protesting. 'Bad girls' reciprocated and dallied by the garden gate until called in by an irate father who would ask 'whatever would the neighbours think?' Or say 'that's the way girls get pregnant you know!'

It was the 1950s. Amongst my friends both at school and in the church group, each week's Goon Show was a much anticipated radio program. The antics of the Goons were discussed and analysed at great length to discover the real meaning of each improbable episode.

Like many parents, my father didn't understand the Goons' off-beat humour. He said the show was dirty and full of double meanings. When I challenged him he could not explain what was dirty, but was sure it must be or the young people wouldn't laugh so loudly at things he didn't understand.

The disc jockey was Adrian Kerridge. He was not good looking, but he was tall and every girl hoped he would notice her. He was slightly older than most of the gang and worked as a recording technician at the BBC. Each week Adrian recorded the Goon Show on a large reel to reel tape recorder and would play the program to the youth group at our 'prayer meeting' on Sunday evening. The girls would blush and smile as the boys guffawed loudly at every joke. All the girls hoped that Adrian would escort them home.

At the Thursday hop Adrian would play requests, often just hinting at who made it and identifying the recipient, or naming the requestor but saying that the recipient would know who the song was meant for. Requests were made by boys. Girls would be thought too forward if they made one.

Most of the evening comprised rock 'n' roll and jive, which was mainly to show off agility and style. But quite a few long legs, stocking tops and suspenders could be glimpsed amidst a swirl of heavily starched petticoats displaying a sexiness that could be seen but not touched.

By the time the lights were turned down for the last waltz most of the young people had been paired off and so knew who they would be walking home with. The waltz was an opportunity for the closeness, sweaty touching and heavy breathing that was frowned upon earlier in the evening.

ONE EVENING just before Christmas, Adrian played 'Sposin' I should fall in love with you' and looking straight at me said it was for a very special girl who knew who she was. That evening he left the playing of the last waltz to the youth club leader and asked me to dance with him. On walking me home, he asked me to go to the New Years Eve dance.

I was petrified. Adrian had actually asked me out! What would he expect me to wear? I decided to buy a length of felt and make a circular skirt. Peacock blue or shocking pink were all the rage, but which? At the Christmas church service I asked what colour suit he would be wearing to the dance. "Brown," he said. "Then my skirt will have to be peacock blue," I thought.

I scraped together all the money I could find and bought a length of felt. Cutting it out carefully on the living room floor I told my mother I had been asked out to a New Years Eve dance. "You'll have to be home by 9.30," said my mother. "I'll speak to your father. He likes Adrian. His parents have a car and always go to church."

I had to work at the shop on New Years Eve. The shop closed at 5.30. After they had cashed up and tidied their counters the shop girls were given a small glass of sherry to toast the new year. I hurried home to get ready. Adrian was to pick me up at 7.30. Reaching home at 7 o'clock, much to my annoyance, Mr Richardson the insurance man was taking tea with my mother.

"Mr Richardson has come to pay out a policy that we took out when you were born. We've been paying sixpence a week since then and now you will be 15 next year we are getting £25 which was to set you up when you start work. Mr Richardson has suggested that, as you aren't going to leave school yet, you take over the payments and you might get £35 by the time you are 18. I told him that you want to go to university and he said that would help to pay your university fees."

I was annoyed. I hadn't realised that my parents had been paying out money for me all those years but sixpence was a lot of money and I didn't want to pay that out each week in the hope of getting £35 in a few more years.

I took out the ironing board and ironed my white blouse while my mother and Mr Richardson lectured me on the benefits of saving for the future. I put the ironing board away and left them still extolling the virtues of saving, through insurance policies of course.

I was tired and lay down on my bed for a few minutes. I fell asleep. When I woke it was daylight. My peacock blue felt skirt was carefully laid out on the bottom of the bed. My sugar starched many layered net petticoat was hanging on the wardrobe door. My carefully ironed white blouse had fallen onto the floor. How long had I been asleep? Why was it daylight? I was sure it had been pitch dark when I went to get ready. It was dark by 3.30 in the afternoon in winter.

My little sister, who I shared the double bed with, stirred. My sister had been in bed asleep when I slipped quietly into the room to get dressed for the New Years Eve dance. What had happened? Had it all been a dream? My mother bustled into the room and opened the curtains. "Wakey, girls!

"Well, you're the clever one," she said to me. "Adrian won't ask you out again. He was here promptly at 7.30. He's a very nice young man. Mr Richardson liked him and he's a very good judge of people. He sat and had a cup of tea with us but when you didn't come down after a quarter of an hour he asked me to go upstairs and tell you to hurry up. You were sound asleep on the bed and I didn't like to wake you."

I could have wept. Adrian would have found another girl to dance with. He nearly cancelled the date with me when I told him I had to be home by 9.30 but said he'd just slip out for a while to take me home then go back to the party.

ON THURSDAY evening I went to the youth club as usual. Adrian didn't even glance at me. even though I was wearing my fashionable peacock blue circular skirt with all the petticoats.

A quiet, studious, dark haired boy asked me to dance. Like most boys at the club he was concentrating too hard on his steps to speak while he was dancing. At ten minutes to nine I said I would have to run home. "But it's not 9 o'clock yet," said the nice young man. "Where do you live?" I told him. "That's just down the road. I can have you there in less than five minutes on the back of my motorbike."

I had never ridden on a motorbike. I heard myself saying, "No, I'd rather run and it's all downhill."

"Come and see the bike anyhow," said the young man." I gazed at the big shiny black and silver motorbike. "Why don't you run and I'll ride along beside you," said the young man. "I don't like to think of you going home by yourself."

He revved up the bike. It made a horrendous noise and sounded as if it would run off by itself. I ran and the young man rode alongside. As I said goodbye my father came out and shook his fist at the young man on the motorbike. "I won't have you going out with boys on motorbikes," he said.

“Motorbikes are dangerous. Who is he anyway? He can’t be one of the youth club boys with a bike like that. Have you been to the jazz club?”

The Harrow jazz club had a bad reputation for loutish behaviour and Teddy boys. Although some girls from the district went to the jazz club nice girls didn’t go.

“Dad! The jazz club is on Tuesdays. I was at the church youth club.”

“Who is he then?“ said my father. “What’s his name? How old is he? How come he can afford to run a big bike like that? It’s an AJS 600 twin. They cost as much as a car.”

“Why didn’t Adrian walk you home?” my mother chimed in. “He’s a nice boy. Mr Richardson liked him and he’s a good judge of people.”

I had to confess that I didn’t know the young man’s name or age or where he lived or whether his parents went to church or how he could afford a big bike. “It’s boys like that who get a girl into trouble,” said my mother. “If you hadn’t fallen asleep Adrian would still be interested, he’s a nice boy. His parents go to church.” I wondered why my parents judged ‘nice boys’ by whether their parents went to church. My parents didn’t go to church. Would my brother, Richard, be judged a ‘bad boy’?

AT CHURCH ON Sunday I found out that the nice young man with the motorbike was called Richard. He was an apprentice at de Havilland. He was 16 and had only just left school. He asked to walk me home from church. “Better not bring your bike right up to the house. My Dad doesn’t like motor bikes,” I said.

“Will you ride pillion? I’ve brought an extra helmet,” said Richard. “I’d rather not,” I said, “I’d like you to meet my parents. Could you come round for coffee after church next week?” said Richard.

I had never been asked to meet parents before. Did this mean I would have a ‘real’ boyfriend? This handsome young man seemed very serious. “I’d like that,” I heard myself saying.

At the Thursday dance Richard tried to dance every dance with me. At 9 o’clock he walked me home. He seemed only to talk about motor bikes and aeroplanes. I listened.

What should I wear to meet his parents? Apart from my school uniform and my new peacock blue felt skirt I only had my confirmation skirt that had been made from white parachute nylon provided by a neighbour who had saved it from his wartime job. With a white school blouse, it looked smart but hardly seemed right. I decided to buy some black velvet ribbon and sew three bands round the bottom of the skirt. Adding a little black bow at the neck of the white blouse and my black school belt I was quite pleased with the transformation.

"Come on," said Richard after church. "Please ride pillion to my house. I'll drive very carefully." Although scared, I climbed on the huge bike. Richard drove very carefully but I felt very vulnerable and much less safe than I felt on my pushbike.

We were soon at Richard's. He lived in a large semi-detached house near the park just about five minutes' walk from my house. As we pulled into the driveway Richard's parents opened the front door and held out welcoming hands. I hopped off the big bike as if I was used to riding pillion. To my horror I felt a cold draught round the top of my legs and looking down saw that my skirt had shrivelled up to the waist on one side. Richard looked embarrassed.

"Your skirt must have caught in the exhaust. I didn't know it was nylon," he said. I was mortified. "I just want to go home," I said. "I'll get my husband to drive you home in the car," said Richard's mother.

The next day, when I got home from school, the vicar was taking tea with my mother. He jumped to his feet and stood stiffly. "I have something dreadful to tell you Ann," he said. "That nice young man, Richard, who you seemed to be friendly with was killed this morning on his way to work. Nasty things these motorbikes," he said to my mother. "The funeral will be later this week."

I didn't go to the funeral. I'd never been to one and wasn't sure I knew what to do. Prayers were said at church on Sunday. I wrote a 'sorry' note to his mother. I didn't go to any more Thursday dances.

A FEW WEEKS later there was a knock on the front door. Opening it, I saw a rather plump boy scout. "It's not Bob-a-Job week, is it?" I said.

"No," said the Boy Scout. "My name is Alan Leach. I was Richard's best friend. He told me all about you and said you were his girlfriend. I didn't see you at the funeral, you must have been too upset. I just came to say that if you want someone to take you out I'll do it. No strings!"

I looked at the Boy Scout. He was quite a bit shorter than I was and had very hairy knees showing between his long socks and long shorts. He was carrying his scout's hat and had unfashionable slicked back dark hair. It was kind of him to call but I couldn't imagine myself going out with him. I thanked him but said I had a lot of studying to do for the School Certificate year.

"I'm doing my School Certificate this year too. Maybe we could study together," said the scout. "What are you doing?"

"Maths, science, geography, history, religion, French, English literature and English language," I said.

"Me too," said the scout.

I felt uncomfortable. The young man was trying hard to be pleasant. I heard myself say "I must be going," and felt a real heel. The young man smiled. "Oh well, if you change your mind," he said and was off.

How funny. He didn't even tell me how I could contact him. It was obviously his good deed for the day. He called a week later with an invitation to the pictures. I said I was busy studying. He called two or three more times. Each time he smiled pleasantly and said he'd call again. I found out that he was a student at the boy's grammar school. He looked taller and slimmer in his school uniform.

Eventually, I felt sorry for him and accepted. We went to see Judy Garland in 'Born in a Trunk'. We had coffee later and talked about the future. I said I was going to stay at school until I was 18 then go to university. Alan was aiming to leave school at 16 and get an apprenticeship, he hoped at de Havilland like Richard.

5 The Met Office

THE LAST MILE to the aerodrome was all downhill. I asked the RAF guard on the gate for the Meteorological Office. I was directed to an old hangar that still had brown and green camouflage markings from the War. Once inside, I asked for the duty officer. A young man in a knitted fairisle pullover looked up from a chart.

"Hello," he said, with a big smile. "So you're the young lady who wants to join the Met Office? I was told you were coming. What can I tell you?"

"Everything," I said.

"Well we are what's called an outstation," said the young man. "We provide local forecasts for this aerodrome. We take readings for the local records every three hours. Would you like to see our instruments?"

He took me outside to the weather station. There was a white painted box with louvered sides about 3 feet by 2 feet and 4 feet high standing on white painted metal legs. The hinged sides swung open to reveal wet and dry bulb thermometers to measure humidity, a normal thermometer, an aneroid barometer with a pen trace chart and other gadgets and gauges I did not recognise.

"Over there is our anemometer," said the young man, pointing to a pole with three little cups on sticks on the top that were whizzing round in the stiff breeze. "That measures wind speed. It's linked to a chart inside the hut. To measure wind direction we look at the windsock over there. And to measure rain we have a rain gauge," he said, pointing to a black pot in the ground a short distance away.

"This is what all the girls like," he said pointing to what looked like a witch's crystal ball on a concrete plinth.

"What is it?" I asked.

"It's a sunshine recorder. The ball focuses the sun's rays and burns a trace onto a card behind the ball. We have a 'sun profile' to show objects that get in the path of the passage of the sun across the sky at different times during the year. For each day we know how many hours of sun we could get as opposed to what we do get. We're lucky here. There is very little blocking the sun because the aerodrome is flat, but in the winter the sun rises behind that clump of trees over there so we lose about an hour of sun each morning.

"We also have to record cloud type and height. Sometimes you can estimate cloud base and height but often we let off a weather balloon to get a more accurate reading of what the wind's doing at higher altitudes. Today, we've got some cumulus, those big fluffy clouds up there. I bet they'll turn into cumulonimbus later this afternoon and we might get thunder."

"What do you do with the information?" I asked.

"Well our real job is to give local forecasts for the pilots who are flying in and out of this aerodrome or local businesses. The information all goes to Head Office every three hours by teleprinter and they use it to make long and short term forecasts for the whole country and provide statistics for companies and other government departments. You see the forecasts in the newspaper and hear them on the radio.

"Why do you want to work for the Met Office?" he asked me.

"Well I'm going to be a scientist. I'm going to go to Oxford or Cambridge and get a PhD. My parents couldn't afford to send me to university. I have a younger twin brother and sister and Mum and Dad need me to bring in money to help with the household bills. I found out that the Met Office gives you time off to get a degree. I've got my 'O' levels, I've got to get my Advanced level GCE yet but I'll get it. Then I'll get into university and do a maths degree."

"How old are you?" asked the young man.

"I was 17 a few weeks ago," I said.

"Come on, it's time to put the kettle on for a cup of tea. We drink lots of tea on outstations," said the young man.

I RACED HOME on my bike. It was uphill for the first part and the wind was against me. I could see the storm clouds gathering. I arrived home flushed from the ride. I told my mother I'd decided to take the job with the Met office. My brother and sister, the twins, were eight years younger than I was and idolised their big sister.

"I'm going to be paid about £6 a week," I told my family. "That's much more than the 15 shillings I'm getting at the shop for my Saturday job. I'll be able to give you at least a shilling each pocket money." Their eyes brightened and they smiled. Their big sister always looked after them.

"Don't be giving your money away too soon," Mum shouted from the kitchen. "Now you've got a real job you'll give me your pay packet each week just like your Dad and I'll give you back your pocket money. The twins are getting bigger and they cost us a lot to feed and keep."

I had already crossed my mother by insisting that I kept all the money from my Saturday job. My mother had retorted that if that was the way I wanted to play it I'd not get a penny for clothes or school outings or anything else I needed. I had existed for the past two years on that Saturday money. I thought myself fortunate that I was given samples of makeup and perfume and even belts and scarves from the store where I worked. I was also given odd lots of wool from which I knitted fairisle jumpers, gloves and hats for myself, and the twins and ends of material from Miss Errington's dress-maker from which I made dresses and skirts.

"I won't be getting a weekly pay packet," I said. "I'll be paid monthly."

"So you'll expect me to keep you in your first month," my mother retorted. "Well consider yourself paying board in arrears, Miss smarty pants. If you're getting £6 a week, you can give me £4."

"Well it isn't £6 a week. It's about £24 a calendar month and I'll have tax deducted and maybe other things. I can't agree to anything till I see what I get."

"I'm not having that," said my mother. "I want to know where I stand. It'll be £4 a week every week, or you'll find other digs. I can't think of anyone who would take you in for full board and lodging for £4 a week."

I FINISHED school at the end of July 1956, just after my 17th birthday. It felt odd – most girls left when they were 16. Those who stayed after 'O' levels would usually stay a further two years to complete 'A' levels and go on to university.

I had tried to leave school when I was 16 like my friends Pat and Babs, who had both gone to secretarial school for six months to learn shorthand and typing. They both now had jobs as secretaries. Pat was working at the BBC and Babs had a job at the Design Centre. I had been offered a proper job working for the department store where I worked on a Saturday. I was to train as a buyer, like Miss Errington, but when I tried to leave school the headmistress had called my mother to the school and persuaded her to keep me at school until I was 18 and then go to university.

"She's much too bright to work in a shop," my headmistress said.

"It's not really working in a shop," I said proudly. "I'm going to train to be a buyer."

"I worked in a shop," said my mother, not letting on that she had worked in a shop for all of three weeks.

"Ann is made for better things," said my headmistress. "We don't often get girls to Oxford or Cambridge but both Ann and Kathleen will get there, you'll see."

"We'll let her go another year and see what happens," said my mother. "I've got twins to support you know, and one is a boy. He's the one who should be going to university. The girls will get married. They don't need education. Boys don't like girls who are too smart."

But a year later, despite protestations from my headmistress, I left school in late July. I applied to join the government's Meteorological Office, always called the Met Office, and was accepted. I didn't start work until mid August, much to my mother's disgust. "I need a couple of weeks to get some new clothes made," I said.

ON MY FIRST day at the Met Office I cycled to work with Alan, who I now considered my boyfriend. He had left school at 16 and was working as a management trainee at the Kodak factory, right next door to the Met Office. The five miles from my house to work took about 20 minutes.

The last quarter mile to the entrance gate was along a dreary concrete driveway always in deep shadow from the tall Government Stationery Office building on the left-hand side. On the right-hand side, behind a high mesh wire fence covered in morning glory, steam trains belching black smoke and hot cinders puffed their way north to England's Midlands, leaving black smuts on people walking or cycling on the driveway. People who didn't cycle to work travelled by train or bus and walked up the long, bleak driveway. Very few people drove to work in cars. In the mid 1950s few people in England had cars.

As with every other Air Ministry building, passes were checked at the gate by two uniformed officers. If you forgot your pass you had to be signed in by the supervising officer, who resented having to leave his desk. Records were kept and transgressions noted and mentioned in annual appraisal reports along with records of lateness and other misdemeanours.

On my first day I had no pass. I didn't know the procedure. At the gate I told the duty officer that I was starting a new job and showed my appointment letter.

The two guards smiled. "It'll be nice to have a young lady here," said one. "I'll call the recruitment lady. I'm sure she'll sign you in."

A rather stern faced woman in a grey skirt, white blouse and navy blue cardigan signed me in. "The first thing we'll need to do is to get you a temporary pass. I'll get one of the men to take your photo for an official pass but it will take about a month to arrive. You mustn't give your pass to anyone but must keep it with you at all times when on Air Ministry premises.

"You can be challenged to show it at any time. First you have to sign the Official Secrets Act. I'll get someone to witness the signature. As a member of the Air Ministry staff you may handle secret documents or see or hear things that are important for the defence of our country. There are always people wanting to buy secrets, but remember you would be in prison for life or even executed for giving up official secrets!"

After the formalities I was taken up a flight of concrete stairs and along a gloomy corridor. The lino on the floor was grey. So were the brick walls. The corridor had no windows and light bulbs without shades hanging on twisted wires from the dirty white ceiling.

I hadn't realised the place I was to work would be so gloomy. My interview had been conducted in London in an elegant office in Holborn. We stopped by a grimy off-white door. The recruitment lady knocked.

"Come in," said a man's voice.

Inside the room were four desks. Two were face to face by the window with a third one facing those two. Between the cluster of three and the door was a desk that had been cleared. The walls of the room, like the corridors, were grey brick. The walls of this office were covered with charts and it was brightened by the pale summer sun that shone through the dirty windows, creating sunbeams in the dusty atmosphere. I noticed that where the walls met the ceiling they seemed to be set in a groove rather than being fixed to the ceiling as walls usually were.

"This is your new Scientific Assistant, Mr Browning," said the personnel lady, and she left.

The two men in the desks by the window jumped to their feet.

"Hello," said one, holding out his hand. "What's your name?"

"Ann."

"We can't call you that Miss ... er" said the man. "I'm Mr Browning so you will be Miss ..."

"Miss Hill," I said. "But I'd rather you called me Ann."

"That wouldn't do," said Mr Browning. "We can't be that informal. You're part of the Air Ministry professional staff. Only the cleaners, the tea lady and the industrial staff are called by their first names." I felt very important and very grown up.

"This is Mr Johnson and this is Mr Overton," said Mr Browning. The other two men in the room nodded. "You've come at the right time. I can hear the tea lady. We have to go to the end of the corridor to get our tea. Have you brought a cup?"

"I didn't know I had to," I said.

"You can have the visitor's cup today but see you bring your own tomorrow," said Mr Browning, giving me a grimy chipped mug just like the one at the aerodrome.

After collecting their morning tea and buttered buns, the two older men read newspapers and Mr Overton took out a maths book. I bought tea, which was a penny. Buns or rolls were tuppence extra. Morning tea lasted 15 minutes then the books and newspapers were put away.

Mr Overton showed me how to read a sunshine card. I was pleased I had seen a sunshine recorder at my 'interview' at the aerodrome. Each site had a profile that indicated where the sun was blocked from the recorder by trees or buildings. The profiles fitted over the card and the percentage of the scorch on the card to the possible sun scorch was calculated for each day and entered on a sheet. Mr Overton showed me that there appeared to be much more sun at Rhyl than at the nearby RAF station up the hill at Prestatyn.

"Rhyl's been burning their cards again," he announced. The two other men came and inspected the card carefully. "You can see the scorch is much darker and deeper and has square ends."

"Why would they do that?" I asked.

"Rhyl is a seaside place and boasts it's very sunny to attract the visitors, but we can check with the RAF station at Prestatyn up the road. Many of the seaside places burn their cards to pretend they have more sun than they really have, but we usually catch them."

Mr Overton checked each card. He sat very close to me and breathed his foul smelling breath all over me. I was very glad when Mr Browning said it was 12 o'clock and he was going to wash his cup.

Lunch was taken in the canteen. Staff queued up. It was like a school lunch, with meat and two veg with jam sponge and custard for pudding. Lunch was ninepence. The four of us from my office sat together and the men made polite small talk, mainly about the weather and the cricket.

AFTER LUNCH THE men went into the garden and read their newspapers or books until the lunch break ended at 1.30. I noticed there were some girls sitting chatting on the garden seats but none as young as I was.

Back in the office, I heard female laughter from the adjoining room. The door opened and two women in their early 20s came in.

"We heard you've got a new girl," said one. "Hello, what's your name?"

"Miss Hill is our new Scientific Assistant," said Mr Browning.

"Do you play netball? We play on the roof at lunch time. We usually bring sandwiches from home or get a roll at morning tea and eat after we play. The canteen is stuffy and it's nice and sunny on the roof. My name's Iris," said one of the girls.

"This is Mrs Jameson and this is Mrs Shelley," said Mr Browning sternly. "They are statisticians. They keep our records. They've been quiet this morning but they usually make so much noise we can hardly work in here."

"We've been down in the basement filing," said Iris.

"Well thank you for the visit ladies. Now we all have to get back to our work," said Mr Browning.

Mr Overton and I returned to the sunshine cards. Mr Browning was reading a book while Mr Johnson poured over a chart.

That afternoon Mr Johnson said he thought I needed a break from sunshine cards and he had a little job for me. He took me to a room at the end of the corridor where there were shelves of stationary. He pulled out a few postcards and some envelopes.

"Our volunteer observers send us temperature readings on these cards," he said. " Someone ordered the cards bigger than the envelopes so each card needs about a quarter of an inch cut off it. Here is a guillotine. It's very sharp. so be careful. Just chop as many as you can. Be careful not to ruin the cards — they cost money." With that he was gone.

I examined the cards and the guillotine. I chopped a few singly. I chopped a few in twos then in threes. I found that if I hopped up on the table and sat next to the guillotine I could put more force onto the handle of the guillotine and thus chop ten at a time. The pile of chopped cards mounted quickly.

Mr Johnson popped his head round the door. "How's it going?" he grinned. I leapt off the desk. Slivers of my skirt fell to the floor. I stood red faced with a large chunk of my skirt on the floor in pieces at my feet.

"I thought I was doing so well," I said.

"Mmm," said Mr Johnson. "Good job it's time to go home. I'll fetch you some bulldog clips to hold your skirt together while you go down the corridor. I'll get your bag from the office so you don't have to go in there. I'll tell them you finished and I sent you home a bit early, this being your first day."

I was mortified. My first day at real work wasn't anything like I expected. The people were stuffy and the work wasn't very interesting. I was worried about how much I would have to spend on food and now I'd ruined my skirt. I slunk down to the bike racks glad I was going home early so people wouldn't see my cut skirt.

Alan was waiting at the end of the driveway. I cried. "It was horrid and I've ruined my skirt," I said.

"My first day wasn't much fun either," he confessed. "The men kept sending me errands for stuff that didn't exist and then they laughed at me. I've been there a year and it does get better. Come on, I'll race you home."

IT DID GET BETTER. I was sent on lots of courses to learn about the weather, which I found fascinating. I learned statistical techniques such as correlation and regression analysis. I met the Chief Climatologist, a middle aged Scottish woman called Miss Dingle, who worked three offices away along the corridor and was a qualified forecaster but did not want to work on an outstation. I found out there were only two qualified women forecasters and because the rules said women had to work in pairs on the night shift, and neither of them wanted to do shift work, no women worked on outstations. "Perhaps you'll be the first, deary," said Miss Dingle.

Miss Dingle took me to the basement to see the archives. It smelt musty. There were records going back hundreds of years. It gave me a thrill to hold notebooks from the 1600s. The people who had written in them seemed very real. There were notes written in scrawly, copperplate writing. One stated 'The water in the water closet was frozen for the 10th day'. Others recorded the winter when the river Thames was frozen over and there was an ox roast on the river. Information on weather was set down amongst details of expenditure and what the writer had for dinner.

I met Dr Aloysius Bleasedale, the Head of the Met Office. He was a tall thin man with a hooked nose. I also met Major Thompson, who shared an office with Miss Dingle. He had spent most of his life in India and had been posted back to England for medical reasons. I made friends with the young women who worked in the next office and played netball with them at lunchtime. Sometimes I cycled with them to the local shops.

I learnt from Iris and Rita that it was not good to be left alone in the office with Mr Overton because he could not be trusted. He 'goosed' the girls. I found out that goosed meant putting his hand up the girls' skirts and groping, although he never tried to do it to me. I also saw that he watched the girls playing netball at lunchtime in their divided skirts.

"He's horrid," said Rita. "No one would ever look at him twice and he smells awful. We have complained many times that he tries to touch us, grabbing at our breasts when he thinks no one is looking and pushing himself against us but the men say we ask for it by wearing short skirts to play netball. They say it arouses the young men.

"When we tell the recruitment officer she says we have to put our complaint in writing in triplicate to Dr Bleasedale. Then they'd hold an inquiry and we'd end up being blamed anyway. They might even stop us from playing netball at lunchtime."

6 Alan Leach

I **WAS DETERMINED** to get my 'A' level GCEs in the same time as the girls at school and to start university when I was 18. I could take Geography at Technical College in Harrow and managed to pass by the end of first term, six months ahead of the other girls at school.

I had to choose a continent to study, so I went to the local library and found that books on Europe took up a whole bookcase. Books on India took up three shelves, as did Asia. North America took nearly as much space as Europe but South America took up just one shelf. I decided to make my major area of study South America because I felt I could read all those books, I passed Geography with distinction and dreamed of someday going to see the wonders of South America.

The nearest Technical College where Pure Maths, Applied Maths and Physics could be taken was in Acton, a 40 minute cycle ride from work. I was allowed to leave work early so that I could get a meal before the class started at 6pm. The class finished at 9pm so I didn't get home till just before 10pm.

I decided that evening classes on four nights a week plus homework and my Saturday job was too much so I dropped Physics and took only Pure Maths, Applied Maths and Geography. This would still give me the 3 'A' levels I needed for university entrance.

BY CHRISTMAS I really felt part of the Met Office family. At the Christmas party I was amazed to watch many of the senior staff singing a mock opera they had written themselves. Several of the staff who played instruments formed an orchestra which accompanied the singers.

On Saturdays I still went to work for Miss Errington. On Saturday evening I would go to the pictures or to a dance with Alan. Sometimes we would meet with others and go by train to a coffee shop in London. The favoured coffee shop was the Heaven and Hell in Soho. Upstairs was full of light and brightness, painted white with lots of angels and gold trimmings. Downstairs was very dark and the walls were painted red and black. I always had to be home by 10pm.

On Sundays Alan and I usually went to early morning communion. After breakfast we would go for a cycle ride, sometimes with a group of people but more often just by ourselves, we would take a picnic and our books to study. Alan was studying for his City and Guilds exams. In the evening we attended evensong, then walked home together. It was a comfortable relationship. We liked the same things and helped each other to study.

We planned to cycle to Lands End for our two week summer holiday. We would stay in youth hostels. My parents were horrified. It was not done for a girl and boy to go on holiday together except in a group like the church cycling group, which my parents did when they were courting.

What would people think? I might get into trouble, then who would marry me? They were already worried I was too bookish. I sat in the corner of the lounge room studying on the nights I was home. I couldn't study in the bedroom because my little sister went to bed at 7pm.

"Blue stocking, blue stocking," my father would shout. "No boy will ever want to marry you. You've always got your nose stuck in a book."

"You should be going out with a proper boyfriend and enjoying yourself like other girls of your age," my mother would add. "It's not right you going round with that Alan. He only comes up to your shoulder. You look very silly together. If God had meant you to be boyfriend and girlfriend, He'd have made him taller than you!"

"I like him," I said. "He's kind and clever and helps me with my study. We enjoy the same things and have lots of fun cycling."

"Oh let them go," said my father. "They're only kids. Nothing will happen. They're both too young to know what to do."

But my father was wrong. It was more than just friendship. Even before I left school, at the boys' school dances couples paired off and scurried into the dark of the unlit classrooms. There was the hissed 'go away' from couples who thought they had found a classroom all to themselves. There was much giggling as those hunting for a quiet corner of their own tripped over couples on the floor. There was the contented sound of heavy breathing once newcomers had settled. Every now and again there was a sharply whispered 'No!' or a softly sighed 'Don't stop now ...'

Afterwards the girls compared notes. No girl but the most forward made a move on a boy. It was her place to feign horror at what the boy was trying to do. It was also her place to cry 'stop' when it looked like he was going too far. It was her fault if he did.

If the boy somehow just slipped it in there was the possibility of getting him to pull it out before anything happened, but that was risky. The girls knew that just one drop of semen even on a lavatory seat could make you pregnant. Pregnancy brought shame. There were many young marriages with babies born soon after in the 1950s. I liked being cuddled and kissed. I liked the touching in the dark. Alan was a good boy. He wouldn't go too far.

JUST BEFORE Christmas a new girl, Ena, joined Rita and Iris in their office next door to ours. Ena was beautiful. Her smile brought sunshine into every room. Her sing-song voice made people smile. She was large and round and very black. I hadn't been that close to a black person except for the beautiful Indian girl in my class at school who people whispered was an Indian princess. Rani, the girls had found, was Hindi for 'queen'. But Rani was at our school for only two months. Rumours were that she had gone back to India to get married. Rani wasn't really black but a pale coffee colour. Ena was shiny enamel black.

She was from Jamaica. She was a qualified weather forecaster and had come to England to be with her boyfriend, Hector, while he studied at the London School of Economics. Hector was the son of the Jamaican Prime Minister. I found out that although Ena and Hector were not married they shared a flat. I was too embarrassed to ask if they shared a bed. Ena was a churchgoing Christian so of course they wouldn't share a bed! I had my suspicions though.

Ena sang like an angel at the Met Office choir at the Christmas party and had introduced me to the very handsome Hector. Hector was tall and lean and not quite as black as Ena. He held Ena very closely as they danced and looked at her lovingly whenever she spoke. Ena said they would go back to Jamaica when Hector got his Masters degree at the end of the year. They would have a huge society wedding.

After Christmas I asked my mother if I could bring my new friends to Sunday tea. When Ena and Hector knocked at the door I welcomed them warmly and took them into the lounge room to meet my parents. They recoiled in horror. I realised I had not mentioned they were black. Ena held out her hand and turned on her big sunny smile. My mother tentatively took the hand limply and was horrified that Ena came close and kissed her warmly on the cheek. Hector offered his hand to my father and said, "Nice to meet you, Sir," My father seemed to stand taller. He wasn't used to being called Sir.

My mother and father bustled out of the room, my father to his shed and mother to get the tea ready. Ena offered to help with the tea.

"No, you just stay there and talk to Ann and the twins," said my mother.

"I've heard all about these twins," said Ena. "We might have twins, Hector, it would be lovely. I want lots of your babies."

My mother busied herself with the high tea. Ham salad with bread and butter and home made cakes and jam tarts. She called Dad from his shed and sat the twins at the table. The twins just stared at Ena and Hector. How would these strange looking people eat their tea?

My father tried to make conversation by saying he worked at Lyons. Where did Hector work? I was going to say Hector didn't 'work'. Hector saved the day by saying, "Joe Lyons? Me wok dere mon, at the Corner House."

"What do you do there?" asked my father.

"Me wash up on a Saturday night. They let me off tonight cos I said I was visiting you. You must be very important cos they said I could have the night off."

Ena giggled. I didn't understand but Ena put her finger to her lips and said, "Hush chile. Eat up ya tea, Ann. It's a very nice tea Mrs Hill. Me Mum makes good home bake food. I miss me Mum."

My mother and father visibly relaxed. These two black people were obviously like the heathen children that they gave pennies for in my Church Missionary Society moneybox.

As soon as tea finished Ena and Hector insisted on washing up. "It's what I do," said Hector. "C'mon Ann, you can dry."

As soon as they finished washing up, much to the relief of Mum and Dad, Ena said they needed to get off home.

"Well, they seemed quite nice," said Mum when they'd gone. "And she smelled of perfume. Most of those black people smell of sweat."

"I didn't like him," said Dad. "Slimy bloke. See how he tried to crawl to me by calling me Sir? Fancy bringing a black boy who washes up at Lyons to our house, Ann."

I could contain myself no longer. "He's the son of the Prime Minister of Jamaica and is here on a scholarship to the London School of Economics."

"And I'm King Tut," said my father. "You're so gullible, Ann. You'd be taken in by anyone and you think you're so clever. All your schooling at that posh school and those books you read don't even give you normal common sense like most folks."

I WAS NEVER very sure what the ladies in the next office, Rita and Iris, actually did. I asked several times as we ate our sandwiches together after netball on the roof.

"You wouldn't want to know, Ann, it's very boring. Anyway, we're trying to forget that and enjoy a break in the sun," they would say.

But one day Rita and Iris told me that they joined the Met Office as Scientific Assistants but had to resign when they got married and come back as wages staff. They knew they would never get promoted and were not allowed to continue to study for Assistant Executive Officer grade, the theory being that they would soon get pregnant and have to leave the service. No young women with children worked at the Met Office, although it seemed that older women like the tea lady were allowed.

Whenever I went into their office, Rita and Iris seemed to be knitting or laughing over letters in a women's' magazine. Often they wouldn't be in their office at all. "Probably in the basement filing," I would tell myself.

Sometimes one or the other would be madly pounding an adding machine that made a dreadful noise. I prided myself that I was able to add up correctly without using a machine, although I'd never used one. When I took 'the figures' to the accounts department in the store I worked in on Saturdays I watched the clerks using an adding machine.

One day Iris asked Mr Johnson if she could show me how to use the machine. It seemed very simple, just enter the number and turn the handle. I found that turning the handle backwards subtracted the entered number. Turning the handle several times multiplied the number by the number of times the handle was turned. Moving the number to the left a place and adding multiplied by 10 times the multiplier; moving the number two places and turning multiplied by 100.

This was all magic. I even found I could do long division by continued subtraction. Previously I had only used log tables at school to do arithmetic on big numbers. This adding machine was very clever. I loved the delicious way the answer register could be set to all 9s then, when 1 was added, all the digits rolled over with a ripple effect to all zeros.

Iris and Rita could operate the adder very quickly. They showed me that although they were fast, calculations had to be done twice by two different people to ensure accuracy.

MY FIRST YEAR at the Met Office was exhausting. There was so much to learn; so many people to learn about. At school there were only two types of people, girls and teachers. Outside school there were boys who all seemed to be slightly different. There were those you liked and those you didn't. And then there were parents. There seemed to be two types of parents, those who were like your own and those who were different.

But at work there were many different types of people. The professionals were called Mr or Miss. Non-professionals, known as wages staff, were people like the tea lady, the gatemen and the mechanics, who wore brown lab coats and mended meteorological instruments in the basement. They were all called by their first names. Wages staff bowed their heads or the men tipped their caps when greeting the professionals. It made me feel very special to be called 'Miss'.

Some professionals were very important people like Dr Bleasdale, the head of the Met Office. On the rare occasions when Dr Bleasdale visited our office the men all stood up. Dr Bleasedale would speak only to Mr Browning. It was as if the others in the room didn't exist.

When Dr Bleasdale left the room we all resumed our seats and Mr Browning would tell us what Dr Bleasedale had said even though we had all heard. Then he would then tell us what Dr Bleasedale had meant by what he said. We all agreed it was very good of Dr Bleasedale to come to our office rather than calling Mr Browning to see him.

Whenever the men left the office they would put on their suit jackets. The Major and some ex army types wore a regimental blazer outside their office. In their own offices some men wore white cotton jackets, and some worked in just their shirtsleeves. The men didn't bother to put their jackets on to go through the adjoining office door to the office where Iris and Rita worked, but of course they were wages staff. I noticed that when Ena joined Iris and Rita, even though she was an Assistant Executive Officer and a qualified forecaster, the men still didn't wear their jackets.

The etiquette surrounding the wearing of jackets puzzled me. I discussed it with Miss Dingle. She always wore suits and always kept her jacket on. Sometimes she would wear a twin set with pearls and a skirt, but that was very rare.

"You're a young lady, Ann. So long as you are neat and tidy and don't wear shorts or trousers or a blouse with a low neck you'll be fine. It's important that young ladies don't wear anything that provokes men to think of them as anything but a work colleague. I worry that you girls wear shorts when playing netball on the roof at lunchtime. It leads the men on and takes their minds off their work. It's not fair to their wives.

"You always look very nice, dear, in your waspie belt and tight sweater. I know it's the fashion and I suppose you can't help being pretty and having a small waist and a big bust, but being the only young lady here you have a duty not to be provocative."

It had never occurred to me that I might have given offence. At the shop on Saturday, all the girls had to wear plain black dresses and were sent home without pay to change if the dressed inappropriately. After my chat with Miss Dingle I tried to moderate my dress. I owned a suit but that was for

Sunday church. I bought a twin set and tried to look like Miss Dingle. Iris and Rita laughed.

"Old bat. No one would look twice at her, except the Major. That's probably why she never married. She was probably born in a suit. Wear what you like, Ann. It's the men's fault if they get all hot and bothered if they see a pretty girl at work. Tells you a bit about their home lives and what their wives look like!"

7 Sunshine to rain

I TOOK MY Pure and Applied Maths Advanced Level GCE in June, just as the girls who had stayed on at school were doing. I was confident of passing 'A' level Geography which I took and passed at the end of the previous year.

But Maths at night school was much more difficult. I had to cycle ten miles on a busy road, do a three hour class and cycle home. I didn't get home until 10pm and was often too tired to eat. I was looking forward to our holiday.

Alan and I had planned our two week trip well. We would cycle to Lands End in ten days and come back by train. The weather was good until we got to our second night's stop at Corfe Castle, then the rain started.

The next day was bright and sunny. We rode the A30 on the crest of the hill along the south coast of England. The views were spectacular. The blue sea sparkled and the wind was at our backs. We took side trips down the steeply sloping roads to explore the tiny villages nestling in the sleepy coves. We ate a lunch of fresh baked bread and local cheese on the beach below beautiful Lulworth Cove with its great sea sculptured arch.

A short ride further and we walked along the pebbles of Chesil Beach. By late afternoon, we arrived at the Litton Cheney youth hostel which was an old cheese factory. Originally a single room, the hostel was now divided into three parts by flimsy hardwood partitions. The girls' dormitory was at one end, the boys' at the other. The mid section, where the warden slept, was the communal area with sitting and dining areas.

The hostel was full. There were a couple of girls we had met at the Basingstoke hostel where we'd stayed on our first night out from home, and a group of Canadian university students on a walking holiday.

It was a lovely warm summer night. We all decided to go to the local pub. At the pub we ordered half pints of scrumpy. The Canadians asked what scrumpy was and were told that was cider, fermented apple juice, and that all the drips from the overflows from the pub's glasses go into the scrumpy vat.

"Sounds harmless," said the tallest of the Canadian men. "Give us all a big glass of your quaint old English apple juice."

We tried to tell the Canadians that scrumpy was very alcoholic, but it was a hot night and they were thirsty. Soon they were very drunk. The tallest Canadian tried to grope me. I told him I was with my boyfriend.

"Are you married?" he said. "Are you on your honeymoon?" Backing away and searching the room for Alan, I said, "No."

"Oh, a sort of little honeymoon before you get married!" he leered. "Come on, leave her alone," said Alan. "You're drunk. Better go back to the hostel and sleep it off."

We made our way noisily down the road towards the hostel but the hostel door was firmly shut. It was after 10pm. We banged on the door but the warden refused to open up. "Psst," came a noise from the open window in the girls' dorm. It was the two young girls, who had gone to bed early. "The girls can get in through the window."

The boys wanted to get in through the window too but the girls were adamant. They would probably get their YHA membership cancelled if boys were found in the girls' dorm. The boys slept outside on the grass but it was a noisy night as the drunken Canadians kept trying to get in through the girls' window.

THE NEXT STOP was Ottery St Mary, just outside of Exeter, an old rectory which was supposed to be haunted. Then came the gruelling ride up to Dartmoor. The wind and rain were now driving directly into our faces. We were very pleased to arrive at the next youth hostel just as low cloud was settling into the valleys between huge piles of mossy boulders.

The whole place was shrouded in an eerie fog. We were greeted by the two young girls who had let me in to the dormitory the night before. The hostel had a part time warden who came only to open the youth hostel and cook the evening meal.

The two young girls had arrived earlier in the day. "The prison is just a few miles away," they told us. "If the fog hadn't come down you could see it from here. We're not keen on leaving the main door open, but the warden said to leave it unlocked. Dartmoor is a prison for the criminally insane. People do escape, and we'd rather they didn't escape to here."

The girls had eaten so we took stew from the big pot left on the stove. After washing up we all decided to turn in. The next morning we woke to the bright call of the warden. She had come to get our breakfast. It was a bright sunny day and soon we were off downhill and into Cornwall. We passed close to the prison and stopped for lunch on an ancient clapper stone bridge where wild Dartmoor ponies ate our spare stale bread.

Cornwall was more pretty little villages. We stopped the night at Lostwithiel, then cycled on to Mevagissey, Polpero, Helston and Mousehole. We walked across the causeway at low tide to St Michael's Mount. Then it was on to Penzance.

Lands End was rough and wild. The sea crashed onto the rocks. There was a signpost showing the distance to London and other world capitals. We took some photos, bought some ice cream, then it was back to Penzance for the night and the train back to London the next day.

When we arrived back home we felt a real sense of achievement. We had cycled to Lands End. It would be John o' Groats the next year, at the very north of Scotland.

MY GCE RESULTS were waiting for me on my return. I was pleased to see I had passed Applied Maths but was disappointed, although not surprised, to have failed Pure Maths. I would have to continue night school at Acton Tech. Maybe I could take Pure Maths in October.

The first day back at work there was a tap at the office door. Dr Bleasedale popped his head in. Everyone stood up. "It's Miss Hill I want to speak to," he said. This was a real surprise. Usually he only spoke to Mr Browning.

This time Dr Bleasedale spoke directly to me. "You might have noticed we've had a wet summer," said Dr Bleasedale. "There is now more work in hydrology than here in sunshine. So my little ray of sunshine will have to become a raindrop. Mr Browning, please take Miss Hill down to Dr Grindley in Hydrology. He's expecting her." With a flash of a benign smile towards me, he was gone.

Mr Johnson and Mr Overton started talking together as soon as Dr Bleasedale had left the room. "She's our Scientific Assistant. Who will do her work if she goes?" Mr Browning said he hadn't been consulted about the move so didn't know the answer to their question. He promised to go to see Dr Bleasedale after he'd taken me to Dr Grindley.

"I don't want to go," I said. "I like it here. Dr Grindley is supposed to be very grumpy. He never smiles when we stand in the queue for tea or lunch."

"But you don't have a choice," said Mr Browning. "Dr Grindley isn't that bad and he's supposed to be very clever. You'll see another side of the Met Office. Get your things together and we'll walk down the corridor."

Mr Browning knocked on the door of Dr Grindley's room. There was a gruff 'Enter' from inside. The room was the same layout as all the offices but there were only two people in the room. Dr Grindley sat in the senior's position that Mr Browning occupied in his office. Both the desk opposite Dr Grindley and the desk on the end were unoccupied.

At a desk sat a tall, pale faced lad with dark hair. Mr Browning introduced me as Miss Hill. To my amazement Dr Grindley stood up and extended his hand in welcome.

"Ann isn't it?" he beamed. "This is your desk." He motioned to the desk opposite his own. "And this is Mr Lloyd, our Scientific Assistant." Mr Lloyd stood up and shook hands formally. Mr Browning nodded to Dr Grindley, turned on his heel and was gone.

I was amazed to be given the coveted '2IC' desk by the window, opposite the senior officer. How was this going to work? Surely Mr Lloyd was more senior than I was. And where were the other officers?

"Brian, show Ann how to plot up this month's rainfall," said Dr Grindley when the door closed. Brian Lloyd took out a large printed map of the British Isles and a box full of postcards.

"We get rainfall readings from about 500 amateur observers all over the British Isles," he said. "These are plotted on the map in addition to results from official weather stations. We also get travelling sheets from local councils."

The travelling sheets were foolscap pages kept together by a tag through a hole punched in the corner of each sheet. I learned that after plotting on the map, there were returned to the owners for the next month's records.

Brian started plotting the results in pencil. "Dr Grindley checks them, then I ink them in. Sometimes the observers get their readings wrong. If they are wrong too often we send an inspector out to check what they are doing.

"On the moors, hikers often use the gauges as a place to spend a penny. They seem to think that's what they are for. In other places, a gauge can get knocked over by a cow or wild animal or a plant can grow up and cover the gauge with its leaves. The observers are supposed to make notes of things that could affect a reading but they often don't."

"How do you know where to plot the figures?" I asked.

"All the observing stations are plotted on that map on the wall but you soon remember where they are. I rarely look at the wall map now.

"When we've plotted all the observations, Dr Grindley draws isohyets to connect places of equal rainfall. He can tell if a reading looks suspect and sometimes we telephone the observer to check. There might have been a thunderstorm that dumped a lot of rain in a very small area but more usually the observer has not read the gauge properly.

"We use the maps to calculate how much water has fallen in each catchment area and, taking into account the evaporation and seepage, we can calculate the water that reaches the rivers. We sell a lot of the data and provide information that assists with the siting of new reservoirs."

"Why has he let me sit in the desk opposite to him and where are the others from this office?" I asked when Dr Grindley left the room.

"You'll find out soon enough. He'll try to get you to do his work because he's writing a book. He tried to get me to do it but my Mum said I wasn't to do it. He's a Senior Executive Officer, and that's several levels above us.

"He gets paid much more than we do. He's probably getting paid for writing his book too. My Mum says that's stealing and he'll be found out and get the sack.

"Mr O'Kane is also part of this office but he spends most of his time out in the field checking up on the observers, so we rarely see him. Dr Grindley goes out inspecting too but not very often. His book is overdue and he gets cross if the work interferes with his writing."

I scurried down the corridor to tell my friends I'd been moved. "What's Dr Grindley like?" they asked. "He always looks so grumpy."

"He seems very nice," I said. He's put me to sit in the 2IC desk. I thought Mr Lloyd would be cranky but he doesn't seem to mind."

"He's a real mummy's boy" said Iris. "It's 'Mum says this' and 'Mum says that'. He'll never leave home and get married."

When I got home I told my mother I had a new job. I described Brian Lloyd and where he lived. "That mummy's boy! His mother is a real harridan. She's big and fat and never wears makeup. She's so bossy and her husband is a little runt of a man. Henpecked, too, I bet," said Mum.

I FOUND WORKING with Dr Grindley opened up a whole new world. He was writing a book on statistics for the Chinese market. I didn't ever find out why he was writing the book or how he had learned to write in Chinese.

He patiently taught me how to do his work, including how to calculate the flow of the river Thames over Teddington Weir that was published each month in the Times newspaper, how to calculate the water to be collected in a catchment area to site a new reservoir, how to tell if a particular rainfall reading was suspicious. I felt very proud that 'my' information was published in the Times. I learnt how to apply the calculus I had learned at school. Mathematics had become real, and useful.

I watched Brian stick carefully to his routine of plotting rainfall on the monthly map and posting traveling observations back to the water corporations. I wondered why he hadn't chosen to stretch himself and do the much more interesting things that Dr Grindley gave me to do.

Brian, for his part, constantly berated me for doing Dr Grindley's work and said that both he and his mother thought Dr Grindley was wrong to be writing a book and I was wrong in letting him get away with it. We both noticed that Dr Grindley kept a large blotter on his desk that he used to cover his manuscript when more senior members visited the office, so we both realised he didn't want his writing to be discovered.

One day the department took delivery of a new Monroe electronic calculator. This was very different from the mechanical calculators the department was using. It plugged into the electric power and calculated sums of squares as well as addition, subtraction, multiplication and division.

This magic machine cost £400, as much as a three bedroom house. At first only seniors were allowed to use the machine. Once he had read the instruction booklet, Dr Grindley taught me how to use it, but did not teach Brian. I was thrilled to watch the answer register roll over to all zeros on the hand calculators but watching this process on the Monroe was even more exciting. The whole carriage seemed to make a series of jumps until it settled with a quiver to its final resting place.

Dr Grindley was invited to India to forecast the onset of the monsoon. The Met Office was in quite a flurry, it was a real honour that one of their own had been invited to go to another country as a British expert. While he was away Brian and I were left to run the hydrology office.

I still had to calculate the flow of the Thames at Teddington Weir for the monthly Times statistics. Instead of using the mechanical calculator, I decided to use the Monroe. The final answer came to 5 followed by several zeros. 5 what? I was used to a result with several significant figures. I knew where to put the decimal point when there were several significant digits but I had never had an answer that gave just a 5.

If Dr Grindley had been available I could have asked him for help. If I had been more experienced I might have redone the calculation on the mechanical calculator. Somehow I felt that using the mechanical calculator was a backward step. I decided to send the figure 5 to the Times. They'd know how many zeros to put after the 5. The people at the Times simply printed the 5 as 5 million gallons a day flowing over the weir that month. During the next week there were several letters to the editor questioning the veracity of the number.

When Dr Grindley returned he was met with a pile of newspaper cuttings of the letters from Times readers and a request to retract the incorrect statistic and replace it with the correct figure. He roared with laughter.

"How did you get it so wrong, Ann? Well at least we know people read our statistics."

I felt foolish. "Never mind, Ann. You do your work and mine and, on the whole, you do it all very well. We're all allowed to make a mistake every now and again. The only people who don't make mistakes are those who will never learn anything new or are dead." He winked and nodded towards Brian as he spoke.

Later that day, Dr Grindley gave the department a talk about his work in India. He had developed a new forecasting method and had used it to forecast the onset of the monsoon to within four days, a great improvement on earlier forecasts. The Major remarked loudly to Miss Dingle that the natives could predict the onset of the monsoon to within half an hour. He said they would be sitting in the marketplace and would gather up their belongings and head for shelter, then you knew the rain would come. No one seemed to take notice of the Major. He was old style Met Office staff. Dr Grindley was their new hero. I felt proud to be working with him.

8 Trouble at home

MY HOME LIFE was becoming more difficult. It was hard to study at home and I hated the constant ridicule from my parents. "I don't know why you can't behave like a real girl Ann," my mother would say. "Most girls would be out dancing and finding themselves a husband. You'll be left on the shelf. That Alan Leach doesn't come up to your kneecap. You look very silly together. All that studying can't be good for you. All those numbers and those sums you do make you very boring."

The Met office tea lady, Mrs Rose, was a tiny wizened old woman who bustled and busied herself to serve everyone with tea and treats twice a day. She knew everyone's business. As a 12 year old girl she had been sent to work as a live in maid at Grimsdyke, the big house owned by WS Gilbert of Gilbert and Sullivan. She was at the house when, in 1911, WS Gilbert had been found in the lake in the grounds where he drowned following a heart attack while rescuing a young girl.

She could talk for ages about the parties at the big house, about the ladies dresses and the handsome men. She was left a legacy in WS Gilbert's will and had bought herself a large rambling house with the money. There was much speculation about why he had left her so much.

The house had eight bedrooms and she took in lodgers. Most were occupied long term by single men working at the Met Office. But there were always a couple of rooms left for young people who were sent from country weather stations to Head Office to prepare for exams.

Mrs Rose charged £3 a week for board and lodging. That included full bacon and egg breakfast each day, a cooked dinner each night, and lunch or sandwiches on Saturday and Sunday. There was a cosy formal drawing room with a large open fire where the lodgers could play cards, listen to the radio or watch the tiny television. Lodgers were not required to do any household chores except keep their rooms tidy for the cleaner. They could study all night if they wanted to.

I was giving my mother £4/10 a week and was expected to help around the house and wash up after the family meals. I could only study in the lounge room where either the radio was on or my mother was playing the piano. My parents were constantly bickering and I often received a slap across the head for misbehaving. I shared a double bed with my little sister. Life was far from tranquil.

I decided to pack up a few of my clothes and move in to Mrs Rose's big house. I did not to tell my mother I was going to move out because I felt sure she would find a way to stop me. I dare not tell my father because I was sure I'd get a good hiding. I didn't tell my brother and sister because I knew I couldn't face their sadness and apprehension that they would now bear the brunt of my father's nastiness.

I felt comfortable from the first day I arrived at Mrs Rose's house. I loved having my own room. It was sparsely furnished with lino on the floor. where my bedroom in my parent's house had carpet, but the bed was soft and the room was all my own. I could study all night if I wanted and there were no arguments.

THREE DAYS LATER, when I returned home to Mrs Rose's after work, as I put the key in the front door I was met by a very serious looking Mrs Rose. "You've got visitors, Ann. I've put them in the drawing room," said Mrs Rose.

I was apprehensive. Who could it be? Opening the door to the drawing room I was met by my mother and my brother and sister. My mother was dressed in her best coat and hat. She had a twin in each hand and they were crying. "Come home, Ann. Why did you leave home? I'm sure we can make you comfortable. The twins are missing you terribly. They cry all the time. Your Dad is furious and I need the money to help feed the family."

I was taken aback. I thought I had escaped to a better life. I didn't want to go back home. I didn't want to face up to a furious father. I had an extra £1/10 a week to spend and I got much better meals at Mrs Rose's. And I didn't have to wash up afterwards. I could study as much as I wanted to without ridicule and was enjoying a life without tension and bickering.

But I looked at my brother and sister and felt I had left them exposed to all that unpleasantness. They couldn't escape and at least when I was at home I could protect them from the worst of my father's bad temper. Reluctantly, I asked Mrs Rose if I could go back home. I had paid a month's board in advance. It had been hard saving the £12 and now I'd lost it but because I had paid my mother in advance at least I had a few weeks to make up the loss. I still had my Saturday job so life wouldn't be that hard. I packed my small suit case and went home on the bus with my mother. "I'll get my bike another time," I told Mrs Rose.

By Christmas tension in the household had become unbearable. The arguments between my parents got more and more bitter. Although my father never raised his hand to my mother, the twins were beginning to receive the odd slap about the head which had previously been reserved for me. They were ten years old now and about to sit for the entrance exam for secondary school. I was now treated less harshly as both parents feared that I might choose to leave home again.

Richard had a bad stutter and endured constant gibes from my father that he 'talked like a girl'. These were often accompanied by a thump to the head. Rosemary was made of sterner stuff and stood up for herself but she also took the odd slap across the head.

One time we were eating Sunday lunch in the usual complete silence (no one was ever allowed to speak at meals) with family favourites playing on the radio, she was slapped by her father for 'chewing in time to the music'. I protested but it was of little use.

ON CHRISTMAS EVE it all fell apart. My parents had an enormous argument. My sister and I huddled together in the double bed listening to raised voices from both parents. We heard our father say he was going throw himself under the train nearby.

I heard the front door bang and crept downstairs to see what was going on. I found her mother sitting on the lounge room floor surrounded by Christmas presents that she was trying to stuff into the pillow cases the twins had hung up for Santa.

My mother was red eyed. "I can't go on like this. I feel ill. I'm going to bed. You'll have to be Santa this year, Ann. Remember to eat a bit of mince pie and drink a bit of the port the kids left out for Santa." With that she went upstairs to bed.

I filled the pillowcases and went back upstairs looking in on Richard, who was sound asleep and tried to comfort a fretful Rosemary.

"Maybe Santa won't come," sobbed Rosemary.

"He will," I said. "He's been already and left full pillowcases. Now go to sleep or he'll send his fairies to take away all your presents and they won't be there in the morning."

The twins woke early. Mum and Dad were nowhere to be seen. "Mum wasn't well last night so we'll let her sleep," I said.

"Where's Dad?" asked Richard. I said, "I expect he's having a sleep in too."

The twins opened their presents. I got them breakfast. I laid a tray with tea and toast for my mother. Opening the door to my parent's room, I was surprised to see my mother sitting propped up on pillows with a trickle of blood at the corner of her mouth. This was serious. I tried to shake her awake, with no success.

I took the hand mirror from the dressing table and held it close to my mother's mouth, like I had seen done in the movies. A faint mist showed on the mirror, which meant my mother was still alive. Pills were strewn across the bed. They were the ones my mother took for her 'nerves'. I had been to the chemist earlier in the week and got a new prescription for my mother. The box said '100 tablets, one only to be taken each night. Keep out of the reach of children'.

I scooped up the tablets lying on the bed, the bedside table, on the floor and those left in the pill box. Only 15 left. Did that mean my mother had taken 85? I hurried downstairs, took two pennies and the list with the doctor's phone number from the phone pot by the front door and went to the public phone box on the opposite street corner.

I rang the doctor who appeared annoyed to be called early on Christmas morning. I sobbed my way through the story. My mother was hardly breathing and about to die.

"Where's your father?" the doctor asked abruptly. I told him he was nowhere to be found, not wanting to tell him about my parents argument.

"I'll be over when I've finished my rounds. See no one disturbs her and keep her warm," said the doctor. "She'll be dead by then," I sobbed.

"No she won't," said the doctor and hung up.

I returned to the house. The twins were playing with their Christmas presents and seemed not to care that they hadn't seen either parent. I went back upstairs. Mother hadn't moved.

I wondered if I should brush her hair and wash her face but thought better of it. I pulled the bedclothes further up towards her chin and sat on a chair by the bed watching my mother, who seemed to be made of wax and didn't look as if she was breathing. I tried the mirror trick again. There was still mist on the mirror.

By midday there was no sign of the doctor or our father. The twins would be getting hungry and expect Christmas dinner. I went downstairs and put the pork roast in the oven. I looked in on the twins who were still playing happily. The clock showed nearly 12.30. No doctor. Maybe I hadn't made it sound serious enough.

I wondered if I should call in help from Mrs Robinson across the street or Auntie Louie and Uncle Bill Wilburn from further down the road but thought our father might come home any time and be angry. I didn't know where to find a phone number for Auntie Eleanor and Uncle Joe in Newcastle, the only relatives with a telephone. Anyway they were 300 miles away.

AT 1PM THE DOCTOR'S big black car pulled up. The lace curtains across the street at the Robinson's twitched. I opened the front door. "Where is she?" the doctor asked brusquely. I led the way upstairs and opened our parent's bedroom door.

The doctor stood formally at the foot of the bed. "What brought this on?" he asked. I retold the conversation I had overheard. It sounded so silly. Had I heard it or dreamt it? "What shall we do with your parents, Ann?" said the doctor. "They behave like children."

The doctor made no attempt to examine mother. "Maybe she is dead and he knows that from looking at her," I thought. I had never seen a dead body.

"These are her extra strong pills," I said, worrying. "I got a new lot at the chemist only a few days ago. I picked up the ones I could find on the bed and the floor but it looks as if she might have taken about 80." The doctor laughed. He picked up the box and held it out to me. "Here, have some," he said.

I recoiled in horror. This must be a dream, I'd wake up soon. The doctor tipped a few pills onto his hand and threw them into his mouth. "Sugar pills," he said. "I've been giving them to her for years but you're not to tell her. You're old enough to understand."

He started writing a prescription on a pad he took from his bag. "I'm writing another prescription. It's for more sugar pills but a different colour. We'll tell her she's been a naughty girl and I've had to take her off her 'strong' ones because she tried to kill herself.

"I'll tell her she can't kill herself with her new ones. You must say the same and tell your father the same story. She'll sleep for about 24 hours. As soon as she wakes call me and I'll come round. If your father comes back tell him not to call me out again today and that he'll have to sleep somewhere else tonight."

With that he was gone. The twins looked anxious. What was the doctor here for?

"Are you hungry?" I asked them. "I'll just need to put some potatoes and carrots on for our dinner. I think there is Christmas pudding too but I don't know how to make it hot. Maybe we'll just have Christmas cake for pudding."

There was a knock at the front door. A very worried Mrs Robinson asked why the doctor had been called on Christmas Day. "Mum's had one of her turns and she's asleep," I said.

"Can I speak to your Dad?" said Mrs Robinson. "He's cooking dinner," I said. "Best not disturb him, he's a bit flustered. I think he drank too much beer last night." Mrs. Robinson tried hard to see past me but the kitchen door was closed. She thought of pushing in to see what was amiss but thought better of it.

"Call me if you want anything," she said and was gone.

After dinner the twins and I played some board games. We didn't dare to put the wireless on for fear of waking mother. I crept upstairs several times but she was still in the same position. I took a face flannel and gently washed the trickle of blood from my mother's mouth. She didn't stir.

It was 8pm when our father returned. He wasn't wearing his pyjamas, just his old gardening togs. He looked cold and hungry. "The twins are in bed asleep. Mum's got one of her headaches and gone to bed early. She said not to wake her and you are to sleep downstairs tonight," I said.

Dad looked sheepish. "I'll just go up and say hello," he said.

"The doctor has been and he says Mum's not to be disturbed," I said. "He gave her some sleeping pills and said you are not to talk to her until she wakes up. He'll come back tomorrow."

Dad looked like a little boy in trouble. "Okay," he whispered. "She must be bad if she called the doctor out on Christmas Day."

I asked him if he had eaten.

"No, but I'm not hungry," he said. He sat in his big chair by the fire and was soon asleep. I went upstairs and looked in on my still sleeping mother before sliding in bed next to my little sister.

THE NEXT DAY I got up very early. I looked in on mother. She was still asleep. I crept downstairs. Dad was still asleep and snoring. The fire was out and the house was cold. I crept back into bed. When it was nearly light the twins started to wake.

"You better play in here until I find out what mood Dad is in," I said. "I'll go downstairs and get you some toys."

Downstairs, Dad was nowhere to be seen. The drawing room curtains had been drawn back and a new fire was crackling in the grate. Looking into the back garden I could see him in the garden shed. I brought the twins downstairs by the fire and gave them breakfast. I looked in on mother, who had slumped down the bed, covered herself with the eiderdown and was now snoring. I crept out to the phone box and rang the doctor.

"I'll be right round," he said, much more brightly then yesterday. "Is your father home yet?"

"He's in the garden shed. He came home late last night," I said.

Soon the doctor's car pulled up and he hurried up the stairs. I followed. He took mother's hand and patted it until she woke up.

"You've been a very silly girl," he told her. "You tried to kill yourself by taking too many of your strong pills. Fortunately Ann found you in time and we pumped your stomach out. I gave you a sleeping pill to settle you down.

"Ann's a good girl, she's looked after you and the twins very well, more than can be said of your husband. But he's back now.

"I can't have you doing that again so I've taken your strong pills away. Ann has a new prescription for some pills for you that aren't so strong. She'll get to the chemist when the shops open again. In the meantime here are a few I have in my bag."

He got out a small pill box and handed it to me. "These won't kill you how ever many you take, they'll just make you sick if you take too many so only take the dose prescribed." He winked at me. "Stay in bed today and let the family wait on you. You'll be alright tomorrow."

"Thank you, doctor," said Mum. "I'd like a cup of tea please Ann."

"Water only for you today my girl," said the doctor sternly.

He followed me downstairs into the kitchen. "I'm confused. You said she wasn't ill," I said.

"She's not. But the trick is to tell her she is," said the doctor. "Where's you father?"

"I'll get him." Father came sheepishly out of the shed and bowed his head formally to acknowledge the doctor.

"You and your wife have both been very silly," said the doctor. "You've got everything you need, a nice house, good children but your silly behaviour nearly killed your wife. If Ann hadn't called me as an emergency she's be dead now." He turned and winked at me again.

"Sorry doctor," said father, "but she does wind me up sometimes. I don't know how to stop her. It just makes me so angry. Other men would get drunk but it's not my way and we can't afford it anyway."

"Just learn to grow up. Sleep downstairs again tonight. Leave her to rest and don't take your temper out on your children." With that he was gone.

That was the first time I saw my mother try to take her life. It was to be a regular pattern which was to last for many years.

9 The accident

ON MONDAY I opened Dr Grindley's post as usual. "He uses you like a secretary," said Brian Lloyd. "My Mum says you do too much for him. You're a Scientific Assistant, opening post is a clerk's job."

I kept my own counsel as usual when Brian taunted me about helping Dr Grindley. I smoothed out an official looking letter, read it and realised it was meant only for Dr Grindley. I replaced it in the envelope and put it on his desk with an 'urgent' note on it.

When Dr Grindley returned he threw the letter back at me. "You look after this, Ann. My book's late. I don't have time to answer letters. Draft a reply and get the typing pool to type it. I'll sign it if I have to."

"It doesn't need a reply" I said. "It says you have to go on a week's training course at RAF Bletchley."

"A week! That's impossible. I can't take a week off from my book. Draft a letter to say I give you permission to go in my place," said Dr Grindley.

"I think you really should read this. It says that all Senior Executive Officers must attend. The Met Office is going to buy a computer and the course is to learn how to use it," I said.

"Who's it from?" roared Dr Grindley.

"It's from Dr Bleasedale," I said.

"Give it here. I'll go and sort it out with him. I'm not going, you're going," he bellowed. With that he raced out of the office clutching the letter and slamming the door behind him.

"He's done it now," whined Brian. "He'll get into trouble. He won't be able to explain why he can't go on the course without telling Dr Bleasedale about his book. He'll get the sack. My Mum says he deserves to get the sack."

"Don't be silly," I said.

Dr Grindley came back with a face like thunder. "Evidently the course is for the five SEOs. I've told him you are far better at maths than I will ever be but he says I have to go.

"I told him I don't want to learn how to use a computer. You do all the stuff we need on the calculating machine. We don't need a computer. I understand it's a bigger, better calculating machine as big as a room. We don't need that! Anyway, it's not till September and it's only June now so we have plenty of time to get him to change his mind."

"Remember I go on holiday in August," I said. "I'm cycling to John o' Groats with Alan.

“You’ll arrange to be back by September so you can go on the course,” said Dr Grindley.

After a few weeks argument that seemed to revolve around the fact that I wasn’t yet a qualified forecaster and didn’t have a maths degree, Dr Blease-dale gave in and said I could attend the course, on the understanding that I would get my forecaster qualifications and my university entrance and actually be enrolled in a maths degree by September.

“Make sure you pass that last ‘A’ level,” said Dr Grindley. ‘Have you completed your university entry application? Can I write you a reference?”

I assured him my application was ready to go and I had been provision-ally granted a place at Sir John Cass College, subject to passing my third ‘A’ level.

“And your forecaster exams, how much more have you got to go there? I can help. Let me know what you need. Why would I want to learn about computers? It’s a much more suitable job for a girl.”

I assured Dr Grindley that I would complete my forecaster exams by the time I went on holiday. I was a little less confident about passing my Pure Maths ‘A’ level exam.

I TOOK MY MATHS exam in the vast halls of the University of London external examination rooms. It was hard but I felt I might have just scraped through.

I felt nervous about going on the computer course. I wasn’t sure I knew what a computer was. How could a calculator be as big as a room? Why did we need one that big? The Monroe did all the calculations we needed. Alan told me that a computer was like the giant electronic brains we had read about in comics and in the newspaper. These brains could think like people but were many times more clever. One day they would take over the world. You could ask them any question and they would give you the answer.

Maybe the course was to learn to speak their language. Maybe the one the Met office would buy would be able to forecast the weather better than the current forecasters who were always getting it wrong.

I went into Harrow Library. There were three books on computers. I read each one. So computers were not like brains at all, they were more like servants. Someone called a programmer told them what to do and they did it very fast and accurately. They never made mistakes. You didn’t talk to them in a language but gave them mathematical equations to work out.

That meant that instead of doing some calculations on the Monroe and writing the results on paper then putting the results back into more equations as you did when working out a correlation, if you could describe the whole calculation in an equation or string of equations the computer just gave the answer. It appeared that you communicated with the computer by punching the equations on a teleprinter tape or for some computers, on cards. The answer came on paper tape which was printed on a teleprinter.

I couldn't see how a computer could ever calculate a weather forecast. Although some parts of a forecast were mathematical to a point, a human was needed to interpret what it all meant. Surely no computer could ever do that? Maybe the Met Office just wanted to do lots more correlation and regression analysis and the computer would save staff. Maybe women like Iris and Rita would lose their jobs.

I passed my forecaster exams and would get a promotion to Assistant Executive Officer (AEO) and a salary increase when the Promotions Board next met. Dr Grindley wrote me a glowing reference. Dr Bleasedale was sure I would get accepted into a maths degree course. There was no more talk of Dr Grindley going to Bletchley.

ALAN AND I checked our bikes and packed our panniers ready for our trip north. It was a much longer trip to John o' Groats than to Land's End but the route we had chosen looked reasonable. We had checked youth hostels along the way and at long last we were off.

We followed the Great North Road to Peterborough as first stop. It was a long first day but with the early start it was well within our limits. From Peterborough we made for the youth hostel at Ilam Hall, where I had once been with a school party. The first two days were long and hard. We wanted to be in York by the fifth night but the third day was only a short ride to Buxton from Ilam. We had learned that the highest inn in England was the Cat and Fiddle just outside Buxton. It would be a hard ride up to the top of the moors but it would be a great achievement.

The road up to the Cat and Fiddle was narrow. It was the height of the holiday season and there were many cars. With three gears on our racing bikes we managed to get to the top of the moor without dismounting. It was very windy at the top but the view was magnificent. The pub wasn't open but there was a café at the side where we could get cups of tea. The café was full so we sat outside admiring the view while waiting for seats.

"It's going to be a really fast ride down," said Alan.

We drank our tea and headed off down the hill back to Buxton. The ride was exhilarating. We bent over our drop handlebars to reduce wind resistance. It was very different from the hard, hot climb up to the top of the moors. The countryside spread out below us in ever changing patterns of green fields enclosed by low, grey dry stone walls.

In the distance we could see high purple hills. The string of cars still toiled up the steep incline on the other side of the road but on our side there was very little traffic. We were traveling at about 50mph, so few cars overtook us and we could ride two abreast. There was a steep drop on my side but Alan left me plenty of room.

Then I glanced down at the road. There was a large stone right in front of me. It must have been knocked off a dry stone wall by a sheep and rolled almost all the way across the road.

I hit it and suddenly it was like watching a movie. I saw someone lying on a stretcher being carried into the Cat and Fiddle café. The patrons gasped. They got up from their seats slowly, mesmerised by the body lying prone on the stretcher, forcing themselves to look at the face.

I could see the face too. I knew it was my own face but somehow I was both the observed and the observer. I could see myself lying on the stretcher. My face was gone. In its place was a mass of lumpy red jelly. No eyes, nose or mouth. Just lumps of red jelly.

WHEN I WOKE UP I was in a bed in a room I didn't recognise. I looked around the room slowly. It seemed to be spinning. There was a face I knew. It was Alan.

"Hello," he said. "So you're back with us. You'll be alright but I have to just go and get a doctor."

A worried looking man in a white coat put his face close to mine and gazed intently. "Can you hear me? Can you see me?" said the man. I tried to sit up but found I couldn't. "Don't try to move, just lie still," said the man.

"Where am I? What happened?" I asked. "You had a very bad accident," said the white coated man who I assumed was a doctor. "You've got a nasty bang on the head. You must lie still." I reached up and put my hand to my face. It didn't feel like my face. It was rough and prickly. "Don't touch. You've got lots of stitches in your face," said the doctor. "Just lie there and I'll get some others then we can examine you."

The doctor left and Alan's face came into view. "What happened?" I asked.

"You hit a large stone and fell off your bike coming down from the Cat and Fiddle. You went over the handlebars. We were going very fast and you hit the gravel with your face."

A memory of the faceless body on the stretcher came to me. “Did I give everyone in the café a fright?” I asked.

“You were unconscious. We thought you were dead but the man in the café called the ambulance and the doctor confirmed that you were alive and brought you here to Buxton hospital. They’ve been very good. You’ve been out for ages,” said Alan.

“What about our holiday? What about our bikes? Did I hurt you?” I was confused. All I could see was the image of that red jelly face. I put my fingers to my face again. “Can I have a mirror? What’s happened to my face?”

“No you can’t young lady,” said a different doctor. “You just lie there. We’ll look after you.” He was bending over with his stethoscope on my chest.

“How long have I been here?” I asked. “Don’t worry about anything,” said the doctor. “Your young man has been here with you. He’s sat by your bed night and day.” I asked for a drink of water.

“Not yet,” said the doctor. “We need to do more tests.” I slipped back into a deep sleep. When I woke Alan was still sitting by my bed.

“Sorry for falling asleep. What happened? How long have I been here? When will they let me out? How soon can we get on with our holiday?”

“The holiday is over, I’m afraid,” said Alan. “You’ve been really ill. I’ll let the doctor tell you what’s wrong. I’ve told your parents. They say they can’t afford to come up here and I’m here anyhow. Kodak will give me time off work until you’re well enough to go home.”

“How long has it been? It sounds as if I’ve been here a while if you’ve done all that. What’s going on?”

“Just don’t worry. Lie still. The doctors here are good people. You’re their star patient. They don’t often get anyone as bad as you. They’ve given you your own room so you don’t frighten the other patients,” said Alan.

I was worried. How long had I been there? Why would other patients be frightened? I saw the red jelly face again. I felt my own face.

“I need to see my face,” I said.

“You’re not allowed to. They say it will set you back. I’ll take a photo. When you’re better we’ll laugh at what you looked like. You do look a mess but they tell me you’ll mend,” said Alan.

I tried to sit up. My head hurt. What was going on? What had happened? What were my injuries? A nurse came in.

“They say you can have some sips of water but you must stay lying down. You mustn’t move,” said the nurse. She gave me some water from a cup with a teapot spout. “Just a few sips.”

"I've got things I need to do. I'm going to leave you for a while but I'll be back," said Alan. The nurse smiled at him. "I'll sit with her. Your boyfriend has been wonderful. He's watched over you night and day. You've had us all very worried but you're going to get better now." I drifted back into sleep.

WHEN I WOKE AGAIN I was alone. I looked round the room. It didn't look like a hospital room. There was a dressing table and a wardrobe and lace curtains on the window. Perhaps I had only dreamt I was in a hospital.

The dressing table looked odd. The mirror had been flipped over and I could only see the plywood back. I put my hand to my face. It felt prickly but didn't hurt. I was determined to get up and look in the mirror. I tried to sit up. My head hurt. It felt as if something was loose. I lay back on the pillow. What was wrong with me?

I remembered I must get to university to do a maths degree. I tried to think about maths questions I must solve. Integral calculus. What was that? I knew the name but couldn't think what it meant. Differential calculus? Why did that come into my head? What was it? Algebra? Quadratic equations? How did that relate to a Quadrille, that was a sort of dance, a sort of Alice in Wonderland dance wasn't it? My mind went back to the time I'd played the Mock Turtle in an Alice in Wonderland play. 'Beautiful soup so rich and green'. What did that mean?

Quadrilateral, that was geometry. QED, pons asinorum, the Bridge of Asses. What did they mean? Equilateral triangles, what were they?

Maths. Maths started with arithmetic. One and one make two. Two and two make four. The inchworm song! But what did one and one actually mean? Tables, times tables, that was maths. Twelve twelves are 144. That was a gross. I'd bought a gross of bridal headdresses, what for? I saw Miss Errington's face smiling. There were other times tables but I couldn't recall them.

I counted to ten. That was alright. I could do that. I tried counting backwards from ten. Ten, nine, seven, six. What next? Try again. Ten, eight, seven, six. How did you get to one? One was the last number. Or was it the first number? I started to cry. I couldn't stand up. I felt wobbly. My head hurt. I couldn't understand maths anymore. I'd never get to university. Why was I in this strange bedroom?

A doctor rushed in. "What on earth are you doing sitting up? Where's the nurse? Here, I'll help you back into bed," he said. He noticed I was crying. "What's wrong? Does your head hurt? You're due another injection. I'll call a nurse."

"I can't count backwards from ten," I said. "I was going to go to university and get a maths degree and be a scientist but I can't count backwards from ten."

"Show me," said the doctor. I tried but gave up after two failed attempts.

"That's fine. You've fractured your skull but you're going to be alright. The fact that you know you're not counting backwards properly tells me you're going to be alright. If I'd asked you to count backwards and you didn't know you were doing it wrongly I'd worry. But the fact that you know you're wrong means you're okay."

The logic was lost on me. I lay back in the pillows. A nurse was giving me an injection. I hated injections but this one was lovely. It made me feel warm and sleepy. I was floating. Nothing mattered at all.

I found out I was in a private ward in Buxton Hospital. I didn't know how long I'd been there. As I slept less, the days got longer. Alan came and played cards with me. I learned he was staying at the local youth hostel.

There were pills to take and lots of injections. I hadn't been allowed to see my face but everyone assured me I would be alright. My face didn't feel prickly any more. Alan said that was because they'd taken out the stitches.

"Do I really look awful?" I asked Alan.

"Yes, dreadful, but each day you look a bit better," he said.

"No one will want to marry me now," I said.

"I will," said Alan. "You're on!"

"I'll hold you to that," I said.

10 The recovery

FINALLY THE DAY CAME when I could go home. We were taken by ambulance to the station. "Where are our bikes?" I asked. "They've been sent on ahead," Alan told me.

I didn't remember much of the journey but soon I was home. My mother looked concerned. "We were very worried about you, Ann, but I couldn't leave the twins and we couldn't afford the fare up there. Anyhow, Alan was with you and he phoned us at the phone box each day at 7pm to tell us how you were.

"You're to go to bed and I will call the doctor. He's had reports from the hospital and he knows how to look after you. I've told the twins they've got to be quiet and not bother you. I've bought two single beds for your bedroom so you won't have to share a bed with Rosemary any more. You should be more comfortable."

The doctor came later that evening. "What have you been doing to yourself young lady? You gave us all a fright. I'll give you an injection for the headaches. I'll come in each morning and evening until you feel strong enough to walk to the surgery."

I remembered I hadn't seen my face yet. I looked in the dressing table mirror. The image that looked back at me was fuzzy but it looked alright.

"What exactly is wrong with me?" I asked. "I was told I'd had stitches in my face but it looks alright," I said. "I still can't count backwards from ten and I can't remember much maths. I have to remember because I'm going to university if I pass my last 'A' level."

"You've had a very bad skull fracture," said the doctor. "Your memory will come back but it might take a while. I've written to the University. Your mother opened your letter offering you a place and brought it to me to ask what to do. I understand they have written back saying they will hold your place open until you are well enough to study."

"How long have I been off work?" I asked. "I was going on a computer course when I got back from holiday."

"I've written to them too. They have been sending your pay home. Your Mum has your letters. You'll be off work at least two years. They know that and will hold your job open for you."

Two years? I couldn't believe my ears. "Why so long? I thought I was better."

"You've got a long way to go yet," said the doctor. "It's late now. Let me give you your injection and I'll discuss this with you tomorrow. You'll be tired after your long journey."

I watched him give me an injection. I suddenly felt very tired. I still had lots of questions but couldn't be bothered to ask now.

IN THE MORNING my mother was standing by the bed with a breakfast tray when I woke.

"Rosemary has gone to school," she said. "Poor little thing, she was very quiet getting into bed last night so she wouldn't wake you. You were asleep by the time the doctor left. You didn't even have any tea. You must be hungry. The doctor said he would be here this morning but you're not to get out of bed except to go to the lav. I'll bring you a wet flannel to wash your face."

The doctor came mid-morning. By that time my head was beginning to throb. "I'll give you an injection first," he said. I couldn't understand why I didn't mind getting an injection. Usually it made me squirm.

"What is the injection?" I asked.

"You're to have a quarter of a grain of morphine morning and evening, according to the hospital. We'll see how you go. You might not need it all that long, then we can give you pills. But I want to observe you myself before I make a change," said the doctor.

"Now," I said when the injection was done. "What exactly is wrong? Do I remember you said I'd be off work two years? I must have misunderstood."

"You've had a very bad bang on the head. You've fractured your skull and damaged your brain. You're lucky to be alive or that you're not a vegetable. We've got to take things slowly. these things take time. We're not sure how badly your brain is damaged but it's not as bad as we feared."

"But I've got to go to university," I said.

"Forget that m'dear. It will be at least two years before we can even think about that or about going to work," said the doctor.

When the doctor left I asked for my post. There was a huge mountain of it. Lots of get well cards from aunties and uncles and people at the Met Office. There were cards from the church and from Alan's Mum And Dad.

TIME DRIFTED BY. Each day I got a little stronger. I spent less and less time in bed. I even managed to walk to the doctor each morning and evening to get my injections in his surgery. My head felt less fuzzy. I could read a newspaper. I didn't care that I couldn't remember how to do maths.

My pay cheque came every month. I had even tried to go to work but everyone seemed too busy to talk to me. Brian Lloyd had moved to my desk and Dr Grindley seemed busy. They were nice to me but I felt out of place.

I enrolled in a revision maths course at Harrow Tech. Alan mended my bike. I was cycling to the Tech one day when I blacked out again.

I woke up with my face buried in black fur. I could hear a woman's voice. I drew my face away from the fur. There was blood all over it. I could see it was a fur coat. The woman was looking down at me.

"We've phoned for an ambulance," she said.

"I'm sorry about your coat," I said.

"Don't worry about that," she said. "My husband was sitting in the car and you cycled right into it as if you hadn't seen it. You ended up on the bonnet and broke the windscreen. We were frightened you had really hurt yourself. You were out cold when we brought you into the house."

I could remember nothing. The ambulance took me to the hospital. I had broken my nose. They called my doctor.

"What on earth were you doing riding a bike?" he said. He took me home in his car. "Stay in bed until I say you can get up," he said.

I wrote to University of London. I explained my situation and asked if they could lend me some books on computers. They said they had ten. I read them all. I could tell I was getting better.

ONE DAY IN the New Year, about six months after the accident, I was walking to the doctor's surgery for my injection. I felt as if I was walking in warm water. The injections felt good. They made me feel warm and sleepy but this wasn't a life.

One evening I had tried missing out on an injection, telling the doctor I'd forgotten but by the next morning my head hurt very badly and I craved the warmth of the injection. Today I was going to ask the doctor how much longer I had to live in this twilight world.

The doctor listened. "You're very lucky, Ann. You could be a vegetable. Every day I see an improvement."

"But how much longer?" I wailed. "I want to be better to go to university after the summer. I want to go back to work. I only see my family, you and my boyfriend."

"I've been reading about some work they've been doing on brain injury at the National Hospital for Nervous Diseases in Golden Square in London," said the doctor. "I'd like to send you to see them. Your mother should be able to take you on the train. You're a bright girl. They might take you on as part of their research work."

At the hospital I was asked to do some tests. Next, they asked me to lie on a bed in a tiny room with a window into the adjoining room. They attached wires to my head with bits of wax.

"We're not going to give you electric shocks. We're measuring the electric activity in your brain. It won't hurt at all but we have to put you in this soundproof room so you have few distractions. We can see you and you can see us through that window. We'll speak to you through this speaker in the room."

I was asked to 'clear my mind'. My mind kept churning. What would they find? They might find that my brain would never work. Did I want this?

"Try thinking of a colour you like. Don't imagine an object in that colour, just think of the colour. See the whole space in front of you painted that colour. Better still, close your eyes and only see that colour."

I thought of green. My mother wore a green hat that I didn't like. I tried to put that out of my mind. "Better," said the voice.

"Now raise your right arm," said the voice. A few seconds break. "Ann, can you still hear me? Raise your right arm."

"I am," I said. A face appeared at the window. "Look at your arm. You're not raising it." I looked. My arm was still by my side. I concentrated more and my arm rose. "Good. Now put it down again and close your eyes again. Lift your arm."

There were more instructions. Things to think. Things to do. When the session was over the doctor came into the room and the nurse started to pick the terminals off my head. The wax had stuck in my hair.

"Very interesting," said the doctor. "We'd like you to come every week so we can watch the process of your brain repairing itself. It's obvious that some parts work well and others aren't working at all."

"Which bit is damaged?" I asked.

"It's the front part, but we're not sure exactly what that part does. Hopefully, your injury will help us find out," said the doctor. I felt useful for the first time in a long while.

I FOUND MYSELF looking forward to the Monday trips to the hospital. Sometimes, afterwards, I would wander round Soho or look at the shops in Oxford Street. I was beginning to feel human again.

I had asked the doctors why my head still hurt so long after the accident. They didn't know but thought they might be able to teach me to self hypnotise. The process was similar to the 'thinking of nothing' exercise that always started the session. I found that if I imagined myself on a beach in a deckchair with blue sky and sea and yellow sand I could almost fall asleep while being awake.

The doctors tried the technique while I was hooked up to their marvellous machine, which I had learned was called an electroencephalograph. I could see my pain responses dropping as I practiced the technique.

The machine produced a series of traces on a graph, one from each contact point on my head. They showed me how they could see when I blinked or when an area of my brain wasn't doing anything even though I thought it was.

The self hypnosis was very valuable and meant that I could stop the twice daily injections and take tablets when headaches got unbearable. It would be very useful in times of stress throughout my life. I missed seeing my doctor twice a day but was pleased that I could manage the pain myself.

ONE DAY IN MARCH 1959 Alan called round after work clutching a piece of paper.

"Here's just the job for you, Ann! You know you keep saying you want to go back to work. I think you're fine. The doctors are just treating you as an interesting experiment and a willing subject for them to work on their pet theories. They are keeping you wrapped up in cotton wool for their own purposes.

"I was looking at the situations vacant notice board in Kodak. This ad has obviously been there for ages because it's all curled up and it's gone brown in places. I took it to show you. It's right up your alley."

It read: 'The Kodak company has a job opportunity for a Statistical Computer Programmer to work in the Quality Control area. Must have a maths degree. Training provided. Salary on application.'

"I can't apply for this," I said. "I'm not a computer programmer and I don't have a maths degree."

"But you know all about computers, you've read all those books," said Alan. "You can do statistics and you've been accepted for a maths degree. I've never heard of anybody who is a computer programmer. I bet they haven't had any applicants. It can't hurt to apply."

A new world was about to open up.

11 Kodak moments

I WAS SURE I wouldn't be considered for the programming job but I was fed up with doing nothing. I was surprised when I had an immediate response to my application letter calling me in for an interview.

My Met Office interview had only been with someone from personnel. At Kodak I was taken into a room with nine people around a large table. They all looked very stern.

They told me that they had read from my application that I was not a programmer but I had read several books on computers. Which books? I took out my list. They spoke amongst themselves discussing which of the books they had read and what they thought about it. I sat and watched.

There were eight men and one woman around the table. The woman seemed to be joining in the conversation in the same way as the men. Her views seemed to be accepted, unlike the Met Office where women held back from giving their views.

"You say you have done some statistics," said a man with a completely bald head. "What have you done and which calculators have you used?" I explained regression and correlation done by hand with an adding machine and log tables then as done on the Monroe. I also told them I could use a slide rule. There were nods and smiles of approval all round.

The woman explained a problem they had at Kodak. It involved something she called diagramming and finding faults in film. She asked me how I would go about trying to get the best of the good bits out of a 42 inch wide roll of coated but not yet slit and chopped film with faults.

I thought it sounded like my experience of cutting out dress patterns from material with faults or stripes or a pattern which had to be matched on the final garment. My mother often bought faulty material at South Harrow market from which we made dresses.

I said I didn't know if film was the same as dress material but if you had to get a dress out of faulty material this is the way you'd do it. I added a bit about watching for where the pattern matched too. The woman sat back in her chair and clapped her hands. "Someone who can understand diagramming. Hooray!" Everyone smiled.

I was asked sit outside the room. I could hear vigorous discussion but couldn't make out the words. After about fifteen minutes the woman who had asked the diagramming question came out and said I would have to take an aptitude test. They would organise that and ask me back to sit the test.

THE TEST WAS EASY and fun. Two weeks later I got a letter saying I would be given a job as a trainee programmer subject to a medical. The annual salary of £500 was nearly twice what I was getting at the Met Office.

"That's more than your father gets," said my mother. My father was less than pleased. "Dreadful place that Kodak. You'll have to work in the dark. During the war men and women worked in the same dark rooms and got up to all sorts of dirty larks."

But how on earth would I pass a medical. Would they want a letter from my doctor? He would tell them I was too ill to work. And they would see the scars on my face.

I discussed my fears with Alan. "Just be yourself," he said. "We have a mini hospital at Kodak with four resident doctors. We have lots of industrial accidents and we can act as an adjunct to the main Harrow hospital if there was a disaster.

"When I had my medical they just took my height and weight and asked me what childhood illnesses I'd had. They looked down my throat and in my ears and hair and checked my eyesight. They made me drop my pants and cough but they won't ask you to do that."

The medical was just as Alan had predicted, without the dropping of the pants. No one asked me how I got the scars on my face and I didn't volunteer the information. I couldn't yet see very well out of one eye but read the board with the same eye twice, hoping the doctor wouldn't notice. I was pronounced fit and sent along to the personnel department to get a start date.

"How much notice do you need to give to the Met Office?" said the personnel manager. "Is it two weeks? That's all right then!" I didn't know how much notice I had to give but I didn't think anyone at the Met Office would care. I felt they'd given up on me anyway.

But what would I do about the hospital visits each Monday? I decided to stop going. They wrote me letters saying how important it was for me to continue the tests. They wrote to my doctor. He was very angry that I had taken a job without consulting him.

"On your own head be it," he said without realising the irony of his statement. He suggested that I could suffer seizures or brain tumours in later life but nobody could predict an outcome. He asked my mother to persuade me to at least keep going to the hospital each week.

"I can't do that" I said. "Explain that I need each Monday off to see if my brain is working? What do you think they'd think of me?"

"You think you know it all, Miss Clever. You wait till you're 40 or 50, my girl. It will all catch up with you," said Mum sternly.

It was to be the mid 1980s before I found out that frontal lobe damage usually resulted in an inability to plan, strategise and think logically. It was to be after the year 2000 that I would read of research that found that people with frontal lobe damage were often unable to choose a suitable life partner. It would be 2005 before I learned that research had found that brain damage like mine often led to 'confabulation'. Do I confabulate? Looking back, my whole life seems to be a confabulation.

ON MY FIRST DAY at Kodak I was taken to the Finishing Department. This meant walking the whole length of the factory, nearly a mile, past buildings where machinery clanked and interesting chemical smells wafted out. In the Finishing Department I was taken into a room where there were two girls about the same age as me, an older heavily pregnant woman, and another woman about the same age as my mother. At a desk by the window sat the bald headed man who had been at my interview. He jumped up.

Hello, I'm Peter Denton." He held out his hand. He held me by the shoulders and turned me towards the other women, keeping his body pressed against me. "Everybody, this is the Ann I told you about. She's a very bright young lady. She got the highest mark anybody in England has ever got in the programmer aptitude test. We're lucky to have her. She's going to be a computer programmer so you won't have to do all those statistical calculations by hand."

"So we'll lose our jobs, more like," said the older woman in a whisper loud enough for everyone to hear.

"Now Grace, you know Kodak policy. Even if your job goes we'll retrain you and give you another one. You won't be out of work. This is Grace, Ann. She's been here over 20 years. This is Gwen. She's the head girl in the room. You can see she won't be here much longer. She'll teach you her job then you'll be the head girl. And this is Evie and this is Kath.

"Evelyn, if you please," said the beautiful dark haired girl with flashing eyes in a strong Irish accent. "And it's Kathleen, Peter," said the other girl without turning to face him. What was wrong here? The atmosphere felt heavily charged with bad feelings.

"Come and sit by me Ann," said Gwen. "We'll share a desk till I go. I'll clear out a drawer for you. I can't wait to get out of this place," she grimaced towards Peter.

Peter returned to his desk. He appeared to be intently reading some foolscap sheets. The phone on his desk rang. "I'll be there right away, Sir."

As soon as Peter had left the room the girls seemed more relaxed. "Do you know what your job is Ann?" said Grace. "I applied for it but they said I was too old."

"And they wouldn't consider it for me because I got pregnant," said Gwen. The two younger girls had taken out women's' magazines to read. "Best keep them hidden. We don't know how long Peter will be," said Grace. "We don't care," they said in unison. "He can stick his job," said Evelyn. "He's awful Ann, You'll find out."

THERE WAS MUCH to learn. The girls spent most of their time analysing customer complaints and quality statistics from the production departments. Most of the information was coded and punched onto cards. Gwen was very adept at replugging boards for the card sorter which, in addition to sorting and counting cards, did some simple statistical calculations on the data like T squared analysis and standard deviation. Correlation, regression and other statistical techniques were done by hand, using log tables or a fairly primitive calculating machine.

They all hated Peter Denton. "He makes me squirm," said Kath. "He always stands too close to me and his hands are always hot and sticky." "That's because he's just been having a wank in the toilet," said Grace. "Ugh!" the girls screeched in unison.

I soon found that Peter would send all the women on 'jobs' for him then would come over to my desk and lean very close. He almost whispered in my ear that he knew the girls were lazy and it was my duty to make them more productive. If I felt I couldn't do that I had to ask him to help but that would affect my bonus. I could feel his hot breath on the back of my neck.

He would invite me to share his desk. "No, not opposite, Ann, come and sit round this side. I've got something to show you." Then he would draw his chair closer to mine and put his arm round my shoulder to 'help me to see what he saw' in the statistics. "Look at this graph. What do you deduce from that?" I felt trapped.

The women were interesting. Grace spent most of the day when Peter was out of the office dispensing wisdom on sex. I had never heard my mother speak about sex. I couldn't imagine my parents 'doing it' and yet Grace was about the same age. The younger girls listened intently eager to learn. Grace had heard that a contraceptive pill had been invented. She would volunteer to test it but they only wanted people under 40.

"Do you have a young man, Ann? I see you cycling home with a lad from Emulsion sometimes," said Grace. I told them about Alan and that he had asked me to marry him. I stopped myself from telling them why he'd offered to marry me. Better not talk about the accident. "Why don't you have a ring?" asked Kath. "I'd expect a ring when someone asked me to marry him."

I explained that we hadn't told my parents yet. Alan was a management trainee and didn't earn very much. We'd get engaged formally when we thought we could afford to save for a house.

"I live in a council house," said Grace. "You don't need to own a house, you can rent." Evie and Kath said they agreed with me, they'd want a house. Anyway they were both Catholic so couldn't use 'things' and would expect to fall pregnant as soon as they married.

"But you might be like me," said Gwen. "I thought I'd get pregnant but it's taken seven years. Still it's enabled us to buy and furnish our house."

A COUPLE OF MONTHS after I started work at Kodak, the disgusting Peter Denton came into the office with a letter in his hand. "I've got approval for you to go on a programming course at Ferranti to learn how to program the Pegasus," he said to me. "It costs £100 for the two weeks so we need to discuss what you will achieve on the course."

He told me that I had to develop a program to calculate Chi squared analysis. Helen Kleineke, who was working in Kodak's newly established Operations Research group was also to go on the course. Helen was an Austrian woman in her 40s with a heavy accent. She was neurotic and overly concerned with her health. She had a tablet for every human function and was continually popping pills. There was never any mention of a husband.

I was overwhelmed by the beauty of Ferranti's Portland Place facility in London. The elegant Georgian terrace house had been carefully restored. The computer room on the first floor had beautifully painted pictures on the panelled ceilings and a highly polished sprung floor that had been used as a ballroom. The Pegasus computer occupied half the large room.

There were ten people on the course. Helen and I were the only women. The trainers included Bill Payne, Bernard Swann, Conway Berners-Lee and George Felton, who later gave his name to Ferranti's 'George' operating system. The trainers, who were Ferranti programmers, spent their time in rooms at the top of the house, which had been the servant's quarters. This space was known to all as 'The Zoo'. With its low ceilings and tiny windows it was quite different from the opulence of the computer room.

The course taught us to write in machine code. I was fascinated by the complex patterns I saw in the code. Helen found the course difficult. One afternoon, in a lecture by Conway Berners-Lee, she whispered to me that the man was an idiot and she couldn't understand a word he said. She took some pills, put her head on her arms on her desk and fell asleep. After quite a while, the lecturer noticed he had lost one of his students.

He came over to the front row where I sat next to Helen, knelt on the floor in front of her and said gently, "What is it, little girl?" Helen lifted her head and in her thick Austrian accent said," I don't understand a word you are saying!" It caused much laughter in the class but that didn't deter Helen from resuming her afternoon nap.

I loved programming from day one. I felt it was like solving complex maths puzzles. Much to my mother's concern, in that first week, I worked through the night every night trying to write the Chi squared program.

ON THE FRIDAY at the end of the first week we all got a turn on the computer to run the test programs we had developed during the week. These comprised simple learning exercises and were supposed to calculate the amount of grass seed needed to make a lawn with flowerbeds in it, or how long it would take to fill a bath with taps delivering a specified volume of water but for which the plug was leaking giving water loss at the other end. A 'very complex' exercise could be to calculate the date of Easter to the year 2000.

Test programs were punched onto paper tape. I punched up my Chi squared analysis program and it was obvious to all from the size of my roll of paper tape that my program was many times larger than everyone else's. Bill Payne took me to one side to find out where I'd gone wrong.

Probably because I was by far the youngest on the course and a pretty young girl with the then fashionable huge full skirts over starched petticoats, Bill took pity on me. I had obviously misunderstood how to write my test program. I explained to Bill that my boss expected value from the course and showed him my program.

He was horrified. It was huge and very complex. Bill pointed out that the program wouldn't work because it needed a routine we hadn't learned yet. I started to cry so Bill quickly wrote the 'extracode' needed and tacked it on the end of my program.

Everyone else's program worked, maybe not getting the correct result but at least getting to the end. Mine took ages and looked as if it had got into a loop. We had been taught to watch the row of tiny dancing dots on the cathode ray tube. These showed, in binary, the instruction that was currently being processed. When the line of dots looked as if it was static, that usually signified that the program had got into a loop or had stopped completely. The address of the instruction could be determined by looking at the address register. We were also taught that setting various hand switches allowed the cathode ray tube to display information on the drum. This was called peeping, but the dots were very faint.

I worked on my program all the weekend and was certain that my code was correct so it must have been Bill's bit that was wrong. On Monday, I confronted him and he laughed.

Later in the week, we learned how to write the code for the function Bill had written for me and I was then sure he had been wrong. I added my new code to my program on the last day of the course when we had another go on the computer.

I insisted on running my program again. Because it was so large, I had to wait until the other students had run their programs. They each ran in about a minute and were all correct. Mine ran for half an hour and I was threatened with having to take it off. At that time, in 1959, Pegasus time cost £50 an hour. The program was allowed to run to the end and was correct. My Chi squared program joined the other statistical programs in the Ferranti Library.

Programmers willingly shared new programs they had developed with each other even if their companies were commercial rivals. Something like a new faster sort routine was greatly prized. The news soon spread when an improved technique was developed. Paper tapes were duplicated and given to all who could make use of them.

12 Operations Research

KODAK UK'S Finishing Department was the largest in the company, with 600 people. John Croston, its young and charismatic manager, was very proud that his department was pioneering the use of computers and achieving good results. This brought him to the notice of Kodak's Board of Directors both in the UK and at Head Office in the USA.

In August 1959 he decided that all programming would be done by his newly formed Operations Research (OR) group, which was located next to his office on the top floor of the Finishing Department. The group comprised Derek Trigg and Barbara Bubb, who had both been around the table at my initial interview, and Helen Kleineke, the Austrian woman who had been on the programming course with me.

Derek was a handsome, dashing Oxford graduate in his 40s who had married a beautiful girl who had danced at the Moulin Rouge in Paris. Barbara was an unmarried woman in her 30s. With her scraped back hair and owlish glasses, she looked like the stereotype spinster. She was studying externally for a maths degree from the University of London, rarely smiled and lived with her elderly father. I joined their team. It was good to escape from Peter Denton.

The work of the Finishing Department comprised several production steps. Firstly, rolls of coated film, which were 40 or more inches wide and 2000 feet long, were received from the coating department. These were slit and chopped to the correct size, taking account of manufacturing faults on the film, quality of the film and finishing production estimates. 35mm roll film and movie film were perforated with holes along one or both sides to facilitate the carriage of film through a camera or projector, then spooled onto metal or plastic spools or cassettes.

Sheet film, like X ray and professional sheets, were interleaved with special paper or foil ready for packing in boxes or envelopes. The products were finally packed with instructions and labels and sent to the Distribution Department for shipment to retail outlets or directly to customers.

At each stage, quality control samples were analysed by the OR department. Less than acceptable quality at any stage could result in total wastage, or a product might be reclassified as a lesser quality or even, in rare circumstances, recut to a different size. The further along the finishing process, the more costly the product became as the cost of labour and finishing materials were added to the cost of coated film.

There were also special orders such as plates or specially manufactured film for motion pictures or special cameras. Much of the process was carried out in the near complete darkness of pan lighting, or the faint orange glow of ortho lighting for less sensitive film.

MOST OF THE WORK of the Operations Research group focussed on the optimisation of the production process and estimating product sales so that the appropriate amount of each type of product was finished to meet demand. Product estimates were exploded into the components needed to finish those products.

This comprised getting accurate information on the components used in the Finishing Department. Surprisingly, this information was not written down and there were many opinions on what comprised a product that had to be agreed upon before components could be typed onto a list, which was called a recipe. Recipes were punched onto paper tape ready for entry on the computer. Estimation was Derek's area. He was experimenting with a new technique called exponential smoothing.

By that time there had been about four sets of estimates: sales estimates, management estimates, Finishing Department estimates and the workers' estimates of what they thought they could produce. There were no statistics on wastage.

Barbara and Helen worked on programs to manage the recipe file and exploding product estimates into numbers of each finishing component, while Derek and I worked on finished product estimates and programs to calculate optimum stock levels and order quantities of components.

It was a culture shock when the workers found the computer could tell them how many of each product to finish to meet targets and how much of each component was needed for each product. We programmers worked with production personnel to understand the production process and suggest changes, wrote our programs, punched them on paper tape and ran them on the Pegasus computer at Portland Place.

THE PEGASUS computer was gradually upgraded. Drum storage was supplemented by magnetic tape and more memory was added so programs ran more quickly and could be more complex. Time on Pegasus was usually booked by the half hour during testing or longer for a production run. At £50 an hour, care was taken that all programs were thoroughly desk checked before they were tested on the computer. Desk checking comprised developing test data and results and following the logical steps in the program by hand to ensure the correct results would be achieved.

But Pegasus was a hard taskmaster. If errors could be determined while testing was in process and the solution was simple, changes could be set on the row of binary hand switches on the console. At other times, it was possible to use the hand switches to jump out of the faulty routine to a later stage of the program.

Paper tape was read by an optical reader. When there were too many corrections to be entered on the hand switches, brown masking tape was used to block holes in the paper tape and we hand punched new holes. It was exciting to go into London to use the computer. Portland Place was near the BBC and I could meet my old school friends for lunch.

Babs was working at the Design Centre just off Oxford Street. She was a secretary to three managers, including Anthony Armstrong Jones, who was about to marry the Queen's younger sister, Princess Margaret. She said that one day when taking dictation she realised that her chair was left warm by Princess Margaret's bottom!

Pat worked at the BBC as secretary to David Attenborough, a scruffy young naturalist making wildlife films for television. He had a famous film star brother, Richard. Kathleen was at the London School of Economics. She had completed her first degree with Honours and was studying for her Masters.

London was an exciting place to be. It was the start of the Swinging 60s. The girls were earning good money and enjoyed shopping in the big stores in Oxford Street or walking in Carnaby Street, which was just off Regent Street and was the place to see the bright young things in the latest fashions.

Although I still bad headaches they were less frequent, and I had learned to use the relaxation techniques the hospital and taught me. But life was too exciting to waste time being ill.

Alan and I were managing to save for a deposit for a house. We thought it was time for him to ask my father for my hand in marriage. When Alan knocked at the front door, all polished and in his best suit, my father kept him on the doorstep.

"Come back when you get your nappies off," was my father's shouted response to Alan's request and the door was slammed firmly shut. "Little twerp," he said as he slumped in his chair by the radio. "I don't see what you see in him, Ann. If God had meant you two to marry He'd have made him taller than you," said my mother.

The time was not yet right. I thought about asking to return to university but the two years suspension was not yet up. But I would be 21 next year and a married woman soon, and married women didn't go to university.

JOHN CROSTON'S Operations Research group was doing so well that it was decided we should have responsibility for improving all business processes in Kodak's UK operation. John himself would be in charge of the new group which would report to Norman Brick, Board Director responsible for UK Operations.

Our group moved to the factory management building, an old ivy covered house just inside the front gate of the factory. It housed the Managing Director and other senior managers.

Norman Brick was an enigma. A tall powerful man with a shock of unruly hair, he was like a perpetual child, forever bouncing into the OR office with new, crazy ideas. He was saving for a sailing boat. The weekend came when he had enough money and went to Cornwall with his wife and a large bag of cash to buy a boat and sail it back to London.

On Monday he returned crestfallen. When the boat sellers discovered he intended to sail for only about seven days each year they suggested he rent a boat for that time and keep his money. Now he had money and nothing to spend it on. He decided to buy a second-hand Rolls Royce Silver Ghost.

Derek had a new house and invited Norman and his wife to the house-warming to impress his new neighbours that he had a friend with a Rolls Royce. Norman turned up in his wife's red mini. Asking for the toilet but finding it occupied, he decided to pee on the garden from the first floor balcony in full view of all. So much for impressing the neighbours!

One day Norman explained to the group how he ran his household finances. He said they ran on the sock drawer principle. He put cash in the family sock drawer where his wife put the clean socks. Everyone took out money they needed for living, including the children. The person who was about to take out the last amount of money told him and he put more in. I was amazed to learn how people lived who owned big houses and were rich and powerful. Their lives were very different from mine.

WITH OUR NEW responsibilities the OR group moved backwards through the manufacturing process to apply our techniques to the Coating and Emulsion departments whose processes fed into the Finishing Department. We were amazed to find that each department set its own targets without reference to any other, and in that each department had many different estimates of all materials. There was no optimisation of stock to be held or for ordering quantities for raw materials like chemicals and film base.

Logic told us that the whole system should be integrated and manufacturing should be based on one common set of estimates. Better flow-through would, theoretically, mean less stockholding between processes, lower holdings of raw material and less wastage and downtime. But the system was too complex for integrated planning to be done by hand.

Derek had learned of a system called PERT, Project Evaluation and Review Technique. Being a classics scholar, he enjoyed the clever play on words as pert originally meant skilled and was derived from the Latin *expertus*. The technique had been used to optimise the very complex manufacture of Polaris submarines. In that project the 'P' stood for Polaris.

I was sent on a course to Sir John Cass College at the University of London to learn more about OR techniques including PERT, Games Theory and linear programming. I set about writing a PERT computer program for Pegasus. In preparation for running my PERT program, each activity in the production process had to be identified and given an estimated duration. A network of activities had to be developed showing the relationship between activities, which could logically come before and after each activity and the dependencies each had on others.

FOR THE FIRST TIME, Kodak had a map of all production processes. The system would work out a schedule for all tasks based on that map and taking into account production capacity at each stage and raw materials available. The system immediately saved Kodak UK many millions of pounds. My PERT program was added to the Ferranti program library for others to use, just as my Chi squared program had been.

But wastage from film with manufacturing faults was still costing Kodak considerable lost revenue. Products with known faults had to be analysed in an attempt to optimise final usage. This had been tried by hand with limited success. X-ray film was the most expensive and was often subject to defects caused by static electricity from machines spooling the fast rolling film base, which generated sparks of light during the coating or slitting processes.

A computer program was written to produce a diagram on how to cut coated rolls with known faults so the resultant product was fault free and brought maximum value. This had been the problem that I had been set at my interview. Faulty X-ray film often ended up as dental X-ray because it was the smallest sheet and did not require the really high quality needed in larger sheets for, say, chest X-rays.

There were other trade-offs to be considered. Larger sheets produced more profit and dental X-ray film was more costly to pack so produced less profit. There was also consideration to be given about the capability of the machines that slit the coated roll to final widths and chopped that to final sheet sizes.

Our systems got more ambitious and complex. We were really pushing the limits of Pegasus. As soon as the new Ferranti Mercury computer became available Derek and I moved to that, renting time on Shell's machine in St Mary Axe or Oxford University's Mercury, and later another at the University of London.

With this new computer, programs could be written in Mercury Autocode instead of machine code. At £100 an hour, Mercury was more expensive but programs ran many times faster than on Pegasus. Other programming languages were also available on Mercury. Fortran for scientific programming and ALGOL for mathematical programming.

Derek was brilliant. I often had difficulty understanding the concepts he was developing. Just as I had done with Dr Grindley at the Met Office, I would say I didn't understand and ask him to explain. Just as Dr Grindley had been, Derek was very generous with his time in helping me to understand what he was trying to do. I noticed that few others ever asked Derek to explain what he was talking about but would often ask me to explain. I got a reputation for being able to interpret Derek's ideas.

I especially enjoyed the trips to Oxford with Derek in his shiny red sports car. We lunched at the best hotel in town and Derek showed me round the colleges and his haunts from student years. He told me that five years after getting his Honours degree, he would don a gown and attend an annual Gaudy, which was a dinner for graduates. In his college, attendance at five annual Gaudies gave the graduate a Masters degree. Derek could then if he wanted study for a PhD.

Even at £100 an hour, time on the Oxford University machine was always difficult to come by. If we were running over time, Derek would get me to chat up the next person booked in the hope that they wouldn't notice the overrun.

Derek had started leaving all the programming to me. He would give me a tiny tape with a mathematical formula punched onto it. I would add code to handle input and output, error checking and error messages. The resultant tape would be many times larger. Derek never seemed to understand how the programs grew so large under my care but was pleased they worked well.

The Shell Mercury computer was used mainly for large linear programs which scheduled oil tankers. These systems were run overnight every night. In the morning, radio messages were sent to the tankers on the high seas often instructing that they be rerouted across the world to refineries with appropriate capacity to optimise profitability.

IT WAS DECIDED that it would be a good idea to develop a course to help all workers understand more about computers. I was asked to give the course as it was thought that if a 'young girl' explained computers attendees would feel more able to understand. I modelled my course on the one that I had attended at Ferranti but used Fortran as the programming language. Any employee could book to attend, from the cleaners to the Board members, and many did.

My biggest problem was teaching the arithmetic that was needed to understand the simple problems. Each course ran for four consecutive Friday afternoons. One unfortunate outcome of the courses was that a brilliant young accountant was so enamoured with programming that he asked to become a programmer. He found the job much more difficult than he ever imagined and sadly hanged himself in the male toilets.

The OR department was seen to be a very valuable group. Derek wrote papers for the prestigious OR Journal and gave talks at conferences in the USA and Europe. Norman Brick would often accompany him. Derek complained to the group that Norman always insisted on going to the best night clubs like the Crazy Horse in Paris, but always left Derek to pay the bill for them both out of his own expense allowance.

Before I was 21, I was promoted to the senior staff with a salary of £1000 a year. Senior staff members were usually men with degrees in their late 30s. I was the youngest member of Kodak's senior staff, and for a woman, that was remarkable. Barbara had been promoted to senior staff the year before but she was in her late 30s and had nearly completed her degree. At that time, few other women ever made senior staff.

To my parents, and to my father in particular, it was unimagined riches. "I've worked my fingers to the bone all my life and never got half that salary. What on earth do you do? It looks like rows of boring numbers to me!"

I tried to explain but didn't get very far.

13 Married life

IN JULY 1960 I would be 21 and could marry without my parent's permission. It was time for Alan to ask my father again for my hand in marriage. This time Alan was welcomed into the sitting room. My mother, the twins and I scurried into the kitchen but left the door ajar so we could listen to the conversation. The radio was turned off.

"We thought you'd never ask," Dad said to Alan with no apparent irony. "About time you made an honest woman of her."

We were called in from the kitchen and it was smiles all round. The wedding would be next year when Alan finished his management training and would start to get adult wages. By that time we would have enough saved for a deposit on our own house and Alan would be earning enough to get a mortgage.

My salary would not be considered when the mortgage was calculated. I might get pregnant and my earnings would cease. In any case, a mortgage was for 25 years and no one expected a married woman to work for that length of time. The ring was to be one of my Great Aunt Polly's rings with a new diamond set in place of the ruby that had fallen out. No good wasting money on a brand new ring.

I was introduced to Alan's cousin Tony, who was to be his best man. He was good looking and fun. I almost wished it was Tony that I was about to marry. I discussed my feelings with my friends who assured me that Alan was just right for me. When my feelings got stronger I discussed them with the vicar who told me that many brides get cold feet but that Alan and I were the perfect couple and would have a good married life.

We had saved hard and had enough money for a deposit on a new £2000 three bedroom semi detached house in Tring, which was about an hour's drive from our work. Houses closer to Harrow were out of our price range. But as the house would not be ready by our wedding, we searched for somewhere to rent in the meantime. Flats for rent were either expensive or really horrid. At one, we were only allowed a bath on a Friday night. We settled on a share arrangement on the ground floor of a large detached house with a huge garden just a few minutes from Kodak.

I called in on Miss Errington to buy my bridal headdress. She insisted on designing my dress herself, picking silver white slipper satin, and having it made up by her French dressmaker. I tried many headdresses and chose a short silk veil held by a single white silk rose. I worried about the cost but Miss Errington insisted on paying for the whole outfit as her wedding gift.

"You think more of that woman than of your own mother who brought you up," was my mother's snarky remark when I told about the gift. She went on to say "You'll find out what marriage is all about, Miss Clever. That Miss Errington doesn't know about that. She's a frosty old spinster. You have to put up with a lot. Men do things to you that are nasty and messy but you'll have to put up with it. You'll find out!"

WE WERE MARRIED on 18 March 1960 at the big old Norman church on the top of Harrow Hill. Babs and Pat and my sister Rosemary were my bridesmaids. My best friend Kathleen said she didn't want to dress up as a bridesmaid but would of course be at the wedding.

We all got together before the wedding in the tiny bedroom that I still shared with my sister. I had thought that bridesmaids were supposed to help the bride get ready but Babs and Pat seemed happy to spend their time making each other look pretty.

John Croston, Barbara Bubb and Derek Trigg from Kodak were invited but my mother had said she couldn't afford to invite their partners. Alan had a large extended family of aunts and uncles, while we only had my god-mother and godfather (Auntie Bess and Uncle Jim who my parents had lived with when they first came to London) and my mother's brother Jimmy and his wife and two children.

My mother said she couldn't even afford to invite Miss Errington, even though she had paid for my dress and veil. I thought that was mean. John Croston made a 16mm film of our wedding and one of Alan's friends took the photographs.

The reception was at a local pub. The food was dreadful. Stale bread rolls with fish paste or a sliced tomato on top and horrid cheap wine. I was very embarrassed. I had offered to help pay for the reception but my mother said it was better to put the money towards buying our house. So long as I paid for the bridesmaids' dresses and Alan paid for the church, the cars and the photographer, Mum and Dad would pay for the reception.

I was now Mrs Leach. On our wedding night in a hotel in the middle of the New Forest, I thought about my mother's words. We had booked the best room with a four poster bed. After we had made love for the first time, I thought it wasn't as bad as my mother had made out. Messy, yes, but I could go into the bathroom to wash.

The next day we drove to Bournemouth in our newly purchased Issetta three wheel bubble car. We got the car ferry to France and drove to the Costa Brava in Spain for our honeymoon.

We returned two weeks later. My life was becoming every young girl's dream. I had a handsome husband who had a good job. We had our own cosy flat where we could entertain our friends. We had enough money to eat out in restaurants and see the latest West End shows.

Although we only had a bubble car, it was new and most people, my parents included, still didn't have a car. Alan's parents had a motorbike and sidecar. Our house would be ready soon and we could move in and start a family. I enjoyed my job but I would soon have to give it up and become a wife and mother.

MUCH TO EVERYONE'S surprise, as soon as she finished her degree my workmate Barbara, the boring spinster, treated herself to a Greek cruise where she met and subsequently married a retired military man. Once engaged, she became a different person. She had her hair permed, wore make up and high heels and became a pretty, giggly schoolgirl again. After she got married she left Kodak to keep house full time for her father and her new husband. And then my other colleague Helen decided that programming was not for her and she also left Kodak.

Ferranti was developing a new computer, the Atlas. It was to be the most powerful computer the world had ever seen and was developed largely for the defence, nuclear energy, and space programs. It was the early 1960s. Men had already soared above the stratosphere atop rockets and had even circled the earth. There was much talk about landing a man on the moon.

It was the height of the cold war, with Russia and America each vying for supremacy in the race to amass nuclear weapons. It was the time of MAD, Mutually Assured Destruction, first described by United States Secretary of Defense, Robert McNamara.

MAD was an appropriate acronym. It meant that nuclear nations either had first strike or second strike capability. A nation with first strike capability would be able to destroy the entire nuclear arsenal of another nation and thus prevent any nuclear retaliation. Second strike capability indicated that a nation could promise to respond to a nuclear attack with enough force to make such a first attack highly undesirable. The arms race was in part an attempt to make sure that no nation gained first strike capability.

In Britain nuclear power stations were being built that promised untold amounts of cheap electric power, but they had to be carefully designed to prevent the reactor becoming critical and turning the whole plant into a giant nuclear bomb.

All these new technologies needed access to powerful computers. Ferranti's Atlas computer held that promise. It would sell for £3 million, an enormous amount of money in those days.

There was much excitement in Portland Place. There was much talk that Ferranti would sell its computer division to International Computers and Tabulators (ICT). ICT was formed from the joining of the British Tabulating Machine company (BTM) with accounting machine company Powers-Samas in 1959. GEC's computer division was acquired in 1961 and EMI's computer division in 1962. When Ferranti joined in 1963, ICT became the largest computer company in Britain.

(In 1968 the Government would force the merger of ICT with English Electric and Elliott to form International Computers Limited — ICL. The rationale was that the merged conglomerate would ensure the British computer industry would be the most powerful in the world. It didn't work out that way).

The excitement at Portland Place was because ICT paid commission to its salespeople, while Ferranti did not. Commission on a £3 million Atlas sale would bring untold riches. I was in the Zoo at Ferranti one day when the discussion, as usual, revolved around the proposed merger with ICT and commission on Atlas.

Bernard Swann, Ferranti's chief salesman, brought a reality check to the group by saying that Atlas was so complex that it would need the skills of a whole team to support a sale. He predicted that few would be sold and said, "If three were sold to the Russian Government they would satisfy all their computing needs to the year 2000!"

Although it was then the most powerful computer in the world and was physically huge, Atlas had about the capability of a desktop PC in the year 2000. As it turned out, only three were ever built, plus three more Atlas 2s, which were also called the Titan. None were sold to the Russians.

At Kodak's OR Department we were looking forward to using Atlas to crack some of the complex problems we were increasingly being given. Atlas was the first computer in the world to have what would later be known as an operating system. This powerful piece of software, called a 'supervisor' on the Atlas, would manage the computer and allow many programs to be run at the same time.

It would contain the drivers for all the peripherals like printers, magnetic tape units, card and tape readers and punches. These drivers had previously been separate subroutines that were stored in the library and called by a program when needed.

The core memory was called the primary storage and the drum was called the secondary storage. The memory was notionally divided into pages, and the Atlas supervisor would move pages between the primary and secondary storage as needed to maximise performance. This would later be called 'virtual memory', and Atlas was the first computer in the world to use it. New terms like 'paging' and 'swapping' were invented to describe how it worked.

ALTHOUGH THE DESIGN of Atlas was exciting and people felt it was getting closer to the futuristic 'electronic brain', it was proving more difficult than anticipated to make the supervisor work. Prospective customers were lining up for trials. The oil companies were first in line after government agencies. Royal Dutch Shell in particular was keen to run several simulated transportation systems overnight to select the most favourable rather than just running the one which was all they had time for on Mercury.

Kodak seconded me to Ferranti to help to get Atlas working. I worked on the drum learning program which was part of the virtual memory and an important component of the supervisor. It was exciting, but Atlas was being built at Manchester University, 200 miles from London. I used the teleprinter to converse with the Manager of Ferranti's Quay Street office in Manchester, Martin Booth.

His messages on the teleprinter were very friendly. He said he was looking forward to showing me round Manchester and Liverpool and taking me to some local clubs and out to dinner. I arranged to fly up to Manchester on the first plane on Monday and return on the late afternoon plane on Friday. Noman Brick offered his Rolls Royce and the Kodak driver to take me from my house to the airport. I felt like a princess.

The trip from London to Manchester in an old DC3 plane was very bumpy. It flew so low that I could watch the cars on the roads below. Each time the plane flew over a factory belching smoke it would be carried up in the thermals then drop back down, making me feel quite sick. When I arrived at Ferranti's Quay Street office I was surprised that, although I was welcomed warmly by the receptionist, I was kept waiting in reception for over an hour.

I could see the staff through the glass partition that separated the reception area from the office. A wave of disgust rolled over me and made me shiver. Surely that couldn't be Peter Denton I saw through the glass? Surely I would have heard if he had left Kodak to work at Ferranti? My mind conjured up the sickly smell of stale semen and the feel of hot sweaty palms that the thought of Peter Denton evoked.

And where was Martin? He had sounded so much fun on the teleprinter and in the brief phone calls we had made. He had offered to come out to the airport in his car to pick me up but I took a taxi. I now regretted not checking into the Midland Hotel where I had a booking before coming to Quay Street. I could have left my case and freshened up after the journey. Eventually 'Peter Denton' came into reception and limply extended his hand.

"Ann is it?" he said. "I'm Martin Booth." His voice sounded flat, not at all as it had sounded on the phone. He took me to a desk. "You can work here during the day. The programmers get to work on the computer after 11pm when the engineers leave. The engineers have the computer from 8am to 11pm. The programmers get what's left. You might like to go to your hotel for a nap so you'll be fresh for the night shift."

I thanked Martin but said I was quite ready for a shift on the computer as soon it was available but I would just desk check my program again to ensure it would run okay tonight. I worked through the day. Although I could see Martin from my desk in the open plan office, he rarely came out of his glass panelled office. Lunch time came and went.

NO ONE ASKED IF I wanted lunch and Martin stayed in his office with the door shut. By 5pm, most staff had left. I wondered if I should go to the hotel and eat there but I didn't know how to get to the building in Manchester University where the computer was located, and in any case Martin had said he would take me to dinner and then on to the university where he promised to introduce me to the programmers from the other companies.

At 6pm he came out of his office. "I suppose you want dinner? Did you get lunch?" he sounded gruff and uncaring. I said I hadn't eaten since breakfast and was thinking of eating in the hotel. "I suppose I better take you to dinner. You are a customer and so I can charge it on my expense account."

I asked if we would go straight on to the university after dinner. I asked if I could go to the hotel to freshen up before dinner.

"Which hotel are you staying at?" he asked.

"The Midland," I said.

"That's just across the road. I'll wander over about 8 o'clock and we'll take a taxi from there. I'll just tidy up here and book dinner. See you at 8 in the foyer of the Midland," Martin said.

Had I misread Martin's eagerness to meet me when we'd spoken on the phone? Had something happened to him? Was this the same man I had been flirting with on the teleprinter? My own feelings about Martin were coloured by the fact that he looked like Peter Denton. But he wasn't Peter Denton.

As I changed for dinner and took a short rest on the bed in the hotel I wondered what Atlas would look like. I packed my briefcase with programming paraphernalia. Martin was waiting and we took a taxi to the Casa del Vino. Martin told me this was the best restaurant in Manchester and the place where most of the companies working on Atlas ate. He told me that as everyone was on expense accounts, each company took turn to entertain the others.

The food was excellent. As we chatted about the marvels of Atlas and Martin drank more red wine, he seemed to get a hint of a twinkle in his eye. Over dessert he suddenly looked up abruptly, grabbed my hand across the table and spluttered an apology for keeping me waiting in reception that morning.

"I was so looking forward to you coming up but when I saw you I just couldn't face you. You looked exactly like a girl I'd been going to marry. She jilted me six months ago."

I told Martin that I had had a similar shock when I had seen him. He looked exactly like a boss I had hated. The tension between us lifted.

"Now that we've got that over, we need to have some fun. There are lots of good night clubs in Manchester and more in Liverpool. What sort of music do you like? Jazz, good. Modern? Even better. We're going to have great fun," Martin said. "But first I need to show you Atlas."

After dinner he took me to the Computer Centre. The place looked like a mad magician's workshop, with wires snaking across the floor and backs of cabinets open to allow the engineers access to the inner workings of Atlas. It was very much an engineering research lab and nothing like the tidy commercial computer rooms I was used to.

MY DAYS AND WEEKS took on a fairly regular pattern. Fly to Manchester on the early plane on Monday morning and back home on the late plane on Friday afternoon. Work in the Ferranti office from about 9am to 6pm. This comprised discussing the previous night's results and strategising new designs where old ones had proved unworkable. then writing and checking new code ready for that night's tests. Back to the hotel to freshen up.

Dinner at Casa del Vino or another top restaurant, courtesy of the Ferranti salesmen or one of the companies waiting to trial and buy an Atlas.

Sometimes a jazz club or bar until 11pm. Taxi to Manchester University Computer Centre where the Ferranti engineers, who had had the machine all day, gave up their struggle and went home to sleep about midnight. The programmers could then use the machine until it broke down, which was usually between 2am and 3am. Then it was time to sleep.

There was one very old brown leather armchair in the computer room, with the horsehair stuffing bulging out. I was the only female programmer, so the men usually let me have the chair while they slept on the floor. At 6am the taxis would call to take us all to our hotels. Because it was located in a rough area of Manchester, taxis wouldn't go to the University Computer Centre between midnight and 6am. Once back at the hotel, the programmers would shower and perhaps sneak a couple of hours sleep on top of the bed until it was time to go back into the office.

It was exhausting. The work was hard and we got very little sleep. The programmers who had been sent by their companies to help get Atlas working were the best they had. We all had a healthy respect for each other and worked well together, excited to be working on the most powerful computer in the world at that time. At the same time we had great fun and played hard.

The Casa del Vino was the favourite eating place. Chateaubriand was the favoured dish. It was expensive, but who cared when the companies were paying, and anyway the cost a £3 meal paled into insignificance beside the £3 million cost of the computer.

At other times we went to Liverpool, which wasn't far away, to a dimly lit club called The Cavern. In years to come we could tell our children that we were at The Cavern and saw the Beatles before they were famous.

At the weekends all I wanted to do was sleep. There was washing and ironing to do and maybe a visit to my or Alan's parents for Sunday tea. The parents sucked on their teeth and commented that it was a very funny way to start married life. They realised that they wouldn't get grandchildren as quickly as they had hoped.

14 My first child

WE MOVED INTO our house at the top of the Chiltern Hills north-west of London just before the very hard winter of 1962-63. The snow lay deep for several months. Like many other people outside the main towns, we had no electricity supply for several weeks and were told that unless there were old people or new babies in the house there was no date for repairing the service.

It was the coldest winter in Britain for hundreds of years and came to be called the Big Freeze. Just before New Year a blizzard swept across England and South Wales. We froze.

Our new house was at the top of a steep hill. The coal truck could not get up it to deliver coal for our boiler, which heated the water and a couple of radiators in the house. The only heat came from the gas oven in the kitchen. Water for washing was boiled in pans and kettles on the gas stove top. Light was from candles in jam jars.

One night we found the hot water bottle still in the bed frozen solid. Not since 1947, when my brother and sister were born, had I experienced such a cold winter.

Now we were in our own house our families anxiously looked for every sign of a grandchild that would be the first for both families. But I was enjoying work and I was still only in my early 20s. Time enough to have a baby when I was 25.

We wondered if it was good time to start a family. It was the height of the Cold War. Alan's mother was the clerk responsible for officers' files at the War Office. As these were top secret she wasn't allowed to read them but had to ensure she booked them in and out of the filing room correctly, that the people who requested them had the necessary clearance, and that they were delivered by secure courier to whoever had made the request.

When the Russians and the Americans locked eyeballs over the Cuban missile crisis in 1962, Alan's Mum told of the increase in file requests and predicted the onset of World War III. She made the same comments when President Kennedy was shot a year later.

Alan and I shared the car journey to work with another couple from Kodak. The discussion during the hour long journey often turned to what would happen if the bomb were to be dropped today. The possibilities seemed very real to us back then and a lot of people were talking about it. It was a very scary time.

THERE WAS LITTLE time to meet with my friends. Babs had married and moved to south London. Kathleen and Pat had both moved to America.

Pat's introduction to life in America was horrendous. It was the time when many young Americans saw life through a drugged haze. Free love was the norm. Shortly after her arrival she went to a party where her drink was spiked. She found herself pregnant with no knowledge of the event that had caused her condition. She was too ashamed to go back to Harrow to live with her parents so continued to send letters home describing the wonders of America.

She and Kathleen had rented a flat together in Boston. Kathleen was working as a high powered economics specialist with management consultancy McKinsey while completing her PhD at Harvard. She was earning enough money to support them both. Kathleen told Babs and me about Pat's misfortune, swearing us to secrecy. She had no private medical cover and had to deal with the American public hospital system.

Three weeks before the baby was due she felt no more movement and was told the baby was dead in utero. Expecting to be taken into hospital to have the baby removed, she was told that as the situation was not an emergency she would just have to wait until labour happened naturally. Four weeks later she went through a painful labour without drugs. Not a good introduction to a new country.

Kathleen loved the USA. For a girl who was beautiful, intelligent and very well paid, the America of the early 1960s was a good place to be.

A NEW MAN came on the scene at Kodak. Recruited to establish a Computer Department, Len Thorpe had been an accountant. He wanted Kodak UK to buy its own computer and install it in a special purpose computer room.

He suggested Kodak look at EMI's new 1100, called the Emidec, which was one of the first fully transistorised computers. Transistors were more reliable than the valves and the core memory was much better than the nickel and mercury delay lines of the early Ferranti computers. Transistors also used less power and generated less heat.

The OR group was invited to go with Len to EMI's factory at Hayes near London Airport to see a demonstration of Emidec. Until that time EMI had largely manufactured records and small electrical goods like record players, radios and television sets. The prototype Emidec, surrounded by a 6 foot high wire cage, stood on the rough concrete floor in the middle of the factory. There was no protection from the dust and dirt of the normal factory environment or from windy gusts that blew in through the large open doorway that led into the factory yard and further on, to the main railway line, where steam trains still ran.

After the demonstration, which was little more than watching the flashing lights on the console and listening to the salesman droning on about what Emidec could do, we were ushered into the boardroom for afternoon tea. A typical English tea lady brought tea and biscuits on a trolley. Derek asked for tea with sugar but finding it was not sweet enough asked for a teaspoon to help himself to more sugar.

The salesman looked worried. "Please don't ask for a teaspoon. We had a bad experience here last week. We were demonstrating to the Coal Board who thought they might buy three of the larger Emidecs, a really big order. Their Chairman, Lord Robens, asked for a teaspoon to stir his tea."

Lord Robens was a Labour peer and had a working class accent.

"The tea lady said 'spoons, spoons! We don't give spoons to the likes of you. You'll put 'em in your pockets and take 'em 'ome!' We haven't heard from the Coal Board since."

There were many meetings to discuss the purchase on Kodak UK's first computer. The OR group wanted one which was mathematically oriented, and suggested buying 10% of the time on the University of London's Atlas, which was now fully operational.

Len Thorpe wanted a commercial computer that could be programmed in the COBOL language that had been developed especially for commercial applications. It could perform arithmetic calculations on pounds, shillings and pence in addition to decimal arithmetic. John Croston and Len argued their cases until they were red in the face and at times shook fists at each other across the meeting room table. They almost came to blows.

Len reported to Kodak's Chief Accountant while John felt he could pull rank because he reported to a Board member, and so had the support of the Board. They each brought their supporters and their managers to the meetings to support their arguments but few of their supporters had enough knowledge to argue on technical points.

Eventually, in 1963, Kodak bought an Emidec and Len set up his Computer Department. His staff had fancy titles based on their skills. There were managers, systems analysts, programmers, computer operators, punch operators, data entry people, data designers and computer engineers. He suggested that the only people who would be allowed to work on computers should be working in his department, but the OR department managed to escape his clutches for another year.

John Croston wrote to Kodak in the USA to get permission to buy 10% of the University of London Atlas. At that time, the Kodak in the UK was well ahead of the USA in terms of the application of Operations Research. The reply from the USA stated that buying into Atlas would not be permitted because Kodak was going to standardise on the new IBM System/360 world-wide. The S/360 was a family of computers, upgradable and capable of sharing peripherals. The first S/360s weren't very powerful, but the concept was to revolutionise the computer industry.

The OR department asked to see the specs of the IBM S/360 and quickly concluded that we could not do our work on it. We asked Kodak in America what they were going to use it for. We were told the IBM S/360 would do invoicing. Invoicing! Kodak UK had a typing department to do invoicing.

John Croston was so disgusted that he left Kodak and took a position as CEO of Hoover UK. I was sent to work with Len Thorpe's department as a programming manager. My job was to convert all the OR systems that had been developed for the Ferranti Atlas to work on the Emidec.

I protested that the systems would not work on the Emidec, or that if they were converted they would take up all the capacity available. I was told to do my best. Derek was now the only person in the OR group. He had negotiated that I would continue writing programs for him and that we could continue to use Atlas even though time cost about £1000 an hour.

I THOUGHT THAT as I was now nearing 25 I had better get on with the job of having a baby. I told Len and he explained to the department that as I might be leaving soon, I had to teach everyone in the department everything I knew.

Apart from Len, who had a big office, everybody worked in what we called cow pens, two people to a pen. These were cubicles with walls about shoulder height with 2 feet of glass on top. When you were seated it was impossible to see if people were in. This led to much standing up like meerkats to look along the row of pens to see if it was worth walking to another pen to talk. Shouting across pens was strictly forbidden.

I was the only female in Len's department. My fellow professionals were unsure how to treat me. They knew I had been working in computers since 1959, which was much longer than any of them. I had also been working in scientific computing, which was alien to most of them. While I was still working in OR, one of Len's managers, John Goddard, had befriended me and taken me to meetings of the British Computer Society. There I had met other programmers but was surprised to see that whereas Ferranti and

Kodak's OR group seemed to have had an equal mix of male and female programmers, the profession was gradually being taken over by men.

I joined the BCS and was seconded to the Programming Language Standards Committee. By the early 1960s many programming languages had emerged. Few people now programmed in machine code unless they were writing specially time critical programs or system software. COBOL was becoming the language for commercial computing with Fortran or ALGOL for scientific and mathematical programming. IBM Autocoder was also popular on the new IBM computers that were gradually taking over the global and British market.

Everyone in the Computer Department knew that I was only going to be there for a short while as I would soon have a baby and 'retire'. Expecting mothers had to leave when they were six months pregnant.

ORDINARY PEOPLE were still overawed by computers. Len Thorpe predicted that soon they would be just a tool of business and support all departments, not just those whose main function was numerical or accounting. To demonstrate his point he decided that Kodak would use the Emidec to predict the outcome of the October 1964 UK election.

The BBC had announced that for the first time they would display data on election results on TV as votes were counted. These would be entered into the BBC's computer to try to predict the outcome of the election. Len felt it would increase confidence in his department if he could develop a system that beat the BBC's computer predictions in both accuracy and timing.

Everyone who could program was dragooned into the project. The fastest punch girls were chosen. TVs were installed. Data collection forms were designed and people co-opted to take down results as they were displayed on TV screens. Dress rehearsals were held. The canteen was put on standby to prepare food for invited guests right up to midnight.

Len invited the Board and all the senior factory managers. The evening was a great success, with Kodak's results showing much earlier than the BBC that the Tory Government would be toppled and Labour's Harold Wilson would be the next Prime Minister. Len had won the race for computer supremacy in Kodak UK.

My pregnancy progressed well. I planned to leave work on 31 December so I would get my bonus. But when the time came, I was working on an especially urgent system for Derek. He sought special permission for me to continue working. After some consideration, it was decided that so long as I had a weekly medical examination by Kodak's own doctors and was pronounced fit, I could continue to work.

The baby's due date was 7 April. I hoped the baby would be born early. When the due date arrived with still no baby, I decided that the one hour each way car journey to work each day was too risky and decided to work from home. Three weeks later, on 30 April, our daughter Claire was born. A first grandchild for both sets of grandparents and born on my mother-in-law's birthday, Claire was a much loved baby.

Home from hospital after ten days, I continued to program for Derek. My job had always been a real pleasure, like being paid for doing something I really enjoyed. I would write programs at home then go into Kodak each week to take in the work I had done, leaving the baby at my mother's house.

At £1 a line of code I was well paid and found that I could easily write 50 lines of code a day. The standard at that time was about ten lines of code a day. But whenever I visited the office I found that decisions had been made to make changes to the system and that these had not been passed on to me.

Everyone was always very sorry but I found the situation unsatisfactory so as soon as I finished that system, when my baby was nearly two months old, I told Derek I would stop work completely and continue life as a wife and mother.

CLAIRE WAS A GOOD baby. I enjoyed meeting with the dozen young mothers who attended prenatal classes together. We met weekly at each other's houses to compare notes about our babies.

Our whole house shone. I felt I had to be a perfect wife. I always had Claire bathed and ready for bed when Alan came home. We would put the baby to bed together then eat the delicious meal I had cooked.

One day in high summer, Alan came home with two surprises. Firstly he had got a job in the OR department working with Derek. Secondly, he had offered to board the young son of the manager of the Kodak France plant, who was going to do work experience at Kodak's UK factory in his summer vacation.

I was taken aback. "But you're a chemist. You don't know anything about operations research," I said.

"I've watched you and listened to what you do," said Alan. "It sounds interesting and it's the way of the future. Your salary was much higher than mine but now I've got a big rise

"And I thought you'd enjoy looking after a young man. It's only for a month and we might get invited to stay with his parents in France some day.

I hear they have a big house in the 16th district of Paris where all the wealthy people live. He's just finished school and been accepted into L'X, the French military academy for officers, like our Sandhurst."

Patrick, the young Frenchman, was delightful, handsome and intelligent. I enjoyed cooking French meals for 'my men'. At weekends we went on trips in the local countryside with the baby and often ate out in local restaurants.

Patrick followed me around like a little puppy. He was very attentive and always concerned about my welfare. One day, when Alan had gone to the shops for some supplies Patrick told me that in France it was a mature woman's duty to 'initiate' a young man. He had not yet been initiated and had hoped I would do him that favour. I was horrified. I told Alan but he only laughed. "He's only a kid. He's probably fantasising!" he said. Nevertheless, I felt comfortable at end of August when Patrick went home.

Although I thought my life was perfect there was something missing. I wanted to leave two years between my two perfect children, so it was time to think about getting pregnant again. But not just yet.

I found myself crying one day because I didn't have enough milk in the house. It would have been very easy to walk down to the village to buy milk but somehow that had not crossed my mind. I decided I had postnatal depression. I consulted our doctor. He listened politely but told me I was missing my high-powered job. He suggested that I should go back to work.

"But I can't, I've got a baby," I cried.

"Yes you can. Leave your baby with your mother. You'll feel much better if you do," said the doctor.

Just before I left Kodak a colleague had given me a press cutting on a new company called Freelance Programmers Ltd, more commonly known as fpl. It was one of the first companies with a lower case acronym, a practice which is widespread now. It had been established a couple of years earlier to employ female programmers working from home.

Four months after the birth of my daughter, I contacted the company's owner, Steve Shirley.

It was to be a momentous decision.

15 fpl

STEVE SHIRLEY founded fpl in 1962. She had been a computer programmer with British Post Office (BPO). At that time, in addition to providing postal services, BPO was responsible for licensing and monitoring radio, television and other telecommunications transmissions. Steve was short for Stephanie. Many people who met her for the first time were expecting a man.

She was a remarkable woman. She was born in Germany in 1933 just after Hitler came to power, and came to England in 1939 as part of the Kindertransport scheme, in which Britain received 10,000 mainly Jewish refugee children who were placed in foster homes.

She was very bright. After the birth of her son Steve offered to work from home part-time for BPO. She was so successful that she was given more work than she could handle by herself, so she asked friends to join her. Other companies heard of the service and so the business grew.

Steve Shirley was to become very well known as a leading British businesswoman and philanthropist. She was awarded an OBE in 1980, was made a Dame in 2000 and a Companion of Honour in 2017.

But all this was well into the future in the 1960s. For the first three years, fpl had been run from Steve's tiny cottage in Chesham, not far from where we lived in the Chiltern Hills. In 1965 fpl acquired office premises up rickety stairs in an old building over a shop near Chesham station. It was there that I was interviewed by Steve just a few days after fpl had moved into the office, although, of course, I did not know they had just set up there.

Everything seemed strange. Where were the staff? Where was the furniture? Steve introduced me to Griff, an elderly man who smoked a pipe. She then took me into an empty room and perched uncomfortably on the windowsill while I sat on a folding chair. I had dressed smartly in a business suit. Dressed very casually, Steve smoked throughout the interview. I was mesmerised by her open toed sandals and brightly painted toenails.

I LEARNED THAT fpl had just been awarded a massive contract of some £20,000, a lot of money in the 1960s, to analyse the black box flight recorder for the Anglo-French Concorde supersonic plane. My experience fitted the requirements of the Concorde project so I was offered a position on fpl's 'professional panel' at £10/6d an hour.

This was much less than I had earned at Kodak but I didn't really need to earn a lot of money, Alan earned enough to keep the family comfortably. I just wanted the job to keep my mind active and I loved programming.

Across the road, in a rented room in a more modern office block, fpl's four managers, two men and two women, sat round one large table. I was introduced to Margaret Mears, manager of the Concorde project.

Margaret told me that because Concorde was the first supersonic passenger aircraft and a revolutionary design, government regulations dictated that it carry a black box that had to be analysed after every flight. If everything seemed correct, the aircraft would be given permission to make another flight. The black box statistics gathered from the early test flights were also used to improve the design of the aircraft.

The prototype Concorde had about 40,000 instruments on the fight deck, indicating such things as altitude, speed, fuel consumption and many other engineering metrics. All the data was stored on magnetic wire. After the flight the data was transcribed onto magnetic tape to be analysed on two purpose built STC computers.

Programs had to be written in machine code so that results could be made available as quickly as possible to minimise the time taken to grant the aircraft permission to fly again. The system had to be completed in a year, as Concorde could not fly until it was operational. There was a £2000 bonus if it was ready on time. My skills fitted the project perfectly as I had experience with both statistics and machine code programming.

fpl's four managers worked normal office hours. They were paid a salary to manage projects and make sales calls with Steve. There were about ten programmers, called panellists. These part-time home based workers were mostly women with young children, who were paid by the hour.

There was tension between the people in the office and the panellists, who saw themselves doing all the work, often under difficult conditions, while the office staff had an easy, predictable life. The office staff were constantly frustrated by the panellists who they saw as inflexible people who put their children and domestic arrangements before work priorities.

Margaret Mears had joined the company when she became pregnant. She was not married and had had her baby adopted at birth without even seeing him. The other woman manager, Pamela Woodman, was an unmarried mother who had decided to keep her baby. The two male managers left the company soon after I joined.

At first only Margaret and I worked on the Concorde project. It was soon obvious more programmers were needed if the project was to be completed on time. More people were recruited and the team comprised up to 20 programmers at its height, and many more for short periods.

Several left because they found the work too demanding. Most testing had to be done late at night on site at Elliot Brothers, a computer company at Boreham Wood in North West London. This was inconvenient for women who were expected to be home to get their husband's dinner and look after their children.

Before the project finished, Margaret Mears left fpl to work for Ferranti at the Weapons Research Establishment, a joint British-Australian defence facility in South Australia. I was the only other person on the project from beginning to end, and I also had had experience managing programmers at Kodak, so I was asked to manage the project. It was completed on time and fpl picked up the bonus. My salary was increased to the princely sum of 12/6d an hour from October 1966.

THE CONCORDE PROJECT was the biggest fpl had completed to that time. It was also the riskiest. It was fixed price, on a computer that was purpose built, and with a very high turnover of programmers and tension between office staff and panellists. I had managed the Concorde project for the last few months, so to address these issues I was appointed as fpl's first home based project manager. From that time, all fpl's managers worked from home, under the same conditions as their staff.

After the completion of the Concorde project in October 1966, I was given six small projects to manage concurrently. By the end of 1966, I was given another rate increase to 14/6d an hour.

There was a tremendous feeling of camaraderie in the company. The women were doing what they loved and had time to devote to their children. Friendships were made that would last a lifetime. Few of the women there worked because they needed the money. Most felt they were maintaining their skills so that they could go back into the computer industry when their children went to school. The technology was moving quickly. It was felt that people who were out of the industry for two years would never catch up and get back into the profession.

With the advent of home based management, Pam, one of the original office based managers, also worked from home. Pam and I were now firm friends. Our daughters were about the same age and played happily together while we discussed our work. At weekends, we went on outings together with Alan and my friend Vivien and her husband and daughter Rebecca, who was the same age as the other two children.

I found I had plenty of spare time. I renewed my interest in dressmaking and smocking and made identical dresses for the three little girls. Most of all I wanted a second baby. I became pregnant again when Claire was 15 months old, right on cue, but had a miscarriage when I fell in the rockery when I was gardening.

Like most of my friends from the mothers' group, Vivien was pregnant. Her second baby was due about the time Rebecca was two. Pam desperately wanted a brother or sister for her little girl, Fiona Jane, but with no likely husband on the horizon she said that she just couldn't face being pregnant again to a man who was not her husband. Might I lend her Alan for the purpose? I couldn't believe what I was hearing but Pam was serious.

I DECIDED TO cut back on work for fpl. My top priority was to get a brother or sister for Claire. I was asked to prepare a manual for fpl's home based managers. Then fpl was asked to provide someone to work on a project with the Economist Intelligence Unit (EIU). The specification of the skills required was fairly nebulous, just someone who was intelligent and had experience in developing computer systems. Steve decided that I would be the best person for the project, which initially was only for ten hours a week, for which I was to be paid £1 an hour.

The EIU was a think tank providing mainly economic advice to government and business. It was based in a large elegant house on the edge of Green Park in central London. Dr Buckland, the Director, explained that when the new Labour Government had handed down its first budget in 1965 it promised to reduce defence spending. But in the budget figures for 1966 defence expenditure and the budget allocation had both increased. This led to a public outcry, so Prime Minister Harold Wilson agreed that if anyone could suggest a project that would make better use of public funds, he would allocate money from the defence budget to that project.

At that time, one of the highest priorities in the UK was the need to build and equip hospitals. Following the baby boom after World War II, Britain's population was growing fast. Early baby boomers were about to become parents themselves. Most hospitals in Britain had been built before World War II and were poorly equipped.

New techniques and materials which had been used to build houses, office blocks and factories had not yet found their way into hospital building. The Assistant Chief Architect from the Department of Health, Robert Radford, was a visionary. He decided that to build hospitals more quickly and cheaply, and to take advantage of new technologies that often arose after the initial intent to build a new hospital, a new approach was needed.

In the 1960s, each hospital was unique in the way it was designed, built and commissioned. A large hospital took at least ten years from site acquisition to commissioning. In that time, building materials, construction techniques, medical techniques, philosophies and equipment could all change radically, rendering the hospital out of date on the day it opened.

Radford's concept was that hospitals could be built using modularised 'activity units'. A 'macro' activity could be a medical unit, say, surgical or maternity. The basic design, shape and size of the unit could be fabricated off site. The hospital could then be assembled on site like Lego.

A 'micro' activity could be hand cleansing which might be done using a hand washbasin, water, soap, taps and a plug. Later this might be performed using just a chemical spray. A computer database could be designed to hold old and new activity records. The consequences of the change could be calculated and design and services drawings updated. Radford had received £3 million to explore his concept and asked the EIU to help.

I was fascinated. The first task was to understand exactly how a large hospital was built. The system was similar in concept to the manufacturing process at Kodak but instead of producing film, the end result was a hospital. This was exciting. It would be easy to build a PERT chart of the process but how could a computer system be built to support the project?

Dr Buckingham was in charge of the project, He was a delightful man. When I visited him, he would suggest that we should walk up through Green Park to take afternoon tea at the Ritz in Piccadilly. One day he suggested that we should call in to see a friend of his on the way to afternoon tea. I was thrilled to see that the tiny, wrinkled and wizened man who opened the door to us was Francis Chichester, who had just sailed round the world single-handed in his tiny yacht, Gypsy Moth, the first person to complete that feat.

The program would be managed for the Government by Solly Zuckerman, a South African born zoologist who was later knighted and elevated to the peerage.

THE PROJECT SUITED me well. Most of the activity, apart from visits to the Department of Health, large hospitals and the EIU, was thinking, which could be done at home. Learning about hospital design and construction was fascinating. As with the early stages of applying computers to processes at Kodak, there were many different opinions about the processes used to develop a hospital. Gaining consensus on which processes provided the best result took much diplomacy and brought together people who rarely communicated or considered others' points of view before this project.

The Government had decided that fpl was a Good Thing as it was conserving programming skills, which were in very short supply in the 1960s. Without fpl, the skills the women programmers had would not be available, so the Government kept giving fpl work. fpl was also attracting good business from large commercial organisations.

The software house concept was growing in the UK, with several companies like CAP and SPL being formed to develop systems for business, government and industry. Most clients expected fixed price quotations. Steve decided that some science needed to be applied to the fpl process and so she employed Kit Grindley to develop a set of project estimating and measurement procedures. Kit was then a consultant with Urwick Diebold and later became the Professor of Information Technology at the London School of Economics, a chair that Steve's company endowed. I was to work with Kit on the project.

Kit also dabbled in interior design and usually pulled up at my house in the afternoon in his red mini with a ladder on the top wearing white painter's overalls. My neighbours were intrigued because I had a child but was still working when my husband supposedly had a good job. They were even more intrigued by the man dressed as a painter who visited three afternoons a week and left before my husband arrived home! I told them about my interesting job but they were very suspicious until an article in the local newspaper described my work with fpl.

Kit and I analysed the data collected from fpl's programmers and identified the significant factors that affected the effort needed to develop programs. We then developed a set of formulas which could accurately produce a fixed price estimate for a project, based on the number of programs in a system, their size and complexity, the hardware type and the programming language.

FROM THAT TIME, all fpl programming projects were estimated using these formulas, which were continually modified in the light of operating experience. Instead of being paid a rate per hour, programmers could now be paid a fixed price for an assignment. Different programmers worked different speeds. Some programmers could earn up to six times the standard rate, while others would be paid only half the standard rate for the same hours worked. The company did not give work to people who produced programs at less than half the average rate.

The effort expended by each programmer was recorded weekly. This data was used to develop a profile for each programmer showing their work patterns. One person might spend a lot of time preparing for coding while another would start coding straight away. The first might then proceed quickly through programming and testing while another could spend much longer testing.

These work profiles were characteristic of the person rather than the task, so a change of pattern could indicate a personal or work related difficulty. An understanding of personal productivity and work patterns also enabled efficient work scheduling. Programmers who produced a completed system quickly could be assigned to a project with tighter deadlines.

The development and maintenance of good performance statistics was essential to estimating project and personal progress when the people on the team were all working from home and rarely seen by their manager. The development and ongoing maintenance of these estimating and project control statistics early in the life of fpl was a significant factor in its success.

The other area of concern was the high turnover of programmers. In the early days when more effort was needed people already on the professional panel were asked to co-opt friends, but by 1967 fpl was growing fast and replacing people in mid project was both expensive and often adversely affected schedules.

Although fpl only had about 150 people on the panel, we had gone through more than 600 people, so we were able develop a picture of the type of person who was comfortable and productive working from home.

We found that if the person was busy and had lots of diverse activities, seeing work as just one of those activities, but being able to successfully plan and co-ordinate between activities, then that person would have a high likelihood of success on the fpl professional panel. Nevertheless, even after careful selection half our programmers dropped out on their first project. Those who remained were good, able workers who stayed with the company as long as they chose.

In spring 1967, Pam married and was soon pregnant with her second baby. She had spent six months as Manager of Systems and Programming in charge of all the home based mangers, so Steve decided to appoint her as General Manager to handle day to day company operations but continued to do most of the marketing herself. I was asked to take on Pam's old role but I declined as my goal was to get a sister or brother for Claire, who was now more than two years old.

16 A growing family

A**LAN AND CLAIRE** and I had moved to a large new townhouse on the outskirts of Hemel Hempstead, one of the 'new towns' built in Britain after World War II to house the country's growing population and people whose homes had been demolished or destroyed in the war.

fpl provided all managers with a portable office which folded up to look like an expensive wooden cabinet. Mine fitted nearly under the open-tread stairs in our smart new open plan house.

I now had a secretary, Anne Duncan, who had been secretary to the Director of the Edinburgh festival. She organised my appointments and files and took dictation. She then returned to her own house, which was only five minutes walk away, to type correspondence for signing later in the day.

Alan and I had spent most of our holidays in Spain since our honeymoon. This year we decided to drive across Europe to Yugoslavia for a holiday on the Adriatic coast. A week before we were due to set off on holiday I found that I was pregnant again, after three miscarriages.

My doctor suggested that I should be admitted to hospital to have my uterus stitched up to prevent another miscarriage, but that would mean missing the holiday, so I took a chance and we had three wonderful weeks travelling around Europe.

On our return my doctor advised me to either give up work or take on someone to look after our daughter and do the housework. An ex nurse replied to an advertisement we placed and Milly became the wonderful support nanny and housekeeper that every working woman needs but can never find or never afford. Both Milly and Anne were Scottish and would carry on about how they missed life in their homeland. Both were very efficient and supportive. My life was very pleasant indeed.

IN MAY 1968 OUR second baby Stephen was born at home. This was quite a different birth. I had made friends with my midwife and was looking forward to having Alan by my side as I gave birth in our lovely big bedroom overlooking the garden. Like Claire, Stephen was very overdue, this time by two weeks. My doctor decided to induce the birth but in the early morning of the planned day I realised that birth had started. I got up, showered and made breakfast as usual, then called the midwife.

Milly got quite flustered when the birth process started. Shouldn't I be in bed? The midwife called round just before noon and told me that the birth would be any minute now. But it wasn't. I was in strong labour when Milly insisted on vacuuming under the bed as usual. I suggested that Milly need not do that today.

"Och, you'll be having visitors to see the baby and I'm not having them seeing fluff under my beds!" she stated firmly.

The midwife and Alan laughed but could not persuade Milly that the bed did not need moving today. By early afternoon, I could hear the neighbours having a ladies' tea party in the sun in the garden next door. Milly had taken Claire for a walk.

The birth was not easy. Stephen was a big baby. Just as he was born, the doctor arrived to do the induction. The midwife had forgotten to cancel it in all the rush. I needed 26 stitches.

Alan phoned our relatives and Milly came back with Claire, who was not the least bit interested in her baby brother because he was in the cot she had been using for her dolls. Just an hour after I had given birth, Steve was standing at the foot of my bed asking me to take up the position of Manager, Systems and Programming and to manage fpl's now 250 panellists and 40 plus projects. I told Steve to look at my baby first.

"Yes, very nice dear," said Steve. "But now will you take the job?"

I agreed.

LATER IN THE afternoon both sets of parents visited. We opened a bottle of French champagne. I felt my life was complete.

Unlike my first birth experience three years earlier, where I had spent nearly two weeks in hospital lying in, I was up and about the day after the birth. The midwife stressed that I should be taking things easy. Stephen thrived and, like Claire, after the first week he slept through every night.

My salary as Manager of Systems and Programming was £1300 a year for a 25 hour week. In addition to Anne, we employed a typist, Jennifer, who lived across the road from my house. On sunny summer days, we all worked in the garden, sometimes with Jennifer and me in bikinis. Neighbours looking over the fence couldn't understand that the ladies seemingly chatting and having fun in my garden were actually being paid for working.

I had not renewed my membership of the British Computer Society when I left Kodak to be a stay-at-home Mum, but now I felt the need to keep in touch with other professionals in the industry. I re-joined the Society and was reinstated with my original membership number of 2791.

I decided to re-join the working group where I had been working on programming language standards up to 1965. But I had become intrigued by a talk I had heard at the National Physics Laboratory in 1966, given by Donald Davies. He described a method for transmitting data across telephone lines which would enable computers to send files of data anywhere in the world. To that time, data exchange had been via card files, reels of paper tape or magnetic tape.

The new concept was called packet switching. The idea fired my imagination. If computers could be linked together across the world then systems would be very powerful indeed. I joined the BCS Technical Board and was nominated as its representative on SC6, the International Standards Organisation's subcommittee trying to standardise data communications.

I also re-joined the Advanced Programming Group, which was focussing on the new science of database management. There was a new Database Task Group. There was much excitement in the industry about how database management systems could increase the power of computers, which to that time had only been able to process files and lists. These two emerging technologies, database management and data communications, would transform business and commercial computing.

Members of the Advanced Programming Group, which was chaired by Ewart Willey from the Prudential Assurance Company, included such pioneers as Maurice Wilkes, Sandy Douglas and Stan Gill. After the monthly meetings, members would go to a seedy pub behind the Pru's head office in Holborn to have dinner and discuss the Next Big Thing in computing.

fpl comprised mostly women, but most professionals in the industry were men, especially those on BCS committees. This gave me a significant advantage, because as I was often the only woman at a lunch or dinner I was usually asked to sit next to the guest of honour. In this way, I met many of the leaders in the industry in the UK and from overseas.

One guest who intrigued me was Ted Codd. Apart from telling me of his love of flying round the world in his own small aeroplane, he described the concept of a method by which business people could present queries to a database in very simple language and get a reply in real time without the need to involve programmers to write the query.

Ted offered to send me a copy of a paper he had written for the IBM research journal called 'Seven Steps to Rendezvous with the Casual User', which explained these concepts. He was later to become well known for his seminal work on relational databases. Computing, or 'Data Processing' as the industry was now being called, was becoming a very exciting profession.

IN ADDITION to my job of managing all fpl's projects, I continued working on the hospital building project, which was becoming huge. The idea of documenting the hospital building process and identifying best practice had caught the imagination of the Department of Health and Social Security (DHSS), which was responsible for the National Health Service. Also, designers were experimenting with best practice design of both micro and macro activity models to support each of the activities in a hospital.

A database was being developed to hold details of suppliers of hospital building products and internal fit-out products like floor tiles, windows, sanitary ware, beds, trolleys and operating suites. Exact specifications for each product were documented, together with price schedules. The project was taken over by DHSS, with the EIU acting as a consultant. More systems analysts and designers, including Sally Wilkinson and Jean Fox, made up a steadily growing fpl team of about ten women.

Other software houses were added to the team, including CAP and SPL. In all, more than 200 companies were involved in the project, including major construction companies and component manufacturers. Each company would assign people to the project. In all over 2000 people were involved. The project was known as CUBITH (Coordinated Use of Building Industrial Technology for Health Programme).

It was easy to see where huge savings could be made by co-ordinating all suppliers to the hospital building process. In addition, hospital design had not been optimum in the past. This had led to women in labour being wheeled through hospitals to get from the maternity unit to the labour wards, which could be located at opposite ends of a large hospital. Similarly, if the morgue and the chapel were not co-located, dead bodies were often wheeled through hospital corridors.

Researchers were beginning to experiment with Computer Aided Design (CAD). A CAD centre was established at Cambridge University, based on an Atlas 2 computer, which was accessed through DEC PDP-4 minicomputers. DEC, which stood for Digital Equipment Corporation, was an emerging US computer company which made computers that were much smaller and cheaper than mainframes. They did not need to be installed in a strictly controlled environment and were often being used in manufacturing to control machines and analyse instrumentation data. They were also used to feed data to the mainframes, in which case they were called front end processors.

CAD was in its infancy. Programs had been developed to support two dimensional design drawings rather than 3D work. Although it was easy to draw a cube using a computer, when it was rotated the lines denoting the sides that should go out of view were still visible. It took quite a while to make this work. Similarly, shading on solid curved sided objects to give the illusion of depth and shadow was difficult to develop. Called grey scaling, this was at first very crude.

All visualisations were in black and white or the strange greeny colour of the cathode ray tube display units. Nevertheless, there was great confidence that if only computers had more power these early attempts at CAD could be improved.

These were the very humble beginnings of a technology that was to become ubiquitous in the 21st century. It would enable the rendering of very lifelike 3D images on games computers, spawning a whole film genre created from Computer Generated Imagery (CGI) and provide trainee pilots with realistic scenery from the their cockpits during simulated training.

The DHSS hospital building team worked with Cambridge University to develop CAD systems to be applied to hospital building. There were dreams that one day it would be possible to 'fly through' a computer generated hospital design to see different views of wards etc. I was happy to see an Atlas computer again. Atlas 2 was a smaller machine which had been developed by Ferranti for Cambridge University, but it was much more powerful than the original Manchester Atlas I had worked on previously.

ALAN AND I MOVED our family to a larger detached house on nearly an acre in the upmarket part of Hemel Hempstead. A gate at the end of the garden opened into a small private wood where the children from the 20 houses on the development could play in safety, as the only access was through the gardens of houses in the group. We planned to have a swimming pool in our garden.

We seemed the perfect family. With both of us earning good salaries and Milly to look after the children and manage the house, we had plenty of time for outings to dinner or the theatre. But something was wrong.

After I had recovered from the birth of my second baby, Alan seemed anxious that I should not get pregnant again. He was horrified by the trauma of the birth. I assured him that the birth had not been that bad. I told him that although the birth had been hard work and might have looked messy, it had not been very painful.

Hormones released during the birthing process erased the memories of most of the pain that a woman might feel. At the moment of birth, when the head popped out, there was the most wonderful feeling of pleasure. Having felt that pleasure, I was sad that most women were given gas and air at that point so missed that experience as I had done when I had Claire in hospital.

"It's nature's way," I told Alan. "If women felt that birth was traumatic they would be fearful of another pregnancy so there would be no second children."

I assured Alan that our family was now complete and I was taking precautions to ensure I did not get pregnant again. But our sex life was almost non-existent.

Discussing this with other women from the mothers' group, most agreed their husbands were less enthusiastic about sex than they had been in courtship and early marriage. Couples were in their late 20s and working hard to bring up children and pay mortgages. Because mortgage repayments were offset against tax, most young couples took out the largest mortgage possible. Husbands were trying to climb the corporate ladder.

MASTERS AND JOHNSON had published their first book on sex in 1966 and information on sexual behaviour was beginning to filter through to women's magazines. Although I enjoyed the closeness of kissing and caressing, our sex life had been exactly as my mother had described it, fiddly and messy. It had never been the joyous thing the magazines now eulogised about. I started to think that my lack of feeling during sex was due to the damage caused when Stephen was born. I coaxed Alan to come with me to discuss my fears with our doctor.

We arrived for our evening appointment at the doctor's surgery during an electricity blackout. I felt uncomfortable discussing such intimate personal matters with a man. I was glad that, with only the light of the tiny night light candle on his desk, the doctor couldn't see me blushing.

After I had described my feelings, the doctor told me I was to come and see him in his surgery at 10am the next day. On the way home I told Alan I knew it was my fault that we couldn't reach the heights of ecstasy I had read were possible. Maybe there would be some medical help available.

In bed that night I agonised about the examination the next day. I felt embarrassed. I had usually been examined by woman doctors, and that was bad enough.

When a male doctor had done an examination during childbirth or pregnancy there had always been a nurse or midwife in attendance too. The idea of being alone in the doctor's surgery in the daylight made me feel very uncomfortable. I now felt it was my fault. There was something wrong with me.

I washed carefully the next morning and wore my best underwear, I arrived at the surgery for my appointment.

"What's wrong with me, doctor?"

"There is nothing wrong with you at all," he laughed. "Is your husband the only man you've had sex with?"

I was aghast. What was he suggesting? "Of course," I said.

"Then the only way you can find out what you might be missing is to have sex with another man," said the doctor.

"But, but I can't, I'm married," I said.

"Oh well, then you'll never know," said the doctor.

"Don't you want to examine me?" I asked.

"No. I can see you're a very normal woman."

I walked out of the surgery stunned. What did all this mean? I had a good life and a good marriage. Who could I discuss this with? Certainly not my mother. Not with my girlfriends either, that would be disloyal to Alan. The doctor must be wrong.

He was trying to fob me off. I should never have started all this. I told myself to settle down. Be thankful for what you've got. You've got two lovely children and a good husband, a superb house, an interesting job any plenty of money.

It was wrong to expect more.

17 A scientific experiment

fpl WAS BEING asked to do increasingly large and complex projects. Many were high profile, such as the first computer based settlement system for the London Stock Exchange, the personnel system for the British Civil Service and a share registry system for Kleinwort Benson, a large merchant bank. Much of our work, as with the DHSS project, was in high-level consultancy and systems design but the company was still called Freelance Programmers Ltd.

Our reputation grew as the industry grew. The company was known as a group of very competent women programmers. The press didn't always help to maintain the image of professionalism that Steve sought. fpl attracted a significant amount of publicity, some of which made us cringe, like the time the Daily Mirror described the system developed to automatically pick pools entries for lazy punters. The article read something like this:

'Every Monday the ladies in fpl leave their washing and baby's nappies to set up their computers to pick your lucky pools numbers'.

The system was only a set of programs to randomly generate results from football games. It was run on the large computer at Littlewoods needing no involvement from fpl after developing the system. But each press article brought more interest and more business.

When clients found out that the women working on their projects were highly skilled and that many had dropped back to programming for their first fpl project but had been managers or systems analysts before they had started their families, they often asked if fpl could help with systems analysis and design. The second project for a client would generally be larger and cover the whole development lifecycle rather than just programming.

The estimating and progress tracking system initially developed with Kit Grindley's help provided accurate fixed price programming estimates and helped to bring projects in on time and within budget. But estimating systems projects was more difficult. fpl tried to charge time and materials as we had on the DHSS project, but some clients wanted fixed price.

The initial estimate for a share registry system for Kleinwort Benson was £25,000, with an option to revise the estimate at the end of the systems design phase. The system was much more complex than we ever imagined. This was because it was the first such system the bank had developed. As they learned more about what computers could do, they extended their requirements. They didn't like the invoices they got but they could see we were working hard and producing good results.

At the end of the systems design phase fpl had already billed nearly £25,000. Peter Marshall, Kleinwort Benson's Manager, said he would now have to put the programming phase out to open tender. fpl could quote but it would be competitive.

Because we had worked on the systems design, we knew the system better than any competitor. Several software houses put in tenders. fpl's tender was £100,000 for the programming phase. We knew several other tenders were much higher. Through contacts in the BCS, I had made friends with many of the owners and top managers in rival software houses. Many of the men gave me more information than was commercially sensible because they thought that as a woman, I needed to be 'helped'. I found out from Alex d'Agapeyeff, CAP's Managing Director, that their estimate was over £250,000.

Because of the business cycle, the system could only be implemented at the start of a calendar year. Try as we might to reduce the elapsed time, fpl estimated it would take 14 months. Starting in January, the project would not be complete until the end of February the following year, meaning that implementation would have to be delayed a further ten months. We tried adding more programmers, assigning the most productive programmers, scheduling tasks in parallel, but nothing could be done to reduce the development time.

The contract went to CAP, who guaranteed to complete the project in under a year. Peter Marshall said he was sorry to see the project go to another company but the design had taken much longer than estimated and the system had to be implemented as soon as possible. I could not see how the project could be completed in under a year. Thinking I would learn where I had gone wrong with fpl's estimate, I asked Alex at CAP how their company would deliver the project in under a year.

"It can't be done," he told me. "That development can't be done in under 18 months."

"But you gave a guarantee of completion in under 12 months," I said.

"Yes, but there will be new requirements or changes in the computer the system is to run on during the development time. This will mean variations. The client will forget the time and see it's not feasible to implement at the beginning of next year."

"But that's cheating. You should have told them that," I said.

"All's fair," was his reply. When I told Steve she asked me why I hadn't thought of doing that.

A few weeks later fpl put in a quotation to develop a stock control system for the Family Planning Association. This time I found out that fpl's estimate was twice CAP's. We were the only two companies invited to tender. fpl won the contract. The client at the FPA said it was much more appropriate for women to be dealing with a system that listed family planning supplies.

Alex at CAP, knowing his company's quote was much lower than ours, asked me if I knew why fpl had won the contract. I told him what the client had said.

'That's not right," he said.

"All's fair," said I.

JUST BEFORE EACH project was due for completion, I visited the client to ask if there was anything else they wanted the team to do before it was disbanded. The usual response from a first time client would be that the quality of work was excellent and the panel members very professional but they didn't like our ethics.

After being told this the first few times and asking why I began to expect the same answer. Clients would tell me that fpl must be a sweatshop and be paying our programmers very little to get that amount and quality of work for such a low cost. The solution was to show our clients of the statistics for their own project and see how much each person had been paid. They then realised that it was the very high productivity that caused the project to cost well below expectation. Our programmers were being paid well but were very productive.

How had this been achieved? I believed it was due to fpl's good project management techniques, especially the metrics used to estimate effort, time and cost and to track progress on the project. Companies asked if we could help them develop a metrics system.

Wherever this was done, the productivity of in-house programmers was only around half that of fpl people working from home. It was becoming obvious that home based working was more productive. Clients usually then gave fpl more work. Eventually 70% of our work was repeat business.

I became good friends with the tall, handsome project manager of CAP's team on the DHSS project, Dick Small. He was a Fellow of the Royal Institution, the oldest and most prestigious scientific association in the world. I was thrilled to know someone who followed in the footsteps of great scientists such as Faraday, Humphrey Davey, James Watt, William Herschel and Charles Darwin. As a schoolgirl, I had visited the Royal Institution with my Physics teacher and had heard a lecture by Sir Lawrence Bragg in the beautiful old fashioned lecture room.

Dick was a qualified astronomer who had used computers for astronomical calculations. He had become enchanted with computing. He was a Senior Partner and a founding member of CAP. In addition to working on the DHSS project, he was working on mathematical programming for the Atomic Energy Authority at Harwell on its Atlas 2. We had an easy friendship and often attended BCS meetings together. He would often suggest a drink afterwards or but I preferred to hurry home to my family duties.

We often got involved in deep philosophical discussions during slow times on the project. There were many such times, waiting to get access to a computer or waiting to see a senior bureaucrat in a hospital or the DHSS.

The project involved a lot of travelling, which was organised and paid for by DHSS. I noticed that Dick rarely joined the team on a train trip or an air journey but preferred to make his own way in his own car, however arduous the journey. If travelling across London he would often walk instead of taking the tube or the bus. Instead of taking the lift, he always ran up and down stairs even in the tallest buildings. He said that was to keep fit. Eventually I challenged him and he confessed he was claustrophobic.

Thinking this must be a tremendous disadvantage in business, I asked if he was getting treatment. He told me he'd been to many psychologists and even a psychiatrist but nothing worked. I was intrigued that someone who seemed so intelligent suffered such a strange affliction.

I read up claustrophobia and found that the current treatment was aversion therapy. I suggested we try taking the tube just one station or taking a lift one floor. It seemed to work. I gave him stones to put in his pocket to hold if he was by himself. He said it worked to a limited degree.

I WAS STILL WORRIED about sex. What was I doing wrong? Was it my fault or Alan's? The doctor's words kept coming back to me. What would sex with another man be like?

I was getting on well with Dick and I plucked up courage to ask him a favour. I asked if he could please help settle my curiosity about sex on one of the occasions we had to stay overnight in Cambridge. This was to be purely in the cause of science, which we both loved and admired. I pointed out it would only happen once and no one was to know.

I immediately realised I had stepped over a line. What was I doing? A 'nice' woman would never ask a man for sex. I was very surprised by Dick's response.

"I thought you'd never ask," he said. "I've wanted to ask you ever since we found out we enjoyed the same things. I never dared hope that it might happen. I never asked because I thought it would ruin a good friendship."

Now I was very embarrassed. "It's not going to turn into anything. It's a one off experiment. I'm just curious," I said.

Dick tried to hide his delighted grin and put on a very straight face. "Of course, but I don't think it would be a good idea to do anything in Cambridge. Several people have already misconstrued our friendship. Several of the men have asked me straight out if we are having an affair."

I was horrified. To think that people thought that about me! Perhaps it would be better to stop this silly idea right here and now. But by now my curiosity had got the better of me. Dick was being very serious and 'scientific' and nice about it.

He suggested that we meet in a London hotel one afternoon for our 'experiment'. That way no one would find out and we wouldn't have to make excuses about being away a night. Dick said I should pick a day and he would make the arrangements.

The day soon came. I booked into the expensive hotel Dick had chosen. I felt foolish using the name we had agreed upon and was told, "Mr Phillips has not arrived yet, Madam." The room was full of the loveliest flowers. I drew the curtains, showered, got into my nightgown and hid under the covers. I could hear my heart pounding. I would have to be brave. This was just a scientific experiment. Dick was a real gentleman. He'd look after me.

The door opened quietly. Dick strode into the room. "Why are you shutting out the sunlight? I want to enjoy this. I want to look at you," he said opening the curtains. I was horrified. This wasn't supposed to be fun!

Dick went into the bathroom. I could hear the shower. Should I just get dressed quickly and leave? This probably wasn't a good idea. The shower stopped. Dick came into the bedroom drying himself on a towel. He looked even more handsome, tanned, slim with no hint of a paunch. I started to feel inadequate about my own body. I'd had two children and my figure was beginning to take on a decidedly podgy look.

He slipped under the bedcovers. "Do we really need these? It's summer, you can't be cold."

"Yes, I'm cold," I said and made my teeth chatter to prove the point. Why didn't he just get on with it? This was embarrassing.

"You're stiff as a board. Relax," said Dick.

"What are you doing?" I said as he kissed and caressed me. "Just making sure you enjoy this," he said.

Then I was floating. I was up on the ceiling looking down at the couple on the bed in the room full of flowers. Don't let this ever stop!

The afternoon sun was growing paler. The shadows on the walls were growing longer. I no longer cared that the bedclothes had fallen on the floor or that I was naked. I felt safe and secure and loved.

Dick was gazing at me, propped up on his elbow. "You're delicious," he said. "You're beautiful.

"Well, I suppose we better be going. I told the hotel that we were celebrating our wedding anniversary and asked them to put all the flowers in the room but I told them we would be out by 7pm. I'm sure they didn't believe me but they played the game. So, 'Mrs Phillips', up, shower, dress and home young lady."

I was in a daze. I was still on cloud nine when I reached home. Milly had prepared dinner and fed Alan and the children. "Thanks for doing that, Milly. I hope you don't mind but I'm off to bed. I've had a big day and I'm tired. Alan, will you put the kids to bed please," I said.

What had I done? Whatever it was, it was very wrong but very nice. Surely Alan and I could learn to give each other the same pleasure. I'd need to read more books. I was frightened I would talk in my sleep. It would be dreadful if Alan found out. I read a book until Alan came to bed then saying I felt much better and I had to do some things to prepare for the next day. I got up and worked at my desk until the early hours.

FACING DICK ACROSS a meeting table a week or so later, I blushed deep red when he smiled and winked. What if he had told people about our secret? Maybe people would 'know' if they saw the wink and the blush. Panic welled up inside. How would I to get through this meeting?

The meeting was over. Dick was moving quickly towards me. "Could we talk about how we ..."

I didn't hear the words. I just wanted to get away but I heard myself say, "Yes. Where? When?"

"No time like the present," he replied. He was actually smiling. This wasn't something to smile about, this was serious. Maybe a meeting would be good. I could reinforce the scientific nature of the 'experiment' and re-confirm the need for secrecy. Yes, a chat would be good.

We found a coffee shop. Dick took my hand across the table. "I haven't stopped thinking about you. I expected you to phone. I didn't like to phone you as I thought that might embarrass you. How are you? Did you enjoy it half as much as I did? When can we do it again?"

I felt embarrassed. "We are both married with children. It can't happen again."

"Why? Didn't you enjoy it? Anyhow, you said it was an experiment. Did you learn anything? Was it different from when you are with your husband?"

"Yes, I did enjoy it but that doesn't mean it can happen again! It was different from when I'm with Alan. It's odd, we see people often but we don't really know what they look like under their clothes. You always come across as smart and businesslike but I didn't realise you had a body like a film star!"

"Thanks for the compliment. You looked lovely to me too."

With Dick there had been no 'fiddling about' and it hadn't been 'difficult and messy'. In fact, I hadn't remembered when Dick had entered my body. I hadn't had to help him, he was sort of just there. I needed to read more, I thought.

"Well although it was very nice, that's it," I said. "It would be dreadful if your wife or Alan found out."

"Jean wouldn't mind. We rarely have sex. She thinks it's just for making babies. We've got two now so although she lets me sometimes it's just to do her duty as a wife.

"She is devoutly Jewish. Do you understand their customs? Probably not. After a Jewish woman has a period, she has to go through a process of ritual cleansing before she can have sex again. Jean always says she hasn't had time to go to the Mikvah and then she's got her next period and of course it's no sex when she's menstruating, that really is against her religion."

"I didn't know you were Jewish," I said.

"So you really didn't look. I'm actually not Jewish, but Jean made me get circumcised before we got married and it was embarrassing and painful. In fact, I don't really know why I married her. Oh, she's a good, sensible wife and she brings up the boys very well. She's a good cook and keeps a good house. She used to make me go to synagogue but she's given up on that.

"I think I really ought to have married her father. He was a great man. He encouraged me through university and, being a Fellow of the Royal Institution, sponsored my Fellowship. His daughter looked like she'd be left on the shelf so he asked me to marry her and settled a goodly sum of money on her so we could buy a nice house without a mortgage. He's been like a father to me and I wanted to please him. I was over 30 and it was about time I got married. I hadn't had girl friends; I'd spent all my time studying."

I was fascinated. I'd known this man for more than two years and yet I didn't know him at all. "How old are you?" I said. "I thought you were about the same age as me."

"I'm 42 and Jean is 52," he said.

I looked again. He was very good looking and fit, but over 40. That was old! And to have a wife who was just a bit younger than my mother? That was amazing.

"Well, I'd like to thank you. You've helped me and given me an experience I might never have had but I'm happily married and that's it. But please can we still be friends? I'd like that," I said.

"You make it hard for a man, Ann, but if that's the way you want it well so be it. Of course we'll still be friends but don't think badly of me if I keep asking you for more."

18 No parents allowed

THE COMPANY WAS going very well but there were growing tensions between Steve and Pam. After six months of marriage, Pam's husband had left her and she was on her own again, happily bringing up her two lovely children by herself.

"Well he did what I needed. Fiona Jane has a brother. Anyhow, there were grounds for divorce cos he didn't like sleeping with six pussycats down the bed and my cats are special. They've always slept down my bed at my feet. It was Jack or the cats. The cats won," said Pam.

Steve's son Giles had always been a source of concern to the fpl women. When he was small, he didn't seem to develop at the same rate as other children. Steve would say, "He does sit up by himself, he's just tired now," or, "He can stand, he just doesn't want to do it right now."

By the time he was four everybody except Steve could see he had problems. Maybe Steve did too but she didn't let on. Like all mothers, she loved her baby dearly. He was very beautiful.

At times when Pam or I or the other women offered to look after Giles for an afternoon when Steve couldn't get a baby sitter, we worried over his temper and his strange guttural noises. Other children his own age were frightened of him. Sometimes he was quiet and would sit silently on the floor tearing paper into tiny pieces. Steve simply shrugged and said he was different and wonderful. Giles was certainly very handsome, with beautiful long eyelashes and a beautiful smile. He was very loving towards Steve and acted almost normally with Steve's husband, Derek.

STEVE HAD LEARNED of a technique to determine whether people were suitable for management roles. Called the Luscher Colour test, it had been developed in Switzerland by a man called Max Luscher. It consisted of choosing a colour from each of several swatches of coloured material and sending the results to Switzerland for analysis, together with a large amount of money.

Steve had done the test herself and felt it had identified her personality perfectly. She gave the test to Pam, who gave it to me. We all agreed that results were very good. It was decided to give the test to all the project managers when they next came to Chesham for a management meeting.

There were about ten project managers, all of them intelligent, feisty women. They were all working from their homes as far apart as Weymouth in the South West to Bradford in the North. During the next monthly management meeting, Pam took the managers out, one at a time, and gave them the test.

As if the meeting was not disrupted enough, my sister Rosemary called me in the middle of it to say that our mother had been rushed to hospital following another suicide attempt.

Rosemary was distraught. I would have to go directly to the hospital. These cries for help had been happening as long as I could remember. Recently they had been getting more frequent. I told Rosemary that I couldn't leave my meeting and that now she was a married woman she needed to start taking her turn looking after our mother at such times. I told Rosemary to go to the hospital and I would come as soon as I could after my meeting.

I had always carried this burden myself, trying to shield my brother and sister from our mother's episodes. But I was fed up with my mother's childish ways, which seemed to be getting worse now that only our brother Richard was still living at home with our parents.

Richard and my father were constantly fighting, often throwing punches. My mother always took Richard's side. She taunted my father that their son was going to be an architect and earn more than he ever did.

Sadly, that would never be so. Richard would never be as bright as his two sisters. In his father's eyes, this made him stupid and effeminate. Not even as clever as the girls!

"You're just a girl yourself," he would say. His frequent outbursts led to my mother getting another one of her headaches and taking herself off to bed. Every few months she would give up altogether, saying life was not worth living and put her head in the gas oven or take an overdose of aspirin. She never did anything too drastic, indicating that these attempts were just cries for help rather than serious attempts to take her life.

After the meeting, I went to the hospital to find that this attempt had been more serious than most. Our mother was very ill. Rosemary looked at me with accusing eyes.

The next day was Saturday, a whole weekend to relax and catch up with the family. I would be expected to visit my mother in hospital. There would be discussions with my father and sister about what had led to our mother's actions this time and how they could be prevented in future. Of course, nothing changed.

SUNDAY BROUGHT more tragedy. Maureen Durham, one of fpl's longest serving and most competent project managers, called Steve to say that her husband Pete had been killed in an accident. Maureen and Pete had a loving relationship and had been childhood sweethearts. They had two lovely young children. Pete was trying to build a chauffer driven car hire company with one of his friends.

It had been a cold evening. Pete and his friend were doing some maintenance on the petrol tank of one of their two cars. They had closed the garage doors against the cold. One of them had lit a cigarette and the whole place exploded.

Maureen told Steve that she didn't want to talk to anybody. She would leave all her files outside the door of her house. The only person she would have pick them up was Gill Ayling, an fpl project manager who lived nearby.

Gill was the wife of the local curate. She was a qualified aeronautical engineer. She was quiet, kind and sympathetic. Maureen had said that Gill was not to knock at the door or try to phone Maureen. Maureen would contact fpl when she was ready to resume work.

Two weeks later a letter was received from the Luscher Institute enclosing a cheque, returning the fee for Maureen Durham's test. The letter said the candidate was so psychologically disturbed that the results would be meaningless. The Institute suggested that professional help be sought and the test redone when the candidate had recovered from whatever was bothering her.

Steve, Pam and I were amazed. Maureen was one of the most balanced people we knew. Surely, the test could not foretell the future? It was the night after the test that Pete had died, wasn't it? Surely Maureen didn't plan Pete's accident. What could all this mean?

The results for the other managers trickled back over the next few weeks. All results seemed to be spot on with the analysis of the personality of each of the other managers. The results from Maureen's test remained a mystery.

At Pete's funeral, Maureen met one of Pete's school friends. They married six months later. Maureen asked to return to work. I told Maureen of her Luscher test results and asked if there had been anything bothering her. Maureen had forgotten the test. I reminded her of the day of the project managers' meeting, the day before Pete's accident.

Maureen was quiet for a long while. "Yes, I remember that day," she said. "I feel ashamed when I remember it. How on earth can a silly colour test pick that up? You might know that Pete's elderly grandfather lived with us. He was quite a burden, incontinent and difficult to feed. I had my work cut out to look after him, the children, and work but Pete's business wasn't making any money and I needed to work.

"On the morning of the meeting, I had to catch the 6am train from Bournemouth so I took Grandad a cup of tea, as normal. He was lying with his eyes open and not breathing. I assumed he'd died in his sleep. My initial reaction was one of relief that I would not have to look after him any more.

"My next thought was that there was little I could do. I needed to be at the management meeting. I just took the cup of tea back downstairs and left the house pretending I hadn't had time to look in on him. I knew Pete would find him and know what to do. Indeed, there was a phone call waiting for me in the office when I arrived telling me to ring Pete. With all the trauma of Pete's death, I'd forgotten Grandad. Of course, we had a dual service for them both and buried them on the same day. It's amazing that the test could pick up my mood. Will I have to do it again?"

Maureen took the test again and her results were the Maureen they knew and loved.

A FEW WEEKS LATER I noticed that my son Stephen seemed to be off colour. Normally an energetic toddler, he seemed listless and off his food.

"He's probably coming down with measles or chickenpox," said Milly.

After a few days, he seemed only to want cuddles from his Mum but when I laid him on the floor, I found him in exactly the same position when I returned. "He hasn't got a temperature," said Milly. "Don't fret. Kids get all sorts of ailments at his age."

I called the doctor. "I see what you mean," he said. "He seems a bit de-hydrated. Try to get him to drink. I can't find anything really wrong, I'm sure he'll get over it. Children do."

After a week, I got really worried. Now Stephen didn't even whimper when left by himself. He would neither eat nor drink. I called the doctor again. "I'm going to admit him to hospital for tests," said the doctor. "It's just a precaution. I agree with you. His systems seem to be shutting down."

We all went to the hospital. I was asked to wait while tests were done. "We need to do a lumbar puncture," said the hospital doctor. "I've put him in an isolation ward. There is something really wrong here."

"Can I see him?" I said.

"Best not. He's really upset by what we've had to do to him already. The lumber puncture is not a pleasant procedure and we can't give him anything to sedate him until we've done that."

"But he's not yet two," I said, crying with the thought of my little boy being hurt and alone and probably very frightened.

"We find it's best that parents keep out of the way. The children soon realise that it's the horrible doctors who hurt them. Makes them appreciate their parents. Go home, have a good night's sleep. Ring us in the morning."

Reluctantly, I left the hospital. The doctors were already taking the attitude that I was in the way and they knew best.

The next morning I rang the hospital to find that they had moved Stephen out into an isolation hospital in the country. "What's wrong with him?" I sobbed. "I'll get the doctor to speak to you," was the curt reply.

"We're not really sure what's wrong with Stephen," said the doctor. "We've moved him out of the main hospital as a precaution. We don't want him passing what he's got onto other patients. We've done tests and it's not until we have the results that we'll know for sure what he's got. But it does look very nasty so expect the worst."

I was petrified. What did that mean? When could I see Stephen?

"We don't encourage parent's visits," said the doctor. "It just unsettles the children and puts an extra load on the staff. The hospital is a long way away. He's in the best place. You can't go into his room anyway, you would have to look at him through a window."

I was stunned. This was serious. I rang Steve and told her I must have time off, as Stephen was very ill. I asked Milly to look after Claire and Alan. I phoned the National Association for the Welfare of Children in Hospital, an organisation I vaguely remembered from talk from a volunteer from the association at a Townswomen's Guild meeting I had attended with Anne.

The association was sympathetic. They told me my experience was shared by many other mothers. The association was trying to get unrestricted hospital visits for parents of children in hospital but was getting opposition from medical staff who insisted they knew what was best for their patients. They suggested that I should drive out to the hospital and insist on visiting Stephen.

THE DRIVE TOOK over an hour. The hospital was in the country, not even near a village. The receptionist was sympathetic. "No one ever visits here," she said. "But I'll see what I can do."

I was ushered into the superintendent's office. He explained that as the hospital was an isolation hospital, all patients were barrier nursed in their own rooms. Anyone going in a room had to scrub up and wear a mask and gown. They also had to scrub after they left the room. Anything taken into the room had to be burnt. The superintendent said that it was distressful for parents to see their children in that state. I asked timidly if I could just see Stephen and give him his favourite bear.

"Not a good idea to leave the bear. Best it's kept for when he gets home. If it goes in his room, it will have to be burned. If he sees it outside the window it will make him distressed."

I felt overwhelmed. I had to see my little boy. "Could I just peep in the window?" I asked, again timidly.

"You won't like it. You'll just get distressed. We deal with this sort of thing all the time. We know what's best," said the superintendent.

"Please," was all that I could manage.

"Well, five minutes. But you'll distress him. We've got him calmed down. We don't want him distressed."

I was taken down a corridor of tiny glass boxed rooms. Each had a cot with a child lying looking blankly at the ceiling. There was no sign of toys or books or pictures. It was difficult to recognise Stephen except for his shock of bright ginger curls. He looked pale and very ill. He looked up at me with big round eyes. There was no smile. He saw his teddy. There was a flicker, a smile, he tried to sit up. I felt as if my heart would break.

"I'm going in," I said. "This is cruel. You're not going to stop me. I'll ring my MP. There will be questions asked in Parliament. I'm the Chairman of the Social Services Committee at the Townswomen's Guild."

"You can go in but you must wear a gown and mask and if you take that bear in it will have to stay here," said the superintendent. "Nurse, we've got a neurotic mother here. Best humour her. She sounds as if she's out to make trouble."

Once in the room, I picked Stephen up and hugged him tightly. "I'm not going to go away again. Here's your teddy. You'll be alright."

"Five minutes only," said the superintendent.

I decided that either Alan or I would be in Stephen's room all the time until he was released from hospital. I was surprised that they now let me have my way. I was worried that if I left the room to go to the lavatory they would find some way of preventing me getting back in. When they seemed to ignore me I tiptoed round the offices until I found a phone. I phoned Alan and asked him to come to the hospital immediately. Fearing the worst, Alan arrived in just under an hour.

The night nurse was on duty. "I can put up with one of you but not two. I'll get killed. What if all the parents wanted to visit their children?" she said. I quickly told Alan that one or the other of us needed to be in Stephen's room all the time. I asked him to go home, get more toys and books, and bring me some food. The hospital had not given me any food.

I slept on the floor of Stephen's tiny glass walled room until he was released several weeks later. I found that the rules of the hospital were mainly for show. Once, when returning from a shopping trip earlier than expected, I found most of the children outside their rooms in the corridor playing happily together. I thought it best not to make this an issue. I seemed to be the only parent brave enough to stand up to the hospital.

Eventually I was told that Stephen had contracted a rare form of encephalitis that had taken a long time to identify. Evidently, few children survived the illness, and of those who did all but 10% were severely brain damaged. Thankfully, Stephen showed few effects of his illness except that when he was returned home he was over indulged by everyone.

I became a vocal advocate for the National Association for the Welfare of Children in Hospital, but it took several years for unrestricted parental visiting to be allowed in British hospitals. Neurotic mother, indeed.

19 The Land of the Free

ALAN WAS ENJOYING working with Derek in Operations Research. He had made several trips to Kodak's head office in Rochester in upstate New York State to explain what the UK factory was doing. He now had an opportunity for an extended stay and wanted to take us with him to show us the wonders of America.

I thought Steve would be concerned about a lengthy absence, especially as I had had so much time off when Stephen had been ill. To my surprise she said the company had worked well while I was away. There were some business opportunities she would like chased up in the USA so she gave me her blessing to go.

It was 1970. Boeing jumbo jets had just started to provide a commercial service. Our family would be one of the first to cross the Atlantic in a 747. Alan said there were three choices of carrier. One had a choice of meals, one had a choice of films and the third had 14 instead of 11 toilets. Having to cope with two young children on the long flight, I preferred the extra toilets but Alan had chosen the carrier with the choice of films.

We landed in New York and hired a car for the drive to Rochester. Once outside New York City the countryside was very pretty. There were green fields and rolling hills as far as the eye could see. It was autumn so we detoured to see the beautiful autumnal shades of the woods in Vermont.

ROCHESTER WAS A company town. Almost a third of the population worked for Kodak. The rest worked for Xerox or one of the smaller organisations like Bausch and Lomb which made lenses for Kodak cameras.

Rochester had seen race riots in the 1960s and much of the town centre had been burned down. Many satellite towns had been established with huge shopping centres and tidy tree lined avenues of large white weatherboard houses with unfenced front gardens.

Alan had arranged for us to stay with Bill and Betty Bolte. Bill was a personnel manager at Kodak. The Boltes had a large house. Their own children had left home so there was plenty of room for us. The house was set on the edge of a forest. Bill was an enthusiastic bow hunter.

"The deer know when the hunting season starts, he said. "I get two weeks before the gun season starts. The deer just stand around and ask to be shot. As soon as they hear the guns, they hide. I get an extra two weeks at the end of the season too. It's as if they just stand thumbing their noses saying 'yah, come and get me'."

Bill and Betty enjoyed having young children in their house again. They did everything they could to make us feel welcome. "Where would you like to go?" said Bill on our first weekend. "We could go to Niagara Falls but that takes a couple of hours and I thought you might like to hire a car sometime and stay over for a weekend."

"I've looked at the map and I'd like to go to the beach," I said.

"That's a very long way away," said Bill.

"It looks close, just on the edge of the lake," I said pointing to the map.

"Well I never. I've never thought of that as a beach. I'll take you, you're in for a surprise. No need to take your bathers," said Bill.

Arriving at the 'beach' on Lake Ontario, we were surprised to see high metal mesh fencing blocking the way to what looked like a pretty sandy beach. A notice warned 'Danger. No Fishing. Eating more than 2 cubic inches of fish a week taken from this lake will lead to severe poisoning'.

"It looks idyllic," I said.

"That's Kodak again," said Bill. "We dump all our waste into the Genesee River. It ignites spontaneously in the summer. It gets into the lake. The Government is trying to get us to clean up our act but all the companies do it, not just Kodak.

"We've started a scheme to try to recover silver from the drains. So far, we've managed to recover half of what we use so it's been cost effective, but they want us to do more and not put any waste into the river. That would make film production uneconomic. The river is very pretty. It flows through a ravine and there are falls. We call it 'little Niagara'. I'll take you there."

The falls did indeed look very pretty. No one was swimming in the river below the falls even though it was a hot day and there were many families picnicking on the riverbank.

THE NEXT DAY, when Bill and Alan returned from work they were deep in conversation. "It will be impossible to run a company at a profit soon," said Bill.

"The Government is ruining industry. I've spent all day arguing against promoting women. Women will work for pin money. They don't want the stress of being supervisors and managers except a few frosty old spinsters.

"The unmarried women usually live with their parents, so don't need money to buy their own home. They inherit it when their parents die anyhow. The Government doesn't understand that the language in our management meetings isn't always suitable for women. Having them there would restrict the men.

"They wouldn't stand for it. Anyhow, as I told the guy from the Government, Kodak does acknowledge women and makes life easy for them. We use a 13 month, 28 day calendar, instead of following the usual calendar month. That fits in with a woman's cycle doesn't it? She doesn't have to remember her red rag days, they are the same each month."

I was horrified. Was this the way men thought about women in management? The men I met in fpl or at British Computer Society meetings seemed to respect the women. The men in client's organisations seemed to welcome the highly efficient fpl female managers. When I was the only female manager at Kodak the men seemed to treat me as an equal.

Bill was still angry. "They want us to send in statistics showing we are promoting women and we have a proportion of women managers. They'll be getting us to do the same with blacks soon." Bill and Alan laughed.

"That will make your job impossible, Bill," said Betty. "Where would you get blacks with the education and intelligence to do management jobs?"

My mind flashed back to my parent's reaction to Hector and Ena when I was at the Met office, and to Rani the Indian girl who was one of the brightest girls in my school. Certainly, there were few black people in significant jobs in England and it seemed it was the same in the USA, even though there were many more black faces on the streets.

KODAK WAS LIKE many of the large companies in the USA. It prided itself in its Christian ethics. Kellogg and IBM were the same. It would be the late 1980s before IBM salesmen were allowed to claim for alcohol when entertaining clients, even though much alcohol would be drunk in such circumstances.

In the USA, Kodak people started the working day with the company prayer. Employees and their families were expected to attend church on Sunday. Going to church in Rochester was a strange experience. Families would drive into the huge car park next to the church, unhook the speaker from the post as they would at the drive in movies, turn the speaker down low and continue their conversation, or even play bridge.

They would know when the service finished by the loud ringing of the church bells. People would then get out of their cars, seek out their friends and shake hands, remarking how good the sermon was. At first, I thought it was only the Boltes who went to church in this way but I soon realised that most other people in Rochester did the same thing

JOHN UPDIKE'S recent novel 'Couples' had shocked all 'good' families in the North East of the USA. Set in New England, Updike's novels told stories of ordinary people, but the God fearing folk who lived in neat houses in the suburbs felt that it in no way represented the way they lived.

Few wives, especially wives of Kodak managers, worked outside the home. There were morning teas and bridge games with the other wives and a bit of charity work. The women were very good at giving each other compliments, but try as I might to think of compliments in return, they always had more to give, making me feel in their debt. Life as a housewife in that era seemed very empty compared with mine as a wife and mother working in a growing and thriving industry.

The men talked patronisingly about their Little Women who kept house for them as if they were a possession or a favoured pet. But they kept quiet about the stolen afternoons with secretaries or other men's wives. Frequent business trips away gave plenty of cover for the sort of forbidden antics that John Updike documented so well in his novels. This was the place depicted in TV shows and films, where everyone played happy families.

After our time with the Boltes we went to Honeoey Falls, a small town 20 miles south of Rochester. The family we stayed with there was not as wealthy as the Boltes and spent much of their time bickering about buying more luxury goods on hire purchase or shopping at one of the shopping malls.

Both parents and their children were out all day, leaving me to walk the countryside with the children. I longed to get back to England and to the work I loved and where people were less materialistic. But Alan loved the country and said he would move to Rochester if a job could be found for him.

JUST BEFORE WE returned to England, Alan suggested that we see more of America. We travelled along the New England coast, stopping in tiny villages in steep coves to eat local lobster, our clothes protected by lobster bibs. In other villages, the local dish was Swedish meatballs or baked clams. There was a different local radio station in each township but they were all playing Cat Stevens' 'Moon Shadow', one of the biggest hits of that year. The large old stone houses on the windswept cliff tops had turrets with widow's walks so that occupants could watch for their sailor husbands and fathers to return from fishing trips in the wild seas.

We drove on to Cape Cod. There the houses were mainly grand holiday homes. Just outside Hyannis Port we thought we had found a quiet, sandy beach only to be confronted by armed guards who came running across the green lawns of the nearby house telling us this was Kennedy family property.

We travelled on to Boston, stopping at Plymouth Rock to see the place where the Pilgrims landed in America. In Boston we stayed with my school friend Pat. She was now married to an executive of a banana importing company and had a new baby.

After dinner, Pat asked what we would like to do. Driving to the apartment, I had noticed a park nearby beside the Charles River, which had been made popular as the 'Moon River' in the film Breakfast at Tiffany's. It was near full moon. I told Pat that I looked forward to walking along the riverbank in the moonlight, looking over at MIT.

Pat looked horrified. "We can't go there. There's a murder in that park nearly every night. We can't go out tonight, it's not safe. I meant what would you like to do in the house. Tomorrow I'll take you to look at my garden. Living in an apartment, we are very lucky to have our own garden," she said.

The next morning, when she woke us with a cup of tea, Pat triumphantly threw the Boston Globe on our bed. Sure enough, front-page news was another murder by the 'stocking strangler' in the park by the Charles River.

I was pleased to see that, after a really bad start to her life in America, Pat had found happiness. She even had a slight American accent. Asked if she ever considered coming back to England, she gave a very definite "No!"

I had been asked by Steve to make contact with a group of women programmers in Boston who, just like the fpl women, were working from home. They seemed very excited to meet and said they had watched press articles about fpl with great interest. But whenever they grew to more than about ten to twelve programmers, the company seemed to collapse.

They were amazed that fpl was now about 300 strong and still growing. I offered to send them the How To manual I had developed for fpl and details of the metrics and project tracking system we had developed. But Steve would not part with fpl's procedures unless the women agreed to work under fpl's management and contractual agreements.

WE MOVED ON to New York. Security at our hotel was much tighter than anything in England at that time. We were told never to open the door to our room unless someone had phoned us first to tell us to expect a visitor. The door had a two-way hatch which could only be opened from one side at a time. Food, newspapers and the like were put in the hatch from the corridor.

It looked like all the hotels I had seen in American films. I expected to see gangsters and a shoot-up in the corridor at any time. Even though the rooms were double-glazed, I was sure I heard gunshots in the night.

We travelled by ferry to the Statue of Liberty and Ellis Island where immigrants had been processed in the 19th and early 20th centuries. We went up the Empire State building and marvelled at the skyscrapers as far as the eye could see, and the tiny yellow cabs on the very straight streets below. Walking up Broadway, we wanted to see Times Square. We asked a policeman for directions and he told us to buy a map. He pointed to a map shop. When we bought a map we found we were actually standing in Times Square. So much for friendly New York Cops.

In Central Park, on a sunny afternoon we had bought nuts to feed the chipmunks and squirrels. I felt proud of our two beautiful children in their Harrods camel hair coats, black patent leather shoes and white socks. We looked every bit an English family on holiday.

Suddenly, as if a whistle had sounded, people started hurrying past us to the park exits. Did the park close at 5pm? Two mounted policemen stopped. G'day madam, sir" they said doffing their caps. "Beautiful children you have there. Are you visitors to our lovely city? It's time to leave the park."

"I didn't see any closing times," I said.

"No, well see here, at 5pm the office workers come out of their offices. The prostitutes come into the park to give them a little fun. The mafia come into the park to relieve the prostitutes of their hard earned. It's not a good place for a nice English family to be."

"And this is civilisation?" I thought.

STEVE HAD RECEIVED a letter from a company in New York which had offered to let fpl sell their software. She asked me to call in and assess them. It was a very hot '90/90' day in New York, 90 degrees Fahrenheit and 90% relative humidity.

Arriving at the company office in an out of town shopping complex, I was surprised when the proprietor held out his hand and said, "Thank goodness you've come. I can't wait to get you home and take my clothes off."

"My husband and children are in the car outside," I said, totally taken aback by this welcome.

"Good, they can follow my car. Come on, it's not far."

We reached an old watermill. It was an idyllic setting. The clear mill pool underneath the working water wheel looked very inviting. Inside the mill, we were welcomed by a huge black woman.

"How's she been?" said the man. "I'm fine," smiled a fragile looking woman in a wheelchair."

"Now you can see why I like getting out of the office," said the man. "I read about your company and thought I'd like to work like that. I could develop software for you and look after my wife. She's got multiple sclerosis.

"I thought if I only told you I wanted to work for your company, you wouldn't be interested. I thought that if I said I had software to sell you'd take the bait. Sorry, I don't have any software to sell but Mammie here makes the best brownies and coffee and you can all skinny dip in my mill-pond."

He was a pleasant man but had very little experience in developing software. Reluctantly I told him that although I'd keep in touch, I didn't really see much future. I offered to put him in contact with the programming women I had visited in Boston. He gave me a 'genuine' Confederate $1000 bill which was hand made on aged parchment. I later found it was a forgery.

"Let's go to Philadelphia to see the Liberty Bell before we go home," said Alan. I just wanted to get back to England.

We had been staying at Howard Johnson motels. They were easy to spot in the towns with their trade mark 'church steeple' rising above an orange corrugated iron roof. They specialised in family rooms and tasty food for the children. Their slogan was 'Happiness comes in 28 flavours' referring to the ice cream for which they were famous.

I couldn't resist sending Dick a postcard with that logo. I didn't write a message or even sign it.

20 Happy birthday!

BACK HOME I settled quickly back into work. Project 727, as the Department of Health hospital project was now known, had grown considerably. fpl now had over 30 highly qualified systems analysts working on the project.

As a separate project, the Oxford Regional Hospital Board had asked fpl if I could design and develop an integrated patient database covering all the hospitals in Oxfordshire. At that time, patient records were held on paper independently at each hospital. If a patient was taken to a hospital they had not attended before, a new record would be started and there would be no link with existing records held elsewhere in the region.

I was also working on another big job. Through the BCS Advanced Programming Group's Database Task Group, I had met a delightful ex RAF officer, Group Captain Peter Bellerby, who was responsible for the huge PRISM (Personnel Record Information System for Management) project, being developed to manage the personnel records and skills of 500,000 British public servants. I had been heavily involved in the early design stage of that system, which was now nearing completion. fpl had high hopes of being awarded the contract for software development.

The individual project managers seemed to have managed their projects well while I had been away, so I decided to concentrate on managing and working on these three interesting projects. I retained the title of Manager Systems and Programming and was available for support and the mentoring of other project managers. My rate was increased to £2 an hour.

Alan seemed unsettled and longed to go to live and work in America. He asked if he could transfer from Kodak UK to head office in Rochester but there was no opportunity at that time. He applied for jobs with the 3M Company, which manufactured the tapes used to back up computer data. He had heard they were experiencing difficulty with coating technologies but found they had an agreement with Kodak not to hire each other's staff.

I was pleased I did not have to face the possibility of moving to the USA. I did not want to raise our children there. It seemed that American society had two sets of values; the squeaky clean public image as seen in TV sitcoms and films, and the way Americans actually lived their lives. I felt that the children especially would find life living under two quite different value sets confusing. In most households, everything was bought on credit so that after the monthly payments were made there was little money left for food and basic necessities. It was a throwaway society. Everything had to be new, the latest. Everything from cars to washing machines and TVs were dumped for this year's model.

FOLLOWING OUR move to the larger house in Leverstock Green, on the eastern side of Hemel Hempstead, my secretary Anne Duncan drove herself and Milly to our new house each day. Anne had never really liked our typist Jennifer, who boasted openly that her two boys had different fathers, neither of which was her husband.

While working in my old house, where Jennifer lived across the road, Anne and Milly would look through the big picture windows and tut, tut, as another 'visitor' would park his car outside Jennifer's house, usually for about an hour. Now Anne was telling me that Alan's car was often parked outside Jennifer's house during the day. I wasn't sure what to think. I liked Jennifer despite her infidelities. Maybe she would help Alan learn new sexual techniques. I'd read about women who did that. Maybe she could teach him some things that we both could enjoy.

A few days before my 31st birthday, in July 1970, I was surprised that Alan had not arranged a special outing. I was even more surprised when there was no birthday card from him. When he arrived home from work on the afternoon of my birthday, he asked if I could organise for Milly to stay late that day, he had something important he wanted to tell me.

"You've remembered my birthday. I knew you would," I said.

"Is it your birthday? Then we'll leave it for another day, sorry."

I was concerned. "You've forgotten my birthday. You didn't send a card. You haven't given me a present. What's going on? You look very serious. Whatever it is I'd rather hear it now."

Alan took me to the bottom of the garden. I sat on the children's swing. It was high summer and still light.

"Sorry to tell you this on your birthday," he said. "But I've decided I want to be a bachelor and live in America. I feel as if I've always been married. We've known each other since we were 15. I know you don't want to live in America. Well, I've decided I do."

I was taken aback. I had thought he might have wanted to tell me about his affair with Jennifer or that he had a job in America but this was totally unexpected.

"Have you got a job in America?"

"No, not yet, but I thought it would take a while to sort things out here and make sure you and the children are settled then if I haven't got a job I'll just go over there. I'm sure I'll soon get a job."

I wasn't sure what to say. I wasn't sure what I felt. I didn't feel anything, not surprised, not apprehensive, not sad, not rejected.

"Say something," said Alan.

"You have to be the one who tells our parents," was all I could say.

Soon afterwards I heard him on the phone to our parents. "Yes, just come over when you've had your tea. Ann and I have something to tell you."

BOTH SETS OF parents arrived at about the same time. I was putting the children to bed. There was much kissing and cuddling from their grand-parents but eventually they each went to bed. Alan busied himself making sure everyone had a drink then stood formally and told the parents he had decided to go to live in America.

"You mean you're all going to America," said Alan's mother. "I thought you might. You seemed to enjoy it but I thought Ann didn't want to go."

"Ann doesn't want to go. She's not coming," he said.

Four pairs of eyes looked disapprovingly at me. "You have to go if you husband wants to go, Ann," said my mother.

"It's not like that, Mum," I said. "Alan, tell them what you told me. Tell them why you want to go," I said.

"Well I don't want to be married," he said. "I want to be a bachelor. Now don't all talk at once. I've spent a long time thinking this through," said Alan as all four parents started to ask questions.

"It's another woman, isn't it?" said his father. "I've had women throw themselves at me. You've got a wife and family, you just have to tell them you're married."

"No, it's not another woman, Dad."

"Well what are you going to do about this, Ann?" Alan's mother said to me. "You just can't take this sitting down. You must give up your job. I didn't get a job until the boys left school. If you don't have a job, he'll have to knuckle down and support you."

My mother agreed with her. "I've never worked. I've devoted all my life to my family. Ann's father and I have always worried about her working and earning as much as the men do. We knew no good would come of it," said my mother.

"Mum, now it's more important than ever that I work," I said. "If I have to support myself and the kids, I'll need to earn well. I'm glad now that I have kept working. Anyway, I love my job."

They poured advice on us. Alan said he would rethink his decision but doubted he'd change his mind. He agreed that we would go to see a marriage guidance counsellor. The parents left.

What did I feel now? I felt empty. I was not sure what the future held. I was earning enough to pay the mortgage and keep the house. I already paid for the groceries and the children's clothes. Life might not change much. Alan was more like a good friend than a husband. It looked as if this was the time that friends were going to part. Friends had gone away before. I felt little different from when Pat and Kathleen had gone to America.

THAT NIGHT I TOLD Alan that I knew about his affair with Jennifer. "Is sex any different with her? Is it better than with me?" I asked.

"Well not exactly better but different. We do oral sex a lot and you and I have never tried it. Would you like to try?"

I had read about oral sex. It didn't sound at all pleasant but I was at the stage in my life when I felt I should at least try other things. Alan started on me. I felt uncomfortable but endured the attention wondering if I would have to reciprocate.

"You're no fun. At least you could try to enjoy it," said Alan. "Jennifer really enjoys it and then she does it to me and it's great. You're too uptight. Sex is to enjoy."

"Well I don't really enjoy that," I said. With that Alan bit me down there really hard and stomped off into the spare room. I went to wash and found that I was bleeding profusely.

When Milly and Anne arrived the next day, they wanted to know what was going on. I told them that Alan wanted to go and work in America and he might go for a trial period.

"Good," said Milly. "That will get him away from that Jennifer. It might make a man of him."

That day I was very sore where he had bit me. The day after I had difficulty walking. When Milly arrived, I said I had to stay in bed because I wasn't feeling well.

"Poor thing, you must be worried stiff with your husband about to leave," said Milly. "How will you afford to pay me? How will you afford to keep this house?

I assured Milly that I could afford to keep her on, and that I would need her even more when Alan was gone.

My mother came over. "You look really ill, Ann. It's not like you. Better call the doctor and get some pills. I take them all the time. They make you feel much better."

The doctor was called. I was embarrassed, but told him what had happened. "You're badly infected. That bite went very deep. What bought this on?" I told the doctor that Alan wanted to move to America. "Well at least get him to use the spare room for a few days. This is very nasty. You won't be able to have intercourse for a couple of weeks," the doctor said.

Dick called several times. Both Anne and my mother were beginning to think there was another side to the story. "He's just a good friend," I said. "Several girlfriends have called and you haven't commented on their calls."

"What exactly is wrong with you, Ann?" said my mother. I told her. My mother was aghast. "What, bit you down there? Well I've read about it of course but nice people like us don't do that sort of thing. You can't live with him now. Just get a divorce. That's grounds for divorce isn't it?"

WHEN I WAS better I met with Dick and told him that I had been too ill to be taken out for my birthday. "We'll give you a good party," he said. "After the next Advanced Programming Group meeting, instead of going to the pub a few of us will take you somewhere great. Just wear your best long dress. It will be somewhere very nice."

I had thought Dick meant that just the two of us would go to dinner but true to his word he organised five of the members to go to dinner. After the meeting, we took a taxi to the Samuel Pepys pub by the Thames.

The upstairs restaurant was called 'And so to Bed' which was the name of a musical about Pepys currently running at a London theatre and a line that he used a lot in his diaries. The tables where draped about with hangings like a four poster bed. We drew the curtains and ate a very good old English dinner of steak and kidney pudding and plum duff and custard, washed down with plenty of good old ale for the men and champagne for me.

"You'll remember today, Ann. It's not every girl who can say she celebrated her 31st birthday with five men in a four poster bed!"

When the dinner was finished, I said I had to get off home. The other four men politely made their exits and left Dick and me to take our port on the balcony overlooking the river. They all seemed sure something was going on between Dick and me.

"I'm embarrassed," I said. "They all think we're having an affair and we're not."

"Let them think that. They're all envious," said Dick. "You look lovely in your pretty blue dress. Don't go home yet, I've organised another surprise."

I was dubious. "No, I'm not going to start an affair. Alan and I are going through a sticky patch but we've decided to go to a marriage guidance councillor and I don't want to complicate things."

"It's not what you think, but it's something I know you'll like," said Dick. We got a cab to the earthworks next to where a new underpass was being built under the Thames near the Tower of London. He asked the driver to wait. The ground was uneven and I had to hold Dick's hand as I clambered over piles of earth and stones, holding my dress so it didn't get muddy. Turning the corner, we came upon a brightly floodlit area.

"They've unearthed some Roman remains," said Dick. "They've been given permission to work at night so they don't hold up the roadworks. I came here a few days ago. It's fascinating."

As we watched, we could see the remains of a Roman wall and some heavy wooden beams. We spoke to the archaeologists and were given a tour of the site. Dick begged a Roman nail as a souvenir.

"I'd love to stay but I must go home," I said. "My mother is staying with us for a while and she is already suspicious about the number of times you've rung to see how I was when I was ill."

With that, I was whisked back to the taxi and driven to my car. The taxi then took Dick on to his home in Essex. "I've had the best birthday ever," I said as we parted.

ALAN AND I booked into a marriage guidance counsellor. After a couple of sessions together, she saw us separately. She was a friendly busty woman. At one stage, when speaking to me alone, with Alan minding Stephen outside the room, Stephen decided he wanted to see his Mummy. He burst into the room with Alan in tow.

Later that evening, Alan told me that he couldn't understand why the counsellor and I had looked so cosy. We were laughing, obviously at him. He also said he thought the counsellor was 'oversexed' because she had a big bust and kept asking him questions about our sexual relationship.

The counsellor told me I didn't have a married relationship. She said it seemed to her that Alan and I were living as brother and sister. I couldn't understand the comment. "And you won't until you fall in love with someone. You'll find that quite a different relationship," said the counsellor.

It wasn't going to work. Alan decided he would definitely go to America. I contacted our family solicitor, Mr Hodge, for advice. A large, elderly, fatherly man, he had always acted for us on legal matters.

"Oh my dear, I'm so sorry. I thought you two were an ideal couple," he said. "Of course I can't act for you both so I'll support you. Now, I think that as you are a young, attractive woman, you should consider a divorce."

He sent a letter advising me formally that he would act for me and not my husband and that he would arrange for Alan to be 'found with a woman'. His fee for that service would be 10/6d. He explained that nothing bad would happen. There were hotels in Brighton that arranged for a woman to hop into a gentleman's bed and a photographer would take a photograph. That would provide sufficient grounds for divorce.

Did I want a divorce? There didn't seem to be any reason unless one or the other wanted to get married again.

Alan moved out and rented a flat near our home. We decided which of the household items he would need to make his flat comfortable. He took the children out on the weekends. After one such outing, Claire said that Daddy's flat didn't look as comfortable as our house. She said his bedroom was all drab and grey. I bought a very regal looking purple and black bedcover for Claire to take next time she visited. Soon Stephen announced that he did not want to go out with his Daddy so Claire made the visits alone.

The effect of the decision on Jennifer was not as I expected. She decided that she wanted to go to America with Alan and take her boys and our children. I asked Alan if that was what he wanted and it seemed it was not.

When Anne Duncan told Steve what had happened, Steve immediately wrote a letter to Jennifer telling her that her services were no longer required by fpl.

21 Career woman

THE COOLNESS AT fpl between Steve and Pam got worse. I did my best to stay out of company politics and immerse myself in my work and my family. I watched as others gradually took sides with either Pam or Steve.

Towards the end of 1970 Steve decided that there was significantly more profitable business in systems and consultancy than in programming. She believed the image of each area was quite different, so she decided to split the company into 'freelance programmers' and 'freelance systems'. But the Trades Practices people would not let her to register a company called 'freelance systems', so she decided to call her second company F2.

She asked me to be Technical Director. Pam was to continue to run fpl as General Manager. Steve would run F2, and be Chair of both companies. In theory, any systems work offered to fpl would be passed to F2 and any programming resulting from systems work in F2 would go to fpl.

F2 WAS LAUNCHED in February 1971 at a grand event held at the Institute of Directors, in a magnificent Georgian building on Pall Mall. Representatives from all our clients, many prospective clients and the press were invited to the launch, together with senior panellists.

In the early 1970s, fashion had moved rapidly from the mini skirt of the 60s to the maxi, where skirts were worn nearly to the ankles. Floor length skirts were also acceptable for daywear. A few brave souls with good legs still clung to the miniskirt and some women were wearing trouser suits for business. There were also hot pants, tiny shorts worn mainly for sports, at the beach or disco but never for work. Steve issued an edict that only maxi length dresses should be worn at the launch. There were to be no miniskirts or trouser suits.

On the day of the event, which was to be held mid morning with a light lunch afterwards, Steve inspected everybody. All passed the dress parade with flying colours. The rehearsal held the previous day had gone very well.

Steve had hired a media consultant to coach the women who were speaking, me included. The consultant decided on the morning of the event that we should each have a small glass of brandy 'to put a sparkle in our voices'.

I was petrified at the thought of speaking before hundreds of people. I said I didn't drink spirits. I was given a small sherry. I had arranged for my secretary Anne to stand at the back of the room and give me feedback by way of hand signals to let me know how my presentation was going.

When it was my turn to speak I lost all my nerves and spoke confidently. Anne even indicated that my usually serious public speaking face had been replaced by a smile. The media manager congratulated the women on their performance and told me he had given me half and half vodka and sherry.

Steve could see a group of clients tightly packed around one of our project managers, the very tall and very slim Brenda Chapman. She looked very demure at the dress parade with a khaki battledress top and long skirt with white shoes peeping beneath the floor length hem. The day had been cold so she also wore a white fur hat and carried a white fur muff.

As lunch was being served, she had taken off her maxi skirt and stood resplendent in tiny khaki hot pants and long white thigh boots. She had removed her fur hat and let her long, blonde hair hang loose to her waist.

Steve was furious. The media manager persuaded her not to make a scene as the clients were obviously enjoying the show. Steve agreed to do nothing so long as he could guarantee that the media would take no photographs.

F2 FLOURISHED. Steve paid me a good salary. Alan was leaving for the USA at the end of the year. He agreed to pay the mortgage on our house until he left. The mortgage was huge. Because interest on a mortgage was considered an expense which could be set against earnings for tax purposes, our house had been mortgaged to the maximum. Many people did that because of the tax benefits. But because I was a female the bank would not allow me to take over the mortgage, even though I was earning more than Alan. So my father had to act as guarantor.

All the relatives, both mine and Alan's, helped with clothes and gifts for the children. I had always bought expensive clothes for the children and passed them on to others, but now the fpl and F2 family offered me hand-me-down clothes for the children. I gratefully accepted.

Separation or divorce was still relatively rare amongst my circle of friends and colleagues. I knew of no woman who had been left on their own unless their husband had died. Although I explained to everyone that the decision to split was mutually agreed, they all blamed Alan for the separation. His own parents refused to speak to him for many years.

Dick and I did start an affair. We started arranging our days so that we could spend stolen afternoons together on the ridgetop on Hampstead

Heath. We made love in the long dry grass which Dick said matched my corn coloured hair.

Afterwards, looking out over London spread out below, we talked about anything and everything. We were both thirsty to glean information about our earlier experiences, and our values and opinions on current issues. Conversations were intense but easy. Why hadn't I met this man before I married? The anticipation of our meetings made my heart race. When we parted it was very painful. Was this real love?

I DECIDED THAT as I was now the breadwinner for my family it was time devote more energy to my career. I set about improving my image, both personally and in the computer industry. I bought designer dresses and arranged to have my hair done at the hairdressers twice a week or before each important dinner or meeting. I visited Elizabeth Arden in Bond Street for their 'top to toe' service every month.

I attended all the British Computer Society meetings and industry dinners I could. Because I was usually the only woman I was often asked to sit next to the guest of honour. To earn additional income, I wrote a weekly article for Computing magazine, for which I was paid £40.

The Department of Health project was a real money maker for F2. The two other software houses involved, CAP and SPL, were vying for bigger slices of the contract but F2 had the lead role and managed the project. We also had the confidence of the Assistant Chief Architect that we were managing the project well.

The head of the Government Audit Department invited me out to dinner several times. I said I never took dinner alone with clients but I promised that when the project was over I would take him to lunch. He could choose the restaurant and F2 would pay the bill. He chose a tiny, intimate restaurant in the upstairs room of a private house in central London.

The room was dark. The rich blood red velvet curtains over the widows were drawn. There were four tables, one in each corner of the room. These were far enough apart to ensure that the other guests would not overhear intimate conversations. The clientele seemed to be wealthy professional men entertaining their mistresses. I wondered if there were bedrooms on the premises and what I would do if things turned tricky.

During the lunch, the waiter joked with the man from Audit, who was obviously a regular customer, implying that I was one of a long line of women he had entertained in the restaurant.

After many courses, each with a different bottle of wine, the conversation seemed to be getting more and more intimate. Eventually he blurted out, "I've always wanted to know, is Steve a lesbian?"

"I'm not sure what religion she is," I said. "I think she's Jewish but I don't think she is Orthodox," I said. Taken aback, he gazed at me through a hazy stupor and called for the bill. When the waiter brought it, he made great show of heaving the 'heavy' bill over the vase of flowers on the table between us and plonked it in front of me.

I turned to the waiter and smiled. "As his wife, I have to pay for this. It's food so it comes out of the housekeeping budget."

The waiter looked embarrassed. "Oh Sir, Madam, I'm sorry. I hope you didn't take offence at my comments." The man from Audit laughed. When we next met, he told me that he'd dined out on the story for weeks.

I HAD BECOME a Fellow of the Institute of Directors, where we had had the F2 launch. It was in a beautiful building and had an excellent restaurant which was a useful place to entertain clients. I could arrange for the bill to be charged to the F2 account, useful in a time when men were embarrassed by a woman paying for their lunch. The Institute also had a very comfortable ladies' room where the few women directors could shower and change for evening events or just rest and read a book between appointments.

I attended the Institute's Annual Conference, which was held at the Royal Albert Hall. The keynote speaker was the Prime Minister of Singapore, Lee Kuan Yu. There was much sniggering in the hall when Prime Minister Lee took the stage resplendent black tie and tails with his wife and daughter in tow in beautiful full-skirted ball gowns with huge puff sleeves.

Whispered comments from the directors, many of whom were ex public schoolboys, implied that one could not expect someone from the colonies to know how to dress for a business event that was held at 10am.

But when Mr Lee spoke passionately of the vision he had for the Singapore economy a chill passed through the room. Was it possible to build a world class economy on a tiny island with no resources? An economy, which this man told us, would one day rival London as the centre of world commerce. We were all very dubious, but all of this subsequently happened.

I was fascinated. How I longed to see the mysterious East. I had been fortunate to see much of Europe and parts of America but the world was a vast and wondrous place. One day I hoped to travel further, like Miss Errington. She had been to Singapore, Hong Kong and Shanghai. I longed to see South America, Persia, Egypt and the islands of the Pacific.

THE SPLIT OF the company into fpl and F2 was not successful. It caused administrative overlaps and confused clients. Many people felt the company had lost its way. Pam was telling clients that F2 was failing and that all business should go through fpl. There were rumours Pam was directing profitable business into her own company. Some senior project managers met with me and suggested we establish our own company.

I felt the concept of the company belonged to Steve and we should not try to steal it from her. Many people felt Steve didn't care about the business anymore. She had moved into a very large house in Chesham which cost over £25,000, a fortune back then. She seemed to spend much of her time in bed.

Dick and I often met at the Royal Institution in Albemarle Street. When I was in the sixth form at school my class was taken by our Science Mistress, Miss Minster, to hear a lecture given by Sir Lawrence Bragg in the old lecture theatre with its high raked seats.

Sir Lawrence had been one of Miss Minster's lecturers when she was a university student. I remembered Miss Minster introducing me to Sir Lawrence, saying I was one of her best students and that I would go on to do science at Oxford or Cambridge. That all seemed so long ago.

Dick was usually late for our meetings. The usher would take me into the members' library. There was a whole section on witchcraft and astrology. Many of the books were handwritten; some dated from 400AD. I was fascinated. This was the origin of science.

I discussed what I had read with Dick. As an astronomer he considered astrology little better than witchcraft. This spurred me on to learn all I could about the arcane craft. When I had read all the books on the subject in the Royal Institution Library, I started to search for knowledge further afield.

I was fascinated to find that many of the ancient civilisations like Persia, China, India and Egypt had used astrology to identify things like the best time for important business transactions or marriages. I also discovered that many modern businessmen in Asia still regularly used astrologers.

I had access to a printed ephemeris that showed the placement of the planets relative to Greenwich meantime. Because I was born in London, I found I could use the printed ephemeris and my newfound skill to accurately 'predict' past events in my own life, like the birth of my children and the date of my marriage.

I asked Dick how I could get hold of an ephemeris for places other than the Greenwich meridian. Ever one for a challenge, and being a skilled mathematician, Dick said he could write a Fortran program to calculate planetary positions, both past and present, for any line of longitude.

Whenever I wanted a chart, Dick would run his program on the Atomic Energy Commission's Atlas computer at Harwell where he often taught Fortran. The program slowed Atlas considerably. When people complained, Dick would say, "Someone must be inverting a large matrix." I learned how to interpret the horoscopes Dick cast. We discussed possibly one day making a living from such a service.

DICK HAD ANOTHER skill with numbers. He worked out the relationship between the numbers on a roulette wheel and the placement of bets on the table. He knew that when the bets on the table were distributed in a certain way, the croupier could place the ball in a part of the wheel to minimise the casino's loss. Placing his bets at the last minute in the place most likely to be where the croupier had placed the ball usually led to a win.

One of the best places to have lunch in London in the early 1970s was the Playboy Club on Park Lane. A prime steak and a glass of red wine cost 10/6d, well below cost, to attract businessmen to gamble at lunchtime. Dick took me to lunch there with a group of partners from CAP and took us all to the gaming room to demonstrate his skill.

Often he would meet me after work and we would drive to a Channel port, take the early evening ferry to one of the French seaports, and gamble all evening. We would then spend the night in a grand old hotel and fly back in time for work in London the next day.

Dick gave me several pieces of beautiful handmade jewellery from our winnings, including a lovely moonstone, which he said was the colour of my eyes when I lay in the grass on a warm summer day. We had the moonstone made into a silver ring. Dick bought a plain silver band to match and called me his 'silver wife'.

The people at the roulette tables fascinated me. I watched the highs and lows of wins and losses. I enjoyed playing but I hated to lose, so rather than playing the numbered squares, I would place an equal amount of chips on black and red or odds and evens, thus always getting a payback. It only equalled what I had bet, unless the ball landed on the zero. But people usually only saw the money you won, not where you had placed your bets.

Seeing I usually got a payout, patrons would ask me how I worked the system. The croupiers gradually worked out how Dick did. It was the same method they had been taught to protect the casino. He was often discretely advised not to go back to the table after a big win.

22 Moving on

IN 1972 F2 AND fpl were joined back together. The experiment had not worked. I was asked to head the Technical Division of the recombined company, which was now called F International, or FI. Pam did not reconcile with Steve and left the company.

The combined company had nearly 400 programmers, who were still called panellists. In addition to the original married woman with children, several men and single women panellists were now working for us.

Many had joined the company because they had special needs which were alleviated by working from home. These included an oratorio singer who wanted large chunks of time off at Christmas and Easter; a man who had been made quadriplegic as a result of a car accident; a writer who wanted to live in the English Lake District, a woman nursing her mother dying of cancer, and people who just preferred the flexible lifestyle that was possible as a panellist.

I appointed one of the project managers, ex IBMer Anne Russell, to be my deputy. Steve seemed to disapprove, saying she could never work with Anne if anything happened to me. Later, I thought I found out why. Anne Russell was a competent, vivacious, dark haired woman married to a man from the IT industry. She made an ideal deputy and was well liked by all the other staff.

Steve's son Giles was growing up to be a handsome young man, but he was very big and strong for his age and definitely had some sort of intellectual problem. Steve had several nannies but most found Giles too difficult and did not stay long.

Steve's sister, Renate, had been working in Australia as a House Mother for Dr Barnardo's, the children's charity. Her marriage broke up so Steve asked her to come back to England to look after Giles. Renate brought her daughter, Clair, who was about the same age as my daughter, Claire. The two little girls became great friends and looked forward to playing together whenever I visited Steve at her home, The Old Schoolhouse, in Chesham.

I BECAME MORE involved with the British Computer Society. It was very much an old boys network. Membership enabled me to gather intelligence on what was happening in the industry. Steve encouraged my involvement as it helped to identify business opportunities for FI.

In October 1972 I was the first woman to be elected to the BCS Council. This caused much comment in the computer press. I spent about one day a week on BCS business but I worked long hours into the night for FI.

I had been elected a Fellow of the BCS in 1970, largely for my pioneering work on the Atlas Supervisor and The Database Task Group. There were very few female Fellows at that time. In addition to chairing the Database Task Group, I was Deputy Chairman of the Technical Board and a member of the Advanced Programming Group, in 1970, I had been appointed the BCS representative on the committee advising the Science Museum on its proposed Computing Gallery.

This last appointment brought considerable publicity for me and for FI. It introduced me to the history of the industry, which I found fascinating. In the early 1970s most people thought computers had been invented by the Americans. US manufacturers, particularly IBM, dominated sales, so it was understandable that newcomers to the profession and the media should have overlooked the work of British pioneers.

The Science Museum had a prototype of Charles Babbage's Difference Engine. Built in 1832, it was a sophisticated mechanical calculator way ahead of its time. But Babbage never finished it, abandoning it in 1834 to work on his much more ambitious Analytical Engine.

This marvellous mechanical machine is considered to be the forerunner of all modern stored program computers. Rather than being built to carry out a specific set of calculations, it would carry out any of a range of calculations determined by setting a number of parameters on the device.

The Babbage machine fascinated me. Its gleaming cogs seemed to work effortlessly and the way they lifted and dropped and carried out their calculations reminded me of the delicious feeling when all the numbers rolled over to zero on the early adding machines and the Monroe at the Met Office.

The Difference Engine had been the centrepiece of Babbage's 'conversation' evenings which he held at his house over a hundred years earlier. Coincidentally he had lived just round the corner from Ferranti's Portland Place office where I had attended my first computer course.

It was at one of these evenings that Babbage met Ada Lovelace, Lord Byron's beautiful daughter, and had started a relationship that was to last until her early death in 1852. Ada was a woman well before her time. An accomplished mathematician, she understood the potential of Babbage's ideas and set about learning all she could and writing a paper on the capabilities of the invention.

Ada's notebooks, along with Babbage's design drawings and notes for his more advanced Analytical Engine, were also owned by the Science Museum. I felt the same thrill when holding the notebooks as I had when I held the weather diaries from the 1600s which were stored in the Met Office archives.

Engineering techniques in the mid 19th century were not up to building a fully functioning Analytical Engine. It would have been capable of carrying out complex mathematical calculations and had many of the components of modern computers, including a mechanical 'mill', which was essentially the central processing unit. Although in the mid 19th century electricity was starting to be used to drive mechanical devices, Babbage's machines were designed to be powered by steam.

Ada Lovelace, now regarded as the world's first computer programmer, died before she was 40, leaving Babbage a disillusioned man weighed down by debt and unable and unwilling to continue his life's work. A working Difference Engine was finally built for the Science Museum in the 1990s, using Babbage's drawings and with funding from Paul Allen, who co-founded Microsoft with Bill Gates.

THERE WERE MANY more delights in the Science Museum. I was shown a range of wooden toys made by King George V for his children. These were based on impinging balls and sloping planes — the elements of my applied maths classes at Acton Tech. When I took my children to the Science Museum, they too played with these priceless exhibits which today could only be handled by qualified experts wearing white gloves.

Although the Museum had been given the early British ACE computer from the National Physics Laboratory, we had heard rumours of very powerful computers used to crack German Enigma codes in World War II. Try as we might, we could not get information on these machines. The technology was still classified as Top Secret. The incredible story of Alan Turing and the part British computers played in codebreaking work at Bletchley Park during the war was not revealed until later in the 1970s.

The computers used by the Americans in the war years were not classified. These were large impressive looking chrome and glass 'electronic brains' like the Harvard Mark I were thought by non experts to be the forerunners of modern computers. Thomas J. Watson, the founder of IBM, reputedly contributed $1 million to Harvard Mark I and was said to have remarked that the world would need only ever need five of them. But they were not proper computers, just large and powerful calculating machines.

The world's first electronic stored program computer was built in Manchester, England and first functioned in June 1948. it was a demonstration machine called the Small Scale Electronic Machine (SSEM), nicknamed 'Baby'. It was not until February 1949 that America's ENIAC, originally operational in February 1946 but as a single purpose computer, was converted to a stored program machine.

Many textbooks conveniently forget that the original ENIAC was a single purpose device, and that it took many hours of engineering work each time a different set of calculations was done. Thus the myth that the Americans developed the first stored program computer was born. EDSAC, the world's first full scale computer, designed as a stored program computer, was built at Cambridge University in the UK and was operational in May 1949.

The world's fourth stored program computer, called the CSIR Mark I, and later renamed CSIRAC, was designed and built by Trevor Pearcey at Australia's CSIRO. First operated in November 1949, it is still in existence, though it is not in working order. All the others have been destroyed.

THROUGH THE BCS I built a good relationship with Group Captain Peter Bellerby, who was in charge of the UK Government's prestigious PRISM project. PRISM was intended to manage the personnel records for half a million British public servants.

Peter designed the database for the system with much help from members of the BCS Advanced Programming Group, especially Peter King, who was a Professor at the University of London, and me. He soon realised that the effort needed for systems development was enormous and would have to be given to a software house.

I had watched PRISM grow from fairly conceptual simple beginnings to a large and complex system that would manage all staff matters in the British public service, from payroll to the identification of personnel with specific skills for specific assignments, overseas postings, and the like. It was the first time the UK Government had attempted such a large systems development project.

Steve decided that rather than risk the project going to another software house with a higher profile than fpl, she would form a consortium of software houses to work on large projects such as PRISM. Thus, in early 1972, ASH, Allied Software Houses, was formed.

ASH comprised FI, Plymouth Computer Systems, CSP (Computer Systems and Programming), ACS (Allied Computer Systems) and Systems Designers. The group had over 170 full time staff, with 400 FI home based professionals as an additional resource. This made ASH the biggest software house with the widest range of skills in the UK at that time. We easily won the PRISM project.

As FI grew, the pressure of running a large vibrant company became difficult to bear. Steve often wanted to talk at 2am and would give me papers late at night to be read by morning. I was still writing a regular column for Computing, a weekly computer newspaper. Milly had decided to go back to full time nursing and I had had a series of less than satisfactory minders for the children. They were now seven and four, and Stephen had started preschool. Maybe it was time to think about getting a more regular job.

FI had been commissioned to develop the software for the Government's Personal and Executive Register. The system provided a job finding service for executives. At the launch, once the Minister had made the speech and cut the ribbon, he asked that the system be demonstrated for him.

Access was via a Visual Display Unit where job applicants could specify parameters for the position they were seeking. None of the very senior men at the launch could use a keyboard so it fell to me, as usual the only woman at the event, to demonstrate the system.

In addition to providing details of skills, academic qualifications, languages spoken, etc. the applicant was asked a number of questions such as the location of the job sought, the salary required, and any other perks like fringe benefits.

I enjoyed using my imagination to describe my dream job. I specified that the job was to be located less than 15 minutes walking distance from my home. I asked for all school holidays as paid leave and requested a salary far in excess of my current salary, non-contributory superannuation and private health benefits.

After the lunch, the manager of the service asked if I wanted him to erase the entry I had made. He said there were over 3000 jobs in the system but as it wouldn't be officially available to the public for another three weeks, mine was the only job seeker entry.

I said my entry should be left in the system to see what eventuated. Little did I know what that would lead to.

A WEEK LATER the system sent me a postcard saying my entry had been recorded. Then the week after that I got another letter that said my entry had been matched with a position.

How could this be? Surely I would know if there was an employer located that close to my home willing to pay such a high salary. Could it be that FI was seeking staff at that level? No, I knew the system didn't match an applicant with their current company. The letter asked if I wanted my data but not my identity, sent to the prospective employer. Why not, I thought.

Then another letter arrived saying the prospective employer wanted to follow the application further. Would I be interested to know who the employer was? In a few days I was told the employer was a company called Computer Technology limited (CTL).

I knew the company. It was a new British computer manufacturer trying to enter the minicomputer market. I knew Iann Barron, the owner, through the Real Time Club, a social group for top people in the industry.

CTL was indeed located just 15 minutes walk from my house. But surely they couldn't afford that salary, and what about the ridiculous fringe benefits I'd specified? I realised that, apart from my initial interview with Steve, I had not attended a real job interview for 16 years. It would be good practice. At that salary, Iann would interview me and we'd laugh about it. Perhaps when he knew my name he wouldn't even want to do it.

I agreed for my name be disclosed to the company. A week later I was asked to attend an interview with Tom Margerison. He was a well-known TV presenter who explained scientific discoveries to the layman. He had founded New Scientist magazine. How was he involved with the company? I looked forward to meeting him.

The meeting was pleasant. Tom told me about the company but it was all stuff I already knew. CTL's main product was the Modular One computer, intended to be a competitor to the DEC PDP range. DEC marketed a range of computers, while the Modular One was claimed to be the computer that could be tailored to suit any client.

Tom offered me a job as a Product Executive in the Marketing Department. My role would be to tell the company what they should be developing to meet customers' needs. I would have no staff except a shared secretary. I was told the starting salary was even higher than that I had requested. Did I have any other questions? I hardly dared ask.

"What about the fringe benefits?" I asked.

"Oh, they are all fine," said Tom. "Even the school holidays?" I queried. "Of course," said Tom.

Tom Margerison commended me for my considerable work for the BCS and said he thought that the contacts I would bring for CTL would be very useful. He asked me to estimate the time my BCS activities took. When told it was about a day a week, Tom had said he thought that very reasonable and urged me to continue.

I was still not comfortable. Why me? Why such a high salary, much higher than normal industry rates? Did I want to work for these people? I had doubts.

"No, I don't think I want the job," I said. "I've heard that CTL is like a mad magician's workshop. I know Iann and he's very nice, but most people I know don't understand what he's talking about," I said.

"Good, good," said Tom. "You are exactly right. That's why I'm recruiting people like yourself who have a very good reputation in the industry. Iann is mad but he is brilliant. We need his flair and brilliance but we are growing rapidly and to extend our customer base successfully and make money we need hard-headed commercial people like you."

"But why will I be working in Marketing?" I said. "I'm a Manager."

"I'm getting a small group of intelligent practical business people to work under me. Like most technical people, Iann thinks his baby doesn't need marketing because it sells itself. I'm out to prove differently."

"But I won't be a salesperson, will I?" I said.

"No, not at all. Think of yourself as a consultant to me," said Tom.

"And what is your position in the company?" I asked.

"I'm the Chairman," he said.

SO I DECIDED to join CTL, and leave Steve and FI after eight very enjoyable years. Steve was very sad to lose me.

Looking back, I have often thought what made fpl and FI so successful. There was no doubt that fpl was founded at a time when there was a severe shortage of programming skills. The concept was supported by the Government and attracted a significant amount of publicity.

The successful identification of people who would perform well when working from a home base was always difficult, and even after many years of operation half those selected did not complete their first project. The general psychological profile of IT professionals is that they have a low need for social interaction. This might mitigate against any feelings of social isolation.

The early establishment of estimating and performance metrics, which I had a bit to do with, permitted fpl to give fixed price estimates to clients and pay fixed price rates to panellists. It also enabled the identification of panellists' uncharacteristic behaviour at an early stage in a project, permitting management intervention and remedial action if appropriate.

Both fpl and FI established a supportive infrastructure which generated a feeling of belonging to a good organisation. There were many social events to bring people together and many panel members formed deep and lasting friendships. They always attracted publicity in the press and they were exciting places to work.

Steve's companies achieved high productivity and a reputation for top quality. There has now been a lot of research on why home based workers achieve high productivity, and also on worker's activities in an office environment. Research shows that about half of the time spent by workers in offices is socialising, game playing and politics.

Steve Shirley retired in 1993 at the age of 60, as she had always said she would. She sold some of the company to her employees but was still a major shareholder when FI was floated on the London Stock Exchange in 1996. She became very wealthy and is one of Britain's leading philanthropists.

She is now Dame Stephanie Shirley and devotes much of her time to her charitable trusts established in memory of her son. Giles was diagnosed with severe autism and died from an epileptic seizure at age 35.

In 2001 FI changed its name to Xansa. In 2007 it was acquired by major French software and systems house Steria for £427 million.

23 The Troubles

I ARRIVED AT THE CTL office in June 1973. I was greeted by the Marketing Manager, Harvey Crammond. I found to my surprise that I was only one of two Product Executives. Harvey told me we would both report to him.

He introduced me to Bernard, the other Product Executive. Bernard was a tall gangly youth who was possibly an albino. His skin was transparently pale, his hair white and his eyes, behind tinted blue spectacle lenses, were a pale pink.

Harvey asked Bernard to go through the things they had been talking about. Bernard introduced me to a secretary we were to share. He pointed to my desk opposite to his own outside Harvey's office. He acted as if he were my superior and spoke in hushed terms about the things Harvey and he had agreed I should work on. The first task was to sort out the salesmen who were selling things CTL didn't make.

I was given the CTL price list and the 35 orders that could not be filled from CTL stock. In most cases the CTL salesman had given a fixed price quote. How could a company work like this? Where was Tom Margerison? Who was Harvey and why was he my manager? I took an instant dislike to Bernard who I felt was slimy and obsequious, like Dickens' Uriah Heep. I decided to speak to Harvey but he was nowhere to be found.

I took the list of items to be sourced outside CTL and saw that most could be purchased from DEC. I rang my contact there and asked for prices. He knew I often asked for prices for equipment for a government department and tried to find out which. I said the client's name was confidential but I wasn't asking for special prices. List prices would do.

Looking at the list of equipment, it was obvious none of the 35 orders could be delivered for the prices quoted by the salesmen. And none could be delivered in the time quoted. Bernard hovered around my desk. He seemed to have little to do.

"Harvey wants that information urgently. Give it to me and I'll check it and give it to him," he said.

"I'll give it to Harvey myself," I replied. When I left that afternoon I took the papers with me. I felt that if I left them on my desk Bernard would claim the work as his own.

Things did not look promising.

WHEN I GOT HOME I rang Dick. "I've made a dreadful mistake," I said. "I hate the place. I hate the work. I hate the people."

"You've only been there one day," said Dick. "First impressions are often wrong. We both like Iann Barron. Have you seen him? Why don't you talk to him?"

"You're right, of course," I said. "I'm being silly. I'm sure it will all work out. The product is good. I can drive the children to and from school myself and the pay and conditions are fabulous."

"Will you be able to get away or have some meetings in London? When can we see each other?" asked Dick.

"I'll still be going to BCS meetings and CTL is keen that I continue with the Science Museum project," I said. "Let me settle in. There'll be opportunities to meet. I couldn't bear to live without seeing you."

On my second day at CTL I gave Harvey the cost of purchasing the equipment needed to make up the CTL orders. I also told him the effect it would have on delivery dates. Surmising that CTL would need a further two or three weeks to ensure that all the equipment functioned well together, I had added a further month to all time estimates.

Harvey was horrified. "I can't tell the Board this. You've got to find alternative suppliers so that all orders can be delivered by the promised dates," he said.

I pointed out that in some cases delivery dates were already in the past, but said I'd try to source alternatives. Most of the items were large disk drives or other peripheral devices which CTL did not make itself. "We might be able to get hold of the hardware but does CTL have software drivers for those devices?" I asked Harvey.

"Why do we need more software? We have a good operating system," said Harvey. "Surely that will do?"

I was aghast. I realised that Harvey was a marketing man, and sales and marketing people in the industry rarely had much technical knowledge as they had had in the 1960s. Many had been insurance or car salesmen. They relied on their technical people to make sure the equipment they sold worked. In general, they just sold items from a pricelist and told the prospective client almost anything to make a sale and get their commission.

Clients buying hardware were mostly business managers or career public servants who again relied on their technical people to get them out of trouble if they bought the wrong thing. IBM was taking a lead position in the industry and even though its hardware and operating systems were inferior to those of most other large suppliers, IBM always seemed to have ways of placating customers at the highest level such that the phrase 'Nobody ever got fired for buying IBM' started to creep into industry folklore.

As it turned out, reliable hardware could not be sourced more quickly than I had indicated. Software drivers had to be developed to access the devices and special engineering was needed to connect the devices to CTL's Modular One computer. Harvey was worried about the situation but delighted when he found that it gave him much more power. It was decided that no salesman could give a customer price or delivery dates unless the order had been checked by his group.

Bernard was up in arms. He wasn't a checking clerk, he had been a salesman and graduated to marketing. In his view, the marketing people told the sales people what to go after. Bernard wanted to focus on manufacturing and steal some of DEC's market.

He had never worked in manufacturing. I tried to tell him about my work in production planning and control and process control in Kodak but he wasn't interested. In his view it was sufficient to find out who DEC's customers were and try to turn them to CTL. Deciding what to sell and checking and producing what salesmen had sold was stuff for young techies. His job was to boost sales. It was the technician's fault if their equipment didn't meet customers' needs.

I pointed out to Harvey that Tom Margerison had said at my interview that my job would be to find out what customers wanted and ensure that CTL had products to meet their need. Through my contacts in the BCS I could find out what computer equipment most companies had and what they thought they needed. But getting CTL to build it was a different matter.

I found out that many CTL products were being built with government funding, and that although funding was sought for one purpose, the money was often spent developing quite a different product. It fell to me to tell them about the change of purpose and persuade them that, as technology was moving so quickly, the funding was much better spent on the product that was being built rather than that proposed. It was not an easy job.

Every few weeks Iann Barron would get the senior staff together to tell us about his latest ideas for computing. One time he told us that one day computers would be the size of house bricks and would be used in cars, lifts and ovens.

CTL's Modular One was the most powerful minicomputer of the time. The processor was about the size of an office desk. Unlike most other computers, the Modular One didn't need a false floor for cables or air conditioning but could be set up in a standard office environment. Computers were getting smaller, more powerful and less fussy about their environment. They were also getting much cheaper in terms of capability. But the size of house bricks? In cars and lifts and ovens? No way.

In 1988, when I again met Iann Barron, I was able to remind him of his prediction and tell him he was wrong. Processors were by then much smaller than house bricks.

I FELT MY PROFESSIONAL life was drifting out of my control. I had more time to spend on BCS activities, which I enjoyed, and more time for lazy afternoons with Dick. But professionally I felt I was just treading water. CTL was not right for me and I was not right for CTL.

Dick invited me to a cocktail party the Operations Research Society was holding at the Zoo. This was the first time the London Zoo had opened its facilities at night for a commercial purpose. Sir Solly Zuckerman, Secretary of the Zoo, would be giving a talk on his work with monkeys and apes.

I looked forward to meeting the man who, as Chief Government Scientist to Prime Minister Wilson, was responsible for funding the work I had done on the CUBITH project applying computing to building hospitals.

The day was warm. I wore a long black muslin dress with large white flowers and green trimmings. Solly Zuckerman's talk was disappointing. He seemed like an old man who was talking about things that had happened a long time ago. The long sunny evening gave us plenty of time to wander round the animals' cages.

On our walk I came face to face with my former colleague Anne Russell, who was arm in arm with one of FI's Directors, Tony Lines. I wondered what Anne and Tony would think about seeing me on Dick's arm. We passed each other stiffly, nodding heads in acknowledgement.

Shortly after the dreamy evening at the Zoo, Dick told me we could not meet again. His wife had found out about us and threatened to deny him access to his sons unless the affair stopped. I was devastated.

MY HOME LIFE was also drifting out of control. In September Stephen started at the same pre-school that Claire had attended. It was very progressive. Claire was thriving in the environment. So long as they spent a short time in reading, writing and maths activities each day, children could choose whether to attend formal lessons. They formed a school orchestra and wrote and performed their own music and plays.

They were collecting money for an in-ground swimming pool, rare for a government primary school at that time. I was Chairman of the Parents

Committee and organised junior discos once a month for the pupils. These were very popular fundraisers.

The headmistress told me that Claire had a fundraising activity of her own. She was collecting butterflies, a skill she'd developed almost as soon as she could walk, and frogs from the school pond. She was selling butterflies for a penny, frogs for tuppence and kisses for sixpence. The headmistress remarked that most of the money was coming from kisses. Claire was eight.

Stephen seemed happy but kept running away from school. At first, he would be found sitting by the school pond. Later he would go to the banks of the Grand Union canal, about a mile from school. They would phone me and I would drive to the canal and find him helping to open and close the lock gates for the boaties. Stephen couldn't swim and I was worried he might drown in the canal. When asked why he truanted he said he didn't know.

One day when my parents were over for Saturday tea, Stephen was playing with his Grandad's steel rule when he lost it in a crack in the floor. I had noticed the gaps in the wood block floor had been widening, but to lose a 3 foot steel rule down one of them seemed impossible. We all looked in the hole. There was no rule to be seen. We got a long thin rod and easily got it about a yard into the hole without touching the bottom. My father removed some of the wood blocks. The crack was long and deep but not too wide.

"Better contact the builder Monday," he said. Dad was by this time in charge of many of the building projects for Lyons, the bakery, hotels and teashop chain where he worked.

I wasn't worried. The house was built by Laings, one of England's most prestigious builders. When we had first moved in, we would hear sharp noises like gunshots in the night and wake to see yet another crack in a wall. The builders had assured us these were 'settlement' cracks and they patched and repainted the walls.

Since Alan had left, the cracks had appeared more often. The company had built about ten similar detached houses in our row. None of the others had problems. The man next door but one was an architect. He told me not to worry. The builder had a good reputation, was one of England's largest. The house had a 20 year warranty. These things happen.

I wrote to the builder. A group of important looking men arrived with many instruments and assured me that they could fix any problem that might occur. The firm's reputation depended on it. "These things are rare but always fixable," they said.

AT THE MONTHLY BCS council meeting in July the President announced he had received a letter from the Belfast branch of the BCS asking him to speak at their inaugural dinner. The Irish Troubles seemed to be escalating rapidly out of control and he said he wasn't prepared to risk his life. He asked if any other council member would go. No one volunteered.

I thought it was dreadful that the people in Ireland had to suffer daily bombings yet no one was willing to speak at their dinner. Although I hated public speaking, I volunteered. It might be fun. The children could stay with my parents for a couple of nights.

The black tie dinner was to be held at Belfast University on 14 September. Arrangements were made for me to stay the night at the University and return home the next day. I flew to Belfast, nervously going over my speech.

We were due to land at 3.30pm. The dinner was to be at 7pm. I was told that BCS members from the Belfast branch would meet me at the airport. I was given several strict instructions. I was not to take a lift from any other person or use a taxi. If I had to use a taxi, I would need to check under the seat for a bomb before I got in. In no way was I to get in a taxi that already had a passenger. As an English person, I might be kidnapped and held for ransom. It all sounded very serious but over cautious.

The plane circled Belfast airport several times. The chief steward announced that a large bomb had been placed in the walkway between the airport terminal and the runways. The plane would land in the middle of the airport and we would be escorted to a safe place where we had to stay until the bomb was defused.

When the plane landed a group of soldiers, guns at the ready, herded us into a large hangar. The doors were bolted shut and there were no windows. Soon the 150 passengers on my plane had been joined by three more planeloads. Initially there had been space to sit on the concrete floor, but with about 600 people it was standing room only.

The air was thick with smoke from cigarettes. There was no drinking water or toilet facilities. More planes landed. People started complaining about the conditions. One hostess said it was better in the hangar than on her plane which held 150 Dutch schoolchildren all suffering airsickness. All the toilets were in a disgusting state and, given cans of Coke to drink, the students were shaking the cans, opening them up and flinging them round the cabin.

Several planes were now parked on the tarmac without enough fuel to reach another destination. An official asked for volunteers to help with the organisation of the stranded passengers. He announced a woman passenger had gone into labour. Was there a doctor present? They'd have to set up a makeshift hospital area in a roped off corner of the shed. A little old lady who was near me announced that she was having a heart attack. Would I take her to the hospital area?

Initially there had been much good-humoured banter. Now cigarettes were starting to run out. Desperately, people who had run out were begging from those who still had them. Finally, all cigarettes ran out and there was an eerie silence in the still smoky atmosphere.

When I took the old lady to the hospital area I seemed to get appointed to the organising group. People were fainting and being sick. Another corner was roped off for people to use as a toilet. People were standing so close that there was no space between them. Although some men gratefully relieved themselves against the wall in the toilet corner, I noticed that others were just wetting and messing themselves where they stood. The area smelled foul. We had been in the hangar three hours.

I TRIED TO practice my speech to myself in my head but realised with relief as the time moved towards 7pm that the dinner would have started and I would not have to give my speech. I would also have had to change into my long blue dress, wash my face and reapply make up. No, there would be no speech tonight.

About once an hour, an airport official gave us an update on the progress to defuse the bomb. Apparently the bomb was very big. They had tried to send in a robot to set off a controlled explosion. It hadn't worked. They had tried to move the bomb, with no success. People were starting to ask why they couldn't just walk across the airport and not go near the arrival and departure hall. There seemed to be no answer.

At about 8.30pm, the official told us that the IRA had agreed to let a bus take out the sick. The pregnant woman was now in strong labour and there were three or four suspected heart attacks, including the old lady who was still hanging onto me.

The man said the bus would be brought up to one of the open side doors and people would have to get in quickly. Also, would the lady from the British Computer Society who was the speaker at the University dinner please get on the bus. I felt bad about taking up a seat on the bus. I was coping well. The same could not be said for those who had been sick, had asthma attacks or were genuinely ill. But I thought of my children at home and decided I would be better safely away from a big bomb.

"I have to stay with this lady," said the old woman hanging on to my arm. "I need her to look after me." It's okay," I said. "I'm the one who has to speak at the University."

When we were all on the small bus, a soldier told us the IRA had let the bus in but might shoot at it on the way out. Armed IRA were all round the perimeter of the airport and on the road into Belfast. They told us to crouch down below window height until they had cleared the airport.

The old lady perked up at the thought of leaving the foul smelling hangar. We crossed the airport and were on the main road without incident. When we got into Belfast, it seemed that the whole city was ablaze.

THE BUS STOPPED at the bus depot. I half expected to be met there but there seemed to be no one about. I was able to get a taxi, ignoring the earlier advice I had been given. Arriving at the University gate, I was met by the Chairman of the Belfast Branch of the BCS.

"We've been so worried about you," he said. "The bomb at the airport has been big news here and in England. It's been on all the radio and TV news broadcasts. "You can wash and change here," said the Chairman, showing me into a tiny toilet.

"If it's alright by you, I'd rather just go to bed," I said. It was past 10 pm.

"But they are all waiting for you," said the Chairman. "They've all heard about the bomb at the airport and want to thank you for being so brave and coming here. We did ask for the President but were delighted when we were told we'd get the first woman on the BCS Council instead. We held off starting the dinner as long as we could. They are just about to serve sweets but I'm sure we can find you a main course."

I decided I would have to put on a show for the waiting dinner guests. Fortunately, I had packed everything in a small overnight bag which I took with me in the cabin of the plane. I changed into my long dress and washed and made up my face as best I could in the tiny room.

Entering the vast hall on the Chairman's arm, the assembled guests rose to their feet and clapped. I was led to a place on the top table on the stage. People fussed around to see that I had something to eat and drink.

Much to my surprise, when I had finished my sweets and coffee was served the Chairman got to his feet and thanked me for coming all the way from England to their dinner. He apologised for the fiery welcome but said that the IRA had put on a special show of force because Prime Minister, Ted Heath, was making a visit to Belfast the next day.

Then he then invited me to speak. I was devastated. I had forgotten what I had planned to say. I had left my speaking notes in my overnight bag outside the hall. 250 faces were turned expectantly towards me. My stomach sank. I felt incredibly tired. I rose to my feet to tumultuous applause.

"Today I witnessed just a little bit of what you people live through every day. I think you are all very brave. I can go home tomorrow but you who live here have to face up to this disruption day after day. It's late now. I'm tired and you don't really want to hear a long speech about the BCS. Just enjoy your coffee and port and your friends." I sat down to a standing ovation.

The rest of the evening, until the finish at midnight, was just a blur. I was shown to a student bedroom and slept soundly.

The next morning I was awakened to a large breakfast. BCS members had called to take me to the airport. The siege at the airport had lasted until well after midnight. Belfast was in ruins. As we drove through the city, they pointed out the significant landmarks that were still smouldering.

When I got to the airport, I was surprised to see a huge crater in the car park where the bomb had been exploded. They had managed to get it away from the terminal but the explosion in the car park had destroyed about 30 cars and left a deep hole the size of three large houses.

I slept all the way back to England. My parents and children were waiting at London airport. When I got home, Dick rang.

"I saw the news about Belfast. How did your speech go? Were you anywhere near the bomb? Did you see Belfast on fire?"

"I thought we weren't to have any more contact," I said.

"But I still worry about you. I think about you all the time," said Dick.

"I'm tired. I'll tell you tomorrow," I said.

This time in Ireland came to be called The Troubles. I sure felt I had a lot of troubles in my own life.

24 Advances in computing

BACK AT CTL nobody seemed to have even missed me. Nobody asked about my trip to Belfast. Nobody seemed to care. Harvey told me I had another duty. The French branch of the company was not doing well. Maybe there were different requirements in France. From now on, until the French were back on track, I would go to Paris for a management meeting every week to find out what they were up to.

The weekly French meeting was at 10am Wednesdays. I flew over every week and was collected at the Paris airport by company car and taken to the office. The meeting lasted two hours. I was then taken to lunch and was free from about 2pm until my plane at 5pm. I rarely had to stay overnight. I was able to act the tourist and visit some of Paris's famous sights.

The language of the company was English but whenever the French realised the questions I asked were too difficult for them they would revert to French between themselves. I didn't tell them I understood French but after a few minutes I would remind them that they should be speaking the language of the company, which was English.

One time we visited prospective customer SNCF, the French Railways. The computer room was over the main concourse at the famous Gare du Nord station. There were big 'Pas de Fumer' notices all over but all the operators were smoking.

I pointed at the rows of disk drives, which at that time were very sensitive to dust particles. I asked how they expected good performance when people were smoking. I was taken round the back of the computer cabinets and told that everything was okay because they had the windows wide open. This was true. The windows opened onto the belching steam trains in the station below.

EVEN THOUGH MY job at CTL paid very well and gave me freedom to do things I enjoyed outside work, I felt guilty about the lack of progress at the company. Staff turnover was very high. I talked it over with Harvey. He said he felt the same but the pay and conditions were very good and he didn't think he could get an equivalent job elsewhere.

I read that Scicon, the large and well-regarded computing consultancy that was a subsidiary of BP Oil, was relocating to Milton Keynes, another new town about 30 miles north of where I lived. I knew Scicon did consultancy in database design and operations research, which I enjoyed. Dick had left CAP and was working in operations research at Blue Circle Cement. I rang him for advice and to see if I could give his name as a reference.

"They're a nice bunch of guys," he said. "I'm sure you'll like working there. Of course I'll give you a reference."

"Could we meet for coffee and talk about it?" I asked.

"I couldn't trust myself. I think of you every day. I feel so miserable," said Dick. "But Jean really means that she'd stop me from seeing the boys and I couldn't bear that either."

In October I applied for a job as senior consultant at Scicon. I took the children out to Milton Keynes to look at houses. The new town was very sterile. Most of the housing in the town was public housing, but there were several small villages in the area which had pretty, thatched cottages.

Houses were cheaper further out, yet it was only an hour to London on an express train and only an hour by car to my parent's house. I could sell my current house and move into something smaller and much cheaper. That would give me a nest egg in case times got bad, or at the least reduce my mortgage considerably.

I got a prompt reply and interview from Scicon. I was offered a job with an even higher salary — though not the generous leave — that I had from CTL. I was told I would get financial help with the relocation to Milton Keynes.

I was worried about the seniority of the position and how the change of employment would affect my work for the BCS. I wrote to Scicon again outlining my current BCS workload. As with CTL, I was told that my work for the BCS would be supported, and indeed welcomed, by Scicon. Everybody seemed to like the fact I made plenty of contacts that way.

It was not a good time to change jobs. A miners' strike caused the Government to announce severe power restrictions. People were allowed to have only one room lit at a time in their houses and only one bar of an electric fire or one ring on an electric stove. Our house ran on gas for heating and cooking so that was not a problem.

There was talk of putting people on a three day week. Many might be laid off completely. My job at CTL was considered an essential industry job so I would stay on a five day week. I didn't know how I would have been able to pay the mortgage on the salary from a three day week.

I took a long time to consider the move to Scicon. I had made a mistake by going to work for CTL. I didn't want to make another one.

THE NATIONAL PHYSICS Laboratory's Experimental Packet Switching Service, EPSS, which had originally been described by Donald Davies in 1966, was beginning to show promise.

Computer generated graphics were still very chunky, mainly based on coarse blocks of colour which gave the resulting images a look of those in a child's comic. There was an effort to link data transmission and computer graphics together with a technology called Videotex or Viewdata, which used data from a central database transmitted over normal voice telephone lines to TV sets in homes. It was eventually launched by the Post Office in 1979 as Prestel and enabled people to check TV programs on their TV sets, make purchases using credit cards, check train timetables, etc.

The Government could see the possibilities of using the new technology to distribute manuals for military purposes from a central point, ensuring that the latest pages were always available and reducing printing and distribution costs. A high level Government panel was established, which I was invited to join.

The public was becoming concerned about the number of databases of personal information that were being developed. Issues of the currency of data, access and most important, privacy were now regularly discussed in the media. The UK Government established a Privacy Commission. I was asked to join one of the committees.

IN OCTOBER 1973 Captain Grace Hopper was invited to England to attend the British Computer Society's Annual Dinner. She and Maurice Wilkes, who had built EDSAC, the world's third stored program computer, at Cambridge, were to be made the Society's first Distinguished Fellows. It was thought appropriate that because I was a woman and a council member of BCS, I should meet Grace at London Airport and escort her to her hotel.

I had read all about Grace Hopper. She was regarded as the mother of COBOL, an early high level programming language. She had coined the term 'bug', referring to computer glitches, when a moth got into the memory of a mainframe computer and stopped it working while she was on shift.

She had also reached the highest level of any woman in the US military. She was to be promoted to Rear Admiral in 1985, the first woman to reach flag rank in the US Navy. Now nearly 70, she was also Special Ambassador for US computer company Univac and toured the world giving lectures about the industry.

I found Grace charming. When we got to the hotel, which was just behind Harrods in Kensington, Grace asked me to organise weak Earl Grey tea and thin cucumber sandwiches on white bread with the crusts cut off while she changed her uniform.

I went into the Salon de Thé but wondered how I would ensure that the tea came at the right time. The manageress told me that Captain Hopper was a regular guest and she knew just what to do. Grace Hopper soon reappeared in a clean uniform. She explained that she travelled with only two uniforms. One to wear and one to be cleaned. She said she never wore anything else.

In addition to attending the BCS dinner, the Advanced Programming Group invited Captain Hopper to speak at one of our meetings. I again picked her up at her hotel. After we had tea, we caught a taxi to the rooms in High Holborn where the Advanced Programming Group held its meeting. She spoke about the development of COBOL. She said that as soon as the US Department of Defense decided to adopt COBOL as a standard, and announced that it would not buy computers that didn't have a COBOL compiler, 250 versions of COBOL were built overnight.

She ended her talk the way she always did by saying, "I've been honoured to be invited to speak to you today but nothing brings me more honour than the uniform that I wear today as a Captain in the United States Navy."

After dinner, she asked if we would like to see one of the new type of computer Univac had just loaned to her. She dived into her large Navy issue handbag and brought out an object about the size of a cigarette packet.

"That's a computer?" we asked, amazed.

"No, that's the box," she said. Opening the box, she brought out an object about the size of a matchbox. "This is the computer."

"What can it do?"

"Anything you like. It has a 64 kilobyte COBOL complier," she said.

'How do you access it?"

"Well if one of you can bring me a teletype with a printer, I'll show you," she said. Someone was despatched to the Prudential's offices nearby to get a teletype keyboard and printer. From the side of the tiny device, Grace pulled out a fine cable the width of a thick hair with a tiny plug on it.

"But how do you plug that into the power supply?"

Grace dived into her large handbag again and pulled out a transformer with an adaptor for the tiny plug and a normal three pin plug for connection to a power supply. The teletype was connected and the assembled group watched fascinated as Grace developed and ran a simple COBOL program.

We were not to know it then but we had witnessed an early silicon chip based computer. Perhaps Iann Barron was right. Computers would one day be tiny.

Grace told us that in her opinion, the mainframe was dead and would be replaced by 'multitudes of minicomputers' that would be linked by telephone lines and all work co-operatively together. It was quite possible that she had seen a demonstration of the US Department of Defense's ARPANET, the precursor of the Internet.

It would be towards the end of the 1970s before computers shared and transmitted data to and from remote locations regularly and reliably. It would be towards the end of the 1980s that the embryonic Internet would move out of universities and defence into the mainstream. It would be the early 1990s before Tim Berners-Lee developed the World Wide Web, which enabled the development of the Internet browser. It would be the mid 1990s before computers worked together collaboratively.

ONE OF CTL'S TARGET markets was health, particularly hospitals that were using computers for patient records. I visited the Oxford Regional Hospital Board. Their biggest problem was that although they had good systems at each hospital, they had no way of amalgamating records for one patient across the eight hospitals in the region. This led to duplication and errors. Records were also lost when they were sent by courier between hospitals.

A woman in the early stages of pregnancy, taken to an accident and emergency unit in the general hospital following a traffic accident, could have important information about her case in the notes held in the maternity hospital. It could take up to a day to get the notes from one hospital to another.

I thought about Grace Hopper's 'multitudes of minis'. If the Oxford Regional Hospital Board had a database management system and if records held in a central database could be accessed across telephone lines in real time, then the problem could be solved. But the Hospital Board did not have a database management system and remote data access in real time was in its infancy.

One day the BCS received a letter from the wife of the Shah of Iran. She wanted advice on how to build computer systems to store patient records for the hospitals that she was building. Morris Ashill, the secretary of the BCS, felt it appropriate for me to answer the letter because I was a female and an expert on database systems.

It had been rumoured that the Shah was considering remarrying his beloved first wife. Because she could not bear him children, he had divorced her and married his second wife, who gave him the heirs needed to carry on the dynasty. Now that his second wife had done her duty, maybe he was free to go back to the woman he really loved.

The Shah was building huge military systems. His second wife decided that if she established world class, free hospitals for the Iranian people, it might help her to keep her position. She had heard about computer systems that could support hospitals and that was why she wrote to the BCS to find out more. I readily agreed to help.

IN NOVEMBER 1973 I attended an IBM computer user conference in Edinburgh. It was held in one of Edinburgh's top hotels and was a high point in the professional year. The speakers were mainly international experts whose expenses were paid by IBM. IBM and some of their partners subsidised the dinners, leaving participants to just pay their own travel and hotel expenses, most of which would be paid by their companies. Almost all attendees were men, and many brought wives. There was a 'wives' program. In the 70s it was assumed that the only type of partner would be a wife.

Most large enterprises now had IBM hardware and those who did not were prospective customers. All were invited to the IBM user meetings as guests of the company. Government departments were still obligated to buy British unless they made a very good case but they, too, were firmly in the sights of IBM salesmen and so invited to the conference.

Consultants like me who were influencers of hardware purchasers were also invited as guests of IBM. Later, IBM customers would take much more ownership of their own conferences but in the early 70s they were pleased to get all the support IBM was willing to give.

The press was there in force, anxious to cover as much of the conference as possible. There were rumours that the keynote speaker at the conference dinner was to be someone very important and IBM would be making a significant product announcement. Much to everyone's surprise, the computer press was banned from the conference dinner.

The magazine called Computing, which I had written a column for, was at that time the most popular weekly computer publication in the UK. The magazine sent a junior reporter to cover the conference. He was a good friend of mine. I agreed to take him to the dinner as my 'wife'. He was considerably shorter than I was. We made a strange couple walking arm in arm to the black tie dinner. My companion was questioned at the door. I proffered my tickets, which clearly stated that he was my 'wife'.

The dinner was excellent. The keynote speaker gave a talk my reporter friend found newsworthy. He and I were seated with several senior IBM salesmen. Towards the end of the evening, while suitably lubricated, the conversation got round to dossiers IBM kept on people of interest.

"Will there be one on me?" I asked.

"I'm sure there will be," said my 'wife'.

"I don't believe it," I said. "I'll only believe it if you can tell me something about me that is not general knowledge."

Three weeks later, the journalist asked me for coffee. "Remember you wanted to know what IBM had on you? You're not going to like it."

I was intrigued. "Last year you went to Admiralty Underwater Research at Portland Bill in Dorset. On the way home there was a heavy storm and you stopped for dinner with a gentleman who was one of CAP's partners. You spent the night with him in the hotel."

I felt the colour drain from my cheeks. The meeting was about FI's Polaris project, which was Top Secret. Dick and I had driven to Dorset separately in our own cars. He had waited while I had my meeting.

After the meeting, we made love amongst the barley on the beautiful warm summer day. A summer storm sprang up. Driving too quickly on the slippery surface, I spun my car through 180 degrees and although not hurt, I was very shaken. Dick suggested we have dinner in a nearby pub until the storm passed. We both drank too much red wine as the rain continued to fall, so we decided to book into the pub for the night.

How on earth could IBM know about that? We had been very discrete, or so we thought. No one was supposed to even know FI was working on the secret project. Certainly, I did not tell Dick any more than that I had a meeting with the Navy.

I knew I had been checked for Top Secret clearance and that the team members often felt that they were being tailed or that their houses were watched because work was done in their homes. I surmised that in some way IBM had access to MI5 or MI6 files, but how? Maybe IBM ran a bureau service for the Government or had access to sensitive records. I never found the answer but vowed that I needed to be more careful in future.

25 The boy's club

I **DECIDED THAT** I could not spend any more time at CTL. I felt my brain was turning to jelly. I had been afraid to leave the company because it was not restricted to a three day week, but now the miners' strike was over and everybody was back on a five day week.

I'd done my research on Scicon. People who worked there told me it was a great company. I had met several of their Directors and liked them. Their clients spoke highly of them. I was assured that I would not be restricted to a three day week at Scicon if the strikes resumed because I would be working on a strategic project.

I had checked out houses around Milton Keynes and found that four beautiful new executive houses were being built at Woughton on the Green, a pretty village which had been mentioned in the Domesday Book and which was just 15 minutes drive from Scicon's new offices. The Grand Union canal ran at the end of the garden. I told the children we would be able to buy a canal barge.

Well-known musicians Cleo Laine and Johnny Dankworth had a house in the next village of Wavendon. They ran concerts and gave guitar classes for youngsters in the large barn on their property. Claire was keen to learn the guitar. It all seemed right. In March 1974 I left CTL and joined Scicon.

I immediately felt at home, which I never did at CTL. There were staff pension schemes and private hospital schemes, information on how the parent company BP was travelling, glossy brochures about Scicon, and much else. I felt as if I could now resume my place in a large prestigious company.

My handsome manager, Ray Waite, advised me that initially I would work on two projects that were very important to Scicon. Then I would be given a client to manage myself.

The first project was to evaluate IDMS, a CODASYL compliant database management system (DBMS) for IBM hardware which Scicon had been offered the opportunity to sell in the UK. It had been developed for BF Goodrich, the large US tyre manufacturer, by software developer Cullinane Corporation of Boston.

The CODASYL database handling extensions to the COBOL language were well accepted by industry and most hardware manufacturers had developed their own CODASYL compliant DBMS.

But IBM persisted with its own proprietary DBMS call IMS. IBM had taken the same stance with nearly all industry standards. It would take a standard and make it 'better'. In making it better there was then no standards compliance and IBM's customers were locked in to the IBM system.

IBM always provided a migration path when upgrading its hardware or operating systems, but migrating applications software built for an IBM platform to a rival hardware vendor was expensive and difficult. Many IBM customers were looking for a way to use standard compliant systems software on IBM hardware, thus preserving cost effective options for later migration to other hardware platforms.

I remembered speaking with IBM's Ted Codd, who had defined the concept of the relational DBMS. He had spoken about it at BCS Advanced Programming Group meeting. Although it sounded wonderful, the hardware of the day was not powerful enough to drive anything except a very primitive form of relational DBMS.

I told Ray that FI had considered selling products but had decided, that as they were often asked to recommend products, there could be a conflict of interest so had decided to preserve their independence and not to align the business to any specific product. Surely, Scicon should consider this before the product evaluation started.

Ray's usual smile turned to a glower. "Just do it," he said.

FOR THE SECOND project, I learned that Scicon was working on a strategic review of information technology and communications for British Steel. The outcome was to be a recommended architecture that would last for the next ten years. The recommendation was to be based on at least two hardware manufacturers' products.

British Steel had been formed in 1967 when the Government nationalised hundreds of small British steel companies to create one conglomerate. By the early 1970s it was losing money. Although some loss making plants had been closed, British Steel had decided to concentrate steel making in five areas. South Wales for slabs, Scotland for sheet steel, South Yorkshire for special steels, Scunthorpe for tubes and Teesside for bars and rods.

Many of the steel plants had, independently, made good progress in establishing data processing systems. FI had worked on several projects for Tubemakers at Corby and the slab and sheet factories had been automated. But we were now talking about something much bigger. In addition to the mammoth task of rationalising production and personnel, the existing data processing systems had to be reviewed and replaced by systems to support the new manufacturing structure and systems architecture.

I was to work with the team and concentrate specifically on the DBMS strategy, data administration, data privacy and programming languages to be used. The project team had some very able consultants, each responsible for their own area of specialisation such as hardware, communications, operating systems, process control systems, etc.

Our manager was a much older man called Arthur who knew nothing about computing and was forever interfering in our work. Although I enjoyed the camaraderie on the team and respected the expertise of the other nine male team members, Arthur's constant meddling made things difficult. His attitude towards me was that of a father figure who did his best to shield me from the cut and thrust and often bad language and risqué jokes of the other team members.

The project was interesting and involved a lot of travel to see the systems currently supporting the different steelworks. Although the concept of rationalisation was reasonable, the amount of upheaval it would bring seemed unmanageable. Many of the manufacturing sites were to be completely automated. There was promise of no redundancies but the steelmakers who lived in the narrow valleys of South Wales didn't want to be relocated in the shiny new Government houses near the new special steels plant in Yorkshire where more skilled labour was desperately needed.

There were other problems. Steel labelling was an issue, especially in South Wales where there were yards full of slabs for which the exact make-up was unknown. Although these could be analysed and relabelled, they had often been made to special order so after years in the yard waiting in vain for the same type of order, they were usually thrown back into the huge furnaces as scrap, reducing their value and greatly contributing to the company's losses. This made the valuation of stock very difficult, but it was not a problem that could be solved by the current computing systems.

One side benefit of many visits to South Wales was that the four star Dragon Hotel in Swansea, where our team stayed, had very favourable rates for Friday and Saturday nights. The children and I had many pleasant weekends in Wales. I would get home at 5pm on Friday and drive to the new Severn Bridge where we would have tea in a roadside cafe.

I would encourage the children to sleep in the back seat of the car for the journey across to Swansea. As we passed the steel works in South Wales the high exhaust towers belching out flame against the night sky looked to the children like dragons. In the morning, I told them that the boiled eggs, kept warm over low burners on the breakfast buffet, were dragons eggs. We spent many happy days on the superb beaches of South Wales.

AFTER EACH VISIT to a plant, the consultant's trip notes were scrutinised by Arthur. Any spelling or grammatical error would result in a dressing down and an English lesson. These sessions were a total waste of time and seemed to take up as much time as that spent on useful project work. Arthur would relay our findings to Ray, who was often so confused that he would call the individual consultants into his office to find out what was really going on.

I could see that this process was frustrating the team and leading to much higher charges to our client. In one such meeting with Ray, I suggested that I manage the project. I had managed much larger strategic projects before. Ray commented that the client wouldn't accept a woman manager. He said that he had chosen Arthur, even though he was old and doddery, because he had a similar manner and personality to the British Steel manager in charge of the project.

Although Scicon seemed to operate like a large company, I became concerned by the large number of memos about staff changes at the top management level. In May a memo from the newly appointed General Manager stated that as financial results for the previous year had been poor it had been decided not to complete the second building at Milton Keynes and so all consultancy staff would remain in London.

There was uproar. Many of the consultants had purchased houses in Milton Keynes, but due to the poor economic climate following the miners strike the housing market had collapsed. This was good for people buying in Milton Keynes, but selling a house in London or the Home Counties was nearly impossible. Scicon had agreed to pay bridging loans for a while but not indefinitely. For many consultants, this looked like financial ruin.

I considered myself lucky. I had not been able to put our Leverstock Green house on the market because I had felt duty bound to share the cracking problems I was having with the house with estate agents, which meant none of them wanted to sell it. This made me put more pressure on our builder to resolve the cracking problem.

I had carefully documented all my dealings with Laings, the builders, but felt out of my depth dealing with the big powerful company and was concerned that I would lose the house. I parcelled all the documents together and sent them to my solicitor, Mr Hodge. He advised me that I was doing quite well without his help and should continue pressing the builder for a resolution but send him a copy of all documents. That made me feel even more alone.

My father was a senior manager at Lyons, the bakery, hotels and teashop chain where he was in charge of all building and maintenance work. But he seemed not to know what to do. He had been present at one of the on-site visits by the Laings team but he just agreed with everything they said. I felt he was on their side, not mine.

I spoke again to my architect neighbour. He did a thorough inspection, even climbing on the roof. He told me the house was breaking into two parts but he did not know why. He spoke with my father. They agreed there was no way the house could be saved economically. It would have to be demolished. He was sure Laings would pay for our family to stay in a hotel while it was rebuilt. An alternative remedy would be to excavate under the house and pump concrete in under pressure, creating a concrete raft for the house to sit on, but that would be very expensive.

Alan's cousin Tony, who had been best man at our wedding, was working for a current affairs TV program. I rang him and asked if his program would be interested in doing a story on my house. He thought they might be.

I wrote to Laings informing them that the house had been inspected by an architect and a builder. Both had agreed it needed to be demolished and rebuilt. Furthermore, I had a cousin working on the TV program, which I named. They, too, were interested in the story. I copied the letter to Mr Hodge, the solicitor.

This had the desired effect. Laings quickly said they would meet all costs of buying and moving to a similar house. They had determined that the house had been built over a row of willow trees. The contractor should have removed the trees completely but had just cut them down and buried the stumps rather than removing the roots.

In the first season, the roots would have tried to make branch growth, pushing the house up. In the winter, the trees went dormant and the house would have fallen. Eventually, not able to make branches, the roots would have died, making the house fall further. Laings proposed to set up a number of monitoring devices round the house to measure the problem. They would then decide a remedy, which might be demolishing the house completely.

I STARTED TO LOOK for another house in the neighbourhood. I told the children that we would not be moving to Milton Keynes. They were pleased not to be moving away from their school and their friends but sad they wouldn't get a canal boat.

I didn't want to work in London anymore. I might have been better not to leave CTL. The IRA kept leaving bombs at railway stations. There were many bomb hoaxes and false alarms, which all contributed to stations often being closed in the evening rush hour.

The problems were usually resolved by 8.30pm, but that meant that commuters didn't get home till very late. The pubs and wine bars were full of commuters killing time until the stations reopened. People who could afford a hotel for the night often chose to stay in town. Others stayed with friends or colleagues. Many marriages, especially in the computer industry, broke up.

Work at Scicon was not as I had expected. I seemed to be well respected by my peers but the top management seemed to spend all their time jostling each other for position. The British Steel project was interesting, except for Arthur's meddling, but there was a camaraderie within the team that made it bearable.

The team learnt that I was corresponding with the Shah of Iran's wife. One of the team had worked on a contract in Iran and told me about the beautiful county, which, he said, was full of antiquities. Scicon had contracts in the Middle East. The biggest was on computer systems for a hospital in Riyadh, in Saudi Arabia. Maybe I could work on that project?

Scicon management agreed I had the qualifications and experience to work on the Riyadh contract but said that, as a woman, I would have to wear a veil outside the office and would not be allowed to drive so would need a chauffer. I would have to leave the children in a boarding school in England. On balance, they thought it would not be a good idea.

MORE AND MORE women were contacting me, as the only female on the BCS Council, to complain that they were not being treated equally with male colleagues or by male bosses. Many of the stories rang true. I had never felt any prejudice because of my gender. Indeed, I felt being a woman in a male dominated industry was often an advantage. But for many women it was not, which caused them to become bitter or leave the industry altogether.

One example, which I felt was not a case of prejudice, was a young female lecturer at University College London. She felt her boss, Professor Paul Samet, was belittling her because she was female. She told me that she had been asked to take a visiting academic to Marks & Spencer to buy woolly jumpers for his children. She was sure Professor Samet would not have asked a male academic to do such a thing.

I knew Paul Samet through the Advanced Programming Group. I liked him and had never found him at all sexist. I found out that the visitor who needed to buy woolly jumpers for his children was Professor Wlad Turski, a Polish mathematician who was one of the Soviet bloc's leading computer scientists. He had developed an operating system solely through references to papers written by Western academics. I said I would have been delighted to have the opportunity to take Professor Turski shopping.

I suggested to the complainant that Professor Samet had asked her because he felt a woman would be better able to help the visitor to buy clothes for his children. I added that I felt she had missed a wonderful opportunity to meet a great man. It was not the answer she wanted to hear.

I started the search for another house. None was as nice as the house we were currently living in. I also realised that the nearly new carpets and floor coverings in our current house would not necessarily fit into a different house. I wrote again to Laings. They agreed to pay all costs, legal fees, stamp duty, estate agent commissions, removal costs and new curtains, decorating and the like. It appeared they were prepared to do anything to preserve their reputation.

But I was still not feeling comfortable. I simply didn't like working in central London. With the IRA bomb disruptions, I was seeing less and less of the children, usually getting home well after their bedtime. And Scicon seemed to be a boys club. There were no other female senior consultants. The salary was good but I felt I was being pushed further down the seniority stack. The boys were making all the decisions.

Then I received the phone call that was to change my life.

26 Australia calling

ONE DAY IN AUGUST 1974 I got a phone call asking me to meet two men from Australia who wanted help with a database problem. I was now Chair of the BCS CODASYL working group on database design and was recognised as one of the UK's top database experts. I was used to receiving such requests from overseas visitors. Could I meet the Australians at 5pm on Friday?

We met at the New South Wales Information Centre in the Strand. The men told me they worked for the largest computer consultancy in Australia and had a problem with the design of a database management system for their largest client.

They had travelled round the world seeking out the top database designers from the countries they had visited. They had asked for names from Computer Societies, universities and large companies. In the UK, my name had been on every list. They asked if I would consider coming to Australia for two years in the first instance, or longer if I liked it. This was out of the blue.

They were tanned, charming and relaxed. They asked if I had children. They told me the children would love the beaches. When I said that one of our pastimes was walking they said Australia had lots of wilderness where walkers enjoyed bushwalking at weekends. Australia had lakes and mountains, fresh fruit and lots of meat for what they called 'barbies', which I learned was a sort of outdoor cooking process where the men usually did the cooking. The weather was idyllic.

It all sounded too good to be true, especially as the previous winter in England had been made miserable by the lack of electric power and coal due to the miners' strike. Even on my good salary, I could only afford for the family to eat meat twice a week. Fruit meant apples, plums or blackberries picked from local hedgerows.

They told me that their offices were on the North Shore in Sydney. I imagined the sea lapping at the sand across the road from the office. I was not completely happy at Scicon but I told them I could not consider moving to Australia,

England was my home. I had a good support network of aunties, uncles, grandmas, grandads, cousins and friends. It would be too much of an upheaval for the children. In Australia, we would know no one. But I went home on the train in a daze, with images of beaches and sunshine.

THE NEXT DAY was Saturday. There was still Saturday post in England. There on the mat was a letter offering me a job in Australia. I had left the two men about 9pm, so they must have had the letter typed and posted it at the midnight post office in central London. I was flattered.

On Monday morning I got a phone call at work. Had I received an offer letter? They had not had my reply. I said it was too much of an upheaval for the children. One of the men I had met, Paul Stephens, came on the phone. "Is our salary offer too low?" he said.

I told him I hadn't even considered the salary. I had no idea what things cost in Australia so could not comment on the salary level. I just knew I couldn't go to Australia.

"We're going back to Australia tonight. Would you like to have lunch with us at the Ritz?" Paul asked. I agreed.

At lunch, they told me again how wonderful life was, especially for children, in Australia. They explained that Australians travelled a lot so I could easily get back to England when I wanted. They told me the salary they had offered was too low for an expert. They were sorry and would offer more.

The next day another letter arrived. This time the salary was twice that in the original letter. These men were serious. I took the letter to the Bank of New South Wales in the Strand, the only Australian bank I knew.

I asked the clerk what sort of lifestyle I would have on the salary in the letter. He told me to wait. Another man hurried to the counter. He was the assistant manager. Could he help? What was my profession? Was I a brain surgeon? That salary was the equivalent of the salary of a manager of one of the bank's largest branches in Sydney.

I told him I was a computer expert. "They must really want you," said the assistant manager.

Back in the office, I opened a memo from the Managing Director. There had been yet another reorganisation. I would not now report to Ray but to another man I really didn't like.

Was the world trying to tell me something? The house had collapsed. I had my second disastrous job in a year. Women weren't valued in the industry in England. I seemed stuck in a job in London, where I didn't want to be. Now I had a new and unpleasant boss.

But I knew that if I changed jobs again, it would really have to be right. I would have to be much more careful than the last two times. If I went to Australia, I would be burning my boats. I knew no one. There would be no friends or family to support me if I got into trouble. It would be stepping out into the unknown.

THE MORE I thought about Australia, the more I felt excited and terrified, both at the same time. I started making lists of Pros and Cons. I realised I needed much more information. I couldn't afford to be wrong this time.

The big worry was that I would be on my own. I knew no one in Australia. But was that right? Renate, Steve Shirley's sister with the dark haired daughter they had called Clair, had gone back to Australia. I wished I had spoken more to Renate about Australia when she was living with Steve but although Claire and Clair played together, I had hardly spoken to Renate.

Also, the bronzed girl across the corridor at Scicon was Australian. She was called Pat but I had no idea what she did at the company.

My Auntie Joan, my mother's youngest sister, lived in New Zealand. That was near Australia wasn't it? Maybe she could help. I remembered Auntie Joan fondly. She had worked for the British Army in Germany. She was pretty and fun and smelled of expensive cosmetics. She always had handbags and pretty scarves to give away whenever she visited. The last time I had seen Auntie Joan was for my 11th birthday party.

Auntie Joan had come to the party in her uniform, as usual, but had a handsome man on her arm. He was a Major. She shocked the family by saying they were going to live in Australia. Vic, the Major, had a grown up son there. There was much sucking of teeth by family members. There had been no mention of marriage.

From being the blue eyed much loved baby of the family, Auntie Joan was now a Scarlet Woman! I couldn't understand the change. What had Auntie Joan done? All my questions were turned away. "You're too young to know," they had said. My mother and my Nana cried a lot. They would never see Joan again.

Just after they arrived in Australia, a baby was born. There was much counting of months on fingers. Auntie Joan reverted to black sheep status. Good job she had had the sense to go abroad and not bring shame on the family. I was too young to understand what all the fuss was about.

"Joan and Vic must have fallen on hard times," whispered the family, "The baby didn't even have a coach built pram. It was a sort of basket weave thing on wheels. They lived in Woy Woy. What sort of name is that! My mother and Nana were in tears again. What had happened to baby Joan?

To me, Auntie Joan was a very interesting woman. She had upped sticks and gone to Germany at the end of the war. She was very pretty. She had beautiful clothes and silk underwear, not the sensible cotton stuff that most women and girls in England had in the 1950s. Now she had gone with a handsome man, a Major, to Australia.

They later moved to New Zealand and sent back photos of their house by the sea and their bonny growing son, Ian. It was many, many years later that I found out how hard it had been for Joan to settle in Australia. It was only after Joan and Vic's deaths that I found out that Uncle Vic had a wife already when he married Joan so was a bigamist. Maybe if I had had the benefit of the real story, I would have been more cautious about going to Australia, but families often don't tell the truth.

I STARTED BY talking to Pat Bunn, the girl in the office across the corridor from mine. Pat was a pretty, tanned, blue eyed, golden haired athletic Australian with a skin that glowed like burnished silk. She looked very fit and healthy, round and curvy without being fat.

Pat confirmed that life in Australia was wonderful. Like many young Australians, she and her brother were on a working holiday in Europe. She would definitely go back home when she wanted to have children. Life in Australia was perfect and it was definitely the place to bring up children.

If I did go, please would I call in on her parents who were missing her and her brother dreadfully. Please would I tell them she was well and happy and coming back to Australia soon. Pat's parents lived in Chatswood, which was on the North Shore very near St Leonards where I was to work.

I asked about house prices and schools. Pat said houses were much cheaper in Australia than in England. They were nearly all detached single storey bungalows and had at least a quarter of an acre garden. Most people lived only about ten minutes drive from their work. Professional people all lived on the North Shore. I could now see the sea from the windows of my house as well as across the road from the office!

Pat said everywhere in Sydney was near the sea. The beaches were long tracts of golden sand and never crowded. About an hour from Sydney by car, there were high mountains, as high as those in the English Lake district. They were called the Blue Mountains because the haze from oils evaporating from the gum trees bathed the mountains in a blue mist. North of Sydney was a great river, good for boating at the weekends.

In both the southern and northern suburbs of Sydney there were huge National Parks. These were great for bushwalking and full of native wildlife, brightly coloured parrots, kangaroos, and beautiful flowering gum trees. In the winter there were wildflowers, including orchids and wonderful Australian native plants.

The schools were good. The weather was wonderful. In Sydney, it was always warm and sunny, even in winter. There were mountains up to 7000 feet high with vast snowfields, only five hours drive from Sydney, where the skiing was very good in winter.

But then I thought about English people I knew who had gone to live in Australia. They were all 'Ten Pound Poms', people who had gone out to Australia for £10, subsidised by the Australian Government. Most were poor and had failed in England. Was Australia full of failed English people? Would I be considered a failure if I went to Australia?

I SET ABOUT seeing if I could prepare a safe haven back in England if I went to Australia and wanted to return. I started calling in favours from friends in the industry. I told them I had been offered a two year contract 'overseas'. Would they have a job for me when I came back? What sort of job? What sort of salary?

I was pleasantly surprised to find that I was well respected. I was offered several good jobs with high salaries. Most asked me why I wanted to go overseas. Why not just change jobs and come to work with them now? I felt flattered to be in demand but it emboldened me to take a step into the unknown. There seemed to be many ways back if it was the wrong step.

I went to Australia House. Not for me waiting in the long queues with the Ten Pound Poms, I was a 'sponsored expert'. I was only going to Australia for two years and was coming back. I was not going to emigrate.

I asked about house prices. After specifying my needs, I was shown the architect's plans for a new four bedroom two bathroom single story house. It had a double garage and a laundry. It could be built anywhere in Sydney for $40,000.

Where should I build? I was told that a place called Turramurra was very popular with professional people. It was on the North Shore but elevated from the Sydney plain so there were good views of the city and the sea. Also, it got the breezes in the summer. Turramurra, I was told, was aboriginal for 'the high place where tulips grow'.

I was shown Turramurra on a map of Sydney. It looked a bit further from the sea than I had imagined. "Oh yes, about a ten minute drive but it has the advantage that your car won't rust from the salt winds blowing off the sea that you get nearer the coast." It all sounded idyllic.

I asked Laings, the builders, how much my payout would be were I just to accept a cash payout. I told them I was considering going to Australia. The letter back was curt but respectful. "Laings will not pay for relocation to Australia but a cash settlement would be in the region of £63,000." The house had cost only £13,000 five years previously.

£63,000! Even allowing for about £10,000 to repay my mortgage, that was about $150,000 in Australian money. If a house only cost $40,000 and my salary was as high as I had been told I would be rich beyond my dreams. This now needed serious consideration.

My offer letter said the company would pay for all transhipment of household goods and furniture and all travelling expenses for myself and my children. What would there be left to pay for? A car, yes. Legal costs to do with house purchase. School uniforms and different clothes for me and the children. Some new carpets and curtains. New electrical appliances, though I had been told that new house prices in Australia included some kitchen and laundry appliances.

My next-door neighbour was marketing manager for Volvo. A Volvo would be nice but I couldn't afford one in England. My neighbour said he would send a telex to Australia and see what he could arrange. He managed to negotiate a discount for his 'good friend'. A Volvo would cost about $2000 in Australia. He handed me the details of his contact in Australia who happened to be located in Artarmon, the next suburb to St Leonards where I was to work. Everything seemed to fit.

A travel agent put together a wonderful itinerary. Australia was a long way away and we could stop off at many places on the way I had always wanted to see. I wrote to the Shahbanu, the Shah's wife, that I had been helping understand databases on behalf of the British Computer Society, saying I was travelling to Iran and could I pop in for a chat? I got a return letter from a Lady in Waiting saying the Shahbanu would be delighted to see me. Just name the day and come for tea!

The die was cast. We were off to Australia!

27 A journey to the Antipodes

OUR FIRST STOP WAS CAIRO. The captain announced the temperature on the ground as we started our descent as 94 degrees Fahrenheit. When we landed the plane stopped in the middle of the concourse. There was a strike at the airport and we would have to walk to the terminal. There would be no one to offload the luggage from the plane.

The terminal was in chaos. Men, women and children were sitting round on the floor in Arab dress. The noise of conversation was deafening. It was hot and smelly. There was no air conditioning. I couldn't understand anything that was being said. There were broken bottles of duty free spirits all over. I thought that Arabs weren't allowed alcohol.

I was to be met by the official government guide and a chauffer driven car. My guide would know what to do. I made for the exit.

"Where is your luggage, madam?" said the customs official dressed in full flowing robes and headdress.

"I presume it's still on the plane," I told him.

"You can't leave the airport until it's been checked," he told me.

A handsome man in a suit, about my age, let out a string of words in a language I couldn't understand.

The customs official shrugged. "Insha'Allah," he said.

"Welcome to my country," said the handsome man. "I'm not putting up with this. Have you got some money? We'll have to bribe someone."

We bribed the baggage handlers. We bribed the porters. We bribed the customs officials. I learnt a new word: 'baksheesh'. I was to use it a lot over the next few days.

When we eventually got out of the airport hours later our car and driver were waiting. So was our guide.

THE BIG WHITE car smelt of new leather. The air conditioning was full on. This was bliss.

"I am Ali. I am your official government guide," he said. "On behalf of my country, welcome. You are staying in the best hotel we have in Cairo. It's on an island in the middle of the Nile and has its own gardens. You are booked into a bungalow in the garden and will have your own servants. You will be safe there.

"Tomorrow we visit the Pyramids in the morning and the Cairo Museum in the afternoon."

The hotel was indeed luxurious. We were woken by a maid before dawn. Ali picked us up at 5.30am. We set out across the desert to the Pyramids, which we reached just as the sun was peeping over the flat sandy desert.

Ali explained that the Cheops was the largest pyramid. The top was smooth but the sides were rough-hewn blocks. He explained that the Cheops had originally been smooth all over, covered with huge limestone tiles and covered with gold in places but this had been subsequently used for other building projects.

At the Sphinx, we were given the history and shown where the soldiers in World War I had carved their names into the soft stone. The Sphinx looked badly in need of a facelift.

We returned to our hotel for a nap before being whisked through the busy streets to the dilapidated Egyptian Museum, which was a fascinating place. We saw the Tutankhamen relics, so much more impressive than the visiting exhibition I'd seen in London a few years earlier.

Ali then suggested we visit a 'friend' of his to take tea. The man had a shop next to the museum. After offering us peppermint tea in tiny glasses in silver stands, the shopkeeper asked me which perfume I used. He said that in Egypt they could make any perfume in the world from essential oils. I told him I used Chanel No.5. He went into the back of the shop and brought out a tiny sample that I complained smelt nothing like Chanel No.5.

The man hurried back into his shop. He brought out a tiny bottle. "This is pure Lotus oil," he said. It is made from the blossom of the Nile Lotus that only blooms at night." I had been wondering what the beautiful sweet smell was that wafted over the hotel garden at night.

"You only need one tiny drop in your bath and the scent will follow you all day. It will send men crazy just as it did for the wives of the Pharaohs. Only they were allowed to use this very rare oil."

The story may not have been true but it was so romantic and the oil smelt so good that I bought a vial of it for an exorbitant price. But then it did last over 30 years.

Son et Lumiere at the Pyramids that night was surreal. The hot wind blowing off the desert and the ever-changing lights and beautiful music transported me back 5000 years to the Egypt of antiquity. The Pyramids and the Sphinx each told their own story in slow and whispered voices. It could have gone on forever.

Over the next few days we visited the ancient cities of Memphis and Saqqara, we went on a Nile barge, we shopped at bazaars, and visited more museums and splendid mosques. We dispensed plenty of baksheesh, but it was sad when it was time to leave. As Ali said goodbye at the airport, I tried to give him a tip, which he declined saying, "It was a great pleasure to show my country to you and your lovely children. I need no more payment. Your agent has taken care of everything."

The airport strike had been resolved. The airport was as efficient as any in the world. We got on our plane for the short journey to Beirut.

IN BEIRUT WE STAYED at the Holiday Inn, set on top of the highest hill in the city. Everything was polished granite and gleaming steel, the opposite of our antique hotel in Cairo.

I asked the concierge if it was safe to walk in the streets or should we take a taxi. "Madame, everywhere is safe here," was his smiling reply, and it was. We walked down the hill to the St Georges hotel, an older hotel by the port with a private beach. There we had afternoon tea that was set out exactly as it would have been in a good English hotel. The temperature was pleasant. We walked slowly back up the hill looking at the beautiful shops full of gold jewellery, pearls, diamonds and fashionable clothes. No wonder Beirut was called 'the Paris of the East'.

The pool in the hotel was unlike any other we had seen. There was a central bar that the bartender reached through a tunnel from the kitchen that went right under the pool. Guests could swim out to the bar and take their food and drinks sitting on brightly coloured barstools half in the water.

Later, after we reached Australia, war broke out in Beirut. We watched the TV news each night fascinated as the Holiday Inn, the major vantage point in the city, was shown complete with bodies lying around the spectacular pool that we had been swimming in a few months before.

Stephen and I were very ill from food poisoning. We had hoped for a side trip to Damascus, I realised that not only would that be impossible but we would have to postpone our onward flight to Tehran in Iran. I asked the concierge to reschedule our flight then telexed the Shahbanu's Lady in Waiting telling her we were ill and would like to postpone our visit by a day.

The reply came back within a few hours, advising that the day I suggested, 26 October, was the anniversary of the Shah's accession to the Peacock Throne. There would be many overseas dignitaries and parades the whole of the coming week. A meeting would not be possible.

We still visited Tehran. It was fascinating. There were many street vendors selling all manner of sparkly trinkets and magnificent silks in beautiful jewel colours. Men were baking puffy flat bread in ovens that seemed no more that holes filled with fire in the stone walls. The people, men as well as women, were well dressed in western clothes and could have been from any fashionable European city.

The city was in festive mood. The newspapers delivered to our bedroom door had big coloured pictures of the Shah showing his life achievements.

Tehran seemed a very civilised city. The mosques were beautiful and quiet oases of calm after the noise of the streets. We stayed a little longer than we intended when we missed our flight to Delhi. It left after midnight and I got the days mixed up.

We managed to find another hotel and the following evening we took a taxi to the airport early to ensure we would be in time for the flight. At the airport, I looked for food. Claire said she only wanted a drink. I was beginning to worry. It had been a week since she had eaten a substantial meal, although she had been drinking well and did not seem ill.

WE ARRIVED IN DELHI at 4am and took a taxi to our hotel. As we drove through the early morning darkness, it looked as if the pavements were moving. I thought it must be from motion sickness but as the light increased I realised the pavements were covered with sleeping people now waking up.

There were cows everywhere. I remembered reading that in India cows were sacred and allowed to roam the streets freely. The taxi stopped outside our hotel. A family had made a living space for themselves by partitioning a corner from the street with a row of half tyres. Of the six children in rags, two were about the same size as Claire and Stephen. Their parents looked old and careworn.

It was a small but up-market boutique hotel. The manager welcomed us warmly. He was sorry we had had difficulties on our journey and had had to change our booking twice. He thought we must now be very tired and would probably like to sleep.

It was dark when we woke, just after 7pm. We had slept for over 12 hours. I got the children dressed and we went in search of food. The hotel restaurant was well appointed and the menu extensive. Again, Claire only took a drink.

After dinner, the hotel manager said that because our stay was shorter than originally planned, he wanted to ensure we saw the important sights of Delhi, and he would show us the city by night in his own car.

We drove to Raj Ghat, the place by banks of the wide river where Mahatma Gandhi was cremated, and to Nehru's cremation place at Shanti Vana. We were shown the grand government buildings on the Rajpath that would put those in London to shame. We were taken to see the Red Fort built by the Emperor Shah Jahan who built the Taj Mahal for his wife's final resting place.

The roads were broad avenues filled with bicycles, old cars and wandering cows. The manager explained that new cars were rarely seen due to import restrictions. When we got back to the hotel after midnight the streets were still full of people. The little family living outside the hotel was still begging for rice, although their pile did not seem any bigger that it had been in the morning. The adults in the family were awake but the children were curled up asleep on the hard pavement.

I mentioned that the pile of rice looked insufficient to feed the family. The hotel manager said they were not begging for rice but trying to sell rice they had boiled. They would only have the rice water to live on.

NEXT DAY WE BOOKED a city tour. As we left the hotel, I dropped a few coins near the rice pile the family outside were still guarding. I hoped that would enable them to eat the rice themselves. There was much bowing and thanking. Street urchins came from everywhere begging for more coins. I asked the hotel manager if he would give a pair of jeans that Stephen had outgrown to the little family outside.

"They will sell them," he told us. "Anything that looks American brings a very high price here because we are not allowed to import. These jeans will feed them all for a month.

"They are a good family. I should send them away but they have lived there for many years and cause no trouble. They don't beg from my guests. I have told them that if they do they will have to go. Several of the children have been born out there on the footpath. The parents do not cut off their arms or legs at birth as many beggars do. A deformed child brings more money from begging."

I was horrified. It seemed bad enough that these people were desperately poor but to consider mutilating their children to get more money seemed callous in the extreme. I decided we would go for a walk on the street. The hotel manager tried to convince us that it was not appropriate. "Is it dangerous?" I asked. "No, you'll be very safe but you might be distressed by what you see."

I thought it would be good for the children to see how people in India lived. Sure enough, we were only a short distance from the hotel when we were surrounded by begging children. Some of the children had only one leg or arm. One had no legs at all and dragged his body along by his hands.

There seemed to be cows everywhere and the stench was overpowering. Turning the corner, I was horrified to see a dead body lying on the pavement covered in maggots. We turned back to the comfort of the hotel.

That afternoon I visited IBM India for an article for Computing. They told me that when a civil servant had visited the computer centre in preparation for the opening by the Minister, he asked why all the machines did not each have their own servant to look after them. IBM had explained that two operators could run the whole machine from the operating console. They were told to employ at least one servant for each of the peripherals, so each peripheral had a smartly dressed attendant standing by.

I learned that computing was taking off very slowly in India. India had many well-qualified mathematicians and saw little need for computers for engineering calculations that could be done very accurately and much more cheaply by hand.

BANGKOK WAS NEXT. We flew next day and got back on our original schedule. We were booked into the opulent Hotel Oriental. I was becoming very worried about Claire. It was now nearly two weeks since she had eaten anything substantial and she was now refusing to drink. The skin on her arms was hanging loosely. I tried all the medication we had brought from England but nothing worked. She continued to say she didn't feel ill.

We arrived in Bangkok late in the evening. We went straight to the hotel doctor, a beaming old Chinese man. After giving Claire a thorough check, he gave me a tiny cardboard box containing tiny white pills. He told me to give Claire one pill as soon as we got to the hotel and another exactly three hours later. This was to continue at three hour intervals until she asked for food. Then I should flush the pills down the toilet and give her only water for the next 24 hours. She would then be fine.

He made me repeat his instructions twice. He said if she did not show improvement in 24 hours, she should be admitted to hospital. I was alarmed. What was wrong with Claire? Shouldn't she be admitted to hospital now? Why wait 24 hours? Why was the doctor so sure of the remedy when he didn't know the cause of the illness? Should I just take Claire straight to the hospital?

The Chinese doctor looked like a benevolent old man. He patted the children on the head and patted me on the hand. Somehow, I felt he knew what he was doing.

Back at the hotel I put the children to bed and gave Claire one pill. Exactly three hours later I woke her for another one. I then went back to reading the hotel magazines and checked our itinerary for the next day.

An hour after taking the second tablet, Claire woke and said she was very hungry. She had lost much of the pallor but had a dreamy, vacant look. I told her she could only have drinks of water. There was a huge bowl of fruit in the room. Claire begged for at least some fruit but I resisted.

Although it was the middle of the night, Claire started talking about our trip in a very animated way. It was very clear that although she seemed much better, she couldn't remember much about the trip after Egypt.

Three hours after the last pill, I decided to give Claire one more. But I was not going to flush the miracle pills away. We were going to spend three weeks in the South Pacific islands. They might come in handy.

WE SLEPT SOUNDLY but woke when breakfast and morning papers were delivered. We could now see the suite in the daylight. It was quaintly old fashioned, with beautiful carved woodwork screens and furniture. Claire appeared fully recovered. She said she was very hungry but I said she was not allowed anything but water until after midnight.

That day we took a boat up the Chao Phraya River to the King's Summer Palace. We took our seats on the open deck and watched entranced as the boat went slowly up the river.

Huge Thai temples lined the banks. They were covered in gold that glittered and gleamed in the sunlight. We passed the sheds where the King's ceremonial boats were kept. Two long thin boats covered in gold ornaments with dragon's heads on the prow were moored outside. Lunch was served on deck at long tables covered in snowy white linen set with superb china, sparkling crystal glass and bronze cutlery.

Claire begged to be allowed food but was told no. At intervals during the morning, she had fallen asleep, often in mid sentence. An American man sitting opposite asked what was wrong. I retold our story.

"Very interesting. I'm a doctor. I wouldn't dream of trying to advise you but do you still have those miracle pills?" he said. I took the box out of my handbag. The man removed the lid and sniffed the contents, licked his finger, touched a tablet and put the finger back in his mouth. Then he threw the box of pills overboard.

"Hey, I wanted to keep those," I said.

"Do you know what that stuff is?" he said. "It's pure opium. It's an old Chinese remedy. Of course, we're not allowed to prescribe it in the West but it's the very best remedy for what your daughter had. You were lucky to get a Chinese doctor or she would be very ill by now. But if you had given her more than one pill at a time, or more often than at three hour intervals, or for more than 24 hours, she'd be addicted by now. It's nasty stuff. That's why the doctor took time to ensure you knew how to administer it."

My blood ran cold. What had I done? I could have killed my precious daughter. "So what do you think was wrong with her and how did opium cure it?" I asked.

"She must have had a bug in her gut and it was going into spasms. The opium puts the gut to sleep for 24 hours. She'll be fine tomorrow," he said.

During the next few days we had tours of the river and the klongs, the canals that run into it. We were taken to see palaces, museums, working elephants, cockfights and all manner of temples. The world was indeed an exciting place and we were only half way through our trip.

OUR NEXT STOP was Hong Kong, I had heard it was the place to have business suits made so I asked the hotel for a recommendation. The tailor made a good suit in 24 hours for a fraction of what it would have cost in London.

I had arranged to visit the Bank of Hong Kong. The manager of the Bank of Hong Kong received me in the vast banking hall with its very high ceiling and tall black marble pillars.

I asked what sort of computer equipment the bank had. The manager told me they had just taken delivery of an IBM computer for foreign trade transactions but with many highly skilled very accurate clerks, they didn't need a computer for standard banking business. My second article sent to Computing in the UK was based on my visit to the Bank of Hong Kong.

That night we were taken to the floating restaurants at Aberdeen for a Chinese banquet. The next day was to be our last so we took the Peak Tram to the highest point on Hong Kong Island.

From that vantage point, just below the clouds, we could see the typhoon shelters and the junks and the busy ferries on the harbour. The whole area looked peaceful and green. The peak had a few large houses dotted amongst the trees, although the narrow flat edge of Hong Kong Island was covered with tightly packed skyscrapers. On the Kowloon side the hotels and offices were not so tall and patches of green parks could be easily seen. Looking towards the Chinese border, the town soon gave way to the tiny villages and open farmland. There were many uninhabited islands in the bay. Hong Kong had been described as a large city but from the top of the Peak, it looked quite small.

BUT I WAS REALLY looking forward to the final leg of our trip. I had always dreamt of the South Pacific. The trip from Hong Kong to the Solomon Islands in small planes via Manila and Port Moresby took all day. After a very bumpy trip we finally arrived at Guadalcanal, the main island of the Solomon Island group, and came to a stop beside the tin shed that served as the Honiara passenger terminal. Passports were stamped by a customs official in full dress uniform that included a short skirt.

Our host on the island, a handsome Swedish man in his 40s caller Kurt, met us with a four wheel drive car. The place we were to stay was a pineapple plantation established by Kurt about 40km from Honiara. Kurt had built several native huts to accommodate his friends and now ran the enterprise as a sort of rustic guesthouse. The tariff was US$1 per person per day, including meals.

The sleeping areas were simple huts made of woven palm leaves with mud floors. Each hut had four single beds with mosquito nets. There was a primitive shower and pit toilet in a palm leaf enclosure just outside the room. There was a larger hut for communal eating. There was no electric power.

The huts were on the edge of a white sand beach fringed with coconut palms. A coral reef enclosed a shallow aqua blue green lagoon. The sea beyond the reef was bright blue. It was beautiful. This was a real South Sea Island!

We spent most of our time playing games on the beach with the house-boys or watching them catch fish for the next meal. There were plenty of pineapples and other exotic fruits to eat.

When we trekkeed into the jungle I was surprised to find that this peaceful place contained many relics from the war. Kurt told us that the Solomon Islands had been the centre for many fierce battles in World War II.

We were very sorry to leave Guadalcanal. I worried that we had to get to the airport on time but Kurt said we would probably be the only ones on the plane and it would wait for us. He made us sit chatting until the incoming plane flew overhead. Only then did he set out for the 40km drive to Honiara.

We were indeed the only passengers on the tiny plane. We had a good view of clear sea as we flew out. It was very clear and we could see the wrecks of World War II ships, turtles and dolphins as we flew low over the islands.

Our next stop was Port Vila in the New Hebrides, which had a much larger airport. The country is now called Vanuatu, but then it was a 'Condominium' run jointly by France and England. Our hotel was the luxurious Le Lagon.

At that time the New Hebrides was famous for its French cuisine. The hotel was set in the midst of a golf club right at the water's edge. There were tiny straw roofed bungalows by the water but our room was in the main building.

After Guadalcanal, the hotel was luxurious. The tariff included the use of all manner of sporting equipment. We felt no need to go into Port Villa.

Our last stop before Sydney was New Caledonia, which was very French. The offhand attitude of the all the people we met was exactly the same as I had encountered in Paris.

We arrived at our hotel in the late evening and went straight to bed. I asked about the time for breakfast and was told any time before 10am.

The next morning we arrived in the restaurant for breakfast at 9am. The room was empty. There was no service. I asked the concierge about breakfast and was told it finished at 7am.

"But I was told last night it finished at 10am." I wished I spoke better French. It is difficult to sound indignant if you aren't confidant with the language.

"You can have breakfast now if you wish," said the concierge. "What do you want to eat?"

I suggested omelettes. I was sure that word was French.

"No omelettes," said the concierge. "Only toast."

"Then toast and coffee," I said.

"No coffee," said the concierge. "Only whiskey."

"The children cannot drink whiskey," I said.

It seemed amazing to me that the French arrogance could be so like that in France half a world away. I vowed never to return to Noumea. There were much nicer islands with much nicer people elsewhere in the South Pacific.

28 Welcome to Australia

WE ARRIVED IN SYDNEY with great anticipation and much relief. From the airport's information service I found a hotel on the Pacific Highway in Artarmon, which I knew was the next suburb to St Leonards.

We got a taxi across the famous Sydney Harbour Bridge, which looked like a bigger version of the Tyne bridge in Newcastle, where my parents came from. I wondered why there were decorations in the streets, forgetting that it was nearly Christmas.

It didn't feel as if we were on the other side of the world. The people looked and sounded English with an accent I couldn't quite place. The hotel was comfortable. The children were pleased to have familiar food again.

The next morning I phoned CSA. "Where are you?" asked Paul Stephens when I rang. He been one of the two men who interviewed me in England.

"We're in a hotel in Artarmon. My aunt from New Zealand will come over to look after the children. Please give me a few days to get my bearings and I'll be ready for work," I said. "We had a wonderful trip."

"I was at the airport to meet you yesterday," said Paul. "I was going to take you to the hotel we'd booked for you but you mustn't have seen me."

"I've booked in here for two weeks," I said. "We'll have to stay here now. I didn't know you were booking a hotel for us,

"I'll speak to the hotel," said Paul. "Pack up and I'll take you to the hotel we've booked. You'll be more comfortable there."

Paul took us to a hotel in North Sydney where we had a two bedroom suite complete with living room, kitchen and all mod cons.

"I don't think I can afford this hotel," I said. "The one we were in would be fine. We only need a place to sleep."

'We've booked you in here for a month. CSA will pay the bill to enable you to settle in. There is no real need to come in to work before Christmas, so just concentrate on getting yourself a flat and getting the children settled in school. Nothing really happens in Australia in January, but if you can find time we do have things you could be doing. There are Christmas parties for you and the children to attend. I'll see you get invitations."

With that, he was gone. I felt it was strange that now I was in Australia, the pressure to start work seemed to have gone. It was only later that I found that, in the 1970s Australia, December was a month of parties and in January most people took their annual holiday.

Auntie Joan came over from New Zealand and helped us settle in. She was pleased to be back in Australia where she had lived when she first left England twenty years before. I hired a car and we drove to Woy Woy to find the house where she had lived.

Woy Woy seemed a long way from Sydney. Auntie Joan told us that the tiny fibro house they had rented there had been very hot in the summer and cold in the winter, but Uncle Vic could fish from the sea across the road from their house. They had wanted to rent a house in Hornsby in the northern suburbs of Sydney but couldn't afford it.

They had been very poor but had not liked to let the family in England know of their troubles. After a couple of years in Australia, they decided to try their luck in New Zealand where Vic had a grown up son. They were very happy there. She hoped we would be happy in Australia. I told her it would only be for two years then we would return to England.

OUR FIRST TWO WEEKS in Australia were filled with sightseeing; trips on the harbour, to the Opera House, the Zoo, the shops, beaches and the Blue Mountains. I was surprised to find that Sydney was not flat as I had imagined but was quite hilly in places. The countryside, especially the Blue Mountains, was very pretty. The harbour was enormous and very beautiful. The beaches were fabulous and relatively uncrowded. The shops were smaller than those in London and the fashions not as sophisticated, but they were adequate.

I enrolled the children into a school in Chatswood. A local child minding service would look after them before and after school and take them to and from school. I could drop them at 7am and pick them up before 6pm. The childminding centre could also take them full time in the school holidays.

We were sad to see Auntie Joan go back to New Zealand before Christmas. I promised to spend next Christmas in New Zealand. I rang Pat Bunn's parents, who invited us to spend Christmas Day at their house. With the children in school and day care, I could now get on with renting a flat and buying a car.

I looked at several flats for rent and found a good one in Artarmon, near the hotel where we had spent the first night in Australia. The flat was new and clean with a swimming pool in the garden. It was sparsely furnished but I thought that buying some pretty sheets and bed covers would soon make it feel like home for the months we intended to stay. I was disappointed to find that the ocean was not just across the road, but the beaches and CSA's offices were only a short car ride away.

IT WAS NOW TIME to start work. Everyone at CSA seemed friendly. Many were immigrants from England or seconded from CSC in the USA. CSA stood for Computer Sciences Australia and CSC stood for Computer Sciences Corporation. CSA was a joint venture between CSC and AMP, Australia's largest insurance company. CSA was established mainly to run AMP's computer systems.

The AMP Society was the largest enterprise in Australia by far in terms of assets. It owned many of the large buildings in Sydney and other capitals, huge cattle stations and had an impressive share portfolio.

I was given a 'buddy', Susie Johnson, to look after me in the first few weeks. Susie was an American manager from CSC on secondment in Australia for a year with her husband and three children. Susie's husband did not work. He looked after their children and took photographs which he always intended to sell but never did.

I was given a huge office. No one seemed particularly interested in giving me work to do. A man called Digby Pridmore looked in to say he would take me to Canberra as soon as possible to meet the Australian Bureau of Statistics, which was building a huge database and needed some help.

There were several Christmas parties to attend. Some were official CSA parties and others were at people's houses. The Americans, who were being paid US salaries plus expenses, lived in huge houses. Their parties were lavish, with lots of alcohol.

None of the American wives worked. They were tanned from spending all day sunbaking by pools or on the beach. Their hair, makeup, teeth and nails were perfect. I felt very dowdy beside them. Susie seldom attended parties because her husband felt uncomfortable that he was the only man who didn't have a job. I was usually the only working woman in the group.

Unlike parties in England or those I had attended in America, in Australia the wives stayed at one end of the room or garden and the men at the other. I found I had little in common with the women so I was usually the only woman in the men's group. Children were included in every party. Younger children were entertained by older children or by a hired child minder.

The CSA children's Christmas party was very lavish. All manner of food and drink was provided for the children and their parents. The children were given expensive gifts from Father Christmas. It was obvious that CSA was a very wealthy company.

We woke up on Christmas morning 1974 to the news that a cyclone had devastated the city of Darwin in Australia's Northern Territory. TV pictures taken from the air showed that most houses had been completely destroyed. People were being evacuated. Appeals asked for money. On the way to lunch with Pat Bunn's parents, I posted a cheque to the appeal fund.

The Bunn's house was beautifully decorated. A huge Christmas tree in the corner of their living room was heavy with neatly wrapped presents. In the middle of the room was a huge dining table set for a Christmas feast. They explained that they hadn't decorated their house for Christmas since their own children were young. Neither Pat nor her brother had children. This year they were going to enjoy a traditional Christmas.

After a turkey dinner with Christmas pudding and mince pies, Mr Bunn dressed in a Santa suit and handed out presents. The Bunns were a generous, homely couple. The children adopted them as their Australian grandparents.

OUR FLAT IN Artarmon was dark with tiny windows. The front door opened into a large wide room in the centre of the house. There were many doors off the dining room leading to bedrooms, lounge room and kitchen. I learned that the 1920s design ensured that the dining room was cool but with all the doors closed, it was also airless.

After seeing all the other wonderful homes, I felt it was a high priority to buy a house so that at least the children would have a proper home. Our furniture was to arrive in January. The shipping included up to three months storage. We should be in our own home by April.

Most businesses and shops were shut between Christmas and New Year so we spent the time touring the many Sydney beaches. The sun was bright and the sea was blue. It only seemed to rain at night. Meat, fruit and vegetables were cheap and plentiful. Although still apprehensive, I was beginning to feel I had made the right decision to come to Australia.

After the Christmas break, I dropped the children at the childminding centre went to work at St Leonards. I was greeted by Paul Stephens who I learned was the head of CSA's personnel department. He surprised me by giving me a salary cheque for six weeks, backdated to the day I landed in Australia. I felt I hadn't done any work. Who were these people?

There were very few people in the offices. I was introduced to Dr Neville Black, an American, seconded from CSC to head the database group on the AMPnet project. He welcomed me with much reverence. He said he had heard about my reputation and valued my input. He had thought he was developing the database side of the large project for their biggest client correctly but no one else seemed to think so.

The difficulty in Australia was that there were few experts in database management to call upon. He had discussed the project with people he knew in the USA and with Univac, their hardware vendor. They all seemed to support what he was doing. He seemed genuinely interested in my opinion.

AFTER SPENDING the day with Neville and meeting the only member of his team not on holiday, an Englishman called Mike, I left with their database strategy report and the feeling that here was a team of dedicated people doing their very best to meet the needs of their client.

Reading the report that night, I felt the strategy was right. So what was wrong here? The Univac database management system, DMS 1100, was a CODASYL system. The approach seemed fine. I needed more information.

I couldn't find Neville so spent time with Mike trying to find out why someone should think that the AMPnet database was wrongly designed. Mike was a tall thin Englishman with a cut glass accent. He had been in Australia for six months and loved every minute.

He told me that Australia was about ten years behind England in computing. Most people at CSA were very nice but they didn't work very hard. The Americans were mainly highly paid frauds, in his opinion, and didn't know much about computing. Most were administrators or managers and spent their time playing golf or sailing on the harbour and getting drunk in the evenings.

He told me that there were many British people on the project. They were mainly family people. The salary CSA paid was too little to properly support a family but they were trapped. If they left to go back to the UK before they had spent two years in Australia, they would have to pay CSA all the money it had cost to bring them to Australia.

"I'm okay because I don't have a family to support," said Mike.

"You speak as if CSA only has one project, the AMPnet project," I said.

"There are other projects but they are tiny. Most people are working on AMPnet. CSA also runs a bureau service but I don't know how profitable that is," said Mike.

"Do you think the database team is doing the right thing?" I asked.

"Yes, Neville is one of the good guys. He has his wife and two kids out here with him. He's different from the other Americans, much more serious and dedicated," said Mike.

"So where is the problem?" I asked.

"I haven't managed to find out yet. What I do know is that most people round here don't know what they are doing but are too frightened to let on.

There are several teams building applications for AMPnet. They are large teams but they say they can't test until we build the schemas and give them the Data Description Language. Every time we try to run anything on the computer, it fails."

"Why?" I asked.

"I really don't know. I'm not a hardware man but I think it's the hardware," said Mike.

AT LUNCHTIME I walked to the local branch of the Bank of NSW in Crows Nest. I needed to establish an account and deposit my salary cheque. The money I had brought from England was in a holding account at the bank. I had been paying bills with my American Express card or travellers cheques. It was now time to look for a house and get an Australian credit card.

At the bank I was shown into the office of the manager. He was a large man with fair, curly hair and a ruddy complexion. He looked like an overfed cherub. As he came out from behind his big desk to shake my hand, I was amused to see that below his white business shirt and conservative tie he had shorts and long socks. I found out later that this was common business attire in the Australian summer.

I gave him my account number and explained I worked for CSA down the road and wanted to establish an account at the Crows Nest branch.

"Great idea. CSA is my biggest customer. I just need you to fill in some details. We don't seem to have a note of your salary or your address in Australia. We don't even have on record that you work for CSA," he said.

As I gave him my pay slip, cheque and the other details he requested he nodded each time, saying softly to himself, "Good, good."

"Now you said you wanted to buy a house. Where are you thinking of living?"

I explained that I didn't yet know but I had been told that Turramurra was nice.

"Then unless you have more money tucked away, you'll need a mortgage," he said. "Will your husband be joining you soon? I'll need to know his salary for a mortgage."

My heart sank. I had fought this fight in England. At first, when Alan had left me, my father had to be guarantor when I took over the mortgage even thought he earned much less than I did and I was earning more than Alan had earned. I was only allowed to take over the mortgage when I had been paying it for two years.

"I don't have a husband," I said.

"Good, good," was the rather odd reply. "But I thought you said you had children?"

"I do, I have two children," I said.

"Good, good," was the reply again. "I can see from this payslip that you are earning much more than most of the men working at CSA. The bank is beginning to relax its policies towards giving mortgages to women. I have a good deal of discretion now. CSA is a good company. They wouldn't be paying you this salary unless you were worth it. I'll let you have a mortgage."

"But I don't want a mortgage. I'm going to pay cash for my house," I said.

"Then unless you have access to capital that you haven't told me about, you probably won't get one in Turramurra," was his reply. "Anyhow, I don't want you buying a house without having me inspect it. I'm responsible for the bank's money and you don't seem to have a man to help you."

There were lots of things that I wanted to say but I felt it better to just smile sweetly and thank him for his help.

"Would you like a Bankcard?" the manager asked.

"If it's like my Lloyds Bankcard, I would like one," I said.

"I'll arrange that too," he said. "That's also at my discretion but I can see you are a very businesslike young lady who won't go running up bills for things you can't afford so I'll trust you with one.

"I'm sure I'll be seeing a lot more of you. Don't forget now, as soon as you see a house you like I'll inspect it for you. Don't make a commitment until you've got my say so."

Beaming, he came round to my side of his desk, helped me out of my seat and, guiding me by holding my elbow, escorted me to the bank's front door.

"Always ask for me. I'll help you any way I can. I'm sure I'll see you again soon," he said.

Back in the office, I described the meeting to Mike.

"You're very lucky to get a Bankcard," said Mike. "They are very rare. They only started in Australia in August last year. You can get money from a money dispenser outside a bank rather than having to go inside. Some of the managers here have one but I couldn't get one. I wonder why they gave you one?"

THE NEXT WEEK Digby Pridmore came into my office with a pile of reports from the Australian Bureau of Statistics.

"I'd like to take you to the ABS in Canberra. Can you get your children looked after? The trip will take all day. We will catch a plane at 8.30am and be back here by about 5:00pm. Is that okay by you? You'll need to read these reports to understand what the ABS is up to."

We went to Canberra the following week. From the airport onwards, everyone seemed to know him and want to shake his hand. He introduced me to everyone as 'our new database expert from England'.

At the ABS, a group of senior managers were gathered to meet us. After Digby had swapped stories with people who, it seemed, he used to work with, they got down to business. I was worried that I would be expected to make a presentation. I hated making presentations and hadn't prepared anything.

I was very relieved when, one by one, they made excuses and left the meeting until I was left with only the young man they had introduced as their Database Administrator. He said he really didn't have any questions because ABS wasn't ready yet to do any computing with any form of database management system. In his view, they were still living in the dark ages and had converted punched card systems onto a computer but that was all.

For lunch the DBA took me to a restaurant where Digby and the other ABS managers were already mildly inebriated and still telling stories about each other. One of the ABS managers kept hinting that Digby was a womaniser and I should be on my guard.

In the taxi to the airport, Digby told me that I had impressed all the managers we had met. On the journey home, I tried to find out from Digby why CSA should think the AMPnet database was a problem. I told Digby that, from what I knew so far, the database side of the project looked good. Digby advised me to think very carefully before I gave that verdict. They needed someone to make the design right.

I had enjoyed the trip to Canberra, Everything seemed neat and polished. It looked like a toy town model of a city.

DURING A LUNCH BREAK at CSA about a week later, I came across a great bear of a man quietly weeping while trying to thread a needle. He was trying to turn up the hem of a school gymslip. I offered to help. I found that his name was Dr Roy MacDonald Taylor and he was one of the Americans from CSC.

Roy was employed by CSC but had been born in Western Australia and had finished his PhD in the USA. There he had married an American woman and set up home in Orange County near Los Angeles.

He had joined CSC and was delighted to find that he could be seconded to CSA on a very high salary and pay no tax in USA or in Australia. To Australia, he was an American citizen paying tax in America. But the USA counted him as a Visiting Overseas Expert and charged him very little tax. In Australia He also got a living allowance.

Roy's wife had just left him and their six year old daughter Loma. He said he was finding bringing up a girl child by himself very difficult. I said at least I could take up the hems of gym slips and perhaps help with other tasks.

I was surprised to learn from him that I had been appointed at the highest professional grade at CSA, the same level as Roy. There were only four people at that level.

"We all wondered about you. We had heard about this very impressive lady who was coming from England to put the AMPnet project right but we didn't believe you existed because there are no women in Australia on that sort of salary and you took such a long time to get here.

"We all thought you were a boogieman dreamed up by the management to threaten us with if we didn't make AMPnet work," said Roy. "Now you're here you seem very nice and quite ordinary. Why were you appointed to such a top job?"

I told Roy I didn't know it was such a top job until people had started to remark on my salary level. I asked Roy what he did on the AMPnet project.

"Oh nothing really," he said. "I don't really have a specific job. I'm just supposed to know when things go wrong and how to put them right. The managers here seem to think the problem is in the database but I can't see that. Neville Black is a very good guy and seems to be doing the right thing."

"So what do you think is wrong?" I asked.

"I don't know. I've been here over two years and I can't work it out. We've got very bright people, several with PhDs, but no one knows what is wrong.

"It all started out okay but somehow went wrong. My theory is that we've got a duff computer. If you can get a duff car, I'm sure you can get a duff computer. We're told it's okay but I don't buy that."

"So what are the symptoms?" I asked.

"Well, it's just that nothing works. We've now got a very large team. They all seem to know what they are doing. They seem nice, genuine people, but everyone has the same story. Nothing they do seems to work," said Roy.

29 Why doesn't it work?

THE NEXT WEEKEND I went to Turramurra to look at houses. They all seemed to be at least twice the price of those I had seen in the adverts in England. What was going on?

After a while, one of the agents solved the problem. The houses I had seen in the adverts were the building price for new houses. They did not include the price of land. Land prices in Turramurra were more expensive than the cost of building a house. Also, house prices often did not include garden paths or plumbing and drainage work.

I had two options. I could buy a house in Turramurra with a big mortgage or move further out. I looked for houses in the beachside suburbs but found they were about the same price as those in Turramurra. I was keen to settle on a place to buy a house before the end of January so that I could find a local school for the children. Child care in Chatswood was costing half my take home salary for fulltime care. It would drop once the school term started in February but I needed to make less expensive arrangements.

The next weekend, I drove further north of Turramurra. About three miles north of Turramurra we passed a McDonalds. We had often visited McDonalds in the USA but there were none at that time in England. We didn't realise that there were only two in Australia.

Claire announced we should live here so we could go to McDonalds. We were in Waitara just south of Hornsby, which at that time was the northern-most station on the Sydney suburban rail system. To live north of Hornsby was to rely on a car for transport or a much less frequent rail service.

We were shown some not very nice houses by the first Hornsby agent I tried. The second, a woman, was more helpful. After listening carefully to our requirements she said she would prefer not to show any houses that day but would get back to me during the week. True to her word, she telephoned on Wednesday saying she would like to show me two houses that afternoon.

I agreed to meet her later that day. One was perfect. It was a beautiful architect designed house with high ceilings, in perfect condition and ready to move into. The real estate agent explained the house had been built for a young couple, but the wife had taken ill and could not manage the steep steps from the road.

The house just felt right. It was bright and sunny with huge floor to ceiling windows and painted white throughout. The kitchen was huge. All the fittings were top quality. This was the house. But I would need a mortgage. I contacted the bank manager.

"Hornsby? Why go to Hornsby? It's such a long way north," he said, but he agreed to go with the children and me the next day to inspect the house. The children loved it. The garden was very steep and, most of the land was bush and filled with native plants requiring little maintenance.

"Yes, I could live in this house," the bank manager said. "Yes, you can have your mortgage."

I visited the local school. It could take both children and seemed very nice. We retrieved our furniture from storage and moved in. It was the last week in January. There was a public holiday on 26 January for Australia Day, which marked the unofficial end of the summer holidays. School started the first week in February. There were uniforms and schoolbooks to buy and after school childminding to be organised.

I had set myself a target of the end of January to complete the report on the AMPnet Database for CSA. The offices were beginning to fill up as people trickled back from Christmas leave. I met all the database team. They seemed very competent. I wrote a simple report and attached Neville Black's strategic report. I stated that the database group was following the correct design processes and I could suggest no improvement.

MANY OF THE PEOPLE on the AMPnet team were recent arrivals from the UK. The CSA social club had an event nearly every weekend. Most of those who attended the picnics and beach parties were immigrants and their families who had formed strong bonds such that the events seemed more like family gatherings than work related events.

Some of the Americans joined the events but mainly the attendees were Poms, which is what Australians called British people. The children and I quickly formed a friendship with the Ryan family who were also Poms and also lived in Hornsby. Geoff Ryan had previously worked for Shell in the UK and Venezuela. The Ryan's three children played very well with my two.

I found the family living behind our house were more Poms, who had been in Australia for many years. Their teenage daughters agreed to keep an eye on the my children after school. Other neighbours were also very helpful and friendly towards us. It felt comfortable living in such a supportive community.

The children loved the outdoor life and their newfound friends. They loved their school although in the first week when Stephen came home with a bloody nose he said, "I'm not a Pom am I Mum?" He told me that the boys at school had said the Australian cricket team would beat the Poms and he was a Pom.

"You can be whatever you want to be," I told him. From that day, Stephen decided he was an Aussie and would tell the boys at school. There seemed to be no homesickness.

My bank manager invited me out to dinner and events at the Opera House. He explained that he lived with his mother but wanted to escape. A woman with a ready made family had great appeal. So that's why he was paying special attention to me. I told him I wasn't interested.

ON FRIDAY in the second week in February I was called into the office of Bob Kassel, the CEO. My manager Adrian Webster, who was one of the people who interviewed me in England, was also in the office. Bob Kassel got straight to the point.

"We've brought you here on a very high salary because we were led to believe you are an expert in databases," he boomed. "Well you've really let the side down because you've demonstrated that you're not an expert, you're a fraud."

Adrian Webster looked sheepish and angry at the same time. "You've let me down, Ann. I told Bob you'd solve our problems but you're telling us Neville Black is right. I was worried that you had no academic qualifications when we hired you. You've let his PhD cloud your judgement. We were told you know more about databases than anyone in the UK. Surely, you can't think there is nothing wrong here. We all know something is very wrong."

I was mortified. "I know there is something wrong. As you say Adrian, everyone tells me there is something wrong but no one knows what it is. I can assure you it's not in the database area. They are doing fine."

"Well Miss, we've been discussing this difficult situation you've put us in," said Bob Kassel. "We just don't know what to do with you. You seem to have other experience like project management but we don't pay our project managers as much as we are paying you.

"You could just resign. We will agree not to force you to pay back what we've spent in recruiting you. You should be able to find another job in Australia or just go back to the UK."

I was horrified. I was just getting to like Australia. The children loved it. They had just started their new school and made friends with the Ryans. We now had a house. I needed time to think. I took the rest of the day off. I certainly wasn't going to resign.

On Monday morning, Roy Taylor was pacing up and down the corridor outside my office. His normally smiling face was grim set. “What have you been telling the management?” he thundered. “I didn’t think you were the sort who would suck up to management but perhaps that is how you got your high salary. The management here is very weak. I thought you’d see that. Sucking up to them won’t get you any friends.”

The corridor was beginning to fill with people eager to watch a row between two top consultants. I opened the door to my large office and asked Roy in.

“What’s happened?” I asked. “Do you know your precious management asked me to leave on Friday? I’m certainly not flavour of the month.”

“Well Neville Black has been sacked. He was called in to Kassel on Friday afternoon and was given a one way ticket to CSC in the USA for Friday night and told he had to report to his manager there. We high flyers are used to being shipped round the world at short notice to help out in a crisis. He thought this must be one of those and he’d be back here on Monday. He was taken straight to the airport and only had time to phone his wife.

“When he got stateside he was sacked. He was told he must have persuaded you to support what his team are doing. You, being a weak woman, agreed. Kassel and Webster sent a report to CSC that Neville was holding up the whole project. They’d recruited you to set him straight but you weren’t able to do that.”

I was horrified. “But he told me he and his wife had bought a house here and had two young babies. What will happen to them?” I asked.

“Oh, it all turned out alright. He phoned me last night because he wants me to give him a reference. He just walked across the road from CSC to Univac and he’ll get a top job there. Part of the deal with Univac is that they will let him have time to come back to Australia to wind up his affairs here and get his family back to the USA. But that’s not the point. Neville is one of the good guys. What did you say about him to make them do that?”

I was aghast. What was going on? I showed Roy my report. “What shall I do? We were just beginning to enjoy it here. It will cost me heaps to move back to UK and start all over again. I probably won’t get such a good job here after this,” I said.

“Just sit tight. There is definitely something odd going on. Perhaps we can put our heads together and find out what it is. I’ll introduce you to two more of the bright guys on the team. They are PhDs like me but, like me, they haven’t got much experience. You’ve got the experience so it could work out. Maybe we can make you an honorary member of the Doctors Club.”

Just before 12 noon, Roy turned up at my office with two brown paper bags of sandwiches from the canteen. "Come on, the Doctors Club is meeting for lunch on the back deck. You're invited. I got you a salad sandwich. I didn't know what you'd want to drink so we can pick that up as we walk through the canteen," said Roy.

I was introduced to John Kaunitz and David Lawrence. John, a PhD from Stamford, was working on something called TCS. David, who got his PhD in Australia, was an operating system guru. Roy gave told them about Neville Black and that he had read my report and felt I had nothing to do with Neville's departure. Indeed, my job was on the line too.

There was general conversation about how the project was going. I watched the men interact. Roy was a big bluff laid back American. John was a small, dark volatile man with a strong eastern European accent. David was a quiet, serious looking, restrained Australian.

They joked that the Doctors Club had lost a member and maybe they'd have to take Gerry on. I felt a little cowed by being included among such high powered minds but reminded myself that they were really no better qualified than many of my colleagues in the BCS who I had met regularly. But I felt it was politic to keep a low profile and speak only when spoken to.

On the way back to my office I asked why they'd laughed about Gerry Asbell. I had not yet met Gerry but Roy had said he was the project's Chief Technical Officer. "You'll find out," was Roy's reply.

In the meantime I decided to take Roy's advice and sit tight. Nothing happened and I started to breathe a little easier.

SOON I WAS HAVING a sandwich lunch nearly every day with Roy, John and David. It was a very enjoyable hour when we shared views about current world events and information on new technologies. John, Roy and my birthdays were less than a week apart in July.

Gerry Asbell was never invited to the Doctors Club. He was usually tipsy by 10am and spent his lunchtime in the local pub, the St Leonards Hotel, known to the CSA staff as the Blood and Guts. He was back in the pub by 5pm each day.

Women rarely visited the pub. I only went there once but vowed never to go again. It was tiled throughout like a public toilet and stunk of stale male sweat. The floor was covered in sawdust and sticky with spills from beer and the pies with tomato sauce, the only food available at the pub. The men stood closely packed, pie held in one hand, beer in the other.

Roy, John and David encouraged me to continue to participate as much as I could in the AMPnet project. There were regular weekly brown bag lunchtime meetings run by John to which participants took their sandwiches. The meetings were intended to provide a platform for AMPnet managers to describe the part their team played on the project.

John described his project TCS, the Transaction Control System, in detail. Like most software developers, he had given the modules in his system strange sounding names. Asked to explain, John could always provide an acronym to justify the name.

After attending a few of John's presentations, I began to realise that TCS was very fluid. I had been used to watching the programmers develop the complex Atlas supervisor in the 1960s and had understood the details of the operating system developed for CTL's Modular One. John's presentation reminded me that I could see the logic in previous system software development but had difficulty following his presentations.

I discussed my difficulties with Roy. "I'm glad you mentioned that," said Roy. "I thought I was the only person in the room who wasn't following John's logic. His heavy Hungarian accent makes following him very difficult and you'll notice that no one ever asks him questions so we don't get much of a chance for clarification. I don't like to ask questions because I really am out of my depth. I think we need to ask David Lawrence what he thinks. He's a pretty smart guy and operating systems are his area."

The next time John said he wouldn't be lunching with the Doctors Club, Roy and I asked David if he followed what John was doing. David said he'd had concerns for quite a while but that John had much more experience than he did so he didn't like to question John too closely.

"The thing that really worries me is that he keeps rewriting bits of the operating system. He says it's only the interface to TCS, but then when we get patches from Univac we have to retrofit John's changes too. Neville Black used to worry that he was doing the same for DMS1100. I also understand that we can't run a distributed system like AMPnet without a TCS, but maybe we'd be better sticking to batch processing until Univac develops one."

I WAS BEGINNING to think I'd found the weak spot in the AMPnet project. But I needed to collect more information. I asked Gerry Asbell if he could describe the relationship between the different elements of the Univac system software and how they related to the applications. The most obvious sign of AMPnet's problems was that the applications wouldn't work consistently.

Gerry gave me a very basic overview of the system. It was to be a distributed system with DEC PDP-11s in the AMP branches in Australia's state capital cities and New Zealand, and a centralised Univac 1110 mainframe in Sydney to handle batch processing.

The state based remote nodes seemed to be only acting as data capture devices. They did a little data checking but the data could not be fully verified until it reached the central mainframe where the main database was held. Data could be sent up to the mainframe during the day in real time but more was sent in batch mode overnight. Records were to be updated overnight and revised information, branch reports and details of data errors were to be sent back to the branch in time for the next day's business.

Gerry drew diagrams showing that the systems software drove the hardware. On top of that, in his diagram, sat the DMS database, which supported the application systems. Thus, Gerry concluded, the problem must be with the DMS.

Gerry said the engineers vouched that the hardware was working properly and anyway, the CSA timesharing bureau ran on a similar Univac mainframe and that always functioned correctly. They had no complaints from their timeshare customers.

I said I had heard that the timeshare system ran a cut-down operating system developed by CSC in the USA for its own bureau service. Could the AMPnet OS be the problem? Gerry said they only needed a simple OS to support timesharing and that he had been assured that the OS they were using for AMPnet was fine. Several of Univac's American customers and other Univac users in Australia ran the same system without problems.

I asked where Gerry thought TCS fitted in. He told me I'd have to ask John. I approached John with caution. I liked him. He was an honest, intelligent, hard working manager with a highly qualified team. He had left Hungary at the age of six just before the revolution in 1956 by walking out over the mountains with his grandmother.

He had always been a bright student and easily gained a university degree. He had joined the Post Master General's department as a cadet engineer and had been given a scholarship by the PMG to Stamford University in the USA where he gained his PhD.

John explained TCS in detail, drawing his sprawling diagrams across several whiteboards. I asked about the interfaces with the OS and DMS1100. John explained he had found the correct places to interface with both systems and the DEC PDP-11 operating system, and had provided subroutines to link to those systems. He said the links worked and did not corrupt the other systems.

I asked how John had learnt how to design a Transaction Control System. Was it at Stamford? I mentioned that the UK Government had been developing the Experimental Packet Switching Software, EPSS, but didn't really have it working in a commercial form yet. I mentioned that I had been working on the UK Government's Videotext committee.

John looked relieved. "You understand packet switching?" he asked. "Very few people do. Did you know that the PMG has been working with Univac in Australia to build a packet switching system called CUDN, the Common User Data Network? I was on that team. It's about to be dropped.

"It might still be developed as a research project but it won't be available to Australian business for many years. I'm convinced I can build that here at CSA. I heard about AMPnet from Univac. When I joined I was pleased I could go on doing just what I was doing at the PMG."

I decided it would be best not to discuss the subject further. I knew that some of the best minds in the UK were working on EPSS at the National Physical Laboratory. How could John and his team build a system like that in Australia, however brilliant his team was?

I decided to turn my attention to the applications development aspect of AMPnet. "Where are the business people who write the business specs for AMPnet?" I asked Roy.

"They are at head office at Circular Quay. But we don't need business specs. We've got plenty of programmers who have worked on insurance systems. These systems are very simple.

"Anyhow, although most of the AMP people are very nice they all started work at AMP when they left school and have never worked anywhere else so they don't have much experience. Their own systems are very old fashioned. That's why they've hired CSA to give them modern systems."

I was beginning to see what the problem might be.

30 Sticking my neck out

I **WAS ENJOYING** Australia. I realised that professionally I was in a privileged position at CSA. Very few people in Australia, men or women, were being paid the sort of salary I was on. I was lucky to be working with a group of bright people even though I knew instinctively that the AMPnet project was in trouble. It was very worrying to think I might lose my job at any time but no one at CSA seemed to care what I was doing.

I attended some Australian Computer Society meetings. They weren't anything like the BCS meetings. It seemed to me Australia was about 15 years behind the UK in terms of computing.

I discovered that the twelve nice business suits I had brought to Australia were far too formal for life at CSA. They were hardly used except for visits to Canberra. People in Australia dressed very casually for work. I discussed my clothes with my neighbour Sheila.

She asked to see my suits and immediately asked if she could have one for an upcoming wedding, saying she'd never be able to afford anything that good in Australia. One by one most suits found new owners.

I had also brought six evening dresses from England but had hardly worn any of them even to parties. I always felt wrongly dressed. If I wore a long dress, other guests were dressed in jeans. If I wore jeans, the others were more formally dressed.

My social life was very pleasant. Now settled in a house with good neighbours and lots of friends, home life was much less stressful than it had been in England. Weekends were spent out in the fresh air at the beach or the countryside. There were no duty visits to be made to relatives. Many of the CSA people were in the same situation so we formed our own 'family'. Few looked outside that group for companionship. CSA was very generous in providing funds to the social club for outings.

I CONTACTED RENATE, Steve Shirley's sister, and found she lived in a charming house in Mosman, on the North Shore about four miles from the centre of Sydney. She seemed a very different person from the quiet, withdrawn woman I had met in Steve's house in England. Renate explained to me that she had gone to Australia after a failed affair with her professor at Oxford.

In Australia she got a job at Doctor Barnardo's homes. She had married on the rebound but found that she could not have children. She and her husband Peter boarded three Barnardo's boys who had been forced to leave the children's' home when they reached 16. They had adopted Clair as a baby, and when Clair was two they had adopted a second daughter, Juliet.

Their marriage broke up soon after and, as was usual practice, newborn Juliet was placed with new adoptive parents. It was only Renate's previous experience in Barnardo's that prevented two year old Clair also being taken back into public care.

Renate had been heartbroken and when Steve had asked her to help with her autistic son Giles. She had decided a spell with her sister in England would help her to sort out her life.

Renate lived near Balmoral Beach. The children and I spent happy afternoons on the sheltered sand. My fair haired Claire and Renate's dark haired Clair soon renewed their friendship that had started in England.

Roy was very attentive. People at CSA were beginning to see Roy and me as an item. My children were wary of Loma, Roy's daughter. They saw her as a spoilt brat. Roy was delighted that the group could take trips together and said Loma had always wanted a sister and brother.

THE MORE I thought about the AMPnet project, the more I felt it was headed for disaster. I now realised that AMPnet employed over three quarters of CSA's staff. If it failed, CSA would fail or at the very least would undergo severe staff reduction. In either case, my job was in jeopardy and I would have great difficulty getting another job in Australia.

I knew AMP was pressing hard for results. The project cost was so far twice the agreed budget and there was little demonstrated progress to date.

CSA staff briefings were held monthly. These were usually addressed by Bob Kassel, the CEO, although other managers also spoke about their own projects and the CSA social club gave information about upcoming events. The meetings ended with drinks and nibbles and a chance to meet the very few other CSA staff from non AMPnet projects like the ABS.

Bob Kassel had been an officer in the US Navy. He had been in the first submarine to travel under the ice to the North Pole. He spoke to us like a commander rallying the troops. He paced to and fro in front of his audience constantly clicking objects in his pocket, a bit like Captain Queeg in the Caine Mutiny. His eyes blazed and his nostrils flared. He looked like a man under pressure.

After Easter, I felt that I would have to return to England. I wrote to colleagues who I had approached for jobs before I left England. Was there still a job for me? All the letters came back with job offers.

I started totting up costs. I had spent half the cost of a house getting to Australia but house prices in Australia had risen slightly so I would not lose much money when I sold our Australian house. I would have enough money for a deposit for a house in England and would have to get a mortgage. Well, I told myself philosophically, it has been an experience.

I decided before I left Australia I would have to tell AMP that in my professional opinion AMPnet would never be successfully completed. I rang the General Manager of AMP. I came up against a very professional secretary who wanted to know, in detail, what I wanted to discuss with her boss, Keith Steele.

I felt my message was too complex to leave with a secretary. Best meet the man face to face so I could explain my feelings because they were only gut feelings. I had no concrete proof.

In England I was well known. I had often been mentioned in newspaper articles and had made quite a name for myself through my BCS activities and involvement in government committees. But I could not get past Mr Steele's secretary.

I decided to try the Deputy General Manager. I was most surprised when, after leaving a couple of messages, the Chief Actuary's secretary rang to set up an appointment.

I dressed in one of my formal business suits. I arrived a little early and was shown into a huge office on the 25th floor of the AMP building at Circular Quay. It had at one time been the tallest building in Australia, but was now eclipsed by many others in Sydney's sprouting skyline.

The secretary announced me but there was no acknowledgement from the oldish man sitting hunched over the large antique desk writing intently. I was taken aback. These were very peculiar people yet they were running the largest enterprise in Australia.

I saw a large antique, high backed chair against a wall facing the desk. I dragged it nearer the desk. There was not a flicker of acknowledgement from the man at the desk. He did not look up from his writing.

"This is a game," I thought. "Then I'll use it as an experience and just observe." I decided I would not speak until the man first spoke to me.

After what seemed like an age, he stopped writing. He carefully replaced the top on his fountain pen and set it down on the desk. He leant back in his chair.

He looked at me over his spectacles. “Yeeees?” he drawled.

“Good morning Mr Wheatley,” I said brightly.

“Before you speak young lady let me tell you I know all about you. I hear you were brought out from England at a very high cost because you are some sort of computer expert but we’ve found out you’re not an expert you’re just a fraud and you’ve come here to make trouble. Well if you make trouble for AMP, I warn you you’ll never work in Australia.”

“I don’t want to work in Australia. I’m going back to England,” I said. “You’re all mad here, it’s probably because you’re all upside down on wrong side of the world and the blood is running to your heads. I’ve just got a question to ask you. Why is it that the budget approvals for AMPnet are $6 million yet the spend to date is nearly $12 million and the project will never be completed. Good day!”

I got up and left slamming the door behind me. I did not even acknowledge the surprised secretary.

“I’VE DONE IT NOW,” I thought. “I’ve burnt my bridges. Now I’ll have to go back to England.”

Without telling the children or Roy or Renate, I continued to make plans to return to England. I did so with a heavy heart. I had grown to love Australia. It was a beautiful country. I had made lots of friends and felt at home. I never felt homesick for England. I thought of Auntie Joan and how she had struggled in Australia at first. Other CSA people had confided they found the move difficult. Should I just accept my lot and try to make a go of it?

A week later, I got a phone call from Mr Wheatley’s secretary. Would I please take morning tea with him?

“Why not?” I thought. “Let’s see more of the game.”

I dressed smartly again and arrived on time. Mr Wheatley’s secretary welcomed me warmly. I was ushered into the room. This time Mr Wheatley jumped up from his desk and shook my hand.

“I believe you like this chair,” he said with a smile, lifting the big heavy chair alongside the desk. He rang a bell. The tea lady, complete with trolley, appeared as if by magic.

“I had the kitchen make scones with cream and jam for morning tea. I understand you English people like that for morning tea,” he babbled. The tea lady asked me what I would like and served coffee, scones, cream and jam. When she had served Mr Wheatley, she slipped silently out of the room.

I decided that, once again, I would only respond to questions and let Mr Wheatley take the lead. We discussed the weather. Mr Wheatley asked if I and my children were enjoying Australia. I replied politely to his questions.

"You asked me a question last week," Mr Wheatley said. "I've only got one question for you. How come my managers don't know what you told me?"

"They do know, but they are too scared to tell you," I said.

"I know it's the truth and they know it's the truth," said Mr Wheatley. "I've had them all in here one by one and they all tell me you're right but they have a difference of opinion with one thing you said. You said the project would never be completed. They tell me it's 90% complete. Can you prove what you say?"

"I can't prove it," I admitted. "I'd need to do a lot more digging to really prove it. It's a gut feel but the project isn't 90% complete, of that I'm sure. It's more like 10% through."

"You know you're a very impressive woman," he said. "I've had people check your references in England and you're very well respected. AMP is a very wealthy company. We can afford to bring experts from anywhere in the world but I need to inform the Board and tell them how much the project will cost. I'll ensure you have access to any papers you want. Can give me an estimate? How long will it take? Will you help us get the project back on the rails?"

I thought for only a short time. This would be an interesting little project. I really did want to get to the bottom of why AMPnet wasn't working. As a professional, I should take the challenge and help these people. I'd done investigations like this before and prided myself in my ability to estimate.

"I think there are two main areas of concern," I said. "CSA is building a Transaction Control System because Univac doesn't have one. Because the system is decentralised with computers in state branches sending data to head office in real time, it needs a TCS. But I'm not sure you need data sent from branches in real time. Do you know the answer?"

Mr Wheatley looked puzzled. "The reason we established CSA and gave them the job of building our new system was that they promised a world class system. If that's the sort of system other insurance companies have we can't afford to be left behind. But you said there were two areas of concern. What is the other?"

"I'm concerned that your business people don't seem to be involved in defining the requirements of the system," I said.

"I'm assured by CSA that they've hired the most experienced people in the world to build our system," said Mr Wheatley. "I've met some of them. Very nice young men from America, England and Europe and well qualified too. If you're an example of the expertise they can bring to work for us we must be in very good hands."

"I'll do my best to give you an estimate," I said. "But it will have lots of provisos. We really need to get back to your requirements and that would take quite a while."

"We haven't got a 'quite a while'. This will get out and I need to ensure I have answers when the Board asks questions," said Mr Wheatley. "I'll arrange for my secretary to set up an office for you next to mine. You only have to ask for resources and I'll see you get them. But let me stress, we need an answer quickly. I'll speak to Mr Kassel. He wants this project to be a success.

"I didn't know the project was running over budget and neither did the Board, but that's not really the main issue. We need to know how long will it take to complete AMPnet and how much more will it cost."

WHEN I GOT BACK to CSA there was a note on my desk to see Mr Kassel urgently. I made my way to the 5th floor executive offices with much foreboding. Had I done the right thing? What would Bob Kassel say?

The secretary asked me to wait in the anteroom to Bob Kassel's office. Adrian Webster arrived grim faced and went straight in to the inner sanctum without looking at me. There was another short wait. I could hear voices from Bob's office but could not hear what was being said.

Bob Kassel opened the door and ushered me in. He was red faced and looked furious.

"I knew you were trouble," he said as soon as the door closed. "We should have sent you packing when we found you weren't the database expert you claimed to be. We made a mistake there didn't we?" he glowered at Adrian.

"Against my better judgement, I was told you would be useful on the MANDATA project the ABS was setting up. Digby said you'd impressed them, but we haven't got that business yet.

"Now I hear you've been sneaking off to our client telling them silly stories that the project is over budget and will never be completed. Well let me tell you, Miss Smarty, you'll prove it actually is 90% complete and it will finish soon.

"We know it's over budget but that's because they want the best system in the world. Well they'll get the best system in the world. We've got the best people in the world working on it. When they see the system working they'll forget the cost. They can afford it anyway. Do you know they are the richest company in Australia?"

I watched as he paced backwards and forwards clicking whatever he clicked in his pocket with a greater intensity than I had seen at the monthly meetings. I looked around the room. It was at least as big as Mr Wheatley's huge office. It, too, had an antique desk with an antique lamp and an imposing leather chair. There were comfortable chairs set in front of the desk for visitors and a small side table with four easy chairs where we were currently sitting.

"For this project, you will report directly to Adrian Webster. You are not to give any information to AMP unless he approves it. Do you understand?" he said.

I felt it best not to comment. I was asked to leave the room while Adrian and Bob discussed the details.

"Boy, you've done it now," was Roy's comment when I found him sitting in my office when I got back. "What made you do it? Webster and Kassel are spitting chips. They asked me if you were all there. You know what happened to Neville? You'll be back to the UK on the next plane."

"I don't think so," I said. "I've been told I just have to prove the project is going okay. I have to report to Adrian Webster. Bob Kassel told him it was his job to help me prove everything is okay."

"But we know it isn't. They'll use you as a scapegoat," said Roy.

"It's okay," I said. "I've already decided I don't want to work here. I'd like to live here but computing is so far behind the UK and everyone is so peculiar. I've been making plans to move back to England for a while now."

"You didn't tell me. I had hoped we'd make a go of it. Loma likes you. I like your kids," said Roy shaking his head.

"I'll do this estimate then go back to UK. I'd like to find out just what is going on here for my own benefit," I said.

"Watch your back," was Roy's parting advice as he left the office still shaking his head.

31 An inconvenient truth

WHEN I GOT BACK from my meeting with Bob Kassel there was a note on my desk to ring Alan Wheatley, saying he had made arrangements with Mr Kassel. The note said I could go and do the work at head office as soon as I was ready. I rang Mr Wheatley and told him about my meeting with Bob Kassel and Adrian Webster.

"Oh no, we're not going to accept your findings filtered by CSA management. You report to me on this study and no one else. I want you working here so I can keep an eye on progress," said Mr Wheatley.

"I'll have to do some work over in the CSA offices. I need to talk to people. I can't just pull information from paperwork," I said.

"Well just do what you think right but report to me if you get any roadblocks. And I want to hear how you're getting on weekly and I want an estimate within a month," said Mr Wheatley.

"I don't want to promise what I can't deliver," I said. "All I can promise is that I'll do my best, I'll keep you informed. I'll ask for help when I need it and I'll be as quick as I can."

I started with John Kaunitz. I told him I had been asked by AMP to come up with an estimate for AMPnet completion and future cost. Could he give me an estimate for TCS. John said he was confident that TCS would be completed very soon. He showed me that recent tests had been going well. He needed to keep his team of 15 people together for about a year but that was mainly for insurance. He could deliver a working system very soon but knew there would be changes needed as Univac and DEC hardware and system software changed and new requirements came from the applications.

It sounded good but I needed a crosscheck. There was a senior programmer in John's group, a tall, beautiful dusky skinned woman from Barbados called Pam Douglas. She was quiet and competent. I had travelled home on the train with her a few times and had tried to get her to comment on TCS. She wouldn't be drawn except to say that she had every confidence in John.

I invited her for a coffee. I asked Pam if she could give an estimate for TCS completion. Pam's wide eyes opened even wider. "Why don't you ask John?" she said. "I have asked John. He tells me the first version will be ready very soon. I'm just trying to get a second opinion," I said.

"It's a well designed system, I can tell you that. John's very intelligent and knows his stuff, but he keeps tweaking it. If he'd only stop making changes and get version one stable then the applications could get going.

"The problem isn't really John's TCS, it's the changes we make to the OS or the DMS. They don't always work so that causes the applications to fail. I think we should develop applications on the plain vanilla OS and DMS and add TCS later when we bring the branches in.

"I know that's not what we promised, but it will get all those applications programmers doing productive work," said Pam.

NEXT I TALKED to the applications teams. All the teams had many developers, and they were building complex systems. One of the worrying things was that the applications were supposed to work together but were all being built in isolation. None of the applications teams spoke to the others.

The project was huge. When the system software support teams, the operators and the database team were added together it looked as if the project couldn't go live in anything other than batch mode with stand-alone applications in under two years. That included time allowed for user testing by AMP business people.

I contacted Ewart Willey, Data Processing Manager at the Prudential Assurance Company in the UK. He was Chairman of the BCS Advanced Programming Group. I also had discussions with Marian Tribe, who was also a member of the APG and chief programmer at the Pru.

The Pru was much bigger than the AMP. It had about 20 million life policies at that time, whereas the AMP had about 2 million. The raw number of policies should not change the development costs. That would be based more on policy variability and complexity and other support systems like investment management or accounting systems.

The number of policies would determine the size of computing equipment, not the effort needed to develop systems. There was no way I could compare the type of policies written by the Pru and the AMP. The Pru was building a batch system on an IBM computer and was not trying to build a TCS or change the operating system and DMS.

The Pru had decided to reduce the complexity of its new system by not including the programming needed to process their very old polices. Their solution was to employ retired members of the Pru to manage their oldest policies, about 20% of the total, by hand and not convert these to the new system. The theory was that the retirees would be able to work until the old policies 'died'.

Ewart was very helpful in providing guidelines for the effort estimates. He said they had experienced problems in converting from a flat file to the IMS database system.

He stressed that it was imperative to include business people in the project development. He had worked for the Pru since he left school and was familiar with their administrative processes before he became involved in computing. But he said the business systems were fast changing and even he hadn't kept up with the business changes.

I now needed to convert my rough estimates to financial consequences. I asked Adrian Webster for CSA's charge out rates. He told me to just give him effort estimates and he'd manage the financials.

CONTRARY TO MY first impression I found that Alan Wheatley was a delightful man. Soon after starting my work, I found that his hobby was making homemade jam. I had made my own jams and pickles for years so we were soon swapping recipes and samples.

I told him that I had nearly finished with my estimates but just wanted time to check them. I asked if I could have a copy of the latest CSA invoice.

"What's the magic number? When will the project be complete?" He asked.

"I can't tell you that until I have the charge out rates," I said.

When I got the latest invoice, I noted that my own charge out rate was four times my salary. In the UK at that time, charge out rates for computing specialists were about three times salary. This was justified by calculating in-house management and overheads for staff as equivalent to salary, the other third was profit. The invoice started with highest cost professionals.

There seemed to be several managers being charged out as fulltime, including Adrian Webster and Paul Stephens. I noticed I had been charged out at 20 days even though I had done no chargeable work on AMPnet that month. Roy and Gerry were also charged at 20 days each at the highest consultancy rate.

I worried about my estimate. I didn't really know what all the people listed on the invoice did. How could I produce a reliable estimate? I still had a gut feel that the project would never be completed. It was too large and all embracing. The biggest worry was whether the systems being built would support the AMP.

I explained my doubts and the inconsistencies to Mr Wheatley. "Yes but how much will it cost and when will we be able to use the system?" he asked.

I drew a big breath. "Based on the current CSA charge out rates and not allowing for increases in rates, I think you will have to spend $60 million more. You'll get the first very simple version in two years time but you won't get a fully complete system for five years. That estimate doesn't include future hardware costs. I see you are still buying hardware," I said.

Mr Wheatley drew his lips together and let out a low whistle. His face went ashen. "I can't tell the Board that," he said, shaking his head. "Are you sure?"

"No, I'm not sure," I said. "I'm very uncomfortable with the estimate and I still have the feeling the project will never be complete. You might get some batch systems. There might be electronic data transfer from the branches but I don't think you'll ever get the system you expect."

"What resources do we need? Do we have to hire more people, better people?" said Alan Wheatley. "Just let me know, we'll hire more experts."

I assured him the people on the project were mostly competent and more people was not the answer. It might even be that they needed fewer people.

"Then why the huge cost?" asked Mr Wheatley.

"The whole project needs to be managed differently. You need to add good AMP business people to ensure the applications are what you need. You need business people to develop test data and test results. No one seems to have given a thought as to how you will convert from existing systems to the new systems. There is a lot to be done before you can start moving forward. There will be a few backward steps first," I said.

"I can see this has been a tremendous effort but I just can't put this to the Board," said Mr Wheatley. "I know you've got young children but the weekend is coming up. Can I ask you to critically review these estimates and let me have a revised estimate on Monday?"

I felt my stomach lurch. I had thought I had got rid of the estimate and could now sleep easy. The work had taken a month. I was looking forward to the weekend. I had put my move back to the UK on hold. I needed to get back to that plan. "Yes, I'll let you have a new estimate on Monday," I heard myself saying.

I spent the weekend going over the estimates. There were so many unknowns. Would AMP be able to find people to work with CSA on the applications? How much of what had already been built would be useful? What would AMP consider a reasonable charge rate for their own people? Would TCS really work? Was the hardware correctly sized?

On Monday morning I called in on Mr Wheatley.

"I've done my best," I said. "I found a few areas where I might have missed stuff. The estimate is now $64 million." (The project was to actually cost $96 million before it was finally abandoned.)

Alan Wheatley's chin dropped. He stood up. "When I said critically review I meant reduce the estimate, not increase it," he said. "Why are you more sure about this estimate today than you were about the $60 million you gave me on Friday? Will it change again if you look at it again?"

I assured him I had done my best. I told him that each time I reworked the estimate it would most probably go up.

He shook my hand rather limply. "Well, it's all we can do," he said.

EVERYTHING AT CSA went quiet. No one spoke to me about what I was doing. I had no more contact with AMP. I continued to eat my lunchtime sandwich with the Doctors Club and attend John's weekly meetings.

Roy tried to persuade me not to return to the UK. It had been a great strain producing the AMPnet estimate on such flimsy information. It would be very easy to take time to relax. My salary was still being paid into my bank account. The children were enjoying school and making friends. The weather was good. The summer heat and humidity was giving way to warm blue-sky days around 20 degrees.

Bob Kassel issued a brief memo on 8 May stating that Adrian Webster was in charge of AMPnet and foreshadowing that he would be reorganising the whole project.

Early on 27 May Bob Kassel called me into his office. This time there were only the two of us in the room. Although it was only 10am, he poured out two generous glasses of whiskey and asked me to join him on the chaise longue. He offered me a glass and took a gulp from his own.

"We've had our differences in the past, Ann. The AMPnet project is huge, probably the biggest in Australia to date. It's got to succeed. The viability of CSA depends on it. We thought the database was the problem but it seems it is not. We rechecked your references and see that you have experience in managing applications. We now think that's the critical area so want you to manage that," he said.

I was taken aback. What had caused the change of heart? Was I being handed a poisoned chalice? Everyone knew none of the applications worked. I said I'd need time to think. I left the room in a daze. I was doing a lot of leaving rooms in dazes.

As a professional, I wanted to get stuck into the applications to prove I could contribute. I wanted to be able to give the AMP something for the $12 million they had already spent on AMPnet. I really wanted to stay in Australia. It was a beautiful country. I phoned Bob Kassel's secretary and left a message that I would accept the appointment.

Before lunch, Bob Kassel issued a memo to all CSA staff giving details of a new AMPnet organisation. Six Senior Managers were to be appointed. All would report directly to Adrian Webster.

Dr Warren Smith was appointed AMPnet Facilities Manager, responsible for operations and system software support. Dr David Lawrence was to head the Technical Department, responsible for all system software developed by CSA. In other words, he would manage John's TCS team. There was no mention of John.

Dr Gerry Asbell was appointed Project Chief Scientist and Mick Norsa was appointed to head a team responsible for project control, documentation and 'participation with AMP in project review activities'.

Ted Jonson was to head the Life and Superannuation applications, which had hardly started. I was to head all the other applications development.

What did all this mean? There was no mention of the review I had done There was no mention of AMP business people working with CSA. Why was there no mention of John? And there was no mention of Roy.

Roy came into my office. "Well, that little exercise you did with AMP doesn't seem to have spoiled your chances at CSA. Do you get a pay rise? Do you think AMP told Kassel to do this? I see Ted Jonson has been given the new applications that haven't really started. You've been given all bad ones so maybe it's commiserations. John is not mentioned at all," he said.

"You're not either," I said.

"Oh, I've been schmoozing up to Ted Jonson. He says he wants me on his team," said Roy. "He knew all about this. He's been working on it with Webster and Kassel.

"He asked me for my opinion on several people. I told him you were one of the good guys but I didn't know he was considering you for this role. He's a helluva nice guy for a Yank. He's bringing his wife and kid over any time now so he's here for the long haul. Looks like you'll be staying now. Loma and I will like that."

JOHN JOINED David, Roy and me for lunch as usual. We could see he was upset. "Why have they put you over me?" he asked David. "Do you have anybody reporting to you other than my team?"

David said it was as much a puzzle to him as it was to everyone. He had not been consulted and had only just seen the memo. He was annoyed that he'd had system software taken off him.

"Hopefully we can work together as friends. Two heads are better than one," said David. "I won't be reorganising your team so it will be just you reporting to me and them reporting to you."

The man who had been in charge of applications was Mike Copeman. I wondered how he would take the change. After lunch, I went to see him. He was clearing out his office. "I'm expecting you'll move in here," he said.

"Do you know where you're going?" I said.

"Yes. I asked for the change," said Mike. "The current project manager of the Mortgage and Investments project is out of his depth. It's huge. It's the biggest of all the applications.

"I used to manage that project until they promoted me to take charge of all the applications. I'm looking forward to being just a project manager again. I've been speaking to Adrian Webster and Paul Stephens about the change for ages."

"Will you let me know if the resourcing on the Investments project is right and if you need anything to help you make it all a success?" I asked. "In particular, do you think it would be helpful to get someone from AMP Investments on the team?" I said.

"The analysts are red hot. Several have worked on investments systems before. They really don't need AMP people. Their systems are antiquated. Our job is to give them systems for the future," said Mike.

"What about testing?" I said.

"Oh yes, we'll bring them in to test," said Mike. "But that's a bit of a way off yet."

"Wouldn't it be good if you could have a look at test data and test results?" I said.

"No," said Mike. "We'd be tempted to build the systems just to give the answers they want. We're going to blow their socks off with the new system. It's going to do stuff they've never thought of."

"Oh dear," I thought. The business people still won't be involved. But I kept the thought to myself.

32 User requirements

LARRY WAS RUNNING the accounting team at CSA. He had several very experienced systems analysts and many programmers. "We've completed stage one of the General Ledger," he told me.

"We haven't managed to test it thoroughly yet, but it's only a ledger so we are confident it will work once the hardware and system software are stable. They've taken John's team out of the loop so maybe we'll test without TCS. Our system is really a batch system. We don't need TCS."

"Stage two is management reporting. Then stage three is to tidy up and add the things they want that we haven't given them," said Larry.

I asked for an estimate for stage two as soon as possible.

"We've never had to do an estimate before," said Larry. "We just ask for staff and get them."

"Well, you'll do an estimate for me in the future and I'll get it signed off by our client," I said. "If you need help, please ask me."

I had five teams reporting to me. I was surprised to find that one was the remote branch software team. These were people who had been in John's team and were responsible for the software on the DEC computers installed at state branches.

Adrian Webster formed an AMPnet Release One team to get as many applications as possible working. The first release of software would be used by the NSW branch and not be offered to other states. The NSW branch PDP-11 was directly linked to the Univac mainframe so did not need TCS.

Adrian also advised that Bruce Paul would be assigned from AMP to work with the AMPnet release one team. The Release One team comprised all reports to Adrian except David Lawrence and would be managed by Dr Attila Kamanitzky.

JOHN WAS VERY WORRIED. He was a good friend of Attila, an American with Hungarian parents. Why wasn't he on Attila's team? John had told a story of how, when Digby Pridmore had taken Attila and John to Canberra to visit the Department of Defence, he had let John talk about his expertise.

Defence expressed concern about having a man with such a strong eastern European accent working on their project. Could he be a spy? John smiled and said his colleague Dr Kamanitzky might be preferable because he had an American accent. Needless to say, CSA did not get a contract.

Attila joined the Doctors Club for lunch. He wasn't clear why John and David weren't on his team. Maybe Univac would be releasing a TCS so CSA would not need to build one. He offered to find out and report back but he never did.

I spent time observing the Investments and Loans On Mortgage (LOM) team. It was a mixed crew. There was a wild Scotsman called Tom. Peter Poten was a tall, handsome American Korean War veteran with white crew cut hair. Everyone said he was a wizard programmer.

Ted Chadwick was a hardworking systems analyst from Lancashire. He led the team of four analysts. Wayne and Robyn were programmers who acted like a pair of star crossed lovers, always seen holding hands and gazing into each other's eyes. Robyn eventually left her husband and married Wayne.

Mike Copeman brought me his estimate for completion of the LOM project. It was his considered opinion that he needed half as many staff again as he already had. That would mean 13 more staff, including Mike, which would bring the team up to 40. With that headcount, he said he could guarantee delivery of release one of LOM in a year.

I told Mike that I didn't think 13 extra staff was right for the project and would he please rework his estimate. A few days later, Mike came back and told me I had been very perceptive. He had redone the estimate and needed to double the team to 52. I asked Mike to review his estimate and let me have a new one on Monday morning first thing.

On Monday, Mike said he'd looked at the estimate over the weekend but could not see anything that needed to be altered. What had I in mind? I said I thought the team should be eight. Mike said in that case he couldn't manage the project. I told him he had that bit right.

I HAD DRAWN UP a list of people I felt were contributing to the LOM project. I went to Paul Stephens, who was now CSA's Personnel Manager, and asked that all those not on the list be removed from the project. Paul said he would have to discuss the issue with Adrian Webster.

I told Peter Poten what I had done and asked him if he would manage the project. He said he'd be delighted. I said I would be asking AMP for a business person from investments to review the project. Peter said that should have been done ages ago.

Adrian called into my office and said he couldn't reduce the project to eight people because the billing would suffer. He agreed to remove Ray, the previous project manager, and Mike Copeman because neither wanted to work on the project. He agreed that Peter could manage the project but said he would not be given a pay rise or a promotion. The rest would stay.

Relaying the story to Peter, he said he was disappointed but would soon find reason to sack several of the team who were not pulling their weight.

I arranged to see the head of AMP Investments Division and the Chief Accountant at AMP, Mr Putt. He was a tall, thin pointy-nosed man with grey hair and a grey suit. I told him that stage one of his accounting system would be ready for testing by his department in a month. Could he please arrange to have test data prepared and test results calculated.

"I have the estimate for stage two. It's $300,000," I said.

"What do I get for $300,000? What is stage one and how much has that cost me?" said the Chief Accountant.

This was worse than I expected. "I've just taken over the management of AMPnet Applications," I said. "Stage one is a standard General Ledger system. I don't know how much it cost. I thought you would have been told. I'm sure CSA has invoiced for it. I'll find out and let you know. Stage two is Management Reporting. One of your staff must have specified what you want. There is also a phase three but I don't have any details yet."

The Chief Accountant's face had gone grey like the rest of him.

"You can't go spending AMP's money like that, young lady. I had no idea I'd spent that money. It's not in my budget. I don't need a new General Ledger. The one we use now is fine. Please assure me you'll spend no more of my money until I've sorted this out. I'll speak with the General Manager and see what he knows. I'll get my secretary to arrange another meeting when I find out what's going on." He showed me to the door.

I was much more circumspect when I met with the Manager of the Investments Division.

"I'm Ann Leach from CSA. I've just taken over management of the Applications team. We are building an Investments system for you. I'm concerned that it might not be exactly what you need. No one from AMP seems to have signed off the business requirements and we have started to build the system.

"I'm from England and we usually get someone from the business to work with the systems analysts to develop the business requirements. Here in Australia it doesn't seem to work like that. We've got very good staff who do understand investments systems so I'm sure it will be alright but I want to be certain."

The Investments Manager looked confused. "I really don't know what you're talking about. I've heard about AMPnet but I thought it was a computer system, not an Investments system. Some insurance companies I've visited in USA have computers to handle their investments but I don't think we need one."

"Well then, it's even more important that we get one of your staff to see what is being done before it costs a lot more," I said.

"I haven't paid anything so far so it can't cost 'more'," he said.

Oh dear. I got a sinking feeling in my stomach. Perhaps I should have gone back to England after all.

I reported my visit to the Chief Accountant to Adrian Webster. "There," he said. "Didn't I tell you the AMP people don't know what they want? It's a simple ledger system for Christ's sake. Of course they need a ledger system. They probably currently use an abacus. They are back in the Stone Age. You shouldn't have gone to see them without me. I wouldn't have gone to see them at all. When they get their new system they will be blown away."

I decided I better not mention my visit to AMP Investments. I asked if I could have the cost of stage one of the ledger system for Mr Putt. "I'll handle that," was Adrian's reply.

A FEW DAYS LATER, I took a call from the Investment Manager's secretary. Bruce Bayliss, an Exec in AMP Investments, was to start a review of the project next Monday. He would meet me in my office at 9am.

Peter and I met Bruce Bayliss as planned. "What exactly am I to do?" he asked. I explained that systems had been built but were not yet complete, and for him to work with Peter and the analysts to ensure the system was what they wanted.

Two weeks later Bruce told me that the planned Investment system bore no relationship with what AMP Investments actually did. He would have to tell his Manager. I said I was sorry, I thought several of the team had worked very hard. It was not their fault.

There should have been business input from the start. As a favour, I asked that the four analysts and Peter be allowed to go and see what the Investments Division at AMP really did. Bruce Bayliss agreed to arrange a visit. When we went there I realised that there were more people on the CSA Investments team than actually worked in AMP Investments.

Ted, the chief systems analyst, asked about the department that handled the complex calculations he had designed. This area made up about one third of the system. We were taken to a very young girl in an AMP uniform sitting behind a typewriter. She looked about 12 years old.

She pulled a child's exercise book out of her drawer. She told us that she had been told that the calculations were very difficult so the men didn't always get them right. When they brought her a set of results, she wrote them in the book in pencil. When they changed the results, she just rubbed the old ones out. When there had been no change for a month, she inked the figures in. When those had not changed for a month, she typed them up and gave a report to the manager. That was the AMP Investments system.

For a while nothing happened. Then Adrian Webster called Attila and me into a meeting with Bruce Paul, the AMP Exec who was supposed to be looking after AMP's interests on AMPnet. Adrian looked haggard as he sat amongst piles of paperwork. Bruce Paul was a benign looking man of about 50 with wavy, silvery hair.

Bruce said he had come to find out how Release One of AMPnet was going. Had there been any meetings about it, if so why hadn't he been invited? Attila squirmed.

There had been several Release One meetings. Attila looked to Adrian for support. Adrian said he wanted his team to get their act together before he asked Bruce Paul to join the meetings.

Bruce asked which applications AMP would get as part of AMPnet Release One and when would they be ready for testing by AMP staff. Adrian looked relieved. "We'll give you good notice but your testing will just be a formality. My staff will have tested the systems very thoroughly," he said.

Bruce again pressed for timing. Adrian looked uncomfortable. "When do you think Attila?" he asked. Attila shrugged.

Bruce said this was not good enough. CSA had been billing AMP for over two years. Without telling AMP, they had overrun all spending approvals by nearly 100%. AMP now wanted answers.

Mr Wheatley's secretary phoned to ask me to take morning tea with him. Once again, he had had the kitchen make scones with cream and jam. When the tea things had been cleared away, Mr Wheatley came round his desk and sat beside me.

"We've been very busy since we presented your estimate to the Board," he said. "I also get stories from the Chief Accountant and the Investments Manager that the systems that have been built for them don't work in the way they should. This has all got to stop.

"We've decided to take over the management of the AMPnet project ourselves. We used to manage all our own computer stuff before we established CSA, you know. We never got in this mess and it didn't cost us as much either.

"We've decided to appoint an AMP manager to manage the whole project. We've got two people in mind. One knows a fair bit about computers but is a very gentle manager, The other knows nothing about computers but is a very strong manager. Of course, both have worked in many AMP departments and know all about our business. They are both in their 50s and have over 30 years service. They've worked for AMP since they left school. Which one would you think best suited to manage AMPnet?"

I did not hesitate. "You need the strong manager," I said. "There are plenty of us who understand computer systems."

IT WAS NOW AUGUST. The mild Australian winter was nearly over. It had been nearly a year since I left England. The winter in Sydney was nothing like an English winter. There had been a few coldish nights but Sydney's winter had more summer weather than an English summer.

Roy was more and more attentive. It was comforting to be able to talk over the peculiar events at CSA with someone who understood the situation. He had asked me to marry him several times but I told him I was not ready to give an answer. He was a nice, gentle, intelligent man but I knew he was worried that his wife might take Loma off him. If he had remarried, he would stand a better chance of keeping custody of his beloved daughter, especially as he could prove his wife's infidelity.

I also knew Roy wanted more children. I wasn't sure what effect more children with a new husband would have on my own two. Roy had said that when we married he would like me to give up work. He had a very good salary. I didn't want to give up work. Everyone at CSA seemed to think it would only be a matter of time before Roy and I would marry.

Roy asked me if I would come to dinner at his house. He explained that Loma was with her mother and if I could get my children minded, we could have a cosy dinner to discuss our future together.

When I arrived at Roy's large but old-fashioned house in Roseville, he went round the house opening curtains and windows. I hated the Australian custom of closing all curtains and windows during the day to keep the house cool. I felt it just made the place smell stuffy. Roy's house smelt worse than most and I noticed that, from time to time, he picked something off the floor and threw it out the window.

"I've got a nice leg of lamb," said Roy, taking the unwrapped lamb out of the fridge by the knuckle end and waving it at me. "It's what I cook best. It will take a while but we can talk as it cooks and I can get you drunk and then you'll agree to marry me."

“What were you throwing out of the window?” I said.

“Oh I’m such a old softy. I’ve got a very old dog. I don’t like to put her out during the day but she shits everywhere. The first thing I do when I get home is to open the blinds and windows and throw the shit out. It makes good fertiliser for the garden.”

I was horrified. Now I placed the bad smell. I realised Roy hadn’t washed his hands before handling the meat. Revolting! No, this certainly wasn’t the man for me, however nice he had seemed. I went into panic mode. I had to get away.

A mangy old dog came for a scratch. “This is my dog. Isn’t she hideous?” said Roy stroking the dog with one hand while still holding the leg of lamb in the other. “I know she’ll have to go. This is one thing I wanted to discuss and I wanted you to see the house and tell me honestly if we should live here or sell up and buy somewhere else.”

“Oh dear,” I lied. “I’ve done a very silly thing. I’ve got my kids minded but I forgot I promised to baby sit my next door neighbour Wanda’s baby while she drives to the airport to pick up her husband. I’ll have to rush off. We’ll have to do this another time.”

“Well that’s good,” said Roy, much to my surprise. “I changed the sheets cos I thought I might get you into bed but my venereal warts are very bad. I was going to tell you about those. My ex-wife used to say they gave her a lot of pleasure and were much better than her vibrator.”

I could hardly believe my ears. I thought I knew this man. This was a very lucky escape! I left quickly.

AS I DROVE HOME, I asked myself again what I was doing here. CSA was certainly on the skids. Although AMP seemed to care, they had done little to change the AMPnet situation, which continued much as it had done before I approached AMP. I was definitely not furthering my professional life.

Although many of the people I had met were very nice, the more I got to know about them, the more foreign they seemed. Australia was a beautiful country and the children loved it but if I stayed much longer would I succumb to this strange culture?

Appraisal time came. For the first time, I got a list of the salaries of all the staff on my team. Salaries did not seem to match staff grades. There was also a marked difference between the salaries of UK immigrants and people who had been recruited in USA or Australia, yet the billing I had seen on CSA invoices was by staff grade. I was horrified by the low salaries that were being paid to some of the most senior analysts. How could they support a family on such low salaries?

I discussed the issue with Geoff Ryan on our way home from work on the train. Although he was not on my team, he told me his salary. It was less than one third of mine yet he had bought a house and had three children to support. He said he just couldn't make ends meet unless his wife worked. Yet he was trapped because house prices in the UK had risen since he came to Australia and he would still have to pay money back to CSA to cover the expenses in bringing him and his family to Australia.

I brought the subject up with Adrian Webster. "They are lucky to be here, Ann. The salaries we are paying are more than they would have been getting in the UK and they have a much better life here," he said.

I argued that although that may be so, I had learned that it cost CSA virtually nothing to bring people to Australia. They came out as Ten Pound Poms. The Australian Government put them up in migrant hostels until they could find somewhere to live. All CSA had done was to recruit them and offer them a job then charge them out at several times their salaries to AMP.

Adrian countered that they were virtually tied to CSA for their first two years. He admitted that they would change jobs if their salaries weren't brought up to market levels, but as people in the IT industry in Australia rarely stayed in a job for more than two years anyway, at least CSA had got value from their acquisition.

I said I thought that was immoral and would expect that the Poms would at least be paid the same as their Australian and American colleagues in the same grade. I proposed salary increases for all those who were underpaid or I would expect them to be charged to AMP at the grade equivalent to their CSA salary. I pointed out that CSA's charge out rate was already four times salary. I suspected that was above industry mark-up and would look into that. Adrian just put his head in his hands and said, "Do your worst."

I REVIEWED THE appraisals from the project managers. Most of the senior people were rated as excellent. The Americans were on a reasonable salary but for all those who had been recruited in UK, I recommended an increase to take their salary to the appropriate level. In some cases that meant almost a doubling of salary.

Adrian called me to his office to review the recommendations. "It's company policy never to award anyone more than a 10% increase unless they get a promotion," he said. "Some of your suggestions are ridiculous. You'll bankrupt the company. Our billings are already considerably reduced due to many of the big projects being closed down. Look at your own salary. It's much too high for the job you are doing. We were paying you as an overseas expert. Now you are just a jumped up project manager."

Was my salary going to be reduced? It certainly was very high compared with other Poms but not compared to the Americans. I was told to leave the decision making to Adrian.

When I got the list of salary increases, they were at the maximum of 10% for those I'd asked to be increased significantly. My own salary had not been changed.

I told all those I considered underpaid that the most I could get this time was a 10% increase but I would continue pushing for more until they got the salary they were entitled to. Trevor Sellers, one of the analysts working on the Accounting systems with Larry, patted his top pocket.

"That's my resignation letter," he said. "I've been checking salaries. I'm very much underpaid. I've got a wife and four children to support and I can't find a reasonable house to buy because the banks won't lend me enough money.

"We all love it here but I'm being exploited. I know what the Yanks are being paid and I'm better than most of them. I was strongly considering going back to England where at least I know what I'm worth.

"If you'd have given me the increase and pretended it was what I deserve, you'd have got my resignation letter. As it is, I'll wait and see what develops."

33 Changing seasons

RATHER THAN SEASONS changing on the equinox or solstice as in the UK, in Australia seasons officially change on the first day of the month before each equinox or solstice. I later learned this was a hangover from convict times, and was when the British Army garrisoning Australia had changed from summer to winter uniforms.

Spring 1975 brought dramatic changes to AMP. On the first day of the season, AMP announced that Phil Grace would manage the AMPnet project. CSA would continue to manage the hardware and system software.

I was called to AMP's office on Circular Quay to meet him. Phil Grace was a large, portly man. I was always to call him Mr Grace. He thanked me for what I had done to draw AMP's attention to the problems on the AMPnet project. He said he would like me to accept a secondment to AMP staff to help get the project back on the road.

"I don't know much about computers, Ann, but if you set up the bullets, I'll fire them. You'll still be employed by CSA but you will work directly for me. I will ask Bob Kassel to second you to AMP."

I agreed at once. Maybe here was the way to get the project back on track before returning to England. Back at CSA there was a message to see Bob Kassel as soon as possible. Although the AMP takeover sounded promising, I still felt fear as I walked into this office.

The door was open. He welcomed me warmly. Putting one arm round my shoulders, he steered me to the chaise longue. The arm remained round my shoulders as he sat close and told me how proud he was that AMP had chosen one of CSA's senior staff to take a top position to help them manage AMPnet. I felt the need to escape and get some fresh air as soon as I could.

This meant yet another reorganisation. A memo that day, signed jointly by Phil Grace and Bob Kassel, announced the new AMPnet organisation would be located in CSA's offices in St Leonards. Each business area was to be headed jointly by an AMP Executive and a CSA Manager.

The Ordinary Life project was to be headed by John Dingle for AMP and Ted Jonson for CSA. Accounting Systems were to be headed by Larry and AMP's Eric Putt. David was to be Chief Technical Officer. John's TCS group and Ed Jansen's branch software group were absorbed into the system software team. I would be seconded to AMP and report directly to Phil Grace. There was no mention of Adrian Webster. In fact, he was rarely ever seen at CSA again.

Phil Grace had firm ideas. He established an administration office headed by an AMP Executive, Anstey Lindsay, and asked me to set up an AMPnet Project Control Office. I decided that there were three main issues to get underway as fast as possible.

Firstly, I needed to develop a PERT chart to show how the different aspects of the project fitted together and to identify dependencies. Only then could reasonable targets for deliverables be set and progress be tracked. Secondly, I wanted each CSA invoice checked thoroughly before it was paid.

Thirdly, in the future, elapsed time and cost estimates would be produced for all new work. These would be checked by the Project Control Office and signed off by both AMP and CSA before work started. I was given two AMP staff members, David Linfoot and a secretary.

I was surprised to be told that AMP paid all CSA invoices without checking as soon as they were received. Changing that process would severely affect CSA's cashflow, but I insisted that invoices be checked in retrospect and errors identified rectified as adjustments in the next invoice.

Work orders would be issued covering staff to be assigned and agreed rates. Changes required a documented request. There was much grumbling from CSA who complained that the project would be over administered and tied up in red tape, which would slow progress. But Phil Grace supported my recommendations.

THE DEVELOPMENT of the PERT chart proved very difficult. Very few project managers had developed estimates. They all seemed to work in isolation and did not understand project dependencies. There were many arguments over how work should be represented on the PERT chart, but eventually a high-level chart showing events and dependencies was developed. Then came the changes. I felt we would never get the diagram agreed.

Roy told me I needed to be very careful. He said most CSA people, especially senior management, hated me as I was seen to be the reason so many had lost their cushy jobs and for all the stupid red tape I had initiated.

I must have been insensitive but I didn't feel that atmosphere at all. I continued to lunch with the Doctors Club each day. In addition to the CSA people I had made friends with, all the AMP people were very friendly and supportive.

I thoroughly enjoyed working for Phil Grace. He was kind and considerate and supportive. The first appraisal I had from him, at the end of November 1975, was excellent in every way. He liked Roy very much. The two seemed very similar on the surface, kind, generous, intelligent, larger than life Australians who were liked by everyone . But I could not erase the images of the leg of lamb and the dog shit that evening when Roy asked me to his house for dinner.

I felt Roy would make a good surrogate father for the children but after much soul searching I reluctantly told him I would not marry him. He seemed very sad but within a year he would be happily married to a nurse who was pregnant with his twins.

CHECKING THE CSA INVOICES, I found so many mistakes that I asked Mr Grace if he would like me to check back into the past to review old invoices. I was told not to worry about that. At least current invoices were being checked thoroughly.

On one invoice there was a charge for 'hardware'. I asked Mr Grace why AMP didn't just buy the hardware itself. He said they got a special discount by buying through CSA. I asked CSA if I could see and check the hardware that was on the invoice. I was told not to worry, but I insisted.

The AMPnet computer room was on the ground floor of the St Leonards building. The building was located on the busy Pacific Highway, the main road going north out of Sydney. The pavement outside was only about two metres wide and there was a slight bend in the highway at that point.

A huge floor to ceiling glass window extended across the whole width of the computer room, which meant that it was in full view from the road. Cars, buses and heavy trucks passed at speed all day and night. I wondered what would happen if a vehicle ran off the road at the bend and into the window.

In the 1960s in the UK it was fashionable to display computer centres to the general public. But as computers were becoming an essential part of a company's operations, and with the advent of bomb threats in the UK in the 1970s, companies were building computer centres that were much more secure and usually out of the public eye, often in the basement.

I pondered these issues as I was shown round the computer room. Each cabinet had a label suspended on chains above it with the name of the component. The purchase item listed on the invoice I was checking was a new disk drive. Looking at the labels hanging above the cabinets, there seemed to be three disk drives. Which was the one on the invoice? As there was no serial reference number given on the CSA invoice there seemed to be no way of telling except that the operators remembered a new cabinet being installed a few weeks earlier.

I discussed the issue with Mr Grace. He surprised me by saying the centre was very secure. He himself had been involved in establishing it in 1970 when he was seconded from AMP to help start CSA. It was the biggest computer centre in the southern hemisphere and AMP wanted it on view so policyholders could see how their premiums were being used to make the company more efficient. He had personally arranged for the large glass window to be imported at great expense from the USA. He told me that it was totally shatter proof and would stop a large tank.

CSA conducted tours for people who wanted to see round the centre. Later I learnt that when a group of boy scouts visited, the operator was explaining how strong the giant window was and invited one of the smallest scouts to kick the window as hard as he could. The tiny scout duly complied and a huge crack appeared diagonally across the window from corner to corner.

I asked why there were no asset numbers. Surely these would be needed for audit and insurance purposes? Mr Grace said that there was several millions dollars worth of equipment and he was sure there would be a complete inventory somewhere.

He sent Anstey Lindsay, his Administration Manager, to check. Anstey found that there was only a list of items with their date of purchase and cost. Also, as far as he could tell, AMP's computers at St Leonards had never been taken into account as an asset in any AMP balance sheet or annual report.

Anstey worried about another issue. He had walked into the computer room without being challenged and there was no bar to entry. The front door of the building was open to anyone off the street.

Security was tightened and AMP's auditors were asked to do a complete audit of the hardware and compile a complete asset register. I went through all the CSA and Univac invoices, which included a unique identifier for each item, to find the date of purchase and the original cost of each.

The exercise revealed that AMP had been charged several times for some items and not at all for others. It looked as if the total hardware value was about $3.4 million but that figure could not be verified with any confidence.

The AMP annual report for 1975 was qualified by a note indicating that the value of AMPnet hardware could not be confirmed. It was the first time AMP's annual accounts had been qualified in over 100 years of operation. It was a blot on AMP's reputation.

Mr Grace decided that in future I would be responsible for all AMP's hardware purchases and Anstey would be responsible for the asset register. He told me that he'd like to know whenever any exciting new product was available in the IT industry even if it didn't really affect AMP so he could show off at his club at lunchtime.

CHRISTMAS WAS coming up fast. We had been in Australia a year. What a year it had been. I was feeling very much in need of a break. We travelled to New Zealand for Christmas with my mother's sister Auntie Joan, Uncle Vic and their teenage son, my cousin Ian.

Auntie Joan and her family lived in a northern suburb of Auckland on the Tamaki River. I was surprised to see how tiny their home was. It was made of weatherboard and only had two bedrooms. The children and I were given a single camp bed which was covered with a single blanket in Ian's tiny second bedroom. Ian slept on chairs in the lounge room. It was obvious that Auntie Joan and Uncle Vic were not well off but the warmth they showed to us more than made up for what they lacked in wealth.

They had an extensive garden full of fruit trees and cupboards full of bottled fruits and preserved vegetables. Uncle Vic had been a motorbike despatch rider in World War I. He had lied about his age, as many young boys had done, and at the age of 13 set off to see the world. He had spent much of his time in the Middle East and North Africa and kept Stephen spellbound with his war stories.

New Zealand seemed trapped in a time warp. It was just like the England I remembered after the war. There was breakfast at 7am, lunch promptly at 12 noon, afternoon tea with small cakes at 4pm, high tea with ham salad at 6pm then supper of welsh rarebit or baked beans on toast at 10pm while we listened to the BBC news.

We had already lived through a southern hemisphere summer, so presuming that New Zealand temperatures would be similar to Sydney's I only packed light clothes. The maximum temperature on Christmas Day was 12 degrees Centigrade. We froze.

New Zealand was lovely. The air was fresh and we were never far from the sea. We drove north to the Bay of Islands in Uncle Vic's tiny car. We were shown the New Zealander's tiny wooden holiday homes, called 'batches'. Prime Minister Piggy Muldoon's batch was about the same size as Auntie Joan's house. Before we left, I treated the family to a smorgasbord dinner at an Auckland restaurant. Claire and Ian tried to outdo each other in the amount they could eat.

I WAS PLEASED to be back in Australia refreshed from our holiday. Few people got back from their holidays before Australia Day on 26 January and Christmas decorations still hung in the streets. Life seemed one big holiday with trips on the harbour or to the beach or bushwalks and barbeques with friends. I was enjoying Australia. The children were happy in their school and looked brown and bonny. I felt I had made the right decision to come to Australia even though the first year had been hard.

After Australia Day the hard work began. Roy produced a work order for part of the Ordinary Life project. He said this was to be the core program and would be 800 lines of COBOL code long. Modular programming was being accepted as the standard, where large systems were broken into many small programs. We had introduced a standard that no program should be greater than 400 lines of COBOL but Roy argued that his program could not be broken into modules or built in less than 800 lines of code.

Looking at the specification, I judged that the program was actually a whole system and would be huge. I asked Roy why the program could not be broken into smaller modules. Much to my surprise, he dug his heels in and said he knew how the system worked and I didn't. He told me just to accept his estimate. He would build the system himself. In fact he had nearly built it already.

I brought the work order to Mr Grace saying I could not recommend that he sign it in its present form as I thought it was significantly under estimated.

"By how much?" he asked.

"It will be at least four to eight times the size. Also the cost and time will increase and the system should be modularised," I said.

He called Roy. "She doesn't know what she's talking about on this one," said Roy. I suggested CSA build the system for a fixed price as shown on the work order. Roy said he'd have to check that out with his manager, Ted Jonson. Ted said he had every confidence in Roy's estimate.

I suggested if CSA was so confident they should do the work for a fixed price of four times Roy's estimate. Ted and Roy refused. Mr Grace picked up the theme. "Do it for eight times as fixed price," he said. Ted and Roy still refused.

Mr Grace said unless they took the work at eight times and fixed price he wouldn't sign the work order. It was duly signed but several months later the program blew out to a very large system of many programs about ten times the size of Roy's original estimate.

It was CSA's first lesson that AMP was not going to accept that they could charge AMP whatever it liked for software development. From that point, unless agreed by both AMP and CSA all work orders and change requests were fixed price.

AMP Managers in charge of the applications had to assure that the work to be done was what was required and that it was cost effective. Also, they had to help me to add the new work to the AMPnet PERT chart ensuring that all prerequisites were acknowledged.

At first, few work orders came in as CSA mangers worried about making mistakes. The work initiated under the old order system started to run down which resulted in staff being taken off the project teams, but gradually and reluctantly CSA Managers complied with the new work order system.

Work orders and change requests were mostly well thought out and well presented, but every now and again there was cause for me to request a review on how the estimates had been derived or to point out ambiguities in specifications.

By now, I really did feel isolated. Roy was much less friendly and I often did not have time to lunch with the Doctors Club. If I did find the time I could feel the strained relationships. The AMP people felt much more in control and welcomed the change, but they were a different type of person to those I was used to working with in the IT industry.

The Ryans were still friendly and Claire and their youngest daughter, Pip, became firm friends. Renate and I took the children to Balmoral Beach for weekend picnics on the many blue-sky weekends as the summer heat gave way to the cooler days of autumn.

The seasons were changing again. So was my life.

34 A man's world

MY NEGOTIATIONS WITH the Australian Computer Society on behalf of the British Computer Society completed successfully, with reciprocal membership agreed. I joined the ACS but its meetings only showed me that Australia was many years behind the UK. There was little discussion about new computing technologies as there had been in the Advanced Programming Group in the UK.

I started to feel that as I had set the AMPnet project on a better path it was now time to go back to the UK. I discussed the issue with Phil Grace. He said he was expecting me to say something about the pressure I was under. He understood that CSA resented the fact that I had exposed significant weaknesses in the AMPnet project and that AMP had taken the project over. He realised that life must be difficult as CSA was my employer and asked if I would like to be employed by AMP.

It was a hard decision. My head told me to go back to England. Staying in Australia any longer would mean I would be so out of date technically that soon I would be unemployable anywhere but Australia. But I had come to love Australia. I had made good friends. The outdoors lifestyle was wonderful. Our standard of living was much higher than it had been in England. The children loved it. They, too, had made friends and I worried how another big life change would affect them. Claire would start high school next year so this really would be my last chance to make a big lifestyle change.

I discussed the possibility of moving to AMP with Roy.

"It won't happen," he said. "AMP people start at the company when they leave school and work their way up. They rarely leave until they retire. Many are second and third generation. They won't take kindly to an outsider being employed at a senior level, especially a woman."

Now I really started to worry. If I wasn't careful I'd end up with no job at all, then I'd have to go back to England. There was so much to do. A house to be sold, a job to arrange in England, furniture to be packed up and shipped across the world. Suddenly it all seemed too hard.

Mr Grace arranged for an employment offer to be made to me by AMP. He said he hoped I'd take it because he would be lost without me. He told me my AMP appointment would be Grade 5, near the top of the Executive range. My salary would be increased and I would be able to transfer my mortgage to AMP and pay only 2% interest. There would be other staff benefits. It sounded too good to be true. I accepted.

WHEN MY APPOINTMENT was announced I discovered that I was only the second person to be appointed an AMP Exec from outside the company. Once settled into the job I found out that I was also the only woman Exec. I was only about 30 people down from the top of what was then one of the largest insurance companies in the world.

We had reviewed the need for John Kaunitz's TCS system and decided that until Univac was able to produce a TCS, the DEC PDP-11s installed in branches would be used only for data input and enquiry. Although these would be connected to head office by telephone lines, data would not be transmitted, checked and processed in real time as originally envisaged.

The main database would be updated in batch mode. Some output reports would be sent back to branches via the phone lines but bulky reports or printing on special forms would be done at head office and shipped to branches by courier as previously.

We wanted to go live with a pilot version of the Ordinary Life system as soon as possible. The NSW Branch was not only the largest of AMP's branches but it was located in the same building as AMP's head office at Circular Quay, so it would be a convenient pilot. Looking more closely at predicted data volumes, we realised that NSW branch would need two PDP-11s rather than the one originally estimated.

I needed to get another PDP-11 as soon as possible. I called Max Burnet, the Managing Director of DEC in Australia. He told me the delivery time for a new PDP-11 was six months. Seeing that DEC's offices were in St Leonards, only a short walk from the CSA office, I decided to go and see Max in person.

Arriving at the DEC offices, I was surprised to see Max sitting at a very small cheap desk in a room with none of the objects of power that were normal for Managing Director's offices. Max was dressed casually in an open neck shirt, shorts and long socks. These Australians!

Max seemed welcoming but told me there was nothing he could do. PDPs were back ordered all over the world. I asked him if it was possible to buy a second hand machine. He said he would see what he could do. A few days later he found one for us.

JOHN KAUNITZ told me that he and his wife Hinda would dearly like a baby but it seemed they would be childless. He said they had made enquiries to adopt but were both too old to qualify. I discussed the issue with my friend Renate who was in charge of NSW adoptions. She agreed to meet with John and Hinda. She liked them and said if they were prepared to take a baby that NSW adoptions might have difficulty placing, she could get them one soon.

They were soon the proud parents of a lovely baby daughter. Leila looked perfect in every way. I asked Renate why she was difficult to place. It was simply that the child had been born to a very young mother. Leila delighted everyone and grew up to be a very talented and intelligent young woman.

Mr Grace often held morning teas for his executive team. As I was a single mother with two children, the conversation at these events would often get around to 'who can we marry Ann off to?'

Whenever the wife of an Exec died, the comment would be, "Wait a couple of months, then we'll have a dinner party and see what happens." They even tried to marry me off to a homosexual Exec because, as the boss said, "You've got two lovely children so you don't need any more of that silly stuff'."

One day I asked Mr Grace why they had never mentioned a man at AMP who was my age, handsome, sporty and unmarried. "Who do you mean?" said Mr Grace. I told him it was Doug Thorne, who had represented Australia in cross country skiing. Doug was a member of the Yeti Lodge in the Snowy Mountains and had invited us the stay there as his guest.

"Oh, you can't marry him," the boss said. "He's not an Executive." I told him that was prejudice. Had I been a young male Exec, he would have been trying to marry me off to a pretty young secretary.

Anti-discrimination laws were coming into place in Australia. My pay was the same as my male counterparts but there were many cases of gender discrimination. Most were because men had little experience of working with senior women.

My Executive package included superannuation and death insurance. The policy stated that on the death of the Exec, a generous lump sum would be paid to 'his wife' and 10% of that sum would be settled on each of the Executive's children. Because I was a single parent, only the 10% would be paid to each of my children.

Rather than point out that this was unfair and that being left without any parent, my children needed more rather than less money to support them, I told our personnel manager that in the case of a husband and wife being killed in the same car accident, 'his' children would only get their 10% each. I added that this would be so if I were to die. The system was soon changed such that the death benefit would be shared between the children.

IN THE MID 1970s computers still used core memory, which was sensitive to heat fluctuations. Just after I joined AMP, our Univac salesman told me that there was a new type of memory called Metal Oxide on Silica (MOS) which was not affected by heat fluctuations. It cost $1.5 million a megabyte.

I told Mr Grace. His first remark was, "What on earth would AMP do with a megabyte of memory? We already have two of the biggest computers in the southern hemisphere, and they each have half a megabyte. Surely that's enough?"

I told him that those computers ran systems developed in the 1960s. These were batch systems based on simple file structures. As the AMPnet system was supposed to be designed to run real time database systems, more memory would be a distinct advantage and I explained why.

He then said, "But $1.5 million! That's a lot of money when our whole system cost less that $4 million. You told us we will have to upgrade the Univac computer and you've convinced me extra memory will be useful so if you ever get the salesman to bring the cost down to $1 million, we'll buy it."

Within six months the price of MOS memory had dropped to $1 million a megabyte and we bought it. I wish I had saved the invoice because it would be of great historical and hysterical value now. Today we refer to MOS memory as computer chips and a megabyte costs a fraction of a cent.

Although manufacturing processes for chips have changed considerably since then, and the chips are now much smaller, they are not very different from that first megabyte I bought for AMP in the mid 1970s.

A few more items were added to the order for MOS memory and the total purchase price was several million dollars. I asked Mr Grace what AMP did to hedge against currency fluctuations as the bill was to be paid in US$. He said he had never been asked but to discuss the issue with Dr Bell, AMP's Chief Economist.

Dr Harold Bell was a tiny round bald headed man with a happy smile. He told me AMP had never bought hedge funds because they would have to pay a brokerage fee. He felt there would be no change in currency in the foreseeable future and if there was it would be less than the brokerage fee on the amount we were considering. I told Mr Grace. He asked me to check the issue with Chief Accountant Eric Putt. Mr Putt agreed with Dr Bell so no forward currency was purchased.

I had decided to send money for my mother and father to come out to Australia from the end of November to the end of March. As I made my way to the airport on Sunday afternoon to pick up my parents the radio announced that there was a significant devaluation in the Australian dollar.

I thought that would be good for my parents as any UK money they brought with them would have a higher purchasing power. But I was worried about the outstanding bill we had for our Univac hardware which, because it was in US$, would cost us about 17% more. When I picked up my parents I was relieved to hear they had travellers cheques in UK pounds. I told them their money was now worth 17% more. We would convert it all to Australian dollars in the morning to get the full value of the changed rate.

When I arrived at work on Monday morning Mr Grace was waiting for me. He looked jubilant. “What about the exchange rate?” he asked, grinning. “It’s awful,” I said. “We should have had currency insurance in place.”

“Yes, the General Manager has just telephoned me to ask if we had hedge funds. I was able to tell him that you had suggested it. We sought advice and followed that advice. We are in the clear, thanks to you,” said Mr Grace. He was bursting with pride and finding it hard to contain his pleasure.

I took my parents to the Bank of NSW in Crows Nest to change their currency before anything else happened. We were told that the old rate was still in force until new advice was received from head office at 9.30. We sat and waited till 9.30 then made a 17% profit on the travellers cheques.

At morning tea Mr Grace told me he had been called to a meeting with the General Manager who had called in the Chief Accountant and the Chief Economist to find out why they had not foreseen the devaluation and hedged against it, especially as they had been asked for advice. I could see that he was very pleased with the whole episode.

I WAS INVITED to the retired AMP women’s Christmas party. There had been articles about my appointment in the AMP staff magazine and there was much congratulation when I was introduced as AMP’s woman Exec. The older women told me that when the men were all called up to serve in the World War II the women ran AMP very successfully but when the war was over they were given their original menial jobs back.

I was surprised to learn that I was not the first woman executive. There had been two others but they were both now retired. They had both been Personal Assistant to Execs and had served in that position for many years. In both cases it was well known that the women actually ran the area in which they worked while their male bosses were ineffectual.

In both cases the women retired a year later. In both cases, although their bosses were Grade 4 Executives, when it was decided to promote the ladies to take their boss’s position when he retired, they were given the lowest Grade 1 position. In both cases when they retired a year later the newly appointed man was back at Grade 4. They did not seem to be resentful about these events, only proud that the women had been made Execs.

35 Working at AMP

I **WAS GETTING TIRED** of always having to ask people to rework their work orders and change requests before they could be included in the AMPnet plan, or directing people to emerging standards in the AMP IT development methodologies manual that we had produced.

In my appraisal at the end of November 1976, Mr Grace told me I had brought good commercial experience to AMPnet in many technical areas and had saved AMP many thousands of dollars in hardware purchases.

But the appraisal also said:

'Mrs Leach's background in a mainly commercial environment has caused her to adopt what might be called a 'hard nosed business attitude' – something that is not always understood or appreciated by her fellow AMP officers or by CSA officers. Mrs Leach will need to take care that her invaluable training and knowledge is not used in a fashion that encourages misunderstandings with her fellow workers.'

I was only doing my job. I asked Mr Grace what I should do differently. He told me I was invaluable and had done exactly what he wanted, but that people resented that after years of doing whatever they liked. It was galling to the managers, all male, to be brought in line by a woman.

Although I had done as Mr Grace asked and lined up the bullets for him to fire, AMPnet staff realised it was I who was preparing the ammunition. He said Australian men were not used to working with a woman who was at the least their equal and often better. But he told me again how much he appreciated what I had done and that he was sure I had a brilliant career ahead of me in AMP.

I mulled over the appraisal. I had enjoyed bringing AMPnet under control. I was proud of what I had done. It had been incredibly hard work, especially as I was also learning how to live in a new country, But I felt pleased to have been able to use my expertise to do a thoroughly professional job. Also, I now had a large circle of good friends and I loved living in Australia.

IT WAS CHRISTMAS AGAIN. The AMP Executive Christmas party was an amazing black tie event. The hundred or so Execs and their wives were beautifully dressed. Our names were announced as we entered the room.

The General Manager Keith Steele and his wife welcomed each Exec formally and said a few words of appreciation to each in turn.

The food was a banquet of lobster, prawns and oysters with all the trimmings. I was congratulated by many of the Execs as the saviour of AMPnet and introduced to their wives as the only woman Exec. It was a heady experience. The children's Christmas party was equally lavish, with no expense spared. I was beginning to understand just how wealthy a company AMP was.

This was our third Christmas since we left England. We were going to have a wonderful Christmas this year. My parents were out for the summer and we were going to enjoy ourselves.

We visited the Blue Mountains and all the beaches. Mum and Dad loved it, especially the casual lifestyle, picnics on the beach and the many barbeques. They thought about moving out to Australia themselves. They could see I was very settled in my new life and had many good friends.

Roy took to my parents immediately and they loved him. He tried to get them to persuade me to marry him and they couldn't understand why I didn't want to. He was good fun and treated us all to many lunches and dinners. Mum and Dad felt Stephen especially needed a father.

Over the break, I had time to consider my future with AMP. I didn't enjoy the feeling of being hated for being professional. I certainly wasn't going to drop my standards so I could become more popular. I considered changing companies but I liked Mr Grace and on the whole I liked AMP. I didn't think I would get such a good job elsewhere and I hadn't met any woman in such a senior position in the computer industry in Australia.

AMPnet was costing more and more, as I had predicted, but no one seemed to care. Roy's Ordinary Life system was now operational in all branches and the accounting systems would be used to process the annual accounts for 1976. Other systems were showing signs of coming to life. I had a very good staff and felt that they could continue their good work with only a little help from me.

LATE IN 1976 Phil Grace had said he had decided that the whole AMPnet team, including the AMPnet computers, would be relocated from CSA's building in St Leonards to the AMP building on Circular Quay. He was looking for someone to manage the move, which would be very complex because now parts of AMPnet were operational the move would have to be made without stopping production.

At the first management meeting in 1977, after the summer holidays, he said he hadn't found anyone to manage the AMPnet move, I decided to volunteer. After the meeting I followed him into his office and said I had something I wanted to discuss.

"I've been dreading this," he said. "You've decided to go back to England with your parents. I thought you were less stressed after your holidays."

I assured him that I had decided to stay in Australia. Indeed my Mum and Dad were considering staying here too. He looked visibly relieved. "I couldn't do without you," he said. "So what do you want to discuss?"

I told him that as no one had offered to manage the move to Circular Quay, I would do it. I said I'd love to take on the technical challenge of moving the computers without stopping production. He looked even more relieved. "Have you done this sort of thing before?" he said. I told him I hadn't, but was there anyone else he preferred to appoint?

He thought for only a few seconds. "You've proved yourself to be an excellent manager so I have every confidence in your ability. But this move is outside your experience, indeed no one seems to have this experience in Australia. Let me think about how we can make this a success. I don't want to set you up for failure."

Later that afternoon he called in to my office. "I think the people move can be done by someone else, so you can focus on setting up the computer centre and moving the equipment. Also, we'll probably need to order more equipment to support the move and we'll need the support of all the hardware suppliers. You've built up good relations with them so I know you'll manage that part well."

I suggested that as we now had procedures for most of the tasks in the AMPnet control office, and as my staff were very good, Anstey Lindsey could probably take on that task along with his administration tasks.

"But who can estimate software development as well as you can? How will we know if the project managers' estimates are correct?" said Mr Grace.

"They are getting better and anyway I'm not going away," I said. "I can always be called back to help. They've got to stand on their own feet some time and we can keep a strict eye on how well they go with their estimates."

I HAD BEEN ATTENDING Australian Computer Society meetings and met up again with John Bennett. I had first met him at Ferranti in the UK in 1959 and later in 1974 just before I decided to come to Australia. He was now Professor of Computing at the University of Sydney and told me he had been very involved in establishing the ACS and had been its Inaugural President.

He told me that Australia had just established a Law Reform Commission and the first reference group was to be on privacy.

John said he had read in the British Computer Society literature that I had worked on privacy issues with the BCS, which had led to the British Data Protection Act. He said few people in Australia understood database technology and the issues it raised for privacy.

Michael Kirby, a brilliant young lawyer, had been appointed Chair of the Australian Law Reform Commission and wanted to establish a working group of two computer people and two lawyers to advise him on privacy legislation. Michael had asked John to be on the committee and to select another professional to join him. John asked if I would be interested. I told him I would, but that I would need to get permission from AMP.

I told Mr Grace about my conversation with John Bennett and invitation to serve as a consultant to the Privacy Reference at the ALRC. He was thrilled. AMP had heard about the growing move to introduce privacy legislation. Like all insurance companies, AMP held a significant amount of personal information about policyholders. This was needed to evaluate the Society's risk and therefore premium on life and general policies and to support contested claims.

Mr Grace asked when and how AMP would be told of my appointment. Did AMP need to do anything to make it happen? He said when he told the General Manager, AMP could hardly believe their good fortune in having an opportunity to influence privacy legislation.

I asked John Bennett what more I needed to do. He said it was already done. He knew AMP would give permission and the papers had already been signed by Michael Kirby and the Attorney General. AMP would receive a letter any day now. When I told Mr Grace he was delighted. "I knew you would go far, Ann," he said. "AMP is very fortunate to have you on board."

The academics from the School of Information Systems at the University of New South Wales, led by Professor Cyril Brookes, had formed a group of the top 20 companies in Australia to share their experience in computing. Cyril had been BHP's first Data Processing Manager. BHP was Australia's second largest company. It had large mineral holdings and mining leases, including iron ore, gold, silver and lead. It also made steel.

Each company in the group Cyril had formed sent their Chief Executive Officer and their top computer executive to a live-in two day event held twice a year in Sydney's posh Boulevard Hotel. The cost was $20,000 a year and there was to be a parallel 'wives' program. The Chief Accountant, Eric Putt, was to represent the CEO of AMP and I was to represent the computer side.

THE FIRST DAY of each Forum comprised tutorials from Australian and overseas academics on world trends in computing. Starting after dinner on the first day, in a totally in confidence, warts and all presentation, one company would tell the others all about their experiences in a specific area of computing. The next day, the group would then share their own experiences in that area. There was to be plenty of free time for the attendees to network and share experience.

I was the only woman delegate at the Forum and made several contacts that would be very helpful in my future career. After the success of the first Forum Professor Brookes and his team were often called upon by AMP to provide consultancy advice on aspects of computing.

At the first meeting the Government owned telecommunications company Telecom made a presentation about the problems it was having with a large project. Mr Grace decided to attend the first night dinner and sit in on Telecom's presentation. After the presentation, delegates moved to a comfortable lounge for informal drinks. Mr Grace wanted to know more about the problems at Telecom. In addition to the two Forum representatives, Telecom had brought some of their senior technical staff to assist with the presentation.

After buying drinks all round, Mr Grace started asking fairly simple questions about the issues raised in the presentation. To everyone's surprise, the Telecom techies started to present very different views on what was going on with the project. They even brought out copious reports and printouts to make their point. Mr Grace declared that there was now an unrestricted open bar with all drinks on him.

I watched fascinated. I had never seen this side of my boss. He seemed to be matching the Telecom techs drink for drink yet the more garrulous and drunk they got the more sober he seemed and the more complex his questions became. By midnight, it was obvious that four separate teams in Telecom were each developing their own version of the system. The discussion started to get nasty and it looked as if a fist fight was about to develop. I quietly slipped away to my room for a good night's rest.

The next morning, Mr Grace and all the Telecom techs had vanished. The Forum discussed Telecom's project without reference to the previous night's drunken revelations. I learnt later that Telecom management had suspected what was really going on with their project and why it was taking so long. They were very grateful to Mr Grace for drawing out the truth.

When I got back to AMP, Mr Grace told me he had thoroughly enjoyed himself and hadn't had so much fun for ages. He said it was very useful to him that Mr Putt would report to the General Manager that even Telecom had projects that were badly managed.

I received numerous invitations to dinner after the Forum. One man was particularly attentive and we formed a friendship that was to last over 30 years. Actually, it was more than a friendship. We became lovers.

36 The big move

IN MID FEBRUARY Mr Grace issued a memo naming me as the Project Manager responsible for the move of the Computer Centre. John Kaunitz was to help with technical advice as required. I was to take up my new position by the end of February.

Enough AMPnet staff were to be moved by June that AMP would not renew the lease on the building it had rented when it moved AMP staff to St Leonards. Moving them would be the responsibility of another AMP Exec.

I was told that the first task was to find a suitable building for the new computer centre and support staff. Although AMP owned much of the commercial property in Sydney, the new computer centre did not need to occupy expensive CBD real estate.

Mr Grace told me he had been involved in building AMP's Head Office on Circular Quay. It had been purpose built to include the Society's first computer centre. Opened in 1962, it was then the tallest building in Sydney and had Australia's first automatic lift. It was on the waterfront in the north part of the CBD, looking out onto the main passenger berth where suburban ferries and visiting liners from all over the world docked.

Mr Grace told me that he had arranged for AMP's Property Division to assign a bright young property engineer to my team. He would help with the infrastructure services like power, air conditioning and water.

Jim, the property engineer, had been involved in getting AMP out of a messy situation when it had tried to significantly expand its property empire in the early 1970s. The situation was very similar to that I had found on AMPnet. A single supplier totally out of control, spending AMP's money any way they chose. They were actually borrowing money from AMP to fund the business. Jim had worked for AMP's contractor, Mainline, and had helped unravel the fiasco. AMP had offered Jim a job as their first Executive hired from outside AMP.

WITH THE HELP OF our main computer suppliers and the operations staff involved, I drew up rough specifications of the space and infrastructure we would need for the new centre. Jim, John and I set about looking at buildings that AMP owned or leased, but none seemed suitable.

AMP was part way through the construction of a new 45 floor building next to the existing Head Office. I asked Mr Grace if we could consider this new building as a site for the new computer centre. He told me it was being built for lease and not for AMP's own use. But after much discussion and examining things like access and floor loadings, we decided to establish the computer centre on the third floor of the new building.

John Kaunitz and I set about visiting all eight major Univac computer centres in Australia and New Zealand. We took advice on how well they functioned. We asked what could have been better designed. We asked about companies who had provided infrastructure services.

Each centre we visited had its own unique needs and solutions, but I found two very interesting pieces of information. All the other companies had got special discounts on their purchases. Mount Isa Mines had got a mining discount. The Department of Defence had been given a defence discount. The Australian National University had an education discount. The police centre in New Zealand got a police discount, etc. Indeed, all Univac customers in Australia and New Zealand had got the same discount as CSA did for AMP, so the claim that they got especially favourable discounts for AMP turned out to be quite hollow.

The second piece of information was more concerning. No one in Australia had moved a computer centre without interrupting processing. Indeed, information from Univac confirmed that none of their customers anywhere in the world at that time had ever succeeded in moving a centre without interrupting processing.

WITH THE SUPPORT of Univac's engineers and CSA's operations staff, we set about designing the computer room. We considered how we would actually keep production running during the move. We realised that we would need to acquire extra hardware to provide spare capacity at the new AMPnet Centre at some part of the move so, I negotiated that Univac would lend equipment to support the move.

After we decided the broad strategy we prepared specifications for the infrastructure we needed for the centre. Jim noticed immediately that there was not enough power reticulated to the building to support both the computers and the additional air conditioning needed to cool the computer centre. We also needed to be able to draw power from two independent sources in case one failed. We also needed an Uninterrupted Power Supply (UPS) with back up battery power and our own diesel generators.

We decided we would have to install an extra substation on the roof. The UPS, battery backup and diesel generators would also go there, How would we get heavy, large-scale equipment up to the 45th floor? The services ducts on each floor would have to be drilled to allow for the large cables to be brought from the roof to the third floor and down to the sub basement where the secondary substation was already installed.

There was much to consider. Raised floors, fire safety equipment with Halon gas flooding in an emergency, security devices, air conditioning, access for equipment, goods lift capacity, etc.

Most importantly was the need for the centre to be shielded from Radio Frequency Interference. This last issue was particularly important because at that time Univac did not shield its signal cables. We called in specialists to measure any signals across the frequency band that Univac told us would cause problems with the computers. There were fairly strong signals from the radar from Sydney Airport but these were outside Univac's specified range. There were some weaker signals from local radio and TV stations and taxi and police radio systems.

More importantly, the site was very close to the Royal Australian Navy base at Garden Island, which in addition to generating Australian naval signals was often visited by overseas navies.

We wrote to the Navy and found that using signal detection equipment to pick up naval signals was illegal. AMP's Anstey Lindsay was head of Australia's naval reserve and used his influence to help us. We received a letter from the Navy that told us they would transmit on all possible signal bandwidths for half an hour at a specific time and gave us permission to measure the RFI. After the transmission, they would change all frequencies.

We decided that all we could do was to build a Faraday cage round the centre to screen it from all incoming signals, just as the Department of Defence had done in their centre in Canberra.

We devised a plan to move the applications across two weekends. For the interim week, some systems would run at St Leonards and some at Circular Quay. A copy of the complete AMP database would have to be installed on both sites.

It was now time to draw a deep breath and prepare a timeline and a budget. Jim and I had roughly priced major infrastructure items. Jim decided to engage architectural firm Peddle, Thorpe and Walker, who had originally designed the building, to ensure our plans were viable from an architectural viewpoint. The firm of consulting electrical engineers who had set up the initial electrical services in the building was also engaged.

The final budget looked like $3.25 million with confidence limits of plus 20% to minus 10%. The time would be nine months from when the space was made available to project completion. John, Jim and I checked and rechecked our figures and I presented the plan to the boss.

His first question was that he wondered why I hadn't asked for more staff. Was I sure that just John, Jim and I could deliver the project with assistance from existing staff on an ad hoc basis? I assured him that I preferred to work with a small tight team I could rely on.

Next, was I really sure about the budget? It seemed that most computer related budgets escalated during the course of the project. On this project, my reputation was on the line.

Lastly, it all seemed to take a long time. We'd already spent six months establishing the location, visiting other Univac computer centres, getting test quotes and advice. I pointed out that no one had done what we were trying to do and although we'd done our homework none of us had experience. It would be the biggest computer centre in Australia and I wanted it to be something that AMP could be proud of.

The cost of the project was above Mr Grace's authorisation level and had to go to the Board. I was told the Board thought the expenditure was well worth the amount predicated to get AMP's computer centre and the whole AMPnet project back under AMP's control. We were given the go ahead in September 1977 for completion by mid 1978.

DURING THE FLURRY of collecting information for the move, earlier in 1977, AMP had received a letter from Australian Standards stating the International Standards Organisation was going to hold a major meeting on data communications standards in Sydney. Would AMP fund and host the gala dinner?

Mr Grace asked for my advice. Data communications was a fascinating new field. I remembered Donald Davies' talk on an Experimental Packet Switching System in Britain in the 1960s. Through the British Computer Society, I had been involved in the British Standards TC3 SC6 that was responsible for standards for the bottom three layers in the 7 layer Open Standards Interconnection (OSI) model.

I had also worked on the committee for the Prestel system before I came to Australia. I asked Mr Grace if AMP could afford to pay for a dinner. He laughed and said if I thought the event would bring prestige to the Society, they had significant funds set aside to fund worthwhile activities as part of their role as a good corporate citizen.

I suggested that it might be an opportunity to get up to date with current thinking on data communications. The delegate list included the top communications specialists from all over the world, including Charlie Bachman from the USA, who had devised the 7 layer model for data communications, which was the main agenda item up for discussion. I knew Charlie as father of the CODASYL database standards and looked forward to meeting him again. I asked that I be invited to attend the three day event as an observer.

I was delighted to meet up with Charlie Bachman and colleagues from UK and some overseas experts whose papers I had read or who I had heard give presentations in the UK. I learned that although the lower three physical layers in Bachman's 7 layer model were now promulgated as an international standard and were being implemented round the world, standards for the higher four layers were still not decided.

IBM had brought out its own version of the standard called SDLC, although it did not yet function beyond layer 5, the session layer. During the three days of the meeting IBM lobbied hard for the world to accept its standard. The British had developed a system called HDLC that would be an open standard and lobbied for that. The Japanese delegation told everyone to go with IBM. At that time the Japanese were making IBM compatible computers and successfully making inroads into IBM's market.

A big issue at that time was proprietary standards versus open standards. Open standards meant companies could move applications easily from one supplier to another to take advantage of advances in technology. IBM was moving the opposite direction. It was intent on keeping its 90% share of the world mainframe market. For every standard, IBM 'improved' the functionality so that if customers used the advanced features that IBM had added, they were locked in and changing suppliers was made more difficult and costly. IBM's argument was that proprietary standards could do more.

IBM even had its own version of COBOL, the most commonly used programming language at that time. Instead of adding the standard CODASYL extensions to support databases, IBM developed its own database management software, IMS. Likewise, it had built its own proprietary Transaction Control System, CICS. It wanted to do the same with data communications, although this time IBM wanted to own the standard. This would give IBM the ability to manipulate the standard to suit its own hardware and system software while locking its rivals out.

I thoroughly enjoyed being in the midst of the international computing scene that I had missed since I came to Australia. I had missed working on standards and being able to share ideas and ask for advice from people I respected in the industry. The UNSW Forum was filling that gap to a certain extent but it was good to meet old friends again.

OUR AUSTRALIAN DELEGATION comprised mainly engineers from Telecom except for the leader of the delegation, Matt Cleland, who was the same programmer I had met at the Australian Bureau of Statistics when I first came to Australia.

The engineers kept discussing the bits and bytes of the technology in the lower three layers. Charlie, Matt, and the UK delegation could see further. Their vision was to enable any computer to communicate and interact seamlessly with any other computer anywhere in the world. I shared that vision, although I couldn't quite see how it could be made to happen, especially at the top layer applications levels.

There was much socialising. AMP's formal conference gala dinner went well but delegates, mostly technical people, preferred the informality of pub barbeques. The Japanese especially liked lunch at The Oaks, an all-you-can-eat pub in Cremorne. They could hardly believe they could get as many T-bone steaks as they liked for $6. The head of the Japanese delegation was a huge man known as HB who could eat three T-bones at one sitting. He said that in Japan that would have cost him a week's wages.

On the last day, it was time to decide on the direction of the new standard. The two candidates were HDLC, an open standard proposed by the British delegation, and IBM's SDLC, proposed by the Americans and supported by the Japanese. Both were discussed thoroughly. The convention at ISO meetings was that the host country votes first followed by the other countries in alphabetical order. To my surprise, Australia abstained.

When the other countries had all voted, the result was a tie. The convention was that in a tie, the chairman of the meeting has a casting vote. The Canadian chairman said he found his position very difficult but had noted that the host nation had abstained. Would Australia like to reconsider its vote?

As an observer, I did not have a place at the table but was sitting behind Matt, the leader of our delegation. I whispered to him to support open standards and he did. Thus the world got open data communications standards rather than proprietary IBM standards. I would like to think I had a role to play in that decision.

A new subcommittee was established under Technical Committee 3 (TC3), to bring the standard into being. I was invited to join Standard Australia's SC16. My area of speciality was to be Layer 7, the Applications Layer.

I felt I was back at the leading edge.

37 Allan Moffatt

SEPTEMBER ALSO BROUGHT my annual appraisal. Once again, Mr Grace was generous in his praise for my contribution during the past year but once more there was that warning. But under 'personality' he had written:

'Very good, but needs to consider best means of conveying her well respected knowledge. Her emphasis is on her own experiences and more persuasion of the recipient is perhaps the way.'

Once again, I asked what that meant. What should I change? Mr Grace said it was to do with the fact that I was a woman with lots of experience in what was traditionally a male world. The men just didn't like it.

Was I insensitive? What else could I draw on but my own experience? It was hardly my fault that I had extensive experience. Surely that was what I was employed for. People outside AMP like people at the UNSW Forum, the ALRC privacy expert group and now the standards group valued my experience. Why not the people at AMP?

Also, I had often watched the men around me show off and boast about their experience whenever they got the chance. I didn't do that. Mr Grace said the people who mattered in AMP valued my experience. It was really the people at my own level or underneath me that didn't like having a knowledgeable woman as competition. The comment unsettled me but I didn't know what to do about it except play the dumb blonde, and I wasn't going to do that.

Apart from that niggle, I now felt very comfortable in my new country. The children were thriving. We had a lovely house with a very low interest mortgage and I had just had a swimming pool built, mainly for the children. I had a very good circle of friends. I had an interesting well-paid job. I was involved in three prestigious groups: the Australian Law Reform Commission's Privacy group, the UNSW Forum, and Standard Australia's SC16 on OSI. But there was still something lacking

Whenever I was invited to parties, all the guests seemed to be couples. All my friends except Renate had partners. Even Roy was about to get married. Everyone was very supportive and friendly towards me and I knew that not all the marriages were happy, but I felt left out and lonely. And I still hadn't worked out all the conventions in Australia. For instance, I always seemed to be wearing the wrong clothes at parties. If I dressed up other women were in jeans. If I wore jeans, others wore ball gowns.

At that time most Australian parties split into two distinct groups, the men stood at one end of the room or the garden and the women at the other. Very few of the wives worked, and those who did were secretaries or clerks. None were technical. I had little in common with the women's conversations and preferred to talk with the men, which worried the wives.

I DECIDED TO go to an afternoon barbeque at the local Parents Without Partners meeting. I noticed a handsome, blond, bronzed Aussie with bright blue eyes who seemed to be observing the proceedings. He seemed not to be joining in any of the flirtatious conversations that were going on all around, conversations that made me feel uncomfortable.

It seemed to me a bit of a meat market, with desperate women throwing themselves at the eligible men. The bronzed Aussie came over to me and asked if I'd been to Parents Without Partners before. I told him it was my first time and he said it was his too and he didn't really like it.

He told me his name was Allan Moffatt. He was a probation and parole officer. He had been a career Army officer and had reached the age when he could take early retirement so had decided to get out of the military. He had four children and his wife had just divorced him. He said he missed his children. He seemed nice.

We exchanged phone numbers and agreed to meet again. I felt it must be difficult living without your children. He had said his youngest was four. During the week, I invited him to a barbeque at my house a couple of weekends ahead. I wanted to see how he got on with my friends.

Almost as soon as Renate had been introduced to Allan she surprised me by taking me to one side and saying, "You're not going to have anything to do with that man are you?"

I told her we had only just met but he seemed nice and was fitting in well with my friends at the barbeque. She said, "I'll never sleep under the same roof as that man. He'll kill us all in our beds!"

I couldn't believe what I'd heard. Renate and Clair often stayed over at my house. She was one of the most level headed people I knew. She didn't make judgements quickly. Perhaps she was feeling that this new man might threaten our friendship. She hadn't behaved like that when Roy had tried to get her to persuade me to marry him. It was an irrational statement to make about a person she had only just met.

Allan had a boat. He said he'd like to take my children and me on the river on the next weekend. I said I would bring a picnic. We had a lovely day on the beautiful Hawkesbury River. Allan introduced me to several of his friends who also had boats on the river. At the end of the day, Allan asked if we could do the same the next weekend and he would to bring his two youngest children. Robbie was the same age as my Claire.

We had several more outings with and without his children and I was learning more about this new man. He was never pushy and always courteous. He fixed a few things up around my house, garden and swimming pool. He was a hit with Stephen, trying to teach him to swim and showing him how to make things out of wood and nails. Claire was more reserved. I had heard that children who had lived with one parent for quite a long while were often wary of a new prospective partner.

One day Allan said he had a day off work and asked if he could take Stephen out fishing just by himself. Stephen was keen to go. When they got home, Stephen was jubilant. He'd caught his first fish! It was small but Allan cooked it on the barbeque and Stephen ate it. When Allan had gone, Stephen related the stories Alan had told about life in the army and flying aeroplanes.

WORK STARTED ON the new computer centre. I had decided we would have Halon gas flooding as a fire protection system. The computer centre at CSA had carbon dioxide flooding which could kill anybody who could not get out of the room before the gas discharged. Halon was more expensive but did little harm to anyone trapped in a room flooded with the gas.

I discussed the issue with Mr Grace. He told me that John Utz, Chairman of Wormald, the big fire protection company, was an AMP Board member so we should get Wormald to quote for fire services. Unless their quote was unreasonable we would not need to go out to tender.

We sent specifications for power, air conditioning and a raised floor to several of the suppliers who had done similar work for other computer centres we had visited.

I devised a rating and weighting system by which we would judge the tenders. We asked for responses but we got no replies. I telephoned the prospective suppliers. I was even more surprised by the responses I got. These were big tenders. Most companies I called said they hadn't started on the tender. Were they the only company that had been asked to tender? Who were they up against? Could they have more time, six months perhaps?

What was going on? These projects were worth a lot of money. We had budgeted about $750,000 for air conditioning and a similar amount for power services. Raised flooring was estimated at $100,000. These were significant amounts in the late 1970s.

I discussed the issue with Jim. "You'll have to just ride them hard," he said. "Tell them they will be out of the tender if they don't do what you say. Do you want me to do it? They are probably just playing because you are a woman. Several have rung me and asked who you are. I told them all you are the boss and they have to deal with you."

I was taken aback by this sexist attitude. I thanked Jim for his offer of help but said I'd deal with the situation.

I discussed the issue with Mr Grace. He had also had phone calls from the suppliers saying they didn't like dealing with a woman. I had never met this attitude in England yet I had dealt with some of the biggest suppliers. Certainly that had never been the attitude of computer suppliers. Mr Grace told me not to worry but to be tough and not give any ground.

I sent letters to each company stating that the return date had been extended by two weeks. If I did not receive a tender in that time, they would not be invited to tender again. It was a bold move but might have backfired because the pool of firms was quite small.

The only tender I had received in the originally allotted time was from Wormald. Mr Grace asked me to now request tenders from other fire prevention companies who would hopefully not be as good as Wormald so at least we could say we had selected Wormald if anyone asked.

Much to my relief, the other tenders came in within the extended time. We evaluated them as quickly as we could and got our decisions to the boss for confirmation. All were within the budgets we had set.

We had already lost a precious two weeks. Also, it would be Christmas in another month, so we would lose five weeks over the summer break. The project completion date was end of June.

I spoke to the selected suppliers and asked that work commence as soon as possible. I wanted a detailed plan from each to add to my PERT chart, as I needed to understand the interdependencies.

The air conditioning suppliers asked if they could liaise with the electrical supplier and the fire company. Wormald needed to liaise with both power and air conditioning. I set up the cross links and the project was off to what looked like a good start. The raised floor could not be imported until after Christmas but even that fitted in with our schedule.

AFTER HAVING A difficult sexual experience with my first husband and a fabulous experience with Dick, I decided I would have to experience sex with any man I might consider marrying but it had been more than five years since I had had sex with anyone.

I decided I better get prepared as the relationship with Allan was deepening. He had often asked if he could stay the night. But I wasn't yet sure and Renate's words rang in my head whenever I thought about it.

By now, I had met some of Allan's work colleagues. They all seemed to respect him. His two children seemed nice even if his youngest, Belinda, did seem a little spoilt, But she was not as spoilt as Roy's Loma had been and his son Robbie was a delight.

Stephen had really taken to Allan and I could see he really needed a father. Claire said she thought we'd be better by ourselves but at nearly 13, I realised that teenage hormones were beginning to cut in and I could expect her to be moody.

I took myself to the family planning clinic and was prescribed the contraceptive pill. I was warned to take other precautions for the first cycle.

I was all set. We had a relaxing Saturday on the river. Allan was staying for dinner. I asked if he'd like to stay the night. He took no second asking. The night was everything I could have wished for. When we awoke on Sunday morning he asked if he could move in and I agreed.

The children made no comment at breakfast. Allan went and got his belongings from his lodgings. The next weekend he brought both his children. Robbie said he definitely wasn't going back home. Belinda said she wanted to go back to her mother's.

To my surprise I didn't get my next period on time. I had allowed a whole cycle on the pill as I had been instructed. Maybe my body was just reacting to having sex again after so long.

I waited a couple of weeks and went to the doctor. I was pregnant. Now I panicked. What had I done? I didn't want to be rushed into anything but I had to make a decision. I told Allan. He was delighted. He said he thought it was the best thing that had ever happened and he would love to have a new baby. We should get married at once.

I wasn't so sure. I didn't like the idea of having an abortion. This was a life. Although the sex was good, I didn't know Allan well enough to commit to marriage. I didn't want to have his baby without being married to him.

Another thing bothered me. He had dreadful nightmares. He shouted and thrashed about in his sleep. I just held him close and he usually settled without waking. I discussed the issue with him and he told me that was why his wife divorced him. He told me he had done and seen things as a soldier that frightened him and came to him in the night. One day, he promised, he'd tell me about them. He said he'd been reticent about sleeping with me in case my reaction was the same as his wife's had been.

WHAT SHOULD I DO about my pregnancy? The decision was made even more complex because Alan Leach's parents were coming to stay for three months after Christmas. I was still wondering how to tell them I had a new man in my bed. But I was still officially married to Alan Leach, so I needed to get a divorce. No fault divorce legislation had come into force in UK in 1976, which made things much easier. Alan Leach agreed to the arrangement and it was all done by post.

But situation was still very difficult for me. I had really only planned to try sex and yet I had taken pity on Allan Moffatt and it looked as if he was here to stay. I didn't really regret my decision but I wished things had not happened so quickly. I had to sort this all out.

I didn't want another baby. I would be 40 soon and I had two lovely children and it looked like I would have to take on at least some of Allan's children. I decided to have an abortion. I told Allan. He said it was my choice and he would support me. Maybe when we settled down and got married we'd have another baby.

The abortion was done in a swish private hospital. It was a very short procedure and only took a morning. I went to work at the usual time and came home at the usual time. Allan got our dinner that night but that was not unusual, he often cooked our dinner. I didn't tell anyone.

Renate and Clair came for Christmas dinner but didn't stay over. I was sure Renate noticed that Allan was living at my house but she didn't repeat her warning.

In early January we all went to the airport to pick up Ma and Pa Leach. The children were pleased to see their Grandma and Grandad. I introduced Allan and Robbie. It all seemed very easy. Allan charmed them both just as he did everyone he met. Ma Leach told me she was pleased I had found someone. We spent lazy days at Sydney's lovely beaches and on Allan's boat. The Leaches were just as entranced with Australia as my Mum and Dad had been and told me they could see why we'd decided to stay.

The more I got to know Allan, the more it felt right to share my life with him. He wanted to show me Malaya where he had spent most of his time in the Army. Although he said he had also served in Vietnam and Borneo, he was mainly part of the British Commonwealth peacekeeping force in the Malayan Emergency. I also learned he had a pilot's licence and was a crack shot with a rifle.

38 Mission completed

THE FIT OUT OF the AMPnet computer centre was going well. It was important to get all the noisy construction work completed as soon as possible because tenants were starting to move into the building.

To maximise security, I wanted our floor to look as uninteresting as possible. There was to be no entry on the tenant list and no sign on the floor itself. There was to be a simple keypad entry at the lift and on the third floor. I discussed this with Mr Grace and to my surprise he agreed.

Getting power from the new substation, the backup power services on the roof and the secondary substation meant drilling large access holes in the utility ducts on each floor. We got a quote for the work. It was $50,000 including the hire of an expensive drill with a diamond cutting head.

The contractor judged that each solid concrete floor would be at least a foot thick and each floor would need three large cable access holes. The work could only be done at weekends. It was urgent as we could do very little until we had sufficient power to the floor.

Coming into work early on the Monday morning following the weekend allocated to the job I was pleased to see piles of concrete cores in the loading dock ready for disposal. I picked one up thinking it would make a good souvenir.

The cores were only two to four inches long. I had supposed they must have broken into short lengths during the drilling procedure but they looked smooth on each surface. Looking again, there certainly weren't 150 feet of cores which I would have expected from drilling nearly 50 floors. Maybe the drills had broken and the work wasn't complete.

I went into the computer centre floor. There were three neat holes in the duct. I put my hand in the access holes. I could curl my fingers under the ceiling and the hole was only the length of my fist to my wrist. I went to another floor; the same depth of hole, and so it was on the several floors I visited. Back on the computer floor, the contractor was waiting, smiling. I still had a core in my hand.

"Well, we finished," said the contractor.

"But the cores aren't a foot long," I said holding mine up.

"Nah, they broke up. I knew they would," he said.

"But there aren't any more than 50 feet of cores on the loading dock," I said.

"Yes, that's just the last lot. We shipped most of the rubbish out yesterday," he said.

"Well, when I put my hand in the holes I could curl my fingers up underneath and the floor only came up to my wrist," I said.

"You shouldn't have worried your pretty little head about that. Some floors are thicker than others and anyway that's not a very scientific way of measuring the depth of core," he said, still smiling.

"Okay. Then I'll bring my tape measure in tomorrow and we'll measure each hole together," I said.

"Tape measures aren't very accurate," he said.

"Then you bring the measure," I said.

"Most of the cost is in hiring the drill," said the contractor.

"Okay, you split the drilling from the drill hire and tell me the actual cost," I said. The contractor was angry but he finished the job and we got the $50,000 reduced to $20,000. I still think he made a good profit.

The story obviously went round the other contractors because I was often asked 'got your tape measure, luv?' The contractors were beginning to understand that a woman could manage a large, complex fit-out project just as well as a man.

MA AND PA LEACH were returning to England at the end of April, Allan and I decided to get married on 30 March. I felt it was a bit rude to ask my former in-laws to look after my family while we went on honeymoon but they were delighted to be able to help. Allan wanted to see Malaya again, and I had always dreamed of going to Bali, so we planned a week in each place.

Tenants were starting to move into the new AMP centre. The new Sydney registry office where we got married was on the second floor of the AMP centre. We had only a few guests: our children including Allan's daughter Anne, Ma and Pa Leach, Renate and her daughter Clair, Allan's friend Mal, Allan's mother Edna, and his brothers Neville and Brian with their wives. After the brief ceremony we went to lunch in the revolving restaurant in Australia Square on top of the tallest building in Sydney.

In the plane on the way to Singapore, Allan said he was looking forward to going to Bugis Street to drink Tiger beer. I wore my pretty long blue dress for dinner in the lovely rooftop restaurant at the Hilton. After dinner Allan hired a cycle rickshaw to take us to Bugis Street.

We seemed to go a long way and I was worried that the bandy-legged wizened old rickshaw man running in front of us would collapse but Allan assured me the man would be pleased to have such a long hire.

Bugis Street was nothing like the place Allan had remembered. He said it used to have lots of little bars. Now tall glass and concrete skyscrapers towered above the street. We found one tiny bar full of decrepit old men. Allan ordered Tiger beer but he said even that didn't taste the same.

A creepy looking young man sidled up to Allan and whispered in his ear. Allan shooed him away. I asked what he wanted. "He's selling dirty post-cards," Allan said. "Let me see," I said. The man looked at me sideways. "You don't want to bother with those," said Allan.

"Yes I do. I've never seen dirty postcards," I said.

Allan motioned to the man to show me. "They all boys," he said proudly as he showed his wares. They were lovely. They could have been beautiful young models. "Lady boys," Allan said. "Singapore is famous for them."

The street vendor moved closer. He seemed to feel he might make a sale. "All boys," he said again. "I'm a boy," I said, playfully. "You crazy," said the vendor pointing his twisted finger to his head while running away quickly.

"You certainly scared him off," said Allan. "Let's go back to the hotel. Tomorrow we are going to drive through Malaya. That will be very different." I was surprised to see the rickshaw driver still standing outside the bar ready to run all the way back to the hotel for us. "I told you he was glad of the fare," Allan grinned.

THE NEXT DAY we hired a car and drove across the causeway to Johor Bahru in Malaya. There were brightly painted, onion domed palaces that looked as if they were taken right out of the Arabian Nights and plantations on each side of the road.

Allan said we should make for Malacca and stay the night there. He was constantly being surprised because what he had known from his time in Malaya had vanished. Nearing Malacca, he described a picturesque rickety old wooden bridge across the river. When we reached the river, a wide new concrete bridge had replaced the old one.

We stopped at a restaurant by the side of the road. I went in search of a toilet. What I found was a room almost ankle deep in raw sewage with no sign of any of the ceramic furniture usually found in a toilet. Outside, I found Allan looking very glum.

"This place stinks," he said. "We had better drive on to KL." We arrived in Kuala Lumpur just after midnight. We booked into the Hilton Hotel and were told we should not have travelled on the road especially at night because bandits often held up travellers, took their car and murdered them.

The next day we read in the newspaper that bandits had held up a tour bus on the road we had just travelled. They had taken everything valuable from the passengers and left them with only their underwear. Allan decided we would fly to Penang but first we would see KL.

Allan now seemed to be in his element. He shouted loudly at waiters and taxi drivers, calling them all 'John'. I could see the concerned looks on the faces and suggested carefully that perhaps they didn't like being called John. Perhaps customs had changed too. He insisted he knew the customs better than I did and reverted to speaking in Malay and shouting even louder when the people seemed not to understand.

"It's all changed," he said. "I'm sorry I brought you here."

At dinner in the Hilton, Allan said tomorrow he would go to the local aero club and see if he could borrow a plane to fly us to Penang. Penang would be better, he promised. I was surprised that even though he didn't have his pilots' licence with him, Allan managed to talk one of the very English locals to lend him a plane to fly to Penang.

We flew over some lovely country in a little two seater plane. Allan flew low over the Batu Caves then over the beautiful pale blue of the lakes in the tin mines at Ipoh. He said he was going to get to Penang as soon as possible to avoid the afternoon storms. I was grateful. I didn't want to be in a thunderstorm in a tiny plane.

Penang was no better than KL or Malacca. We visited a filthy, smelly turtle temple where the turtles seemed to slide and wallow in years of their own excrement. Then on to a sacred snake temple where we both had photos taken with snakes draped round our necks.

That night he said Malaya had been a mistake. We were going take the borrowed plane back to KL then go back to Singapore until it was time to set off for Bali. I was relieved. In our extra days in Singapore, we went to all the tourist spots including Raffles Hotel, which was splendid. We went to see where the guns set up to protect the island in the second world war had pointed out to sea. The guns had remained silent as the Japanese invasion came down from Malaya and across the causeway.

Bali was everything Malaya had not been. The island itself was still unspoilt. I bought some lovely large shells from the little beach traders who quietly offered their wares. There was no hustle as there had been in Malaya. We spent lovely relaxing days driving through lush green hills of terraced rice paddies or touring the little villages, each specialising in their own crafts like silver or woodcarving or setting precious stones.

We went up the volcano in the centre of the island and visited quaint Hindu temples. At night, we watched local dancers. Beautiful, graceful Balinese girls wore ornate tinkly gold headdress and had long, long fingernails. The Gamelan tinkled unforgettable sounds on the warm air. I came back very rested and very happy.

WHEN WE GOT BACK to Sydney it was kisses and presents all round. Ma and Pa Leach said they had enjoyed their stay and would certainly be back. As we waved them off at Sydney airport, we were sad to see them go.

Work on the new computer centre had progressed well. We were still well ahead of schedule and under budget. Silver foil now covered the windows and blocked the lovely harbour view. It couldn't be helped, we had to block the stray RFI signals. The room would now have to function with artificial light so I ordered some heavy bluey green curtains to hide the ugly silver foil.

The raised floor had been laid. Some of the tiles had been left open and I was crawling under the floor to inspect the earth mat when I heard a feeble male voice saying 'hello' somewhere above my head.

I politely told the elderly gentleman who owned the voice that he was in a secure area and I had to escort him out of the room. I asked him how he got in and he said the door was open. I took a note to myself to smarten up on security.

"May I ask what this is going to be?" the visitor asked politely. "I'd heard it is something to do with AMP. As a policy holder, I'd like to see how my money is being spent." His eyes twinkled.

I told him the vast space was to be AMP's new computer centre but it was supposed to be a secure room and he would have to leave. "Then where are the computers?" he asked. I told him they were not yet delivered. We had to get the room ready first.

"Good work," he said as he left.

Later in the day Mr Grace came over to see how the centre was progressing. "I heard you had a visitor this morning," he said. I said I was sorry because it had shown up our lax security but I'd since tightened up. I said I didn't quite know what to say when the visitor had said he was a policy holder.

"You did very well," Mr Grace laughed. "That was our Chairman, Sir Vincent Fairfax. I'd invited him to take a look at what we are doing and told him how to get in. He said he met a charming young lady who treated him very courteously. Well done!"

ROADS ROUND the building were closed on a Sunday so that huge cranes could lift the new substation and diesel generators onto the roof. The air conditioning and fire services were installed and all were now ready to be tested.

Jim got the air conditioning tested and it worked exactly as specified. When I arranged for the fire services to be tested, I was advised that testing was usually done with carbon dioxide, as it was much cheaper than Halon. I asked how much Halon cost and was told it would be $9000, while carbon dioxide would cost $1000.

I told the Wormald manager that as we were going to install several million dollars worth of equipment and as AMP now was relying heavily on its computers to run its business, the $9000 was money well spent. We would test with Halon.

Evidently no one had yet tested an installed Wormald system with Halon. Mr Grace said he'd had a phone call from John Utz, the AMP Director who was also Chairman of Wormald. Was it right to test with Halon? Mr Grace asked for my reasoning and agreed with my conclusion.

He told me that Wormald wanted to use this test for training and publicity. They would send a crew in to film the process and John Utz himself was to be present. "If he's going to be there, I suppose I better be there too," said the boss. "When is it going to be tested?"

I said we'd yet to set a date but it would have to be at the weekend. Tenants would have to be informed because we were going to do a whole drill with all building fire alarms sounding and it would have to be soon.

We arranged for the test to be done on a Saturday. We had designed the system such that air conditioning would shut off as soon as the alarm started. Then 30 seconds would be allowed during which the flooding could be stopped if the people in the room felt they could put out the fire without full flooding using hand held extinguishers. There were big red buttons at intervals through the room to shut off different systems. Some sectors, like the printer paper store and the shift leader's offices, were on separate systems so these all had to be tested separately.

The fire detectors were triggered by sensors detecting excessive heat, particulate matter or smoke in the room. Due to a Sydney City Council regulation we had been forced to install water sprinklers but we had got agreement that these would not activate in the first 30 seconds and could be switched off after an alert by people in the room so water would not wreck our equipment. I had watched the engineers test the system by checking timings on the electrical circuits.

We had developed a script for all procedures. The Project Manager from Wormald would talk through the process as it was recorded on film. Most of the observers stood outside the huge room, looking in through the glass windows. The Wormald Project Manager lit a cigarette and held it under a sensor head. He started counting seconds. At 20 seconds he hit the big red button that stopped the release of Halon and the water sprinklers.

Test 1 functioned perfectly. Test 2 would stop the water sprinklers but allow the Halon to flood the computer room but not the offices etc. Again, a lighted cigarette started the process.

The count started. Water sprinklers were deactivated at 20 seconds. At 30 seconds, nothing happened. The count got up to 60 seconds. Still nothing. The test was stopped. It was concluded that the timing mechanism for triggering Halon had been set incorrectly. The Wormald engineers made adjustments and the test started again. This time the count went for two minutes. Still the Halon flooding did not start.

We all agreed that further adjustments needed to be made. The test was rescheduled for the next Saturday.

Even more people assembled for that test. The event was taking on a party atmosphere. At 31 seconds one of the Halon dispensers made a sort of pfffft noise and a dribble of liquid trickled out. Adjustments were made. On the second test more of the sprinkler heads discharged a trickle of liquid.

John Utz looked red faced. He turned to Mr Grace and said, “I guess we’ll have to come in again next Saturday, Mr Grace.” I interrupted and said there would be no more testing until the fault was found and rectified.

It turned out that the small explosive device that was supposed to cut through the metal on the top of the Halon canisters to release the gas to the system was not strong enough. When the canisters had been examined it was noted that the explosive charges had triggered but only some had slightly ruptured the canisters.

John Utz said he was embarrassed. Wormald had installed Halon systems in several computer rooms but had never tested them with Halon. The carbon dioxide canisters used for testing were weaker so had always discharged their gas in a test. If the news got out to customers Wormald’s reputation would suffer, although he pointed out that his engineers would have to replace the weak explosive charges on all installed Halon systems.

Mr Grace congratulated me for sticking to my guns and demanding that the test be done with Halon. He said he hated to think what AMP’s liabilities would have been if the fire equipment in those other computer rooms hadn’t worked when there had been a real fire.

ONCE ALL THE fire and security systems were fully operational, dedicated data lines for telecommunications were installed and tested and the room was ready to receive the hardware.

I advised Univac that we were ready to accept the loan hardware from the USA. I was told that it would come by Flying Tiger airlines, a leading specialist hardware transport company. I was told that it was very important that the equipment should not get into the customs store where it could take up to six months to clear.

If we played our cards right we could arrange for customs to be cleared on the plane before the gear was taken off. It could then go straight into our vans and to the computer centre. I was told that this was a very difficult procedure and rather than hire a customs agent, it would be best for me to manage this myself.

I went out to the cargo part of Sydney Airport to find out how this procedure worked. Several of the men in the customs gave me advice and said they would help on the day. They told me I should get to the airport well ahead of the plane landing or customs would take over. I decided to watch several planes arrive before ours so I could see exactly what happened.

The day before our cargo was due, I took Stephen out to the airport. The men in the cargo area were fantastic. They showed Stephen how they monitored the planes and gave him several promotional goodies like mugs, pens, pencils and hats. They even took him inside a cargo plane to watch the unloading of some especially large freight. They explained that they often had to ship large animals in crates. Stephen was fascinated.

The next day as Stephen and I watched the huge Flying Tiger 747 land. Everyone helped with processing our shipment. It was amazing to see the inside of a stripped out 747 fitted out with rollers and lifting devices.

By the end of the day I was able to tell Mr Grace that our shipment was on its way to Circular Quay, where John and Jim were to receive it and see it was safely brought up to the computer floor and secured ready for installation over the next few days.

The new loan equipment was installed and tested by the Univac engineers and our operations staff. Now everything was ready for our dress rehearsal, where we split the systems and moved some computing to the new equipment whilst keeping the remaining systems working at St Leonards. The dress rehearsal went exactly to plan. We were tempted to leave the transferred systems at the new centre but as that had not been the plan we transferred them back to St Leonards and checked that everything still worked, which it did.

Next weekend we transferred the same systems and left them to run at the new centre. The weekend after that we had to transfer hardware and install it at the new centre, leaving the residual systems to run on a smaller system at St Leonards. Everything went to plan. The last job was to transfer the last of the hardware from St Leonards and extract the loan hardware to send back to the USA. The general conclusion was that we had had such good luck that it would be best to keep all the loan hardware for a while.

It had been a long and difficult project, but enjoyable. I was sad to see Jim go back to Property Division. Jim, John and I had made a good team.

The project had come in on time and under budget. The boss was very pleased. He felt AMPnet was on the right track and moving forward so his job in computing was now complete and he would go back to General Management. He asked me what I would like to do next. He told me I could choose any job I wanted and before he left the division he would make sure I got my wish. I said my greatest love was running application teams and cleaning up messes. He said he was sure he could find some of those.

Cecil Potter, always called Ces, replaced Phil Grace as Data Processing Manager. Ces had joined AMP straight from school. He had served as a Japanese interpreter in the war. When AMP established CSA, he had chosen to join CSA. He was part of the management team at CSA but had now chosen to return to AMP to take up his new post.

I was worried that, as part of the senior team at CSA and being friendly with Bob Kassel, he would take the opportunity to pay me back for my perceived disloyalty to CSA. It sounded childish, but I mentioned my fears to Mr Grace.

"He wouldn't dare to do anything to you," said the boss. "He knows how much AMP thinks of you and I will still be here. I'll be Ces's boss so don't you worry."

But I did worry.

39 Sorting things out

MY HOME LIFE was going very well. Allan's 14 year old son Robbie was now living with us. I was concerned Robbie could not read or write. Allan amazed me by remarking that Robbie was an idiot and would never make anything of himself. He was put into the bottom class at school.

Allan's eldest daughter Kathy, who was 19, was living with her boyfriend and they were about to be married. His second eldest Anne, who was 18, stayed with us from time to time. She couldn't seem to get a job, so she offered to stay at home and manage the house. That included doing the housework and washing and being at home when the children came home.

That arrangement suited me very well. But I didn't really trust Anne and knew she spent most of her day by the pool. After six months, Anne went back to live with her mother. Allan tried to get custody of his youngest daughter, Belinda, who was five, but much to his annoyance, custody was awarded to his wife. Belinda came to us every other weekend and for half of each school holiday.

Shortly after we were married, Allan took us all down to Yass near Canberra where his father lived. His father, 'Feather' Moffatt, was an amazing man. Tiny and wizened, he had been a boxer and was, for a time, the featherweight champion of New South Wales, which is how he got his nickname.

In the 1930s, he became a member of Jimmy Sharman's boxing troupe travelling to country shows and taking on all comers. He had been banned from all four pubs in Yass because he liked to arm wrestle the young bloods. This, and the associated betting, usually ended up in fisticuffs.

Most of Allan's cousins still lived around Yass. His cousin, Billy Privet, was chief stockman on the Merryville estate, a prize sheep station. Billy had nine children, eight boys and a girl. Claire and Stephen loved going to stay in Yass. Claire could ride the horses and, as Billy was the chief fireman in the district, he let all the children drive the fire truck across the fields.

On the first visit to the Privets, Stephen spent the night in the garden sleeping in a tent with the Privet boys. In the morning Stephen came into breakfast with black eyes and a bloodied nose. The eight Privet boys had bashed the pale ginger headed Pom in the night, although Stephen swore they did not. Grandad Feather took charge and spent the morning teaching Stephen how to defend himself and give as good as he got. Feather reprimanded the Privet boys for an unfair fight. The Privets said Stephen did very well and was now one of the Privet gang.

In Yass it sometimes snows in the winter. The prize sheep never went outside but were kept in centrally heated pens with slatted floors through which their droppings fell into flowing water. The radio played classical music to them all day. All they had to do was grow prize winning fleeces.

The lesser quality sheep did spend their time outdoors. The baby lambs were born in mid winter. The sheep were shorn before lambing and provided with plastic jackets to keep off the worst of the weather. Billy and the boys got up each dawn and checked the lambs. They helped any sheep having trouble giving birth and picked up the dead lambs, which were burnt so as not to encourage feral animals.

In September Allan and I took the whole family to the Snowy Mountains for a skiing holiday. We stayed at the Yeti lodge as a guest of Doug Thorne's club as Claire, Stephen and I had done in previous years. Allan and his children soon picked up cross county skiing. We all skied the ten miles there and back to Kosciuszko Chalet and had a great time tobogganing down the slope outside Yeti and building a snow cave.

ON RETURN TO WORK John and I were tidying up some of the paperwork left over from the AMPnet Computer centre project when Mr Grace came in. He told us that AMP's soon to be appointed General Manager, Alan Coates, played tennis every Saturday morning with Allan Moyes, who was the Managing Director of IBM. Last Saturday they had agreed that AMP would return to IBM as their major hardware vendor.

It was our job to make the case. Even though Ces Potter was now Data Processing Manager, we would continue to report to Mr Grace, the work was to be treated as highly confidential.

AMP had been only the second commercial organisation in Australia to install a computer. It had installed an IBM 650 in 1958, which was replaced three years later by an IBM 1401. In 1965 two IBM S/360s were purchased and were still in use. The AMPnet system started development to replace the IBM S/360s with Univac 1100 equipment in 1973.

It was easy to make a case for the change to IBM. Firstly, most of the world's insurance companies ran on IBM gear. This would enable us to share experiences. Secondly, there were many application packages written for IBM. This would enable us to buy software instead of building it ourselves.

But I thought the most compelling reason was that IBM was strong enough not to allow AMP to tinker with the basic system software as we had done on the Univac computers. By now AMPnet had cost $94 million, much more than the $66 million I had estimated, and it was still not complete.

We added some detail about what other companies in the insurance industry were doing on IBM computers and gave a list of packages, like accounting packages, that we thought AMP should purchase.

I estimated the number and cost of staff we would need compared with AMPnet. I based my estimate on the number and type of staff other insurance companies using IBM gear had. I used my contacts in the British Computer Society and the Australian Computer Society to find out details about the staffing levels of each of the insurance companies I had contacted.

After looking at several different companies I found that data processing staff numbers roughly correlated to size of company in terms of policies in force. I got in contact with people I knew at IBM to get similar statistics for US companies and found out that these fitted the model I had developed.

I decided to make a similar model for insurance companies using Univac computers but could not find enough to draw any statistically significant conclusions. My findings showed how few insurance companies used Univac machines and that pro rata staff costs on IBM platforms were a good deal less than they were on AMPnet.

The boss was thrilled with the report. He said we would present it to the AMP Executive Committee before they sent it to the Board for ratification. The Executive Committee comprised the General Manager Keith Steele, the soon to be appointed General Manager Alan Coates, Mr Grace as Chief Manager of Corporate Services, the Chief Actuary Noel Taylor and the Chief Accountant Eric Putt. I was asked to help Mr Grace present the findings.

Mr Grace had given my report to the committee. They said they had all read it so he just presented the conclusions and recommendations. They all agreed with the findings then Mr Steele asked if I had anything else to add.

I said, "Just because the letters on the side of the box are IBM doesn't mean that things can't go wrong. I'm sure IBM will be stronger than Univac and won't allow AMP to do anything too silly but you have to take responsibility for the management of your own data processing."

Mr Steele thanked me for my comment and congratulated me for an excellent report then to my amazement he said, "Gentlemen, this is the first time a lady has presented to the Executive Committee. I think this calls for celebration. I declare this meeting closed and suggest we go to the board-room and break out the champagne!"

On the way out Mr Grace said it was convention not to say anything when the General Manager asked for comments.

"NOW WE HAVE to work out how we shall announce this decision," Mr Grace said. "Even though it has to go to the Board for ratification, the news is bound to get out so we will have to move quickly.

"I suspect Mr Coates will tell Mr Moyes unofficially but we shall need to keep Univac sweet for a few years yet. I don't want them to hear on the grapevine so we should speak to Bill Wells as soon as possible. I want you to sit in on these meetings with me."

He telephoned Bill Wells, who was General Manager of Univac Australia. He impressed on Bill that he had an important announcement to make and wanted a meeting as soon as possible. He stressed that Bill was to come alone. It was a rather peculiar request but Bill said he would drop everything and hop in a cab. He would be in Mr Grace's office within 30 minutes.

Over coffee, we chatted about the next steps in the conversion to IBM. Mr Grace said he expected IBM would have some suggestions. He was sure they had customers who had converted from Univac to IBM before.

Mr Grace's secretary announced Bill Wells' arrival. He was shown into the office and offered coffee. He was a tiny, dapper man in a smart pinstripe suit and round thick-rimmed spectacles. His thick black hair was held in place with brilliantine.

Mr Grace stressed that what he was going to say had to remain confidential until ratified by the Board, but he wanted Bill to hear the news directly rather than on the grapevine.

When we told Bill the news he said he wasn't surprised. He had watched AMPnet struggle and had not known how to help. CSC, the American parent of CSA, was a big Univac customer. Bill was torn between keeping CSA/CSC sweet and serving AMP as best he could.

Bill surprised us by saying that actually AMP could help him. He told us that Univac was bringing out a new range of computers that were more economical to run and much more robust than the current 1100 series. He said it would help him enormously if, when AMP announced the decision to move to IBM, they could announce that as they would take, say, five years to convert, they would be installing the latest Univac equipment.

He would give AMP the new equipment totally without cost as he thought it would help him to sell more of the new machines in Australia. He said the move to the new machines would require no changes to AMP's software and would all be done by Univac specialists at no charge.

Mr Grace said it was a very generous offer which he would gratefully accept on behalf of AMP. When Bill Wells left Mr Grace seemed very pleased with the arrangement and raced off to tell the General Manager.

Next, we had a meeting with IBM. Interestingly, the GM, Allan Moyes, did not attend but sent his team of 'conversion specialists' It was obvious most of the team of six were salesmen.

They were sworn to secrecy until Board ratification but had obviously been told the news before they attended the meeting. They were good actors and pretended the decision was news to them. They told us they had a team of specialist converters in the USA and would get them to visit as soon as possible so that we could get on with developing estimates and plans.

On 28 October a special AMP all staff bulletin was issued saying:

'The AMP Society has invited two major data processing equipment suppliers to submit proposals to satisfy AMP data processing requirements until the late 1980s'.

The bulletin stated that AMP was only planning to change the 'central site' computers at Head Office and went on to outline AMP's computing history. It also said that AMP was undertaking a strategic review and that the AMPnet concept was to be retained.

I read the bulletin with interest. It was obviously a face saving exercise. I knew that the decisions had already been taken. I couldn't see IBM allowing the PDP-11s at branches or the CDC VDUs used for input and enquiries to stay for long. Soon everything would be badged IBM.

TRUE TO HIS WORD, Mr Grace arranged for me to manage three of the application systems. He said I'd asked to be given messes to clear up and these three projects were the worst messes AMP had.

The first system supported AMP's General Insurance business. It was a batch system developed for the IBM S/360 computers in the 1960s. No attempt had been made to convert it to be part of AMPnet. It hardly ever ran on time and whenever it did run, the results were not very reliable.

Most of the staff working on the system were CSA staff. The AMP manager was a Grade 4 Exec called Alan Smith. The CSA manager was George Garrard. As soon as I took the system over, George was promoted to a Grade 7 position with AMP to take charge of all AMP's computer operations. I was only a Grade 5. George was the third AMP Exec to be appointed from outside the Society.

The second system was built to support the Collector business. Collector insurance premiums were collected by the rep who visited the policyholders at their house or workplace. The costs of this business type were escalating. The computer system was costing too much to run and costs needed to be reduced significantly.

The Collector System also ran on the IBM S/360s. The AMP man in charge was Arthur Pynor, a Grade 5 Exec. The team was a mixture of AMP and CSA people.

The last troubled system was the Property system. It was an AMPnet system that was several times over cost estimate and well behind schedule. The team was largely CSA. With over 200 properties to manage, AMP needed the system to be working as soon as possible.

The nearly 100 staff on my new team were located on the 17th floor of the old AMP building at Circular Quay. My office was right in the middle of the front of the building. It had a magnificent view looking out over Circular Quay and across the harbour to Sydney's North Shore.

NOW THAT I had moved to the AMP's Head Office building, I was beginning to understand AMP's formality and tradition. Office size was determined by Executive Grade, not by job need, so everyone knew which Grade an Exec was by their office size. I was Grade 5 so my office was 6ftx10ft. Grade 6 officers had 6x12; Grade 4 offices were 6x8; Grade 3 and 2 had 6x6 offices. There were no Grade I Execs.

Just like the Met Office where I had worked in the 1950s, AMP men worked in their offices in their shirt sleeves but donned their jackets when outside their office or when they held a meeting in their office. What protocol was I, a woman Exec, supposed to follow? I decided it was all too hard and I would please myself just as I had at the Met Office.

I started to review the General Insurance system. The AMP manager, Alan Smith, told me that although he was in charge, he didn't understand how the systems worked. His young ginger haired assistant, John Meadows, was keen to help and get the system working as well as possible. It seemed to me that John did most of the work and CSA staff did as little as possible.

Now George Garrard had gone, the CSA manager, Trevor, spent most of his time managing a rock band. He had a large office next to mine. Every time I went to speak to him he was either not in his office or sound asleep on his desk. He had no idea about the system or what his staff were doing and referred me to John Meadows to answer any questions I had.

John told me that the system was too big to run on the computer as one system so it had been broken into two parts called Premiums and Claims. The Premiums system processed new business, kept records of policies in force, their cover, and policy payments. The Claims system recorded claims made and listed money to be paid to policy holders so that cheques could be issued. The problem was that the two systems used different master files and did not communicate with each other. It was possible that claims were being paid where there was no policy in force.

I found that there were two Premiums systems and five Claims systems. They all processed the same data and were run until one of them got to the end without failure. It was crazy.

Each weekend the systems took all the capacity of both IBM S/360 computers and often overran the weekend timeslot. They produced stacks of printed output that was split up by branch, and used to answer queries or produce claims cheques in each branch General Insurance department. At the end of month, all policies were listed and AMP's total liability calculated. This report produced 12 boxes of paper.

I said from now on, only one Claims system and one Premiums system would be run. The team could select which of the many systems should be retained and which thrown out. We would then concentrate on getting the two chosen systems correct. We would then see about making the systems run together off one master file.

Everyone said they couldn't choose which system to keep. They each had good points and bad points. I said then I would choose. Whenever I chose one system I was told that was the worst choice I could make. I gradually whittled the systems down to one for Claims and one for Premiums. I was told by all the staff that the ones chosen had been the worst choice I could have made but I stuck to my guns and had all other systems trashed.

ALTHOUGH THE SPACE my staff worked in was beautiful, it seemed a little cramped. The building had a footprint the shape of a capital H, which provided maximum window space. I walked round the floor but found that one of the arms of the H was blocked off by floor to ceiling partitions and a locked door.

I asked my staff what went on in that area and was told that was where the industrial staff packed up output to send to branches. Industrial staff at AMP were janitors or cleaners or messengers. They were usually oldish men who wore brown lab coats.

I said that if they were my staff I wanted to meet them. I was told I shouldn't really do that. They were very smelly and sweaty and often worked in singlets and shorts because the area was so hot, it was not a fit sight for a woman. I said again they were my staff I wanted to see them. My words fell on deaf ears. This all seemed very odd.

I stayed late one night and went to the main janitor's office, I said I was the new Management Exec on the 17th floor, which he knew through the internal publicity following my appointment. I said I'd left my key to an area at home and did he have a master key?

We went up to 17th floor. The door was unlocked. To my amazement inside the area was a tower made of the cardboard centres of rolls of photo-copying paper. The tower was floor to ceiling and took up nearly the whole area.

The next day, I asked John Meadows if he knew the tower was there. He said everyone knew. It belonged to a CSA programmer called Jim Donovan. I was told that there were similar towers being built in offices all over the world. Jim's was nearly the biggest. At that time, AMP had a photocopier on each floor that used photosensitive paper. When the copier was about to run out of paper, a red mark appeared and they loaded a new roll of paper. Evidently Jim had people stationed near each photocopier to watch for the red mark and rescue the cardboard centre.

Jim was on my budget as a senior programmer. I called him to my office. I said I was having the tower removed and the space made available for staff. I sent Jim back to CSA. The next CSA staff magazine carried a photo on its cover showing a proud Jim standing beside his tower which was claimed to be the largest in the world. I also saw him many times on the TV news because he was the organiser of cyclist's blockades of the Sydney Harbour Bridge campaigning for more cycleways.

I told Trevor that he was going back to CSA and gradually, over a six month period, reduced my 100 staff to 50, mainly by weeding out the non-performing CSA staff. The AMP Execs were each sent back to their business departments. The systems all ran more effectively than they had ever run.

40 A world trip

MY NEW MANAGER WAS an ex AMP salesman called Ross Middleton. Everyone called him Ross Muddleton because he seemed totally out of his depth. No one could understand why he had been appointed. He greeted me warmly and said he was very glad I was on his team. He had heard all about me from Phil Grace and looked forward to my help in running his area.

Ross had three teams reporting to him. The Deposit Administration team headed by Ken Harrison built systems to manage AMP's Superannuation business. These were still being built for the Univac, with a largely CSA team. Life Insurance systems were managed by AMP Exec Tony Cuneo, who also had very little data processing experience. And the Accounting systems had been taken out of the Data Processing Division and were managed by AMP Exec Ross Gordon, who reported to the Chief Accountant.

I had been out of the mainstream for 18 months when I was planning and building the new computer centre and writing the report on moving to IBM. I had reported directly to Phil Grace and had not concerned myself with the politics and comings and goings in the Data Processing Division.

When CSA was in charge AMPnet was in a mess. But many of the AMP Execs now in charge had very little data processing experience. Talking about this to people outside AMP, at the UNSW Forum or ACS meetings, I found many other companies were using non DP people to manage their data processing. It seemed to me that the pendulum had swung too far from technical people in control to business people in control. Neither was ideal.

I tried to be supportive of Ross Middleton, but I could not see why, with no relevant experience, he was my boss and two grades above me. Also, with the General Insurance system in such a mess, I could not see why George Garrard was promoted to be two grades above me. I couldn't see why Ken Harrison and Tony Cuneo were the same grade as I was.

APPRAISAL TIME WAS here again. Rather than being appraised by Ross Middleton, I was called to Ces Potter's office to be given my appraisal. He said Mr Grace had given me a glowing appraisal for the delivery of the new AMPnet Computer Centre and for my work on the study to move AMP back to IBM. He felt that as I had only been in my new position for a few months, it was too early to judge my progress so I would not get an appraisal for 1978.

Ces said he really only wanted to ask me how the job was going and what plans I had for my future at AMP. I said I was enjoying the challenge of my new position. He looked at me over his spectacles and said he felt he had to ask me because my personal situation had changed. I was now married and had the responsibility of more children.

I asked if he had asked Tony Cuneo that question because Tony had five children. He answered that Tony had a wife to look after the children. I asked if he thought Mr Grace had asked Anstey Lindsay that question because Anstey had four children. He looked puzzled and answered that Anstey also had a wife. We both sat silently looking at each other. Ces looked puzzled. I'm sure he meant his enquiry kindly but the inference was that now I was married I should stay at home and look after the children. Phil Grace had never asked or even hinted at that issue.

Finally Ces got to his feet and said "Oh Well. We shall have to see," and my 'appraisal' was over. I took only a short Christmas break so that I could be on hand for the end of year runs for the Collector and General Insurance systems. Property was still far from ready to go into production.

I noticed that John Meadows was in the office at all hours and most weekends. I asked him when he had last taken annual leave. He said he had not taken leave or had a weekend off for four years. He was the only one who could get the systems through.

He told me he had taught himself COBOL and often made changes to the systems himself to get the runs through. The CSA team confirmed this and said they had given up making changes as John usually reversed them out.

This raised two questions. Firstly, why was John making changes when he wasn't a programmer? More importantly, what on earth did the large CSA team do? I found that there was no documentation for the systems, so I started the CSA team documenting the programs, a necessary task hated by most programmers. I told John that he was not to make any changes to the systems unless he asked me first and told me exactly what he planned to do and why.

I checked for procedures for getting changes into the IBM S/360 systems and found that no one had bothered with procedures. John even operated the computers if things were not going well. This was serious. It seemed to me that John had made himself indispensable. What would happen if he took ill or left AMP? John assured me that would not happen.

We got through nearly a month with John assuring me that changes had to be made and me forbidding them to be made. The month end was difficult but the systems limped through.

I told John he was to have the next week off. He said he dare not take time off. I said I'd be grateful if he was available by phone if we needed help. The systems worked without too much help from the programmers.

I told John to take the next week off. His wife rang to ask if he was going to lose his job. I told her he was our most valuable staff member but the systems had to work without him. He took a third week off. For the fourth week he asked if he could take his family away on a short holiday but still be available by phone. I agreed but said I wanted him on deck for the month end run. That too went smoothly.

When John came back to work after that month off he looked years younger. He said his home life had improved considerably and never again did he want to get into the situation in which he had found himself. I said it had not been his fault. I felt his management had been poor and most of the staff just plain lazy. I promised him that things would change. I asked Alan Smith if John could be transferred to my staff and he agreed.

I worked with John to get the CSA team down to a small number of hard workers. The rest were sent back to CSA. I appointed John as manager of the team. There would be no CSA manager, just one combined team with John at the head. I said I would send John on a management course.

I told John Staveley, Managing Director of AMP General Insurance, that I could support the General Insurance systems satisfactorily if I had a team of four good people. I asked if I could have permission to hire contractors rather than rely on CSA to provide staff. I did not ask Ces because I was sure he would say no.

To my amazement John agreed and told Ces I was going to pioneer hiring contractors from the general market. Ces was not happy. CSA was not happy.

DURING MY WORK on my application teams, Mr Grace had often asked me to sit in on meetings with IBM. They had found a company in America with good experience in migrating systems from Univac to IBM. They brought Tony Brown, one of the directors of the company, to AMP to meet us. Tony told us that the company had also worked with some insurance companies and had very good references. Mr Grace said I should go to San Francisco to meet with the company and check them out.

AMP's General Insurance said it could no longer limp along with its current system. Now AMPnet was going to be phased out, maybe they could use an off the shelf system. They had already been approached by a Sydney company that had the Australian franchise for selling a General Insurance System used widely in USA. Mr Grace said Alan Smith was being sent to the

USA to talk to insurance companies about their use of the system. He said I should go with Alan to check out the technical aspects of the system.

Mr Putt, the Chief Accountant, said that NCR, the company that supplied the mechanical accounting system used in his department, now made specialist data entry computing equipment that linked into IBM mainframes for further processing. He asked me to visit NCR in Dayton, Ohio and provide feedback on the suitability of the equipment for AMP.

I told Mr Grace that I would like to visit the Prudential Assurance Company in England to find out how its new system was running. It had been developed for IBM equipment and was a fully fledged real time on line database system.

The trip would take the whole month of March. I saw an opportunity to take Allan to visit my Mum and Dad in England and got permission to add a week's holiday to the trip. AMP was still flying Execs First Class so I could trade my ticket for two economy tickets for Allan and myself. Allan's mother Edna agreed to look after the children.

Just as I was about to leave an announcement was made that my boss, Ross Middleton, would be going back to the sales department. He had been In the Data Processing Division for six months. There was no goodbye party but he left me a card showing a pea pod with a pearl in place of one of the peas. He had scribbled 'you are that pearl' on the card.

Well, I thought, at least I made an impression there. I went away feeling sure that when I came back I would be asked to fill the vacancy left by Ross.

ALLAN WAS VERY EXCITED about the trip. We were to travel right round the world and he had never done that. He said he didn't like the idea of letting me go off on a trip with Alan Smith, although when he met Alan Smith the two acted as if they had been long lost blood brothers.

We set off on 2 March 1977. We were greeted at San Francisco airport by Tony Brown and his wife. They were a delightful couple. The next day I visited Tony's company. He said that while converting systems from Univac to IBM, his company had developed software that did most of the conversion automatically.

Tony told me that the skill came in planning for the conversion, establishing the test data and results that were to prove the conversion, and redeveloping the Job Control Language (JCL) that enabled the systems to operate smoothly. JCL was something most programmers hated writing but it was essential as it was the script that described system operation.

Tony helped me understand how to estimate conversion costs. He said his company would help but to do that he would have to take a team to Australia for a month to examine AMP's systems. His wife Kathy had been brought up in Queensland and would love an excuse to visit Australia.

The next stop was with NCR in Dayton, Ohio. A model of the Wright Brothers' Kittyhawk plane was hanging from the ceiling in the airport, reminding passengers that the men who had made the first powered flight, came from Dayton. The plane seemed so tiny and so frail.

At the exit a smartly dressed and very tall and very black chauffer was holding a card with my name on it. He said he was the personal chauffer of the CEO of NCR and had been sent to take us to our hotel. He had parked the car right outside the exit doors. It was a huge elegant metallic blue beast with baby blue suede seats. The chauffer said he would be at the hotel at 7.30 in the morning to take me to the plant.

When he picked me up next morning he held the back door of the car open for me, but I said I preferred to sit in the front. He raised his eyebrows but opened the front door for me. I was welcomed at the plant by the CEO himself. He said he was delighted to receive a visitor from Australia. AMP was a valued customer and NCR was now moving into computers. He was sure I would like what they had to offer.

I was ushered into a room filled with people. They gave me a slide show about the history of Dayton and of NCR. They explained the vast factory was serviced by underground tunnels that ran from building to building. They then briefly described their new product. The slides didn't look real to me. They looked as if they were made out of rather crudely painted cereal boxes.

When I asked to see the product I was told it wasn't quite ready. I said I hoped I hadn't come all the way from Australia to see pictures of badly painted cereal boxes. The leader of the group looked sheepish. He said I would have to sign a Non-Disclosure Agreement if I was to be shown the product. I said I would expect that.

Coffee was brought and after much whispering and toing and froing I was led into an office to sign the Non-Disclosure Agreement. It looked as if it had just come off the typewriter. I was then led to what looked like a workshop. An attractive young woman was sitting at a device that looked like a typewriter. It had a teleprinter attached. As the salesman talked through the process, the young woman started typing. I asked if I could operate the machine. The salesman looked awkward but agreed.

I noticed the device seemed to be held together by lots of elastic bands and paperclips. I asked why. I was told there were numerous safety devices.

The machine didn't work when they were operational, so on the prototype machine, several mechanical gates had to be held open with elastic bands.

I said I didn't believe they had a real product. They all looked relieved and agreed they didn't yet have a product but they would soon. They said they had been most embarrassed when they had been told I was to visit, they knew it was far too soon but hoped I would be just a very senior manager on a junket who was unable to ask technical questions. They seemed nice people, and genuine.

NCR had laid on a special lunch for me. Over lunch they asked that I don't judge them. NCR did have some very good products under development. They promised next time I visited they would have something really good to show me. The chauffer whisked me back to the airport in the big blue car. What a strange visit!

AT 4PM THE NEXT DAY we flew to Columbia in South Carolina to visit the company that developed the General Insurance system for IBM computers. There we met a very professional team offering the software called PMS (Policy Management System). That was also the name of the company.

After running through the basic features of the product they listed about a hundred general insurance companies worldwide who had bought the system. There were none in Australia but the company told us they had appointed an agent in Australia. Alan Smith was impressed by the list of companies. He said we were to visit several of them on our trip. The company volunteered to arrange for us to meet or speak to any of the companies we chose.

After the peculiar visit to NCR, this company was refreshingly open. We asked how the system could be modified for Australian conditions and were told that we would have to discuss that with the Australian agent but that several custom modifications had now been made and all worked satisfactorily.

At lunchtime we were joined by some more senior managers and taken to a luxuriously appointed club. While the men were signing in there was some whispering between the staff and one of the PMS people. He turned to me and said, "I'm sorry. I had forgotten this club does not admit women. We have to leave." We walked round the back of the club and entered again through a back door and up some narrow stairs. We were ushered into a private dining room. "Sorry again," said the top man.

"If we are discrete they will let us eat in this private room." I had forgotten that some places in America still had such old fashioned rules. I wanted to ask if they allowed black people to lunch in the club but thought the question might offend.

In the evening, Allan Moffatt joined Alan Smith and me plus more people from PMS. We felt easy with the PMS people. Their attitude and product had certainly impressed us so far.

WE FLEW ON TO Toronto in Canada where we were to visit four insurance companies who were using PMS. We had arranged to arrive in Toronto late on Friday night so that we could go to Niagara Falls over the weekend.

When we woke on Saturday morning the temperature was well below freezing. AMP gave a clothing allowance to Execs visiting the northern hemisphere. I had used mine to buy myself a fur coat. Alan Smith had bought himself a fur lining for his Burberry raincoat so we were both well prepared for cold weather.

We hired a car and set off for Niagara. While Allan Moffatt drove the car to the falls Alan Smith and I walked through the park above the falls. I remembered visiting with my first husband and dropping a leaf into the rapids above the falls. As the river picked up speed it had had a mesmerising effect on me as if it was asking me to throw myself into it.

I remembered the distant roar of the falls and that roar getting louder and louder as we walked through the park above the falls. As we set off, the snow was falling lightly and it felt as if we were in a winter wonderland. The closer we got to the falls, the more the air filled with spray. The spray settled on us as ice. By the time we reached the falls both of us were covered in ice.

Alan Smith and I visited four large insurance companies in Toronto using PMS. They were on the four opposite corners at a major crossroads in the centre of the city and could be reached by walking along underground, heated walkways.

The companies had nothing but praise for PMS and the people who sold it. I gathered lots of statistics about how the system ran on IBM S/360 (now renamed S/370) computers. Everything we heard impressed us. It seemed the product had no competitors and had gained a large part of the market in USA, Europe and South Africa.

We visited Cigna Insurance in Philadelphia then went on to Boston to visit New England Life and John Hancock, two of the largest insurance companies in the world. On the journey from Philadelphia to Boston we passed over the Three Mile Island nuclear power station.

The film The China Syndrome had just opened. We had seen the long queues for the film outside all the cinemas in each city we visited. We had not yet seen the film. Little did we know that only a week later the world would be holding its breath while the news of a disaster at Three Mile Island made the China Syndrome a real possibility.

John Hancock and New England Life were both very impressive companies. They supported everything we had heard from other companies we had visited. PMS was the only General Insurance system to buy and that it was very good.

I WAS BEGINNING to worry about Allan. He seemed to change during this trip. His night terrors seemed less but he and Alan Smith played up in many of the places we visited, stealing little souvenirs and annoying people in the hotels. When I mentioned the behaviour, Allan said I should relax, that was the way all Australians behaved overseas.

In Boston, we said goodbye to Alan Smith. He felt the visit had been entirely worthwhile and was looking forward to reporting his findings to his boss, John Staveley, the Managing Director of AMP Fire and General, AMP's General Insurance arm.

We arrived in London in the early morning. We went straight to the Royal Garden Hotel in Kensington. We had a beautiful room on the third floor. It was huge and overlooked Kensington Gardens. We hired a car and drove to my parents' house in Harrow. They said we should stay at their house. I knew it wasn't really big enough for us all but they insisted and Allan agreed that it would be much nicer than staying at the hotel.

We visited all the tourist spots in the London area. As usual, Allan charmed my parents and everyone else he met. We visited Ma and Pa Leach who said they were glad we were still so happy.

I visited the Prudential Assurance Company. It was good to meet DP manager Ewart Willey and Marion Tribe, the Chief Programmer, again. Over lunch we reminisced about the old days at the Advanced Programming Group of the BCS and all the now famous people we had met. The Pru seemed very satisfied with its IBM systems. They had all heard that PMS was very good but didn't use it, as they had already built all their systems themselves by the time PMS was available.

I had a phone call from Ian, AMP's Fire and General's re-insurance expert, based in London. I had been told he was one of the best in the world and that he actually made more money for AMP through reinsurance than the company made from premiums.

Ian asked if I would like to visit Lloyds with him. Lloyds had just moved into their amazing new building in the City. Ian was obviously well known.

He was on first name terms with all the ‘names’, as the partners were called. I was interested to see how business was done.

There was a conversation, an agreement and a handshake. Business worth millions of dollars was done in a very short time with no paperwork. Ian said he did make notes for his own purposes, and probably the ‘names’ made notes for themselves, but business was done largely on an honour system.

Our week in England went too quickly. I would have loved to show Allan the Lake District and other parts of England but there wasn’t time. My parents said they would be over in Australia again soon.

On the way home, we stopped off in Bangkok. Allan changed to the person he had been in Malaya on our honeymoon, calling hotel staff and taxi drivers ‘John’. I could see them cringe.

We stayed at the Hotel Oriental, which was still listed by American Express as the best hotel in the world. When we got home, I was horrified to find that Allan had souvenired towels and a towelling dressing gown. He said that hotels expect pilfering and it’s what Aussies do.

My concerns were mounting.

41 Allan off the rails

I **WORRIED THAT** Allen's son Robbie, now 15 and dying to leave school, could not read or write. He seemed intelligent to me. On Saturday afternoons I baked cakes and biscuits and prepared some meals for the week ahead. Robbie loved cooking with me and had recognised that the words in a recipe for flour or sugar were the same as those on the jars containing flour or sugar.

I discussed Robbie with John Bennett on a plane trip to Canberra for a Privacy meeting. John said one of the professors at the University of Sydney had a son who couldn't read and write as a teenager. The boy seemed intelligent, as I thought Robbie was.

The family had sought advice from SPELD, and organisation for people with special learning difficulties. After the boy had been assessed, they were shown how to teach him to read. He ended up going to university.

I discussed the issue with Allan. He said Robbie was an imbecile and would never learn to read. Nevertheless, I took him to SPELD where his IQ was judged to be just above average. I discovered that when he was five he had a Malay nurse who spoke and read to him in Malay. No one seemed to notice that Robbie wasn't learning to read in English.

Initially, I struggled to find written matter that was simple enough for Robbie to read but interesting enough to hold his attention. As Robbie badly wanted a motorbike, we started on the road rules and never looked back. Within six months he was reading fluently.

Success teaching Robbie to read led me to think we might be able to cure his bedwetting. Allan was adamant that he knew all about stopping bed-wetting and he had tried everything. I asked our doctor for advice. He suggested we hire a pad and bell.

Allan scoffed. He said he had tried that. Robbie was just thick. I reminded him that Robbie had an above average IQ and I was going to try that method. The first night Robbie used the pad and bell his bed was dry and he never wet the bed again even when I removed the pad and bell.

I HAD TIME to meet Allan for lunch almost every day. He often brought one of his Parole Board clients to lunch. He had been in court with them all morning and they had been given into his safekeeping until the afternoon court session.

Allan's area of responsibility was Kings Cross, the red light area of Sydney. Many of his clients were young prostitutes. They were often very beautiful, under 20 and quite well educated. I couldn't understand why young women with such promise ended up 'on the game'. Some told me it was because they spent most of their earnings on drugs.

Several young girls told me that men often paid for services but didn't want sex. This was especially so with groups on a buck's night when the bridegroom would beg the girl to pretend they had had sex but ask her not to come near him in case he caught something and passed it on to his bride.

Football grand final nights were also very lucrative. A girl would be hired for a night at a hotel for about $2000. The men would take turns to go into her room but again, most would beg for the girl not to touch them but to pretend they had had a good time.

Allan would sometimes walk me through the red light district. The ladies would call out, "Is that your wife, Mr Moffatt? Bring her in for a cup of tea." Some of the girls were especially beautiful and it seemed that whenever I asked why on earth such a beautiful girl was on the game, Allan would say, "It's a fella!"

ALLAN CAME WITH ME once to the UNSW Forum. He was the only male partner and got quite friendly with the accompanying wives. While delegates attended an evening session, he took Cyril's wife on a tour of the red light district and introduced her to several of the ladies. She asked to see inside the brothels and came back from her evening visit very excited.

At the next Forum, she promised to take Allan into her world. She took him to an opera at the Opera House. Just before interval, as the lights were coming up, he playfully put his arm round her and pinged her bra strap. When the lights were fully up she was embarrassed to find the members of her mother's group in the row behind. She and Allan came back very flustered eager to tell Cyril in case he found out from another source.

At that Forum, one of the managers spent the whole of one dinner telling Allan about an especially tricky situation he had on his plate at work. I listened as Allan used the ELIZA technique on him.

The technique was named after an interactive computer program developed by a psychologist to elicit responses from a client. It was a very simple early attempt at Artificial Intelligence. It had been developed when research had shown that clients would often answer questions more openly and fully to a computer than to a person, especially when the questions were of a sexual nature.

The ELIZA program relied on a number of simple open-ended questions and phrases such as 'what happened next?' or 'what did you think about that?' typed onto a teleprinter, which was the human computer interface. When the client stopped answering reasonably the computer would type 'and what do you think your mother (or father) would think about that?'

The next morning at breakfast, the man asked me which company the man he had been speaking to last night was with. Before I could answer that Allan was my husband, he said the man had been a brilliant consultant and had given him wonderful advice that would solve all his problems!

IN JULY 1979 I turned 40. I organised a simple lunch at home for my friends and colleagues. I had catered for much larger parties but felt apprehensive about my 40th because Allan was starting to act very strangely. It was funny at first but got very wearing.

He also started being rude to friends and neighbours. Many of them told me that although they still wanted to be friends with me they didn't feel comfortable with Allan. I decided to join the Vietnam veterans wives' association. After attending several meetings, I found that many had similar experiences to mine. Many had much worse stories to tell.

On one occasion I organised a Sunday barbeque and bought good quality steak. The day before the barbeque I cut it into portions, put it into a large dish to marinate in red wine and spices, covered it in plastic wrap and put it in the fridge overnight.

The next day I made salads, garlic bread and desserts. I asked Allan to get the barbeque going. Guests started to arrive. Allan offered drinks. I went to get the steak but it was not in the fridge. I asked Allan where he had put it. He said he had not seen any steak in the fridge.

After a while, Allan announced to our guests that he had to apologise for his wife because she had forgotten to buy steak so he would go to Kentucky Fried Chicken and buy enough for everyone. I protested that I had bought steak but it had gone missing. Allan encouraged everyone to laugh at me.

"She is normally so organised at work but she is a dreadful housewife. I keep her because she is good in bed," he joked. I was angry but realised that would only make me look more foolish so joined in the joke. Allan raced off to KFC and brought back enough chicken for everyone.

A few days later Claire told me the toilet in her ensuite was blocked. I tried unblocking it but couldn't move whatever was causing the blockage. I put my hand up the U bend in the toilet. There was something soft and squidgy. My first thought was that it was a rat but as I pulled blood came into the toilet pan.

I assumed one of the girls had put sanitary towels into the toilet, but the thing I was pulling seemed more solid than that. I had a horrible feeling that one of the girls had got pregnant and had aborted into the toilet. I pulled harder and there was my steak still wrapped in plastic.

Allan denied all knowledge, as did the children. He told me I must have tried to flush the steak away in a moment of madness. He told me I was always doing silly things now but he loved me anyway.

BUT LIFE WENT ON as normal. We visited cousins in Yass and went skiing in the Snowy Mountains. But to preserve my sanity I started keeping notes of unexplained events. Invitations to parties slowed to a trickle and people gave excuses not to come to our house. Allan's night terrors started again.

Allan had always been fascinated by the yellow model Jensen car Dick had given me. Graham Thorpe of Peddle, Thorpe and Walker, the architects for the AMP Centre, drove a brown FF Jensen. I had pointed it out to Allan one day when he picked me up from the AMP car park and joked I really preferred a brown FF Jensen if he was going to buy me one.

The next day, when I got home, there was a brown FF Jensen parked outside the house. I thought Allan must have hired it. He told me he had bought it for me. I challenged him, asking how he could afford it. He showed me a receipt for $3000. He told me that one of his prisoners in Long Bay Gaol had owned it but as he was in for a long stretch he couldn't bear to think his wife would get his car so he sold it to his probation officer, Allan.

I said I was sure probation officers weren't allowed to buy cars from their clients. He assured me his boss had given permission. I said I was sure the car was worth much more than $3000 and I'd check its value with AMP General Insurance. I felt something illegal was happening. I told Allan to get rid of the car. I said If he didn't I'd go to the police.

Allan said we should just take a spin in the car and I'd fall in love with it. He would just drive round the block. Stephen asked to come and got into the dicky seat in the back. As we drove away, Stephen asked why the back of the front passenger seat had been ripped and sewn up. Allan said he didn't know. When we got back I said he should still give the car back or I would go to the police.

The next day I found out the car was worth between $30,000 and $50,000, depending on condition. When I got home, the car was still outside the house. I challenged Allan and said again I'd call the police. The next day the car was gone. Allan told me he had sold it to a car dealership on the Parramatta road for $30,000. He would buy a new boat with his profit.

THAT YEAR WE WENT to the Darlinghurst Police Christmas ball. After the ball a group said they were going on somewhere for drinks. We walked down to Forbes Street and stopped outside what looked like shabby wooden garage doors set in a brick wall with no windows. Someone knocked and announced 'Darlinghurst Police'. A panel in the small door opened just enough to reveal a pair of eyes. The panel shut as quickly as it opened and the small door was opened wide. We all went in.

I was surprised to see a mini casino complete with croupiers, roulette wheels and blackjack tables. It was an illegal gambling club. They were common in Sydney at the time. Was I going to witness a police bust? We certainly had some very senior police in the group.

There was a tiny dance floor. The people sitting nearest to the dance floor were moved out and we were given their tables. Drinks were ordered and we were all given some poker chips. I love to play roulette so I took my chips and played my usual game, placing equal chips on black and red or on odds and evens. One of the drunk police wives came and stood beside me, congratulating me for always winning.

We danced, drank and gambled. About 4am, Allan came to take me home. The woman I had been sitting with said, "Aren't you going to cash in your chips? You've got about $300 there." I told her I thought as they were only plastic they had been given to us to just play with. She looked amazed but quickly popped them in her own handbag.

Driving home in the early hours, I asked Allan how the police were playing in what I had thought was an illegal club. Allan told me the police probably owned the club. "You enjoyed yourself didn't you?" he asked. "Just keep your mouth shut."

On Boxing Day the whole family came over for a barbeque. Allan was his old pleasant self. Had I been imagining the whole thing? Was I just going through an early menopause? I had heard that women sometimes suffered memory loss or have peculiar thoughts in menopause.

In March Alan Leach's Auntie Elsie and Uncle Les came out from England to stay with us. Allan charmed them as he did everybody at first. We took them to the ski lodge and to the farm in Yass. They loved Australia.

But back at home Allan's behaviour became more difficult. At times he ranted and raged. Robbie seemed to get the brunt of his Dad's anger. One Saturday afternoon when Robbie and I were cooking as usual, the phone rang. It was one of Allan's parolees. I was furious. I knew Allan dealt with some very violent people, and although they had completed their prison sentence and were now on parole, I didn't want anything to do with them. I asked the man how he had got our number. He said Allan had given it to him for emergencies. This was an emergency. He was going to kill himself.

I tried to calm him down and asked him not to do anything until he'd spoken to Allan. I told him Allan was out and would be back soon. The prisoner rang several times more. He sounded very upset. When Allan came in I was relieved. I told him about the phone calls and gave him the man's number.

To my surprise, Allan said the world would be a better place if the man did kill himself. He rang the man and told him if he was going to slit his wrists to remember to slit along the arm rather than across it because he'd bleed to death more quickly. I was horrified. Then Allan told me the next day that the man was dead. He had slit his wrists and had taken Allan's advice on how to do it. Surely this was all wrong.

Allan grew very moody. He spent a lot of time by himself. I asked Robbie what his Mum used to do when his Dad behaved oddly. Robbie said everyone just tried hard not to set him off. His daughters Kathy and Anne confirmed what Robbie said but suggested I ask their mother for help.

I rang Allan's previous wife, Grace. She said she had tried to warn me that he was mad before we had married. She told me he had spent time in mental hospitals and had had electric shock treatment but nothing worked. She said he would get worse and start beating me up as he had her. She said he once hit her in the face with a very hot iron and hurt her sexually saying she would never give pleasure to another man.

Grace said she worried every time Allan took Belinda out by himself. She thought he might even murder Belinda to get back at her.

This was getting really bad. Grace had tried to stop me marrying Allan but I thought that was just sour grapes. I remembered Renate's words when she first met Allan. I rang Renate to discuss the matter. She said she had been watching out for signs of instability but hadn't seen any. She said I should get out of the marriage as soon as I could.

I asked Robbie how bad his Dad had got. Robbie said once Allan had tied their two cats' tails together, slung them over the washing line and watched them scratch each other's eyes out. Robbie's eyes shone when he told the story as if he relished the idea.

I was now really worried. Renate had been right.

42 Ruffling feathers

WHEN I GOT BACK to AMP after the big trip to the USA and the UK, I was surprised to find that Ken Harrison was now my boss. He had little experience in data processing or management. Why had he been promoted over me?

I asked Ces Potter. He said Management thought I had enough on my plate as, in addition to managing some of AMP's most difficult projects, I was representing AMP on the UNSW Forum and still served on the Privacy enquiry and the communications standards committee. Also, I now had more family responsibilities and was supporting Mr Grace in the purchase of and conversion to IBM gear. That seemed enough for anyone.

Ken's salary and grade was now one level above mine. If I was so valuable, why wasn't I promoted? I was still smarting from the fact that George Garrard had left the General Insurance Systems in an unholy mess and yet been promoted to Grade 7.

I asked Mr Grace what I had done to be treated the way I was. He said Ces had told him the men wouldn't stand for a woman managing them. Was this payback by Ces for exposing the AMPnet fiasco? I wasn't sure what to do. I was well paid. I loved my job. Really that should be all that mattered, but it still rankled.

THE COLLECTOR AND PROPERTY systems were now running smoothly. I had appointed Peter Whalan as manager of the Collector systems. He was a quietly spoken, competent man and all anyone could wish for in a manager. He was the son of John Whalan, who was head of the AMP sales staff.

Peter worked closely with his father to develop systems that really did serve the business areas well. He also understood the need to keep costs reasonable and ran a small competent team of AMP and CSA people. The Collector systems still ran on the IBM S/360 computers. I made Peter my deputy and he had looked after my area very competently while I was away.

The Property team comprised almost all CSA people. I was pleased to discover that Ted Chadwick was on the team. Discussing the Property system with him, I asked why it was so far over budget and well behind schedule, and which of the people on the team were any good. He said that most of the problems were caused by CSA trying to build a system without discussing it with AMP. This was a familiar pattern.

AMP did not like the fact that the IBM contract was based on US law. Mr Grace suggested we get the AMP and IBM legal teams together over drinks late in the afternoon and work it out.

Alcohol only seemed to make the lawyers on each side more intransigent. The sun set, the wine flowed. I suggested that we do away with the contract and work under common law. Both sets of lawyers turned towards me.

I felt I must have said something stupid but much to my amazement they agreed, shook hands and swiftly left. Mr Grace was delighted. “Where did you learn that one?” he said. I told him I had seen it done by the UK Government when dealing with IBM. AMP ran for many years with no formal contract with IBM.

We decided to put the new IBM computers in the computer room built for the IBM S/360s. Being largely solid state, the new IBM 3030 computers, which followed on from and were compatible with the S/360s, had a much smaller footprint and drew much less power than the older computers.

Extra space was taken up by the ever increasing disk farm that replaced magnetic tape drives but they would also get smaller as disks became more dense. Because the computers generated less heat, they needed less power for air conditioning.

NOVEMBER WAS APPRAISAL time at AMP. Ces gave me mine this year. I didn’t ask why my manager, Ken Harrison, hadn’t done my appraisal. Ces said everyone was delighted with what I had done in the year but he had something to say to me that he knew I wouldn’t like.

He said that a year earlier I had inherited 100 staff. The three systems I had taken over were in a mess and they were now all working even better than anyone had ever thought possible but I had reduced the staff under me to about 50. With 50 staff, I was only entitled to a Grade 4 Executive rating.

I couldn’t believe what I was hearing. I pointed out that George Garrard had left the General Insurance systems in a mess and had been appointed as Grade 7 when he transferred from CSA to AMP. The other Execs who had been running Collector and Property were Grade 4 and had been doing a poor job. Ross Middleton had been my boss at Grade 6 and I couldn’t see what on earth he had contributed.

I had represented AMP on the UNSW Forum. I had helped Phil Grace with the IBM purchase. I served on the Communications Standards and Privacy reference committees. Why was I being judged as Grade 4? It looked like a demotion to me and would look that way to everyone else.

Ces looked hurt. He said he knew I would be angry but I had got it all wrong. I wasn't being demoted, I would still be a Grade 5 Exec, it was the job that was a Grade 4. I would still have the same status and pay.

I was fired up. I didn't know what to do. I loved my job and I was well paid, but I felt undervalued and cheated. Ces spoke first. "If I could do anything about it Ann, I would," he said. "What can you suggest?"

I told Ces that there were several other projects in his division that were in a mess. Why not give those to me to sort out and make my staff up to 100 again? Ces looked relieved. "Can you really take on more?" he said. "I admit there are some messes and I don't know what to do with them but I don't want to overload you."

I smiled sweetly and told Ces I'd love to help put more projects right. He said he'd discuss it with Mr Grace and let me know. Within a week I'd been put in charge of systems for the Investments Division, the Accounting Division, the Personnel Division, including payrolls, and the Sales Division in addition to General Insurance, Collector and Property.

I was now in charge of all AMP's systems except Life and Superannuation. I had 125 staff. Of course there was no suggestion I should be put up a grade, but I knew I wouldn't make any attempt to reduce my staff levels. I was beginning to see how the game was being played.

Ces had been trying to get control back into the Data Processing Division in case other divisions decided to take their systems away from the DPD. As soon as Ces told Eric Putt, the Chief Accountant, that I would manage his systems he agreed to give responsibility back to the DPD, The systems were all running very smoothly.

Work on the Investments systems hadn't really started. I would have to select a new team for those systems. I had Ted Chadwick from Property in mind but needed him to deliver the Property systems.

A new man called David Stubing was been appointed to take charge of the new General Insurance system. He came from South Australia and his reputation came before him.

John Staveley, the Managing Director of General Insurance, told me that David was very competent. He had been very involved in the settling of claims for Cyclone Tracey that had devastated Darwin in the first Christmas that we arrived in Australia.

His colleagues in South Australia branch thought him anything but competent. They had nicknamed him 'Stupid'. I thought I should reserve judgement until I met the man.

David Stubing was tall and handsome with greying hair. He looked every inch the manager. He made sure that everyone knew he had gone to St Peters, a very old and prestigious private school in Adelaide. He seemed to spend most of his first week in John Staveley's office.

EVERYONE DECIDED THAT although the PMS system seemed ideally suited for our General Insurance Company, we didn't like the company that was selling it in Australia. Try as we might to get the parent company in the USA to deal with us directly they wouldn't do that.

Eventually we decided we would have to buy from the company we didn't like. They would make all the modifications needed for Australian conditions and run the system on their bureau machine for the first year, then we would take it in-house.

Just as we were about to sign the contract, David Stubing spoke up. "There's an alternative. A company in Melbourne has built a General Insurance system specifically for Australian conditions. It was built for Palmdale Insurance but they went bankrupt so the people building it bought it from the receivers."

I knew the system David was talking about. "Yes, I know it but it doesn't work," I said. Two young programmers from CSA had left to build Palmdale's system but Palmdale had gone broke. I said that before they folded Palmdale was only about a tenth the size of AMP General Insurance.

John Staveley was nodding. The system wasn't built for IBM computers. Ces relaxed and said, "Oh well, that's out."

But David persisted. "I think the software is very good. They came to Adelaide to speak to me but I said I had to find out what AMP was doing before I could agree to buy their system."

Mr Grace scowled. "You don't make that decision," he said. He then asked me what sort of computer the system was built for. I told him it was a Perkin-Elmer computer. Perkin-Elmer was a company that specialised in process control and monitoring systems. They weren't in insurance or other commercial systems as far as I knew.

"Why on earth did Palmdale pick those systems? No wonder they went bankrupt," Mr Grace said. "We've just decided to focus on IBM. We can't reverse that decision."

David Stubing said they had chosen Perkin-Elmer because it was a good product. Perkin-Elmer had invented a process that made computer systems easy and cheap to build and easy to change.

John Staveley looked interested. In the current market, ease of change was most important to the General Insurance Company. The latest type of contract they wanted to introduce was estimated to take twelve people nine months to build.

Mr Grace said AMP must do everything it could to save money. “Ann, you have three months to review this system and report back.”

THE NEW SYSTEM was called POLISY, which stood for Palmdale On Line Insurance SYstem. It had been developed in Melbourne by two ex CSA people, David Albert and Adrian Brooks. Their tiny company was called Inscom. David was the technical man and Adrian the smooth salesman.

I contacted Adrian Brooks and told him that POLISY had been discussed at AMP and I had been given the task of evaluating it on behalf of the Society. Adrian said he and David Albert would come to Sydney the next day to tell me all about the system.

When we met them they explained that the most important aspect of their system was SMART, which stood for Systems Methodology Application development in Real Time. SMART seemed to be a ‘meta language’ in which insurance contracts were described and converted into program logic. This sort of application specific development language had been mooted since the 1960s. Many had been described at the Advanced Programming Group at the British Computer Society.

“So really there is no ‘system’ as such,” I said. “You just provide the tools to develop one.”

“We’ve used the tools ourselves to develop stuff for Palmdale but they collapsed before we could test our code,” they said.

“Why pick Perkin-Elmer computers? Why not develop the system for IBM?” I asked.

David told me that Perkin-Elmer computers were especially designed to process small, simple transactions in real time. Although there were no real commercial systems developed for Perkin-Elmer computers, in Australia, they were used in betting systems.

The Australian Jockey Club had installed two Perkin-Elmer computers in a huge semi-trailer that was driven between the three different race courses where the AJC ran racing in Sydney on race days. Adrian said the computers were very robust and rarely broke down. They were also used to support betting through the TAB. They were used in the gaming industry because transactions were small, simple, high volume and needed to be processed very fast.

I asked David how long it would take a good programmer to learn how to use SMART and build something useful. He said they would gladly demonstrate the system and let my staff use it to build an insurance contract.

I had a brilliant young programmer called Patrick on the General Insurance team. Patrick was unconventional and dressed in a very flamboyant, effeminate way. His hair was long and often untidy. He liked to work from dusk to dawn. His productivity was phenomenal and he was very smart.

I ASKED PATRICK if he would like to spend a week in Melbourne working on a new computer. I told him I wanted him to learn how to use the system and let me know how easy it would be to build insurance contracts for AMP using the system. We got him on Friday's early afternoon plane and told him to take a taxi to St Kilda where POLISY had an office.

On Monday, Patrick rang to say he loved the system. The company had looked after him well and he had built a very complex contract. He had built 'Select a Cover' insurance on a block of flats and added marine cover to make it more complex. This was amazing. My team were in the middle of building 'Select a Cover' insurance. It was estimated to take twelve people nine months to build.

I told Patrick he was pulling my leg. He said the POLISY people had started to teach him about SMART as soon as he arrived mid afternoon Friday. He was so fascinated that he worked on the system the whole weekend only going back to his hotel to eat and wash. He hadn't slept.

I said I would send down one of our most pernickety business people from AMP Fire and General to test the system. I would be very cross if it didn't work. Patrick assured me it would. Bruce Arthurson was despatched on the early afternoon plane. Next morning he rang to say the system worked perfectly.

I was sure there was something wrong. I told them I would get on the next plane and test the system myself. By late afternoon, I had put the system through its paces and couldn't fault it.

Bruce, Patrick, David, Adrian and I sat in POLISY's tiny office in disbelief. David and Adrian were thrilled their system had been used by real insurance people and it had worked on a very complex contract. Bruce said it would make a tremendous difference to General Insurance that new contracts could be built so quickly and cheaply.

I returned to Sydney. I reported our findings to John Staveley and David Stubing, who looked very smug. I told Ces and Mr Grace. They worried about Perkin-Elmer. They told me to find out more from Perkin-Elmer's other customers. They asked how big the POLISY company was. I told them it was very small.

There was a lot to consider. We might have to support ourselves if the company went broke. How viable was Perkin-Elmer? What would IBM think? Most of all, whatever we did would have to support AMP Fire and General properly and be cost effective.

I asked Patrick, John Meadows and Bruce to try to build more of the AMP system for Perkin-Elmer using SMART just to see how long it would take to build the whole system. I also asked that they think about the data file structure and how we could convert current IBM S/360 files to POLISY.

I contacted Perkin-Elmer. The company's one salesman in Australia told me the best thing he could do was to take me to see his two main customers, VicTAB and the Australian Jockey Club. He suggested we visit the AJC next Saturday, when the weekly races were at Randwick, where the AJC was based. He would organise tickets for the Members' Stand. How many would I like? I decided to take John, Patrick, Bruce and Allan.

THE NEXT SATURDAY we all met at the restaurant in the members' stand at Randwick. We lunched on lobsters and champagne. While Patrick and John talked to the AJC programmers and operators inside the huge semitrailer, I was taken behind the scenes to be shown how the betting system worked.

A row of women sat behind safety grills selling betting tickets. I was told it was most important that queues of punters were served as quickly as possible. There were only eight races a day, and once a race started, there could be no more bets on that specific race. Similarly, when the results from a race had been announced it was imperative that winning tickets and payouts be identified quickly, because punters would probably put some or all of their winnings on the next race.

Even with the calculations needed to compute the fast changing odds and print the betting slips, the system seemed fairly simple. But transaction volumes were very high and all transactions were processed in real time. In 1980 such systems were rare.

Next week we visited VicTAB in Melbourne. This was quite a different setup. The betting process was largely the same but on a much larger scale than the AJC. VicTAB covered bets from races all over Australia and some from overseas, so had to calculate the odds and payouts on many races simultaneously.

All bets were made by phone. Punters set up accounts and the system had to check they had sufficient funds to cover their bets. Like the AJC system,

VicTAB had to ensure that winnings were returned to customer accounts as soon as possible after the result of each race was known.

Hundreds of women were seated in tiers round the windowless room taking bets by phone. They each had headsets and microphones and were speaking animatedly while entering data. The supervisor explained that as the punters were remote and couldn't be given a betting slip, all conversations were recorded so as to resolve any disputes.

I was shown the bank of Perkin-Elmer computers that supported the enterprise The Data Processing Manager told me the system was very reliable. He told me that Perkin-Elmer support in Australia was very good indeed.

The Perkin-Elmer salesman was very different from salesmen from other companies. He was more like the salesmen I remembered from the early days. He was knowledgeable about his product and intent to help his clients get the best possible service.

I asked for a list of all Perkin-Elmer customers in the world. I rang several of them and although their applications were very different from AMP's, they all told me Perkin-Elmer products and support were faultless and the computing systems were very cost effective, especially when compared with other computer manufacturers like IBM and DEC.

I wrote a short report for Mr Grace saying it looked as if the POLISY system would indeed support AMP General Insurance very well but I needed time to estimate costs and negotiate terms with Perkin-Elmer and the POLISY people.

THE TERMS I NEGOTIATED with POLISY were that David Albert would provide training and support for my staff until we could support ourselves. I made it clear that my aim was that we would be self-sufficient as soon as possible and would not rely on David as he had no back up.

I said we would expect to pay no fees for POLISY until we had satisfied ourselves that it was right for AMP. If after a year we disliked anything about POLISY, even if we didn't disclose why we didn't like it, we would pay nothing.

Much to my surprise, Adrian and David agreed, so long as AMP agreed not to disclose the contract terms and that POLISY could tell other prospects that AMP was evaluating the system. I said that would be okay so long as POLISY did not refer any prospects to AMP for comment. POLISY had not developed a contract so it was agreed that AMP legal could draw up a simple document that David and Adrian agreed to sign.

I felt that first step, although successful, had been fairly easy. Adrian and David obviously had little commercial experience and seemed eager to sign or do anything to be able to use the fact that AMP was evaluating POLISY to help them sell their product.

I thought Perkin-Elmer would be more businesslike and not so generous in their dealings with AMP. To my surprise, they agreed to my opening position that Perkin-Elmer should supply hardware, training etc. at no cost to AMP for a year, after which the computers could be returned at no cost to AMP if we decided not to proceeded with POLISY. Again, they asked if they could announce that AMP was evaluating Perkin-Elmer computers to support POLISY.

In just over a month from the first meeting at which POLISY was mooted, Mr Grace called another meeting of Ces, John Staveley and David Stubbing at which I presented my findings. In my report, I stressed that although the POLISY proposition looked cost effective and achievable, AMP had taken the strategic decision to base its computing on an IBM architecture and we should consider very, very carefully any move away from that decision.

I WAS SURPRISED at the commotion the decision caused. Brian Pollard, the AMP Account Manager for IBM, asked if he could host a lunchtime meeting to discuss our decision to evaluate POLISY. Mr Grace had told him the basis of our contract with POLISY and Perkin-Elmer.

I got a call next day from the Managing Director of the company selling PMS in Australia. He knew I was busy but wanted to discuss why we had started to evaluate POLISY and how he could make us change our mind. He suggested I go to his office after work, say 5pm.

On being ushered into his large office, I was offered a comfortable chair while he sat behind his large desk trying to look impressive. After some small talk, he went over to an impressive drinks cupboard and offered me anything I would like. I chose orange juice. He poured himself what looked like a huge whiskey. As he drank, he relaxed. It was fairly obvious he had been drinking before I got into the room.

He told me he would lose his job if AMP continued with POLISY. He had ordered larger IBM computers on the basis that AMP would be running PMS on his company's computers for the first year. Other General Insurance companies used his bureau were already considering POLISY.

He poured himself another large drink and tried hard to get me to take an alcoholic drink. I stuck to orange juice. Looking red faced and going back behind his desk, he said he was feeling very hot. He removed his tie and jacket. After making himself another large drink he stood up and unbuttoned his shirt revealing a very hairy chest and a huge gold medallion. As I watched in amazement he continued to unbutton his shirt then start to unzip his trousers.

"I'm a married woman, I've seen all that before," I said and left, slamming the door behind me.

THE EVALUATION of the POLISY system went very well. My team built the replacement system within the year and we agreed to pay for the package and the Perkin-Elmer Computers. During our year of evaluation, David and Adrian had managed to sell POLISY to most of the other large Australian General Insurance companies and were trying to break into the UK market.

Both had bought large houses in fashionable parts of Melbourne. Adrian had upgraded his sports car to an expensive foreign model.

Testing by AMP Fire and General was complete and we now had to convert the existing General Insurance systems to POLISY. To the General Insurance Company I was a hero but more and more I was being left out of meetings inside the Data Processing Division, especially those organised by IBM to discuss technology futures and new products.

My other business clients like the Sales Division and Accounts were still pleased with our services but I felt ostracised by my peers. I felt that they thought I was a traitor to IBM and if they got too near to me, whatever affliction I had would rub off.

They seemed to have no understanding that IBM computers were not the best for every application or that Perkin-Elmer computers fitted the POLISY system like a glove, and were in many respects better than IBM's current computers.

43 Management training

IN 1980 I WAS DELIGHTED to learn that AMP had appointed another female Exec. Marea Stephens was a fully qualified solicitor who took a Grade 4 position in AMP's Legal Division. Marea and I made friends immediately.

She was a tremendous support and someone from inside AMP with whom I could discuss the issues I was confronting. Most specifically, the strange attitude some people in my division seemed to have towards me, which I now felt sure was because I was a woman.

The technical press at this time was full of articles about personal computers, or PCs. There were even articles in the mainstream press. To people in the computer industry, they seemed to be toys of little use in our commercial world, but I remembered Grace Hopper's comment that one day big mainframe computers would be like dinosaurs and would be replaced by 'multitudes of minis' linked by communication lines.

From my membership of the UNSW Forum, and other links I had established with people and companies outside AMP, I was gaining good information about what was happening in computing in other Australian companies and overseas. The technology was evolving quickly.

When Phil Grace was head of the division, he saw to it that the information I had was distributed to the division's managers. I kept Ces informed, but he did not suggest the information be more widely distributed.

I decided to hold a lunchtime meeting once a month so people from the business divisions could hear about the latest developments in the world of computing. I invited the heads of the divisions and their staff. I also invited Ces and Ken Harrison but neither attended. Ken told me no one would come and that the whole idea was a waste of time.

We got companies making personal computers or business oriented software to provide demonstrations. I got Professor Cyril Brookes from UNSW to present information gleaned from the Forum and from his overseas trips. Because the attendees were from several different divisions of AMP, my senior staff and I took the opportunity to tell them what we were doing for all the areas I was responsible for.

I followed up the meetings by asking the divisional heads to fill in simple questionnaires about how they viewed the presentations and the services we provided. I was pleased to see that the meetings were very well attended and the divisional heads rated our services very highly.

I TOLD ALLAN I wanted to go away for a short holiday with just my own two children because it might be the last time I could do that. Claire was talking about leaving school, though I wanted her to stay on and go to university.

Allan wasn't happy but couldn't do anything to stop me. In August I took Stephen and Claire to Queensland. We had a wonderful holiday except that I tried to do the trip on a shoestring. I had thought I had better start conserving money just in case.

When I got back home I confronted Allan. I made sure he was well fed and a bit drunk and relaxed. I said his wife had contacted me to discuss something about Robbie and had mentioned he had electroshock treatment. There had been rumblings about the use of this treatment at Chelmsford Mental Hospital in Sydney, where it was rumoured that several people had died under treatment. The full story didn't come out until much later when there was a Royal Commission and the treatment was stopped.

Allan admitted he had been in Chelmsford and had been given the treatment. He said it had a very bad effect on him. I felt sorry for him. I realised he must have suffered in the war and the treatment had made it worse. I said we needed to get him help. He said he could get unlimited help from the medics who looked after ex soldiers. He would contact someone tomorrow. I was relieved. Perhaps everything would be okay.

IN NOVEMBER it was time for appraisals again. I decided to get my staff to appraise themselves and me. I said their appraisals of me would be confidential and anonymous. My staff were slightly disconcerted by both suggestions but soon warmed to the notion.

Without exception, they all appraised themselves much more harshly than I would have done. But their attempts gave me an insight into how they saw themselves and an opportunity to help them get the support they needed to enable them to be the best they could be. Their appraisals of me were supportive of what I was doing for them. Without exception, they all suggested I get a better spider to help me write more clearly! These two-way appraisals were later to become common practice in business.

Ces appraised me again and thanked me for another good year. He told me I had been selected to go on a live in management course for a month in February. Traditionally, AMP sent Execs to Mount Eliza in Victoria, then the pre-eminent management school in Australia, when they were due for a promotion to very senior management.

My hopes rose. Perhaps they were considering me to replace Ken Harrison who was still notionally my manager, although he rarely spoke to me. Perhaps Ken had been put in his position as a way of getting an insight into data processing before being promoted to manage a branch.

Ces brought me back to the real world by saying he had discussed the matter with Phil Grace and they had decided not to send me to Mount Eliza but to the advanced management course at Macquarie University that was only a few miles from my home on Sydney's North Shore.

He handed me the course brochure. After glancing through the outline the course seemed very similar to the Mount Eliza course so I asked why not send me to Mount Eliza. Ces said he thought it would be better because I would not be so far away from my children. I pointed out that both courses were totally live in with no home leave.

Ces said AMP had been considering the Macquarie course for a while and would like me to evaluate it for AMP. I asked if I could be given the chance to choose which course I went on and was told it was now booked in my name. Even though I subsequently reported that the Macquarie course was excellent, all the AMP Execs after me were still sent to Mount Eliza.

THE GENERAL MANAGER'S Christmas party was spectacular, as usual. Allan escorted me proudly. He loved dressing up in a dinner jacket and looked very handsome. He was now seeing a specialist regularly and taking medication. He seemed much calmer. Perhaps life would get better.

Sadly, Claire decided to leave school. She was 15. I really wanted her to go to university. She was a very bright girl but seemed to me to have got in with the wrong crowd. At least she got a good School Certificate so she could go to university later. She worked in our local Turkish restaurant for a while and loved cooking. Now she started to work in a hot bread shop, getting up each morning to catch the 4am train and leave work at midday.

It was not what I would have wished for my beautiful, brilliant daughter, but I had seen the results of parents taking decisions for their children against their wishes. It seemed to me it was best to allow children to follow their own path and to support them as far as possible in their chosen career, and when or if they changed their minds.

The break from normal work to go to the management course at Macquarie University was like a breath of fresh air. We had a good mix of people on the course: trade unionists, a man from China, a man from Africa and several very high-powered executives from Australia's top companies. There was one other woman, Celestine Michelle, who was one of IBM's Execs. I didn't find out until later that she and I were the first women to attend that course.

Celestine was in charge of IBM's PC business in Australia. As PCs were becoming more powerful, some business people were buying them and either using packaged application software, developing systems themselves, or hiring programmers to build systems for them outside data processing divisions. These systems were built without all the red tape and complex, costly procedures that had been established inside data processing divisions, which meant they were often built more quickly and at less cost.

IBM could see these 'business built' PC systems taking processing away from the big mainframe computers and so had established a Personal Computer division. They had staffed the new division with young staff, no one over the age of 35. Thus Celestine was a very young manager to be given responsibility for a division of IBM Australia.

Being from the younger set, IBM's PC people in the USA decided they could disregard IBM's antiquated rules and write their own. One rule was that all managers from one division could not travel together by air. Tragically, by ignoring that rule, the entire US PC management team died when the aircraft in which they were travelling crashed.

Days on the management course were long. We started at 6am and did not finish until after 10pm most nights. Then there was private study needed to prepare for the next day. There were many group tasks to achieve and set projects that had to be completed outside teaching time, so some nights finished very late indeed.

We slept in student quarters. They were comfortable single rooms with narrow single beds and shared bathroom facilities. Allan managed to get into my room most nights and stay till the early hours of the morning.

We found out the Chinese man was a professor from a Beijing university. He was over 70. His English was excellent. He told us many stories about life in China, including the suffering during the Cultural Revolution, which had not long finished. He never took tea or coffee but spent each break doing Tai Chi. When we were given the results of our fitness tests he far exceeded anyone in the class, having a fitness age of about 40.

44 I married a psychopath

ALLAN SAID HIS DOCTOR wanted me to accompany him on his next weekly visit to his military doctor. He turned out to be a psychiatrist. I later found out that he was considered the best military psychiatrist in the country. The visit seemed to go amicably. It was really just a chat. I said very little. Allan and his doctor seemed to have built up quite a good rapport.

The doctor asked if I would book a time to see him on my own. At my visit the next week the doctor asked how I thought Allan was going. I said I felt he had been better since he was seeing the doctor and thanked him. The doctor surprised me by leaning forward and taking my hand.

"But he isn't any better and he never will be," he said. "Allan is a psychopath!" I was taken aback.

"He can't be a psychopath," I said. "If he was he'd be locked up."

"No he wouldn't," the doctor said. "There are many psychopaths in our society. They are usually butchers or surgeons or work in abattoirs, and there are many in the military. I see them every day."

I was confused. "So how can you tell?" I said. "Allan has told me some of the things he's done in war and that must be a dreadful weight on anyone's conscience." I went on to tell him how I believed we sent men to war then rejected them when they came back damaged.

"That's not the way it is," said the doctor. "If you or I had done those things we'd feel bad about it. Allan's problem is that he loved what he did and feels no remorse. You're a young attractive woman. Leave him while you can. Things will only get worse."

I remembered Renate's words when she first met Allan. How did she know? Was there some literature on how to identify a psychopath? Renate had probably read something in one of her professional journals or had learned about psychopathic traits on a course.

But I felt I couldn't abandon Allan. I had faith that things would improve, but they didn't. Robbie had left school and started work. He had also started to show some of his father's characteristics. Allan still treated him as if he were an imbecile. The look in Robbie's eyes frightened me. He asked to live with his sister Kathie who was now married, so I let him go. He often came back to see us but I felt much safer at night with Robbie out of the house.

CLAIRE LEFT HOME, saying she didn't want to live in a madhouse. She moved in to a shared flat in Hornsby. I called in often and took some groceries. One day I got a call from Hornsby hospital to come at once because Claire had been admitted. There was an emergency.

Suspecting a traffic accident, I hurried to the hospital but when I asked for her at reception, I was surprised to find that she had been taken to the psychiatric ward. When I got there she was very drowsy as she had taken an overdose of some sort of medication.

My baby! My precious, beautiful daughter. What had I done? I could see trying to live in her own flat was a strain. The cupboard was often nearly empty as I slipped groceries into it but she was 16, and I had left home at 16. I went back home after that. Perhaps Claire would too.

The doctor told me they had got to Claire in time and pumped out her stomach but needed to find out more about her state of mind. They told me that they had sedated her and I should go home and come back the next day.

The next day Claire was not in her bed. I was told she had gone for a walk in the grounds. They told me that she couldn't get away. She was in her nightclothes and slippers and the grounds were secured.

The woman I had seen the night before, who I thought was a psychiatrist, was actually a psychologist. I didn't know the difference. We chatted. They said Claire was worried about my safety and didn't like Allan. I told them about Allan and gave them the phone number of his psychiatrist. The hospital psychiatrist said he knew Allan's man and that he was one of the best. He said he'd call him later.

After a while, they asked if I would like to take Claire back home. I said I wanted that very much but perhaps she wouldn't want to come. They said they would make it a condition of her release that she live at home. If I agreed, she could go home with me today. I said of course I would agree and signed some papers for her release.

As they sent someone to find Claire, the psychologist said, "Claire will be fine but I'm not so sure about you. I can authorise a course of six sessions with me if you like. It might help you to sort yourself out."

Me? What was wrong with me? I agreed.

Claire came home with me. She told me she had not intended to overdose but was had been very tired and had just wanted to sleep. The next day I rang Allan's psychiatrist. He'd had a call from the psychiatrist at Hornsby hospital. He said he was sorry about Claire but repeated things would only get worse, without saying exactly what would get worse. He said he thought it was time for him to suggest to Allan that he put himself in a psychiatric hospital. He said as we had private medical cover Allan could go into a very nice private hospital in Lane Cove.

My life had been turned upside down. My husband and daughter in a psychiatric hospital, and I also needed treatment. What on earth was going on? I realised that I needed to do something. Most of my friends and all the neighbours were frightened of Allan and had drifted away. I couldn't see why but he must have done something or said something without my knowledge.

I had once caught him threatening the neighbours with a gun because their dog was barking. Maybe it was over the top but I was sure he wouldn't use the gun on the dog. Now I was not so sure. I wasn't sure about anything. I was beginning to think the strain with Allan was causing me to perform badly at work and no one had told me. Was that why I was being passed over for promotion again and again?

A couple of weeks later Allan came home with a long face. He had been collecting his trailer boat from where he had taken it for a fishing holiday. On the way back, a wheel had fallen off the trailer and he had left the boat by the side of the road. When he went back the next day, the boat was gone.

He collected the insurance money and bought a bigger boat. A couple of weeks later, exactly the same thing happened. A wheel came off the trailer and he had to leave it beside the road. When he went back it was gone. I knew that losing two boats in the same way in two months looked very suspicious, but I still didn't doubt what he had said.

A few days later two policemen came to the house looking for Allan. He tried to tell me it was something to do with his work but something in his voice told me that wasn't true. Allan said it was all too much and he was going to admit himself into a psych hospital.

I later found that he had gone back to the people he had bought the boats from to get them to alter the receipt to show he paid more than he did. The insurance company checked the first loss and found he had done the same thing for that boat. This was insurance fraud. I also wondered if he had arranged for one of his criminal clients to steal the boats.

I RENEWED MY FRIENDSHIP with Renate. It was like old times. She was a great support. She was delighted to have been proved right about Allan but still worried that I had not divorced him. She said she had been worried that he had hurt Claire or approached her sexually in some way. She said she had spoken with Claire about her fears and found that they were groundless. I was relieved. I had wondered the same thing but had not had the courage to discuss it with Claire. Was I frightened about what I might find out?

I longed for things to be different. I could not bring myself to end my marriage. When he came home from hospital on the weekends, Allan tried hard to please us all and looked so vulnerable. He was scared he would be 'scheduled' and have to live the rest of his days in a psych hospital.

It all got too much. A long weekend was coming up but I had to work Monday. Renate asked us to stay with her. She suggested I ask the psych hospital to keep Allan in for the weekend. I felt bad about that, but the hospital said they were often asked to keep a patient over the weekend and they had procedures set up to do just that. I still didn't feel good

We had a lovely weekend. On Sunday Renate said I looked much less stressed. She suggested we stay another night and I should go to work straight from her house in Mosman. She would take the children to the Zoo, which was nearby, for the day and I could pick them up after work.

My neighbour was feeding our cats. I said that as I had planned to be back on Sunday night, I had only left enough food for the cats until then. Renate suggested I call the neighbour. Surely she could find something to feed them for one more night.

I rang my neighbour. She asked me if I was sitting down. She said Allan had come with a large removalist's van and taken all the furniture. I said that couldn't possibly be, he was in his hospital. She said no one dared approach Allan but they knew it was him. There was no name on the van but she had noted the registration number and, through a relative who worked for the motor registration authority, had got the address of the van owner.

This sounded very odd. I thought we must have been burgled, probably by one of Allan's criminal mates. That, too, seemed implausible because the furniture was removed in daylight. I rang the psych hospital. They assured me that Allan had been sedated for the weekend and was still in bed sound asleep, as he had been all weekend.

Renate and I drove to my house and see what was going on. We called in at Hornsby police station on the way and told them what had happened. The policeman on duty looked disbelieving. He rang Allan's psych hospital. He got the same story that Allan was still in bed and sound asleep and had been all weekend.

The policeman agreed with me that it probably was an ordinary burglary. It was now nearly 10pm. The policeman asked if there were any guns in the house. I told him Allan had several guns. Shooting was one of his hobbies and he was a very good marksman. He had won trophies. The policeman said it would be best if the police went to the house the next morning. We went back to Renate's house and slept.

IN THE MORNING Renate and I called in at the police station just before 6am. We all went round to my house. The front door was wide open. The police went in first and told Renate and me to stay well back. When they came out, they said all the furniture was gone and the house was in a real mess. There was no sign of a break-in.

We went into the house. There were obscenities scrawled all over the pale cream walls in blood. Downstairs in the lounge room, my white shag carpet was covered in shit. So much shit that I wondered where it could have all come from. I walked through the rest of the house. All the furniture had gone except in Stephen's bedroom, which was untouched. I noticed a little note on Stephen's fish tank. In Allan's handwriting it said 'I fed the fish'. I pointed it out to the police who were busy taking fingerprints and photos.

"Allan must have been here," I said. I phoned the psych hospital again. They suggested that Allan must have recognised the different medication given to him with his nightcap drink on Thursday evening. It was supposed to sedate him for the whole weekend.

They said he must have pretended to be asleep but slipped out and put a pillow in his bed making it look to the casual observer like a person. Or maybe he got another patient to sleep in his bed. When he had returned on Sunday afternoon he must have taken the tablets because they now couldn't wake him. I handed the phone to a policeman who was also told the story.

I rang AMP to tell them I wouldn't be in at work that day. I spoke to John Staveley, GM of AMP General Insurance, and told him I had been burgled but that a neighbour had the number of the van and the address of the owner. By 10am, John rang me back to say they had located all my furniture in a second hand furniture shop in the Sydney suburb of Enfield.

The police were still taking statements from neighbours and searching the garden for clues. They immediately put an order on the shop that the furniture not be moved until further notice. They were pleased the burglary had been so easily solved. They were worried they found no guns but sent a policeman to sit by Allan's bed to question him as soon as he woke up.

Renate and I tried to clean up the mess in the house. I didn't want the children to see it. I realised that the blood on the walls had come from frozen meat that had been taken from my freezer. The police found the remainder in the garden. I had no idea where all the shit had come from. As the police were saying their goodbyes, one tripped over a hand grenade in the hall. He looked horrified.

"Don't worry about that," I said. "Those are just Allan's war souvenirs. The kids play with them." I picked up the chromed hand grenade and showed him the engraving on it that showed where it had come from. “We’ve got lots of those,” I said.

The police said it was illegal and I should find all the others. I went into Stephen’s bedroom and brought down a couple of mortar shells. Again, they were chromed and dated. I said there were probably more in the loft and promised to bring them to the station when we had finished cleaning up.

The police left and neighbours came to help with the clean up. The lounge room carpet had to be thrown out. They brought us snacks and lunch and told us that Allan was mad. They had always known he was mad. Renate agreed. She told them that he was in a psych hospital and would probably be kept there for a long time.

Before I left the house I telephoned Ces. I told him that John Staveley had found my furniture but the house was a mess. I said I’d need the week off to get myself straight again. He readily agreed.

It was a long day. We got the house more or less tidy. I had found more grenades and war souvenirs and took them to Hornsby police station. The policeman on the front desk looked unimpressed. “These are someone’s war souvenirs,” he said. ”We don’t want them here.”

A voice from a back room shouted, “Is that the woman with the bombs? Clear the front office.” He appeared at a side door and ushered us into the yard at the back of the police station. There, surrounded by 2 foot high walls of sandbags, sat the chromed hand grenade the police had taken away in the morning. We were told that the bomb squad was on its way to collect and dispose of any more of the explosives we brought in. Although the detonator had been removed from the hand grenade, it was still full of explosives that could be unstable and go off at any time if dropped or mishandled.

They asked if there were any more explosives in the house. I told them that Allan had been an explosives expert and had more plastic explosives in the loft but I thought he knew what he was doing. I told them that he used explosives in the Snowy Mountains where he would let them off in a stream and catch the dead fish as they surfaced.

Renate looked incredulous. “He’s a psychopath in a psych hospital. I learned yesterday that he is a crack marksman who keeps guns at home. Today I hear he has gelignite stored in the loft. Isn’t that all dangerous?” she asked no one in particular. She turned to me. “You knew all this and still you stayed with him! What were you thinking?”

I left my front door key with the police, explained how to get into the loft, and drove with Renate to her house.

WHEN I GOT HOME the next day the neighbours told me excitedly that I had missed all the fun. About an hour after we left, a police car with a screeching siren came down the hill followed by an army truck which presumably held the bomb squad, followed by another police car with siren screaming. The neighbours all came out to see what all the fuss was about but were told to go back to their houses as there might be an explosion.

The police told me that enough plastic explosive had been found in the loft to blow up our house and those on each side. It was evidently very unstable and, had the bomb squad not taken great care, it could have exploded. I had lived in this house with an unstable madman with high explosives. I was jolted by the reality of it all. I now had to do something about my marriage.

I imagined I would get my furniture back in a few days and could return home. Meanwhile we could stay with Renate. But it was not that easy. Both Allan and the furniture shop insisted that the furniture had been sold and it was just being stored in the shop overnight. Allan produced a receipt saying he had sold the furniture to a Mrs E M Smith of Toronto for $1.

The whole seemed crazy. I looked up Mrs E M Smith of Toronto in the phone book. I had thought the name 'Smith' had been a fabrication but sure enough, there she was in the listing. I couldn't resist making a telephone call. I enquired about the delivery of some furniture from Sydney. The male voice on the line said, "Are you the police?" I assured him I wasn't, to which he replied, "Leave me alone. Everyone is ringing me about this. I wish I hadn't got involved," and slammed the phone down.

The next day, I rang my solicitor and told him I had found that E M Smith was a real person. He said I shouldn't have interfered. He said that Mrs Smith was mother of one the patients at the private psych hospital where Allan was staying. The patient was a murderer. Allan had told her that as a probation officer, he could prevent her son from going to prison by agreeing to look after him. Mrs Smith just had to buy a load of furniture from him for $1 and give him a receipt. She willingly agreed.

I realised that life was not going to be as easy as I had thought. Allan had discharged himself from the psych hospital and said he was going to live with his mother in Redfern. Now I was really worried for the safety of my children and myself. I took out a restraining order to keep him away from the children and me but realised that it probably wouldn't stop him from finding us if he wanted to. I told Claire that she should call the police if Allan came anywhere near her. I decided to keep Stephen off school for another week while we stayed with Renate.

WHEN I WENT BACK to work after the week off, I told Ces what had been going on. He was most compassionate. He said AMP would look after me and provide all the assistance I needed. Did I need money? I told him I had plenty of funds but was worried about our safety. He insisted that I have two weeks compassionate leave. I said I was much less stressed now that Allan was out of my life but he insisted, saying it was in AMP's interest as well as my own. Maybe I didn't feel stressed but I might not be able to handle difficult situations that might arise.

I began to realise what it was really like to be a top executive in a large company. Ces said AMP had arranged for me to live in an AMP executive flat in Cremorne until I could return to my home. It was right by the ferry terminus across the harbour from AMP. It was ready now. We could move in tonight if we wanted to. He gave me the keys.

He had arranged for me to put my car in the AMP car park under the building and said I should use an AMP car until things settled down. AMP security had been informed not to allow Allan into the building. Could I let them have a recent photo of Allan? Until then everyone would be stopped and checked on entering the building.

When I said that was a lot of fuss, Ces said AMP was pleased to have the opportunity to test their security systems. He said it was not widely known that a few weeks before a man with a gun had got into the General Manager's office. Security had been increased after that.

Evidently the man simply wanted to talk to the GM about his insurance claim. The GM had been trained to handle such a circumstance and had remained calm and friendly until security came to take the man away. The top executive floor now had security on the lifts and all the offices were behind bulletproof glass.

We moved into the delightful flat in Cremorne. A member from AMP Personnel whose job it was to see that visiting Execs were comfortable in their accommodation greeted us. She told me that AMP had about 12 flats they used for the purpose. She opened the kitchen cupboards and showed me she had done our first week's grocery shopping and had filled the fridge and freezer. There were even cans of Coca-Cola for Stephen and a bottle of wine for me. I asked if I could pay for the food but she insisted that AMP would pay for everything.

I thought over all the times I had thought AMP was acting stupidly but now realised that they were a very caring, compassionate company and I was very lucky to be working for such a generous employer.

I returned to work after three weeks off feeling very refreshed. It was late May. I decided that, apart from getting Claire back to live at home, more than anything I wanted my parents to visit us for Christmas. Without telling them of the traumatic experiences we had been having, I sent them money for the plane tickets.

Much to Renate's relief, at long last I had started divorce proceedings. By the end of July I was divorced.

The months moved on. We heard nothing of Allan except through numerous exchanges between his solicitor and mine. Our furniture was still in the shop in Enfield. The owner of the shop kept phoning and begging me to collect the furniture as it took up all the room in his tiny shop and he was unable to do any business.

I found out that the man who owned the shop was an ex-parolee of Allan's. I was worried that he might do something silly with our furniture. AMP assured me that the furniture was fully covered by my insurance policy so even if the shop burned down, I would be covered.

My friends rallied round. We went camping with a large group in mid winter. It was good to have friends again. At last I got frustrated and asked the courts if I could at least move the furniture to a Grace Brothers storage facility but it was six months before we were back in our own home with our undamaged furniture.

The neighbours were all very supportive when we moved back into our house. They told me to never hesitate to ask for help. I bought a big German Shepherd dog. I had been advised that it would be the best deterrent to keep Allan or any of his associates away from us.

45 Dealing with the men

DESPITE ALL THE UPHEAVALS at home, my professional life seemed to be running smoothly. We were starting to make headway by choosing and installing application packages for Accounting and Payroll on the new IBM computers.

POLISY was almost ready to go into production. Each time we thought we were ready to go the General Insurance company decided to introduce more features. I would have rather installed a plain vanilla system and got that running smoothly. I knew that once we installed the system changes would be requested but felt we needed to install the system as soon as possible.

It was appraisal time again. Again Ces gave me my appraisal. I wondered if my personal difficulties would have an effect on my promotion prospects. I didn't really care. Allan was out of my life. I felt a great lightness as if I'd escaped from some dreadful nightmare. Work was fairly easy and I was well paid.

Ces said he had had no idea that I was living under such difficult circumstances and congratulated me for not allowing my private life to affect my performance at work, which he said had again been outstanding.

He told me that he was retiring at the end of the year and Morris McLeod would be taking over as the Manager of the Data Processing Division. Oh dear, I thought. Morris was another manager who knew little about current computing technology and practice.

Morris had been one of three people to program AMP's first computer in 1958. I wasn't clear about how long he stayed in the computing field but I knew he had not chosen to move to CSA in 1970. He had been doing an administrative job for at least the last decade. Why didn't AMP appoint someone with more experience in computing?

I had now given up all thought of being appointed to the position but surely someone could be recruited from outside AMP. Someone who would understand the issues and complexities we faced.

MY MOTHER AND FATHER would be arriving soon. I wanted the house to be ready for their visit. I hadn't told them about the upheavals with Allan. I wanted to tell them face to face. I decided to go into the loft to see how the bomb squad had left it. Discarded kids toys and spare carpet were still there as I had remembered. There was also a bundle of manila folders tied together with an old cotton strap secured with a rusty buckle. They looked official. I had never seen them before. I took them into the kitchen. They were Probation and Parole files. I started to read some of the entries. I recognised the names on some of the files as Allan's clients.

The files were fascinating. One was for a prisoner in Long Bay Gaol for murder. The notes indicated he was the nephew of a senior NSW politician. The notes stated that if he paid his parole officer $10,000 and said he had found God in prison, he would get parole. The price was usually $20,000 but it had been agreed that an exception would be made because his uncle was in a position to help further.

At the time, there was a lot of discussion about the politician in the press saying he was the Mr Big of crime in NSW. All the files had notes about how to get money out of the prisoners and their families.

I rang Ken Lukes, Head of Probation and Parole. He asked me to tell him the names on some of the files. He sounded astounded. "We wondered where those files had got to," he said. 'Where are you?" I told him I was at home and had found the files in our loft.

"Don't let them out of your sight. I'll send a car round to pick them up immediately," he said. I said I could easily bring them in to work with me the next day and drop them off at his office. He said that would not be appropriate and that a car would be at my house within the hour.

Sure enough, a big black chauffer driven government car arrived soon after. The files were handed over. I heard no more. The politician whose nephew had been the subject of one of the files resigned soon afterwards.

While Mum and Dad were in Australia we went out nearly every weekend. They loved being with my group of friends and really enjoyed our visits to the Blue Mountains and to the Snowy Mountains to see the wildflowers. By the end of their stay in February, they decided they would like to live in Australia. When they left they were going to see how they could arrange their finances to allow them to emigrate.

DIVISIONAL BUDGETS were introduced at AMP. The total for the Data Processing Division for 1982 was just over $15 million, which included hardware purchases. My own area of responsibility was for just over $2 million. It did not include hardware purchases, which were all in the computer operations budget. I was surprised to see that mine was by far the largest budget for a single manager.

At first I had decided not to trim the staff I inherited when I took over the second group of business areas, but some were totally non productive and I gradually let them go and had not replaced them. I fully expected Ces to tell me, as before, that because I had reduced the number of staff reporting to me my position would be downgraded, but he didn't.

The second highest budget, at $900,000, was for Life systems. But all four business systems managers were on Grade 5. Why hadn't I been promoted beyond Grade 5 when I had the largest budget and the most staff? Also, my area was more complex because we were supporting several AMP Divisions whereas Life and Superannuation each only supported one Division. Indeed, Superannuation had been split into two groups and both the managers were Grade 5 Execs.

A new CSA man joined the team. He was tall, slim and good looking. His name was Johnathan Harrison. One of the first things Morris did when he took over the Division was to tell me that Johnathan needed a project to run and that I had to give up my Property project. Property was now running very well and I resented having it taken from me when I had sorted out a mess. But Morris insisted.

Over the next year I watched Johnathan increase the team numbers significantly and become the Golden Boy of the Division. How could that be when he was only responsible for a small part of what had been my empire? Why wasn't I treated like that?

I was very proud of the team I had built to support my business divisions. The turnover of staff in my group was very low, too. In the early 1980s, most computing professionals changed jobs every two years or so. The people in my group rarely moved outside the group.

The other groups referred to mine rather scornfully as the 'little United Nations'. I had professionals from India, Vietnam, China, Thailand, France, Germany, the Scandinavian countries, and of course the UK and Australia. We had slightly more men than women and I had a woman junior manager, Rhonda Ellis, reporting to me. The other groups had few women professionals and most were white Australians who were either born in Australia or had migrated from the UK. None had female junior managers.

I valued diversity. My group worked very well together. One of the projects generated by the UNSW Forum was to develop productivity metrics for computer development and maintenance based on statistics from the member companies in the Forum. This interested me as we had developed metrics when I worked for fpl in the UK. Metrics was a significant research interest in the UK but was very new to Australia. By the metrics developed from the 20 largest Australian enterprises that were members of the Forum, my team's productivity was very high.

I told my staff that I could not possibly have as much intelligence or experience as they had collectively so their job was to support me and keep me from looking foolish. My job was to support them and ensure they had all the resources they needed to provide the best possible service to our business divisions. The group sometimes socialised outside work. We had family picnic days with sports, usually some sort of cricket.

SHORTLY AFTER HIS APPOINTMENT Morris was taken on a six week IBM Chief Data Processing Executive world trip to be brought up to date with computing technologies in the IBM world. To our astonishment, he took Johnathan Harrison with him. This was most unusual, especially as Johnathan was a member of CSA and not AMP. IBM lent Johnathan an IBM PC for the trip, one of the first of IBM's portables, but it was large and heavy so called by the industry a 'luggable' computer rather than a portable.

After they returned Johnathan gave many talks about their visits. Morris sat in on the talks, often falling asleep. Johnathan was careful to say that Morris had done most of the work on their trip. On one occasion Morris woke up with a start, apologised for falling asleep and said, "Johnathan said I often asked the most intelligent questions while I was asleep."

Was this a new way of working with IBM? They seemed to have Morris eating out of their hands. I had supported the move back to IBM because I thought IBM would be strong enough to stop AMP from doing silly things, even though their technologies were not as good as those of their competitors. But it now it looked as if IBM was running AMP just as CSA had done.

Talking to other big companies, especially those in the Forum, it seemed this was the pattern in many of them, especially if they had IBM computers. The Data Processing Manager had little understanding of computing but followed IBM's directions.

IBM now had nearly 90% of the world market in mainframes. There was little competition except from the Japanese who were building IBM clones for a lower price, but the Japanese didn't offer the same level of support services offered by IBM. The industry joked about 'Snow White and the Seven Dwarves' or 'IBM and the BUNCH'. BUNCH stood for Burroughs, Univac, NCR, Control Data and Honeywell.

There were other computer companies but they were seen as specialists and no competition for IBM. DEC was seen as a specialist in manufacturing, process control and computer aided design (CAD). Cray provided specialist supercomputers largely for research. Perkin-Elmer and Hewlett Packard specialised in process control computers. Many new suppliers were entering the market, but they were very small. PCs were still seen largely as toys.

Even though many of IBM's competitors' products were technologically superior, IBM was judged by many to be the only 'safe' company making computers for large commercial enterprises and government. The saying in the industry was that no one ever got fired for choosing IBM.

Morris said he had been told that POLISY had been purchased because it would be easy and quick to develop but it was taking far too long. I told him that David Stubing kept delaying the start because he kept finding new functions to add to the system, while I preferred to install a plain vanilla system and add to it later. I didn't point out that most of the new IBM systems at AMP like Life and Superannuation were way over budget and much later than first forecast, and were not nearly as complex as the General Insurance System, which was AMP's first real time system.

Morris said he had decided that I should concentrate on getting POLISY installed and I would have all my other systems given to other people. I went cold. I felt I was being 'punished'? I suspected this was payback from IBM for supporting the purchase of Perkin-Elmer systems that took at least two thirds of AMP's total compute load away from IBM.

Morris said I would no longer report to Ken Harrison but would report directly to him because he wanted to keep a close watch on what I was doing. I was outraged. What on earth did he think he could do by watching what I was doing? I took a deep breath and smiled sweetly.

I asked if I was being demoted. Morris said quite the opposite. Senior management believed that development on the Perkin-Elmer was much more difficult than working on IBM systems with all the support IBM gave. So IBM was behind this! He said I would retain my Grade 5 Exec position and later would probably be promoted. I could almost hear the addition of 'so long as you make it fail and get General Insurance back to IBM'. Well if that was the game, I'd make it work so well it would never fail.

DAVID STUBING became even more obnoxious. He seemed to think that he was now my manager and that he could tell me what to do. He was still a Grade 4 Exec working in a different division. He knew that I reported to Morris but really wanted the General Insurance company to take over its own computing. I thought maybe that would happen but realised that it probably wouldn't as the real game was to get the General Insurance systems back under IBM control.

A competition was held to find a name for the new General Insurance system. It was decided to call it FIREMAN. My load was considerably lightened. I had a good team working on FIREMAN so I felt I could now take things more easily. The only battles were with David Stubing, who kept insisting on larger and more extensive changes to FIREMAN. I tried drawing analogies such as likening changes to FIREMAN to operating on a patient. I stressed that operating on the brain and the heart at the same time could kill the patient. David taunted me by saying if I was as good as I thought I was I would be able to do anything he asked.

We listed all changes requested and estimated each individually in terms of cost, effort and elapsed time. The change requests came so thick and fast that one of my senior staff was occupied full time just on estimating. Looking at the costs of changes implemented, I reckoned that we had rebuilt the system three times. Whenever I pointed this out to David Stubing I was told to mind my own business.

Weekly meetings about which changes should be done during the next week were always unpleasant. They nearly always ended on a sour note because David Stubing felt he had not got things all his own way, when my team insisted on only building in the changes we considered would not unduly destabilise the system.

One of the programmers on my staff, Dave Nichols, seemed able to manage David Stubing's expectations quite well. Dave would go and speak to David Stubing and as if by magic we would get a cohesive group of changes which were exactly what we had suggested instead of the hotchpotch of disparate changes which could cause extensive and destabilising change on all parts of the system.

Dave was a contractor. He was often drunk and did very little work. By my usual standards I would have terminated his contract, but his ability to pour oil on troubled waters made him worth his weight in gold. David Stubing asked that Dave be promoted to Project Manager but Morris, who had often caught Dave drunk at work, would not hear of it. I had to keep defending Dave's presence on my team to the teetotal Morris.

David Stubing was really abrasive. He lectured my team on computing. He would tell us of innovations he had read about in the newspaper or heard about from his mates at the golf club then ask why we weren't using those on FIREMAN. Told the cost of a particularly large change he would tell us that his son, who now had a PC, could build the whole of FIREMAN in a week on that PC. Such comments only made my team ask me how he kept his job and no one now wondered how he had got the nickname Stupid.

Contrary to usual executive practice at AMP, unless I had a confidential meeting I kept my office door open. One day I was on the phone when David Stubing barged into my office. Seeing I was on the phone, he turned on his heel and shouted at my secretary, "When that woman gets off the phone, tell her to come to my office."

I quickly put down the phone and called after his retreating form, "David, you wanted to see me?" I ushered him into my office and shut the door. I stood very close to him making him retreat until his back was against the closed door. "If you ever try that again, I'll knee you in the balls and smile while I do it" I said. I opened the door and smiling sweetly said, "Goodbye." He looked flustered but never again called me 'that woman'.

Morris kept giving me tips about how to gain respect as a manager. One day it was that if I keep my office door open to everybody I wouldn't be respected as a manager. On another occasion he told me that if I let my staff to call me by my first name, I wouldn't have their respect.

This last comment amused me. All Morris's six direct reports called him by his surname yet the staff didn't respect him. Behind his back, they thought he was a bumbling clown. I noticed that although all my staff called me by my first name, when they spoke about me to people outside our team, they always referred to me as Mrs Moffatt.

46 Equal opportunity

I WAS CALLED TO NSW Police Headquarters. Two detectives introduced themselves and said they were working on an investigation into Probation and Parole. They said they wanted to ask me some questions about Allan Moffatt but could not force me to answer because I was his wife. They did not seem to know we were now divorced. They asked me if anything strange had happened while I was living with Allan.

They knew about Allan's psychological problems and the explosives found in the house and that he had had my furniture removed. First they asked if I could tell them anything more about the explosives. Where had they come from? Had I ever seen them used? I told them that Allan had used them to kill fish in the Snowy Mountains. They said they were both trout fishermen and that was a crime, but not the sort of thing they were interested in for this enquiry.

I mentioned the brown Jensen and the sewn up rip in the back of the passenger seat. They looked more interested. When did this happen? Did I know the car registration number? Did I know which prisoner Allan bought the car from? Did I know where the car was sold?

All I could remember about the prisoner was that his solicitor was called Phil Murphy. They asked me how I knew. I said I had a manager on my staff called Phil Murphy and that was the name on the receipt for $3000 Allan had shown me. After an animated conversation they decided the solicitor must have been Chris Murphy, who was well known for representing many prominent criminals, so that was not a way of identifying the prisoner.

I mentioned that Allan had collected the car from the police compound in Gosford. They phoned Gosford. The Jensen was easy to identify, it was the only one they had ever had. That gave the investigators the name of the prisoner and the registration number of the car.

Next they asked the Gosford car pound if the car was car damaged in any way. In particular, had the passenger seat been repaired? Evidently the car was perfect when it had left Gosford. There was no repaired tear in the seat.

One of the investigators left the room. When he returned he said that a car dealer on Parramatta Road now owned the car. They phoned the dealer to ask where the car was. He said he drove it to work each day, it was in his car lot. They told him the car was now impounded and must not be moved. The police would be round to get it.

They thanked me for my information and said they would call me when they had any information or needed to question me further.

A few days later they told me the car had belonged to a heroin dealer. They found traces of heroin inside the car seat. They surmised that Allan had picked the car up and on the trip from Gosford to my house the heroin had been removed and the car seat repaired. They had suspected for a long time that Allan had been supplying heroin to prisoners in Long Bay. I was once again astounded that I had lived with this man for more than two years and not really known him at all.

IN NOVEMBER I was walking in the Royal Botanic Gardens in my lunch break when I saw a man sitting near Mrs Macquarie's Chair weeping. He looked a little older than me, with brown hair that was obviously dyed, and wore a peculiar suit that was a cross between workman's overalls and a pilot's jumpsuit. I asked if he needed help.

He told me his wife had just left him. He was an academic in engineering at the University of Technology Sydney .We chatted a while and found that we lived only a few miles apart. We exchanged telephone numbers and he promised to phone. His name was Walter.

The land between our houses was steep, dense bush. One Sunday we pushed our way through the bush and walked from my house to his. He seemed pleasant enough but I wasn't sure I wanted to get involved with anyone. Certainly I would take Renate's advice before I went any further.

I invited Renate and her daughter Clair for Christmas lunch. My Claire came too with her new boyfriend John. Walter seemed to have nowhere to go for Christmas lunch so I invited him too.

I was busy cooking in my huge kitchen surrounded by the family. Renate and Walter were deep in conversation downstairs in the lounge room. I called them for lunch but they didn't answer. When I went to get them they were sitting very close together on the lounge speaking in very animated German. They both looked up as if they were not expecting to be interrupted.

Excitedly, they told me they had both been Jewish refugees from Germany and had been sent to England just before the outbreak of World War II on the same Kindertransport scheme run by the Quakers. They had both been diagnosed with suspected tuberculosis and had both been sent to the same hospital on the border of England and Wales. They had both been in the same ward. When Renate had been in the ward it was a girls' ward. Two weeks later when Walter was in the same ward it was the boys' ward.

Later in the day Renate told me Walter would make a very suitable husband. I told her that the relationship was nowhere near that stage. She told me Walter had told her it soon would be.

Meanwhile Allan Moffatt applied for half my property and part of my income as maintenance, stating that he could now not work at all and that he had paid considerable sums of money towards my house. His claims were not substantiated but because he was getting Legal Aid he could call as many court hearings as he chose, but fortunately I did not have to attend them. Apart from quite large solicitor's fees; the matter was settled to my satisfaction. Allan got only a very small payment.

Claire was now working for a local French patisserie. She asked if she could come back home to live. I was delighted. She told me that she and John intended to marry in the next year so he moved in too. Later in the year Walter moved in. We decided to sell both our houses and buy something we chose together but after looking for a while, we decided to sell my house and extend Walter's. We would build a flat under the house for Claire and John.

1983 WAS DEDICATED to training General Insurance staff ready for the implementation of FIREMAN later that year. We did several dress rehearsals of the conversion from the IBM systems that were over 20 years old. It had been a miracle that we were able to keep the old systems fully functional and up to date with business and government changes while building the new system.

NCR had now perfected the cash receipting hardware that I had initially seen in prototype when I was in the USA in 1978. Eric Putt, who had then been AMP's Chief Accountant, had now replaced the retired Phil Grace as Manager Corporate Services and was now Morris McLeod's manager. Anstey Lindsay had been appointed Chief Accountant. AMP now decided to buy the new NCR systems to process all the company's income, some $10 million a day.

Anstey Lindsay asked Morris to assign my team to build the new cash receipt system based on NCR computers. There was little Morris could do but agree. The systems were successfully built, tested and installed in six months. IBM did not make specialist income accounting systems and so lost another very important part of AMP's business.

The FIREMAN system went live on 5 April 1983. It was an instant success and AMP's first real time system. I got congratulations all round but was told that because there would be lots of changes I would remain Data Processing Manager of the General Insurance Systems division for another year. The

General Insurance people tried again to move Data Processing into their division but were not successful.

I didn't really care. It was now nearly ten years since we had came to Australia. During that time I had worked very hard. I felt I deserved a lighter load at work. Anyway, I had Claire's wedding and a house move to organise. My parents and Alan Leach's parents would be coming over for Claire's wedding. It was to be on 4 August, which was also my parent's 50th wedding anniversary.

1984 BROUGHT EQUAL OPPORTUNITY for women legislation into operation in Australia. To redress the inequality of women in the workplace, companies with over 500 staff had to report the proportion of women in senior positions and show that they were being paid equally with men for equal work. If they did not meet the recommended criteria, they would be 'named and shamed' in a report for Parliament. Penalties were to be introduced at a later date. AMP was proud that it now had three women Execs out of 120, but that was far below the Government's expectations.

Interviews for executive positions in the Australian Government had to include at least one 'outsider' and one woman on interviewing committees. Those appointed had to be earning more than the salary offered for the position under review. Although not compulsory, this was also adopted by many large non-government enterprises. Because I fitted all three criteria, I was often loaned by AMP to sit on interviewing panels.

One episode involved the appointment of the Data Processing Manager for the Australian Broadcasting Corporation. It had been decided that every five years, all positions in the ABC would have to be recontested. The positions would be open to existing staff and applicants from outside the ABC. The interviewing panel was the Director of Technical Services at the ABC and the Personnel Director, both of whom were men, and me.

The first candidate was the existing Data Processing Manager. He spent his half hour telling us just exactly what he thought of a system that made him reapply for his existing job. He was obviously very angry and used very crude language to describe ABC management.

When he left the room, the other two members of the panel asked me what I thought. I told them I thought his behaviour and attitude was inappropriate but we should not use that to judge his competence for the job. As he had been in the job for five years they would have to make a judgement based on performance.

The second candidate was the deputy Data Processing Manager. He spent his time telling us what a fuckwit his manager — the man we had just interviewed — was and that he should be given the job. When the interview ended I was asked to give an opinion. I said it was the same as for the manager we had interviewed first. I could not judge.

Eight other candidates from outside the ABC were presented. We rated each against the job description and required attributes. After two days of interviewing we had to make a choice. There was much discussion. I noticed the two men on the panel never made comments about Jane Busby, who I believed met all criteria and was by far the most appropriate candidate. She was also the only woman.

I said we should discuss Jane. The two men stated firmly that Jane could not do the job. I asked why. I was told that Jane wouldn't be capable of handling ABC politics. I said that I had seen no mention of ability to handle ABC politics in the job description of required attributes. The selection process took another whole day. By the end of the day, the panel reluctantly agreed that Jane was the best candidate.

Many years later, I checked on Jane's progress with the ABC. I was told that she was an excellent manager and had changed the departmental character so much that politics rarely interrupted their work. Productivity and quality had increased tremendously. Jane had built a very diverse team including several women in senior positions.

I am certain that had I not been on the selection committee, Jane would never have been considered as an appropriate candidate.

Shortly after the interviews, AMP received a cheque for $1200 from the ABC made payable to me. I took it to Morris. I hadn't realised companies paid for my services. To my surprise, Morris said, "I know your daughter is getting married soon. Put the money towards the wedding. You deserve it."

THE AUSTRALIAN Law Reform Commission had decided to adopt the OECD Privacy Principles, so its work was coming to the end. The International Standards Organisation had published the initial reference model for Open Systems Interconnection, so I decided that after many years of reading standards documents, I could now leave that committee.

I had more time to get involved with the Australian Computer Society. I was elected to the NSW Branch Executive in charge of organising branch meetings. I realised there was real need to help the general public, especially women, to understand more about computers.

There was much discussion about introducing PCs into schools. I was appointed to represent Australian Business on the 20 person Government Committee established to set policy in the area. Again, AMP was delighted that one of its Executives was appointed to such a high profile committee.

The other members of the committee were all government employees, mainly bureaucrats working in the education area. The first task of the committee was to draw up a list of reasons that computers should be introduced into schools. As the only outsider, I listened while reasons were given and debated. It was nearly lunchtime and we had agreed 19 items. I caught the Chairman's eye and suggested that one reason could be 'to fit our students for work after school'. Chaos broke out. Committee members pontificated that it was obvious I was not an educationalist. Education was not to fit a student for work. It was an end in itself.

The Chairman glanced at his watch and stated as it was nearly lunchtime and I had heard the feelings of the meeting, I might like to withdraw my suggestion. I said I would not. I represented business and I am sure that was what business wanted. I asked the Chairman to take a vote. He said I would have to move a motion.

Fortunately, I had just joined Toastmasters and had been taught formal meeting procedure. I put the motion. The Chairman asked for someone to speak in opposition. The previously vocal delegates were silent. The Chairman asked if anyone would like to discuss the matter further. No takers. He said he would then put the matter to a vote. The motion was carried by one vote.

Although in the initial published list of reasons for Computers in Schools my item was at the very bottom, in the years to follow, I noticed that my item worked its way to the top of the list.

47 Extracurricular activities

THE UNIVERSITY OF NSW School of Information Systems, that under Professor Cyril Brookes had been running the successful Information Technology Forums for the top 20 companies, decided to organise an International Conference in April and bring top speakers from all round the world to Australia.

Cyril Brookes was to chair the whole event and Professor Ross Jeffrey was to chair the Papers committee. They asked me to chair the organising committee. The whole conference was to be held under the auspices of the prestigious International Federation of Information Processing (IFIP) Technical Committee Number 8, responsible for standards for Information Systems. Cyril was Australia's representative on that committee.

The resulting JISIS (Joint International Symposium in Information Systems) Conference was a great success. We brought top speakers from round the world, many of whom I had met in my previous 25 years in the industry and others that I had simply read about. I organised tours and dinners for speakers, who all told us it was the best conference they had ever attended and that we should organise another one for next year.

People thought we must have put enormous effort into organising the event, but we had only had the three committees. Ross and I were on Cyril's committee, Cyril and I were on Ross's committee and Ross and Cyril were on my committee. We had great fun organising it. It was oversubscribed and made $30,000 profit for the Australian Computer Society, even though we paid travel and living allowances for many of the speakers.

I WAS BEGINNING to think it might be time to leave AMP. It seemed I would never get any further in my career. AMP had been very good to me, but I had also worked hard and made a significant contribution. What did I want to do next?

I thought I would like to run a software house with flexible work options like F International. I wrote to Steve Shirley suggesting I establish a branch of FI in Australia. She was not interested.

The very intelligent Australian Computer Society office manager, Ann Reynolds, had worked with us on JISIS. She was a superb administrator. I told her I was thinking of setting up a software company and asked if she would like to join me. She jumped at the chance.

Meg Alexander was also interested. She had been NSW Branch Chair of the ACS and had excellent marketing skills. She was currently working for Computer Power, one of Australia's leading software houses.

Pam Birkett, who I had met at a Computers in Schools meeting, seemed to me to understand how Australian Government worked. I thought she would be an asset in helping us to get access to some of the NSW Government funding currently on offer for start-up Information Technology companies. Pam, Ann, Meg and I met once a week over dinner after work to discuss strategy and develop a proposal for funding.

As a separate initiative I realised that the senior teachers I was meeting through the Computers in Schools initiative seemed to have little understanding of computers. Many were terrified that school children understood more about computers than they did. I organised a one day seminar to increase their understanding. Many of these women were in their 40s or 50s, and were now head teachers in schools.

I asked several PC suppliers if they would lend us the PCs and the people to demonstrate them. Given the audience and the tremendous market there would be for computers in schools, they all supported me. The seminar was a great success, some of the attendees even used the PCs that were loaned to us. AMP was delighted to be involved in the initiative.

MY MUM AND DAD came to Australia for Claire's wedding. They stayed three months. Claire and John decided that instead of moving into the flat Walter and I were building for them, they would move in with John's mother who was living by herself. Stephen was delighted because he would now be able to live in the flat himself. He was 16.

Alan Leach's Mum and Dad came from the UK for the wedding. Claire asked me if I would mind if she asked her Dad to give her away. I said of course I didn't mind. It was her day and she should do what she wanted.

I had encouraged the children to keep in touch with their Dad. After all he would always be their father. Nothing could change that. I sent him photos and copies of their school reports fairly regularly but I knew his parents and his aunts and uncles still thought he had done the wrong thing by leaving me to bring up the children, no matter how often I told them that our split had been a mutual decision. Alan made only a flying visit to Australia for the wedding.

My parents found out that Alan was going to give Claire away only the day before the wedding. Both they and his parents declared that they would not attend the wedding if he came. My mother said my father was expecting to give Claire away and had bought a suit the same as John's and the groomsmen's. I wondered why he had bought a pink shirt and light beige suit!

I reminded them it was Claire's day and she wanted Alan to give her away. The storm blew over but Alan was given a frosty reception. On the morning of her wedding, 19 year old Claire told her grandparents that she was going to be married for 50 years like they were.

After the service, at which the vicar also blessed my parent's wedding of 50 years, Alan congratulated me on bringing up such wonderful children. He had not seen them for over ten years. I reminded him that they were his children too but he said he never felt that.

I sold my house and moved into Walter's house. We arranged our finances such that we each owned a half share of the house and had no mortgage. I really did not want to get married again. Walter had been married four times before. I had just got out of a disastrous relationship. I didn't want to risk marriage again but neither did I want legal problems if it didn't work out. I got a very good lawyer to draw up a contract on our arrangement in the event we did want to split again. Walter agreed.

IN 1985, ALTHOUGH I was still notionally Data Processing Manager for AMP General Insurance, my workload seemed lighter. I was appointed Chairman of the NSW Software Industry Association. AMP seemed happy for me to spend most of my time on outside activities. At first I thought this was strange but learned that AMP saw this as part of their good corporate citizen obligations and felt it was a good opportunity to keep their name in front of their policyholders.

I had always been terrified of public speaking and had avoided it as much as possible. Now I needed to speak in public often. AMP sent me on a public speaking course and gradually I trained the butterflies in my tummy to fly in formation. The prestigious positions I had involved speaking with all levels of government. I was often invited to represent the IT industry and the computing profession at important public events and dinners.

To mark the close of the first year of equal opportunity for women, AMP decided to hold a seminar for their senior women. We now had five women Execs and five other senior women managers. The ten of us were each invited to bring along a male colleague. The day was to be facilitated by an outside consultant, one of the many women who had become instant experts in helping companies treat women more equally.

I decided to bring Ken Harrison, who had been my manager for several years. I felt he needed to understand how to manage women. When he had been my manager, he had never even acknowledged that I was on his staff.

The day consisted of lots of roleplay and advice to the men on what women want. The women were coached to learn how to stroke men's egos while standing up for their rights and getting what they wanted in the workplace.

At the end of the day we were put in two lines, sitting on chairs, the men on one side the women on the other, knees touching. We were asked to each speak in turn about what we had learned from the day. Most people gave rather bland and non-committal replies but when it was Ken Harrison's turn he was very aggressive.

He sneered. "Look at you lot. Trying to play managers. Well it doesn't work for me. At least my wife is female. She sits by the pool getting brown or plays tennis most days. She is there for me looking beautiful when I get home from work and when it's time for bed she is ready for sex."

There was a stunned silence. Rhonda Starkey, one of the senior personnel managers, looked up and down the row of women and said, "Ooh, who brought him girls?" The meeting ended in laughter. Ken slunk out of the room with his tail between his legs. I think he realised he had gone too far.

THE NEXT YEAR would be my tenth year at AMP. I was due three months paid long service leave in addition to my four week annual holiday. Walter wanted to visit his many relatives in USA and I wanted to take my long dreamed of trip to South America.

We planned to take four months to travel round the world, including England to visit Walter's mother and brother and my parents and other relatives, plus in-laws from my first marriage and friends.

At the end of the year, Stephen decided to postpone university for a year and look for a job in accounting. It was traditional for AMP Exec's children to be given a job at AMP. Stephen applied and was given an interview. I coached him on how to conduct himself.

After the interview he came to my office, excited he now had a job. He told me the interview had been nothing like my description. The interviewer had just wanted to discuss the football, then told Stephen he had a job and that it would mean he could come to work by car with me. Stephen said he had told the interviewer that wouldn't last long as I was planning to leave AMP to set up my own software company. I was aghast that he'd let the cat out of the bag.

A few days later Morris called me in. I thought this was it and news of my plans had got back to him after Stephen's indiscretion. But he said nothing and just reminded me my long service leave was due. He said he had problems getting his staff to take long service. I told him I had no problem and that Walter and I would take a four month holiday starting in April 1986.

Morris congratulated me on completing the FIREMAN project. It had now been running successfully for over a year. He said he was beginning to appreciate the difficult task I had developing what was still AMP's only real-time system on a platform where the manufacturer provided little support for commercial development. The teams developing Life and Super-annuation still had not completed their projects and they were developing on IBM's latest computers with all of IBM's vast resources at their disposal.

I didn't argue. I didn't tell him that Perkin-Elmer computers were far superior to current IBM computers for developing real time systems, which was why POLISY was being adopted by many General Insurance companies all over the world. I did tell him Perkin-Elmer had given us great support. He didn't believe me. He was now thoroughly brainwashed by IBM, as most Australian data processing managers were.

He told me that from the beginning of 1986 I would no longer be in charge of data processing for AMP General Insurance. AMP had decided to appoint a technology futurist. The job was mine if I would like it. Initially, the position would report to Morris as computing and communications technology futures seemed to be the most important currently. Later the role might extend to other technologies.

The job would be to find out what was happening in research establishments and universities all round the world and how these developments would affect future products and provide advice on the way technology was developing such that AMP would not cut itself off from future opportunities.

Johnathan Harrison had transferred from CSA to AMP, where he was in charge of technology strategy for the next five years. My brief would be to look beyond that period. My first task would be to write a management report on Fifth Generation computing and how AMP could benefit from it. It sounded like an exciting job. Perhaps it was a reward for all my hard work.

The newspapers and technical journals were full of articles on the amount of money being ploughed into Fifth Generation computing. There were multi million dollar projects in USA, Europe, Britain and Japan. Fifth Generation Computing would be based on the knowledge industry and Artificial Intelligence but there were few details of exactly how this would help business.

AT THE END OF THE YEAR Meg Alexander said she had met a multi-millionaire at a Christmas party. She had told him about our software company and he had agreed to fund it. There would be no limit to the funding. He just wanted an equal share with the four of us. She would arrange a meeting.

I liked Meg's friend Peter when I met him. He was charm personified. A tall handsome eastern European, he had come to Australia as a refugee with nothing, made good in the technology business and now drove a dark green Bentley. It was fairly obvious that he and Meg were more than just friends. Meg said it would make no difference to our company.

But then she started saying things like 'Peter and I have decided' or 'Peter said we must do this'. I started to feel uncomfortable. I told Meg I wanted time to think. I was going overseas for four months and would make a decision when I came back.

I had been elected Chair of the NSW Branch of the ACS for 1986 and 1987. Most computer companies, including IBM, sent letters of congratulation on my appointment. NSW was by far the biggest ACS branch in Australia and most computer companies and large computer installations were based in NSW. Chairing the ACS's largest branch was a position of some influence with government. 1986 was going to be a busy year.

In preparation for Professor John Bennett's retirement from the University of Sydney at the end of 1986, and to ensure John left an enduring legacy in his name, a group of computer professionals had founded the Research Foundation for Information Technology at the University.

I was appointed Chair of the Research Proposals Evaluation Committee at the University. We were responsible for receiving proposals from the academics and deciding which were worthy of funding. These would be sent to the main committee to decide how research funds would be distributed.

Following publicity about my appointment as AMP technology futurist, hardware vendors and universities were eager to show me their latest products and research and tell me what they imagined the future would be. DEC was pioneering Artificial Intelligence in Australia. Some of the universities were pioneering robotics, and hoped that AMP would fund some of their research.

I had heard about the amazing innovations at Xerox PARC (Palo Alto Research Center) in the USA. Apple and Microsoft had both based their Graphical User Interfaces (GUIs) on the work pioneered at Xerox PARC. I could see that would be the way of the future and had heard that Xerox had developed some interesting applications.

Xerox's Australian head office was on the Pacific Highway in Gordon. It was on my way home from work. I set up a meeting for 3pm on a Friday so that maybe I could beat the Friday traffic going north for the weekend and get home a little early.

After discussing some of the splendid screen based graphics Xerox had developed, and some of their advanced printing facilities which they thought might be useful for developing marketing material, they showed me a system they had designed for the US Government to track 'spooks and crooks'. They had a dataset online with the details of households all over the world.

From an image of the globe I could zero in on any city and get statistics on population size and make-up, income, crime, employment, etc., at almost any level down to a specific street. I could get city plans too for any city in the world including the names of buildings and the companies located in them. I could get statistics at an individual household level, although not the names of people in the house. But I was sure there would be a link to other databases which would provide this information.

I was having fun looking up places we were going to on our long trip. I noticed it was dark outside and I remarked we would get storms for the weekend. The Xerox man helping me use the application asked why I thought we would get storms. I replied because it was getting dark outside. He told me that was because it was 8pm! I had been so fascinated with the application that I had lost all track of the time.

FIFTH GENERATION technology was supposed to draw together all the disparate technologies that had been developed in parallel in the past and, by synergy, produce a new, better type of computer system more like human intelligence which would quickly surpass human capabilities.

The Japanese Ministry of International Trade and Industry (MITI) was the first to announce a Fifth Generation project in 1981. It involved Japan's eight top technology companies working collaboratively rather than competitively. To that time Japan had largely been a follower of technology, with Japanese companies copying products developed in the West and selling them at a lower cost. In 1982 Japan established ICOT, the Institute of New Generation Computing Technology, to run the Fifth Generation project. The initial budget was US$700 million.

In the USA most IT research projects were being run by the military, many through DARPA, the Defense Advanced Research Project Agency. Many individual computer companies also had large research budgets. IBM alone had a 1984 research budget of US$4.5 billion, and Bell Labs US$2 billion.

As a direct response to the Japanese Fifth Generation project, Britain started the Alvey Project. In the 1960s and early 1970s the UK computer industry was well ahead of Japan and the USA, but this advantage had been whittled away by 1980.

Europe's answer to the Japanese Fifth Generation project was called ESPRIT (European Strategic Program on Research in Information Technology). Funding for the initial pilot phase was US$20 million.

Iann Barron and Philip Hughes were both members of the UK Alvey management Committee. I had worked with Iann at CTL and knew Philip through the UK Real Time Club. I proposed to contact them in the UK.

Walter's cousin Arno was head of Bell Labs in New Jersey so I thought I could discuss the Fifth Generation project with him while we stayed with him and his wife, Ann when we were in the USA.

The real challenge was to get into ICOT in Japan. I wrote stating I was the futurist at AMP and I was researching the Fifth Generation project. I said I was intending to travel to Japan and asked for a visit to ICOT. I gave a brief outline of my career, plus information about AMP. I added I was Chair of the NSW Branch of the ACS and would also like to gather information on their behalf. My request was politely turned down.

I contacted colleagues and found that it was almost impossible to get into ICOT. I spoke to another AMP Exec about my trip and the fact that I really wanted to get into ICOT. He suggested I contact a neighbour of his who worked for JETRO (Japanese External Trade Organisation) in Sydney. When I visited him, the JETRO official looked at the copies of letters I had sent to ICOT and their refusals.

He said there was one attribute I had not listed, and he thought that he could arrange a visit. He said I should contact him again in 24 hours. True to his promise, when I contacted JETRO the next day, my visit had been approved. I asked what the extra attribute I had not included was.

I was told I had not mentioned I was female. Dr Fuchi, head of ICOT, liked women.

48 The Fifth Generation

IN APRIL 1986 we set off on our four month trip. We had organised it very well. In San Francisco we stayed with Tony and Kathy Brown, who had helped AMP convert the Univac Systems to IBM. Walter wanted to make some visits to pursue his research interest into Urban Traffic Systems. In San Francisco he had arranged a tour of the BART, the Bay Area Rapid Transport system. That night at dinner he was remarkably quiet about his visit to BART.

When I asked what he had learned he said it was interesting that the Chief Engineer, who had been his guide, was black. He had a PhD but was black! We cracked up. The only thing Walter and I ever argued about was his strong feeling that black people were an inferior race.

We hired a car and drove to Los Angeles to stay with Walter's friend Don, an ex naval commander. He was a member of the America's Cup organising committee for the 1987 race being organised by the San Diego Yacht club.

Australia had won the Cup in 1983, breaking the 132 year record that had been held by the USA since they took the cup from the UK. The 1985 race was won by the San Diego Yacht Club. We teased Don by saying that if the Aussies won the cup back, we would turn it into a hub cap. He thought we were serious and got very worried. Don took us onto the big US Navy base in San Diego. He had a badge on his car and it was interesting to see the naval people jump to attention and salute as his car passed.

FROM LOS ANGELES we flew to Lima in Peru. We took a train up the highest railway journey in the world that went over the Andes to 17,000 feet. Fortunately some locals on the train gave us coca leaves to chew so we were not too affected by altitude sickness.

On reaching Huncuayo, the little town at the top of the Andes, our hotel suite, at the best hotel in town, cost US$10 for the night. Our dinner, five courses plus wine, cost US$2 each. Walter ate guinea pig, I had trout. The trip, in a very luxurious first class carriage complete with green velvet upholstered seats and fine wood carving, took eight hours each way and cost us US$8 each return.

It was the time of the uprising of the Shining Path guerrillas in Peru. There was a curfew in Lima after 8pm and the night resounded with gunshots. The beauty of the Andes was in sharp contrast to the squalor of people living in cardboard boxes by the side of the railway. We visited many historic places in Lima including the fabulous Gold Museum.

After Lima, we took a plane to Cusco to see more Inca remains and take the train trip to Machu Picchu. We stayed the night in the hotel right on the ruins on the night of the full moon when there was a total eclipse. An American TV team was there to film the eclipse over Machu Picchu. We watched the eclipse sitting on the top of the altar stone, the highest part of the complex. It was very beautiful but very spooky.

After Peru, we visited Bolivia and travelled by boat on lake Titicaca to the sacred island where the Inca were supposed to have emerged from the lake. We saw people living on islands made of floating rushes and the ancient rush boats on which Thor Heyerdahl based his boat for the Kon-Tiki voyage. In La Paz, every other person on the street seemed to be selling coca. That is the leaf from which cocaine is made and which the Bolivians chew to aid stamina and ward off altitude sickness. During our four day stay, the banks all closed while the currency was devalued 30%.

At 12,000 feet above sea level, La Paz has the world's highest airport. We took a small plane across what was left of the Amazon jungle to Rio de Janeiro.

The headlines on the newspapers being read by our fellow passengers screamed in large black headlines that there had been a nuclear disaster and the world was doomed. We couldn't read any more of the Spanish or Portuguese text but were eager to find out what had happened. When we got the English newspapers the next day we learned that there had been a nuclear accident at Chernobyl in Russia.

FROM RIO WE WENT to Iguazu Falls. The main waterfall is wider than Niagara and deeper than Victoria Falls. To get to it we walked for about a mile through the jungle past over 70 smaller individual falls. The jungle shed a greenish glow over everything and the air was filled with huge bright blue butterflies. The noise was deafening. It was spectacular.

We flew via Sao Paulo to Brasilia, the very modern capital of Brazil, where we had dinner with the Australian Ambassador. He lived in a house that was surrounded by a very high wall with barbed wire and broken glass on top in an up market suburb of Brasilia. We asked why all the security. From what we had seen so far, Brasilia was a sparkling clean, very modern city.

The Ambassador told us there was a large underclass of homeless people in the city and a lot of violent crime fed by a thriving drug trade. The Ambassador had a pet monkey that ruled the household and was adored by his master who constantly fed him titbits. The maids seemed less fond of the animal as they were kept busy cleaning up the monkey's frequent deposits.

The next day the Ambassador took us to his gem merchant. He explained that he had some very important visitors who wanted to buy high quality gems for a good price. I bought a five carat aquamarine for US$40 which was valued at US$500 by AMP's valuer when I returned to Australia. For a further US$8 I bought a beautiful yellow topaz for Claire, and a melon stone, a type of tourmaline that was green edged with a pretty pink centre and looked like a slice through a watermelon. For my mother I bought a 22 carat amethyst. There were also emeralds, rubies and diamonds for sale at ridiculously low prices.

We flew to Manaus where the Amazon River is over 1000 miles from the sea and already over ten miles wide. We took a boat to the joining of the waters where the black water of the Rio Negro joins the yellow waters of the Solimões River. For many miles the two rivers intertwine making amazing swirly patterns as the waters mix. We walked for a full day in the jungle. Being on the Equator, it was very hot. When we reached a pond I threw myself in to get cool. Our guide said, "Madame, there are piranhas in there." By then I was so hot that I didn't care.

We spent a month in South America. It was all I had dreamed about and more. It was a tremendous adventure.

NEXT WE FLEW BACK to the USA. Most of Walter's large Jewish family had fled from Germany to America just before World War II. His father's family had ten children. They all escaped except the youngest who, along with her father, was sent to a concentration camp and never heard of again.

Walter had worked in the USA for many years before he moved to Australia so, in addition to his relatives, had lots of friends living there. We visited many cities. In Washington, while we were staying with the family of one of Walter's ex-students, Walter had arranged a visit to the President of the soon to be opened Metro train system. He returned sooner than we expected telling us that the President of the Metro had been called to the White House to advise the President of the USA on a transport matter so must be very important. He had arranged to see Walter the next day.

The next day, Walter didn't seem eager to talk about his visit. When I asked him about it he said it was a waste of time. The Metro President was obviously a political appointment, he said. "He wasn't black was he?" I asked. "Not only black but a woman!" was Walter's terse reply.

Most of Walter's family lived near New York. I looked forward to meeting his famous cousin, Arno Penzias, who had received the Nobel Prize for detecting the echo of the Big Bang, thus proving that was the origin of the Universe.

Arno was Director of Research at Bell Labs, the inheritor of the Thomas Edison tradition. He met us at JFK airport in his chauffer driven car and took us to his office at Bell Labs in New Jersey. He showed me an experimental fibre optic cable that he said could carry all the phone calls made in New York at any one time, even at peak times. He said it was finer than a human hair and I pulled out one of my hairs to check. I had read about fibre optics. This was an amazing development and would revolutionise telecommunications.

In the foyer of Bell Labs, Arno showed us the transistor that had been invented by Bell Labs in 1947 and revolutionised the electronics and computer industries. I was allowed to play with Belle, which was at that time the most powerful chess playing computer in the world and a good example of an 'intelligent' computer, even though its intelligence was limited to chess.

Arno asked if I liked to play chess. He promised to show me his own chess computer and give me a game. That night we played chess till the early hours of the morning. I asked Arno what there had been before the Big Bang.

He said, "For a very intelligent woman, you ask a very silly question showing that you don't understand what the Big Bang was. Before the Big Bang there was nothing." Scientists now think this may be wrong and are trying hard to find out what came before the Big Bang.

Arno had arranged that we spend a day at the Metropolitan Museum in New York, but I said that after all the travelling we preferred to get some exercise. We spent a very pleasant afternoon at Arno's luxurious sports club, swimming and using the gym.

When we got back to Arno's office he said he just had to check his email. He seemed very excited and made several phone calls. We asked what had caused his excitement. He said Bell Labs had had an application from a black PhD. They were as rare as hen's teeth. Getting one to work at Bell Labs would make a tremendous difference to their relations with the US Government.

I remembered reading about how Bell Labs had refused to employ Jewish people for many years. Arno was of course Jewish. It was interesting to see how far equal opportunity had come since the 1960s when the arguments in the USA were all about equal opportunity relating to women's employment.

I asked Arno about the Japanese Fifth Generation project and what the USA was doing in that area. Arno told me that in March 1983 President

Reagan had announced the Strategic Defense Initiative (SDI), better known as Star Wars.

He said much of the new research into IT and communications was being done under the SDI program. The main thrust of the program was to build an 'umbrella' over the USA to protect it from foreign attack. Arno thought that SDI would never work but was pleased to have access to the funding.

He said he thought the USA had lost its way in research in general, especially in computer research. Bell Labs had made many very important discoveries and researchers there had won six Nobel prizes for physics. They relied on hiring bright minds and providing excellent research facilities. Researchers had largely been left to their own devices.

Now the emphasis was on applied research. This meant researchers had to provide solutions to known problems that could be developed into products. Arno felt that only undirected pure research would bring the innovations needed for the Fifth Generation of computing.

Arno said the US Government was scared stiff of rising Japanese expertise in computing. In the USA research was too fragmented with each company competing rather than collaborating. There was too much focus on space and military research, with the hope that useful commercial products would result. He looked forward to hearing more about my visit to ICOT.

WE FLEW ON TO ENGLAND. We were met by Walter's brother Rolf and visited his 93 year old mother. Together with my parents, we travelled round England visiting people and places I had loved. The Lake District was just as magnificent as I had remembered.

I visited my friend Kathleen who, when we were both five years old on our first day at school, had held my hand and walked into school with me. She now ran a swanky antique shop in the High Street in Harrow. She was still tall and lovely. Her long hair had gone grey. She had never married.

I asked how someone with a PhD who had travelled the world as a top management consultant came to run an antique shop. She told me that when her father died she came back to Harrow to help her mother. The shop was for sale. She had plenty of money so she bought it. She said she was now making much more money than she ever had. She and her mother lived above the shop. She loved going to sales in great English country houses and haggling over prices with the other dealers. She seemed very happy.

Two years later both she and her mother were found dead in the shop. They had taken an overdose of sleeping tablets in glasses of brandy. No one knew why.

I contacted several colleagues about the Alvey project and what England thought about the Japanese Fifth Generation project. They seemed to think that England had lost its place in the computer race and the power was shifting to Japan. Interestingly, they too thought that the USA had lost its way. After too short a stay in England we left for Germany.

THE ATMOSPHERE in Germany was very subdued. They were not allowed to drink milk or eat fresh vegetables because of the radioactive fallout from Chernobyl. Driving through the Black Forest, I noticed that at least a third of the trees were dead. I asked Walter's relatives what people thought about the dead trees. They said it was as if a family member had died.

We stayed with one of Walter's cousins who told me that he had been a conscientious objector during World War II. After a spell in prison he was sent to work as a teleprinter operator. I discovered it was an Enigma machine, not a teleprinter, which he never realised. He told me that every day at exactly the same time, two officers came in to the room and sent him out.

He knew they did something to his teleprinter but had not discovered what. Occasionally they came in later in the day and do something else. He had realised it was something to do with the wheels on the machine but apart from that he had no idea what he was operating.

Knowing the story from the British point of view, I told him about the British code cracking activities at Bletchley Park, which had now been de-classified, and how the Enigma machine was used. He was amazed. It was a real thrill to meet a German who had operated an Enigma machine.

Walter had arranged a visit with the Research Director of Mercedes Benz, Hubertus Christ. I was given the opportunity to talk to the CAD team there. I was amazed and delighted to see how far the technology had developed since my CUBITH days.

Over lunch Dr Christ told us that Mercedes had developed what we now call a GPS system, such that cars could be directed by an automated mapping system linked to a satellite. Knowing that Walter was going to see fully robotic manufacturing in Japan at Toyota, I asked if Mercedes used robotics.

Initially, Dr Christ said Mercedes prided themselves that they turned out a high quality product using very skilled German craftsmen. When pressed he said they had whole factories that were totally lights out operations run entirely by robotics. But if the unions found out they would bring Mercedes to a standstill.

ON TO FOUR WEEKS exploring beautiful India. We stayed in Maharaja's palaces that had been converted into luxury hotels. We travelled through the foothills of the Himalayas and spent time on the lakes in Kashmir. We shared our houseboat with a man who had marched with Ghandi on the salt marches. He had also been a Member of Parliament and the editor of one of India's largest newspapers.

I loved Jaipur the most, with its marvellous Astronomical Observatory and pink stone buildings. We were shown the sights of Jaipur by a very handsome local doctor who knew his city very well and took a pride in showing it off to visitors. Walter was ill when we visited the huge Maharajah's palace. When we left Walter to recover by himself, the doctor seemed to delight in seeing me blush while he told salacious stories about life in the harem.

He asked if I was afraid of the dark. When I said I wasn't he asked me to trust him while he showed me one of the Maharajah's wonders. He took me into a small room. When he shut the door it was pitch dark. He asked me to lie on the floor with him then he struck a match. The whole tiny room came alive as hundreds of jewels fixed to the walls and ceiling glowed and sparkled in the light of the flickering match. He said this was the room where the Maharajah deflowered new ladies brought to his harem.

In Udaipur, we stayed at the Lake Palace, another converted palace on a beautiful lake that was used in the James Bond film Octopussy. Walter had planned our trip to Agra to coincide with the full moon. The Taj Mahal was spectacular by moonlight.

FROM INDIA WE travelled to Japan, where I had been looking forward to my meeting with Dr Fuchi at ICOT. A young lady who said she was Dr Fuchi's personal assistant met me. She said her job was to ensure I knew all about ICOT so Dr Fuchi did not have to waste his time providing basic information.

After her very formal presentation, Dr Fuchi came into the room. I told him I had just come from Bell Labs where all the researchers had PhDs. I asked how he selected people to work at ICOT. Dr Fuchi said he didn't believe in working with anyone who had more than a first degree. Several of his team had no formal qualifications. No one in his team was older than 28 except him. He himself was just 35. He said he needed bright young minds that could think unencumbered by other people's ideas.

My overall impression of ICOT was its unrelenting greyness. Staff sat in two rows of grey desks that faced each other. There were short, grey fabric screens in front of each desk such that the people sitting at them could only just see over the top to the person opposite. The room in which they worked had a grey tiled floor and grey walls.

Except for Dr Fuchi's office with its magnificent views of Mount Fuji and lavish displays of gifts and thank you letters from visitors, there were no individual offices and none of the personal touches such as family photos or mascots on the desks. The grey people hunched over grey terminals at grey desks looked bored. The men all wore the same grey suits like a uniform. There were only two women.

I asked Dr Fuchi if he could demonstrate any of the research outcomes ICOT had attained so far. After all, it had been in operation for over four years. He said the work was confidential but would be published in papers later. I got the distinct impression there was nothing really innovative happening here. I was told that it was just about time for the current participants to go back to their companies and make way for a new group of researchers. It was all a great disappointment.

Back at my hotel, I was surprised to get a phone call from the Australian Embassy. They said they had not heard from me. When was I going to call into the Embassy for a debrief on ICOT? I said I hadn't planned to visit the Embassy, but I was told that all Australian visitors to ICOT were expected to meet Embassy officials to tell them what they had learned about the place.

I went there immediately. The Australian Embassy was magnificent. It was in an old house set amongst extensive gardens. I was told it was often used for weddings. An official asked what I had learned from ICOT.

I told him how disappointed I was. He was very surprised. He said most people thought ICOT was doing great things. He gave me papers to read from academics who had visited. I felt as if I was reading the Hans Christian Andersen tale about the Emperor's New Clothes. I was asked to write a short report about my visit for the Australian Government. I said I'd write it when I got back to Australia.

49 Set up to fail

FOUR MONTHS WAS A long time to be away. I called in on Morris to tell him I was back. He seemed pleased to see me.

I contacted several of the academics who had visited ICOT. I wanted to find out what they had learned that I had not, and why. They all told me that their findings had been very similar to mine, but having read reports from other colleagues they felt their visit must have been on a bad day so wrote in glowing terms about ICOT.

So I was right. It was all a fairy story. Later reports showed that ICOT had not discovered anything really new and that the eight companies sent staff to ICOT only because they hoped to find out what their competitors were doing. They were still working competitively.

I wrote up my trip report and finished the Fifth Generation report. Morris gave it to Johnathan. I thought that would be the first step in making me report to Johnathan but I was wrong. My career was about to change again.

I was now being included in all divisional meetings, including special meetings held regularly by IBM to explain new computing techniques to the Execs in the Data Processing Division. I can only describe these meetings as brainwashing, but I kept quiet knowing that I now had contact with some of the best minds in computing and heard about new computing trends and technologies long before IBM told us about them.

At one IBM session when we were being told about a new IBM product that, if implemented, would lead to AMP buying much more computing power, I was surprised when Johnathan Harrison questioned the need for that product at AMP. I also thought the suggested product was not needed at AMP but kept quiet. Talking to other Execs after the meeting, they, too, felt AMP did not need the IBM product being touted.

There were eleven AMP Execs at that meeting. I was sitting next to Johnathan. After some discussion with the IBM Manager proposing the product, the IBM man came and knelt in front of Johnathan and said very quietly, "Before you dismiss this new product, think of who influences your salary increases." It was a remarkable comment. Johnathan just shrugged and no more was said.

I didn't like this new atmosphere where IBM seemed to be forcing its products onto clients rather than letting them make decisions based on needs and product suitability. I was not surprised to learn Morris had appointed a team to look into rewriting FIREMAN for IBM computers. The team was much larger than my team which had developed the system in the first place. I was told not to approach or influence that team and they were told not to discuss their project with me.

I asked John Staveley, Managing Director of AMP General Insurance, if he knew about the rewrite of FIREMAN to IBM. He said he would allow it only if the move would lead to a more cost effective outcome. He said he was very pleased with FIREMAN and was regularly in touch with other companies in Australia and overseas who were also very happy that they had chosen POLISY.

The FIREMAN conversion team eventually told me the architecture of the Perkin-Elmer computer was years ahead of IBM in terms of supporting real time systems. But if IBM could get AMP to convert, there was a high likelihood that other General Insurance companies using POLISY would move back to IBM.

Talking to other professionals, there seemed little chance of ever getting away from IBM's control except perhaps by buying a Japanese lookalike computer, such as were now being offered by Fujitsu. They were cheaper and more robust but would not come with IBM's extensive support. I had hoped the Japanese Fifth Generation project would lead to a company to rival IBM but after my visit to ICOT I feared I was wrong.

At the first meeting of the University of Sydney Research Proposals Committee we had a proposal to develop a GPS map and tracking system, now known as a Satnav, for cars and trucks almost identical to the one I saw in preproduction at Mercedes Benz. The researcher said his invention was unique and would generate millions of dollars for Australia and the University. I asked if he was in touch with other researchers working on the same type of project. He again said his idea was unique and he didn't want anyone else to know about it in case they started working on the same thing.

I had signed a Non-Disclosure Agreement at Mercedes so I couldn't tell him that was where I had seen his idea nearly ready for market. I suggested he contact research organisations in large car and truck manufacturers to ensure no one else was working on the same system. Until that was done, I would not put his idea forward for funding. He was very angry.

Another researcher simply demanded $100,000 to buy new computer equipment. I asked what he proposed to buy and how it would help his research, and until I had that detail I would not consider his request further. The other proposals were not worth considering at all.

I was told that academics were not used to being asked questions about their projects, they just expected to be given the money. I stressed that was not the way the committee would work while I was Chair.

At the next meeting the academic who just wanted money came with a costed list of equipment that totalled $300,000, but with no detail of his research. He simply said he could do better research with more equipment. The man wanting money for his GPS system never did contact anyone else about it. Even when I gave him Hubertus Christ's card at Mercedes he continued to say his system was unique.

ONE DAY MORRIS called me to his office. He said the most important thing he had to do was to get the size of the AMP's computing facility right. For the previous three years it had needed to be upgraded mid year, blowing his budget and disrupting many of the systems. He thought the increase in demand by the business divisions had caused the problem.

Morris realised that, having provided simple end user languages and PCs to business divisions, they had found they could build many systems for themselves more quickly and often more cheaply that those built by Data Processing Division. IBM was driving this facility because it helped them sell more computing equipment, but the whole thing was getting out of control.

Systems developed by business divisions were often not documented and did not follow Data Processing Division standards. When the original developer left AMP, no one else was capable of taking over their systems so they were often rebuilt or discarded altogether. This was a problem faced by most large enterprises in the mid 1980s.

John Kaunitz had left CSA in the late 1970s to take up a position as a lecturer at the University of Technology Sydney. He came back to work for AMP about five years later. Morris told me that John had built a complex mathematical model for calculating compute capacity, but although it had been used for the previous two years it still seriously underestimated growth. Morris said I was to find out from John how his system worked and use it to estimate the compute capacity needed in 1987.

John would not be available to work with me as he had been assigned to another project. I would have an assistant who had worked with John and knew how to use John's system. I had three months to produce the right answer for the 1987 budget then I would get a new and exciting assignment.

Logic told me that if John's system had given the wrong result in previous years, if we used it again we would still get the wrong result. The system seemed overly complex but was really only using past statistics of usage to mathematically predict the next year's usage.

I realised that with end user computing flourishing and more PCs being connected to the IBM mainframe there had been a step change in usage. This change in computing, especially where business people could develop their own complex requests for reports from corporate databases, had led to significantly more load being placed on the mainframes.

The feeling of people and researchers from overseas who had presented papers at JISIS was that as PCs became cheaper and more powerful the mainframe would be mainly used as a database manager and for routine transaction processing. Data manipulation and analysis would increasingly be done by business people using their own PCs.

Examining the systems being built on business PCs showed there was much more data held by business divisions than that currently stored on mainframes. This data was essential to the business and should be part of the corporate database. Although there was significant research into expert systems and intelligent Knowledge Based Systems, these usually fell well short of business expectations.

I felt we needed one-on-one sessions with each business division to tell them about the style of computing that was becoming possible, putting them in touch with companies doing new things, and then finding out what new things they thought they would be doing in the next year. My overseas trip and my ACS connections put me in an ideal position to do this. I would need to estimate the cost of new technologies and get business divisions to calculate the benefits, then modify their future plans accordingly.

Morris asked me why I hadn't sent round the forms John had developed for collecting data and asked for past usage statistics. I told him what I proposed to do. He was furious and told me John's system had cost a good deal to build and had to be used. I told him if we used the old methodology we would get the same unsatisfactory results, but I was unable to persuade him to let me try a different method. I felt I was being set up to fail.

I read all the papers I could about capacity planning and asked all the experts I knew for help, including Cyril's group at UNSW. They all backed my method. I took the responses to Morris. He was furious that I had discussed the matter with people outside AMP. He told me IBM had approved John's method and it must be used.

I asked my assistant to issue John's forms and get hold of previous capacity statistics, while I started using my methodology in parallel. The business people seemed to like being asked what they wanted to do and being told about new computing possibilities. They started asking their colleagues in other companies what they were trying and what had been successful.

It was easy to judge what the consequences of new practices would be. At times, the costs seemed higher than they expected and compromises were reached. For each division, I wrote a thumbnail sketch of what they planned to do and the things they wanted to do but which had been rejected on grounds of cost.

I presented my findings to Morris. He couldn't believe the massive increase in mainframe compute power and in PCs needed to meet the plan. Additionally, most business requests were for PCs with colour screens that cost much more than the monochrome screens in use in most areas of AMP. Nothing more was said about John's methodology, which gave a far lower increase in compute capacity at a much lower cost.

Morris said he would have to think about what he would do about my findings. I was sure this meant discussing them with IBM. IBM would be delighted.

SINCE I HAD RETURNED from my trip there had been several more speaking engagements and press and radio interviews to give as Chair of the NSW Branch of the ACS. I was now much more relaxed about public speaking. I found I liked impromptu speaking on the radio or to newspaper reporters or in answer to questions after my speech. The thing I really hated was giving a speech. I felt that no one was really interested in what I had to say.

John Bennett was due to retire at the end of 1986. He had been Australia's first Professor of Computer Science and had worked at Sydney University for over 30 years. He was very well respected. He had been a pioneer and Maurice Wilkes' PhD student in England, where he had worked on the world's first full size programmable computer. He had been the inaugural President of the Australian Computer Society and had served on many committees of IFIP, the International Federation for Information Processing,

The Australian computer fraternity arranged a gala dinner for John, to be held in the Great Hall of University of Sydney. I was to give a speech on behalf of the Australian Computer Society.

On the night, the Great Hall looked magnificent. All the professors of Computing and Information Systems in Australia attended. Most had been John's students. There were also several important guests from overseas. Walter and I sat at the top table. I sat next to Sir Harry Messel.

I was petrified. Although I had continually rehearsed my speech I kept re-reading my notes under the table as dinner started and drank only water. Harry Messel was very kind and, sensing my nervousness, kept telling me that everything would be all right. He tried in vain to persuade me to throw away my notes and have a glass of red wine.

When the time for speeches came, all the electric lights were turned out. Only the candles on the tables and spotlights shining on the beautiful carved roof lit great space. Before dinner, I had checked out the speaking position. There was a small light on the lectern but as the lights were turned off the lectern light was also off. I was even more petrified. I wouldn't even be able to see my notes. Fortunately, the electricians managed to get a small light to the lectern before it was my turn to speak. It all went very well. The audience even laughed at my jokes!

AMP'S DATA PROCESSING DIVISION had appointed its own personnel manager because it felt that AMP's personnel department did not have the skills to choose appropriate IT professionals, and because IT salaries did not fit the scales for other AMP staff. The division's manager John Wheatley was always drunk in the afternoons and would keep his office door tightly shut. Everyone knew not to try to speak with him after lunch. John reported directly to Morris and I was surprised that Morris tolerated the situation.

Morris told me that we needed 200 more professionals to meet the division's strategic plan for 1987, at a time when there was a significant shortage of IT professionals. Morris said that as I was now getting to be well known from my radio broadcasts and my photo was often in the newspapers, he would like me to recruit the 200 staff needed by the end of the year. It was then the beginning of December. I could see this was another situation where I was being set up to fail.

I asked Morris when I would get the exciting new assignment he promised for when I had completed the 1987 capacity planning. He said that was still in train but he really needed my help to get more staff. He knew John Wheatley was incapable of getting them.

I took stock of the situation. AMP had been very good to me when Allan Moffatt had trashed my house and taken all our furniture. The company had allowed me time to pursue outside activities, and I was well paid. AMP was a good company, but I still felt I was being used.

I felt that it was because I was a woman, or because I'd made POLISY successful where it had been expected to fail. I had watched men much less capable than me promoted to jobs I would have liked to have done.

But I knew Morris was right. If anyone could get the people AMP needed, I could. I doubted AMP needed 200 extra staff. Most projects were overstaffed and there were many tiny one person special tasks that seemed to me to be not worth the cost. Our business divisions were complaining about all the overhead costs that were being loaded on them. I sympathised. I was sure I could run the department more efficiently.

Advertisements were put in the leading computer newspapers and in the IT sections of major newspapers asking applicants to respond to me. I sent out a memo asking project managers to list the staff they needed. I was amazed to get memos saying things like 'Ten programmers, no women, no Asians, no one over 30'. The first such requests surprised me but when all were very similar I realised that I needed to take a different tack.

I sent out another memo saying I wanted professional attributes and skills listed, not personal ones. I was bombarded with comments saying if I didn't get the type of staff requested, then their teams just wouldn't work. People would leave and we would be in a worse situation. I took the issue to Morris. He said he had had similar complaints about my 'attitude'.

I reminded him AMP called itself an equal opportunity employer. I would choose staff based on skills and merits. Of course personality played a part but I would check staff skills and I would need a very good reason not to appoint a person with the right skills. Any manager rejecting staff on spurious grounds would not be offered any more candidates and Morris would have little chance of getting another 200 staff by January.

I interviewed all applicants myself and listed the technical attributes of candidates I thought would be suitable. I published numbered lists without names, ages or gender. Project managers soon asked to meet numbered candidates. Many were Asian or women or over 30. Few were rejected after an interview. Managers who rejected people on inappropriate grounds were not offered other candidates.

One position was for a senior manager reporting directly to Morris. I selected three capable candidates and asked Morris if he'd like to make the final selection. He said he'd leave that to me. My preferred candidate was a Hong Kong Chinese man. Morris said if he was the best just appoint him. AMP had never had a Chinese staff member at that level before. I felt I was doing something towards staff diversity and our equal opportunity policy.

Imagine my surprise when visiting AMP ten years later the man thanked me profusely for giving him his start at AMP. He was now a senior manager with over 90 staff. He asked me to visit his empire. I was amazed to see that almost every face was Chinese.

BY CHRISTMAS I had recruited 80 staff. Morris gave me an excellent appraisal for 1986 and reiterated that he had a very good new position for me that would mean a promotion to Grade 6 Exec reporting to him. He would tell me about it after Christmas.

Most of the new recruits had come via recruitment consultants, commonly known as head hunters. Several had invited me to Christmas lunch. One, Mike Singleton, asked me if I had ever thought of leaving AMP. I said I had often thought about it but after 12 years, I would probably stay with AMP for the rest of my working life.

He said if ever I felt I'd like a change I should contact him. "In fact," he told me, "I have two very interesting positions I could offer you right away." He said he would send me the details.

The first company Mike suggested was offering a very high salary and the position sounded interesting. But it had a poor reputation in the industry. I remembered my experience at CTL and Scicon in the UK.

But the second was intriguing. The separate Australian state based stock exchanges were being amalgamated into one Australian Stock Exchange (ASX) by an Act of Parliament in 1987. The job was to bring their computer systems together and to produce a strategic plan for replacement technology to take the ASX to the year 2000. I would be responsible for a team of about 70 professionals, split between Sydney and Melbourne.

I had not known the stock exchanges were structured by state but I was not surprised. Many things in Australia were state based, a hangover from when they were separate colonies before Federation in 1901.The states even had different railway gauges.

The other thing I knew about the Stock Exchange was that the Australian Financial Review, the national financial newspaper that all AMP Execs had delivered to their desks every day, was always referring to 'Joke Net', the name they gave the current Stock Exchange computer system. This was a word play on the name the Stock Exchange used for their existing system Jecnet, which stood for Joint Exchange Computing Network. Joke Net was always failing.

This sounded like a situation I could help put right. I asked Mike to set up a meeting for me. He said it would be after Christmas.

I was ready for the next phase of my life.

50 Goodbye AMP, hello ASX

JUST BEFORE CHRISTMAS 1986 Walter retired and my father died. I didn't go to England for the funeral. I had made a decision not to go back for funerals but to travel to England occasionally or pay for close relatives to come to Australia as often as they could. I promised my mother I would come to England and take her on a good holiday in about six months, when her grief might have lessened and she could enjoy the trip.

Mike Singleton wrote to the Stock Exchange on 31 December enclosing my resume. I had two interviews in January and on 6 February I was offered the position as ASX National Development Manager, on a salary twice what I was getting at AMP.

The first interview was with Rory Collins. Rory was tall, dark and suave. He had a strong English public school accent. He showed me internal memos explaining to staff how the new national ASX would come into being but not when. The memo stated that ASX would be incorporated by an Act of Parliament by the end of 1986 or early 1987.

Rory sketched out an organisation chart showing the structure of ASX. It was run by what he referred to as the Gang of Four, or G4. They reported to the ASX Board. Beneath them came Rory as General Manager of the Information Systems Development Division (ISDD) and another position of General Manager, ASX Clearing.

It looked to me as if the GM of ISDD controlled most of the systems while the GM of Clearing had very few responsibilities. Rory said he was also responsible for a Strategic Planning team consisting of Geoff Reynolds and Phil Mason. They were responsible for developing a plan for a computer system to take ASX into the next century.

As National Development Manager I would report to Rory and manage nearly all the staff in ISDD except the Strategic Planning team. I would also be part of the Strategic Planning team. I would not have anything to do with 'production', which I understood to mean computer operations.

Rory sketched out the different computer systems I would be responsible for and the number of staff in each team. It was all very confusing except that I noted that the existing state stock exchanges seemed to have just about every computer manufacturer's equipment except IBM's.

I was also given a printed organisation chart that showed that Angus Richards was National Development Manager and Rory was responsible only for production and strategic planning.

I was about to ask who Angus Richards was and how my position related to his when Rory said, "Angus has been at the Stock Exchange for ages. He is very overloaded and you will see the shape of the department will be very different when you take up your position. Anyway, Angus will need to meet you before we can make an appointment."

This all smelt to me like office politics. I knew I wasn't good at politics but the job looked very interesting indeed. We set another meeting date for me to meet Angus Richards.

BACK AT AMP Morris offered me the 'exciting new job'. He told me he had watched how I worked and noticed I was very good at administration. What he needed was a good Admin Manager who would be responsible for Budgets, Personnel, Planning etc. It would be Grade 6 and there would be a significant pay increase.

I was horrified. Yes, I was good at administration but I didn't want that to be my sole job. Yes, Morris needed an Admin Manager but it wouldn't be me! I felt he was pushing me into a 'girl's job'. He saw me as a Little Woman who could keep the department neat and tidy.

I thanked Morris but told him that wasn't the sort of job I wanted to do. I didn't mind helping out if the situation demanded it. I had produced a good computer usage forecast for 1987. I had also helped with staff recruitment. What I wanted was to manage a group of professionals and develop and maintain useful and cost effective systems for business. Morris told me the men didn't like being managed by a woman. I told him that was discrimination and that AMP had committed to being and equal opportunity employer. He shook his head and said if I didn't take the job offered he didn't know what to do with me.

I was furious. I had served AMP loyally for 12 years. I had seen others get the jobs they wanted. I had seen lesser qualified people promoted over me. George Garrard was a dunce who was promoted to Grade 7 in charge of all production after I relieved him of his position as Manager of the Fire and General systems. Everyone knew he was a waste of space. John Wheatley was a Grade 5 Exec and was drunk every day.

The Exec team all treated George Garrard. as a joke, a man to be humoured or avoided. He should never have been promoted to the position he held. Rumours were that he was kept in his position by IBM, who had him doing anything they asked.

George had started acting quite peculiarly towards me. Whenever the Exec team met together, he would work his way round the group until he stood next to me. He would then just cup my buttock with his hand. Nothing more. No squeezing or rubbing, just holding. I would ask him to remove his hand but he only grinned. I would stomp on his foot with my high heels but he would take no notice. I would ask one of the other managers to ask George to remove his hand but again he would just grin.

I had taken the issue up with Morris, hoping to get something done. Morris just said, “Well don’t encourage him.” I spoke to AMP personnel. I know they spoke to George. The behaviour continued. I was asked if I wanted to make a formal complaint but I thought that was going too far. It became a departmental joke.

At one stage we needed George to do something he didn’t want to do. The Exec group was discussing how we would persuade George to do what we wanted. Someone said, “Ann should ask him nicely, he touches her bottom and she lets him.”

What could I do about Morris’s offer? Nothing much. There were no other female managers in our division. I would just have to wait until Morris was replaced but his replacement would most likely be just the same. I could not expect things to change.

It was time to get out.

I HAD NOT YET had a formal offer from the ASX. I still had to meet with Rory and Angus Richards. That meeting was similar to the first meeting with Rory, just a chat. I mentioned that I had various professional commitments mainly relating to my position as Chairman of the NSW Branch of the ACS. I asked if I should resign from them. Both Rory and Angus said I should carry on doing industry related things as it helped with making contacts in the Industry.

I told them my father had just died in UK and I had promised my mother I would take her on holiday around May or June. I said I would need three weeks’ leave which I would take without pay. Rory said he quite understood. His mother in UK was a widow and he had done the same thing when his father died. Rory rang me after the meeting and said Angus was impressed. There was an offer letter in the post.

I was supposed to give a month’s notice to AMP but I persuaded them to let me take leave owing and leave within a week. I could almost hear Morris heaving a sigh of relief that the ‘difficult woman’ was leaving.

I decided I needed a real break between AMP and ASX. Walter and I spent a weekend being pampered at the most expensive health resort in Australia. It was like beginning a new life.

I STARTED AT the Stock Exchange on Monday 9 March 1987. My letter of appointment had come from the Sydney Stock Exchange as the ASX was not yet incorporated. Rory seemed pleased to see me. He introduced me to my office. I was surprised when he told me he didn't want me to have responsibilities for staff yet, he just wanted me to get to know the place and see how the staff reacted.

Oh dear. What had I done? I asked him what would happen if the reaction of the staff wasn't good. Rory said he was sure it would be. He issued a memo stating that my position was National Development Manager. What had happened to 'Gus' who held that position on the printed organisation chart, I wondered. Rory's memo said I would work with the project managers to develop manpower budgets for 1987 and 1988. How could I do that? I had no idea what they were doing. Had Rory been speaking to Morris and learned that I was good at budgets?

My second task was to review salary scales to ensure the annual review process in July reflected current market rates. The memo ended with a comment that these two tasks would give me 'the opportunity of gradually assuming more direct project responsibilities'.

Well. I had obviously made a mistake. This wasn't the job I wanted at all. It was too late to regret what I had done. I would just have to make the best of it. I was being paid handsomely. If things didn't improve I'd ring Mike Singleton later in the week.

I started reading the pile of staff Policies and Administration procedures. I noticed I had to seek permission to make comments to the media. The media was now constantly contacting me for comment. This could be a real nuisance. I sent a formal memo to Rory seeking blanket permission to make media comment so long as this did not implicate the Stock Exchange. Rory granted permission instantly.

I was delighted to see that several of the people who had worked for me at AMP were now working at the Stock Exchange. These included Dave Nichols who had worked for me on FIREMAN and Perry Gretton who had worked in standards. Dave was still drinking too much and disappeared before lunch each day. He could be found in the pub if required. He worked for 'Gus' who I discovered was the Angus Richards I had already met. I asked Dave about the relationship between Rory and Gus. He said it was friendly rivalry but Gus seemed to be losing out.

On the Thursday of my first week, Rory invited me to a meeting with the two strategic planners, Geoff Reynolds and Phil Mason. They made what seemed to me a very well prepared, professional presentation. Seemingly for no reason, in the middle of the presentation, Rory screamed at them to get out of his office. He said he would terminate their contracts. He was red faced and obviously consumed with anger. He reminded me of my father in a rage.

Geoff and Phil quickly backed out of the office. I got up to go but Rory put his hand on my arm signalling me to stay. "Who do they think they are?" he spluttered. "Cheeky young things. They think they know it all. Well it's easy with hindsight. Just leave me to sort this out," he said dismissively. He calmed down and it seemed my cue to leave.

I went to Phil and Geoff's office. I entered cautiously, half expecting to find they had been thrown out or that Rory was with them. They welcomed me in. "What was all that about?" I asked. "Do you still have a job or have you been sacked? Does Rory often behave like that?"

They told me Rory had worked for the NSW Stock Exchange in the 1960s. He had had just returned after about ten years away. They realised that he must have worked on many of the systems they were criticising. I said perhaps they should preface any criticism with 'with the benefit of hindsight' or 'of course things are quite different now.' They both agreed. They were sure Rory would calm down and they would keep their jobs.

What on earth had I got myself into? I felt sure that if Rory ever shouted at me like that I would just curl up in a little ball and die, or resign. I couldn't stand being screamed at like that. It frightened me just as my father's rage had done. The week ended quietly but I was really apprehensive about what the future would bring.

THE NEXT WEEK also started in conflict. Rory said he had noticed in my resume that I used to buy all AMP's hardware. The Stock Exchange now needed 300 more IBM compatible PCs for the introduction of SEATS, the Stock Exchange Automated Trading System. He asked me to buy them. I asked if there was a file on the subject I could read to see what had been purchased before. I wanted to know if the PCs had been purchased from IBM or if clones had been bought from other suppliers, and to see any quotes that might have been given for previous purchases.

Rory's secretary gave me a file. I noticed the last batch of PCs had been bought from Compaq, one of the major clone companies. The price looked very high. I rang Compaq and other companies including IBM to get their best prices. They were all lower than ASX was paying, except for Compaq. Prices of PCs were dropping rapidly so I expected to be given better prices. Compaq must just be high priced at present. I drew up a short list for Rory.

He glanced at my list and asked me why I had bothered to get quotes. He said the Stock Exchange bought from Compaq because they were reliable PCs. He said the Q in Compaq stood for quality. I said I would try to talk them down. He told me not to bother and just pay what they asked.

This seemed odd to me. I contacted a colleague in the industry and found the Compaq PCs his company bought cost at least 20% less than I had been quoted. The Stock Exchange was a prestige customer and 300 PCs was a good order. I would have expected to get a significant discount. I went back to Rory. He got angry.

"Just do as I asked," he roared. I said I couldn't do that. If we were audited, I would be asked to explain why I had paid more than market price for the PCs. Rory looked worried.

"Do you think we could get audited?" he asked. I told him there was always a possibility. He pouted. "Then do what you think is right."

I didn't try to get a discount because I was still very new to the ASX, but I was confused. I asked Phil and Geoff over lunch if I'd done the right thing. They told me they thought Rory's brother-in-law was near the top of Compaq. That was why he was so put out.

The ASX came into being on April Fools' Day 1987. The newspapers were full of articles about it. Rory was quoted as saying the state exchanges had let their grip on technology slip over the previous decade but the new ASX was working hard to bring the systems up to date. SEATS was due to go live on 1 July and would greatly improve the situation.

IT WAS A BUSY TIME to be Chair of the NSW Branch of the Australian Computer Society. Apart from the annual PC Show in February, at which I gave the opening address, and presentations about computer education in schools, I was also involved with the Australia Card debate.

The Government was trying to introduce the Australia Card, which was to be a national identity system to link the disparate databases held in each government department. Technology did not yet allow these to be linked in any other way than by using the same PIN (Personal Identification Number) in records in each database. That meant everybody in Australia being given a number, much like the Social Security Number in the USA. The Government envisaged considerable savings by matching tax, health and benefits files. All in all, eleven departmental files were to be linked.

The Australian Government had been lax in passing privacy laws. Privacy advocates like Roger Clark and Graham Greenleaf spoke strongly against the introduction of the Australia Card before appropriate privacy legislation was enacted. The ACS also took a strong stand against the introduction of the Australia Card on privacy grounds. The NSW Branch of the ACS ran several meetings to stop its introduction. The bill was withdrawn on 2 April with the excuse that a drafting error had been identified.

In early April, a month after I joined the Stock Exchange, Rory gave me responsibility for the 30 staff in Melbourne. When I visited them they seemed a close knit group who were sure I had been hired to close Melbourne down. I told them I had heard nothing about that.

Peter Cheers was in charge of the Melbourne staff. He seemed joined at the hip to Ros Crawford, the Exchange's Database Administrator. I wondered if they were having an affair. They were always together and often spoke in unison. They told me they had worked together for many years.

Ros seemed very professional and said she was pleased to see another woman manager at the Exchange. But I couldn't read Peter. It was obvious that he resented the visit and the fact that he no longer reported to Rory. The printed organisation chart Rory had given me at my first interview showed Ros reporting to Gus. I asked her what had happened. She told me she didn't know. The organisation was always changing.

I was spending more and more of my time with Phil and Geoff, the strategic planners. They had prepared a strategic review process with four phases: Develop a business strategy, assess the current business and IT positions and define any shortfalls, formulate alternate IT scenarios and select the most appropriate to meet ASX's business needs, and prepare a migration strategy.

The major issue decided under Phase 1 was the concept that the systems should be divided into two types, essential services and support services. Essential services were those that were required for the business functions of ASX, such as Trading and Settlement. Support services were those that could be provided by other enterprises outside of the ASX.

This led to the establishment of a policy that ASX would provide its own support services only if they were commercially viable and offered on a 'user pays' basis. At the end of this phase, a report on the findings was sent to the General Management of ASX, the 'Gang of Four', for ratification. G4 approved the concepts.

Phase 2 was to assess business and technology shortfall. Ros Crawford had developed what came to be known as the 'spaghetti diagram'. It showed the links between all systems across different platforms. The diagram clearly supported the view of member firms that current technology across many disparate hardware vendor platforms was not supporting ASX adequately.

Phase 3 was to identify a technology solution for the merged ASX. Several different computing scenarios were considered and evaluated against a set of critical success factors that included flexibility, likelihood of success, responsiveness to change, and the suitability to the ASX environment.

We decided that ASX's business needs were best served by the adoption of a Common Operating Environment (COE) concept for essential services. The COE defined a coherent set of interworking systems software components including operating systems, database management systems, communications systems and applications systems residing on one or more physical computers.

We knew SEATS was a hot potato, and that including it in our plan would lead to difficult political issues. We decided that SEATS should be defined as an 'experimental prototype' and developed unhindered for three years before needing to be integrated into the standard systems architecture.

It was now time to select a hardware vendor capable of meeting these requirements. We complied a shortlist of possible vendors. It comprised DEC, Tandem and IBM, with the proviso that if IBM was selected then IBM plug compatible mainframes would also be considered.

I knew that once we approached hardware vendors, IBM for one would start lobbying the ASX Board and people who they thought might be able to influence the decision.

It was imperative that the vendor chosen should be based on logic rather than politics. I suggested we make our decision and seek Board approval by August 1987 but tell vendors the decision would not be presented to the Board until November. That should give us clear air to make decisions before the lobbying began.

We drew up a list of 94 items we considered needed to meet ASX's requirements. These included such things as the availability of off the shelf applications like acquiring the settlement system from the London Stock Exchange, price, ease of development, skill availability, whether ASX already used the hardware and system software, etc.

We closely guarded this list of items carefully lest the vendors get hold of it. Each item was given a weighting indicating importance. We would then evaluate vendors' proposals against these items giving each vendor's product a score of 0-5 where zero meant the vendor did not meet the item and 5 meant it was met completely. Multiply the weightings by the score and the result should identify the best vendor.

51 The Gnomes of Zürich

IT WAS TIME TO GO to England and take my ageing mother for a holiday. I decided to take Claire. She had been planning to go to Europe in 1988 with her new husband, John, but he decided he didn't want to go.

Claire and John were now living in a caravan in a mango plantation in Bowen in Queensland. They had been doing itinerant work picking, planting and packing. My lovely, talented, intelligent daughter was living a gipsy life. She told me they were enjoying life and making lots of money. They were certainly seeing Australia and seemed very happy.

I was about to book the tickets when Rory called me into his office. "How would you like to go to Switzerland?" he asked. I told him I was just coming to ask for time to see my mother.

"That's good. The Stock Exchange can pay for that," he said. "We'll send you First Class. I need you to attend the FIBV in my place and go to the London Stock Exchange to see how they are getting on with building their settlement system.

The FIBV — Federation de International Bourses de Valeurs — was the worldwide industry association for stock exchanges. Rory told me that every year or so the FIBV met in Switzerland to discuss issues relating to their work. Each country sent a technical representative and a management representative. Rory should go but couldn't spare the time. I couldn't see how I could represent ASX. I didn't yet know enough. Rory said just watch and learn and make contacts.

I asked if I could do as I did at AMP and trade my first class ticket for two business class, one for me and one for Claire. He agreed. Claire insisted on paying $1500 towards her part of the costs.

I WAS BEGINNING to see what was going on. There was a power struggle between Gus and Rory, and Gus was being sidelined. I suspected Rory didn't want to go to the FIBV because he might lose out by being absent. Rory seemed overly polite to Gus whilst Gus seemed to me to be a tired old man. Gus now had responsibility only for the new settlement system. Although he had a small team working on a prototype, rumours were that ASX would buy the system developed at the London Stock Exchange.

The SEATS project was another power group. In the organisation chart that Rory had shown me at my first interview, SEATS was one of my responsibilities, but now I was told I must not talk to the SEATS team. The reason given was that the project was to go live on 1 July and nothing must prevent its introduction.

I learned from the two strategic planners that the new system was needed urgently because trading volumes had greatly increased since the state stock exchanges had been amalgamated. The 12 digit docket numbers used to identify each trade were now being repeated in under a month, even using the digits 0-9 and the 26 letters of the alphabet.

This was causing problems within the rest of the system. The programs in this area had been written in a much earlier time when identity numbers were restricted in length to save computer space. The docket number was used as a key identifier throughout the system. Program documentation had not been kept up to date so identifying areas for change would be time consuming and costly.

I noticed that one of the people I had worked with at AMP, Jack Russell, was shown on the organisation chart as the manager of the SEATS team. I asked Jack if he would like to meet for a drink after work. Jack told me that the SEATS team were not allowed to speak to anyone. The system had to go live on 1 July. There had been several earlier published start dates.

I asked what the delay had been. Jack said their manager Ian Macauley had been sick and each time he had been away he had new ideas when he returned. I asked what exactly would SEATS do. Jack said it was a fairly simple system that was a front end to the main Stock Exchange systems and simply matched bids and offers and generated a trade docket.

It was really like a game of snap. Brokers entered bids and offers on a stock. When they matched, the trade went through. The SEATS system replaced the 'chalkies' who wrote bid and offer prices on chalk boards on the exchange floor in the current 'open outcry' system.

A thought struck me. "How many digits do the dockets generated by your system have?" I asked. Jack asked why it mattered. He said the big topic at the exchange was the need for a bigger docket identifier so SEATS generated 36 digit numbers but it could generate larger ones.

"I would do the same," I said. "But the back end systems that I'm responsible for aren't built to work with 36 digit numbers."

"You'll have to change them," he said. "Or you will have to change SEATS to match the back end systems."

"You won't be allowed to change SEATS," I told Jack. "It would take untold time to change the back end to match SEATS.

"That's your problem," he said.

GINGERLY, THE NEXT DAY I told Rory the dockets generated by SEATS would not be able to be processed by the back end systems. He looked scared.

"There must be something we can do," he said. I told him we could alter SEATS. He said the brokers had been promised a brand new system where the docket problem would be solved.

I asked if I should get an estimate for changing the old systems and Rory could get an estimate for changing SEATS so a decision could be made. Rory told me not to bother with an estimate, just get on with making changes. I asked what would happen if we couldn't make all the changes in time for the launch of SEATS on 1 July. I thought he was going to explode.

I asked Ros to use her spaghetti diagram to identify where the docket number was accessed by each system. I asked Peter Cheers to estimate time needed to change them all to 36 digits. We also had to discover if this change would need a hardware upgrade.

At the end of April Rory gave me responsibility for many more systems, including DBCA (the Distributed Broker Client Accounting system). Oddly, although he said I was responsible for the project, the project manager Ian Jackson would continue to report to Rory.

Ian Jackson was the very image of a project manager, tall and good looking. He looked very efficient. His area was covered with impressive charts showing various aspects of project progress. One chart showed changes made each week and bugs found. The two lines on the graph followed each other perfectly.

I asked why changes had to be made every week. Ian told me his business sponsor insisted on it. I asked how changes were tested. Ian said they had some production data that they used. I asked why they had not developed structured test data that tested all aspects of the system.

Using production data, as every programmer knows, is dangerous because it rarely includes every case and so cannot guarantee that a system will handle any expected case correctly. I asked how the new changes were introduced into production. Ian just looked blank and said his team made the changes themselves.

Checking with Peter Cheers, I found that his team also used the previous week's production run to test changes. There was no testing by business people. Peter's group also had access to the production systems and put changes into production themselves.

This seemed dangerous. Current best practice was that both the development team and the business unit responsible for the system tested the changes. Then they were given to a production integration team which was responsible for seeing that the operations staff could deal with the changes before they were introduced and all systems would continue to process successfully.

Issues such as changed operations procedures, operator training, ensuring sufficient hardware capacity for the changes, and ensuring the change did not adversely affect other systems all had to be considered before changes could be introduced into production. All these were missing at ASX. No wonder the system often failed.

I introduced improved testing procedures and suggested to Rory that we needed a production integration process. Ian was furious and said I was undermining his authority. But I was able to show that it was his changes that were generating the errors.

Once my new procedures were in place, we had fewer errors and only monthly releases. I explained the difference between correlation and causation to Ian and his charts were removed.

CLAIRE AND I LEFT Australia on 23 May 1987. Although I had been at ASX less than three months, it felt like a lifetime. The task ahead looked enormous but the job was challenging and it used all the technical expertise I had gained over the previous nearly 30 years in the computer industry.

We had business class seats so arrived in England refreshed. As we were travelling Air New Zealand our first stop was Auckland then over the North Pole to London. Our route took us over polar ice caps where we saw herds of reindeer, then on over fields yellow with rapeseed flowers right down the backbone of the British Isles. I hired a car and we drove to my mother's house in Cambridgeshire.

With my mother we travelled all over England, visiting relatives and friends. I had plenty of money so we stayed at five star hotels. Our visits were interspersed with professional visits to invite speakers for the ACS 1988 Annual Conference and to catch up with the progress of the UK's Alvey project. The following year, 1988, would be Australia's Bicentennial. Many special events were scheduled. People were very pleased to be invited to Australia to speak at ACS 88.

Alan Leach's parents had their golden wedding anniversary on 7 June. We left my mother in Cambridge and drove to London. We were to be the surprise guests at the lunch given by my first husband Alan and his brother Brian to commemorate their parent's anniversary.

We arrived as the guests were about to have lunch. All the aunties and uncles and cousins had been invited. Grandma and Grandad Leach didn't know we were in England and couldn't believe we were actually in the room. Claire had been a very special first grandchild as she was born on Grandma Leach's birthday. Grandad Leach took hold of Claire's arm and wouldn't let her go. I sat on a table with cousin Tony and his family. At the end of the party Claire went off with Alan and Brian and their parents while I went to Essex to have high tea with Tony and his family.

Many people I met said life in the UK was grim under Margaret Thatcher. I didn't feel it myself, but then I was a tourist with plenty of money. I did notice that most of the five star hotels we stayed at were nearly empty and there were few guests in the restaurant for dinner.

When I joked with my sister that she was wearing my old coat that I had left her when I left the UK 13 years before she had said, "This is my only coat." My sister and her husband were comfortably off but I was shocked that she had not been able to buy a new coat in that time.

THE DAY BEFORE I was due to fly to Zürich for the FIBV, I visited the London Stock Exchange. Many people I had known when fpl had developed systems for the LSE in the 1960s were now in senior positions. Most were also going to the Zürich conference. I was given a tour of the new Stock Exchange building. It was interesting to see the trading floor empty now that the LSE had implemented automated trading.

The LSE started automated trading in October 1986, but although bids and offers were placed from brokers' offices by computer, confirmation had to be made by phone to complete the trade. In Australia the system was to be fully automated, with no confirmation phone call. The ASX would be the first exchange in the world to install fully automated trading.

The British system was called the Big Bang because the switchover was instantaneous. All stocks were traded on the new system from the first day. Several major regulatory changes were introduced at the same time. Australia was intending to trade only the top 20 stocks initially.

When automated trading was introduced at the LSE the system had failed for many of the first few days. The people at the LSE told me they made a couple of serious design errors.

Firstly, they had underestimated the number of brokers who would sign onto the system on the first day so the system was very overloaded. They advised me to ensure there was enough capacity to support all initial users or to restrict usage at first. They thought it was bad PR to restrict usage.

Secondly, the system created a transaction each time someone pressed the enter key. On the first day when the computers were overloaded and the service was slow, brokers kept hitting the enter key in an attempt to get the computer to process their transaction. Each single transaction often turned into 10 or 20 as it was entered several times. This further overloaded the system. This was valuable information.

They told me they were developing a settlement system based on IBM computers. They were happy to negotiate a price for the system for the ASX. Settlement was a real issue at the ASX, as it had been for the LSE. Currently settlement took about a month and some transactions were not settled for over a year. This tied up significant funds and led to errors. The aim was to settle in three days, or even the same day.

CLAIRE MISSED JOHN terribly so decided to cut her trip short and not come with me to Switzerland. I had arranged for us to stay for a few days at the Hotel Oriental in Bangkok on the way home. American Express still rated it as the world's best hotel. Claire said she would still stop over there on her way home.

Zürich is a beautiful old city on the shores of Lake Zürich. It is the centre of banking in Switzerland. I met with Bruce Shepherd, the senior broker representing ASX Management. We were taken on a visit to the Zürich Stock Exchange. Although still an 'open outcry' Exchange like ASX, the Zürich Exchange worked in 'rings', as did all Swiss Exchanges at that time.

Each ring bought and sold a specific range of stocks like industrials or financials. A specific stock was traded at a specific time of day. Brokers wishing to trade that stock, whether to buy or sell, called out their orders across the ring. When an agreed price was reached a clerk at the centre of the ring recorded the transaction and dockets were produced. The Swiss Stock Exchange was planning to automate as soon as possible.

The next day Bruce and I took a taxi to Bürgenstock, where the FIBV conference was held. It was a pretty drive past lakes, through Zug and on to Lucerne. Bürgenstock is a five star resort set 3000 feet above Lake Lucerne. It is one of the most luxurious resorts in the world.

I was given a suite complete with huge bedroom, sitting room and an enormous bathroom. The view was across fields full of alpine flowers to high snow clad peaks. It was all rather old fashioned but the height of luxury. I walked round the resort looking at the beautiful views across Lake Lucerne and trying to find my way round the vast complex.

When I returned to my room there was a box of Swiss chocolates and a letter from the President and Senior Vice President of the Basel Stock

Exchange inviting me to cocktails on the terrace followed by a boat trip with dinner on Lake Lucerne.

It was a perfect evening. I met up with the group from the London Stock Exchange and the years rolled away as if we had worked together only yesterday. They told me a lot more about their settlement system. Although they were supposed to be offering it for sale to try to recoup some of the development cost, confidentially they did not recommend it.

After the boat trip, we talked well into the night over drinks in the hotel bar. The LSE people all seemed very keen to learn more about Australia. With the problems in Thatcher's Britain many were thinking about moving there. Back in my room, there were more gifts from the other Swiss stock exchanges and more invitations to parties and dinners. They all seemed to be trying to outdo each other.

THE NEXT DAY started with a special session for technical delegates. The LSE people and I put forward a motion that, as all exchanges were moving to automated trading, we should agree that the ISO OSI standards be used for all communications. The issue was debated and the motion was put forward for ratification at the next plenary session.

After morning coffee there was a plenary session with a speaker. The man demonstrated a system he had developed that was intended for clients who regularly traded several millions dollars of stock at any one time. I thought of AMP and how they regularly traded large parcels of stock.

The scheme would be open to a restricted number of members from all over the world who would buy and sell stock only to each other, bypassing all brokers. The membership fee was $1 million. Stocks were traded by computer in a real time auction. The group owning and operating the system would offer a stock for sale for a specified time period, say five days.

Buyers would place bids knowing only the name of the stock but not the size of the parcel, the name of the member offering to sell or the value of other bids. At the end of the time period allotted the auction would conclude. Those members making the best bids would be successful. They would receive the amount of stock they requested until the parcel was sold and they would learn the prices of all other bids. Members' identity would be known only to the system owners. All monetary transactions would be with the system owners. The system owners would take a 0.25% management fee.

While the presentation was in progress you could have heard a pin drop. When the presentation finished there was uproar. It seemed as if everyone in the room was shouting the same time. This was an outrage. These people were stealing the most lucrative part of their business.

On the surface the system looked very good. The brokerage costs were well below current levels. I thought the speaker was going to be lynched but suddenly we heard a whirring sound and looking out of the window saw his helicopter take off. He was gone. No chance for questions!

The hubbub didn't die down. Was this legal? What were the stock exchanges going to do about it? This could be the end of life as we know it! Should the FIBV get legislation changed in each member country?

I never heard of the system again.

THAT AFTERNOON we went on a trip to Engleberg by train, then up to the top of the Mount Titlis glacier by chairlift and rack and pinion railway. The view from the top was stunning. From the end of the railway we walked through ice caves lit by fairy lights to get to the restaurant that was on a large open deck. At over 3000 metres the view was spectacular.

Back down from the mountain we visited an ancient Benedictine Abbey with beautiful painted murals, then back to Bürgenstock by train and taxi. The Swiss trains were spotlessly clean and arrived and departed at exactly the time shown in the timetable.

That night we had the first dinner at the hotel. The men brought their partners, not all of whom were wives. They dripped with real diamonds and all looked like French models in perfect couturier gowns, hair and makeup perfect. So these were the famous Gnomes of Zürich! Over dinner I discovered that the Swiss brokers were also bankers and were incredibly rich.

The rest of the conference was a mixture of short presentations and long lunches and dinners. It seemed to me that the main purpose was to make or renew contacts. The Technical Director of the London Stock Exchange and I put our motion that all members of the FIBV use ISO OSI standards for computer communications. It was adopted but that seemed to be the only motion put to the meeting.

I flew back to Australia via London, not stopping in Bangkok.

52 The crash of '87

IT WAS MID JUNE 1987. The ASX now realised that there was no way SEATS would go live on 1 July. Another launch date had been missed. I felt that Rory and the management of ASX was blaming me for all the delays. Ian Macaulay, the Project Manager for SEATS, delighted in telling everyone that the system was ready and the delay was because it was my systems that couldn't cope with his new baby.

The general perception still was that ASX was getting a brand new system with SEATS. Few realised that it was just a simple-minded front end system and that the real processing was still being done on the very old systems that made up about 98% of the processing at ASX.

I could still not understand why management didn't realise that SEATS had to fit in with the existing back-end systems. I asked Peter Cheers and Ros Crawford. Surely they understood. They told me they had told management but no one listened to them.

I was still not allowed to speak to the SEATS team, so I had to find more areas where SEATS and the back end systems were not compatible by taking Jack to the pub. Peter Cheers and Ros Crawford identified areas where there might be a conflict so I could ask Jack what SEATS did in that area. It was slow progress and I dare not tell Rory each time I found a discrepancy. I told Ros and Peter to just make the changes as we found them.

Mark Wales was a young programmer who had worked at the Exchange since he left school. He had a good grasp of what the systems did from a business viewpoint. I arranged for him to develop end to end test data and results to test the ASX systems, including SEATS.

ON 1 JULY I WAS surprised to get a very nice letter from Rory thanking me for my work and giving me a pay rise. So he wasn't cranky with me. Yes, he had a temper but he had never turned his rage on me. Maybe I had misjudged him. I had probably been wrong to not keep him advised of all the problems we had found in integrating SEATS with the core systems. I would try to do better in future and behave more like a grown up.

As part of our vendor evaluation process we asked the hardware vendors and their customers, especially other stock exchanges, many questions. We told each vendor that we would not consider any component, be it hardware or system software, that had not been in commercial use for at least a year. We carefully guarded the list of 94 items we were evaluating.

When we felt we had collected as much information as possible we offered each vendor a day when Rory, Gus, Phil, Geoff and I would do or listen to anything the vendors wanted to tell us before they presented their recommended systems. The reaction of the three vendors was very different.

The DEC salesman, Mick Duncan, said he could see we were all busy people so he gave his day back to us. Mick had been a wonderful salesman. We all felt he had been scrupulously honest. He produced all the information we requested quickly and in the exact form we had asked for. We knew Mick's Manager Lyndon Lane and the DEC's General Manager Frank Wroe were supporting Mick but they trusted him sufficiently not to interfere with his interaction with us.

Tandem used its day to provide polished presentations. Managing Director Ray Whiteside led his very professional team. Tandem thought it had the edge on the other two vendors for two reasons. First, as Tandem was the most recently purchased hardware installed at ASX, with the exception that the yet to be installed SEATS system which ran on DEC computers, the application software running on Tandem computers would not have to be rebuilt, thus saving ASX considerable migration cost.

What they did not know was that those applications had been ported across several hardware platforms and were originally designed in the 1960s, so needed to be completely redesigned and rewritten.

Second, Tandem was famous at that time for its 'non stop' architecture. All transactions were duplicated across two processors in parallel so if one stopped the other could function alone until the failed processor was repaired. For this reason alone many Stock Exchanges around the world were buying Tandem computers. But we had specified a relational database system and Tandem's was not yet in production.

IBM brought a team of 'experts' to run through why IBM computers would serve ASX best. Their team was led by Paul Hunter. Many stock exchanges used IBM computers but IBM was the only type of hardware never installed at ASX. IBM was losing ground globally to Tandem and badly wanted to win the ASX account.

IBM thought its trump card was that we would purchase the London Stock Exchange's Settlement System, which had been developed for IBM. It did not know that the LSE technical manager did not recommend his own system.

One of the IBM people was a software engineer called Stefan who had worked on the AMP account. We had specified a relational database system but IBM was still selling the non-relational IMS database management system. IBM insisted it did have a relational system. It wasn't quite ready but it would be when the ASX wanted it.

I knew IBM did not follow the ISO OSI communications standards we had specified as mandatory. Paul again said they would include these in their tender. I asked Stefan why I didn't know these existed. Did they exist? He shook his head.

Again, Paul said these would be made available specifically for ASX. IBM offered to fly us anywhere in the world at IBM's expense to meet any of their customers we would like to meet. We told them we didn't have time. We thanked them for their presentation. I never saw or heard of Stefan again.

We took the tenders and each of us evaluated them against our list. We discussed our evaluations and reached compromise scores where we did not agree. It was rare that we disagreed on any score.

After scaling again to make the scores more easily understood, DEC scored 100, Tandem scored 95 and IBM 40. One of the major reasons for choosing DEC was that because the design was based on minicomputers it could be scaled up quickly, fairly cheaply and easily if trading volumes increased, whereas buying a new mainframe like an IBM 3030 or a Tandem mainframe to handle increased trading was a large incremental cost.

IT WAS NOW AUGUST and our decision had to be put to the ASX Board. Rory decided to make the presentation himself. He was very nervous. He wrote his speech and presented it to Phil, Geoff, Gus and me. Phil and Geoff produced some very impressive graphics. Rory asked me to sit in on his presentation to the Board to answer any questions he could not.

After his first presentation to us I told Rory that I was a Toastmasters' evaluator. I asked if he would like me to help him polish his speech. He agreed. We worked late into the night and he improved considerably.

The day of the Board meeting came. Rory was still very nervous. I took him for a cup of coffee in Australia Square to try to calm him. The ASX Board members were all principals of the major banks and brokers. For some reason the Westpac Bank Board member, Kevin Troy, scared Rory. His name only had to be mentioned and Rory's face turned white. I noticed he was one of the 24 men sitting at the long boardroom table.

One of the Board members was also on both the IBM Board and the AMP Board. He suggested that the Board could not make a decision on vendor until we had worked out the cost. We said that working out the cost was a huge task and rather than work it out for three vendors we wanted the Board to ratify our decision then we would calculate the cost.

The Board thanked Rory for his presentation and asked us to go outside while the matter was discussed. After a while ASX Managing Director , Ron Coppel came out and congratulated Rory. He said the Board agreed with our recommendation. All we had to do now was to calculate the cost of the migration and the hardware needed.

We called in the three vendors separately to tell them which we had selected. Rory asked me to sit in on the meetings with him. Firstly we called Mick Duncan from DEC. Rory held out his hand in welcome and said "Congratulations Mick. You won". Mick said, "Won what?" We told him the ASX Board had that morning approved that DEC should be our chosen vendor.

"I thought you weren't going to the Board until November," Mick said. He said he would have to tell his GM right away.

Next we told Ray Whiteside from Tandem. He said he didn't think Tandem would win because its relational database system wasn't ready. When we told him he only just missed out and that IBM was a long way behind he seemed pleased.

IBM's Paul Hunter was the next to be told. He looked at me and said, "Ann, I thought we were friends. Why didn't you tell me our tender wasn't good enough? We could have made it better." Did IBM have a hand in getting me the job at ASX in the hope of getting their hardware chosen by ASX? Paul went back to IBM and resigned.

THE NUMBER OF TRADES per day was increasing rapidly. From the average of 5000 trades a day in January, some days the system was processing 30,000. Alan Bond was often in the market. He was a multi-millionaire who was known as a corporate raider and asset stripper. He would gradually buy stock in a company until he got near the 19.5% level where he would have to declare his holding. He would then rapidly acquire the whole company.

As soon as the general public saw Bond was in the market, the 'Mums and Dads' (which was what the press and the brokers called the general public) followed him, buying up the stock, which by this time was rapidly increasing in price, thinking Bond was on to a good thing.

Once Bond acquired the whole company he would strip it of its most valuable assets and transfer them into his private company, Dalhold. The original company would then be worth far less and the stock price would fall rapidly. The losers were usually the Mums and Dads, yet they kept up the game of hanging onto Bond's coat tails in the hope of also getting rich.

If a company knows of anything that could change the value of a stock it is legally bound to advise the ASX before giving the information to anyone else. Such advice is called an announcement. While there was still a trading floor, ASX had the option of announcing the information over the loudspeakers on the floor or just sending the details to the brokers and others, like the press, who subscribed to the announcements service. As trading increased it became it impossible to announce them all on the floor of the Exchange.

Alan Bond meticulously sent ASX formal announcements at each stage of acquisition and asset stripping, yet these announcements were only rarely made formally on the floor of the ASX. Members of the Exchange, the Brokers, the pundits and ASX staff could all get access to these announcements. I thought that as ASX was duty bound to provide a fair and open market, it was important, especially in the Bond case, to enable anyone to have access to announcements.

I told the Chairman of ASX, Laurie Cox, that as every announcement was entered onto the announcements database, it would be easy to set up PCs in the front hall of the exchanges where members of the public could search the announcements database by company name or date. They could ask, for example, for all the Bond announcements from this date to that or for a specific company. I told the Chairman it would only take one of my staff about two man days to set up as all announcements were entered into the ASX mainframes.

His reply surprised me. "But you wouldn't do that would you, Ann?"

"Wouldn't I?" I replied.

"No you wouldn't," was his stern reply. It was obvious there was a two tier system, one for insiders and one for everybody else.

DBCA WAS NOW READY to be made available to the brokers. DBCA would be widely used but was not deemed an essential service. The Hewlett Packard computers it used would be purchased and installed in brokers' offices. Had we developed our current business strategy before work on DBCA started there would have been little doubt that ASX would not have embarked on that development.

We were helped in the final stages of DBCA development by McNalls, a large broking firm, which had offered to rigorously test the system for us and to use it for a running in trial. It performed beautifully.

Just before DBCA was launched, Ian Jackson announced he owned the software and had the right to sell it to the brokers. Rory asked me if this could be true. I asked him what sort of contract he had with Ian. There was no contract. I asked if anyone had ever given Ian the rights to DBCA. Rory mumbled that he might have given Ian that impression.

I suggested we contact Philip Argy of Stephen Jaques, who was at that time recognised as the best IT lawyer in Australia. AMP regularly used Philip for work on IT contracts. Rory asked me to go and see Philip immediately. Philip gave me a strategy for buying the rights to DBCA from Ian Jackson for $1. I followed Philip's advice and handed over $1 on behalf of ASX then got Ian to sign the document Philip had drafted giving all rights to ASX.

I went to see Rory in his office showing him the signed document and telling him that ASX now owned all rights to DBCA. Rory was delighted and immediately went to tell the story to Ron Coppel, the ASX Managing Director. Ron Coppel reported the event to the next ASX Board meeting.

The Board responded by asking if ASX owned SEATS. I think the Board still thought SEATS was much more complex than it really was. Rory was called to front the Board meeting and told to ensure ASX did own the software and not to return until he had fixed it. I was again despatched to seek advice from Philip Argy. This time it was not so easy. SEATS Project Manager Ian Macaulay had drawn up a contract which gave him copyright to the system. It was signed by the Managing Director of the now defunct Sydney Stock Exchange, Peter Marshman.

Philip again suggested a strategy that I carried out. I was able to tell Rory that ASX had full rights to SEATS but Ian was allowed to sell it to other stock exchanges. Indeed he had already entered negotiations with the Swiss Stock Exchanges. The Board was not happy but had to accept the situation. Ron Coppel was told that all contracts had to be sent through ASX legal in future.

THE BOARD WANTED to know when SEATS could go live. I was getting the strong feeling that I was being blamed for the delay. Three launch dates had come and gone and although the existing system rarely failed now brokers were looking forward to screen trading. They had all been trained to use SEATS and thought because they were all trained on PCs and they had been installed in their offices, that was all that was needed to run it. Ian Macaulay still did not tell them the new system had to link seamlessly with the old systems.

It was decided that only 20 major stocks would be traded on SEATS at first and that the system would not be fully automatic. Brokers would have to confirm a trade by telephone before it went through.

I was sure that we had done all the testing we could possibly do on the back end systems without using actual data from SEATS. I asked Ian Macaulay to provide output from a SEATS test run so that it could be input to the back end systems. Ian provided us with a magnetic tape. Apart from a few tiny changes, I was able to tell Rory that our test had worked.

"Excellent," said Rory. "I can now tell Ron Coppel and the G4 that we can launch SEATS."

"Not just yet," I said. "We need the brokers to test the system from end to end just like we did for DBCA. We need to stress test the system by generating high volume transactions. We can write a simulation program to do the testing but we need real people to do the broker tests."

"Well maybe McNalls will test it. They tested DBCA for us," Rory said. I said that DBCA was not an 'essential' system by our new definition, and whereas DBCA had only been taken up by a few brokers, when SEATS was launched the eyes of the world would be on us.

Rory thought I must be crazy. We were in the throes of a strong bull market. Trading was fast and furious. The brokers were making lots of money and were working all hours keeping up. No broker would have time to test a computer system they would expect it to work. That's what we had IT people for. I reminded Rory how I had had to find out how SEATS fitted with our back end systems and said I was still far from confident that the systems would perform as they should.

Rory suggested another test with a different magnetic tape from the SEATS team but I was adamant. We needed real brokers to test the system. I could see Rory's patience was wearing thin. He had nearly been out the door to tell G4 that our test had worked and now I was telling him the system still wasn't ready.

"Well when will the damn thing be ready?" Rory bellowed. I suggested we find out how soon we could set up broker testing and how long that would take then allow two more weeks to make the inevitable changes the brokers would demand. Then allow another couple of weeks before going live.

Rory rolled his eyes. "It's the end of August now. It sounds to me as if you are saying it won't be ready before next year." Rory articulated his words very carefully, his voice was surprisingly soft and calm but I could see he was about to explode. Nevertheless, he agreed.

FOR THE TEST we planned to back up the production system at the close of business at 3pm. We would then mount a test database with the 20 stocks. From 5pm the brokers would trade from their offices using SEATS for two hours. At 7pm we would reload the production backup and run the overnight processing. We would provide champagne and savoury snacks in the brokers' offices and they would trade against each other.

The test would run for three consecutive evenings. The broker who made the biggest profit would be given a gold bar. The two runners up would be paid in gold coins. Brokers would be asked to let us know if they found errors or wanted anything in the system changed. The idea caught their imagination. This was like betting. This is what they did. This was a good game. The three test days took on a carnival atmosphere.

As I had predicted, small errors were found. Changes were requested to both SEATS and the back end systems. G4 fought very hard to minimise changes because they now understood that 'that woman' would expect time to test the changes and may even want to get the brokers involved again. That was obviously impossible.

I pondered why I had such difficulty getting ASX to understand the rigour needed to ensure the software was as bug free as possible. I deduced that the cultures of stockbrokers and IT professionals were very different. Brokers happily bought and sold millions of dollars of stock often on no more than a handshake. IT professionals agonised over the minutiae of computer code knowing that one tiny error could bring disaster. For brokers near enough was good enough. For IT people perfection was never enough.

SEATS would go live on Monday 19 October 1987. We didn't realise what was about to happen to world financial markets.

There had been a strong bull run for over ten years. In December 1976 the main ASX index, the All Ordinaries, stood at just over 100. In January 1987 it was just over 1400, and by October it was over 2200. On 18 October the respected financial newspaper, the Times on Sunday, asked brokers, financial institutions, industry and academics to predict where the All Ordinaries, would be by 30 June 1988.

The brokers were very bullish. All except one predicted rises of up to 20%. Only BZW Meares forecast that levels would not rise further. The forecasts of financial institutions ranged from the Macquarie Bank predicting a fall of 15-20% to Equilink predicting a rise of 25%. Academics all predicted falls of up to 30%.

They couldn't all be right. But none of them predicted what was about to happen.

IN MID OCTOBER there were tremendous storms in the UK and across Europe. A severe cyclone hit England on the evening of Thursday 15 October. There were reports of 300 year old English oak trees being uprooted in the parks in London and severe flooding made transport difficult. It was so bad the London Stock Exchange did not open on Friday 16 October.

That week there were significant drops on Wall Street, but that was not unusual. There had been some bad economic news and changes to the US tax system that made mergers and acquisitions less profitable. By the week-end there was pent-up demand to sell.

The ASX was the first major stock market in the world to open on Monday 19 October. The SEATS launch on went off without a hitch, though it was initially only for the top 20 stocks. The previous week's falls on Wall Street did not affect the Australian market significantly. The ASX closed by the time the London market opened on what was to be called Black Monday.

When the LSE opened it fell heavily. The closure on Friday meant it had not been able to account for the drops on Wall Street the previous week. Then the New York Stock Exchange, which opened a few hours later, also fell heavily. The Dow Jones index fell by 23%, one of the largest one day drops in history. Both exchanges had to stop trading when their systems could not cope with the increased volume of transactions.

The New Zealand Exchange was the first stock exchange in the world to open on Tuesday 20 October. Bets were made at the ASX to forecast the extent of the drop on the NZX. At 8am Australia time, when the NZX opened, it lost over 25% of its value immediately. It was down nearly 1000 points. The closest bet had it going down only 40 points.

Global interest turned to Australia. I went onto the trading floor to watch the opening. There was chaos. Trading was frenetic. Even though brokers could now trade the top 20 stocks from their own offices, they had sent their young traders onto the floor to trade in open outcry.

I was sure the system would not hold up. We had stress tested it, but there was no way we would have introduced the extensive changes that were needed to implement SEATS had we known the volume of transactions we would have to process. But the system performed faultlessly.

I went back on the trading floor just before the 3pm closing bell. The floor was ankle deep in pink transaction slips. The market had fallen 25% in one day. The only brokers on the floor were the Principals and Senior Partners. They were all looking shocked. It was very quiet.

Tokyo, Hong Kong, Singapore, the big European exchanges, London and the big American exchanges all failed under the high volume of transactions.

In a post-mortem, high trading volumes were blamed on programmed trading, a newly introduced function where computer generated algorithms were used to make decisions to buy or sell. Because most computers used one of a limited number of similar algorithms, programmed trading spooked the market and made the falls deeper than they otherwise would have been. It was a vicious circle.

Many markets shut down their computers to slow the fall. Most large markets fell by 25% to 40%. The Daily Mail reported the Queen lost $240 million. There were jokes that every Porsche in the City of London had a For Sale sign on it and that all the lifts in City offices were empty because people were leaving by jumping out the windows.

It was reported that in Hong Kong an investor asked his broker to step outside for a quick chat and shot him. Initially we thought it was also a joke, but it was true.

The next day there was more mayhem. Johnnie Walker's Steak House was one of the favourite lunch stops of ASX staff and brokers. During the lunch recess, people were offering a Porsche for a lesser car or a holiday house in Fiji for cash to help with debts. My own broker, a very conservative single woman with young children, lost her house. Like most brokers, she had been borrowing to play the market. Most thought the bull run would never finish, or at least not yet. They were smart, they thought, and they would see the signs and get out in time.

At the ASX I was treated like a hero. Few knew of my many overnight vigils to make sure SEATS would work, but they could see the results. We had been the only large stock exchange in the world to keep processing on that very black day. The G4 now realised that testing and caution did pay off.

I had drawn on all my years of experience to make it happen. It felt good.

53 A quieter time

IT WAS TIME TO TAKE STOCK. I now loved my job at the ASX. The seven months I had been there had been hard but they had stretched me. The three week break I had in May and June to go to England and Switzerland had set me up perfectly for the hard work ahead.

It was difficult having half my staff in Melbourne. It meant I spent two days a week in Sydney and three in Melbourne or vice versa. I felt there was considerable animosity towards me in Melbourne. I wasn't sure whether it was because the Melbourne staff still felt they were going to be closed down or that Peter Cheers resented reporting to a woman. I noticed whenever Peter came to Sydney, his first stop was in Rory's office where he spent a long time with the door shut.

But my nights in Melbourne brought pleasures to release the tensions of the day. I always stayed at the Hyatt on Collins, a luxurious five star hotel. Rory preferred the Windsor, a comfortable but slightly old fashioned hotel.

After a 12 hour day at the Melbourne Stock Exchange, following a 6am flight from Sydney on the first day, I would get to the Hyatt at about 8pm. First stop was a good massage by their excellent sports masseur. I then swam up to half a mile in the hotel pool.

Back in my room, I would order titbits from room service. Never a proper meal, just the things I really liked. Next I would either watch silly programs on TV I would never confess to watch at home or even to my best friends. If my special friend from the UNSW Forum was in town we would make lazy love until the early hours of the morning.

My relationship with him had gradually changed from a professional relationship, where I sought a sounding board from one of Australia's most experienced IT professionals, to deep friendship, to afternoons and nights and of wonderful slow lovemaking.

When I married Allan Moffatt I reluctantly told this lovely man that our stolen pleasures would have to stop. He just looked at me quizzically and said, "You'll come round." As life with Allan Moffatt became more and more difficult I turned again to my friend for solace. I think it kept me sane.

We were both very careful not to reveal our relationship. He was very married and very rich. I often met him with his wife at IT events. She was always pleasant towards me but I felt sure she knew about us. If she did she never let on to either him or me. He had told me she didn't like sex but saw it as only a way to get babies. Indeed when a conversation at a dinner once turned to breast feeding she shuddered and said she couldn't imagine it. All her babies had been bottle-fed.

When I decided to live with Walter, I again said the relationship would have to stop. My friend just smiled and said, "We'll see."

Now the relationship was just part of my life. It had been going for twelve years and would continue for as long again. We stole weekends in luxury resorts or afternoons and nights at the Regent Hotel in Sydney. He listened to my stories about my work. I listened to his. We were comfortable just lying by a pool in the sun reading books or I could take up my embroidery if he had to finish a report for his Board.

So going to Melbourne wasn't ever too much of a chore. In the mornings I would get up at the hotel at 6am, go to the gym for an hour, grab a quick breakfast, take a taxi to the Melbourne Exchange and start work at 8am. I was so glad I hadn't taken the safe route of accepting Morris's boring Administration Manager job at AMP.

CLAIRE SEEMED HAPPY. I worried that she wasn't reaching her intellectual potential but she was still young and, as an itinerant agricultural worker, at least she was seeing lots of Australia and seemed to have enough money. Most importantly, she was making a life of her own choosing.

Stephen was well regarded at AMP and getting good appraisals. When my job at ASX came with a luxurious Ford Fairmont Ghia car, I gave Stephen my Ford station wagon. He still mixed with his friends that he had known from school when we first came to Australia. They spent noisy evenings in his flat below our house. Several of his friends were attending university but Stephen still didn't want to go, even though AMP would have given him generous time off to study.

Walter had retired. He seemed to be very set in his ways but he, too, enjoyed his life. He read and swam in our pool. He went to lunch with his friends and played table tennis regularly.

I had a comfortable life. My term as Chairman of the NSW Branch of the ACS would finish at the end of 1987. That would reduce my public speaking load. There was another JISIS conference to organise for February 1988 but being the second conference, we could just invite our speakers from the first conference plus a few new ones. I had agreed to assist on the 1988 ACS Annual Conference but we already had some good speakers lined up for that. The Australia Card debate was still hot and involved me in press comment and radio interviews, but the load was beginning to lighten.

IT LOOKED AS IF life at the ASX would be easier now too. I had good staff, They were following the IT principles I had laid down. Perry Gretton was working on Quality Assurance standards with Mark Wales and Ann Stuckey. Perry was a very valuable right hand man and a stickler for excellence.

Phil Mason, Geoff Reynolds and I worked on a migration strategy and a five year plan for the ASX re-equipment program. During the strategic planning process we had managed to elevate the importance of the functions of what we had come to call the core systems at ASX.

The G4 now realised that the systems they had called the back-end systems were really the engine room of ASX and high profile systems like SEATS and DBCA were merely the froth on the top of these heavy duty systems. SEATS and DBCA had simply had the benefit of self promoting prima donna project managers while the staff working on the core slaved away on outdated equipment patching ancient computer code.

The objective of the migration strategy was to implement the key essential systems of Settlement and Trading at the earliest possible time. We concluded that the critical path for improving the settlement systems was not developing new software but the extensive regulatory and legal issues that needed to be resolved, including the possibility of new financial legislation. We also understood that the establishment of a powerful, flexible network based on published international standards was paramount to the success of the whole operation.

We proposed the rationalisation of all ASX IT staff and functions and the establishment of a software house concept where all development was based on the provision of cost, effort and elapsed time estimates that could be tested against estimates from competing outside software developers. These estimates could then be used to track the progress of our projects.

I SENT MUM a Business Class ticket to come to Australia for the English winter. She arrived just in time to attend one of our now traditional Iron Butterflies lunches. The dozen or so senior women of the IT industry got together about twice a year for lunch and provided informal support to each other when needed.

A newspaper reporter had paid for one of the lunches on the understanding that he could listen in and report on the conversations he heard. He concluded that we were a tough bunch of very feminine ladies and he gave us the 'Iron Butterflies' nickname. He remarked that our lunch conversation was much more interesting that an equivalent male get together would have been.

This November the lunch was held in the Premiers' Room at the prestigious Hotel Intercontinental that had once been the old NSW Treasury building. I could see my mother was very impressed. Her daughter was now part of this group of very professional, beautifully dressed women.

The next weekend brought the ASX's traditional Sydney versus Melbourne IT sports weekend. It was held at the Lake Hume Resort at Albury on the NSW Victorian border. Mark Wales and Ros Crawford were the chief organisers. They had designed the games' T Shirt as the graph of the index at the crash with the motto 'I survived the 1987 crash'.

Rory, my mother and I had been given the best accommodation at this rather tatty resort. It was a dilapidated cottage. As my mother and I were making a cup of tea on the Sunday morning in our dressing gowns Rory appeared in his own dressing gown looking the worse for wear after a big night at the rock 'n' roll party the night before.

Rory was charm personified. He really played up to my mother. who loved it. He told her he missed his own mother in England dreadfully. My mother said I had paid for her and my father to come to Australia nearly every year to escape the English winter. Rory sang my praises. My mother bristled with pride.

Driving back to Sydney, my mother talked incessantly about Rory. She thought he was wonderful. She also thought he fancied me and that I should have an affair with him. She had read about women having affairs with their bosses. She said she didn't like Walter. He was no fun.

Claire and John came for Christmas. There were weddings and parties and theatre outings. Mum had a wonderful time. Just after Christmas, Walter went on a round the world trip by himself to visit his relatives.

THERE WAS A significant shortage of IT professionals in Australia. There was a lot of focus on the low proportion of women in the industry. Published Australian statistics showed only two other women at the salary level I enjoyed and very low numbers of women at all salary levels throughout the Western world.

Labor was in government. Industry Minister Senator John Button was trying to develop policies to elevate Australia's position in IT. The trade deficit in IT was large and increasing. One initiative was the BITS program, in which large companies like AMP, BHP, Westpac paid towards university scholarships to attract more people into the industry.

The first intake was strongly contested. About 30,000 people vied for about 120 places. The University of NSW, the University of Technology

Sydney (UTS), Monash University and the Swinburne Institute of Technology each had about 30 places.

Cyril Brookes from UNSW rang me. He said there was a problem selecting the first batch of students. The top students were all girls! I laughed and asked him if he would have been phoning me if the top students were all boys? Had the selection process been fair? Why was he ringing me?

Cyril then saw that the selectors didn't have a problem. Sadly, when the top girls were offered places only three quarters of them accepted, leaving the way open for the addition of some boys. At the end of the first year half of the remaining girls dropped out, leaving an equal number of males and females to graduate. A further five years after graduation half the female graduates dropped out. This was to be the pattern of female education and employment in our profession.

I have often wondered why so few women join the IT profession and why those who do often leave within five years. Computing is an excellent career for women. In general, women make very good programmers because they understand the value of neat, tight code, catering for all eventualities, good documentation and thorough testing. Women make good analysts and designers because they really listen to business needs and provide optional design solutions where possible.

I have known some very good male programmers, but in general males concentrate on the main route of a program and do not take into account all the possibilities. They do not test as thoroughly as women. Male analysts feel they know what business people want so don't listen so closely to their needs. They rarely provide options and are reluctant to demonstrate alternative solutions.

So why so few women in our profession? I believe is a reflection of the status of women in all professions. This is so even in the 21st century. Many women blame a break for child rearing but I think it's more likely that people choose people like themselves. Most of the people choosing places for higher management are men, and men tend to choose other men.

I have observed another peculiarity. When women do get to the top, many do not promote other women. When I speak to them about this they tell me that having males reporting to them makes them look more powerful.

54 Bicentenary

THERE WERE MANY issues surrounding computer education in schools. I thought that PCs should be used as a learning tool and incorporated into all subjects. Too often, teachers felt threatened by computers. They felt the students knew more about them than they did. This was probably true, but as a consequence it was only the younger and more enlightened teachers who used computers.

In the late 1980s the Australian Government gave the states over $6 million for computer education in schools. Many states spent their money on PCs, while NSW spent the money in training teachers to use computers. NSW achieved a much better outcome. Although Prime Minister Bob Hawke said the vision was that there would be one computer for each student, this would not be achieved in Australia until well into the 21st century.

Another issue was whether students should be taught how to program computers or how to use them as a tool. I tried to help by visiting as many schools as I could, helping teachers overcome their fear of technology. I also gave talks to students, especially girls, about careers in computing.

Often university graduates are over-qualified for the programming work they are given when they start work in the industry, yet most employers asked for a candidate with a first degree. Wealthy companies like AMP, the big banks and the ASX can afford to attract and hire graduates, but they are usually put to work patching old code, which usually causes them to move elsewhere after a year or two.

If well-trained vocational education students had been hired they would have been pleased to do maintenance. Their pay would have been less than that for a graduate and IT costs would be lower. Graduates could then work on new systems. In any case, about half of the professionals in the industry in Australia did not have any tertiary qualifications, and still don't.

IN JANUARY 1988 I started to recruit the team to build the new core systems for the ASX on the DEC platform. The estimates given in the Strategic Plan were for 64 additional people. We saw we might never need that many as we might purchase some off-the-shelf software or find that productivity on DEC computers would be better than anticipated. It had been difficult to estimate staff numbers and staff costs because although there were plenty of program development metrics for IBM computers, there were few for DEC.

We had been told that programmer productivity was significantly higher on DEC computers, but as we had no firm basis for that we cautiously used the IBM metrics for our estimates. All new positions were open to current staff members but we had to be careful to leave sufficient skilled staff to support and maintain the existing core systems until the new systems were ready, estimated to be about September 1989.

Space was tight in the Australia Square Plaza building where my current Sydney staff were located. The DEC redevelopment team was to be based in Sydney but as there was no room in Australia Square, we found space for the new team in the old Univac building in the North Shore suburb of Chatswood. This was conveniently near to DEC Australian's head office where all the staff training was to be done.

The positions and salaries we offered were attractive so we had many good applicants. I needed a good deputy. Peter Cheers assumed he would be it but I wasn't sure of his loyalty. I told him he would be manager of the Melbourne team and that seemed to satisfy him. Perry Gretton would have made a good deputy but he said he didn't enjoy management.

Pedja Paskutini had come to Australia as a refugee from the wars that were raging in Yugoslavia. He was a 45 year old who had responsibility for computing in a large government department in Yugoslavia that ran on DEC Equipment. Pedja impressed me as a person who had worked his way through all stages of the industry as I had done. He understood programming and the procedures for delivering high quality systems. I was concerned about how I could verify his excellent references that had been written by DEC's manager in Belgrade. Fortunately, DEC Australia was able to verify Pedja's position and references.

Pedja had applied for a job as a programmer, imagining that he would have to start at the bottom in a new country and work his way up. He was delighted when I suggested that he might like to consider a position as my deputy. Rory bristled when I introduced the short, fat, moustachioed Yugoslav who smelled faintly of garlic.

I pointed out that I had checked his references and we were very fortunate to get a man with such a depth of experience on DEC gear. The government department Pedja had been responsible for in Yugoslavia was much larger than the ASX. I would not get someone so experienced in Australia. Rory shrugged and said it was my decision.

Gradually the team came together. I decided to start with 36 people and add more as the team settled. Looking at my team, I realised I had created another 'little United Nations' just like the team I had at AMP.

1988 WAS AUSTRALIA'S BICENTENARY. The big day was Australia Day, 26 January. One of my camping friends, Colin Burns, was Company Secretary at Bridge Oil. Their boardroom was on the top floor of one of the highest buildings in Sydney with spectacular views over the harbour. Colin arranged for us to spend the day in his boardroom. Everyone brought champagne and other goodies.

My mother was entranced not only to be in a prestigious boardroom with good friends, but also to watch the pageantry on the harbour as tall ships mingled with the Sydney ferries and sailing boats to celebrate the great day.

In February my son Stephen went on holiday to Queensland. His car was stolen with all his clothes and $2000 of camera equipment plus his windsurfer. He decided to use the insurance payout to buy himself a new car.

My cousin Ian was visiting us from New Zealand where he was now Chief Vehicle Inspector. He helped Steve buy a bright red second hand sports car with only 200km on the clock. We were fascinated when Ian insisted that the car be put up on the ramp so that he could do a complete inspection. A sports car with only 200km on the clock didn't sound real. But Ian was able to confirm that it was indeed a real bargain.

I decided to throw a party for Mum before she returned to England. I arranged a splendid buffet in the Royal Botanic Gardens on the edge of Sydney Harbour. We started at 7pm so that we could watch the sky over the Sydney Harbour Bridge change colour from bright blue, through greens and pinks, to the bright red sunset that Sydney is famous for.

I invited all the people my mother had met during her four month stay in Australia. It was to be a surprise so I arranged for my friend Myrna to take my mother for a walk round the harbour to see the sunset. My guests and I hid when we saw Mum and Myrna approaching and jumped out to surprise her just as she noticed the buffet tables. To her surprise Claire and John came down from northern NSW where they were working on a cotton farm.

The JISIS conference in February went splendidly, although it did not make as much profit as the first one had made. Many of the international speakers agreed to return to Australia to speak at our ACS Annual conference in September. It was interesting to reflect on how things had changed in IT in the four years since the first JISIS conference. It seemed to us all that we were in the most exciting industry at the most exciting time. Professionals from all round the world agreed that we were all getting very well paid for having great fun.

In May Walter and I decided to travel to northern NSW to visit Claire and John at Colly Farms near Collarenebri in outback NSW, where they were now working, It was one of the largest cotton farms in the world and Walter was keen to see all the large equipment Claire and John had told us about.

The day before our trip, John rang to say Claire had been in a dreadful accident and might not live through the night. She had been working in the new cotton gin when she got stuck in the ram on the baler that pushed the ginned cotton into hessian sacks. The supervisor who was driving the gin had done a 12 hour night shift and was working on until his replacement came to take over the day shift.

The supervisor should have been watching Claire as she tried to extract the batch number from the cotton just before it was baled. He should have stopped the machine when she was taking too long, but he was tired and got distracted. The emergency stop should have halted the process when the pressure in the ram built up, but it didn't. The pressure pads on the floor surrounding the baler should have stopped the process because someone was standing too close to the bailer. They also failed. Claire got caught in the machine, which tried to ram her onto the baler as if she were cotton.

Walter and I drove madly through the night to get to Claire, expecting the worst. In the early morning, on dry roads with good visibility, I was stopped by the traffic police doing 133 km/h in a 100km/h zone. I told the police we were racing to see my daughter who was very ill. They gave me a speeding ticket but sympathetically told me to appeal the fine.

When we reached the tiny Collarenebri hospital, Claire was in intensive care. Her doctor, the only one for at least 100 miles, told us she had survived the night and now he wasn't even going to take her temperature. If she survived another day she would be fine. I asked if we could get her evacuated by air ambulance to a major hospital. The doctor said as she had punctured lungs and ruptured kidneys even the change of pressure in a helicopter flight could kill her. All we could do was wait.

Walter wanted to see where the accident happened. He thought the whole setup was an engineering disaster. He demanded to see the man in charge. We were taken to see Ron Jett, a larger than life American. Walter blasted Ron for his incompetence. Ron said straight away that he was very sorry. He had been anxious to get the new gin online and had not completed all the safety checks. The accident was entirely the fault of Colly Farms. Claire would be compensated and all her medical expenses would be paid.

Walter continued to rant about incompetence saying he was a qualified engineer and a senior academic at a university. He would immediately get on to this and that government department.

Ron kept saying he was sorry and all the blame was his. What more could this man say? I was anxious to get back to Claire. Then I looked at the pictures on Ron's office wall. There was a sketch of the USS Nautilus, the first submarine to go under the North Polar icecap in 1958. The names of all the men on board were written below the sketch, including Ron's. Bob Kassel's name was not there.

"When I worked for CSA, the Managing Director used to tell us he was on that voyage, but his name is not on the list," I said.

"What was his name?" Ron asked, relieved for the change of subject.

"Bob Kassel," I replied.

"He was one of our officers," said Ron. "His name is on the back." And there it was: Lieutenant Robert Kassel. The USS Nautilus was the first ever nuclear powered submarine and that voyage to the North Pole broke many records.

We hurried back to Claire. She was propped up on pillows looking very pale. The doctor told us she was very lucky. Her body had hardly any fat so her cell walls were very strong. The crush of the ram in the cotton baling machine would have killed most people.

Collarenebri is a tiny town with only about four shops and a pub. Everyone in the town seemed to have heard of Claire's accident. John told us that they all thought it was a miracle she survived. People greeted us as we walked round the town, they were all anxious to hear how Claire was progressing. After a few days she was well enough to get out of bed but it would be two months before she was fit to go back to work.

I wanted Claire to come back with me to Sydney to be checked by a specialist but she told me she had tremendous faith in her doctor. Being the only doctor for miles around he had to deal with every type of emergency and illness. He was an elderly man and knew his stuff. He had been on the phone to experts all along to discuss her case and had treated her very well. In any case, she didn't want to leave John.

Back in Sydney, I rang every day to see how she was progressing. The Collarenebri telephone exchange was one of the last manual exchanges in Australia. The operator would tell me how Claire was today before putting me through to her.

John hassled Claire to move on to their next job but she wanted to rest. She was lodging with a local family and still felt too exhausted to move on. When she was fully recovered Colly Farms offered her the job as cook for the single men's quarters. Claire had always loved cooking so gladly took on the job. John wanted to move on. They broke up.

WE ALL NOTICED Rory was acting strangely. Most people thought it was because he was out of his depth. Several people asked me what Rory did. He only had two direct reports, his secretary and me. I wasn't clear who Phil and Geoff, the two strategic planners, now reported to. Their work was really over and they were both looking for new contracts.

I told people who queried this that when I had been hired Rory had said he wanted me to manage the technical side of the department while he handled all the external interfaces with the brokers and ASX senior management. I had agreed readily because I enjoyed the technical side of things and felt Rory would be handling all the politics.

I noticed Rory was now spending much more time with Peter Cheers and Mark Wales. While I had little worry about Mark, except that he was sycophantic and would probably agree with anything Rory said, he was a good worker and Perry, who was Mark's manager, seemed to have him under control.

I wasn't so sure about Peter Cheers. He now knew all the IT staff would work in Sydney and that the Melbourne group would be gradually closed down as the new core systems were built. The Melbourne staff had the option of moving to Sydney with generous relocation packages, but Peter couldn't see his place in Sydney, especially as Pedja was now formally confirmed as my deputy. Pedja told me to watch my back and that Peter was after my job.

Rory was drinking more. All the senior brokers seemed to drink heavily at lunch. Rory usually lunched with them. Ever since I arrived at ASX, his work pattern was to get to work early in the morning and go to lunch at noon. We then rarely saw him until about 6pm unless he had an important meeting in the afternoon. He would then work through until about 10pm.

55 Thanks for nothing

IT WAS INTERESTING keeping up with international financial markets. There seemed to be new things to learn every day. Following the October 1987 crash trading volumes and values were down but there was still an air of optimism in the future for those who were now called Masters of the Universe. The 1987 movie 'Wall Street' had made the financial markets seem a very exciting place to work. Gordon Geko's mantra, "Greed is Good' seemed to me a very good summary of market behaviour.

There was much talk about new financial instruments initially called 'synthetics' but later called 'derivatives'. Here, instead of a stock representting a share in a company, the new instrument would be made up of sliced and diced parts of stocks and bonds. These were then sold as a hedge against regular stocks. They were claimed to be safer than normal stocks because they represented a balanced instrument where the risk was evened out.

I just couldn't see anyone wanting to buy an instrument where it would be impossible to get at the fundamental basis and value of the product. I mentioned my thoughts to the ASX Chairman at a lunch. He told me that the brokers were clamouring for new products to sell and they thought this new instrument would make a valuable contribution to their offerings. Of course it was these derivatives, and derivatives of derivatives, that were to be the main cause of the Global Financial Crisis in 2007.

DEC HAD ASKED ME to be the keynote speaker at its annual conference at the end of July, at the new Fairmont Resort in the Blue Mountains. The resort was not yet open, the DEC event would be its first function.

I hesitated because I still wasn't entirely comfortable speaking to a big audience. DEC wanted me to speak about the strategic planning process at ASX and why we had chosen DEC. Geoff Reynolds, Phil Mason and I had written a paper on the Strategic Planning Process at ASX for the Australian Computer Society's Annual Conference to be held in September 1988. It had been approved by ASX. I thought I could probably use that as a basis. I spoke to Rory about it.

"I wasn't asked," he growled.

"I don't know why they asked me then," I said. "I thought they must have asked you and you'd turned them down. I know you don't like public speaking."

"No, I wasn't even asked," said Rory grumpily. "I'll have to check it past G4." The management group gave their permission.

I contacted DEC and was told that they wanted this year's conference to be spectacular. They had had many good wins in Australia and overseas and could afford a very good conference to thank the salesforce for their efforts over the past year and to set them up for a good 1989.

The main speakers would be Managing Director Frank Wroe, Australian Sales Director Nick Ramensky, and me. We would have a speaking coach and a professional to develop our graphics. The first planning meeting would be held in a few days.

The first presentation rehearsal was held in a TV studio complete with cameras and screens so that we could see every aspect of our performance. Our coach was Paul Griffiths, one of the ABC's top presenters. I was nervous. I had practiced my speech but I was sure I wouldn't perform as well as the other two speakers, and speaking in front of Paul Griffiths was daunting.

We were first asked to read through our speeches. I was set at ease when Frank dropped his papers all over the floor and Nick seemed to have lost one of his pages. Paul tried to put us all at our ease.

The second read through went better. We all laughed at our little quirks and ticks as shown on the TV playback. Paul rehearsed us twelve times in all. In the end we were all much more confident and polished. It was a tremendous opportunity to improve my presentation technique.

The graphic designer took our rough images and turned them into a mega production on a dozen large screens that would run automatically behind us during our presentations. We were told not to worry. The audio visual technicians were well rehearsed and knew when to change the slides.

Walter and I were given the best suite at the beautiful new resort hotel. There were chocolates, fruit, flowers and champagne waiting for us. I decided to make full use of the spa and have a facial, manicure, pedicure and massage, thinking I would feel more confident if I knew I looked my best.

There were over 400 people at my presentation. At the end they gave me a standing ovation. I even managed to answer a few questions. I felt very good about myself and went to the hotel shop to buy myself a memento.

I had started buying myself a little brooch or something tiny whenever I spoke in public and felt I had done a good job. It really built my confidence. On this occasion, I bought a very expensive hand knitted jacket. Every time I wore it in the future I remembered how good I felt when I bought it.

Throughout the four days of the conference I was treated like royalty. DEC even paid for my spa treatments.

THE DATE 8.8.88 was fast approaching. The number 8, and more importantly the number 88, is regarded as auspicious in many cultures, especially in China.

There was much speculation about what the day would bring. Rory had been twitchy all week. He said it was his son's 21st birthday party on the weekend before. On Monday morning, 8.8.88, Rory's secretary was waiting outside my office door. She said Rory had asked me to join him in Ron Coppel's office.

What could this be about? Was Rory going to resign? Was I going to be given his job? Rory was now hardly mentioned in the press. Most journalists came straight to me. I was always careful to ask Rory for permission to answer press questions and to give him the opportunity to speak first. He would just shrug and say, "They asked for you."

Similarly, ASX managers would ask me things they should be asking Rory. They would tell me they could never get hold of him. I always followed up with a memo confirming conversations, copy to Rory.

Rory was sitting outside Ron Coppel's office looking glum. He always reminded me of Eeyore the donkey in the Pooh books when he looked glum. One of his favourite sayings in meetings was "Slow down, I'm a bear of very little brain." He would remind us that he was brought up on A. A. Milne's Pooh books and lived near the Hundred Acre Wood (which in real life is actually called the Five Hundred Acre Wood) in the south of England when he was a boy.

We sat in silence. Ron Coppel opened his door and ushered us in. There was no offer of coffee that would be usual early in the morning. Rory and I sat down.

Rory turned to me and said, "This is very difficult. As you know Ann, the volume and value of trading through ASX has halved since the crash so we can't afford to continue with the re-equipment. As we hired you for that job, we are making you redundant."

This wasn't meant to happen. Certainly not on 8.8.88! I felt as if I was in a bad dream and would soon wake up. Ron Coppel thanked Rory and asked him to leave us. Ron asked me if I would like coffee. I could hardly speak but I said yes, thinking it would give me time to gather my thoughts. What had I done? What had caused this decision? Would others be made redundant?

I asked Ron, why me? He handed me a typed letter. It was a reference dated 8 August. It was glowing. It set out all my achievements and apart from some slight typos everything was in order.

Coffee was brought in. Ron came from behind his desk and sat next to me. He said these things happen. They are difficult and I should try to maintain my dignity. I thought he thought I was going to cry. Well I wasn't going to cry. I was angry. I had worked very hard. I had made a significant contribution. The reference letter acknowledged that.

He said I was the only person to be made redundant. The reference letter said there was no other position in ASX with such seniority so redundancy was the only option. Why me? Why not Rory?

Ron said I should refer people to him for references, not Rory. That seemed odd. I needed time to think.

I WENT STRAIGHT TO see Ron Hawthorn, the Personnel Manager, and told him what had happened. He said I couldn't have been made redundant. He would have been involved. I had been working hard. Would I like some time off?

I showed him Ron's letter. He looked shattered. He said he just couldn't understand why he wasn't involved.

Next I went to see Phil and Geoff, the two strategic planners. They, too, were shocked. Phil said Rory had gone bonkers. The whole thing would collapse if I left. Rory certainly couldn't manage the technical side himself.

I thought through what had to be done. I wanted to say goodbye to my staff. I had agreed to negotiate a price for three large Hewlett Packard computers. We were nearly there. The final meeting was to be tomorrow. Neither Rory or Ron had said anything about timing or handovers.

I went back to my office. My secretary was sitting at my desk crying. Rory's secretary was sitting at my secretary's desk outside my office. She told me she had been asked to get me to clear my desk and leave without speaking to any of my staff. Is this how it works? What was to be my compensation? I asked to speak to Rory. His secretary said he was very upset and had gone home. I told her I would be back tomorrow for the Hewlett Packard meeting and asked her to organise my final pay.

I started to clear my desk. Perry came in. The news had started to circulate. He said let them stew. I would easily get another job. I wasn't so sure. I was 49. Jobs at the top were few and far between, especially for women. Perry said Pedja was waiting to be called in and made redundant. He knew Rory didn't like him. I said Ron Coppel said I was the only person to be made redundant. I wrote a short letter to Ron Coppel asking to be told why I had been made redundant. Then I left. I still had my ASX car. No one had told me to hand it in. This was all very odd.

THE NEXT DAY I drove the ASX car into the office as usual. My secretary welcomed me with coffee. There was a letter on my desk. A casual glance told me it detailed my compensation payout and how my car could be purchased, and other administrative matters. I decided not to read it immediately. I needed time to go though it carefully

The Hewlett Packard salesman came in. We concluded the deal for the purchase of three computers very satisfactorily. I phoned Rory, his secretary answered and said he was unavailable. It was all as if nothing had happened.

There were so many loose ends to finalise. I was deeply involved in the ACS Annual Conference planned to be held in September. I was to give the paper written by Geoff, Phil and myself. I had had an invitation to attend the opening of a new facility at UNSW by the Federal Minister for Education, John Dawkins, later in August. I had been invited to the 1988 post budget dinner where the Prime Minister, Bob Hawke, was to speak about the budget. There was so much to organise.

When I got home, still with my ASX car, I had a good look at the letter and the compensation payout. It was for only three months. That didn't seem enough to me. The summary of my entitlements made no allowance for my superannuation. I had clearly remembered that although it was part of my package and was non-contributory that minimised my tax, superannuation was my money and should have been included.

I rang Ron Hawthorn. He agreed that the compensation amount was much less than it should be. He said he had been told not to speak to me and that all contact had to be only with Ron Coppel. That seemed ridiculous. I rang my friend Marea, the lawyer at AMP. She suggested a good redundancy lawyer, who said I might not benefit from making a court case for wrongful dismissal and would only get more compensation if I could prove I could not get re-employed.

He said with my reference and experience, I should easily get a good job but he agreed to write a letter demanding my superannuation payout and stating that I was entitled to 12 months redundancy pay, and also that we still might sue. The amount came to another $44,000 plus superannuation. I also had expenses I had not claimed and I still had the ASX car.

The negotiations with my solicitor were handled by Ron Hawthorn. The final payout was very generous and entirely to my satisfaction, although it all took quite a while. The ASX also paid my legal fees.

My staff organised a splendid goodbye lunch. Peter Cheers did not attend, although most of my Melbourne staff did. But I still did not have a job and thought I had few prospects of getting one.

I DECIDED TO ATTEND as many events as possible to try to see what opportunities were available to me. The UNSW event was to establish a joint venture with IBM where UNSW would deliver IBM's customer education. Many of the IT Managers from large IBM customers had been invited. It seemed a good place to check out employment prospects.

The UNSW initiative was one of Senator John Button's Partnerships for Development ideas. An offsets program had been in operation in Australia for many years whereby major importers of technology were supposed to establish manufacturing facilities or develop products or services in Australia. The value of the offset was a proportion of the value of their imports. For example, Australia made the wing assembly for Boeing 747s.

The differential between imports and exports in the IT industry was too large to be covered by small schemes. Most big companies, IBM being the largest, did not discharge all their offset obligations but the Australian Government was reluctant to enforce penalties. The Button PDP initiative stated that unless importers met their obligations, their import licences would be curtailed.

IBM established a manufacturing plant at Wangaratta in Victoria to assemble PCs. It also gave all its customer education away to universities. The UNSW scheme was one such. Cyril Brookes had been given leave of absence from his position as Professor and Head of the School of Information Systems to run the new facility that had been established as a subsidiary of Unisearch, the commercial arm of UNSW. It was located in elegant new offices at Bondi Junction and was called The Institute of Information Technology.

It was a good scheme for UNSW. At that time academic pay was low compared with salaries in the IT industry. It was difficult to attract and retain good quality academics, especially those with industry experience. Academics teaching IBM's courses were granted leave and paid $1500 a day. That supplemented their income and helped with staff retention. Profits from the scheme went into the UNSW coffers. Cyril Brookes also had plans to develop better IBM courses, provide consultancy to IBM customers and fund more IT research at UNSW.

I WAS A BIT MORE concerned about attending the Hawke Budget night dinner. I had been invited by one of the industry's leading head-hunters, John Price. I was sure I had been invited because of my position at ASX. I rang John and told him I would not attend as his guest because I was no longer working at ASX. I had been made redundant.

John was very sympathetic. He said senior executives were made redundant more often that I might realise. Usually the parting was due to incompatibility with the Board or senior management. John said he usually placed these executives very successfully; it was often just a case of cultural incompatibility. Would I like him to help me?

I thanked him but said I'd already asked Mike Singleton, who placed me at ASX, for his help. John said I should attend the dinner because I would find out that nearly all the successful executives he had invited had been made redundant or had left their employers at some time in their career.

"It's alright for them," I thought. "They're part of the old boy's club. It would be much more difficult as a woman to get another senior placement." I was beginning to regret leaving AMP. At least AMP was safe and would never make someone redundant. At AMP, Execs had a job for life. I probably should have taken up Morris's offer and just bided my time.

John's table at the dinner was directly under the speaker's lectern. Everyone at the table knew everyone else except for one man who nobody knew. John politely asked him if he was at the wrong table. The man told us he was Bob Hawke's bodyguard. We jokingly asked him to show us his gun, which he did.

All the major TV stations were at the dinner waiting to film the Prime Minister's speech. The Hawke table was, unusually, in the middle of the room. As he passed me to take his place at the lectern, Bob Hawke squeezed my shoulder and whispered in my ear that he admired my bright red suit.

There had been considerable speculation in the media about whether Bob Hawke would hand over the Prime Ministership to Paul Keating who was the Australian Treasurer and Deputy Prime Minister. It had become a major issue, with Keating claiming there had been a deal that he would take over. Hawke started by laying aside his prepared speech and stated that he was not intending to hand over to Paul Keating. There was uproar for a few minutes. All the TV cameras and other media left immediately hoping to meet print deadlines or get vision out on the 10 o'clock TV news.

The speech was something of an anticlimax. Most of it had already been widely debated as the budget had been delivered on the previous day. As Bob Hawke passed me on the way back to his table, he again squeezed my shoulder and said, "Love the suit."

John had arranged for his guests to circulate round the table. I collect dinner menus signed by the other guests at my table. Asking for signatures, I was able to tell people I had been made redundant and ask for advice. John was right. Most had at some time been made redundant and were generous with their advice. Most told me to let everyone know and hold my head up high. I would soon be snapped up. I had a high profile in the industry. It was beginning to get easier with each person I told but I still felt bruised.

I asked the bodyguard if he would get Bob Hawke's autograph for me. He told me that Bob loved being asked for his autograph and I should ask him myself. The dinner was coming to an end. People were mingling. Mr Hawke was standing at his table talking to a group of people.

I gingerly went and stood near the group. Hazel Hawke, the PM's wife, was standing nearby. No one seemed to be talking to her. I asked for her autograph. She said she had never been asked before and duly signed my menu. She tapped Bob on the shoulder and said there was a woman who wanted to speak to him. He turned to me and said, "Lovely suit. Lovely colour. I could see it from my table. You look wonderful." From the Prime Minister!

He went on to ask me my opinion about Chinese students coming to Australia to go to our universities. He seemed to ignore the other guests and spoke only to me for what seemed ages. I hardly said a word but listened intently. He seemed very pleased with himself. He signed my menu.

There was a tall, portly man standing next to Mrs Hawke. I asked if he would like to sign my menu too. He did. I asked who he was. He said he was the Editor of the Financial Review, which sponsored the dinner.

I went home feeling very uplifted.

THE NEXT MAJOR EVENT was the ACS Annual conference. Things were not going well. Although we had a good line-up of speakers, bookings were slow. We were to hold the conference at the new Darling Harbour Convention Centre. It was supposed to be finished by Australia Day in January 1988 but it was way behind schedule.

We decided to hold sessions in smaller rooms, but in an effort to extend the building contract until Christmas 1988 so that the builders would get their Christmas bonuses, they had removed the roof of the building and hoisted large pieces of earth moving equipment through the roof onto the carpeted floors of the conference rooms below.

I worked with the company leasing the Conference Centre to get a curtain made to partition off part of the large auditorium so that the conference looked better attended than it would have done in the large hall. The curtain cost us $10,000 and I had hopes, but no promise, of selling it to the leasing company after the conference. The facility itself cost $10,000 a day to hire. It was a three day conference.

The ASX sent a letter to the ACS saying it was withdrawing its permission for the presentation of the paper that Geoff Reynolds, Phil Mason and I had prepared. It had already been printed in the conference proceedings. I couldn't see why it could not be presented. Cyril Brookes was conference Chairman. He advised me not to fight the matter as it might affect any reference I might want ASX to provide for me. I knew he was right but it was just one more little hurt.

The conference was a nightmare. There was still a lot of building noise. Electricity and air conditioning was cut off from time to time. I spent all my time trying to smooth out problems, but it was still very unpleasant for all attending.

But attendees thought the content and speakers at the conference were very good. We had speakers from all over the world. The speakers' dinner at the Regent Hotel was a splendid affair. It was good renewing acquaintances with people from the UK, especially with my old boss from CTL Iann Barron, who had just invented the Transputer that was a complete and powerful computer on a single chip. He was now married to a famous novelist and lived in Bath.

I hoard interesting newspaper cuttings. I had saved one with a picture of Iann in a hipbath at the exhibition where he had first shown his Modular One computer. I gave him the cutting. He was delighted. He had not saved that one himself.

The conference looked like making a substantial loss for the ACS. I was beginning to think that everything I touched was going wrong. But we were able to negotiate a total rebate on the room hire fee so the conference just broke even.

56 On the train to nowhere

I DECIDED TO GET AWAY from Sydney and visit Claire. She had recovered from her horrific accident in May and had been given the job as cook for the single men at Iffley cotton farm in far northern NSW, which had just been acquired by Colly Farms. She told me that there had been a party to farewell the previous cook. Everyone had got very drunk and had thrown spaghetti and salad into the ceiling fan in the kitchen. The kitchen walls and ceiling were covered in the residue from the prank.

Claire was trying to find time to clean the kitchen in addition to feeding the 60 or so men in the quarters. The job of cook came with a nice little demountable house. Claire had previously been living in a converted bus. John had left to continue his life as an itinerant worker but Claire said she now wanted to stay in one place for a while.

The countryside was beautiful on the ten hour drive to Iffley. It had rained and the sides of the road were covered in wildflowers. I helped Claire clean the kitchen. I peeled mountains of potatoes and washed up.

I didn't tell Claire I had lost my job. I just said I needed a holiday. As I scrubbed floors and peeled potatoes I cried into the buckets of water telling myself this is what I had come to. The only job I could now get would be peeling potatoes or washing floors. I felt very sorry for myself.

But I enjoyed life at Iffley. Claire's 'boys' were an odd group but there were some interesting men amongst them. They were all hardworking farm-hands. Some were itinerant workers. Some were students backpacking round Australia. The men all seemed very supportive and respectful towards Claire. She did not allow swearing or boots in her kitchen. The men obeyed.

She cooked delicious meals. One man told me Claire was a real restaurant cook. I was proud of her. The nearest town was a 300 km round trip. Meat, milk, bread, fruit and vegetables and other groceries were delivered only once a week.

Claire told me the farm often got flooded in for up to six weeks so she had to order sufficient supplies to cater for any eventuality. It must have been very difficult to keep preparing delicious meals for hungry men in those circumstances with no help.

The men worked 12 hour shifts. Claire cooked breakfast, prepared food for the men to make their own packed lunches, and cooked dinner. During the cotton harvest, the men worked night and day. They had tremendous appetites, often eating three large T-bones at one sitting. We got up at 4.45am and were in bed asleep by 8pm. It was a good life.

Colly Farms was huge. Iffley alone was about 100 km by 100 km. There was another, larger quarters about 70km from Iffley with more men. Some of the men were skilled mechanics who worked in the vast sheds used to repair and store an extensive variety of machinery. The farm had three large storage lakes that were filled with waterbirds. The cotton fields were laser levelled and irrigated with reticulated water supplemented by water from the storages. It was one of the largest cotton farms in the world.

Claire and I took a short trip to the Warrumbungle National Park in northern NSW. But then I had to go home.

WHEN I GOT BACK to Sydney I was amazed to find twelve job offers waiting for me. The news of my departure from ASX had been front page news in the computer press. Several companies had contacted ASX for references and had written offering positions at salaries equal or higher than my salary at ASX or asking me to state the salary I would like. I couldn't believe it.

I thought carefully about what sort of job I wanted. I would be 50 next year and expected my next job to last ten years until my retirement. I decided I enjoyed life most when I was managing software development teams.

I chose to join a large software house called DMR, a French Canadian company which had a large Australian operation. I knew Managing Director David Major well and liked him. DMR had a good reputation in the industry. I contacted David. We went to lunch and discussed how I would work with DMR, I was then interviewed by David's Director of the Sydney office, Ted Wilkes.

I liked Ted, who was to be my boss. The salary offered was better than I had at ASX and there was a car and other fringe benefits. The letter confirming my appointment detailed my duties. It was all I could have hoped for. The people I met at DMR were friendly and welcoming. I agreed to start work on 1 November 1988.

I worked with Ted Wilkes to find out as much as I could about how DMR operated. I learned that DMR had been founded in Montréal and that D and M and R were the initials of the three founders. Three days after I joined I was invited to dinner with David Major and Tom Moore, the M in DMR, who was visiting from Canada. David had invited several senior DMR people to meet him.

They were an impressive group of people. I met Tamara Selnick, who was a Director of DMR Sydney. She had joined when the company she worked for was taken over by DMR. Tamara was one of the few people in the company who had an office. Most consultants and managers had desks in the open plan area but they spent little time in the office. Mostly they worked on site with their clients.

Every time I went into Ted's office he seemed to be laughing at me. Thinking I must be imagining it, I asked Ted if he was indeed laughing at me. He said he wasn't laughing at me but just smiling to himself wondering what I would think if I knew what he knew.

This was an intriguing statement. I asked Ted what he meant. He asked if I could keep a secret, then told me that all the time he was talking to me about a job at DMR he was being interviewed for a job at AMP.

So that was why he kept asking me about AMP. I asked him what he was going to do. He said he had now been offered the top job in IT at AMP and was considering the offer. I asked if he would be replacing Morris McLeod. Ted said he would be Morris's boss.

Now he asked me openly all about computing at AMP. I said I had always thought AMP really needed an IT head who was an IT professional. I asked what had happened to Johnathan Harrison who Morris was grooming to take over the division when he retired. Ted looked at the IT organisation chart he had been given and said Johnathan's name wasn't on it.

A MONTH LATER Ted left DMR to join AMP. The new head of the Sydney DMR office was a slight and weedy looking Chinese Australian called Mark Lo. He was very aggressive and very abrupt. Gradually, I was dropped from the weekly management meetings, as was Tamara.

I had been working with another senior DMR consultant, David Savage, trying to win a contract for the NSW State Rail strategic review. It sounded interesting and, as David Savage was running another large project, I assumed if we won the contract, I would manage the project.

We won the contract. Mark Lo thanked me for my contribution and told me he would now find something else for me to do. He had taken David Savage off his own project and given him the State Rail project to manage. Mark told me it was about trains so needed a man to run it. But a couple of days later I was called into Mark's office to be told I was to manage the project because it reported to the only female Director of State Rail. He thought she might prefer to work with a woman.

It was an interesting project. Everyone knew NSW State Rail was in a mess. The project was to assist with the rationalisation of State Rail then develop a strategic plan to redesign and redevelop their IT systems to support the rationalisation. It was like the work I had done at ASX. Meetings with Fay, the NSW Rail Director, and her team were held in their grand old fashioned marble offices above Central Station in Sydney.

Fay and her team had evaluated all State Rail stations and decided which should be kept open and which closed. Fay showed me the list of stations to be closed. I was concerned that station workers who had spent their lives working for State Rail would now be made redundant. In small country towns it would be difficult for men in their 50s to get a job again.

Fay laughed. She said many redundancy payments were in excess of $250,000. This was a fortune to someone living in a country town. She told me there was one station where trains never stopped. It always won the best garden competition. She had found out that all of the four staff at that station had jobs in the town. The Stationmaster was the local butcher. They took turns selling tickets for the buses that took passengers to the next station to board their train.

I asked why there was a station at that town and was told that if ever the Queen came to Australia and travelled by train she might want to stop there. Another story involved 500 km of track in the Outback where the only train that travelled it was the track inspection train. Fay said she had no hesitation in closing down inefficient stations.

MY MUM WAS COMING to Australia again for four months to miss the English winter. I had negotiated with DMR when I joined that I could take a short break after Christmas to take my mother to see Claire on Colly Farm.

Mum and I set off on Boxing Day. Mum loved the trip into Outback Australia and was proud to see her granddaughter cooking for so many men. One day we decided to go into town. The nearest town was Moree, 150 km from Iffley. Claire put some small turkeys on a low heat in the gas fired commercial oven before we left.

When we got back to cook the vegetables and turn up the heat to brown the turkeys, Claire saw that one of the banks of gas jets had blown out. This caused the other set to burn fiercely to try to keep the oven on the selected setting. One lot of turkeys was burned black and the others were still raw. The men were due in for their dinner in an hour. I asked Claire what we should do.

She said, "The first rule, mother, is don't panic. You take the burnt turkeys, pick off the burnt bits and remove the bones. We'll chop them up and curry them so they won't taste burnt. I'll cut the raw ones up and deep fry them."

The men said the curried turkey meal was one of the best dinners they had ever tasted and teased Claire for trying to put on a good meal to impress her mother and grandmother.

Work continued on the State Rail project. David Major asked me to write a report on IT in Australia for the Canadian Government. DMR Canada was writing a similar report for the Australian Government about IT in Canada.

Mark Lo asked me to set up some strategic relationships with hardware suppliers so DMR could provide consultancy and development work to support their sales. In the late 1980s hardware vendors only sold and installed hardware. They hadn't yet branched out into the more lucrative area of software and services delivery. Although I assisted on many successful proposals, I was not given any of the resultant projects to manage.

I started having memory lapses. I read that memory lapse was one of the symptoms of menopause. I was nearly 50. But this was getting really bad. I found that unless I wrote down my destination, by the time I got from the 8th floor where I worked to the foyer of the building I had forgotten where I was going. I would read a page of a technical report and not be able to recall any of the information by the time I got to the bottom of the page. It reminded me of the feelings I had after I'd fractured my skull when I was 18.

I went to the doctor and asked for hormone replacement medication. I had read that this eased the symptoms of menopause. The doctor told me I didn't need medication. So what did I need?

The State Rail project was still gathering statistics. I wondered when the information about station closures would be made public. I was told the information I had seen was to be kept secret until the NSW State Government agreed it could be disclosed.

I was asked to gather information on ticket sales at small rural stations. The group responsible for this information was located in a city office block. When Fay and I visited the Departmental Head welcomed us and introduced us to his two deputy heads.

He showed us his staff of 64 in a large open plan office. He explained the system of data collection. He said each station sent eight pieces of data each month, for the number of tickets sold for each of four ticket types, and the total amount collected for each of them. The information was transferred by hand onto a large sheet and totalled for each category. The totals were sent to State Rail management at Central Station by the end of the month.

The Head of Department addressed me gruffly and said, "I know what you're thinking. You're thinking this could all be computerised. Well it can't. We've tried that."

I wanted to tell him that a schoolgirl with a desk calculator could produce the figures on a Friday afternoon but I kept quiet. I tried to find the person in State Rail head office who received the report. I found that no one even knew of its existence.

I called back to the department that prepared the report. The secretary looked surprised to see me. There were no staff in the office at all. The secretary told me they were all on an RDO (Rostered Day Off). She said I should make an appointment if I wanted to visit again.

I visited a week later, still no staff. Again, only a secretary was on duty, a different one from before. She told me the staff were all on an RDO. I asked how could that be. They were on an RDO the week before. I thought they only got one a month. She told me staff could borrow an RDO from the next month. I visited again a week later. Again no staff. This time I was told staff could take an RDO saved from the previous month, so three RDOs in a month was quite possible. I suspected there were more.

Fay told me all the staff in the department had other jobs outside State Rail and were collecting two salaries.

IN MAY MY SON Stephen was 21. We had a sumptuous party at the Wentworth Hotel in Sydney. Stephen still says his was the best 21st of all his friends. Claire brought her new man, Noel. I was pleased that they were able to get to Sydney for the party.

In July the State Rail restructure was all over the press. There was uproar as 8000 jobs were cut. Fay was reprimanded for flying to each location to announce the redundancies instead of taking the train. The Government now had to approve the strategic review and re-equipment strategy.

Meanwhile at the ASX news of computer glitches was almost an everyday occurrence. The brokers were questioning the value of SEATS.

My camping friends and I drove to Queensland as far as Fraser Island. On the way back we spent time on houseboats on the Manning River. Walter had gone to the USA to visit his relatives and didn't come on our trip. I would have my 50th birthday while we were away and I couldn't understand why Walter wouldn't come with us and would miss my 50th birthday.

While we were on the houseboat I was playing Scrabble with my friend Val when suddenly the whole board didn't make sense to me. None of the words were correctly spelt. I couldn't make any words from the tiles in my tray. I felt sick and had to stop playing. Val accused me of giving up because I knew I couldn't win. This was very worrying. I tried to tell Val about my memory lapses but she didn't want to listen.

My friends had organised a 50th birthday party for me on the trip. But when I got back to Sydney I found that Walter had organised a much larger party for my 50th. There were people from many areas of my past life. I don't know how he managed to find them all. Val told me Walter had been planning the party for six months.

I told my doctor that I was sure I had early onset Alzheimer's disease. I told him that my grandma and two aunts had ended their days with Alzheimer's. He told me he was sure I didn't have Alzheimer's but would send me to a gerontologist who would confirm I didn't have the disease.

Dr Jeneke, a psychiatrist and gerontologist attached to Hornsby hospital, told me he spent his days with Alzheimer's patients. He said I didn't have the disease but he realised there was something wrong with me. He needed to do more tests. I asked him what he thought was wrong.

The test results showed I had very low serotonin levels. These are usually found in people with severe depression, but I wasn't depressed. He said the problem could be solved by taking tablets that would increase my serotonin level, but we really should find out what was causing the problem. He said he spent his life with old people. Mine was an interesting case. If I would allow him he would like to take me on as a patient with weekly visits.

I received a lovely note from David Major about my Canadian report that he thought was excellent. He also congratulated me on my work on a tender for a strategic review of IT for the Singapore Government.

Even so, I was not comfortable at DMR. David seemed to be taking me under his wing directly which was nice, but Mark Lo was an unpleasant chauvinist pig and he was still officially my manager. What had I done? I had been at DMR less than a year. I had been made redundant from the ASX. My mind was going. Perhaps David Major was just being nice to me because he had hired me. It was all a mess.

I realised DMR had probably hired me because I had good contacts in industry and government. They wanted me to open doors and identify potential projects. It was really a marketing job. I hated marketing. I also hated Mark Lo, but what could I do? I'd been at DMR for less than a year. I'd just have to stick it out and hope life would improve.

Fortunately a new door was about to be opened.

57 University at last

AT THE END OF JULY Cyril Brookes rang me. He said his Institute of Information Technology (IIT) at the University of NSW, which was the joint venture with IBM to deliver IBM customer and internal staff training, was going very well. But he wanted to leave to pursue his research and develop the software he had designed to assist managers to make decisions. It was called Grapevine.

Cyril had been telling me about his software for years. It was a brilliant concept but few people understood what it did. He said he wanted a good manager for IIT. He was proud of what he had built and didn't want to give his baby to just anyone. Would I like to run IIT?

Of course I would! It would get me out of DMR. Maybe I could start work on a first degree that would lead to a PhD. I had never received real academic qualifications. I imagined I would have to take a pay cut. I was sure that a university wouldn't be able to pay me as much as a job in the IT industry would pay, but I didn't mind. I could manage easily on less money.

I told Cyril I'd love to run IIT. He reminded me that IIT was part of Unisearch, UNSW's commercial arm, and the ultimate decision about my appointment would have to be made by them. He said he would tell them I was his choice of manager and that he thought they were lucky I was available because few other people could do the job.

Cyril said he would appoint himself Chairman of IIT and establish an Advisory Board of Directors. He had been meaning to do that for a while. Now seemed to be the right time. I would be Director and report to Cyril. It all sounded fine and was subject to an interview with the Head of Unisearch.

The Head of Unisearch was taking a sabbatical so Cyril arranged that the Acting General Manager, Ross Lewis, would interview me over lunch with Cyril. We lunched at a fish restaurant in Kensington High Street. It was close to the University of NSW and also near Randwick Racecourse. I remembered Allan Moffatt telling me that it was frequented by criminals and was where all the big deals were done.

We had a pleasant lunch. Cyril did most of the talking, telling Ross all about my career and my professional activities with the Australian Computer Society and other committees I had served on.

At the end of the lunch, Ross said he was sure he would be able to appoint me. He just had to discuss such a senior appointment with his Board. It was a done deal.

THREE WEEKS LATER I received a letter confirming my appointment as Director of IIT. I resigned from DMR immediately. On 24 August Cyril wrote a memo stating that he would take up the role of Chairman of IIT on 2 October and I would take up the role as Director from the same date.

IIT's offices were on the 15th floor of Bondi Junction Towers. My huge office had views across Sydney and out to Bondi Beach. I spent the first few weeks getting to know the staff and meeting the academics who were delivering IBM's courses. I also met the IBM staff who were running their education department within IIT.

Cyril gave me some background about UNSW's relationship with IBM. He had been Head of the School of Information Systems within the Faculty of Commerce. UNSW also had a School of Computing Sciences within the Faculty of Engineering.

Cyril wanted his students to work on the computer platform that they were most likely to meet when after they finished university, which meant IBM. The academics in the School of Computing Sciences wanted their students to use computers that were the most advanced the University could afford. At the end of the 1980s, IBM computers were nowhere near the leading edge in computing.

Richard DeLamarter's book 'Big Blue: IBM's Use and Abuse of Power' was published in 1986 detailing IBM's tricks for maintaining its pre-eminent place in computing. IBM computers were used in over 80% of all large commercial companies in Australia and throughout the world. There had been an antitrust case against IBM in the USA, but this had been terminated by the business friendly Reagan administration in 1982, leaving IBM to continue its practices unchallenged.

Richard Delamater had been the senior economist for the US Department of Justice. He worked on the US Government case against IBM for eight years. He had access to all the material discovered during the case. His book revealed how IBM had carefully created an image of excellence when the truth was that it maintained its place in the industry through FUD (Fear, Uncertainty and Doubt) about its competitors' products. IBM's products at that time were generally inferior to those of other computer manufacturers in the market, as most IT professionals had long suspected.

WHEN UNSW NEEDED to acquire a new computer to support academic and student work Cyril recommended they should buy an IBM. The School of Computing Sciences said it could not teach or do its research on an IBM machine. Also, they wanted their students to be able to discriminate between good and bad computer architecture. In their opinion, IBM's computers were outdated technology.

Two groups formed, the Red team and the Blue team. The Blue team supported the acquisition of IBM computers. (People in the computer industry often called IBM 'Big Blue'). Cyril and his staff and supporters formed the Blue team. The Red team comprised the computer science academics and their supporters. Academics from the Red team, Professors Graeme Helestrand and John Hiller, presented papers at conferences on how poor IBM computers were. The UNSW Business School, the Australian Graduate School of Management, (AGSM) supported the Red team.

Cyril told me that the University decided to settle the matter in a way only a university would choose. They would hold a debate. The debate was to involve the Vice Chancellor, the two Pro Vice Chancellors and the Deans of the 13 Faculties. Cyril spoke for the Blue team and Jeremy Davis, who was then Dean of the AGSM, spoke on behalf of the Red team.

As he was not a Dean, Cyril was not allowed to vote. Jeremy voted against buying an IBM machine. All the other Deans and the VC's group voted in favour of buying IBM. Jeremy Davis immediately said he would resign his position as Dean of the AGSM.

UNSW bought an IBM machine. When IBM gave away their customer and internal education to Australian universities as part of their Partnerships for Development Program, those chosen were UNSW, Curtin University in Western Australia, Swinburne Institute of Technology in Victoria, and the University of Queensland.

Curtin decided to deliver only PC courses. UQ and Swinburne chose to deliver only courses for IBM's AS/400 minicomputer range. UNSW could deliver all IBM's courses and also took over courses in the other states that the other universities chose not to deliver. As NSW was by far IBM's biggest customer for IBM courses, UNSW's portion of the IBM education pie was about 90% of the whole.

THERE WAS A LOT of publicity in the computer press about my appointment at UNSW. I met Geoff Reynolds from the ASX for coffee. He told me my staff at ASX were pleased I had done well since I left.

He said he was telling Rory about my latest appointment when Rory exploded and said, "Ann, Ann, Ann, everyone keeps telling me how well she has done. She made me feel like my mother did when I wet my trousers when I was a little boy!"

This was a very telling comment. It reinforced my theory that I was made redundant at Rory's request not for something I had done but for who I was. He had often told me how competent his mother was. He must have had difficulty relating to a competent woman.

When I started taking medication to boost my serotonin, my memory lapses ceased. I enjoyed my weekly visits to Dr Jeneke, but we just seemed to chat about life in general. He hadn't found out why my serotonin levels had dropped so low.

I was driving one day when I distinctly heard my mother's voice saying, "You think you're so clever, my girl, wait until you're 40 or 50, it will all catch up with you!" She had said this when I got my job at Kodak and decided to discontinue weekly visits to the National Hospital for Nervous Diseases to check how much of my brain was working again.

I was eager to tell Dr Jeneke. He surprised me by saying "You've told me that story three times already." He said now I had realised the effect my mother's words had had on me when I reached 50, my serotonin levels would go back to normal. I asked him why he hadn't told me I had told him about my mother's comments.

He said I had to realise myself that that was the cause of my memory lapses. He said when he asked me how my current memory lapses felt I had told him I felt like I did when I couldn't remember things after my skull fracture when I was 18. He said if he had told me that it was my mother's words that had caused my current problems I never would have believed him.

I told him Geoff's story about Rory's outburst. He said Rory's problem was similar to mine. Rory's mother, who he obviously adored, had told him he was a failure, even if it was only when he wet his pants when he was a young boy. Every time he met a competent woman, he was scared she would expose his inadequacies. It all made sense to me now.

Dr Jeneke asked me how I felt when I had been made redundant. I said I felt inadequate and incompetent. He asked me if I felt angry. I told him I didn't get angry because my father had always got angry for seemingly no reason and I thought anger was a waste of energy.

Dr Jeneke then got angry with me. He said he thought my treatment by ASX was outrageous. He had read my reference and couldn't imagine why they let me go. He now understood and it made him angry. He explained that anger was good if used properly. He encouraged me to try it. He said suppressed anger turned to resentment.

I stopped taking the serotonin. I had no more memory lapses.

I ASKED THE PEOPLE at UNSW what they liked and did not like about the UNSW-IBM joint venture. They told me they did not feel comfortable having a commercial relationship with just one supplier. Everything else was okay.

I asked Frank Wroe, DEC's Managing Director, if UNSW could deliver his customer and internal education to help him meet his PDP commitments as we were doing for IBM. Frank said DEC preferred to do its own customer education but it did need help with its PDP commitments.

He reminded me that I had said it was difficult to get metrics for software development on a DEC platform. Would UNSW like $500,000 to develop metrics for DEC systems? Also, DEC was considering closing its Artificial Intelligence group but would like someone to keep an eye on AI research and advise DEC Australia if there was anything they might be interested in. This could be called research and would contribute to discharging DEC's PDP load. Of course I said we would be delighted.

Professor Ross Jeffrey of the School of Information Systems, who was considered to be Australia's expert in software development metrics, was delighted to get $250,000 to fund research into DEC metrics.

I knew that Dr Claude Sammut from the School of Electrical Engineering was researching AI and expert systems. He was developing an expert system that would significantly reduce the cost of pathology testing in Australia. Pathology tests on blood and urine samples were largely automated such that each sample was subject to a wide range of tests. But doctors ordered each specific test by name on a separate request sheet.

Pathology labs were bound by legislation to do each specifically requested test separately. Claude thought that if a doctor could be presented with an expert system that listed the tests that were run together, doctors could then just signify which of the results they were interested in, thus significantly reducing the number of tests and cost of testing. I asked Claude if he would like some funds to help with his research and, in return advise DEC on the status of current AI research. He gratefully accepted.

I also asked IBM what they did and didn't like about the joint venture. They told me they were sure that academics could not satisfy their customers as well as IBMers could.

I asked IBM how they measured customer satisfaction with education services. They told me that when they had delivered education, every customer evaluated each course. But evaluation forms weren't always filled in for IIT courses. I told them that from now on I would ensure attendees would evaluate each class and we would endeavour to exceed IBM's own performance in education delivery.

I WAS CONCERNED about the stories women in the IT industry told me the way they were treated. I certainly saw some unfair treatment, as in the ABC incident. I also felt I had been unfairly treated at times because of my gender. I couldn't quite put my finger on the reasons. Other women told me they had the same feelings but found it difficult to be specific.

I felt if we all shared our stories with each other we could develop strategies on how to handle different situations. We might be able to find out what works and what doesn't and help redress unfairness in our industry.

Less than one quarter of professionals in the industry were women, so I wanted to encourage more women into the profession. I tried to do this as I talked to girls in schools but we needed more women to help.

At the end of January 1990 I called a meeting of 16 senior women from the industry to discuss the matter. We all agreed that we wanted to help, but we didn't want to form a women's society or a women's lobby group and we didn't want to set up a formal structure with presidents and secretaries. We just wanted to form a self-help network. We established three objectives:

- To encourage women in IT to reach their potential. We realised that not all women wanted to get to the top. But they did want to feel they could reach the level they were comfortable with and not be held back because of their gender.
- To encourage more women to join the profession.
- To help all women, in every walk of life, better understand IT.

We decided we would run the group as a network, not a hierarchy. And because women often have little spare money, especially if they are single mothers or women in low paid positions, we would not charge a membership fee but women attending events would pay their share.

We had two top women computer journalists in our initial group, Helen Meredith and Beverly Head. They started seeking publicity for our group. After a few attempts at variations on 'Women in IT', which could be shortened to WIT but changed into halfwit, we decided to call ourselves FIT, Females in IT, to embrace the fitness craze.

I ENJOYED LIFE at the University. It was a stimulating environment and there were always dinners and lectures to attend. Every day there were new things to learn. The Campus Conference held on the last weekend in March showcased research being carried out by UNSW academics. My staff were nearly all excellent. Several were retired UNSW staff and worked at the same leisurely pace adopted by many of the academics I met. IIT also had several instructors who were not academics but taught courses and assisted with the running of IIT.

The man on my staff who impressed me most was Paul Boer. I appointed him my deputy. Cyril remarked that Paul was a nice enough fellow but not a person who would set the world on fire. It sounded to me a very good attribute for a deputy. Paul was also very intelligent and often won IBM's Lecturer of the Month prize.

Cyril had offices in the IIT space and was assisted in developing his software by what he called his Chinese laundry, a group of exceptionally bright student programmers from the School of Computing Science who were mostly of East Asian origin. It was a very happy working environment.

The two Professors from the School of Computer Science, Hiller and Helestrand, who had been the leaders of the anti IBM Red team, wanted to teach for IIT. IBM expected people teaching for them to wear the standard IBM smart dark suit, white shirt and tie. Hiller and Helestrand taught in scruffy jeans and sweaters and refused to wear suits. Also, they had little respect for the IBM course material and wanted to teach their way, which included throwing chalk at inattentive students. Yet they also wanted to earn the $1500 a day that we paid academics to teach for IIT.

I refused to allow them to teach unless they conformed to our standards. They took their case to the Vice Chancellor who told them I was running a commercial unit and 'What Ann says goes'. They didn't like it and started asking why this 'pretty blonde woman' who didn't even have a Bachelors Degree was being paid more than they were. Time, I thought, to get some academic qualifications myself.

THERE WERE SIGNS that IBM's supremacy in the computer industry was beginning to decline. The antitrust case the US Government had brought against IBM had been thrown out, but the bad publicity from DeLamarter's book, and IBM's hubris, was starting to hurt.

An antitrust suit was also brought against the Bell Telephone Company. It was broken up into regional 'Baby Bells', separate companies that would compete against each other. The move was disastrous for Bell Labs, which now had to exist on commercially funded research. The once great research laboratory, which had won seven Nobel prizes for pure research, now had to work on applied research.

We got in touch with Cousin Arno at Bell Labs. He told us that, although this meant less pure research, it was not all bad news. Before the divestment Bell was overburdened with bureaucracy and unprofitable. The Baby Bells were all trimmed down and eager to compete in the open market. They grew rapidly and most were very profitable, and gave Bell Labs plenty of research projects.

It might have been better for IBM if it had been forced to restructure. In the early 1990s its revenue and profitability started to decline. The company's aura and the IBM FUD factor were beginning to wane. The IT industry was changing, but IBM was not.

Other computer brands, especially the Japanese 'IBM clones', were far superior to IBM in terms of quality and price-performance. These machines, from Fujitsu, Amdahl and Hitachi Data Systems, were all doing well, in Australia and internationally, and knocking IBM out of many accounts.

A new breed of powerful but inexpensive minicomputers were starting to replace mainframes. IBM had failed to gain a significant share of the PC market and its software was losing ground to competitors. IBM was fighting, and losing, on many fronts.

A nice little story in the press in 1990 told how IBM Canada had ordered parts from a Japanese company stating that they wanted only 1.5% defective parts. This was a very high standard at that time. The Japanese firm shipped the goods with a note saying they didn't know why IBM wanted 1.5% defective parts but they had packed them separately for convenience.

58 Meeting life head-on

I PICKED UP MY NEW CAR at the University. I had been driving an IIT Holden Commodore but now I would have my own Ford Fairmont Ghia again. I drove home very carefully because I had a new car and it was raining heavily. I had just been to a fairly boring lecture about the UNSW dinosaur dig at Riversleigh. It was 11pm. Just after I crossed the Harbour Bridge, I saw undipped car headlights coming straight at me at tremendous speed. The traffic was heavy and there was no space in the line of cars to my left to cut into. The traffic was bumper to bumper in both directions.

Thinking I must have fallen asleep and was on the wrong side of the road, I glanced down to see that the line in the centre of the road was clearly on my right so I wasn't on the wrong side. Before I had time to take evasive action, the other car hit me head on.

There seemed to be no noise. There were lots of people milling around and all the traffic stopped. No one was taking any notice of me. I could see smoke coming out of the crumpled bonnet of my car. I thought, "I must be dead. This must be what it's like to be dead. You can see stuff going on but no one speaks to you because they know you are dead."

There was a man standing in the teeming rain next to my car. He was speaking on a mobile phone. I couldn't move. I couldn't get my car door open. My hands were locked by my sides. I thought that I could just about reach the car's horn with my nose. If I could make the horn sound then they'd know I wasn't dead.

The car horn blared. Once I managed to make it sound it wouldn't stop. In slow motion, the man bent down and looked through my broken car window.

"What's wrong love?" he said.

"I can't move and I think the car is going to catch fire," I said.

"Yes, we know," the man said. "We've tried to get you out but we can't. The emergency services are coming."

Just then everything seemed to speed up. A young couple said, "The car is about to go up. We can't just leave her there. Can you reach the car keys with your teeth? We think we can get the back door open and get you out that way." My new car was a station wagon.

I managed to get the keys out with my teeth and drop them out of the window. The young couple got in the back and hauled me over the backs of the seats. People were saying they were very brave and very crazy. Someone found a fire extinguisher and put the fire out.

The rain was still coming down in torrents. The road was blocked in both directions. It was a major road out of Sydney and even at 11pm the traffic was still very heavy. There were crowds of people milling around. I couldn't feel anything from my waist down but I wasn't in any pain.

I was carried onto the road and laid on a stretcher. There were five ambulances with their headlights on spotlighting the five stretchers lying in the road. There seemed to be three men and a woman lying on the ground on the other stretchers. The woman looked in a bad way with a drip and blood transfusion lines hanging round her. One of the men had a large bandage covered in blood on his head.

Why weren't we being put into the ambulances? Why were we still lying on the road in the rain? I heard someone on a two way radio. "We are completely full. We can only take them if they have life threatening injuries."

Then I heard someone calling Westmead Hospital. That was about an hour's drive away! There were many closer hospitals. I sat up and said to an ambulance man talking on a two-way radio, "That woman will never make it to Westmead. What's the hold-up?"

The man told me all hospitals were completely full due to a train crash the day before that killed several people. I remembered that the TV news had said there were over 100 casualties. Suddenly we were all put in ambulances and we were off. I couldn't see much but it felt like I was being taken back over the Harbour Bridge into Sydney.

I ARRIVED AT SYDNEY HOSPITAL, the city's old original hospital, on the edge of the CBD. Walter and Stephen were sent for. There were gunshot injuries and heart attacks all around me in the casualty ward. I kept on insisting I had no pain so more urgent cases were treated ahead of me but I still couldn't feel anything below my waist. My neck and spine were X-rayed. There seemed to be nothing wrong. I still couldn't stand or walk. At about 3am the doctor thought I was just suffering from shock and sent me home. He gave me some painkillers just in case I needed them. He told me to walk about and not stay in bed or I would stiffen up.

I got home about 4am and woke just before noon. I still could not stand or walk without hanging onto something, and I still had no feeling from my waist down. I rang UNSW to tell them I had written off their car. The man who managed the car pool told me not to think I had the record for writing off UNSW cars. A professor had wrapped one round a telegraph pole just 20 minutes after he collected his new vehicle

We called our doctor and he visited telling me I was just suffering from shock but might get some pain later. My friends Geoff and Val said they would call over to see how I was and bring dinner. Around 6pm I was sitting in a chair when a wave of intense pain hit my whole body. I took pain killers but they had little effect. I resisted calling the doctor again as it was getting late and I had been told to expect pain.

I had a very unpleasant night. The next day our neighbour who was a nurse visited. She remarked that my feet were very swollen. They were about twice normal size and very black and blue. I persevered with the painkillers for another few days, walking as much as I could.

About six days after the accident we called the doctor again. He looked at my swollen feet and asked if the hospital had X-rayed my feet. They had not. The doctor sent me straight to see an orthopaedic specialist.

More X-rays were taken. They showed I had compound fractures in every metatarsal bone in my right foot and stress fractures in every bone in both ankles. The specialist said no wonder I was in pain. The injuries were similar to those I would have got jumping out of a 6th floor window onto concrete. My bones were very strong. It would have been better had I broken my legs.

They told me that probably most damage had been done in pulling me out of the car rather than waiting to be cut out. But then the car looked as if it would catch fire so what else could have been done? Also, walking on badly broken feet and ankles for six days hadn't helped much.

From that point I was not allowed to walk at all. After several visits to specialists I was told I might never walk more than a few steps again. Being a bushwalker this was devastating. No more trips to the Snowy Mountains or bush walks with my camping friends.

AFTER THREE WEEKS at home, I felt well enough to go back to work. It was hard being in a wheelchair. The only wheelchair accessible toilet was on the first floor. It was kept locked so I first had to get the key from the janitor on the ground floor and return the key after.

I took taxis to and from work. Getting a taxi to take me home was difficult. If we tried to book a wheelchair taxi none would come. My secretary Ellen would stand on the taxi rank. When a taxi was available I would emerge from a nearby doorway and the taxi, once hired, had to accept his fare. Still several claimed not to be able to get their boot open so could not carry my wheelchair. I was beginning to realise how difficult life was in a wheelchair.

IBM established a teaching facility with North Sydney TAFE College. I was invited to the grand opening by the State Minister for Education. I arrived 30 minutes early so I could find out how to navigate the building and find the invalid toilets. The carpet on the floor was so thick that it was impossible to use a wheelchair unaided.

The toilets had a wheelchair enabled cubicle with a wide door but someone had decided to add a panel to make it a 'normal' door. They had also decided the huge space in the toilet needed to be filled up and had affixed a large waste paper towel basket in the middle of the room, making it impossible to accommodate a wheelchair.

The Director was proud of his new facility. I pointed out the problem. He told me the architect had specifically designed the building to be wheelchair friendly. What could they have done better? I suggested they should hire a wheelchair and try it themselves.

After six weeks the specialists suggested I could try going back to work for a couple of days a week. When I told them I had already been back full time for three weeks they were amazed.

Deborah, the young woman who ran her car into mine, was a student at UNSW, as was her brother. They were the children of wealthy Chinese parents who lived in North Sydney. She was in hospital for three months. She had broken her jaw in several places and fractured her pelvis in addition to suffering several internal injuries. Her brother, who was also in the car, fractured his skull.

When the parents found out I had a senior position at UNSW they asked me not to expel their children. I told them I had no power to do so. Deborah remembered nothing about the accident. She was banned from driving for ten years.

ONE DAY BY CHANCE I bumped into Lyndon Lane, who had been Mick Duncan's boss at DEC. Mick sold the DEC computers to ASX. Lyndon said she had decided to leave corporate life.

For some time I had been toying with the idea of establishing a software house or consultancy as part of IIT to give work to people who wanted to work from home on a flexible basis. I thought it might help women during their child rearing years, just as working for fpl had helped me. I thought Lyndon would be just the person to run that organisation. I put the suggestion to her. She accepted.

I was feeling better. Unisearch renewed my contract for three more years. Lyndon Lane also wrote to tell me she would like to run IIT Services. Just a short while later I got a significant salary increase.

We launched IIT Services at a breakfast in the Royal Botanic Gardens in Sydney on 4 December 1990. Lyndon had prepared a very professional launch that was well attended. She had organised golf umbrellas for the guests with the new IIT Services logo. The morning had been sunny but just as guests were leaving and being handed their umbrellas, fine rain began to fall. I told Lyndon that she couldn't have planned her launch any better. We both thought it was an omen of good things to come.

Mum came for Christmas again. We did the usual pre Christmas round of parties and theatres. Just after Christmas, Walter decided to go to USA to visit his relatives. Mum and I went to the Snowy Mountains with my friends. It was frustrating for me because I couldn't join in on the walks but neither could Mum so we took the ski train and chairlifts.

We visited Claire at Colly Farms and met her new boyfriend, Rodney. We asked Mum if she would like to go in a helicopter. Colly Farms had several helicopters. The pilot would take visitors for a joy ride for a slab of beer. The pilot assembled the helicopter before our eyes. When he was nearly ready he asked if we wanted the doors on or off. I asked Mum. She said just do what we usually did. I said, "Doors off."

Mum asked where the helicopter was. I looked at her in amazement. She had watched the pilot get it ready. It was whirring its engine in front of us. Mum looked at the tiny bubble fronted helicopter and said, "When the US President gets into a helicopter there are steps leading up to the doors and lots of men get in."

I assured her this was the helicopter we were going to ride, without doors. She had a great time flying low over the cotton fields chasing mobs of kangaroos and didn't want the trip to end.

BACK IN SYDNEY my feet and ankles were still very painful. I could walk about 100 metres with a stick but I thought I did too much while we were away. I went again to see my specialist and was told that one day my ankles would just crumble into dust and I would no longer be able to walk. It was not a happy prospect.

When Walter returned to Sydney, before I could tell him my news about my feet and ankles, he informed me that he wanted me to leave our house. While he was in the USA, he had met a woman who had been his mistress when he was younger. She was married and would not leave her husband but he had died and Walter had invited her to come to Australia and live with him.

What a shock! Just like that, out of the blue! I asked Walter not to say anything to my mother who was to leave in a few days. I didn't want her to be upset. Walter said I could stay in 'his' bed until his new lady arrived in three months. Then, if I hadn't found anywhere to live, I could move into the spare room. I reminded Walter that the house was jointly owned and I would take my share and leave as soon as possible.

The Sydney housing market was very depressed at that time so I easily found a brand new 'executive villa' with a small garden that was just right for Stephen and me. It was all on one level and easy to navigate in a wheelchair.

The economy was depressed largely due to the first Gulf War and the increasing cost of oil. The IT industries were in free fall, but IIT and IIT Services continued to thrive. I was appointed as a Director on the Advisory Board of the Institute of Administration at UNSW. It was a prestigious Board that included all the top Execs at UNSW.

IBM HAD ANNOUNCED its first UNIX computer, the RS/6000, would be built in Australia as part of its PDP obligations. This was IBM's first move into the UNIX environment. IBM's version of UNIX was called AIX. It was almost plain vanilla UNIX, and although IBM had stated on many occasions that it supported the adoption of open systems there was a suspicion that AIX would be 'enhanced' so that it would become an IBM proprietary system. This would bind customers more closely to IBM and make a change away from IBM more difficult for their customers, just as had been done on other IBM computers.

The RS/6000 computers would only be built at IBM's Wangaratta plant in Australia, in Japan and the USA. Australia would supply all Asian countries except Japan. Previously, Wangaratta had been one of only four plants producing IBM PCs.

David Bolt was the IBM Exec in charge of RS/6000s and UNIX. He said he was so impressed with IIT that he asked us to deliver all IBM's UNIX education in Australia and Asia except Japan. This was a tremendous vote of confidence in our capabilities and fitted well with UNSW skills. It enabled us to bring instructors from the School of Electrical Engineering into IIT.

It was also an opportunity to include the School of Computing at the Australian Defence Force Academy. ADFA is part of the University of NSW but based in Canberra, at Duntroon Military College. Jenny Seberry, a senior lecturer at the University of Sydney had just been appointed at ADFA as Australia's first female Professor of Computing.

I was surprised when Jenny welcomed me warmly and then burst into tears. She said her appointment to ADFA had been the worst thing that could have happened to her. ADFA was totally male dominated culture and the men were horrible to her. They kept digging holes for her to fall into. Jenny had been used to the supportive, inclusive environment at the University of Sydney under John Bennett, where her expertise had been highly valued. Jenny had been given many high value research grants for her work on telecommunications for which she was well known in Australia.

I told Jenny, welcome to the real world. She said she was going to take sick leave or quit altogether. Jenny had a brilliant mind and charming personality. She was a large woman who rarely bothered with female trappings like makeup and sophisticated hairstyles and clothes.

After lunch, I had a meeting with Jenny's lecturers. They told me they knew I was a friend of Jenny's and that she was dreadful. She was totally unfeminine and should leave ADFA. I told them they were lucky to have an academic with such a high standing in the IT industry and who brought such high value research to ADFA. But after only six months she took up a temporary post in the USA. When she returned to Australia it was as Professor of Computing at the University of Wollongong.

We reorganised the classrooms in ITT and established a large RS/6000 UNIX laboratory. I contacted Peter Ivanov, who was in charge of computer support in the School of Computer Science. I asked if he could organise a team of computer scientists that could deliver UNIX education. This would involve trips throughout Asia as well as all over Australia.

Peter chose some of his colleagues in Computer Science and a brilliant PhD student, Ashley Aitken, who became one of our best instructors, regularly winning IBM's Instructor of the Month prize. Peter asked me if he could invite his friend Chris Doney, who was in charge of computer support at the AGSM. Chris ran a DEC UNIX shop. He and his staff were all familiar with UNIX and readily adapted to teaching IBM's AIX.

IN MAY 1990 IBM renewed its contract with IIT for a further three years. This time, the contract was for the whole of Australia, and for all Asia in the case of RS/6000s. IBM said it liked dealing with IIT but didn't like dealing with the other universities. But IIT could outsource training to them, so long as quality and customer satisfaction levels were met.

IBM itself was changing. Margins on hardware sales were very thin. IBM announced a new strategic direction, saying it would move into the delivery of applications software and services.

Soon after, I was waiting by the lifts at IIT when a man who had been hanging around in the foyer tried to push open the main door. He seemed annoyed when it wouldn't open. I asked if I could help him. He said he was looking for the IBM training centre. I offered to show him round. He was very brusque. He asked me how much money the centre made for UNSW. I told him that was confidential but he might get the information from UNSW. He walked off looking very disgruntled.

Two weeks later, the man presented himself at our reception again asking for me. He informed me his name was Richard Kaan and he was the new head of Unisearch, which meant he was my new boss. He said now would I tell him how much IIT made for UNSW. I said that information was still confidential and he would have to ask UNSW or Unisearch.

I rang Ross Lewis, the Acting Head of Unisearch, and asked him about Richard Kaan. I didn't know Unisearch had been looking for a new boss. Ross said he hadn't been consulted and had only just been told himself. He said, "Watch out for Richard Kaan, he's a nasty piece of work."

The next time I visited Unisearch Richard Kaan was in the Director's office and Ross Lewis had been relegated to a tiny office at the back of the building. This was not good.

59 The Land of the Midnight Sun

I **WAS INVITED** to represent Australia and give a paper on women in IT in Australia at the first IFIP women's conference that was to be held in a tiny town in Finland just north of the Arctic Circle. My paper was to be given on 1 July.

I was very excited. This was just a week after the summer solstice on 23 June. I had always wanted to see the Midnight Sun. There was also to be an overnight boat trip to St Petersburg and a day visiting the famous Hermitage Museum, then back to Helsinki by boat. St Petersburg was another place I had always wanted to visit.

IBM had also been asking me to visit head office at Armonk north of New York in the USA. IIT was now well exceeding all IBM's own quality metrics and IBM corporate now wanted to know how a university could deliver IBM education better than IBM staff. I thought I could also visit my Mum and perhaps take her on holiday for a week or so.

My trip was approved by Ross Lewis and Cyril. IBM was paying my Business Class fare. I had booked my ticket. I advised Richard Kaan I was going overseas. He said he wanted to see my itinerary. He said I could go to IBM in the USA as they were paying my fare but I could not go to a 'silly women's junket' in Finland nor could I visit my mother in England.

I pointed out that it was an honour to be invited to represent Australian women at IFIP. I had been selected by the Australian Government and had agreed to give a paper. He grudgingly said I could go to Finland but I had to choose between going to St Petersburg and visiting my mother. If I visited my mother, I could only spend five days including a weekend.

I couldn't understand why this man was being so unpleasant. Cyril contacted him on my behalf and said I was due leave. IIT had exceeded all its targets. Cyril would deputise for me while I was away. Richard Kaan told Cyril that if that was the game he would cancel my trip altogether. Cyril said I should tread carefully until we found out why he was being so unpleasant.

THE IFIP WOMEN'S conference was not as well patronised as expected, probably because of the global downturn in the fortunes of the IT industry, so the conference was transferred to Helsinki, where we were billeted at the University. Even though Helsinki was below the Arctic Circle, I still might see the Midnight Sun.

There were about 100 women from many countries. On the night before the conference, the Finnish Government arranged a reception given by their deputy Prime Minister. We were taken by bus to a large old house in the country. The countryside was beautiful. The hedgerows were full of pink dog roses and lilac. The warm summer air was filled with perfume.

When we arrived at our destination, after some short speeches, we were told there was to be a Finnish barbeque. The house had a large sauna and was by a lake. Until dinner was ready we were encouraged to use the sauna and lake. The Finnish women explained the procedure. We were each given two large towels and escorted to the sauna. The Finns discarded their towels and went into the sauna naked. Most women were more modest.

The woman from India and others from South-East Asia remained fully covered. When we could take no more heat, the Finnish women, still naked, led the way to the lake and jumped in. The rest of us were more modest and covered our bodies with towels, especially as the way to the lake was past some men barbequing our dinner. The men took no notice at all of naked women running past them.

Some of the women wouldn't go into the lake. Some tried to keep their towels round them. Some kept their towels on until the last minute. The lake was freezing. I swam to one of the Finnish women, my teeth chattering. She told me the ice had melted on the lake only three weeks earlier. In the winter they jumped through the ice. It was invigorating!

When it was time for dinner we were all very chatty. We ate dinner in the twilight by the lake. It was a wonderful introduction to a new country.

The next day I gave my paper. I outlined our objectives in FIT to increase and support the number of women in IT in Australia and to ensure that all women better understood IT. I also spoke about my own career in IT and how working for fpl while my children were young had helped me get back into the industry at a senior level. I told them I had started a similar enterprise in Australia.

That night we went to the Skylight Bar. It had a glass roof. I sat with colleagues until midnight. I could still read a newspaper without the aid of artificial light.

The next day we went to the lovely harbourside markets. I was surprised to see huge strawberries and peaches and all the summer fruits and vegetables I associated with the south of France, all grown in Finland.

Next day I flew to London. I was sad to only have a few days with my mother but she was very pleased to show off her globe trotting daughter to her friends in the retirement home where she had a small flat.

THEN I FLEW TO NEW YORK and travelled up to White Plains, about a hour north of the city and near IBM's headquarters in Armonk. When I got there I met IBM's Head of Learning worldwide. He congratulated me on breaking all customer satisfaction records for course delivery and asked me how we managed it.

I told him that all my instructors were practicing IT professionals as well as tutors. IBM's customers rated each IIT course they attended. I told all my instructors I expected them to achieve above satisfactory ratings. If any student rated the course lower I phoned them to find out why. Sometimes they said it was IBM's course material. Rarely it was IIT's facilities or organisation.

If it was because they rated the instructor poorly I would meet with the instructor to try to find out why. Instructors knew that if they got three ratings that were only satisfactory I would not allow them to teach for three months. One more satisfactory rating and they were off the team.

I had over 70 instructors who were all keen to find out about real life issues in the IT industry. They told their students that if they had technical problems at work relating to the products described in the course they were taking, then the instructors would stay back at the end of each day to try to help them solve their problems.

If we were asked questions about IBM products we gave honest answers without disparaging the product or IBM. As an example, I said that IBM's current version of DB2, its relational database product, did not support all 12 of Ted Codd's principles for relational database design. IBM instructors always argued with students telling them DB2 supported Codd's ideas exactly. The IBM Learning man took frantic notes.

He took me on a tour of IBM's Learning facility. Many of their regional Learning centres in the USA were video linked. This technology was very new. Just before the prolonged airline pilot's strike in 1990, IBM Australia had established its ISEN (Interactive Satellite Education Network) to link its education facilities in all Australian capital cities. IIT's instructors had done some teaching via the new ISEN located at IBM Australia's teaching facility in North Sydney.

ISEN classes were taught under TV type lights and instructors had to wear full TV makeup. Most didn't like getting made up but two of our instructors were into amateur dramatics so loved the process. The ISEN system was two way for sound so students could ask instructors questions, but it was only one way for video so instructors could not see if students were present or not.

The service was especially popular during the airline pilot's strike because students could not easily travel and ISEN classes were held in every state capital city. Before ISEN, customers had to travel to Sydney for some of the more advanced courses and so there were accommodation costs in addition to travel costs.

In the USA, the IBM video system was also used to bring short talks by university lecturers to IBM customers. In Australia, IBM's customers were encouraged to use ISEN for company meetings, but few did.

I was interviewed on IBM's internal TV and taken to meet other IBM executives to be told about IBM's future strategic direction and new products. I had mentioned that we were doing some research for DEC, although I said the work we were doing was confidential. I was taken to the famous Thomas J. Watson Research Center at Yorktown Heights.

The Yorktown Heights facility compared favourably with Bell Labs. It was out in the countryside. Staff were more casually dressed than other IBM staff who still wore dark suits, white shirts and conservative ties.

I was taken to see the processor farm. I had been told that pure research demanded high compute power and complex maths facilities. The processor farm was rows of IBM 303X computers. I said these could not possibly be used for high compute work. I expected to see Cray computers. I was assured IBM did all its research on these machines.

I WAS INTRODUCED to an Australian, Dr Greg Rose, who had lunch with us. He was working at the Thomas J. Watson Research Center on a sabbatical. I asked him if he knew Dr Greg Clark, who was then IBM Australia's Chief Scientist. Yes, he did. Greg Clark was researching neutrinos and was a friend of Paul Boer, my deputy at IIT, who had shared rooms with Greg at Uni. Greg Clark and I often discussed his research. He was fascinated to discover I knew Arno Penzias at Bell Labs, who was one of his heroes.

Over lunch I again said IBM couldn't be doing advanced research using 303X machines. Finally, after lunch, I was sworn to secrecy and taken to see the GF9 computer. It was in the dark in a tiny back room. It was an array of DEC Alpha computers! It was called the GF9 because it delivered 9 billion floating-point operations per second. Now that sounded more like it.

IBM also showed me the work it was doing in parallel processing. The researchers said they had managed to link about 250 processors in parallel. The computers they were using were Transputers. They were amazed when I told them I had worked for its designer Iann Baron and he had spoken about the Transputer at our ACS conference in 1988.

They asked me if UNSW would like to do research for IBM. Greg Rose was due to return to Australia soon. Could he continue his research at IIT? We would be the first university outside USA to be given some research. Would US$2 million do for a start? I said I'd be delighted. They said they would get the paperwork ready and send it to Brian Finn, head of IBM Australia. It would also help IBM Australia meet its PDP obligations. Greg Rose thought it was a splendid idea. He was wondering what to do when he got back to Australia. He was enjoying working on his current project. Now he could do it back home.

IBM then suggested I visit Cornell University in upstate New York. IBM had a special relationship with Cornell. It was one of five universities in USA that did research for IBM. My trip was arranged for the next day.

Cornell University is one of the old Ivy League universities. The buildings actually were covered in ivy and looked very old but were not. Cornell had its own five star hotel that supported their Hotel Management studies. As a guest there, I was made very comfortable.

The man in charge of IBM relations was my guide. He said he couldn't tell me what they were doing for IBM Research but it was always interesting work and brought a lot of prestige to Cornell. He also showed me the hardware IBM had given them to support their research. He told me Cornell ran a series of IT courses for schoolchildren in the vacations. These were very popular. I thought it was something that IIT could run for UNSW.

BACK IN AUSTRALIA I told Cyril I had managed to get US$2 million research from IBM. He told me DEC was now ready to give IIT all its customer and internal training. Cyril arranged a meeting with the Vice Chancellor and the other top Execs at UNSW to share the good news.

Cyril and I then went to tell Richard Kaan. On the way to visit Richard, Cyril told me he had found out why Richard was so horrid to me. Richard had been recommended to Unisearch by his friend Jeremy Davies, who was Cyril's sworn enemy after the debacle of the debate on IBM computers that made Jeremy resign as Dean of the AGSM and take the more lowly position as Professor. Richard was not against me personally, but was determined to close IIT to get back at Cyril.

Cyril said he had discussed this with the Vice Chancellor. The VC said Richard wouldn't be able to close IIT. We had a three year contract with IBM. Cyril said now we had DEC training and research as well as IBM's and Richard just couldn't just shut us down.

It was time to start on my journey to get a PhD. I planned to complete before my 60th birthday so I thought I better get started. I contacted Professor Ross Jeffrey, who was now the Head of the School of Information Systems at UNSW. I asked if I could enrol in a first degree. Ross laughed and said he wouldn't take me into a first degree. I knew more than his lecturers. I asked how then could I get a PhD. Ross told me Macquarie University was taking experienced people straight into a Masters program. I applied and was accepted.

I contacted Di Ryall, Managing Director of Apple Computers in Australia, to ask if we could deliver some multimedia training for Apple. She agreed so we established an Apple multimedia lab at IIT.

It was a time of deregulation of telecommunications in Australia. A second carrier license was to be let. It would be competition for Telstra that had, up to that time, been the sole government owned telecommunications company. The second carrier was called Optus, and was made responsible for Australia's domestic satellites, which were privatised, to get it started. There were two consortiums bidding for the Optus licence.

One group preparing for the Optus bid occupied the floor above IIT at Bondi Junction. Optus was a consortium of companies including Bell South, Cable & Wireless, DEC, the large Australian transport company Mayne Nickless, and insurance companies National Mutual and AMP. I started building a relationship with them to try to capture their training if they won the bid.

Australia was in recession. The Treasurer Paul Keating got a lot of bad publicity by saying it was the 'recession we had to have'. All the IT companies were hurting. In October IBM announced its profit had dropped by 85%. But IIT's revenue for 1991 increased to 130% of 1990 and was well over $4 million a year.

In November I was asked to join the Australian Information Industries Association delegation in a meeting of ASOCIO, the Asian-Oceanian Computing Industry Organisation in Kuala Lumpur.

At ASOCIO, countries of the region showcased their IT skills and discussed how trade between them could be improved. It was great fun and very stimulating. I was amazed at how much KL had grown since I had been there on honeymoon with Allan Moffatt.

At the end of 1991 IBM decided to close the joint venture it had with NSW TAFE. It had been established with funding of $12 million, $8 million from IBM and $4 million from TAFE. It was based on AS/400 computers, IBM's business oriented minicomputer range. Most companies running AS/400s ran packaged software so needed little staff training. Swinburne Institute of Technology ran IBM's AS/400 education in Victoria and the University of Queensland in that state. The contract in NSW had not been let as part of the initial IIT deal but that was of no concern as IIT felt there was very little need for AS/400 training in NSW.

IBM had predicted that 1100 students a year would graduate from the TAFE/IBM facility. But since it opened early 1990 it had graduated only 49 students. The prospects for 1992 and beyond looked no better.

I agreed to take over the facility as long as it did not cost IIT any money. We would supply instructors and train in the TAFE facilities but only when there were sufficient students to at least break even. Although we worked very hard to make the venture a success it finally closed at the end of 1992.

CLAIRE AND HER NEW MAN Rodney came to stay for a few days in August. They had just got engaged. They were going on a round-the-world trip. Their first stop would be to visit Claire's Dad, Alan Leach, who was still working for Kodak in Rochester. While they were there they got married in a ceremony hosted by Alan. They visited my Mum in England and showed her the beautiful wedding dress that Alan's wife had bought for her. My Mum asked if they had told me they were married but they said they were saving that until they got back to Australia.

Rodney's Mum and Dad were upset that they had not been invited to the wedding. Rodney was their youngest and much loved son. Claire was much older than Rodney. I think they thought she was cradle snatching. When they arrived back in Australia they gave a real Australian party for all their friends and relations.

My mother came again for four months over the English winter at the end of 1991. I was pleased that I could still afford to pay for her to come Business Class. We had the usual round of parties and theatre outings and went to see Claire and Rodney.

Mum looked very frail when I took her to the airport for her return trip in February. Sadly, she died about ten days after her return to England. It was a good way to end her life. She was 81, had had a very good time in Australia and was fit and well. When she left us she looked tanned and bonny and she died without pain.

60 Management problems

ON NEW YEAR'S DAY 1992 Grace Hopper died. She had made it to Rear Admiral in the US Navy, the first woman to reach flag rank. I remembered her prediction that mainframe computers would eventually be replaced by 'multitudes of minis'. It hadn't yet come true but the research we were doing for IBM was part of the journey. What sort of 'minis' did Grace Hopper have in mind when she made the prediction in the early 1970s?

As time went by I thought she meant PCs. But they were still not very powerful, even though they could now be linked using ISO standards or the newer, more simple TCP/IP that had been developed to link computers on the Internet. The embryonic Internet had been functioning since the late 1960s using the Experimental Packet Switching Service (EPSS) developed at the National Physics Laboratory in the UK.

During the 1970s and 1980s most Internet users were in the US Department of Defense, led by DARPA, the Defense Advanced Research Projects Agency and the universities. They passed messages and exchanged files, usually research papers. In the late 1980s big technology companies like IBM established their own global networks to transfer files of data and email messages. The Videotex System I had worked on in the UK in the mid 1970s was an experiment in networked shopping and information exchange in UK. But these networks were unreliable and slow.

In the early 1990s the Internet was opened to commercial users. But it was only when the World Wide Web, which made it much easier to navigate between Internet addresses, and web browsers became widely available after 1993 that the Internet really took off.

In the early 1990s PCs were still very clunky. In business they were mainly used as 'intelligent terminals' linked to private networks connected to large mainframe computers, or as stand-alone word processors, or for spreadsheets and to prepare slides for presentations.

Most PCs used MS-DOS, an operating system that was full of bugs and hard to use. The 'MS' stood for 'Microsoft'. IBM lost the opportunity to own the PC space when in 1981 it paid US$32,000 to a small company called Microsoft for a PC operating system rather than develop its own, which would have taken much longer.

That meant Microsoft owned the PC operating space. Software standards were becoming more important than hardware standards. Ten years later

IBM finally built its own PC operating system called OS/2. It was a better operating system than MS-DOS but it was all too late. In the meantime Microsoft founder Bill Gates became the world's richest man.

Apple presented an alternative to IBM and Microsoft. Its computers were elegant, with a simple operating system based on UNIX. The design was based on the Graphical User Interface (GUI) software built at Xerox PARC. The screen images were based on bitmap technology and scrolled smoothly. Apple had modified and improved that software, developing windows that overlapped and could be seen as folders lying on a desktop. But the market saw Apple computers as toys for hobbyists or arty types.

THE RESEARCH WE DID for IBM was much more like Grace Hopper's 'multitudes of minis'. By the 1990s, universities and researchers were using fairly powerful desktop workstations from DEC or Sun Microsystems. These were inexpensive enough to be purchased as PCs but were much more powerful. They were usually linked to the Internet, which enabled communication with other users.

But sometimes researchers needed extra compute power for a short time. Conversely, researchers were often not using their computers for periods of time if they were away at conferences, or on sabbatical or holidays, or lecturing or at weekends. Or they might not be using the full compute power and some could be put to good use by others.

The University of Wisconsin developed a concept it called Condor, which harnessed available compute power and lent it to people on the network who needed more power. Condor was based on a thought experiment developed by Maurice Wilkes for sharing processor capacity on the Cambridge Ring system developed at Cambridge University in the 1960s.

The University of Wisconsin people conceptualised a condor, a giant bird of prey circling over the network, taking spare capacity and giving it to anyone on the system who needed more. The management was very complex, because the moment capacity was taken away, it could be that the very next instant it was needed by the user from whom it was taken. This was complicated further if charge-out between users was involved.

IBM saw an opportunity to sell powerful workstations networked through an IBM propriety network where a computer owner would contract to make any spare capacity available to others on the network. The big challenge was the management of the system so that each user got the capacity guaranteed within their contract.

This management issue was the challenge Greg Rose had been working on at IBM's labs and for which UNSW was given research funding to solve. IBM called its system the Farm Project because it called the gathering and sharing of capacity 'farming'. The new RS/6000 workstations were ideal for the purpose.

By the late 1990s many hardware suppliers and system providers were working in this space. The concept was then called Grid Computing. Later in the 2000s and into the early 2010s these systems were usually referred to as Grid Cloud Computing, or just Cloud Computing. This collaborative and cooperative computing using powerful workstations was just what Grace Hopper had envisaged.

I decided to try to mend bridges with the Australian Graduate School of Management and Jeremy Davies in particular. I asked if we could establish Greg Rose's Research work in the AGSM. Of course they were delighted. The launch of the initiative was held at the AGSM.

Head of major Australian software and services company Computer Power Dr Roger Buckeridge attended the launch, though he had not been invited. He was an officious man who said he now represented ACCI, the Government's Australian Computing and Communications Institute. He told me that IBM had promised to give ACCI any research it might do in Australia. I told him the research funds we had been given came direct from IBM in the USA. I thought he might make a scene at the launch but he didn't.

EARLY IN 1992, after its first loss in decades, IBM abandoned its 'no layoffs' policy. It also restructured into three divisions and divested itself of many business areas that were no longer profitable. Industry watchers said that had IBM been forced to restructure under the antitrust case as Bell Labs had been, then this 1990s restructure would have been less painful and the company might have been more profitable. Pundits were predicting the death of the mainframe and proprietary systems and the rise of powerful workstations and open systems.

Several IBM staff decided to enrol in tertiary courses for a year or two, after which they thought the market would have recovered and their services would be in demand. Several IBM Execs joined the Masters program I had enrolled in at Macquarie University. In our first lecture the young lecturer told us how to analyse computer performance. What he was saying was totally incorrect.

One by one the IBM Execs stood up and told him he was on the wrong track. They were told to sit down. I decided to keep my head down in class and act the naïve student but in our break I told the lecturer that the IBMers were correct. He asked me who I thought set and marked my exams, and told me to listen very carefully to what he said.

At the end of the lecture we were told to read the relevant chapter of our textbook. The book confirmed what we already knew about analysing computer performance. During the week students phoned each other to ask if they had read the chapter. At the start of the next lecture the six ex-IBMers confronted the lecturer and used the chapter to support their argument. The lecturer replied that he had now read that chapter and they were correct. He confessed he was only one chapter ahead of us in the textbook.

Nothing I was told in the three years I spent on that Masters degree had any bearing on anything I had done in the previous 20 years working in the industry. The students who did well were those who had not worked in the industry but who regurgitated what the lecturers fed them. But it was a hurdle I had to jump to get into the PhD program. Fortunately, after reaching diploma level, halfway through the Masters, I was allowed to transfer to the PhD program.

IBM CONTINUED TO HURT, all around the world. Its share price dropped to its lowest for over ten years. IBM blamed its woes on the fact that capital was tight and companies were just not buying large mainframes. It retrenched over 40,000 employees worldwide.

In September 1992 IBM Australia announced it would probably make a loss for the year. In the 1980s the local operation had moved into impressive new custom-built headquarters at West Pennant Hills in the north-west suburbs of Sydney. In 1992 these were sold and leased back to free up capital. At year end over 1000 people in Australia took up IBM's generous redundancy offers and left the company. Brian Finn, head of IBM Australia, announced the company's emphasis would shift from selling hardware to the more lucrative and faster growing services business.

It was true that the world economy was suffering a downturn, but IBM itself was suffering far more. It had lost many loyal mainframe customers to the Japanese clones and had never really gained a decent share of the PC market. Now it was desperately reducing prices to maintain position, but this was eroding profits and not really helping to gain market share. IBM needed a drastic solution or it would vanish.

Cyril and I were called to West Pennant Hills to meet Brian Finn. He said he realised that IIT had a three year contract and he acknowledged that we were providing outstanding service to his customers, but because IBM was reducing margins it also needed to reduce costs. He suggested IBM pay us a flat $400 a day for delivering its education.

To that point our rates were based on days per student. IBM retained a small proportion of the fees for marketing, administration and course material, and paid travel and living costs if we had to send instructors outside Sydney. We paid our instructors $1000 a day. In addition, we had the cost of running the Bondi Junction facility, purchasing new hardware when necessary and training new instructors.

Cyril and I were horrified. We doubted that our instructors would take a huge pay cut. At $400 a day the university would be subsidising IBM. IBM was not going to reduce fees to customers but just take the margins and force IIT to take a loss.

Cyril and I relayed the information to the Vice Chancellor, who agreed IIT could not subsidise IBM. We then told Richard Kaan, who of course said IIT should be closed immediately. We told him we had plenty of other offerings and IIT Services was coming along nicely. IBM had only made a proposal. They hadn't insisted we take a revenue cut. We needed time to negotiate.

I was contacted by Bell Labs, which wanted to establish a research facility in Australia as a joint venture with a university to help it penetrate the Asian market. I contacted the Dean of Electrical Engineering. He was delighted to be included in meetings with Bell Execs from the USA. The research Bell wanted to do in Australia involved GPS (Global Positioning System), the technology I has seen at Xerox and Mercedes.

UNSW had been approached by Tata, the huge Indian conglomerate. Tata wanted to establish a University of Technology in India that specialised in IT, computer science and communications. Initially the only students would be the sons and daughters of Tata Execs. They envisaged sending the students to UNSW in Australia for the first two years of study and back to India for their third year when UNSW lecturers would teach in India. Degrees would be conferred by UNSW.

Richard Kaan asked me to manage the discussions with Tata and liaise with UNSW to organise teaching staff. I couldn't understand why he had asked me to manage what seemed to be a very lucrative initiative until we reached the point of signing a Memorandum of Understanding (MOU) that outlined and confirmed the agreement.

The MOU was signed by the Vice Chancellor on behalf of UNSW and the Tata people organised a dinner to celebrate. Richard was asked to deputise for the VC. I watched with interest as he squirmed while being spoken to by the Indians and ensured he sat quite a distance from them. The next day he told me he hated Indians. They always smelled of curry!

Richard started insisting that he tell IBM he was closing IIT. We had quite a bit of difficulty preventing him from doing so. He finally decided that he would close IIT Services. Lyndon Lane had managed IIT Services well and the business was profitable.

Without my knowledge, Richard called her to a meeting and fired her. There would be no severance pay as she had been with us for less than a year. A furious Lyndon berated me for not warning her about the meeting and she accused me of sacrificing her to save my own job. No matter how much I assured her that I had no knowledge of what Richard intended to do, she was sure I had a part in her removal and left IIT in high dudgeon.

SOME SENIOR IBMERS from the USA came to UNSW to talk about more research in the UNIX space. They were very pleased with the work Greg Rose was doing. They made a presentation about the new work at a morning tea hosted by the VC. The Deputy VC of Research, Cyril, Richard and I were invited but Richard decided not to attend.

The new research sounded exciting. After the meeting I suggested they meet Chris Doney at the AGSM. who was now head of our RS/6000 AIX educational team. I wanted them to tell Chris about their new research. Although I could tell Chris about the meeting, I thought he would like to hear it from the specialists.

On reaching the AGSM, I called Chris to join us for coffee. He wore a dirty T-shirt and very short black board shorts with a large tear in the backside revealing he was not wearing underpants. I just smiled sweetly and expected Chris would dazzle them with his brilliance. The visitors regarded Chris strangely but soon relaxed when I told them Chris was in charge of their RS/6000 education for the whole of Asia.

Part way through the meeting, Chris realised he was not dressed correctly for an IBM meeting. Although IBM had relaxed their dress standards in the RS/6000 and PC divisions, allowing staff to grow their hair and wear jeans, they still expected us to stick to their dress code while we were teaching.

Chris stopped the IBMer in midstream and apologised for his dress. He said he had been rebuilding the comms network and crawling under the floor. I knew this wasn't true. He had just come back from surfing at the beach.

Chris said, "Ann expects us to follow IBM dress standards when we are teaching but when we get our first overseas gig we go to a tailor in Hong

Kong who runs us up a dark blue pinstripe mohair suit and throws in two white shirts for $400. We share a rack of ties." Chris looked pleased with himself. The IBMers looked astonished.

I WATCHED THE ACADEMICS at UNSW play politics. It was much worse than anything I had encountered anywhere I had worked before. Their behaviour was destructive and unpleasant. I surmised this was because they had plenty of spare time on their hands although they always made out they were over-worked.

I had managed to avoid getting involved in politics in all the companies I had worked for although I had observed how they were played. I didn't understand them and didn't think I would be any good at politics anyway. I wasn't ruthless enough. I hated what Richard Kaan was doing to IIT but watched him do the same thing to other parts of Unisearch. I enjoyed being on the Advisory Board of the Institute of Administration at Little Bay. Now the Institute had become embroiled in UNSW politics.

I admired Josh Owen, the Director, immensely. He ran his Institute efficiently and with a grace and generosity of spirit that made everyone who met him admire him for his quiet competence. He was a very dark Malay from Singapore. It was a great surprise to me to be told that the Vice Chancellor was considering closing the Institute down. Certainly the Institute was situated on prime real estate with its own private beach. The buildings were looking a bit tired but Josh had kept refurbishing the facility as far as profits would allow after he had sent a significant slice of profits to UNSW.

Josh sought letters of support for the Institute from Managing Directors of most of Australia's largest companies all of which sent their employees to the Institute. The file of letters was impressive. All the Managing Directors gave glowing reports of the important place the Institute played in developing the education and culture of managers in Australia.

Josh decided to hold a live-in weekend seminar for Chief Executives and their wives to reinforce support for the Institute. The VC and his wife were invited but did not attend. About 50 of Australia's top Chief Execs attended. I was also invited.

It was a splendid weekend. The food and wine were the very best. Josh ran the weekend as a sort of junior management seminar, although there was plenty of time for networking and sports. Josh asked us all to consider our lives and our aspirations for the future.

In one session he asked us set short term six month goals and longer term five year goals. He asked us to write a letter to ourselves as if we were five years into the future congratulating ourselves for achieving all the goals we had set and describing how we had got there. We each produced three copies. One was given to Josh, one to our course buddy, who had been chosen at random, and one for ourselves. Josh promised to write to each of us in five years time to find out if we had achieved our goals.

I thought very carefully about where I would like to be in six months and in five years. My short term goals included standing up to Richard Kaan rather than avoiding him, and making IIT very successful. I would have completed the first year of my Masters degree and been accepted into the PhD program in the next year. I would have started building my new house and have lost 4kg in weight.

In five years time I said I would see my children happy and successful in the things they had chosen to do. I would like to be well on the way to achieving my PhD. I would like to be running IIT as a successful IT services enterprise utilising the skills of professionals working on a flexible part time basis. Finally, I would have built and be living in my new house.

That meeting was life changing for many of the participants. As I came across them in the next five to ten years it was remarkable how many had left the job they were in and were following their dreams. Without exception, they were all happier, more fulfilled people. Josh had worked his magic.

Nevertheless, the Little Bay facility was closed and the Institute was amalgamated with the AGSM. The Vice Chancellor thought the soft management skills that Josh espoused were irrelevant and did no credit to UNSW.

The AGSM was teaching the new scientific and hard-nosed approach to management. It was creating the tough Execs who would be running the businesses of the 21st century. Interestingly, in the 21st century attitudes to management changed after a series of economic disasters and companies started to appreciate the softer people oriented skills that Josh was teaching.

61 My own company at last

THE END OF 1992 was fast approaching. IBM's stock price was dropping like a stone. It had halved since August. IBM looked like making a US9$ billion pre-tax loss, higher than any other company ever. IBM put this down to the cost of staff severances. Worldwide staff numbers had dropped from 407,000 in 1987 to 275,000.

But the industry knew better. IBM had clung on to the margins made from the mainframe market for far too long. It had not recognised the huge technological change towards smaller but more powerful computers and open systems. As IBM's stock price was falling, those of Microsoft and Intel were rising rapidly and their profits were booming. Even Apple was growing rapidly and making huge profits.

I thought my own prospects for 1993 looked good. But after Christmas I returned to work on 4 January to find Richard Kaan waiting. He told me that he had decided to close IIT. He handed me a letter confirming I was now redundant and setting out my severance payout. All the other staff got the similar letters, except John Baker who was to be retained to run a cut down version of the organisation.

John Baker had been DEC's Education Manager. He was near retirement when DEC outsourced all its education to IIT and was given a generous severance payment. After a couple of months, John approached IIT to see if he could work for us for two or three days a week. John said he wanted to run our PC business. It had never done particularly well apart from training UNSW staff and delivering PC courses for Computer Power. John thought he could extend the business to other companies and the general public.

Richard asked me to document what should be done with IIT's current business initiatives. I had known the closure of IIT was possible ever since Richard took over but when it happened I was shellshocked. To be made redundant at 49 had been painful and I felt fortunate to have received several offers of employment but now, four years later, I was 53 and there was a severe recession. Most technology companies were laying staff off. I thought I would never get another job, certainly not a high paying one. The outlook was bleak.

All my IIT staff were very unhappy. Cyril was overseas. It was the January summer break and we had no courses running, so we all decided to take the rest of the day off. Over lunch, we compared our redundancy payouts. My severance pay was far less than that for anyone else. How could that be? I asked if I could take staff letters back to IIT and get copies. I would return them tomorrow.

After lunch I phoned Ross Lewis and asked for advice. He said he would need advice himself soon as he was sure he would soon be made redundant. He agreed with me that my severance pay was totally wrong. He helped me prepare a letter setting out severance pay using UNSW rules. My eventual payout was four times the one given in Richard's letter to me and more in line with payouts for the others.

I wrote a letter to Richard telling him what I thought of my severance pay I sent a copy of Richard's letter and my reply to Alex Ciccinelli, UNSW's head of personnel. He then discussed it with the Vice Chancellor and the Pro Vice Chancellor, Chris Fell. The next day when I handed my letter to Richard, Alex had already told him that the VC was disgusted by his behaviour and he was to pay me an appropriate severance.

By the time I got to IIT, my staff were all waiting. They suggested we should run IIT as our own business. I said that just wouldn't be possible. Running a business backed by UNSW was one thing. Going out on our own in a recession was just not realistic.

The staff asked what I had suggested we do with each element of business. Chris Doney, who was now running our RS/6000 business, said IBM had no one to deliver AIX education. Maybe we could continue to deliver that at IBM. John Baker said DEC now had no one to deliver its training, as we delivered all the company's courses in DEC's own training facility. Surely that could continue.

We were earning $2 million a year from DEC alone. I was sure UNSW wouldn't let us walk away with that. We had over 30 current initiatives. Surely Richard would insist that they be retained by Unisearch.

John Baker said Richard only wanted him to deliver PC education and manage the research contracts we had. John said he didn't know how to manage research and would refuse to do that. We agreed that the researchers should manage their research themselves except that we would take the IBM research away from AGSM and see it went to ACCI. That would be payback to Richard and Jeremy Davies, who was still a professor at the AGSM, for closing IIT.

I CONTACTED BELL LABS. The people there said they would only work with UNSW if I could manage the initiative, so that initiative was stopped. Bell Labs eventually established its own company in Australia. Tata also ended its dealings with UNSW when it was told IIT was closing.

I still thought starting our own company would have many problems. but I asked my friend Marea, my lawyer friend at AMP, to set up a company for us. We called it Technology Solutions. We agreed that all six permanent staff should own a share in the company and I would be the CEO. Paul would be the company secretary. John Baker wanted to be a Director but he did not want Richard Kaan to know.

I discussed the tasks needed to close IIT with Richard. Before we started, I asked if the staff and I could take over IIT and run it ourselves, although we would not take over the offices or the leases on any equipment.

"Do what you like," he said, to my amazement he said. He also agreed to my higher severance payout.

Back at IIT, the staff were jubilant. We agreed that initially we would all work from home and, although out of pocket expenses would be paid, none of us would be paid fees unless we were doing billable work. Chris Doney was still employed by AGSM and the rest of us had good severance payouts, enough at least to support us for about six months.

By the end of the week we had our company established. We contacted our 70 or so lecturers and contractors who all agreed to work for the new company. I contacted all IIT's clients and told them the company was to be closed because IBM had decided to take its education back in house.

No one I contacted was surprised. The technical press was full of reports of IBM's attempts to reduce costs. They were all relieved when I said our services would continue as Technology Solutions and all the staff would be the same. I hinted that rates might even be reduced.

There was initial euphoria as we planned our new company. We issued press statements and sent letters to all contractors, clients and prospects. But I still felt very insecure. I considered what I could not live without if money got tight. I bought what I thought would be three years supply of lipsticks, perfume and pantyhose. I had still not used all my supply ten years later. I suspended my Masters course for six months while I got Technology Solutions off and running.

I realised that I would have to do some marketing for the company until we could afford to hire a salesperson. My stomach churned. I hated sales and marketing, but someone had to do it.

I soon found it was easy. We had built a good reputation through IIT and companies recommended us to each other so it was simply a matter of taking calls and making a short presentation about our capabilities to each new company then listening to their current needs. I could then prepare a proposal outlining how our skills could meet those needs.

I JOINED THE East Coast Business Women's' Network. Initially, I thought I had nothing in common with women who were selling lipsticks or writing books, or who were TV presenters, or one person businesses, or women who were importing goods or making tablecloths for David Jones. But at each month's meeting I realised that running a technology company was very similar to running any other company.

At the first meeting I exchanged business cards with Linda Bergin. Both our cards had email addresses, which was a rarity in those days. Robin Henderson, who ran the network, asked how many other women had email addresses. Out of more than one hundred attendees, no one else had one.

At each meeting two women talked about their companies. These were feisty women who were following their dreams and had a will to be successful. They gave me the courage to do the same. We were in a better position than many of them. We had taken over a successful business. We had forward orders to keep us going.

I thought about small businesses such as bread shops with no forward orders. They baked their bread each morning but maybe no one wanted bread that day. Their bread was good and their service was good, but they would have to throw their good bread away and make a loss. Also, a competitor could start up next door. We had few of those challenges. If we continued delivering good service, managing our company well and charging realistic fees we would be successful.

We established a serviced office in North Sydney. We were immediately profitable. DEC made us one of two accredited DEC Training Companies in Australia. We had a lucrative contract with the Australian Army to deliver UNIX training. We delivered AIX courses for IBM in Manilla and Shanghai.

WITH THE ECONOMY still contracting, companies were looking for new ways of saving money. Several who had reduced staff found that their offices were often only half occupied. Many found that hot desking, or assigning desks to people as they arrived at work rather than giving each employee a permanent desk, could save expensive office space.

IBM led the way by renting a huge warehouse to seat people who were not out working with clients or out selling. It then let out a proportion of its swanky head office at Cumberland Forest in West Pennant Hills.

'Teleworking' or working from home, was another way of cutting down on expensive office space. In the USA, it was as also seen a way to conserve petrol and reduce pollution. I had run the technical division of fpl in the 1960s so had experience of managing home-based workers. I emphasised in all our publicity for Technology Solutions that our people were all working from home. I was asked to make comments about home-based working in two ABC radio programs. This brought Technology Solutions more publicity, and more enquiries from both workers and prospective clients.

In April 1993 I was asked to make a presentation on teleworking to the Information Technology Management course at Macquarie University's Graduate School of Management. They presented me with the latest edition of the Macquarie Dictionary and when I returned home, I found a nice letter and a cheque for $1000 tucked inside. In early June, I was a speaker at a government symposium on teleworking.

By the end of June we had been trading for five months and had made a profit of $13,400, even after all our setup expenses. Chris and Paul were busy teaching, mainly for IBM. Paul was also handling all our accounting, sending out assignment letters, invoicing and paying contractors and other bills. Chris was still supposedly full-time at the AGSM.

I was also doing some consultancy. The Australian Information Industries Association (AIIA) asked me to do a report on the number of women in technological positions in their member companies, which included most of the largest IT companies in Australia.

I DECIDED TO VISIT Claire and Rodney for a week. They had left Colly Farms and moved into a new house in Moree. Rodney had a job as a mechanic and Claire was office manager in a car dealership. I took the paperwork from the AIIA survey to work on while I was there. Claire had had a disagreement with the firm that laid her carpet so her floors were just bare concrete. She was working in a local restaurant at night, getting home around midnight.

I was working on my computer waiting for her to return home. I heard her car and jumped up to open the door for her. Unfortunately, I got my feet tangled in the power cord of my PC and fell a heavily on my face on the concrete. I heard the bones in my arm break with two loud cracks. I lay on the floor trying to work out how to get up. When Claire came in she had heard what she thought were two pistol shots, saw me lying on the floor with my eyes open and thought I had been shot.

I was taken to Moree hospital. It was after midnight. The one doctor on duty told us he had just put a motorcyclist back together and would prefer to attend to me in the morning when he was fresh. He was sure both my arms were broken but had sent the radiologist home so would not know the full extent of the damage until the morning. I was sedated and put to bed.

After X-rays in the morning I was told that I had complex compound fractures in two places in one arm and in four places in the other. Claire told the hospital that I had top medical cover so wanted a top orthopaedic specialist. We were told that the theatre was booked for the next two days for emergencies. If I wanted a specialist my bones would probably have set and have to be broken again. Best get them done straight away. We agreed.

I was given pre-meds ready for theatre. The day passed with nurses and doctors telling me they had more accidents to attend to so my case had been delayed. They gave me more painkillers. By the end of the day the original doctor apologised for the delay but said he would like to set my bones under a local anaesthetic. Would I mind?

I was assured that it would not hurt but I might not like watching. I agreed. The effort to get the bones realigned did not hurt but the pushing and pulling and grinding of twisting bones was gruesome. I had plaster casts from my fingertips to well above my elbow. I was in hospital for another night then Stephen flew to Moree to drive me and my car back to Sydney. It was a ten hour drive.

Apart from the work I was doing myself, I had several sales calls organised. Chris had gone on holiday to Hawaii for a month, Paul was teaching in Tasmania for a month. It was a bad time to be running a new company with two broken arms.

I had a nurse each day to shower me. Friends and neighbours pitched in and fed me. Stephen cooked, shopped and cleaned our house. I asked one of the FIT group, Sue Meyer, to help me complete the AIIA survey report. The seven weeks in plaster soon passed.

Technology Solutions was going from strength to strength. I wondered why I had ever doubted that we would be successful. It was exhilarating to be running my own company at last, even with two broken arms.

IBM WAS STILL HURTING. Its loss for their first quarter of 1993 was US$S8 billion. This was almost as much as the loss for the whole of 1992, which had been the largest corporate loss ever. More people were laid off. More research was stopped completely. Support for universities was stopped. It was a bloodbath. The industry was appalled by stories that IBM had bought its own shares at double market price to shore up its stock price.

A final report on ICOT, the Japanese Fifth Generation project that I visited in 1986, had been released. ICOT was to be closed. It was judged to have made no contribution to IT whatsoever and to have been very badly managed. This was more or less in line with my feeling when I visited, and quite contrary to the glowing reports by most visitors. I felt vindicated.

Teleworking had become the flavour of the month. Technology Solutions was held up as a shining example of the way most people should be working. In December Australia hosted an international conference on teleworking with speakers from all over the world. I was a keynote speaker.

The Government had started to fund Telecottages, local technology centres established to support teleworkers. In January I opened the Lismore Telecentre and visited another in nearby Byron Bay when we made a one hour TV program about teleworking. It seemed that every week I was asked to speak on radio or TV about the subject.

ON THE AUSTRALIA DAY weekend in January 1994 my camping friends and I went to the Snowy Mountains bushwalking. I had been told my feet were getting worse and I would not be able to walk for much longer. I asked the specialists if there was anything I could do to retard the degeneration and was told just to continue to build core body fitness and strength for the day when I would not be able to walk. Meanwhile my arms were also mending.

We walked up the old road from Charlotte's Pass to the base of Mount Kosciuszko, the highest mountain in Australia, but only a little over 2000 metres tall. It was an easy 16km walk there and back. My feet hurt but I had got used to the pain. The alternative to pain was to do nothing.

I decided not to turn back to Charlotte's Pass but continue on the Five Peaks walk, which takes the best part of a day. All my friends found reasons to not come with me. I carried on. Soon my feet hurt no longer. I just couldn't feel them as I doggedly put one foot in front of the other. When I reached the other end, quite exhausted, all my friends were waiting. They had been sure that if they didn't come with me I would be sensible and turn round.

I told them I was sensible. I had asked my doctor if my feet would get worse sooner if I walked and was told they would not, so I decided to do the walk just one more time. Thinking back it was stupid and reckless. I might have needed to be brought out by mountain rescue, especially if the cloud had come down or I had fallen on some of the trickier parts of the walk. This was real wilderness and I didn't see another soul on the walk but it was a lovely fine day and I knew where I was going having walked that track many times before. I spent the next three days in bed.

My specialist couldn't believe I had done the walk. He said most women of my age, 54, wouldn't even attempt it. I told him I might go cross county skiing next season.

62 Shoot the messenger

AT THE END OF JULY I got my first High Distinction in my Masters. It was a unit on communications which introduced us to the emerging World Wide Web and Lynx, Veronica and Mosaic, the first web browsers. It opened my eyes to what the future might be like. This was exactly what I had imagined in the 1960s when Donald Davies had given his talk on Computer Communications that had led to the UK's Experimental Packet Switching Service, EPSS.

We had seen glimpses in IBM's Prodigy System, in the UK's Videotex system and in file sharing through the Internet. The World Wide Web was altogether different. It was truly an open system enabling people anywhere in the world to publish and access information. And it was free.

I learned that Tim Berners-Lee had developed the World Wide Web at CERN. He was the son of Conway Berners Lee who taught me to program at Ferranti back in 1959.

At home we shared a driveway with our retired and rather nosy next-door neighbours. When we first moved in they were pleased to have a professional woman from UNSW living next door. When they saw me wandering round the garden in my dressing gown early in the morning and not keeping business hours they surmised I had lost my job. I told them I had started a new company and working from home. They kept asking me in for morning tea. My status had obviously gone down in their estimation.

ABC TV started a new program about the new technologies called 'Hot Chips'. One of the early programs was about teleworking. They asked if they could film that program at my house. I told my neighbours that the TV people might block the driveway with their recording vans and equipment. If they needed access via the driveway they should just tell the TV people to move. My neighbours looked a little disbelieving. Why my house? They asked if they could watch.

Two large ABC semitrailers rolled up full of recording equipment with large satellite dishes on the roof. The popular TV presenter Graham Phillips paced the driveway in tatty jeans and T-shirt reading through his script. Later in the day he showed up again smartly dressed, TV cameras whirring. When the filming was finished and the vans had all gone, my neighbours came to ask me when the program would be screened. They treated me with much more respect after that. They had a TV personality living next door!

I was asked to join the Council of the Northern Sydney Institute of TAFE. This was the largest technical college in Australia. I was especially interested in their computing courses and in getting more women to train as computer programmers. I spoke on this subject at several TAFE events during 1994.

I was even more convinced that, although we did need educated minds to develop new technologies and to work in research, university courses were not the way to fill the IT skills shortage. Most companies now had huge quantities of old code that needed constant maintenance. Some studies found that up to 90% of programming was maintenance.

I was convinced that most of that work did not need university graduates but could be done by well trained TAFE graduates. Also, about half the professionals in the IT industry in Australia had no tertiary qualifications yet employers still demanded graduates. In many companies, new graduates left after a couple of years churning through companies until they got trapped by golden handcuffs including staff loans and bonuses.

This churn contributed to reduced productivity as employees probably spent the first six months in a new job learning about their new assignments and the last six months of the two years searching for a better job. This reduced the two years of employment to about one productive year.

IN 1994 I STARTED learning Mandarin in preparation for a grand trip to China. Claire started a degree in English Literature. Stephen planned to start a Bachelor of Business degree in 1995.

The first Internet café in Australia opened in Sydney, where people could hire a computer to access the Internet for about $6 an hour. The café boasted high-end Apple Macintosh computers with a 1 Gigabyte hard drive. Similar cafes had opened in London and New York. IBM was still floundering but most companies in the IT industry, especially in the services sector, were booming. At Technology Solutions we were all making lots of money.

In January 1995 Technology Solutions was two years old. In Australia over 70% of small businesses fail in the first three years. Most have closed by the time they reach the age of seven. We were going from strength to strength despite starting in a severe recession.

I organised a competition for the graphic artists at Hornsby TAFE to design a logo for our company. We paid the student with the best design $1000. We now had a characteristic livery themed green and dark blue and using recycled paper, we intended to give the impression of an environmentally conscious enterprise.

In January my brother Richard visited us from England for four weeks. My sister Rosemary and Richard and I had just received about $20,000 each from my mother's estate. I used my money to pay off some of my mortgage and I bought an IBM PC. Richard decided to come and visit me in Australia.

Richard had always been difficult. He was rarely employed and seldom washed. I took time to drive him around to show him the sights but he slept most of the way.

Towards the end of his time, my group of friends and I went to the Snowy Mountains for the Australia Day weekend to see the wildflowers, as we usually did. Three of my friends were nurses. They realised I had had a difficult time with my brother so offered to look after him while we were away. Try as they might, even they had great difficulty to get Richard's dirty clothes off him to wash and to get him to take a shower.

IBM AUSTRALIA established a joint venture services company with Lend Lease, a major Australian conglomerate. It was called Integrated Systems Solutions Corporation, or ISSC. We were asked to work on many of its projects, the biggest being to assist ISSC to implement an administration system for Optus Vision, a pay TV company which was a subsidiary of the Optus telephone company.

Optus Vision was Australia's second pay TV channel. The system was based on the work we had done for Galaxy, Australia's first pay TV company. The Optus Vision system was launched successfully, on time and within budget, in September 1995. We were then asked to implement the same system for ISSC at CETV, Australia's third pay TV company.

ISSC also asked us to rationalise all the UNIX computers at Telstra, Australia's largest telecommunications company. Like many other large enterprises Telstra had treated UNIX boxes like PCs and allowed business units to purchase them without reference to the IT department. This led to a proliferation of non-standard systems that were often poorly documented and unmaintainable after their original owner left the organisation. Many of Telstra's UNIX systems were running mission critical systems.

One of them was the system that supported 000, the national emergency services telephone number. We found that this system was totally non standard and vulnerable to failure.

My consultants working on the project kept telling me how dangerous the system was and that something had to be done. I kept telling them that it was their job to point out areas that needed significant improvement and offer suggestions for that improvement.

Through the ISSC connection we were asked to provide Lend Lease with advice on how to use the Internet for business. I was heavily involved in that consultancy. Mainly known as a building construction and management company, Lend Lease was a very large and diverse company. The payroll systems it ran for many major companies paid nearly 20% of all employed Australians. We were asked to modernise these elderly systems and provide a web based interface.

We continued to provide training for DEC. One large assignment involved teaching Microsoft Office to over 3000 Queensland Electricity Commission employees based all over the state. Paul Boer managed that project and delivered some of the courses himself. Participants evaluated all courses and we got an average rating of 4.85 out of 5.

We delivered all DEC's Microsoft education. That meant we had to pay $20,000 every year in fees to keep our instructors' Microsoft Accreditations up to date. We also delivered training for DEC hardware and software for many other companies. We developed a range of courses on Teleworking for NSW TAFE. These were to be part of the National Curriculum developed for ANTA, the Australian National Training Authority. I also provided consultancy in Teleworking for Optus, Lend Lease and the Australian Government. We were very busy.

IBM asked me to speak at its annual internal and client conferences. In all, I gave presentations at more than 16 conferences in 1995 and many more presentations to individual companies. With all this work and more and Chris, Paul and I being assigned to projects ourselves, we needed more administrative support. We hired an accountant, Bernadette Orr.

IN EARLY 1995 we won a tender for a study for the Rural Industries Research and Development Corporation (RIRDC) on the benefits of information systems for rural Australia. We were one of 47 companies bidding. We were up against some very stiff competition and I wondered why we had won the business. I was to find out later.

The work involved travelling all over Australia to gather data. I worked on the project together with Dr Maarten Stapper from CSIRO and Steve Welstead, who had been Telstra's manager of rural services and now ran the Byron Bay and Lismore Telecottages.

The study was very interesting. We held meetings in every state capital and in some large country towns. Steve Welstead visited an Aboriginal settlement at Maningrida in the Northern Territory that had started selling their art on the World Wide Web. At most meetings we had to start by explaining what was possible with the new technologies. Few people in rural Australia had any idea what the Internet could do for them in distance learning, telemedicine and online business.

Some innovative systems had been developed. The Australian Meat and Livestock Corporation had developed a method of describing cattle, which, together with electronically readable tags on the cattle's ears, uniquely identified each beast in a herd. Cattle for sale could then be individually identified, described and photographed for sale lists, offered for sale via a computerised bidding system and not transported until sold. This cut down the costs in transporting cattle to market and possibly back to the farm if they were not sold and the possibility of damaging them in the process.

We found that the most requested information was good short and long-term weather forecasts. These were available by fax and telex and were a good application to develop for the Internet.

As petrol became more expensive and drink driving laws more stringent, fewer and fewer rural people were driving to sales and country markets and stopping at the pub for a chat and a drink after the sales. Chat groups on the Internet were becoming popular with young people. We felt these could provide a similar service for gossip and information exchange between people in regional, rural and remote communities.

We came up with many applications that could be developed for the Internet that were just right for people in regional, rural and remote Australia. But most Internet Points of Presence (POPs) that country people needed to access the Internet were in capital cities and could be reached only by dial-up phone calls to the city, which could cost up to $45 an hour. The Internet was still very slow and so costs to just access email were still very high for people living outside major cities.

As part of the study we sent a questionnaire to all the agricultural bodies we could find and all the local councils in regional, rural and remote Australia. We also gave it to everyone who attended our widely publicised meetings. We got a high proportion of replies.

I was asked to speak about our study several times on the radio and most local newspapers from the places where we held meetings published reports of the study and the meeting.

DR MAARTEN STAPPER was a plant sciences researcher working at the CSIRO. Originally from Holland, he had pioneered dry rice farming in Australia. We bought Maarten's services from the CSIRO. Although this reduced our margins, he brought added expertise to the team.

Steve Welstead had heard Maarten speak about his visit to Holland where flower sellers and growers were using the Internet to ensure they met market needs. At the end of each day, the flower markets emailed the growers with information on the type and colour of flowers and the number in each bunch that they needed the next day. Flower growers would pick and pack their flowers as required in the early morning to send to market. This meant the flowers were the freshest they could be and, as they were picked to meet market needs, there was very little wastage.

Maarten was going through a messy divorce. Although he ran his meetings splendidly and sent good notes to us, when it came to writing the chapters of the report assigned to him he either chose not to write the chapters or wrote them so badly that Steve and I had to rewrite them. And yet he continued billing CSIRO, which in turn billed Technology Solutions.

In September, we sent a draft of our report to RIRDC. The Director, Dr Roslyn Prinsley, liked the report and said she would just pass it by her Board before it was printed.

We were to prepare two reports. One would be a short report of findings and recommendations that would only be about 30 pages for general consumption. This would be backed by a more comprehensive report with details of methodology, full findings and reasoned arguments for our conclusions and recommendations. We also put all meeting notes in the appendix plus all the replies from our survey.

Also in September, I was asked to present a paper on the findings of our study at the Australian Bureau of Agricultural and Resource Economics' (ABARE) conference in February 1996. This was to be the 50th ABARE conference. In addition to the formal conference at the Canberra Conference Centre, it was to be televised live and broadcast throughout Australia and South East Asia. I asked RIRDC for permission to present the paper at the ABARE conference. As the conference was to be televised, the paper also had to be vetted by the ABC's legal department. All this was done by the end of September 1995.

We were invited to a Board meeting of RIRDC in Canberra. The Board said they were pleased with the way we had conducted our report but did not like the recommendations. We were asked to revise that part of the report. We asked for specific comments but the Board was very vague about precisely what they wanted.

Steve and I redrafted the recommendations and were called to another Board meeting. Again, we were asked to toughen up the recommendations. What did this mean?

CLAIRE AND RODNEY were expecting their first baby, my first grandchild, in October. The baby was a footling, meaning she had one leg stuck in the passage from the uterus through which she would be born. As this would make the birth difficult, Claire's doctor decided the birth should be by caesarean. Thus we knew the exact date and time of the birth.

I planned to go to see my new granddaughter as soon as I could. We were asked to go to Canberra again to discuss the report with the RIRDC Board on the day before my granddaughter's birth. I was very frustrated. I didn't want to drive the 600 km to Canberra and back the day before setting off on the 800 km drive to Moree. Steve Welstead would have to fly from Lismore and stay at my house for the night.

What on earth did RIRDC want? We asked the Director who had seemed pleased with the report. She said she had no idea what the problem was. We had already done much more work than we had billed for. The contract was fixed price but we realised it was an important study so were prepared to do everything necessary to make it a success. Also, Steve and I had had to make good Maarten's work and we had paid CSIRO for what Maarten had billed.

We decided we should confront the RIRDC people and ask exactly what it was they wanted. We had already offered to include or remove any of the recommendations they chose so long as that did not destroy the integrity of the report or contradict our findings. The Chairman reiterated that the Board appreciated the amount of work we had done and our findings, but our recommendations fell short. The Chairman said the meeting would be adjourned for tea and he and I would 'have a little chat'.

He took me to a side room and asked if I knew why Technology Solutions had been given the contract. I said I wondered why myself. He said we got it because I had worked at the Stock Exchange. RIRDC had identified the problem that to make Internet-based systems viable in rural and remote Australia, something had to be done about the costly telecommunications connection charges. He said he wanted me to recommend that RIRDC establish its own private telecommunications system for people in regional, rural and remote Australia, just like the communications system at ASX.

I was horrified. I pointed out that ASX operated in cities. The most remote broker was in Newcastle, 160km north of Sydney, and it used a dial-up line at trunk rates. Running a private telecommunications system was complex and needed significant expertise. In addition, it was very expensive, especially over long distances. I could not recommend that at all. He got very angry and said then he would terminate our contract and we would not be paid our final payment.

Back in the boardroom, the Chairman announced that he had terminated our contract. I asked him to tell the Board why. He said he would tell the Board the reason in private and dismissed Steve and me.

Outside, Steve asked me what happened. When I told him he said it just wasn't fair. I said I would fight for our final payment. I wrote to CSIRO and stated that we would not be paying Maarten's final payment. CSIRO said they would sue.

THE NEXT DAY was the day of my granddaughter Rhianna's birth, I loaded my car with presents and things Claire had asked me to buy in Sydney and left home for the long 800km drive north. By 6pm I was in Moree. My granddaughter, Rhianna, had been delivered successfully. Rodney was busy with his video camera filming his wife and new daughter.

The drama surrounding my granddaughter's birth continued. About 18 hours after she was born she developed a high temperature and spots that looked to me like German Measles. The Moree hospital called for help from the children's hospital in Sydney who decided she needed to be taken to the nearest specialist paediatric unit, which was in the much larger town of Tamworth, about 300km away.

The medevac aeroplane arrived about 2am to take our new baby away. As Claire had had a caesarean, at first they would not let her travel with her baby but she insisted and the plane took off into the night with our precious family. Rhianna looked so tiny and so ill I felt sure we wouldn't see her alive again.

Rodney was not allowed to travel in the plane so I drove him the 300km through the night to Tamworth. We arrived just as dawn was breaking. Our baby had been put on antibiotics and looked much better. A few days later the problem was diagnosed as a golden staph infection picked up in Moree hospital.

As soon as Claire was well enough, about six weeks after Rhianna's birth, she decided to take her new baby to Paris to show off to her Dad, my first husband Alan Leach, who with his wife was now working for Kodak France. Claire and Rodney first travelled to England to show off their daughter to my mother, my sister Rosie and her family. and my brother.

They then visited Alan Leach's mother, Rhianna's great-grandmother, and Alan's brother in England. Then Alan came to take them all through the new channel tunnel to Paris for Christmas.

They returned to Australia on Boxing Day. Stephen and I had a second Christmas dinner with Claire and her family. Rhianna was ten weeks old and had already been round the world.

A couple of days after Christmas I set off to Moree to stay with Claire, Rodney and Rhianna for a short holiday. On the way back to Sydney I visited Chris and his wife who had moved to a lovely house he had had built at Coolum Beach in Queensland.

Chris's dream had been to live near a good surfing beach. He had bought his piece of land a few years before and by the end of 1995 had built a house. Technology Solutions was doing very well and he could afford to leave the AGSM and move to Coolum on the Sunshine Coast in Queensland.

Chris now had a baby daughter, Paige, and was relying on Technology Solutions entirely for his income but as we were all earning considerable sums he felt quite secure.

But there were dark clouds just over the horizon.

62 Rumblings

I **RETURNED TO SYDNEY** in mid January ready to give my presentation at the ABARE conference on 8 February. There was a letter waiting from the RIRDC stating that they would not allow me to deliver the ABARE paper. I contacted the ABC.

They said they had signed a contract with me and I had to give the paper. The ABC was adamant so I had to go ahead.

My friend Dr Phil McCrae was working at CSIRO as Director of Information Technology. He had special responsibility to help Australia exploit the 'Information Superhighway', as the Internet and WWW were beginning to be called, for business purposes. I asked if he could support my ABARE presentation by running examples of interesting websites as background to my talk. This meant my talk had some great visuals.

I presented myself for makeup at 7am the next day as requested by the ABC even though my presentation was not until 11am. It took ages to make me up and get my hair right. I and two other participants were then taken to the 'green room' to wait until our session. There was tea and coffee and several choices of cold drinks and nibbles in the green room but I was too nervous to eat anything. At 10am we were taken back to makeup for a touch up and then we were on.

I had never done live TV before. Halfway through I noticed my excellent visuals weren't being displayed, but I got tremendous applause when I finished. The questions were easy. Some came in from South East Asia. At lunch I was inundated with delegates telling me how important the study had been and requests to repeat the talk at other venues.

Then the ABC producer handed me a fax from my solicitor. It contained a letter from the RIDRC Chairman acknowledging that they couldn't stop my presentation but 'they would be watching my every word'. I felt very afraid but glad I had not known that before I made my presentation.

We heard that our RIRDC study was to be completed by Dr Roger Buckeridge, the same man that represented ACCI when we had launched the IBM research IIT was doing at the AGSM. We were told not to contact him.

TECHNOLOGY SOLUTIONS was now running very well. We had lots of business coming in. Most came to us by recommendation from existing clients. Some came from media exposure, through the press or radio interviews.

In March DEC sold its education arm to an international training company GKN, the Global Knowledge Network. GKN did not like having all its eggs in one basket with only one training provider so started to appoint others. We simply contacted those and arranged to contract to them.

GKN used our services throughout Asia so soon we were training in Malaysia and Singapore. GKN concentrated on Microsoft training. It was difficult for our instructors to keep up to date and pass their accreditation exams but we managed.

DEC asked Chris to develop a system for P&O Ports. Chris convinced two members of his staff at AGSM, Gunther Feuereisen and Tania Edwards, to leave the AGSM and join him on the project. During the time our system was being built and installed there was significant unrest at the ports and a very long strike in which the conservative Howard Government tried several strike breaking tactics. After the system was implemented productivity at Australian ports doubled.

Paul started telling me that Chris was being horrid to him. At first I just said he had to sort out his differences with Chris. Chris had not said anything to me about Paul. Eventually the situation became serious. Paul started crying about the situation whenever we spoke or met.

I had worked with Paul for several years and valued his intellect and management skills. I couldn't understand why he was so upset by Chris. I thought he was just going through a mid life crisis.

Paul had married late in life. Before his marriage he had lived with his mother and had the traditional bachelor's life, running a sports car and being very involved in sporting activities. One year he had come 30th in the Sydney to Surf marathon. The woman he married, Lexie, was quite a bit older than him. He realised he would never have children with Lexie and was beginning to regret that. The company was doing well. Everyone had his or her crises every now and again. I felt we could carry Paul through his.

Eventually I asked Chris what was going on between Paul and himself. He told me Paul was 'a waste of space.' He said Paul didn't pull his weight in the company and should be forced out. I agreed that Paul now didn't often take assignments himself and never seemed to bring new business into the company but he had contributed significantly to our company in the past and had taken on several projects that Chris had left in a mess. When projects had got messy Chris had simply dropped them and said he had too much to do for AGSM. Now Chris had left AGSM he didn't have that excuse. I started to set Paul some mutually agreed goals. He didn't manage to achieve any of them and got more and more depressed.

I was spending more time than I could manage on the Paul and Chris situation. My Masters was nearing the point where Macquarie University agreed I could turn it into a PhD.

FITT had gathered another 'T' in its description and was now Females in Information Technology and Telecommunications. It was taking up much more of my time. I was doing much more public speaking. I was trying to learn Mandarin. I was also very involved with TAFE. I had been asked to join the Visiting Committee for the School of Information Systems at Wollongong Uni. I had quite a few billable consulting assignments myself.

Although I was enjoying running our company tremendously, sometimes I felt all my life was taken up with work. On some nights I worked until midnight. On one occasion when I had deadlines to meet I worked right through the night.

I thought long and hard about the situation with Paul. I didn't want to lose his support and guidance. He had been a good friend and an intelligent sounding board for company matters. Chris was a good technician but was too self absorbed to be a good manager. He was very charismatic and people loved to work for him.

People had warned me about Chris. They said he was heartless and ruthless. Chris had been adopted. His father had run sheep on the hills around Hornsby Heights where we now lived. Cyril Brookes said Chris was one of his favourite students and was very intelligent but everyone modified their comments by saying he was self centred and ruthless.

I asked Paul what his long-term dream was. He surprised me by saying he wanted to go back to Tasmania where he had grown up and spend time golfing and fishing. His mother had recently died and left him her house. He was toying with the idea of running his part of our business from Tasmania.

We set more business goals but by August Paul decided he just wanted to go to Tasmania with Lexie and retire. I later heard he had set up his own business and was working for one of our clients and had involved some of our contractors. His contract with us did not allow that but we had plenty of other business and I felt we owed something to Paul so I let it go. I was sad to see him go.

AS SOON AS PAUL resigned Chris reminded me that John Baker, who had been the Director of Education at DEC and had worked with us at IIT, was still a Director of Technology Solutions. John had been retained to run IIT when the rest of us had left but his job only lasted another six months before Richard Kaan closed IIT down completely.

Chris suggested I contact John and get him to resign as Director. John agreed. That left just Chris and me as Directors of Technology Solutions.

In 1996 IBM turned a corner. Like many IT companies, it decided that the money was in services rather than selling hardware. Because IBM Australia had established ISSC, one of IBM's first services ventures anywhere in the world, the local company was now one of IBM's shining stars. Worldwide, IBM was back in the black. Revenue from hardware was up 12% on 1995 but services grew by 31%.

I met Dr Roger Buckeridge again at a conference. He said he had been asked to take over our RIRDC project and he had been told not to contact Technology Solutions. He promised to send me a copy of his report. He said he was contracted to read all our material and just produce the 30 page report for general publication for which RIRDC had agreed to pay him $30,000 in one final payment. He said our work was very good and he told RIRDC he could not improve on it.

Like us, he refused to recommend that RIRDC be given money to develop a regional telephone system. When he presented RIRDC with his final report the Chairman rejected it and refused to pay him. Roger then sent his draft to several members of Parliament and to prominent people he knew would have an interest in the report stating that RIRDC refused to publish it. They were forced to do so.

His report acknowledged that Technology Solutions had done all the original work, which was excellent. His report was essentially a summary of our report. I immediately wrote to our solicitor with a copy of the new report. He demanded that we be paid our final instalment which RIRDC paid. The total bill for the project was $150,000. I then paid CSIRO what we owed them for Maarten Stapper but stated that as his work was not up to the standard we expected I had withheld some of their fee. They agreed to release us from our commitment. With solicitors' fees we just broke even on the RIRDC project, but we put far more effort into the project than we billed for.

In early 1997 I received a letter from the Australian Institute of Management (AIM). I had been voted their 'Speaker of the Year' for 1996. The award was judged by feedback from members attending AIM presentations and conferences during the year. I got an average evaluation of 9.8 out of 10. I won a voucher for books from the AIM bookshop. My presentation was in Sydney so I was paid to give my talk in other capital cities. The award boosted my confidence no end. I had never thought of myself as a good public speaker even though I was often asked to speak again after I had given a presentation.

In June 1997 Telstra bought 24% of ISSC. IBM still retained a 51% shareholding, leaving Lend Lease with 25%. Telstra's 2800 Information Technology staff and contractors joined ISSC. Telstra was just about to be partially privatised. Throwing its lot in with ISSC seemed a very sensible thing to do with Telstra's funds from the part privatisation and greatly strengthened ISSC's expertise in telecommunications, now a major component of most large IT projects.

I WAS ACCEPTED into the PhD program at Macquarie Uni. I decided to take a break from study. Technology Solutions was going well. I had not had a decent holiday since we established the company in early 1993. My niece Melanie Jane, my sister Rosie's daughter, was getting married in the UK in August 1997, I decided I would go to China for five weeks and on to the UK for her wedding.

Chris's wife's sister, Joanne, was living in Hong Kong. Her husband Mike was in charge of all Honeywell controls for Hong Kong's new airport. They had a flat in the north of Hong Kong near the new airport that was yet to open. Jo had been a staunch member of FITT and was now a senior Exec at American Express in Hong Kong. The UK was going to hand Hong Kong over to China on 30 June 1997, so I thought I would ask Jo if I could stay with her for the handover celebrations. Jo said she would be delighted to have a visitor from Australia.

The handover was amazing. The pomp and ceremony, and the parades, decorations and fireworks were better than anything I had ever seen. On the evening of 29 June the British put on a show. Prince Charles officiated but it rained very heavily. We decided not to go into the city centre but went to a party for expats and watched the festivities on TV. The next day the Chinese took over. Every flat in all the high rises seemed to be flying the Chinese flag or the new Hong Kong flag. The day was bright and sunny. We went to the town centre to watch the pageantry. There were beautifully lit barges on the harbour. The Chinese fireworks were even better than the British ones the day before.

I had booked a luxury five week tour of China. The tour group comprised only six people plus a translator, a guide and a driver. After staying with Jo for a week I joined my tour in Guilin. I had seen pictures of the beautiful karst country around Guilin, with its steep hills and waterfalls, on Chinese scrolls but I never thought it would be so beautiful and so extensive.

We took a two day trip on a boat down the beautiful Li River that was called the band of green silk by the Chinese people. We stopped overnight in a tiny inn and slept on straw bales. The head of the local Communist Party was visiting and all the local people from the minority tribes came out in their traditional costumes. We all danced by the light of the moon and stars till early morning. The next day we walked into the village. I had been told that media in China was heavily censored but a tiny café with a mud floor in the village had a satellite dish on its roof. The patrons were crowded round a TV set watching CNN TV news.

Next we flew to Xian with its huge city walls and ancient bell tower. Xian had been the main city in China until the fairly recent past. We saw the tombs of the famous Terracotta Warriors and learned there were over 200 more tombs in the area yet to be excavated. The Chinese had decided not to unearth more treasures until they could afford to build cover over them as they had the first tomb. There was also one of the best museums I have ever seen showing people had lived in the area for over 6000 years. Their pottery, art and tools looked very modern. People in England at that time were still living in caves.

Xian is also the dumpling capital of China. That night we ate 50 different types of dumplings at a restaurant that specialised in dumplings fashioned to look like the animals that made up the filling. The rabbit dumplings looked like little rabbits sitting in a pasture of wildflowers. The seal dumplings were set in a plate of blue jelly representing the sea with a white meringue iceberg.

From Xian we travelled to Beijing. We toured the Forbidden City, which amazed me by its sheer size. It was my birthday so after a trip to the Beijing Opera, I decided to go into the city centre and eat at the McDonalds that I had seen in the corner of Tiananmen Square. I seemed odd to me to see a very western symbol so near Mao's tomb and the Great Hall of the People. In McDonalds, I was mobbed by students wanting to practice speaking English with me. The food was exactly as it was in Australia.

The next day we walked the Great Wall of China. It had surprisingly steep steps that I navigated on my bottom. When I had told my specialist I wanted to walk on the Great Wall he said that I might stand on the wall but I would never be fit enough to walk on it.

After a week in Beijing we travelled to Wuhan then onto a boat on the Yangzi River. We passed the huge Three Gorges locks and dam that was nearing completion. We were told the resultant hydro scheme would provide one third of all China's electricity needs when completed. We travelled through the Three Gorges and saw many ancient and beautiful cities that would be inundated when the dam was completed.

New cities of concrete and steel had been built over 500 metres above the river, just above the flood line. These would house the people displaced by the rising waters. They had all mod cons with bathrooms and flush toilets but were very different from the rambling old towns they replaced. Our river trip ended at Chongqing. I was surprised to find that Chongqing had a population of over 30 million. It was one of the largest cities on earth and I had never even heard of it.

I CAUGHT THE PLANE back to Hong Kong and then went First Class to London. My sister and her family met me there. I went to see my old secretary, Anne Duncan, from my days at fpl. Anne and I took a trip round the south of England, catching up with old fpl colleagues. We called in on several British Telecottages and the new computer museum at Bletchley Park.

The story of Bletchley Park's involvement in British code cracking in World War II had now been widely publicised. A group of British Computer Society members who were retired engineers and programmers were rebuilding replicas of early British computers at Bletchley. I remembered I was going to be sent to Bletchley Park to learn about computers when I worked at the Met Office but then I fractured my skull and couldn't go. That was over 40 years before.

My niece's wedding was a splendid affair. Her husband Julian was a very bright young actuary who had been the world Rubik's Cube champion before the age of 16. His prize was a Mercedes car with a Rubik's cube painted on the side. Unfortunately, he was too young to drive it.

At the wedding his best man, his brother, stood up to make his speech with a 'This is Your Life' type book. He threw Julian a Rubik's cube and threatened to read Julian's life story from his book until Julian solved the cube. There was much laughter when Julian said he had forgotten how to.

63 Intel inside

WHEN I RETURNED to Australia I was delighted to learn from Chris that our company was still working well. I learned from Tina, our new accountant, that we had made a good profit while I was away. But that profit was slowly whittled away over the next few weeks when unpaid bills surfaced.

At the end of August 1997 I drove to northwest NSW to see Claire and her family and take them the presents I had brought from China. They had a house on a farm in Rowena, between Moree and Walgett. The property was owned by Australia's largest wheat farmer, Ron Greentree, who was to become the Chairman of GrainCorp when the NSW Government privatised its grain distribution the following year.

As I drove north I heard on the radio that Princess Diana had died. It seemed that the whole world was in mourning. The funeral was watched by millions of people all around the world. To many people it was as if a member of their family had died.

Microsoft had largely ignored the Internet. At one stage it made a half-hearted attempt to emulate the system but soon gave up. At the end of 1997 they were in the throes of an antitrust case with the US Government because it now had a monopoly on PC software. Shades of IBM.

In 1993 Bill Gates decided he would get involved with the Web by starting to build a web browser, called Internet Explorer, that he was now proposing to build into the Windows 95 operating system. After a bit of legal pressure, Microsoft was made to decouple its browser from its operating system.

The commercial use of the Internet was growing. Big companies were starting to establish websites but most of these were only online versions of their company information brochures. One company in South Australia had started offering online share trading. Amazon started selling books via the Internet.

The big banks all developed online banking. Our accountant Tina could do all her work at home, but most people were wary of doing their banking over the Internet. The Australian Information Industries Association (AIIA) established an Information Economy Task Force. I was invited to join and given special responsibility for privacy issues in electronic commerce.

One of the first tasks we established was to develop a series of booklets to tell the general public how to use online banking. These were very successful.

1997 WAS DRAWING to a close. It had been five years since I made those five year plans at the CEO seminar at Little Bay. I looked at the goals I had set. I had achieved them all except the move to a new house and it wasn't IIT that I was now running, it was my own company. In the letter I had written to myself five years earlier stating that I had achieved my goals I said I felt good about my achievements, and I did. I might not yet be in my new house but the house I lived in served me well.

Both Stephen and I were working and studying hard. The house was the smallest I had ever lived in except my parent's home, but the mortgage was small and it was cheap to run and easy to clean. It could be made to accommodate guests and parties. What more could I need? I wrote to Josh. He was no longer at UNSW but I had kept in touch. He was pleased to hear I had achieved my goals.

I had been on the Council for the Northern Sydney Institute of TAFE since 1994. In 1998 I was elected Chair. I was surprised to be invited to join the NSW TAFE Commission Board. This carried a stipend of $25,000 a year, almost as much as many people earned for a proper job, yet the appointment only required attendance at ten half day Board meetings a year. I was to find out that I actually spent much more time than that, but the involvement was very interesting and stimulating.

Christmas was with us again. Time for the Messiah and Christmas at the Opera House. Time to go to Rowena for Christmas with Claire, Rodney and my two year old granddaughter. Time to go to the Snowy Mountains to see the wildflowers on the Australia Day weekend.

IN LATE JANUARY I read that David Bolt, who had been in charge of the RS/6000s and IBM's UNIX systems when we were at IIT, had been appointed General Manager of Intel Australia. Intel built the processor chips that powered most of the world's PCs. I wrote a letter congratulating him on his appointment and including some promotional material on Technology Solutions. I was surprised when he rang and said he needed to see me as soon as possible.

He told me Intel was about to launch a worldwide accreditation scheme. Many companies built PCs using Intel chips but some were not built well. Each company using Intel microprocessors was allowed to put the 'Intel inside' sticker on their PCs. The shoddily built ones were bringing Intel into disrepute because when the computer failed people thought it was the Intel chip that was at fault. They had no idea how a PC was actually built and that the microprocessor could be perfect and the problems caused by other components or just a faulty build.

Intel decided not to sell chips to any company or person unless at least two people in the enterprise were accredited to build PCs. It had spent well over US$10 million developing a training scheme that would teach people how to build a PC properly. Next year Intel would spend a further US$20 million on the scheme.

David told me there were 1200 enterprises building PCs in Australia. Many were tiny suburban computer stores. All these had to be accredited. David said he knew my people delivered excellent training and wanted to give us the contract. We had to commit to send a trainer for two weeks on a Train The Trainer (T3) course in Hawaii in a couple of weeks time. Intel would pay all living expenses and we would have to cover the airfare.

I immediately thought of Mark Thomas. Mark had worked for us at IIT delivering RS/6000 AIX courses. He was intelligent and articulate. He had completed his first degree in Computer Science at UNSW then moved to the AGSM to do a Masters degree and finally got another Masters degree from NIDA, the National Institute of Dramatic Art, the performing arts arm of UNSW.

Mark sometimes taught at both the AGSM and at NIDA. His real love was performing arts. He had done some TV work as a producer and had been the First Assistant Director on the first Mad Max film, and then Director of the Queensland Film Festival.

Like most people working in Performing Arts, Mark had difficulty finding continuous work so took up delivering training whenever he needed money. He was an excellent trainer. Mark had worked for me on and off for nearly ten years. He seemed a splendid choice to run our Intel business. At this time he was working on our Vodafone project as Network Manager.

Over coffee, I told Mark about the Intel prospect and asked if he would be interested in managing the project. Initially, I would want him to go to Hawaii for two weeks to do the T3 course. Mark said he would love to run the Intel gig.

I told Chris we would need to establish a training facility initially in Sydney and later in most state capitals. The whole accreditation suite was to be about ten five day courses initially for over 100 people at about $500 a day each. Intel was forever changing its products so accreditations had to be renewed every two years.

This looked like riches beyond our dreams. We would be the only company in Australia to deliver the training. I told Chris we would need a bank loan to set up the training rooms. I would work with Intel to develop a business plan to support the loan.

Mark was very excited about going to Hawaii. When he returned he said he'd had a ball. He had met trainers from all over the world and had made several useful contacts. He had hired a Harley Davidson motorbike and had toured the big island. But he said the training system was far from ready. It was to be launched in USA in March but even that might be postponed. Intel had arranged a follow-up meeting for all the trainers in the USA in March. This time, Intel would pay for everything including the airfare.

Late in February Chris and his family went to the Cook Islands for six weeks. He said it was the best surfing ever. When he returned he insisted that we should register the company in the Cook Islands because we could avoid paying tax. The Intel project looked like bringing us huge profits so we needed to think about tax.

I was concerned. I didn't think the large companies that were our customers would like to deal with a company registered in the Cook Islands. This was the first time Chris and I had disagreed about company policy. Chris sulked. I said if he could find me a good technology company registered in the Cook Islands I'd talk to them and consider it. I also agreed to ask Cyril Brookes why he hadn't registered his company in the Cook Islands. His company, Grapevine, was now very successfully selling his software in the USA. Cyril was usually very canny about dealing with tax issues. I also agreed to ask AIIA if they knew of Australian Technology companies registered overseas.

In March Mark went to Salt Lake City for Intel. Again he had a great time but said the course material was still very poor so the program wasn't ready to launch yet. In April we had to send our second trainer on the T3 course. This time I sent Gunther Feuereisen. The course was for Asian companies only so it was held in Singapore. In July we hosted a T3 course for Asian companies, including some from China, in Australia. The launch had been postponed again but the material was better.

I worked with Intel Australia's manager for the accreditation scheme, a pleasant young American called Stephen. He helped me with costs for running the course that Intel had calculated. One cost was that Technology Solutions needed a website. All the admin for the scheme was to be web based, including student's bookings, orders for course materials and chat groups for students and instructors. Our website was linked to the Intel website and we were allowed to put the Intel Authorised Training Centre logo on our business cards and letterhead. I felt we had really arrived. The income for our first year from the Intel business was projected to be $11 million. Cash flow was negative for the first few months but before the end of the first year we showed a healthy profit.

I took our cash flow projections plus a short outline of the Intel project to our bank to borrow some money to fund our initial cashflow. We had banked with the same bank since we started our company five years earlier. Our account had always been in the black. This was the first time we asked for a bank loan and this to fund a very prestigious project with guarantees from Intel. The bank refused to lend because we 'had no assets', a common problem faced by companies in the IT industry.

FORTUNATELY THERE WAS A WAY OUT. Together with three other out of town universities the University of Wollongong had established a prestigious office in the centre of Sydney. I had been a member of the University of Wollongong IT Committee since 1995 and had just been elected Deputy Chair. Although the committee sometimes met in the Sydney offices, I found out that they were otherwise only rarely used.

In addition to meeting rooms, there were four elegant offices, one for the Vice Chancellor of each university when they visited Sydney. I asked if we could rent an office that we would vacate if it was needed for a meeting. We could then use the address on our letterheads. It gave us a serviced office in the heart of the city for less than we were paying in North Sydney, and included a phone number and message taking facilities.

The University of Wollongong also had a training facility to save students based in Sydney from travelling the 90 minutes to Wollongong. I asked if we could hire a room for our Intel training. I said we could fit the rooms out with top of the range PCs that could be used by the University if we were not using it. They gave us a lovely big room at no cost. Now we didn't need a bank loan at all.

In July, Mark Thomas and I went to an Intel Management conference in Phuket in Thailand. I had been to Phuket with Allan Moffatt and hated the place. Patong Beach was full of young boys selling themselves to rich old American men for $1. The place was full of lady boys, garishly made up young men dressed as women. It was decadent and creepy.

This time Intel paid for everything, including business class airfares for Mark and me. The venue was a six star resort. The other delegates were managers of Asian companies and their chief trainers. Many of the companies manufactured or assembled PCs in addition to delivering Intel training.

My room at the resort was huge. The bathroom alone was the size of a normal hotel room. The bath was sunken into the floor with marble steps leading down into it. Intel was obviously a very wealthy company.

One evening the group decided to go into Patong. I warned them how horrid it was and said I'd rather stay in the resort. But everyone was going so I went along for the ride, saying I'd stay in the bus we hired. The group agreed to return to the bus in two hours but most returned in about 20 minutes, agreeing with me that the place was very seedy.

We worked hard, often working into the night. Intel sent people from their research arm to tell us what they planned for the future. It was great to feel I was again learning about cutting edge technology. It was exciting to meet people from the booming Asian countries and to try to understand their languages and customs.

We were told we should market the courses ourselves, although Intel would put details on the Intel website and advise all their customers about their scheme. Marketing! There it was. I was beginning to feel inadequate again.

I decided to ask Max Burnet to help. Max had been DEC's Managing Director when I first came to Australia. He had been DEC Australia's employee number one. When DEC was taken over by Compaq in March 1998 he decided to retire and not be 'compaqted'. Max had built a museum of DEC computers in the foyer in DEC's Head office. On retirement he asked if he could buy the museum. DEC sold it to him for $1.

The Compaq takeover of DEC surprised everyone. Compaq was a PC company. The industry had been surprised when Compaq had taken over Tandem Computers. In Australia, that meant a takeover of only 144 staff. With the DEC takeover it meant absorbing 1200 staff, many more than Compaq itself had in Australia. The industry likened these Compaq takeovers to a minnow swallowing a whale.

Max said he would be delighted to work with us one day a week to market our Intel training. We hired Gunther's sister Astrid to administer our Intel training project. The initiative was going well all over the world but the Australian Government and a couple of other countries decided that to force people purchasing Intel chips to be accredited was against the Trade Practices legislation. Now it was not compulsory for PC builders in Australia to be Intel accredited. Intel said it would find other ways to ensure their customers in Australia were accredited. It had all been for nothing.

64 The company splits

TECHNOLOGY SOLUTIONS was going well. Our end of financial year income and profit for June 1998 was twice that of June 1997. Although DEC had been taken over by Compaq, it preserved its own identity. We still did the bulk of DEC training in Australia. DEC's major reseller, Integrand, decided to offer services in addition to selling boxes. DEC asked Chris if Technology Solutions could help, so this became another major customer of ours.

Our Vodafone project, which I was managing, was going very well. One of our people, Sue Meyer, had worked her way up the Vodafone hierarchy. She was now General Manager, Information Systems. We were paying Sue $250,000 a year and still making a profit from her services. She asked us for more of our staff to support her so it was a win-win situation.

The big issue in IT all over the world in the 1990s was the problem posed by the upcoming year 2000. In the early days of computing when machines were less powerful and more expensive, to minimise storage space and compute time dates were often stored as dd/mm/yy where the yy was simply the last two digits of the year.

This meant that, after 1999, the years in the 1900s could not be differentiated from the years in the 2000s. No one had expected systems built in the early days to still be functional by the year 2000, or if they were they imagined the date field would be extended during regular maintenance. I remember often suggesting we change old dates to the dd/mm/yyyy format while we were doing other maintenance, but was told we were to get the changes installed as soon as possible. The date issue could be left for later.

Well now it was 'later' and business people realised that there was little time left to make changes in systems that were 30 or 40 years old. There were predictions that air traffic control and banking systems would fail, causing chaos and even death.

Computer people were blamed for allowing the situation to go unnoticed even though many of us protested that we had tried to make the changes. The job of working through millions of lines of old computer code was horrendous, especially because for many the original source code or documentation was no longer available.

Even if the source code was available, few current programmers were proficient in old computer languages. Conferences were held. Governments were worried. Working groups were formed. Automation was suggested but it was realised that such complex logic could not be automated, except maybe to identify where dates had been specified in data.

I thought this was a real opportunity to gather together retired programmers who wanted to work flexibly from home. I was sure they would be willing to spend some of their time identifying and making changes. Pay rates were high. Programmers were being offered up to $2000 and $3000 a day for the work. I contacted IBM to offer our help. I thought it would be their customers who would have the most need. But we never did get any contracts for Y2K remediation, as the conversion was known.

MORE AND MORE services were being offered as part of what was now being called electronic commerce or eCommerce, basically the use of the Internet to buy and sell products and services. The Australian Government established the National Office for the Information Economy, (NOIE) and held a summit in Canberra to discuss how Australia could exploit eCommerce to counter the 'tyranny of distance' from the USA and Europe.

The issue of poor and expensive access to the Internet for people in the bush came up again. More firms were offering online share trading. One online US broker was charging as little as US$8 for a trade that cost US$70 through Merrill Lynch. It was suggested that by 2001 most stock trades in the USA would be online.

By the end of 1998 Technology Solutions had over 100 staff but needed more. We appointed a personnel administrator, Val. Chris built a system for her but it was badly designed and she had great difficulty using it. She preferred the spreadsheets I had designed to keep track of people skills.

Chris had stayed at my house a few times and used my PC. Each time, after he had left my PC wouldn't work for me. Chris said it had worked for him and I probably didn't know how to use it. I called Gunther to fix it and it worked perfectly – until the next time.

Chris was getting increasingly aggressive. We still met for dinner once a month but the atmosphere between us had changed. We decided we needed an end game for Technology Solutions. I would be 60 next year and didn't plan to work indefinitely, although I was enjoying running the company. We decided that we would sell the company after the Olympics that were to be held in Sydney in 2000. I started to find out how much the company was worth. The consensus seemed to be around the $2.5 to $4 million mark.

Mark Thomas noticed the tension and tried to bring Chris and me together. He said we were the 'Mum and Dad' of a great company. He encouraged us both to talk frankly about our differences but we agreed we really had none except that Chris was being paid more than I was. Chris was working almost exclusively on billable work. I was doing some billable work and all the PR stuff, more public speaking, more interaction with the media, etc. and bringing in the new business.

I didn't really mind. I was earning more than ever and I was having a ball. We agreed that as we both brought a lot to the company we should be paid the same. I suspected Chris didn't like all the publicity I was getting.

TELECOMMUTING WAS GAINING POPULARITY. I was still in demand to speak about the subject at conferences. Lend Lease attracted much publicity when it announced a teleworking initiative.

The industry was concerned about the multiplicity of qualifications so established the National Information Technology and Telecommunications Industry Training Board (ITTAB). I was invited to be an inaugural Director. The Board was responsible for approving course material and determining appropriate teaching and testing processes for vocational and university education and training and creating a framework of qualifications.

The ITTAB conceptualised seven levels from Certificate 1, which was very elementary, to first degree. Higher levels up to PhD would be added later. Competencies to be gained were specified for each level. Training programs were then matched to qualifications. This was a huge task. There were many training programs in existence, and agreeing on equivalences was complex.

Chris and I had our usual monthly dinner meeting in March. There had been a shooting in Sydney so all the traffic was gridlocked. I arrived at the restaurant about an hour late, although I had phoned Chris several times to give him an update on the traffic situation.

The restaurant was empty except for Chris. We ordered dinner. Over the first course, Chris said he had something very difficult to say to me. He took my hand and said I was a 'lovely lady' and everyone thought a lot of me but as a friend, and for my own good, he had to tell me I was loosing my intellect and bringing the company into disrepute.

I was stunned. Chris had spoken very softly. He had taken my hand, something he had never done before. His facial expression had been one of sadness and pain. Was he right? My mind flashed back to my memory lapses in my 50s and my skull fracture when I was 18. Had it all finally come to a head? Had people really not liked to tell me?

I pulled myself together. I said to Chris surely I hadn't heard what he had said correctly. If this was true why was I asked to speak at conferences and be invited back again and again. Why was I invited to join the TAFE Board and the ITTAB Board. Why had I been elected Chair of the Wollongong University Visiting Committee and the Northern Sydney TAFE Council?

I stood up and threw my serviette at him. I told him he would apologise to me and stormed out of the restaurant without waiting for an apology. On the way home in my car I was fuming. Was this what Chris had done to Paul? Found Paul's weak spot and pushed him until he cried? Well I wasn't going to cry. This was outrageous! Chris would apologise or else.

Now I saw him as a greedy person, trying to get the company for himself. Well he was trying it on the wrong person. Had he deliberately messed up my PC to confuse me? Was he telling other people I had lost my intellect? I was as angry as I had ever been in my life.

I wished I could talk to Paul about Chris's nastiness and ask Paul to tell me exactly what had happened to him. I'd have liked to apologise for the way I had helped to oust Paul from the company but I had lost touch with him. The next day I phoned Mark and told him what had happened. He said surely I had misheard Chris. I must have been stressed. The company was getting very big and perhaps too big for just Chris and me to manage. Perhaps I needed a holiday. That just made me feel worse. Was Mark trying to tell me that Chris was right?

Mark rang back. He said Chris denied saying anything of the sort. I had just got angry and stormed out of the restaurant leaving him to pay the bill. Had I imagined it all? Was I stressed?

No, I was certain Chris was trying to get me to give up and leave the company to him. I asked around to find out if other companies had difficulties between partners. Most people told me I shouldn't have let the company have only two partners. There should always be at least three. One woman who owned a very large systems services company told me that she and her business partner had not spoken for years. Others told me that was the reason their company had suddenly closed or they had left.

I asked if people really thought I was losing my intellect. Most looked at me strangely. Why the question? They all told me I certainly was not.

I DECIDED NOT TO speak to Chris unless he first apologised. I sent him an email telling him so. I got no reply. Apart from not communicating directly with me, Chis carried on as if nothing had happened. I sent out the agenda for our next monthly meeting stating that I would not meet Chris unless I got an apology first. No apology.

Mark brought us both together. He asked Chris what he wanted to do. Chris said he wanted me to see an industrial psychologist. Mark asked me what I wanted. I said I wanted us to attend a mediation process with a professional mediator I would ask AIIA to recommend. I said I would not attend a meeting with an industrial psychologist unless we both attended. Chris agreed. I then agreed to make an appointment for mediation and Chris said he would set up a meeting with a psychologist.

The meeting with the psychologist came first. He was a weird wizened man aged about 70. He made us play many of the games I'd either played on management courses or read about before. Four blind men trying to identify an elephant by touch showing we all have different perceptions. Making lists of exactly what we wanted and what we thought the other wanted. Prioritising what should be done with the company, etc.

At lunchtime the psychologist announced he was going to break for an hour. He suggested some places nearby where we could get lunch. We were in St Leonards so I knew the territory well. Chris said he had no time for lunch. He just needed somewhere to make phone calls. I went for a walk.

After lunch, there were more management games. I had agreed to do everything that was asked of me so I just played along. At one stage Chris angrily said we were getting nowhere. The psychologist told Chis to just to do as he asked.

Around 4pm, the psychologist's whole body language changed. He looked younger. He sat up straight and barked at Chris, "Well, what are you going to do?" All day he had spoken softly. This was a real change. Chris simply said, "I'm going to let Ann buy me out of my half of the business." The man closed his portfolio folder and said, "Well, that's all. Is there anything you want to ask me?"

Chris said no and thanked the man for his time saying he would write him a cheque for $3000 for his fee. I asked, "How did you do that?" The man said, "I've been doing this every day for longer than I care to remember. The first part of the day is to allow me to assess the individuals then, when I know the answer, I ask the question. I knew what Chris would say before lunch."

I said, "You didn't ask me a question." He said, "I didn't need to."

I thought the day was very strange. Now I had to find someone to buy Chris's share of the company and restructure the new company so that we didn't get into the two partner situation again. We'd had several approaches to buy the company. It shouldn't be that difficult.

IN JUNE I WAS INVITED to join the Australian Government delegation to the APEC Women's Leaders' Conference in New Zealand. APEC, the Asia Pacific Economic Co-operation forum, was founded in 1996. It had been established to foster economic co-operation and development between economies in the

Asia Pacific region. Participants in APEC were referred to as economies, not countries. The delegates to the main meeting were the Chief Ministers of the 21 economies involved.

In 1998, the New Zealand Prime Minister, Jenny Shipley, was the only female delegate at the Heads of Government meeting. She decided that women's issues needed better representation at that forum so the Women's APEC was formed. Jenny Shipley hosted this, the first Women's APEC meeting, in 1999. She promised to take any resolutions we made to the APEC Heads of Government meeting in September 1999.

Each economy sent four women, a woman in government, a woman in commerce, a woman in small business and a woman in technology. I was chosen to represent women in technology in Australia.

Many of the delegates were very important people in their own countries. We had the Vice President of the Philippines and many minsters from other countries. The meeting was held in a five star hotel in the centre of Wellington.

The New Zealand Government paid for everything. It hosted interesting sightseeing events with lots of local culture. On the first night the Australian delegation was invited to the Australian High Commissioner's very grand official residence set in the hills above Wellington with beautiful views of the city and harbour.

There were many protests by local women. Wherever we went we had to have a police escort. The protestors dressed up as cleaning ladies with mops and brooms. They were angry that New Zealand was funding women's APEC when the country was in financial stress. This especially applied to the many women looking after children on their own. They called us Rich Bitches and said we didn't represent normal women.

I presented a paper on the importance of women taking ownership for developments in technology and taking responsibility for their own lifelong education. My speech was well received and resulted in a proposal to the APEC Heads of Government meeting. I met many interesting women at APEC and continued to correspond with several after the meeting.

From Wellington, I flew to an Intel Management conference in Hong Kong. Again we stayed at a five star hotel. All the training companies were working well. Intel was pleased with its initiative.

MY 60TH BIRTHDAY was in July 1999. I asked my two children to give me a black tie dinner for 60 of my friends. I said we would hold it in the dining room at the Ryde TAFE College. Ryde had a renowned cooking school. I had been to several black tie dinners there. They were always splendid affairs and I knew we would only be charged for the food ingredients and the wine. TAFE loved to have events that would allow their students to demonstrate their skills. The dinner for 60 would cost only $1000.

It was indeed a splendid dinner. The food and service were wonderful. The Cordon Bleu school was part of the college. It was one of only two in the world, the other being in Switzerland. They made handmade chocolates for us. The horticultural part of the college put pots of flowering orchids on every table for guests to take home. The whole room was decorated and there were coloured metallic stars on the floor.

Claire had raided my family scrapbooks and made a 'Great Wall of Fame' out of family photos and press clippings plus an area for guests to write comments. It was everything I had hoped for. I had invited Chris and his wife Deb but they neither came nor sent apologies.

A few days later I organised a FITT lunch in the NSW Parliament House dining room. Senator Kate Lundy was guest speaker. She spoke positively about FITT. She congratulated me on my 60th birthday and said some lovely things about me. All the women then stood up and sang 'Happy Birthday'. I was presented with a beautiful crystal glass eagle with outspread wings.

IN AUGUST AND SEPTEMBER I was invited to speak to Women in IT groups at Westpac Bank and at the AMP Society. In August I was a judge and presenter at the Australian Financial Review/Telstra Web Awards in Melbourne.

The awards presentation in the elegant Melbourne Town Hall was televised live. My co-presenter was James Morrison, the famous trumpeter. I loved his music. James did not turn up to the rehearsal in the afternoon, so someone from the ABC stood in for him. I felt slightly cheated because I didn't get to rehearse properly and, as usual, I was very nervous.

The judges were the presenters at the awards but did not present the categories they had judged. The presenters were seated for dinner at a long table in front of the stage. I was seated opposite James Morrison. We chatted as if we had known each other for years. I was an adoring fan and he loved it. I refused wine until after we had done our presentation.

ABC presenter Adam Spencer was the master of ceremonies. He was another radio personality I loved. When it was our turn, to present, by way of introduction, Adam said we all knew James but he wanted to tell the audience of about 1000 people about me. He said some very nice things about me and about Technology Solutions. I don't know where he got his information from but it was very flattering.

The format of each presentation was that the co-hosts just chatted. I had been prepared to chat about the web awards and the technology of the web. James decided he just wanted to talk about me. He said he hadn't realised I'd done all those things that Adam had spoken about. I was embarrassed and kept saying I loved his music. When it was time to open the envelope and announce the winner I was delighted that it was the Australian Broadcasting Corporation.

Back at our table, I could now relax and have a glass of wine. When all the awards had been presented Adam Spencer announced that James Morrison's band would play for us. The stage curtains opened and there was the band. James was still sitting opposite me. After a short while he stood up. He took a trumpet from under the table and started to play. Then still playing he sauntered up to the stage and joined his band. It was a perfect evening for me.

I was also asked to be judge and presenter at the Australian Financial Review's Australian Software Awards. These were not as lavish and prestigious as the web awards but it was interesting judging new software.

The Australian Government had designated 1999 as Online Australia Year. Senator Richard Alston said the year was to build on Australia's information economy strengths by raising national awareness of the economy-wide benefits of the information revolution. Each month was to have a different focus. It was decided to dedicate a week to Women Online.

At the beginning of 1999, the Director of the National Office for the Information Economy asked me to be the advisor for the Women's Online Week that they were going to hold in October 1999. The event was to boost women's use of the information economy and was very successful.

I ORGANISED A MEDIATION day for Chris and I to resolve what was to be done about Technology Solutions. Chris had never apologised to me and we were still not speaking although the company continued to prosper. I had had several offers from people who wanted to buy into the company but Chris had rejected them all. He had suggested that we sell the company outright to a rather unpleasant man. I asked around the industry about the man and found he had a reputation for closing businesses down. I didn't want to see the company that we had struggled to build just closed down.

The mediator asked to speak to me before the mediation. He told me Chris was bringing a solicitor to support him. I asked why did we have to bring a solicitor? The mediator said some people did and if Chris was bringing one it might be useful for me to be represented too.

At the mediation session my solicitor suggested that as the relationship between Chris and me had broken down the best thing to do was to split the company. The rest of the day was spent in discussing how. The company had to be formally closed by an independent administrator. Letters had to be sent to clients and staff. We agreed how this should be done.

Chris's solicitor appointed an administrator but he told everyone our company was insolvent and was being liquidated, which was totally untrue because we had more than $150,000 in our current account. He was replaced by an administrator chosen by my solicitor. Chris then sent unapproved letters to all our clients stating that he was now running the company and had just changed the name. These had to be retracted. It was a messy affair.

Chris and I had agreed to hold a Technology Solutions Christmas party. It was decided that this should not be held but I could not get the deposit back so I held the party for my new company. Many of our panel and staff came to the party. They all said they were sorry to see Technology Solutions split up. I was very sad to see my wonderful company end this way but it had lasted over seven years and that was good for a small company in Australia in the 1990s.

65 Time for reflection

JUST BEFORE CHRISTMAS my son Stephen moved into his own flat near the harbour. For the first time in my life, I was living by myself. There was much to do to get my new company up and running. I chose a name, EXOCAT, EXpertise On Computing And Telecommunic-ations. A new website had to be built to preserve continuity with the Intel business, which was to be mine. New stationary had to be ordered.

Fortunately for me, Chris agreed that I should take over our office plus the phone number and address. Chris would run his side of the business from his home in Queensland.

Christmas 1999 brought more dinners and parties than ever but I did manage to get to Claire and Rodney's place for Christmas. They had moved to a house in Queensland. It had been one of their two investment properties that they had sensibly bought while they lived in houses provided by Colly Farms.

They had gone to inspect their house in Queensland and decided they would like to live there. It was in Burrum Heads, a tiny village where Rodney's family had spent their holidays when he was young. Burrum Heads is on the coast about 30kms north of Hervey Bay near Fraser Island. The house was on a rural block with five acres of garden.

We had about 20 family members for Christmas lunch. Instead of the usual roast turkey dinner we had seafood out in the garden. My grand-daughter Rhianna was four years old and would be going to school soon. Burrum Heads seemed to me to be a good place to bring children up. Claire and Rodney had found jobs easily. Next year both Claire and Stephen would finish their first degrees and graduate.

THE YEAR 2000 was very near. It had seemed such a long way off when the Met Office had told me when I joined in 1956 that although I could retire at age 60, I could be employed until I retired in 2004 at the age of 65

Sydney promised better fireworks than ever to welcome in the new millennium. I had been invited to several New Year parties. One was in Byron Bay with my friend Glen Schaeffer. Byron is the first place on the Australian mainland to get each day's sunrise. Glen told me there would be 2000 drums on Byron Bay beach to welcome the sunrise and everyone on the beach would be mooning to greet the dawn. 'Mooning' is a strange Australian custom of exposing the bare bottom to whatever, in this case the rising sun. It is considered a friendly greeting!

The clocks, and the date, clicked over to 2000. There were none of the IT disasters that were forecast due to Y2K date errors. No aeroplanes fell out of the sky. All banks opened on time although an extra bank holiday was allowed in case banks had problems. Many people said it was a fizzer and the whole thing must have been a scam. I think there were so few problems because the IT industry did such a good job at fixing the problem.

I went to the Snowy Mountains for Australia Day at the end of January as I always did. None of my bushwalking friends felt fit enough to walk so this time I went with Stephen and his friends. We did the Main Range walk. Stephen's friends carried my pack and said they would carry me as well if necessary.

STARTING A NEW COMPANY was harder than I remembered. We had built Technology Solutions over seven years and worked as a team. Now I was trying to do everything myself in three months. Even so, within the first three months we had billed $750,000. At the end of February I went to an Intel management meeting in Singapore. We were still working with them, though the accreditation scheme was not as lucrative as we had hoped. Again Intel paid for everything.

The Australian Government asked me to stay on in Singapore until 8 March, which was International Women's Day. They wanted me to host the Singapore end of a virtual cocktail party for women in IT&T in Australia and in Singapore. They booked me into one of Singapore's best hotels, the Shangri La. I relaxed and was pampered for eight wonderful days. I lounged by the pool, swam, went to the gym, had massages and facials, lived on fruit and took numerous tourist trips round Singapore.

I went to Raffles Hotel and had a gin sling in the Long Bar where women used to be banned. Over the bar was a beautiful painting of a nude woman tastefully draped in flimsy scarves. I went to an orchid nursery and learnt how orchids are propagated and grown.

Singapore had changed a lot since I had last been there. Gone were the death houses I remembered where old people used to sit in the sun and smile at passers by while they waited to die. Gone was the old Arab Quarter when you could buy anything, replaced by modern buildings and fancy shops. I didn't go to Bugis Street where Allan Moffatt had taken me on our ill-fated honeymoon.

The cocktail party was held at the Australian High Commission. Telstra had given us as much bandwidth as we needed. There were huge screens where we could see the people at the Sydney end that was to be attended by women from FITT. The American and Chinese governments found out what we were doing and wanted to join in but there wasn't enough time.

There was wonderful food and wine and lots of lobster and champagne. About 200 women and men attended. The Australian High Commissioner spoke first then I spoke, then the women just chatted across the link. It seemed like the entire world's news media had joined us. The Sydney end was less successful. There was torrential rain in Sydney so only a few people turned up.

During the next week CNBC broadcast the party several times as part of their IWD news. There I was on the TV right after Aung San Suu Kyi from Burma! Many friends from all over the world rang or emailed me to tell me they had seen the broadcast on their local TV news.

I HAD REACHED the part of my PhD where I had to prove my thesis. I had to prove or disprove the idea that 'If we used the strategies needed to make teleworking successful in an office environment, we could increase staff productivity by at least 20%'.

The Director of Research at Macquarie University and I had tried to find a company to lend me 100 people to prove my thesis. I figured I needed two groups of 50, a control group and a group that followed my suggested way of working. First I tried Lend Lease. They agreed and offered $30,000 to the University to fund the research. Then they decided they couldn't cope with a university student working with their staff.

I tried AMP. At first I got a yes, but then they decided they had too much change already and couldn't manage any more. TAFE said I could use their staff but I thought TAFE administrative people couldn't be made to work more productively by any means.

The Director of Research, who was also my PhD supervisor, suggested I go to America to complete my project because companies were larger in the USA so getting 100 people for my project would be easier. I didn't want to go to the USA for the six months that the project would take. How could I leave my business for that long?

He then said, "For goodness sake Ann, just write everything up and we'll give you your PhD. You know more about this subject than anyone else." I was horrified. I thought the purpose of a PhD was to prove or disprove a thesis. I felt if it was this easy I didn't want it. I stopped the PhD.

I WENT TO QUEENSLAND to look after Rhianna while Claire attended a university course. I liked the Burrum Heads area very much. I had planned to retire to Port Douglas in far north Queensland but thought I might like Burrum Heads better, and Claire and her family would be nearby. There was some land for sale so I bought 2.5 acres as an investment. Later I thought I might put a house on it and rent it out.

Then I asked myself whether I really wanted to build up a company again. I counted my money and decided I could afford to retire. The only drawback I could see was that if I moved to Queensland my long affair, which had now gone on for over 20 years, would have to stop. Hmm!

2000 was Sydney's year for the Olympic Games. NSW TAFE was a major sponsor and did all the training needed. TAFE was given tickets for all the major events. Board Members were asked to indicate which they would like to attend.

The Olympics were splendid. Stephen was still working for AMP. He was now in marketing and worked on the Olympic torch relay, which AMP sponsored. We saw several events from AMP's corporate box. We attended the men's water polo final and watched the finish of the men's marathon. I saw the closing ceremony from a party on Observatory Hill in Sydney. There were fireworks over the harbour. The city was packed, and the journey home took ages. No cars were allowed in the city. It took hours even to walk to the train station.

I decided not to try to sell my company. It might take a while and I was eager to start my new life. I just gave the Intel business to the universities, I gave the project work to the people working on each project. Our clients were happy with the arrangements, as were all the staff. Our accountant got a good job locally.

I attended one last FITT meeting at the NSW Parliament House. I was surprised to find that it was not really a FITT meeting at all. My friends had gathered all my professional colleagues together for a farewell party.

WITHIN THREE MONTHS I sold my house in Sydney, built a new one in Burrum Heads and moved to Queensland. Friends and colleagues worried that I was unwell or had gone bankrupt. I knew better. I was off for a better life.

I thought about what could have been. I was sure that if Chris had waited we would now be selling the company and each of us would have pocketed millions of dollars. That was not to be. I have never had vast amounts of money but I have always had enough. I was happy with the future I had chosen. I had had a wonderful career. I felt as if all my life I had been paid handsomely to do what I loved.

I'd brought up my children and they were now successfully living their own lives. Claire was now a teacher. Stephen was doing well at AMP and living in his own flat. My career had enabled me to indulge my passion for travelling. I'd had a ball. I felt blessed.

With the sale of my Sydney house I had a nest egg and a new house just 7 km from a lovely white sandy beach. I had read that the best place to live anywhere in the world was on the sea coast within 200 miles of the tropic of Cancer or Capricorn. Burrum Heads was about 250km south of the tropic of Capricorn. It seemed to me like heaven on a stick.

It has been said that people with frontal lobe damage lose the ability to plan. I'm glad that the accident I had when I was 18 didn't seem to affect my abilities in that area. I think it's vital to plan or it is impossible to achieve all the things you wish to do. It is even more important as you get older and you have less and less time left to achieve your goals.

An Operations Research technique that has served me well is Game Theory. The aim is to conceptualise all the things that can stop you achieving your goals and develop strategies to overcome them. The technique was developed by John Forbes Nash who was the subject of the film 'A Beautiful Mind'. It's been a very useful adjunct to planning.

It took me more than ten years to learn how to retire. Even though I had over two acres of new garden to tame and my granddaughter, Rhianna, to look after before and after school, I found it difficult to let my professional life go. Friends had been surprised when I left Sydney so abruptly. When they visited my new home, they realised how lucky I was to have found such a beautiful place to live.

At first I thought I would help my local community to understand more about IT. I ran a series of Tech Talks at the Fraser Coast Campus of the University of Southern Queensland (USQ) located in Hervey Bay. I invited friends from the industry to come and stay with me and give talks about all things IT, starting with Max Burnet giving his talk about IT history.

In 2001 the Queensland Minister for Education appointed me to the Wide Bay Institute of TAFE Council and the Hervey Bay TAFE College Council. Also in 2001 I was appointed to the Board of the Australian Computer Society Foundation, which sought funding from Australian businesses to provide scholarships for students to study IT at university.

In 2002 my granddaughter Rhianna was seven years old. For her birthday I took Claire, Rodney and Rhianna to Disney World in Florida.

Afterwards Claire and family went to stay with Claire's Dad, my first husband Alan Leach, who now lives in Jacksonville in Florida. I travelled down the beautiful Florida Keys to Key West. I'd always wanted to drink a Margarita in Margaritaville in Jimmy Buffet's club. It was all I had ever imagined and more.

Afterwards I went to Panama for a week and travelled through the Panama Canal by small boat with time to get out and study the locks. What an engineering feat. I travelled through the jungle by train to Colon that was like a lawless, rundown Wild West type of place that must be the arse end of the earth. Panama City was exciting but also very wild.

AFTER I RETIRED and went to live in Queensland I thought I would be forgotten by our industry, but was delighted to be called to Sydney to be inducted into the Australian IT Hall of Fame. I didn't even know the industry had a Hall of Fame.

It didn't, until 2002. In that year, from 145 nominees identified by our industry, three people were selected by a panel from our industry and became the inaugural inductees. In a very male dominated industry, it was a great honour to be the second person and first woman to be inducted. One of the award sponsors was Air New Zealand who gave the three inductees two round the world tickets each. It was a very pleasant reward for a most enjoyable career.

Together with my friend Liz, in 2003 we travelled round the world for nearly four months visiting friends and relations. We stopped off in Tahiti, a place I'd always wanted to see. Apart from seeing where Cook observed the transit of Venus, it was a disappointment. Those French again. Also on that trip we visited my cousin Ian in New Zealand and Christine McKenzie who I had met at the New Zealand women's APEC meeting. Christine lived on a farm at the extreme south of the South Island. We drove through New Zealand's lovely Southland to the wild south coast to stay with Christine and her family for a week.

In 2003, together with USQ, the Wide Bay Institute of TAFE and the Queensland Department of State Development, I established an Innovation and Incubation Centre in Hervey Bay to help local people and businesses use of IT successfully. Also in 2003, I was voted President of our local University of the Third Age. I still teach there regularly.

In 2004 I was appointed Chairman of the Wide Bay Burnet Regional Leaders focus group on Infrastructure. The task took me all round Wide Bay Burnet to meet with and talk to all Wide Bay's leaders. After writing the report of our findings, in 2005 I presented the findings to a conference of over 400 people at the Wide Bay Leaders Group, which comprised all the region's mayors, politicians, business leaders, heads of schools etc. I was asked to give my talk to several other conferences in our region including the Wide Bay Burnet Junior Leaders Conference, where I was keynote speaker.

In 2005 the University of Southern Queensland awarded me an Honorary Doctorate of Engineering. So I got my Doctorate after all. Claire had a second baby, Cassandra, so I now had a new baby to look after. It was such a joy to look after Claire's children. I had been working when mine were young, and I now had time to enjoy small children and watch them grow. It was a pleasure and a privilege.

IN 2006 I WAS OFF again round the world. This time to my nephew Matt's wedding in London. I finally got to St Petersburg. I spent a week there, which was fabulous. My son Stephen came with me and brought his new girlfriend Nicole. In 2008 they married.

In 2009, when I was 70, I retired from all professional appointments to just relax and tend my garden. Ten years after 'retirement' I felt I could live life just for me.

By 2009 I was living sustainably, as I had always wanted. I was almost self sufficient in fruit and vegies, I generated more power from PV panels on my roof than I consumed. I had no reticulated water or sewage service at my house and collected all my water from my roof and treated my own sewage before releasing it onto my fruit trees.

I have had visits from friends from all over the world in my first ten years. There are direct flights from Hervey Bay to Sydney and the trip takes only about 75 minutes. I had many trips to Sydney to shop and visit friends. I even managed to sneak trysts with my wonderful lover until he died.

In 2011, I was amazed to be called to Melbourne to be inducted into the Pearcey Hall of Fame. Named for Trevor Pearcey who developed CSIRAC, the first Australian computer and the world's fourth, this is the highest professional honour awarded to anyone in IT in Australia.

Now perhaps I can relax and just enjoy life.

Postscript

I HAVE HAD A wonderful life and a wonderful career. Like most people, I have had my ups and downs. I'm very glad I have had the opportunity to set it all down. Let me end on the lessons my career and my life have taught me:

TAKE TIME TO OBSERVE

Often a solution to a problem is simple but counter-intuitive. In my experience, it is often the most junior staff, who have time to observe and ask why, who suggest the most successful solutions.

PUT YOUR OWN NEEDS FIRST

This is something I learnt late in my career. We women are often taught to put the needs of others before our own. It seems selfish, but I have found that you are better able to help others if you meet your own needs first.

It makes sense when the flight attendant on an aeroplane announces that you should put your own oxygen mask on first before helping others and it works in life.

TAKE GOOD CARE OF YOUR PHYSICAL AND MENTAL WELLBEING

We each have only one body. It is important that we treat it well and maintain and exercise it regularly so that it will be fit to support us in all we want to achieve in life. I have had more than my share of trauma, physical and mental, and keeping healthy in both areas has helped me a lot.

PROMISE LESS AND DELIVER MORE

In providing estimates for IT projects I have always slightly overestimated. This not only provides a margin for error but it delights clients when projects are brought in under budget and ahead of time.

In my Masters program I was horrified when one student said he always underestimated. If management knew the real cost of projects they would never get the go-ahead. He said once a project was part way through more budget and time would always be allocated. I consider this attitude to be dishonest. It has been the scourge of the IT industry. IT is a service industry. Professionals must learn to provide accurate estimates.

VALUE DIVERSITY

Life is too comfortable when you are surrounded by yes-men and yes-women. We need to be with people who constructively challenge our ideas and recommend alternatives so that in a culture of mutual respect other people's views are heard and the outcome is the best and strongest solution.

APPOINT A COMPETENT DEPUTY

In this way things can continue successfully if you are ever away from work through sickness or on holiday. It also means you have the choice to take on interesting opportunities as they arise.

REWARD YOURSELF WHEN YOU ACHIEVE SOMETHING

I hate public speaking. The first time I made a presentation to a group of over 500 people and received a standing ovation, I bought myself a very expensive hand knitted jacket. Whenever I wear it I recall the event that led to the purchase and I feel a million dollars. Something as simple as a small piece of jewellery or a nice book will serve the same purpose.

MAKE TIME TO PURSUE ACTIVITIES OUTSIDE YOUR CAREER

All work and no play makes Jack a dull boy. And Jill a dull girl. Everybody needs enjoyable interests outside of work.

HAVE FUN

If you do not look forward to going to work each day you are probably in the wrong job. Have the courage to get out of a situation you are not enjoying.

I will leave you with a quotation from the 16th century essayist, scientist and philosopher, Francis Bacon.

'I hold every man a debtor to his profession; from the which, as men of course do seek to receive countenance and profit, so ought they of duty to endeavour themselves, by way of amends, to be a help and ornament thereunto.'

I have certainly enjoyed the fruits of our industry and enjoyed making a contribution to our profession.

Peace.

Made in United States
North Haven, CT
24 September 2026

19102541R00270